Geoff Tibballs worked in television for fifteen years before leaving in 1989 to become a full-time author. He has since had over a hundred books published on a wide variety of topics, including social history, sport, television, and humor. His 1997 book, *Titanic*, written to coincide with the Hollywood blockbuster, was a best-seller. His titles for Constable & Robinson have included *Business Blunders*, *Legal Blunders* and *The Mammoth Book of Jokes*.

For Carol, Nicki and Lindsey

VOICES
FROM THE
TITANIC

**The Epic Story of the Tragedy
from the People Who Were There**

Edited by Geoff Tibballs

Skyhorse Publishing

First published in the UK as *The Mammoth Book of How it Happened: Titanic*, by
Robinson, an imprint of Constable & Robinson Ltd, 2002

Skyhorse Publishing books may be purchased in bulk at special discounts
for sales promotion, corporate gifts, fund-raising, or educational purposes.
Special editions can also be created to specifications. For details,
contact the Special Sales Department, Skyhorse Publishing,
307 West 36th Street, 11th Floor, New York, NY 10018 or
info@skyhorsepublishing.com.

Skyhorse® and Skyhorse Publishing® are registered trademarks of
Skyhorse Publishing, Inc. ®, a Delaware corporation.

www.skyhorsepublishing.com

10 9 8 7 6 5 4 3 2 1

Library of Congress Cataloging-in-Publication Data is available on file.

ISBN: 978-1-61608-605-3

Printed in the United Kingdom

CONTENTS

INTRODUCTION

The morning of Wednesday, 10 April 1912, dawned bright and breezy in Southampton, but the cool spring air was heavy with anticipation. For in a few hours' time, the biggest ship in the world, the White Star liner *Titanic*, was due to set off on her maiden voyage, bound for New York with a passenger list which read like a Who's Who of early twentieth-century society. The great and the good had been captivated by accounts of the ship's superlative accommodation, which likened it to a floating hotel. For those who could afford prices of between £400 and £870 for a one-way ticket, a first-class suite aboard the *Titanic* was the only way to cross the Atlantic. The inaugural voyage of this magnificent vessel was expected to be an occasion that would live in the memory for years to come. And so it proved.

The *Titanic* was born out of entrepreneurial greed – a ruthless desire by shipping magnates to cash in on the lucrative transatlantic routes and to eliminate all competition in the process. The chosen method was to build bigger and faster ships than ever before. The principal protagonists were two British companies, the White Star Line and Cunard, the latter having been responsible for establishing the first transatlantic steamship service via its vessel *Britannia* in 1840. Over the next fifty years trade between the United States and Britain increased sevenfold, not only in terms of tobacco, cotton and wheat, but also in human cargo. Growing numbers of Europeans saw America as the promised land and opted to start a new life there, and, since the only means of travel was by ship, passenger demand rose dramatically. Founded in 1850, when it specialized in carrying emigrants from Britain to Australia, the White Star Line steadily began to challenge Cunard's monopoly on the transatlantic routes and by 1875 had produced steamers capable of travelling at 16 knots, reducing the journey time to less than seven and a half days. All White Star vessels were built at the Harland & Wolff shipyard in Belfast.

Sensing a business opportunity, American financier John Pierpont Morgan decided that he, too, wanted a slice of the action. His company, International Mercantile Marine, bought Inman Lines of Liverpool and started a fierce price war, offering third-class transatlantic passages for as little as £2. He then tried to buy Cunard, but was prevented from doing so by the British government. So he turned his attention to White Star. The chairman of Harland & Wolff, Lord Pirrie, thought that the best way to protect his yard's interests was to team up with Morgan and in 1902 he helped the American acquire White Star, which thus became a subsidiary of International Mercantile Marine. Joseph Bruce Ismay remained as chairman of White Star and all White Star ships continued to have British crews and to fly the British flag. But the real power lay on the other side of the Atlantic.

In 1907, backed by sizeable subsidies from the British government, Cunard launched the *Lusitania* and the *Mauretania*, both of which were capable of an average speed of 26 knots. At the time White Star's fastest ship was the *Teutonic*, at 21 knots. In order to compete with the Cunarders, White Star laid plans for the construction of a fleet of three huge liners, larger than anything which had gone before, and which would offer the last word in passenger comfort. To reflect their size and class, they were to be called *Olympic, Titanic* and *Gigantic*. The design team was led by Lord Pirrie's brother-in-law Alexander Carlisle until his retirement in 1910, when he was succeeded by another of Pirrie's relatives, nephew Thomas Andrews. J. Bruce Ismay approved the design on 29 July 1908 and a contract was signed for the building of the first two ships. Work on keel number 400 – the *Olympic* – began at Harland & Wolff in December 1908; keel number 401 – the *Titanic* – was laid at the end of the following March.

The two sister ships were almost identical, although the *Titanic* was marginally longer at 882 ft 9 in. by virtue of the addition of an enclosed promenade for first-class passengers. Each ship boasted ten principal decks, a maximum speed of between 24 and 25 knots, a regular service speed of 21 knots and what was thought to be the latest in safety features. These included the installation of a Marconi wireless system for telegraphing messages at a range of up to 1,500 miles and a network of supposedly watertight compartments. The *Titanic* was divided into sixteen such compartments, formed by fifteen watertight bulkheads running across the hull. Six of these reached up to D deck, eight went up to E deck, but the other rose only as far as F deck. Each bulkhead was equipped with automatic watertight doors, held in the open position by a clutch which could be released instantly by means of an electric switch controlled from the captain's bridge. In a special issue published in the summer of 1911 *The Shipbuilder* magazine concluded: 'In the event of an accident, or at any time when it may be considered advisable, the captain can, by simply moving an electric switch, instantly close the doors throughout, practically making the vessel unsinkable.'

In concentrating their defences on transverse bulkheads, the *Titanic*'s designers had taken into account the experience of the Guion Line's *Arizona*, which, in 1879, had ploughed head-on into a 60-ft-high iceberg near the Newfoundland Grand Banks. Although her bows were wrecked, the *Arizona* remained afloat and was able to make it safely back to St John's. But the transverse bulkheads, while effective against a blow to the bows, failed to protect the *Titanic* from a side-on collision. The designers claimed that the *Titanic* would stay afloat even if two of the watertight compartments somehow became flooded but, by not extending the bulkheads sufficiently high within the interior of the ship, they left it vulnerable to a sudden inrush of water, which, as it transpired, would flood one compartment, surge over the top and fill the adjoining one.

An even more alarming oversight – and one which would take up countless newspaper column inches – was the issue of lifeboat provision. The outdated British Board of Trade regulations had not been amended since 1894, when the largest vessel afloat was the 12,950-ton *Campania*. The *Titanic* had a gross tonnage of 46,328. Under the regulations, all British vessels of over 10,000 tons were obliged to carry sixteen lifeboats with a capacity of 5,500 cubic feet, plus sufficient rafts and floats for 75 per cent of the capacity of the lifeboats. So, by law, the *Titanic* did not have to carry any more lifeboats than a 10,000-ton ship even though she would inevitably be carrying many more passengers. The *Titanic* had a capacity of 3,547 crew and passengers, yet was required to carry lifeboats for only 962 people.

Alexander Carlisle was so concerned about the lifeboat capacity that his original plans incorporated sixty-four boats, sufficient for everyone on board. However he was forced to revise his ideas because lifeboats took up too much deck space. International Mercantile Marine and its subsidiary the White Star Line demanded that any extra space be used to provide more spacious promenades for the all-important first-class passengers. Such misguided priorities meant that the *Titanic* carried the bare minimum sixteen lifeboats, although an additional four collapsible boats were provided to raise the overall seating capacity to 1,178. White Star prided itself on the fact that the *Titanic* therefore had boats in excess of the Board of Trade regulations, but the figure still represented just 53 per cent of the estimated 2,228 people on board at the time of the disaster, and only 30 per cent of the *Titanic*'s total capacity.

Naturally these considerations had no place in the minds of passengers and crew as they converged on Southampton on that April morning. The first-class travellers, at least, were more concerned with inspecting the ship's much-vaunted facilities, which included a gymnasium, squash court (at 2s 0d for half an hour), Turkish bath and swimming pool. Passenger accommodation was spread among the top seven decks, A to G, and was strictly segregated according to the three classes of ticket. First-class passengers were able to sample private, enclosed promenade decks (to keep out the chill evening air), and a splendid à la carte restaurant, while even the second-class state rooms were the equal of first-class accommodation on virtually any other ship of the day. Similarly, the state rooms for third-class (or steerage) passengers were as smart as second-class cabins on other vessels. At the very bottom end of the scale, the cheapest passage was £7 15s, including meals, where the accommodation for many, especially immigrants, consisted of an open dormitory way down on G deck. While first-class passengers could enjoy the ship's facilities well into the night, White Star encouraged all third-class travellers to retire by 10 p.m. Allegations of preferential treatment given to first-class passengers during the rescue – to the point where steerage passengers were said to have been forcibly prevented from reaching the lifeboats – would be a recurring theme of the *Titanic* tragedy.

White Star had anticipated a huge demand for tickets for the *Titanic*'s maiden voyage, yet the initial response had proved disappointing, mainly because a national coal strike in Britain had seriously damaged the shipping industry. Voyages were cancelled at short notice, leaving customers wary about making firm travel plans. The strike was not finally resolved until 6 April – four days before the *Titanic* was due to sail for New York. Faced with the prospect of a half-empty *Titanic* setting off on her much-hyped maiden voyage, White Star transferred a number of passengers to the *Titanic* from other liners. Most were happy to do so, but a few demurred. They had a strange feeling of foreboding about the majestic new ship.

Southampton Docks were a hive of activity from daybreak on the morning of 10 April. The general crew reported at 6 a.m. and were followed ninety minutes later by Captain Edward John Smith, an experienced seafarer who had been transferred from the *Olympic*. The first passengers started to turn up at 9.30 when the boat train arrived from London Waterloo. Among the 497 third-class passengers who would leave from Southampton were 180 Scandinavians, lured by White Star's aggressive advertising campaign in Norway and Sweden. The vast majority were emigrating to the United States and had booked their passage aboard 'the first available ship'. That ship was the *Titanic*.

The final boat train arrived at 11.30 a.m., carrying many of the 202 first-class passengers who were sailing from Southampton, and half an hour later – at the stroke of noon – three loud blasts on the *Titanic*'s powerful whistles heralded her departure. As she was cast off, eight crew members, who had slipped out for a last-minute pint, dashed along the pier in a desperate attempt to scramble board. Two just managed to reach the gangway before it was raised; the other six were left behind on the dock, cursing their luck.

The first stop was to be Cherbourg in northern France, followed by Queenstown in southern Ireland. From there, it was full steam ahead across the wide open waters of the Atlantic . . . and a date with destiny.

In the immediate aftermath of the disaster – which brought full-scale inquiries both in Britain and the United States – a number of questions needed answering. Had Captain Smith ignored warnings of ice? Was the *Titanic* making a speed record attempt? Why was the colossal iceberg not seen by the lookouts until the last minute? Why were some lifeboats allowed to leave half empty? Why were so few third-class passengers saved? Did officers of the *Titanic* open fire on third-class passengers to prevent them reaching the lifeboats? What was the identity of the mystery ship seen on the horizon? Could hundreds of lives have been saved had the nearby *Californian* responded more quickly? And, most important of all, how did a supposedly unsinkable ship come to end up at the bottom of the ocean? That some of these questions remain unanswered to this day accounts for the enduring fascination with the *Titanic* a hundred years after the event.

The story of the sinking of the *Titanic* has been told countless times since 1912 by authors and film producers alike, but no account is as graphic or revealing as those of the eye-witnesses, from the people who were actually there on that fateful night. Here, via contemporary newspaper reports and survivors' tales – many of which are from rare sources and have therefore never previously appeared in book form – the Hollywood tinsel is stripped away so that the real story of the *Titanic* can be told, step by step, from her glorious launch in Belfast to the sombre burial services for those who perished at sea. The all-too-brief journey takes in vivid accounts of the departure from Southampton (a dramatic affair in its own right), life on board the luxury liner and the moment of impact, described by one Able Seaman as 'just a trembling' while a trimmer on duty in the engine room experienced nothing more than 'a slight shock'. A first-class passenger recalled: 'It did not seem to me that there was any great impact at all. It was as though we went over a thousand marbles.' But while passengers were led to believe that everything was under control and that there was no cause for alarm, it became apparent to senior officers that the collision was infinitely more serious than anyone had imagined. The *Titanic* was slowly sinking.

As the evacuation process got under way, there are powerful descriptions of tearful farewells, panic, bravery, fear, resignation and, ultimately, the frantic scramble for lifeboats. Those who managed to find a place recount the horrendous conditions in the boats, of witnessing the great ship go under, of seeing human bodies bobbing up and down lifelessly in the sea, and of the enormous relief at being plucked from their nightmare by the rescue ship *Carpathia*. Some of the narratives throw up sizeable contradictions, but given the circumstances this is only to be expected.

Initial newspaper reports confidently stated that all on board the *Titanic* had been saved. But within a day the awful truth emerged that over 1,500 lives had been lost. The gathering of information was not helped by a virtual news blackout imposed by the *Carpathia*, but, when that ship docked at New York on the evening of 18 April, the world's press were on hand to describe the arrival and to snap up survivors' stories for exclusives. Many of the most poignant scenes took place at the quayside as friends and relatives hoped and prayed that their loved ones would be on board the *Carpathia*. For although a list of survivors had been issued in advance, many of the names were vague and incorrect. This was the moment of reckoning. For some, it would produce a sense of joyous relief; for others, inconsolable heartache.

The days and weeks that followed brought official inquiries, accusations and denials, reunions and burials. Newspapermen were on hand to record them all, complete with occasional inconsistencies, a spot or two of sensationalism, and their own peculiarly nationalistic slant on affairs. The American press were quick to blame the British for the disaster, citing survivor Bruce Ismay as the villain of the piece and emphasizing the heroism of all the American millionaires. The British press reacted by largely defending Ismay and another target, Sir Cosmo Duff Gordon, while printing allegations of cowardly behaviour by assorted Italians, Germans and Chinamen, basically anyone foreign. Some of these accounts, therefore, have to be taken with a hefty pinch of salt but they nevertheless provide an interesting insight into the prevailing feelings of the day. This, then, is the tale of history's most infamous maritime disaster as it was relayed in all its horror to the world in 1912.

Compiling this book would have been impossible without the help of the staff of the British Newspaper Library at Colindale. I would also like to thank the National Maritime Museum at Greenwich, Nottinghamshire Library Services, and, as always, Nick Robinson and Krystyna Green at Constable & Robinson.

INTRODUCTION

Most of the newspapers and magazines from which extracts have been taken for this book have long since ceased publication but nevertheless I have made every effort to contact any copyright holders. I sincerely apologize for any omissions.

Geoff Tibballs, May 2001

CHAPTER 1

A FLOATING HOTEL

ANOTHER BELFAST TRIUMPH

Launch of the Titanic

Each year the tide of progress rolls steadily on, relentlessly and unceasingly. There is no retardation, no sign of an end. Arts and crafts have reached heights that were undreamt of by the last generation. Science brings forth fresh marvels with each rising of the sun. Thinking men light on new ideas, and in a twinkling these ideas are accomplished facts. Nature has been forced to yield her secrets. Pioneers full of determination march from triumph to triumph. Great feats compel the world's admiration, and then sink into line, and are accepted as ordinary events, while others spring up to take their place. There has been no era like the present one in all history.

Another step on the road of evolution was accomplished today when the *Titanic*, the sister ship of the *Olympic*, which has just completed her steam trials, was launched at the Queen's Island. The triumphs of science and engineering have been many, and Belfast can well support its claim to be regarded as one of the leading pioneers, especially in the matter of shipbuilding. When the construction of the *Olympic* was contemplated doubts were expressed that such a monster undertaking could be carried out, but Messrs Harland & Wolff proved last October that the project was quite feasible, and that they were capable of building such a huge vessel. The *Olympic* and the *Titanic* are not merely ships: they are floating towns, with all the improvements and conveniences that are associated with cities. Both ships are, indeed, marvels of engineering.

The *Titanic* is of the same dimensions as the *Olympic*. The two boats represent the last word in shipbuilding. Messrs Harland & Wolff, by their construction, brought back to Belfast the blue riband of shipbuilding, which was taken from the city when the giant Cunarders, the *Lusitania* and the *Mauretania*, were turned out from yards on the other side of the Channel. The last big vessel built for the White Star Line was the *Adriatic*, which was launched in 1906, but she is easily eclipsed by the *Olympic* and the *Titanic*. Never before have such huge vessels floated on the ocean. A few years ago and anyone who suggested vessels of their size would have been laughed to scorn.

Messrs Ismay, Imrie and Co. have always endeavoured to lead the van with the White Star liners, and the two new giants worthily uphold their reputation as shipowners. The firm was not content to take the second place while other firms forged ahead. They have shown that they are determined to meet enterprise with enterprise. It now remains for some other large firm of shipowners to try to go one better. Messrs Harland & Wolff ably carried out the desire and orders of Messrs Ismay, Imrie and Co. and to them will always belong the honour and credit of being the constructors of the greatest vessels on the face of the globe – the *Olympic* and the *Titanic*. It takes a good amount of imagination to realize the marvel that has been accomplished with these two liners. Not only in size, but in equipment do they stand alone. They mark the beginning of an era.

It is safe to predict that the *Olympic* and the *Titanic* will enhance the great reputation already enjoyed by the line; they are without a peer on the ocean. Though so large, they are beautiful. Everything on board has been well – in some cases brilliantly

– conceived and admirably carried out, and passengers will find comfort, luxury, recreation, and health in the palatial apartments, the splendid promenades, the gymnasium, the squash racquet court, the Turkish baths, the swimming pond, palm court verandah etc. Moreover, the state rooms, in their situation, spaciousness and appointments, will be perfect havens of retreat, where many pleasant hours are spent, and where the time given to slumber and rest will be free from noise or other disturbance. Comfort, elegance, security – these are the qualities that appeal to passengers, and in the *Olympic* and the *Titanic* they abound. The horse has been described as the noblest work of the Creator. A ship may be said to be one of the finest of man's creations. Today ships are amongst the greatest civilizing agencies of the age and the White Star liners *Olympic* and *Titanic* – eloquent testimonies to the progress of mankind – will rank high in the achievements of the twentieth century.

The Launch

The *Titanic* entered the waters of the Lagan as quietly and gracefully as did her sister *Olympic*. The wave she displaced was infinitesimally small, she was pulled up short and sharp, and almost before one could realize that a new leviathan had been launched the spectators were already turning their steps homeward. In this respect those who took the trouble to go to the Queen's Island have ground for serious complaint against Lord Pirrie. So exact is he in his arrangements, and so admirably and completely are his plans carried out, that these big launches threaten to become quite uninteresting. A couple of gun-fires, the turn of a lever, and another floating palace is ready for the final equipment. You don't get that thrill of expectancy born of a doubt whether the vessel will move or not. You are just told to be there at a certain time, and if you are not you have only yourself to blame. Incidentally you have missed the sight of a lifetime. You have missed a thrilling demonstration and how brain and labour, working harmoniously together, can turn out, without fuss or excitement, a wonder of the world.

The *Titanic* looked very big as she lay on the stocks this morning; somehow she caught the eye more completely than did her sister ship. The vessel appeared the embodiment of strength, though at the same time her graceful lines made it difficult to believe that between her closely riveted plates was accommodation for the inhabitants of a respectably-sized town. High up in the air her stem lowered, the men on her deck looking mere specks on the skyline.

There was a big crowd in the yard, and the special stands erected showed a sea of faces, all waiting expectantly for the great event of the day. Within the railed-off enclosure round the ship all was well-ordered confusion. Foremen got their orders from principals, and transmitted them to the men waiting to execute them. Lord Pirrie was the dominant figure. In yachting attire he was here, there, and everywhere, giving orders and inquiring into the minutest detail.

From a quarter to twelve onwards the comparative silence became disturbed by the incessant rapping of hammers, as the final shores were being knocked away. Then again came silence. Rockets went up with two loud reports, and everyone was on the tiptoe of expectancy, for this was the first signal to stand clear, and men were seen scurrying from beneath the great mass of steel. Their work had been completed. The *Titanic* was only held in check by the hydraulic lever.

Then came the final denouement, suddenly, almost unexpectedly, for it wanted three minutes to the advertized time of the launch. Two more loud reports were heard, and almost before the spectators had time to realize that the *Titanic* was about to leave the stocks, the launch was an accomplished fact. Lord Pirrie gave the signal, the releasing valve was opened, and while the crowd still wondered the *Titanic* slid slowly, but gracefully, down to the river as straight as a die between the giant gantries which seemed almost to touch her sides. So far so good. The next question which sprang to mind was, would she be checked safely? This was quickly answered, for the drags and anchors worked with mathematical precision, and the great liner was pulled up within her own length, and rested peacefully on the water until she was taken charge of by tugs and escorted to her berth. The actual time of launch was sixty-three seconds.

A great many brains and hands have been concerned in the construction of the *Titanic* and her sister ship, but, as is well known, the master mind of the whole achievement has been Lord Pirrie, who designed the vessels and has personally taken the responsibility of their construction from keel to truck, also their arrangements, decorations and equipment. It is not often given to a man, even at the zenith of his career, to achieve so notable a triumph as is represented by the completion of the trials of the *Olympic* and the launch of the *Titanic* on the same day, which moreover, by a happy coincidence is the birthday of both Lord and Lady Pirrie. Their many friends, and all interested in the new vessels, will regard this and the beautiful weather under which the events have taken place as a fortuitous combination of circumstances of the most auspicious character.

FROM THE COUNTY ANTRIM SIDE

Thousands upon thousands of people assembled at all parts of the docks near to or opposite Messrs Harland & Wolff to enjoy the sight, but perhaps no finer view was secured than that in the vicinity of the Spencer Basin, which is situated on the County Antrim side of the river. Access to the basin was gained from Corporation Street right down past the timber piles, and from ten o'clock on till near noon, the roadway was thronged with men and women, boys and girls, from all classes of Belfast folk. The weather was brilliantly fine, and the gay colours of the ladies' dresses lent an animated brightness to a scene which on other days of the year is composed of dull piles of wood and stacks of coal, and with everything gay to the eye, and with the expectation of seeing the

Olympic's sister ship take her plunge, everyone was in the best spirits. Down at the basin every possible point of vantage was taken up, the timber piles and coal stacks were utilized as grand stands for the time being, and lorries drawn up alongside the front of the river were also greatly utilized, the carters doing a rich day's work by charging twopence per head for standing room.

(*Ulster Echo*, 31 May 1911)

THE LAUNCH OF THE *TITANIC*

Another Triumph of Belfast Shipbuilding

It took exactly sixty-two seconds for a launching weight of no less than 25,000 tons, travelling at a speed of twelve knots, to slip down the ways into deep water. And the amazing thing about it all was its seeming simplicity. As a nation we do great things quietly; and some of our overseas visitors who saw the *Titanic* enter with such quiet dignity the brown waters of the Lagan on Wednesday last must have thought for a moment that the launch of a 45,000-ton liner was quite an everyday incident in this famous Ulster shipyard. Indeed, it is not, of course, but Belfast is quickly educating us all to the idea that the only insurmountable limit to size in ships is the depth of the sea!

With the experience of the *Olympic* behind them the townsfolk of the Ulster capital took the launch of the *Titanic* almost as a matter of routine. Certainly there was no thought of failure or even hitch, and while there was a most pardonable display of local pride in this latest vessel sent forth from the Queen's Island yard, there was not, perhaps, the same element of novelty about the doings of the day, and the crowds that witnessed the launch were, I think, smaller than when the *Olympic* was waterborne on Oct. 20 last. Even so they were vast and enthusiastic, and the minute of launching thrilled them as before. The day was one of summer sunshine, and the scene was bright with dainty frocks, and with hats which in size paid a delicate compliment to the huge vessel herself.

It was in keeping with the traditions of the yard that there should be as little ceremony about the launch as possible. This rule appeared even to restrain the display of bunting visible within the shipyard itself. Save for the British ensign, the Stars and Stripes, and flags signalling 'Good Luck!' which waved in a line from the landward edge of the gantries under which the vessel lay, there was an entire absence of decorative colour. The enormous proportions of the liner, it is true, did not suffer thereby, while the business character of what was being done gained immeasurably. Everything was carried out strictly to a well-defined programme, for everything was in order for the critical moment. There was no appearance of rush or anxiety, because the thing to be done was too great for any eleventh-hour hurry. Exactly an hour and a half before the vessel moved the clang of hammers under her indicated to the leisurely assembling people that the vessel's minutes on earth were numbered. That reads like an obituary notice; but in truth it is rather an intimation of birth. For every shore that was knocked away the bonds that bound this Titan to earth were being released; only the hydraulic triggers held her in place, and on these the pressure was rapidly increasing.

Meanwhile the stands erected for the convenience of the spectators within the yard were being gradually filled, and there successively appeared within the closely guarded foreground round the ship men of note in the shipping and shipbuilding world. The Right Hon. Lord Pirrie had been in the yard all the morning superintending the final arrangements for the launch of a vessel which owes her design and construction largely to his genius. A few minutes before noon (Irish time) he received the distinguished White Star party in the offices of the yard, and punctually at noon the owners' representatives took their places on the stand reserved for them by the side of the vessel and immediately in front of the mechanism that released her. In addition to Lord and Lady Pirrie and the directors and officials of the shipyard, prominent among these were Mr J. Bruce Ismay, chairman of the White Star Line; Mr J. Pierpont Morgan and Mr E. C. Grenfell (his partner); Mr Harold

A. Sanderson, general manager of the White Star Line; Mr Henry Concannon, assistant manager; Mr P. E. Curry, Southampton manager; Mr E. W. Bond, assistant Southampton manager; Mr R. J. A. Shelley, Liverpool; Mr M. H. Workman, London; Mr Charles F. Torrey, managing director of the Atlantic Transport Line; Mr John Lee, Mr Charles Payne, directors of Messrs Harland & Wolff; Mr J. W. Kempster, director; Mr R. Crighton, director; Mr Wm. Bailey, secretary; and Mr Saxon J. Payne, assistant secretary.

On a final tour of inspection Lord Pirrie left his guests to visit the platforms at the vessel's bows. A few minutes after noon a red flag was run up at the stern as a signal of preparation. Five minutes later two detonators warning the men to stand clear broke upon the hushed crowd to tell them all was ready and the mighty *Titanic* was straining to be set free. At 12.12 the firing of another rocket was followed immediately by Lord Pirrie giving the signal. For a second or two nothing happened. Then without fuss, without hesitancy, with much dignity and with an old-fashioned curtsy as her bows finally left the ways, the *Titanic* was waterborne. The supports that remained fell gently over like a pack of cards, and so smoothly and so sweetly did she take the water that there was practically no backwash. Her launching weight of 25,000 tons was slightly less than that of the *Olympic*.

How easily to the eye of the onlooker was this huge mass of ineffective power brought to! She was motionless apparently in less than her own length from the water edge of the slipway, though it must in reality have been more. Powerful forces were at work, restraining her from going one foot beyond the limits assigned. I understand that Messrs. Bullivant & Co., Ltd., the well-known steel wire rope makers, were responsible for the manufacture of the ropes used in the launch. Six check ropes and two drag ropes were used, each of these being eight inches in circumference and having a guaranteed breaking strain of over 200 tons. In the case of both the *Olympic* and *Titanic* wire ropes for mooring purposes were adopted, and these were supplied by the same firm. These hawsers are of 9½-inch circumference, and were guaranteed, together with thimbles and splices, to withstand a breaking strain of 280 tons. Fussy but vigorous little tugs helped, too; and the well-known Mersey tugs *Herculaneum, Hornby*, and *Alexandra* were soon engaged in hauling the liner to the new fitting-out wharf below the Alexandra Graving Dock, while a score of small row boats were rescuing floating tallow from the water.

And through it all while the crowds cheered themselves hoarse, and while most of the spectators were homeward moving, Mr Pierpont Morgan sat in the owners' stand and smoked a contemplative cigar (brand unknown). Lord Pirrie beamed on all (and there were many) who congratulated him on the splendid success of the launch. These twentieth-century magicians deal not with spell and incantation, yet the magic of their work has surely no equal! than the *Titanic*, Lord and Lady Pirrie, both of whose birthdays, singularly enough, fell on Wednesday, could have had no better present to give to the world of intercourse, whereby seas are made narrower and hand may grasp hand round the wide world. Happy, indeed, were these coincidences, and they may be held to augur well for the future career of No. 401.

(*The Shipping World*, 7 June 1911)

The quarterly publication, *The Shipbuilder*, produced a special issue in the summer of 1911 to describe in detail the sumptuous accommodation provided for first-class passengers by the two new White Star Liners, *Olympic* and *Titanic*.

The restaurant, situated on the bridge deck, will be considered by many competent judges the most enticing apartment in the vessel. It is 60ft long and 45ft wide. The style of decoration adopted is that of the Louis Seize period. The room is panelled from floor to ceiling in beautifully marked French walnut of a delicate light fawn brown colour, the mouldings and ornaments being richly carved and gilded. Large electric light brackets, cast and finely chased in brass and gilt, and holding candle lamps, are fixed in the centre of the large panels. On the right of the entrance is a buffet with a marble top of *fleur de pêche*, supported by panelling and plaster recalling the design of the wall panels. The room is well lighted by large bay windows, a distinctive and novel feature which creates an impression of spaciousness. The windows are divided into squares by ornamental metal bars, and are draped with plain fawn silk curtains having flowered borders and richly embroidered pelmets. Every small detail, including even the fastenings and hinges, has been carried out with due regard to purity of style. The ceiling is of plaster, in which delicately modelled flowers in low relief combine to form a simple design of trellis in the centre and garlands in the bays. At various well-selected points hang clusters of lights ornamented with chased metal gilt and crystals. The floor is covered with an elegant pile carpet of Axminster make, having a non-obtrusive design of the Louis Seize period. The colour is a delicate *vieux rose*, of the shade known as *Rose du Barri*, in perfect harmony with the surroundings.

Comfort has been well considered in the arrangement of the furniture. Small tables have been provided to accommodate from two to eight persons, and crystal standard lamps with rose-coloured shades illuminate each table. The chairs have been well studied, and are made in similar light French walnut to the walls. The woodwork is carved and finished with a waxed surface. The upholstery covering is Aubusson tapestry in quiet tones, representing a *treillage* of roses. For convenience of service there are several dumb waiters encircling the columns and forming part of the decorative scheme. A bandstand, partly recessed and raised on a platform, is provided at the after end. On either side of the bandstand is a carved buffet, the lower portion of which is used for cutlery and the upper portion for the silver service, thus completing the necessities for a well-appointed restaurant to satisfy every requirement ...

Comparing the *Titanic* to its sister ship, the article went on:

The reception room adjoining the first-class dining saloon having proved such a popular feature on the *Olympic*, in the case of the

Titanic a reception room has also been provided in connection with the restaurant, consisting of a large and spacious lounge decorated in the Georgian style. Here friends and parties will meet prior to taking their seats in the restaurant. The elegant settees and easy chairs are upholstered in silk of carmine colour, with embroideries applied in tasteful design. The breadth of treatment and the carefully proportioned panels on the walls, with richly carved cornice and surrounding mouldings, form an impressive *ensemble*, which is distinctly pleasing to the eye.

(*The Shipbuilder*, June 1911)

THE WORLD'S BIGGEST SHIP

A Visit to the Olympic *at Southampton*

The state rooms in each of the three classes are distinguished by being exceptionally large and lofty, while the furnishings are probably without parallel on any vessel afloat. Everything has been done to ensure the comfort of the passenger, and he is given a degree of privacy hitherto almost unknown on board ship. Down to the least detail his wishes have been consulted. The wash-stand accessories are many; his wardrobe convenient to all his immediate needs; his couch the best he could possibly wish for. The popular Marshall 'Vi-Spring' mattresses (formerly known as 'Hare Spring') manufactured by the Marshall Sanitary Mattress Co. Ltd, London, are used very extensively on this ship, as they will be used on her sister ship, the *Titanic*; and in many other respects these state rooms will appeal to all sorts and conditions of voyagers. The second-class and third-class are furnished in a style that represents, without exaggeration, what was thought sufficient for the first-class only a few short years ago; and if there is one thing more than another that should induce second and third-class travellers to patronize this great liner, it is the fact that they share in all the advantages of an absolutely steady, practically unsinkable ship with those who can afford the highest-priced suite of rooms that the *Olympic* can boast. This is a consideration of the first importance to all who are in the least afraid of the sea.

But it is when we reach the public rooms that we best realize what the large vessel means. She is a floating palace; and in three or four of the principal rooms there is nothing to distinguish them from the rooms of some stately country house or elegantly furnished hotel on the sea front. It is difficult to believe we are afloat. This particularly applies to the reading and writing room which Lord Pirrie has confessed is his favourite. Fireplace, bow windows, and the furnishings generally convey an idea of a retreat in some country house amid 'haunts of ancient peace'.

(*The Shipping World*, 14 June 1911)

Ten months later, in the immediate aftermath of the disaster, a number of newspapers quoted extensively from the official White Star brochure to illustrate the splendour that was the *Titanic*. The *Boston Post* from Masschusetts wrote:

Perhaps the best description of the giant *Titanic* is that which was furnished by the officers of the White Star Line at the time of the *Titanic*'s launching on June 15, 1911.

This description, which also embraced the sister ship *Olympic*, was as follows:

In the White Star Line's new triple-screw steamers *Olympic* and *Titanic* are epitomized all the science and skill of a century of steam navigation. The same spirit which actuated the White Star Line in introducing into the Atlantic passenger trade the steamers *Oceanic*, the first steamer to surpass the length of the *Great Eastern* – *Celtic, Cedric, Baltic,* and, latterly, the giant *Adriatic* – has produced these new surpassing ships.

Figures speak most concisely and eloquently of the supremacy of the *Olympic* and *Titanic*. The largest plates employed in the hull are 36ft long, weighing four and a half tons each, and the largest steel beam used is 92ft long, the weight of this double beam being four tons.

Further, the colossal rudder, which is to be operated electrically, weighs 100 tons, the anchors 15½ tons each, the center turbine propeller 22 tons and each of the two wing propellers 38 tons.

The huge after 'bossarms', from which are suspended the three propeller shafts, tip the scales at 73½ tons, and the forward 'bossarms' at 45 tons. It is also interesting to note that each link in the anchor chains weighs 175lb. In each ship the unusually large number of sidelights and windows – over 2,000 – add much to the brightness and cheerful effect of the public rooms and passenger cabins.

As already intimated, nothing has been left to chance in the construction of these superb ships, and besides being the largest and heaviest vessels ever built, they are also undoubtedly the strongest.

Their towering hulls are moulded to battle against the seven seas, and boast, in each ship, the presence of three million rivets (weighing about 1,200 tons) holding together the solid plates of steel. To ensure stability in binding the heavy plates in the double bottom of each ship a half million rivets, weighing about 270 tons, have been used.

The whole plating of the hulls has been riveted for hydraulic power, with an almost entire absence of the usual deafening noises, new type seven-ton riveting machines, suspended from travelling cranes having accomplished this work quickly and well.

Safety Assured
The double bottom referred to extends the full length of each vessel, varying from 5ft 3in. to 6ft 3in. in depth and lends added strength to the hull. The subdivision of the hulls of the *Olympic* and *Titanic* into fifteen compartments separated by watertight bulkheads of steel further assures the safety of the vessels.

The gigantic size of these steamers is best appreciated when it is recalled that in length each vessel overtops by 182½ ft the height of the Metropolitan Tower in New York – the highest office building in the world, and 132½ ft beyond the height of the new Woolworth building now under construction.

Each ship being four times as long as the height of the famous Bunker Hill Monument and 327ft longer than the height of the Washington Monument, their massive measurements far excel America's most famous memorials.

Bilge or fin keels prevent these fine steamers from rolling, and their machinery is the unique combination of reciprocating engines (operating the two wing propellers) and a low-pressure turbine (operating the center propeller), an ideal arrangement which has been tested thoroughly and found most satisfactory from an engineering point of view in the White Star Line's Canadian service steamer *Laurentic*.

Spaciousness and Beauty
A rapid survey of the 11 steel decks of the *Olympic* and *Titanic* reveals the most careful and comprehensive preparations in every department. Three elevators in the first class and one in the second class provide a comfortable means of access between decks, which, on ships so vast as these, saves the passenger much effort.

On the topmost deck – cheerfully named the 'Sun' deck – one finds a commodious open promenade with a large area for deck sports. All the enticing outdoor games that seem exclusively identified with the pleasant hours aboard ship are played here, and the ardent devotee of the putter and the niblick can keep in 'top trim' by assiduous attention to the fascinating pastime, 'deck-golf', with its 18-hole course.

Here also is located the roomy gymnasium with its complete equipment, which will attract many passengers seeking mild and healthful diversion. Forward are the officers' quarters and the wheelhouse and chart rooms.

Comfort and Luxury

On the vast area of the upper promenade deck 'A' just below, the steamer's chair 'brigade' will be very much in evidence, as here are many sheltered nooks and corners where the bracing salt air can be enjoyed with the utmost comfort.

There is also abundant space for promenading. On this deck are situated several of the most charming public apartments. The extensive, richly decorated Lounge, one of the chief social centres, the spacious, elegantly fitted smoke room vie in interest with the exquisitely furnished reading and writing room with its delicate colourings.

All these public cabins have the spacious, graceful windows of the various colonial periods, which easily cause the impression that outside one might see lawns and trees; and, although this be not so, the view is one excelled by no other in the world – the mighty grandeur of the ever-changing sea.

The amateur photographers will be especially pleased with the photographic dark room, which is provided with fittings of the latest pattern, all available without charge.

The palm court and veranda café, where one may while away many a pleasant half-hour, are also situated aft on this deck, and will be found largely reminiscent of the delightful boulevard cafés of Paris and Vienna. The wide outlook from this vantage point adds greatly to the pleasure of those who visit its precincts.

On the upper promenade deck are also a large number of the choicest state rooms both as to location and luxurious furnishings, which are in excellent taste.

A striking and at the same time a pleasant feature of the promenade deck 'B' is the glass-enclosed section. As a protection against inclement weather, its windows make it a pleasing and perfect shelter, while on cold, clear days when the windows are closed to prevent the ingress of icy breezes, the deck becomes a veritable sun parlour, and here at times promenade concerts by the ship's professional string orchestra and delightful evening dances are held with every degree of comfort. Under gleaming vari-coloured electric light bulbs and with gay streamers adding their brightness, one could hardly wish for a more pleasurable scene.

On this deck are also many cabins and apartments de luxe, the latter consisting of several rooms en suite, having their own private bath and toilet arrangements, with rooms for servants adjoining. The beautifully appointed restaurant with its superior à la carte service, seats 160 people and is designed to cater to those travellers who prefer merely to engage their cabins and transportation, and as a separate transaction avail themselves of the restaurant's facilities.

On the upper deck 'C', in addition to the passenger state rooms and apartments de luxe, one will find the ship's inquiry office, where the business of this floating city will be transacted. Aft on this deck an important innovation is the special maids' and valets' saloon, where servants may congregate and where their meals will be served.

The saloon deck 'D', just below the upper deck 'C', has as its most prominent feature that important gathering-place, the grand dining saloon, seating 550 passengers, and extending the full width of the ship, 92½ ft.

Small tables are everywhere in attendance, and the alcoves, which congenial parties will find especially pleasant, lend an air of cosiness to this apartment which is, at first view, so vast and impressive. The large leaded glass windows about the sides of the room are an unusual feature, assisting materially in ventilating and lighting the saloon. On this deck also is the beautifully decorated reception room, whose handsome furnishings and hangings add to it a distinct note of refined taste.

Among many other special attractions for passengers in the first class are the Turkish and electric bath establishment, completely equipped with a hot room, temperate room, cooling room, shampoo rooms and massage rooms, but more notably, the adjoining large salt water swimming pool, of even greater dimensions than that on the company's well-known steamer

Adriatic, which was the first ship to be equipped with these delightful innovations.

The remarkable dimensions of the *Olympic* and *Titanic* have also made it possible to introduce for the pleasure of passengers a full sized tennis and handball court, 30ft long, extending through two decks, where these healthful exercises may be indulged in.

(*Boston Post*, 15 April 1912)

LAUNCH OF THE *TITANIC*

The general arrangements for launching the 45,000-ton White Star steamship *Titanic*, which occurred on May 31 at the Harland & Wolff shipyard at Belfast, were similar to those in the case of the sister ship *Olympic*, which were described in the December 1910 issue of *International Marine Engineering*. The vessel was held on the ways by hydraulic triggers, only requiring to be released by the opening of a valve in order to let her glide into the water. Her launching time was sixty-two seconds, her speed twelve knots and her weight about 25,000 tons.

The *Titanic* is of the same design as the *Olympic*. The following are the leading dimensions:

Length over all	882ft 9in.
Length between perpendiculars	850ft
Breadth, extreme	92ft 6in.
Depth, moulded, keel to top of beam, bridge deck	73ft 6in.
Total height from keel to navigating bridge	104ft.
Gross tonnage (about)	45,000 tons
Load draft	34ft 6in.
Displacement (about)	60,000 tons
Indicated horsepower of reciprocating engines	30,000
Shaft horsepower of turbine engines	16,000
Speed	21 knots

The *Titanic* is a triple-screw steamer having a combination of reciprocating engines with a low-pressure turbine. The reciprocating engines exhaust into the low-pressure turbine, which drives the central propeller. The reciprocating engines which drive the wing propellers are sufficient for manoeuvring in and out of port and going astern. There is no necessity for an astern turbine, which is required in steamers fitted with turbines only. There are 29 boilers for the ship, having in all 159 furnaces. All of the boilers are 15 feet 9 inches in diameter; but 24 are double-ended, being 20 feet long, while five are single-ended, being 11 feet 9 inches long. The shells of the latter are formed by one plate; the others have, as usual, three strakes. At each end there are three furnaces, all of the Morison type, with an inside diameter of 3 feet 9 inches. The working pressure is 215 pounds, and this under natural draft. The boilers are arranged in six watertight compartments, and owing to the width of the ship it has been possible to fit five boilers athwartship. The boiler compartment nearest the machinery space accommodates the single-ended boilers, and these are arranged for running the auxiliary machinery while the ship is in port, as well as for the general steam supply when the ship is at sea.

In each of the five large boiler rooms there are two See's ash ejectors, and in addition there are four of Railton & Campbell's ash hoists for use when the vessels are in port. A large duplex pump of Harland & Wolff's own make is fitted in a separate room in each boiler room, the advantage being that the working parts of the pumps are not injuriously affected by dust. The boilers are fitted with the Ross-Schofield patent marine boiler circulators. The exhaust turbine, instead of being in the same engine room with the two sets of piston engines, as in earlier ships, is accommodated in a separate compartment abaft the main reciprocating engine room, and divided from it by a watertight bulkhead. In the reciprocating engine room there are two sets of main engines – one driving the port and the other the starboard shaft. In the wings there are the main feed and hot-well, bilge, sanitary, ballast and fresh-water pumps, and a contact and surface heater; while on the port side a space has been found for an extensive refrigerating plant under the immediate observation of the engineers.

The two sets of reciprocating engines – one driving each wing shaft – are of the four-crank type, arranged to work at 215 pounds per square inch, and to exhaust at a pressure of about nine pounds absolute. These engines are on the balanced principle. The high-pressure cylinder is 54 inches in diameter, immediate cylinder 84 inches, and each of the two low-pressure cylinders 97 inches in diameter, the stroke being 75 inches in all cases. The exhaust steam turbine, by which the central screw will be driven, is of the Parsons type, to take exhaust steam at about nine pounds absolute and expand it down to one pound absolute. The condensing plant is designed to attain a vacuum of 28½ inches (with the barometer at 30 inches), the temperature of circulating water being 55 degrees to 60 degrees F. The rotor, built up of steel forgings, is 12 feet in diameter, and the blades range in length from 18 inches to 25½ inches, built on the segmental principle, laced on wire through the blades and distance pieces at the roots, and with binding soldered on the edge as usual. The length of the rotor between the extreme edges of the first and last ring of blades in 13 feet 8 inches. There is, as has been said, no astern turbine, as the centre shaft is put out of action when the ship is being manoeuvred. The bearings, thrust and governor are of the ordinary type adopted in Parsons turbines. The turbine can be rotated by electric motor, and the usual lifting gear for the upper half of the casing and the rotor is also actuated by electric motor. The rotor weighs about 130 tons, and the turbine complete weighs 420 tons. The turbine shaft is 20½ inches in diameter, the tail shaft 22½ inches, each with a 10-inch hole bored through it.

The propeller driven by the turbine is built solid, of manganese bronze with four blades, the diameter being 16 feet 6 inches. It is designed to run at 165 revolutions per minute when the power developed is 16,000 shaft-horsepower. As usual with turbine condensers, the inlet is of the full length of the condenser, and is well stayed vertically by division plates. In line with these there are in the condenser corresponding division plates, which secure an equal distribution of steam over the whole of the condenser tube area. The pear shape concentrates the tube surface at the point where the largest volume of steam is admitted where it is most needed.

There are four sets of gunmetal circulating pumps, two for the port and two for the starboard condensers, with 29-inch inlet pipes and driven by compound engines of Harland & Wolff's own make. For each condenser there are two sets of Weir's air pumps of the 'dual' type, both air and water-barrels being 36 inches in diameter by 21 inches stroke.

For generating electric current, both for light and power, four 400-kilowatt engines and dynamos are fitted in a separate water-tight compartment aft of the turbine room at tank-top level. The engines, which indicate each about 580 horse-power, are of the Allen vertical three-crank compound, enclosed forced lubrication type, running at 325 revolutions per minute. Each set has one high-pressure cylinder, 17 inches in diameter, and two low-pressure cylinders, each 20 inches in diameter, with a 13-inch stroke. They take steam at 185 pounds pressure per square inch. The engines exhaust either into a surface heater or to the condenser. Each engine is direct-coupled to a compound-wound, continuous-current dynamo, with an output of 100 volts and 4,000 amperes. Their collective capacity is 16,000 amperes. The dynamos are of the ten-pole type, and are fitted with inter-poles.

In addition to the four main generating sets there are two 30-kilowatt engines and dynamos, placed in a recess off the turbine room at saloon-deck level. Three sets can be supplied with steam from either of several boiler rooms, and will be available for emergency purposes. They are similar to the main sets, but the engines are of the two-crank type. The distribution of current is effected on the single-wire system, and is controlled and metered at a main switchboard placed on a gallery in the electric engine room, to which the main dynamo cables and feeders are connected. The latter pass up through port and starboard cable trunks to the various decks, radiating from thence to master switch and fuse boxes grouped at convenient points in the machinery spaces and accommodation, from whence run branches to the distribution fuse boxes scattered throughout the vessel controlling the lamps and motors.

A complete system of electric lighting is provided, and electricity is also largely employed for heating as well as for motive power, including 75 motor-driven 'Sirocco' fans, from 55 inches to 20 inches in diameter, for ventilating all the passenger and crew spaces as well as the engine and boiler rooms. All the fan motors are provided with automatic and hand-speed regulation.

The shell plating of the ship is remarkably heavy. It is mostly of plates six feet wide and of about 30 feet in length. The width tapers towards the ends. The laps are treble-riveted, and the shell strakes in the way of the shelter and boat decks have been hydraulically riveted. Also the turn of the bilge, where bilge keels 25 inches deep are fitted for 295 feet of the length of the vessel amidships. There are fifteen transverse watertight bulkheads, extending from the double bottom to the upper deck at the forward end of the ship, and to the saloon deck at the after end far above the load water-line. The room in which the reciprocating engines are fitted is the largest of the watertight compartments, and is about 69 feet long; while the turbine room is 57 feet long. The boiler rooms are generally 57 feet long, with the exception of that nearest the reciprocating engine compartment. The holds are 50 feet long. Any two compartments may be flooded without in any way involving the safety of the ship. The two decks forming the superstructure of the ship and the navigating bridge are built to ensure a high degree of rigidity. At the sides they are supported on built-up frames, in line with the hull frames, but at wider intervals. The deck houses are specially stiffened by channel-section steel fitted in the framework, and where, as on the boat deck, the public rooms pierce the deck, heavy brackets are introduced to increase strength against racking stresses when the ship is steaming through a heavy seaway. Expansion joints are made in the superstructure above the bridge deck at convenient points in the length – one forward and one aft, the whole structure being completely severed and the joints suitably covered.

The stern-frame was made by the Darlington Forge Company, and the total weight of the casting was about 190 tons, the stern frame being 70 tons, the side propeller brackets 73¼ tons, and the forward boss-arms 45 tons. The centre propeller, driven by the turbine, works in the usual stern-frame aperture, while the wing propellers are supported in brackets. The stern frame is of Siemens-Martin mild cast steel, of hollow or dish section, in two pieces, with large scraphs, one on the forward post and one on the after post, connected with best 'Lowmoor' iron rivets, two inches in diameter, the total weight of rivets being over a ton. They were all turned and fitted and specially closed with rams. There are in all 59 rivets in the forward and 54 rivets in the after scraphs. In the stern frame there is the boss for the shaft driven by the turbine, the lower portion of this part of the stern frame having a large palm cast on its extreme forward end, to give a solid connection to the after boss-arms and main structure of the vessel.

The rudder also has been constructed by the Darlington Forge Company, Ltd, and is of the usual elliptical type, of solid cast steel, built in five sections, coupled together with bolts varying from three and a half inches to two inches in diameter. The top section of the rudder is of forged steel from a special ingot of the same quality as naval gun jackets. On the completion of the forging an inspection hole was bored through the stock of the rudder in order to ensure that there were no flaws.

There are ten decks in the ship, named from the bottom upwards: Lower orlop, orlop, lower, middle, upper, saloon, shelter, bridge, promenade and boat. The passenger decks – promenade, bridge, shelter, saloon, upper, middle and lower – are named alphabetically A, B, C, D, E, F, G. Two of the decks are above the moulded structure of the ship. The lower orlop, orlop and lower decks do not extend for the complete length of the structure, being interrupted for the machinery accommodation. The bridge deck extends for a length of 550 feet amidships, the forecastle and poop on the same level being respectively 128 feet and 106 feet long. The promenade and boat decks are also over 500 feet long. The first-class passengers are accommodated on the five levels from the upper to the promenade decks. The second-class passengers have their accommodation on the middle, upper and saloon decks, and the third-class passengers on the lower deck, forward and aft, and on the middle, upper and saloon decks aft.

The steering gear is fitted on the shelter deck, and is very massive, the diameter of the rudder stock – 23½ inches – affording some idea of the dimensions. The gear is of Harland & Wolff's wheel-and-pinion type, working through a spring quadrant on the rudder head, with two independent engines, having triple cylinders, one on each side. Either engine suffices for the working of the gear, the other being a stand-by. The gear is controlled from the navigating bridge by telemotors and from the docking bridge aft by mechanical means.

The navigating appliances include, in addition to two compasses on the captain's bridge and one on the docking bridge aft, a standard compass on an isolated brass-work platform in the centre of the ship, at a height of 12 feet above all iron work and 78 feet above the waterline. Adjacent to the bridge there are to be two electrically-driven sounding machines, arranged with spars to enable soundings to be taken when the ship is going at a good speed.

The vessel is to be fitted with complete installation for receiving submarine signals. The lifeboats, which are 30 feet long, are mounted on special davits on the boat deck. The ship is designed for two masts, 205 feet above the average draft line, a height necessary to take the Marconi aerial wires, and to ensure that these will be at least 50 feet above the top of the funnels and thus clear of the funnel gases. The masts are also for working the cargo by means of cargo spans, and in addition there is on the foremasts a derrick for lifting motor cars, which will be accommodated in one of the foreholds. There are three cargo hatches forward and three aft. All the hatches in the after part of the ship are served by electric cranes of the same make; two of these will be on the promenade deck; there being two small hatches to the hold below, so as to form a minimum of interference with the promenading space.

There are three elevators in the main companion-way and one in the main second-class companion-way. For first-class passengers there are 30 suite rooms on the bridge deck and 39 on the shelter deck. These are so arranged that they can be let in groups to form suites including bedrooms, with baths, etc., with communicating doors. On each of these two decks, close to the companion-ways on either side, adjacent rooms are fitted up as sitting or dining room. In all there are nearly 330 first-class rooms, and 100 of these are single-berth rooms. There is accommodation for over 750 first-class passengers.

For second-class passengers the rooms are arranged as two or four-berth rooms, the total number of second-class passengers being over 550. For the third-class passengers there are a large number of enclosed berths, there being 84 two-berth rooms. The total number of third-class passengers provided for is over 1,100.

The first-class promenades on the three top decks in the ship will be exceptionally fine. The bridge deck promenade is entirely enclosed. It is a space over 400 feet long, 13 feet minimum width each side of the vessel, and with a solid side screen fitted with large, square lowering windows. The deck above this is the principal promenade deck, and is entirely devoted to first-class passengers. It is more than 500 feet long, and will form a splendid promenade, the width in parts exceeding 30 feet. The topmost, or boat deck, is also devoted to first-class promenading, and is 200 feet long and the full width of the ship. The first-class dining saloon is designed to accommodate 532 passengers, and ample smoke-room, restaurant, lounge and reading and writing room accommodation is also provided.

The second-class dining saloon is situated on the saloon deck aft. It extends the full breadth of the vessel, with extra large opening pivoted sidelights arranged in pairs. The panelling of this room will be carried out in oak. The third-class dining accommodation is situated amidships on the middle deck, and consists of two saloons well lighted with sidelights and will be finished enamel white.

(International Marine Engineering, July 1911)

SHIPS AND THE STRIKE

White Star to Reduce Speed

The effect of the strike on local shipping, as referred to on our shipping page, where it is mentioned that the White Star Line are confident that the *Olympic* will sail next Wednesday, and that the *Titanic* will commence her maiden voyage a week later. We hear, however, that an order has been given that the speed of the vessels shall be reduced, in order that as much coal as possible shall be saved. The ships are capable of a speed of nearly twenty-three knots, but to maintain this rate the average consumption of coal is about 600 tons per day. A speed of over twenty knots makes a very big demand on the bunkers, but steady steaming at about twenty knots will enable a big economy to be effected. It is the additional knot or two that makes speed expensive. The Company has therefore decided to limit the speed of the *Olympic* and the *Titanic* to twenty knots. It will involve but a few hours extra at sea. It is hoped that whatever else happens the *Olympic* and the *Titanic* will be able to sail regularly, but it is not yet certain whether the *Oceanic* will take her scheduled sailing on April 17. At the moment, this vessel is in dry-dock. She damaged a propeller on her last voyage, and this is now being put right. If the strike ends in the course of a week or so, the *Oceanic* is almost sure to sail on April 17, but at the moment nothing is certain except the fact that the Company are determined to sail the *Olympic* and the *Titanic* on Wednesday and Wednesday week respectively.

(Southampton Times and Hampshire Express,
30 March 1912)

The White Star berth will not be vacant very long after the *Olympic*'s departure on Wednesday, for the *Titanic* is due to arrive here on the same day. Whatever happens in regard to the coal trouble, the White Star Line are as certain as they can be that not only will the *Olympic* get away next Wednesday, but that the *Titanic* will be able to sail on her maiden voyage next week. The *Olympic* has picked up a large quantity of coal in New York, and the *Titanic* is assured of having her bunkers filled. The bookings for both sailings are heavy, and the departure of the two largest ships in the world from the Docks within a few days of each other will be an event of considerable interest.

The officials have had so much worry lately that we gladly acceded to their request for our help in making it known that the *Titanic* will not be open for inspection. Already applications have been received from all quarters for permission to visit the ship, and the courteous 'No' has been so often uttered that it was suggested that the services of a gramophone should be requisitioned at once! There is to be no public ceremony of any kind. The *Titanic* will enter the Solent without the blare of trumpets or the display of the silver oar. A lot of work will have to be done on board the ship during her week's sojourn at the Docks, and it will be impossible to allow people on board 'except on business'.

The statement was made this week that the *Titanic* was a thousand tons larger than the *Olympic*. This is not so. She is a triple screw steamer of 45,000. She differs from the *Olympic* in regard to some features of her accommodation. We have previously referred to the arrangements which will reserve a private promenade for passengers in certain suites of rooms; another innovation is a reception room attached to the restaurant room. The restaurant will be under the management of Mr L. Gatti, late of Oddenino's Imperial Restaurant, London, whilst the squash racquet court, under a professional player, has been adopted, the experience of the *Olympic* having fully justified the experiment. Captain E. J.

Smith, of the *Olympic*, which arrives today, will be transferred to the *Titanic*.

(*Southampton Times and Hampshire Express*,
30 March 1912)

DEPARTURE OF THE *TITANIC*

The White Star liner *Titanic*, which has just been completed by Messrs Harland & Wolff Ltd, left the fitting-out jetty at half-past nine o'clock this morning, and in charge of four tugs proceeded down the Victoria Channel to Belfast Lough, where her trials took place. The stately proportions of the mammoth vessel were greatly admired by the large crowds of people who had congregated in the vicinity of the Twin Islands. The compasses having been adjusted, the speed trials took place over the measured mile. The *Titanic* will leave later in the day for Southampton, from which port she is due to sail for New York on the tenth inst.

(*Ulster Echo*, 2 April 1912)

A WONDERFUL SHIP

In a port where the magnificence of the appointments of the *Olympic* are so well known, it seems scarcely necessary to say much about the *Titanic*. The privileged few who have had the pleasure of visiting the ship since her arrival at Southampton on Thursday morning have been at a loss to express their admiration. One person said that the *Olympic* was all that could be desired, and the *Titanic* was something even beyond that! And if his hearers smiled at his method of putting it, they were to agree that the White Star Line had taken every possible opportunity of effecting improvements, their experience with the *Olympic* having been brought to bear. The *Titanic* had a delightful trip from Belfast to Southampton, and among those on board were Mr Morgan (Morgan, Grenfell and Co.), and representatives of the London and Southampton offices of Café Parisien.

These gentlemen were quick to notice that several changes had been made in the *Titanic*, and particularly was it noticed that increased state room accommodation had been provided. The two private promenade decks were inspected with interest, and they have been instituted in connection with the parlour suite rooms. Then a delightful addition is the Café Parisien which has been arranged in connection with the restaurant. The deck space outside the restaurant has been utilized for it and it represents an entirely new feature on steamers.

The Café Parisien has the appearance of a charming sunlit verandah tastefully arranged with trellis work, and chairs in small groups surrounding convenient tables. It will also form a further addition to the restaurant, as lunches and dinners can be served with the same excellent service and all the advantages of the restaurant itself.

In the first class dining room over 550 passengers can dine at the same time, and a feature of the room is the arrangement of the recessed bays where family and other parties can dine together in semi privacy. The second class passengers have been very generously provided for. The dining saloon extends the full breadth of the vessel, and will seat 400. The state rooms are of very superior character, and the promenades are unusually spacious, a unique feature being the enclosed promenade. The accommodation for third class is also very good, and the vessel will accommodate in all about 3,500 passengers and crew.

(*Southampton Times and Hampshire Express*, 6 April 1912)

WHITE STAR LINER *TITANIC*

The completion of the *Titanic* marks a further stage in the progress of British shipping and shipbuilding, and in the development of the White Star Line. The *Olympic* and the *Titanic* are essentially similar in design and construction, and yet, so rapidly are we moving in these days of progress, that already the experience gained with the *Olympic* is being taken advantage of in the *Titanic*.

Consequently we find that there are several changes carried out in the second ship with a view to meeting even more completely than before the requirements of the service, and the large number of passengers with whom this type of ship is proving so popular.

Beginning with the top deck (the boat deck) increased first-class state room accommodation has been provided. The same applies to the upper promenade deck (A deck) and on this deck ship's side windows are fitted for half the length of the deck from the forward end, this arrangement giving the sheltered promenade, with, at the same time, full view of the sea, so much appreciated by passengers.

On the promenade deck (B deck) there is also increased accommodation, the deckhouse being extended to the ship's side, and two private promenade decks having been instituted in connection with the parlour suite rooms. On the same deck a Café Parisien has been arranged in connection with the restaurant, the deck space being utilized for this, which is an entirely new feature on board ship. A reception room has also been provided in connection with the restaurant, in view of the reception room connected with the first class dining saloon having proved so satisfactory to passengers. The restaurant itself has also been increased in size.

The private promenades are decorated in a style of half timbered walls of Elizabethan period. The Café Parisien is decorated in French trellis work with ivy creepers, and looks extremely attractive.

On the upper deck (C deck), which is the deck immediately below the promenade deck, the first-class accommodation has been increased also; and on the saloon deck (D deck) the reception room in connection with the dining saloon has been enlarged, and additional seating accommodation provided in the saloon.

On the main deck (E deck) increased accommodation has been provided, and generally throughout the first-class accommodation as a large number of wardrobe rooms have been added, also the number of suites of rooms increased, and more state rooms with wardrobe rooms attached provided.

(Cork Free Press, 9 April 1912)

CHAPTER 2

NEW YORK BOUND

Harry Fairall, a thirty-two-year-old married man with three daughters, worked as a saloon steward on board the *Titanic*. He was planning to start a new life in America, and was going to send for his family when he was settled there. Before joining up with a skeleton crew in Belfast, he sent a postcard of the *Titanic* from Southampton, posted on 26 March 1912.

> Dear N. We leave the Dock Station at 2pm today. I will write from Belfast and tell you everything. Yours in haste. H.

Mr Fairall's wife was pregnant at the time and gave birth prematurely after the *Titanic* went down. The baby died six months later.

Joseph Scarrott was born in Portsmouth in 1878. He had worked on a number of other White Star Line vessels, but when he signed on as an able seaman on the *Titanic* on 6 April 1912 (at wages of £5 per month), for the first time in his life he experienced a strange foreboding.

> The signing on seemed like a dream to me, and I could not believe I had done so, but the absence of my discharge book from my pocket convinced me. When I went to the docks that morning I had as much intention of applying for a job on the Big 'Un, as we called her, as I had of going for a trip to the moon. I was assured

31

of a job as a Q.M. on a Union Castle liner, also I was not in low water for 'Bees and honey'. When I went home (36 Albert Road, Southampton) and told my sister what I had done, she called me a fool. Now this was the first and only time that she had shown disapproval of any ship I was going on. In fact she would not believe me until she found I was minus my discharge book.

I was under orders to join the ship at 7am, Wednesday April 10, the time of sailing being 12.00 that morning. The trip was to be a 'speed up' trip, meaning that we were to go from Southampton to New York, unload, load and back again in sixteen days. Although it was unnecessary to take all my kit for this short trip, I did not seem to have the inclination to sort any of it out, and I pondered a lot in my mind whether I should join her or give it a miss. Now in the whole of my twenty-nine years of going to sea I have never had that feeling of hesitation that I experienced then, and I had worked aboard the *Titanic* when she came to Southampton from the builders, and I had the opportunity to inspect her from stem to stern. This I did, especially the crew quarters, and I must say that she was the finest ship I had ever seen.

Wednesday 10. I decide I will go, but not with a good heart. Before leaving home I kissed my sister and said, 'Goodbye', and as I was leaving she called me back and asked why I had said, 'Goodbye' instead of my usual, 'So long, see you again soon'. I told her I had not noticed saying it, neither had I. On my way to join the ship you can imagine how this incident stuck in my mind. On joining a ship all sailors have much the same routine. You go to your quarters, choose your bunk, and get the gear you require from your bag. Then you change into your uniform, and by that time you are called to muster by the Chief Officer. I took my bag but did not open it, nor did I get into uniform, and I went to muster and Fire and Boat Drill without my uniform. 11.45 a.m. Hands to stations for casting off. I am in the starboard watch, my station is aft, and I am still not in uniform. My actions and manners are the reverse of what they should be.

(*Southend Pier Review, Number 8*, 1932)

Mr and Mrs Edward W. Bill of Philadelphia were staying at London's Hotel Cecil with the intention of travelling to Southampton to sail on the *Titanic*. But at the last minute Mrs Bill had a premonition of impending doom and the couple decided to sail on the *Mauretania* instead. On reaching New York safely, Mr Bill revealed:

I had our rooms all picked out on the *Titanic*, and I told my wife that it would be interesting to be on the greatest ship in the world on her maiden trip. Mrs Bill was not very enthusiastic, and when I started for the White Star office to get the tickets, she begged me not to go. She said that she couldn't tell why, but said she didn't want to go on the *Titanic*. I had never known her to object to any plan of travel I suggested before, but this time she was immovably firm, and I yielded to her wishes reluctantly.

Another who was afraid of sailing aboard the *Titanic* was Esther Hart, mother of seven-year-old **Eva Hart**.

We went on the day on the boat train . . . I was seven, I had never seen a ship before. It looked very big . . . Everybody was very excited, we went down to the cabin and that's when my mother said to my father that she had made up her mind quite firmly that she would not go to bed in that ship, she would sit up at night . . . she decided that she wouldn't go to bed at night, and she didn't.

Cornish steward **Harry Bristow** wrote to his wife Ethel from Southampton on the day before sailing:

Dearest Et, I have earned my first day's pay on the *Titanic* and been paid and I may say spent it do you know dearie. I forgot about towels, also cloth brush so I've to buy two. My uniform will cost £1 17s 6d, coat plus waistcoat and cap and Star regulation collars and paper front (don't laugh dearie it's quite true) two white jackets etc, so it won't leave me very much to take up. My pay is £3 15s plus tips. I'm in the first-class saloon so I may pick up a bit. I've been scrubbing the floor today in saloon, about a dozen of us. I lost myself a time or two, she is such an enormous size I expect it will take me a couple of trips before I begin to know my way about here. I believe we're due back here again about the 4th next month. I am not sure though. I've to be aboard tomorrow morning 6 o'clock sharp, means turning out at 5am. You might send a letter to me addressed as envelope enclosed a day before we're expected in so that I could have it directly I come ashore, now dearie with fondest love to boy and self and be brave as you always are, your ever loving Harry.

Harry Bristow died in the sinking. His body was never identified.

Southampton-born **John Podesta**, twenty-four, signed on as a fireman on the *Titanic* on monthly wages of £6. The morning of 10 April 1912 – sailing day – saw Podesta enjoy a last-minute drink in a Southampton public house with watch-mate William Nutbean and fellow firemen Alfred, Bertram and Thomas Slade.

I got up on the morning of April 10th and made off down to the ship for eight o'clock muster, as is the case on all sailing days, which takes about an hour. As the ship is about to sail at about 12 o'clock noon, most of us firemen and trimmers go ashore again until sailing time. So off we went with several others I knew on my watch, which was 4 to 8. My watch-mate, whose name was William Nutbean, and I went off to our local public house for a drink in the Newcastle Hotel. We left about 11.15 making our way towards the docks. Having plenty of time we dropped into another pub called the Grapes, meeting several more ship-mates inside. So having another drink about six of us left about ten minutes to 12 and got well into the docks and towards the vessel. With me and my mate were three brothers named Slade.

We were at the top of the main road and a passenger train was approaching from another part of the docks. I heard the Slades say, 'Oh, let the train go by.' But me and Nutbean crossed over and managed to board the liner. Being a long train, by the time it passed, the Slades were too late, and the gangway was down leaving them behind.

THE DEPARTURE OF THE LINER FROM SOUTHAMPTON

Viewed from Trafalgar Quay, in the brilliant setting of Southampton Water, under a blue sky flecked with fleecy clouds, and the ocean greyhounds of yesterday – the *St Louis*, the *Oceanic*, and many others – dwarfed in the near distance, the scene was tremendously impressive. Within the week Southampton has sent forth the two greatest liners in the world – the *Olympic* and the *Titanic* – a record in itself.

Never before in the history of the mercantile marine has so great a triumph of naval architecture as the *Titanic* left a port. So there was a new sensation in the occasion of this leviathan's movement – a monster, towering to the flags above 160ft, deck over deck, and with a length of 876ft – as she rounded the Test Quay, majestically displayed her lines, and bore down on the Solent.

An officer aboard told me that he had been on the *Titanic* four and a half days and, apart from his own sphere, knew very little about her. In three hours, having walked some six miles, new wonders and improvements revealing themselves in all directions, one was only able to take 'samples' of extraordinary interest in themselves, and of great importance to the ocean traveller. On the *Titanic* sunshine is being taken out. The gloom and depression of November's fogs off the Banks have been annihilated. The first-class passenger sits down to dinner in the splendid saloon, with its windows of cathedral-grey glass, and the attendants switch on cunningly hidden electric lights on the outside. The effect is naturalness itself.

One can engage for £870 the voyage a 'private ocean trip'. There are honeymoon suites, with honeymoon decks set apart for the millionaire brides and bridegrooms of the future; state rooms decorated in every different style and period, with lovely, ample cot-beds in brass, mahogany, and oak; lounges decorated in Louis XVI style; verandahs with climbing plants and ramblers; real coal fires as well as hundreds of radiators; restaurants and cafés; reception-rooms upholstered in the daintiest silk, with gorgeous panels and richly carved cornices – the whole forming an impressive ensemble in perfect taste, satisfying to the eye.

There were but 1,470 passengers, besides the 800 members of the crew and scores of attendants on board today, so that there was no crowding in any part of the vessel. Fully an hour before she sailed the gymnasium, in charge of a professional gymnast, was in working. On one side a lady was having a camel ride and recalling the delights of the Pyramids; in another corner there was a bicycle race; many passengers took their own weights on the automatic chairs, and some had a spin on the mechanical rowing machines. In the squash racquets court two Americans were 'fighting the battle of their lives' – it might have been at the Bath Club, so thoroughly at home did they look.

In the third-class, or steerage, departments, the loveliest linen, glass and cutlery were displayed ready for luncheon, while the easy-chairs, card tables, pianos and settees reminded one of the first-class accommodation on many liners twenty years ago.

But the most fascinating feature, perhaps, of the *Titanic* today was the trips of 'discovery' men and women set out to explore. They were shot into the depths by splendidly equipped electric lifts. They called at the post-office for a chat with the postmaster on the sorting arrangements. They wandered to the swimming baths and the luxurious Turkish saloons. They examined the kitchens, with their 21,000 dishes and plates, tons of silver and cutlery, and acres of glass and linen. They touched the pianos on every deck in every corner of advantage, or listened to the band; scanned the arrays of novels and more serious works in the libraries; and learnt all sorts of wonderful things about the electric buttons which control this 47,000-ton vessel, command its engines and its little army of services alike.

At 11.45 the bells clanged. The visitors wandered down the gangways. Hatchways were closed. The tugs snorted, and the *Titanic* set out on her maiden trip. But scarcely had she moved 600 yards into the bay when it was evident that something unlooked for had occurred.

Among the crowds still waving handkerchiefs there was a sudden silence. The gigantic triple expansion engines had begun to work. Nearby were the *Oceanic* and the *New York* – great vessels in their day – now dwarfed to comparative insignificance. Directly the huge screws of the *Titanic* began to revolve, the suction caused the seven great stern ropes of the *New York* to part, and the American liner's stern swung round into midstream.

All eyes were fixed on the *New York*. It looked as if there must be a collision; but, as a matter of fact, there was no real danger. The *Titanic*'s screws were stopped almost instantaneously, and the *New York* was towed to safety. Then the *Titanic* slowly sped down Southampton Water, the faces of her passengers peering at every nook of the seven tiers along the whole length of the liner, until she melted away in the distance, and her maiden voyage had begun.

(*The Standard*, 10 April 1912)

MAIDEN VOYAGE OF THE *TITANIC*

The departure of the *Titanic* on her maiden voyage on Wednesday was marred by an untoward incident which caused considerable consternation among the hundreds of people gathered on the quay-side to witness the sailing of the largest vessel afloat. By some means or other the passing of the *Titanic* caused the *New York* to break away from her position alongside the *Oceanic* with the result that the *Titanic* and the *New York* narrowly missed colliding with each other. Fortunately, the captain of the tug *Vulcan* was able to take a rapid glance of the situation, and by his promptness and skill in manoeuvring he was able to hold the *New York* whilst the *Titanic* got clear, and a very dangerous episode ended with nothing more than a few broken ropes.

Let it be said at once that the story that the *Titanic* was unmanageable, and that she was the reason for the incident, is absolutely untrue. As a matter of fact, she had got underway beautifully. It is doubtful whether the *Olympic* has ever cleared the new dock in such a splendid manner as did the *Titanic* on this occasion. From the moment she began to move from her berth in that dock she was under absolute control, and she passed out of the dock not only majestically, but also smoothly and calmly. If anything, she was proceeding more slowly than the *Olympic* usually does, and she turned her nose towards the sea with the greatest ease. It was a low but rising tide, with a fairly strong breeze, and if the officials anticipated any difficulty at all it was when she was making her exit from the new dock. But there was not the slightest difficulty. To the writer, who was standing on the quay at the time, the tugs appeared to be working magnificently, and once she had turned round and straightened herself for the Channel a few of the people standing by began to move homewards, some of them being heard to make exclamations of surprise at the ease with which a 46,000 ton steamer could be shaped for the sea.

Indeed, matters were going so well that some of the tugs were able to slacken off. One or two, at least, had left the vessel, and were merely following in her wake until she had cleared the Dock head. But it was at this point that the trouble began. At berth No. 38 the *Oceanic* was moored to the quay-side, and the *New York* was moored to the *Oceanic*. Both those vessels have been laid up on account of the strike, and they were presumably moored alongside each other in order to save quay space. This system of mooring ships together is quite an old one, and no one apparently gave a thought to the possibility of anything happening on this occasion. We believe we are right in saying that the two vessels occupied exactly the same positions when the *Titanic* arrived at the port a week ago. In those circumstances it was, perhaps, forgivable that no one gave them a thought, but what happened will probably bring about an alteration when next a mammoth vessel leaves the port.

It is difficult to convey a true impression of what actually occurred. All eyes were fixed on the *Titanic*; the *New York* was in nobody's mind at the moment, but when the *Titanic* had almost got alongside the American Line's vessel something began to happen which diverted attention to the *New York*. The *Titanic* had just begun to move her propellers, and she was practically in what is termed the 'sea channel'. Without the slightest warning, the ropes which kept the *New York* in her position began to snap. It was suggested that the displacement of water by the *Titanic* had first of all had the effect of increasing the volume of water under and around the *New York*, with the result that the vessel was raised from her normal position, and her ropes were thus slackened. Then as the larger vessel passed on ahead the volume of water decreased in the vicinity of the *New York*, with the result that she suddenly reverted to her former position. This caused too great a strain on the ropes, and they snapped as easily as a grocer snaps a piece of twine with his fingers. The *Titanic* was drawing the water behind her with considerable force, and as the *New York* was now helpless and unmanned, her stern began to move in the direction of the *Titanic*, that vessel being now broadside on.

For the moment it seemed as if nothing could prevent a disastrous accident. We do not believe in using the 'ifs' too much, for the truth is often bad enough without any 'might-have-beens' tacked on, but it was only too plain to those on the quay-side that if the *Titanic* had touched the *New York* the latter vessel might easily have rammed the *Oceanic*, and the slightest touch on her stern must have sent her heavily into the *Oceanic*. Fortunately, however, the worst did not happen. Having got the *Titanic* fairly under way, a couple of tugs hung back, their portion of the work having been successfully accomplished. The two tugs were, however, proceeding along slowly near the stern of the *Titanic*, and when the *New York* began to move it was these tugs – the

Vulcan and the *Hercules* – that went to the helpless ship. It was a smart bit of work. The *Vulcan* got to the *New York* in very quick time, and a rope was speedily put on board. As luck would have it, however, the first rope snapped, but in less time than it takes to tell another rope was thrown. This was made fast by some workmen who happened to be on the *New York*, and by a tremendous effort the vessel was kept from drifting on to the *Titanic*. The *Hercules* and the *Vulcan* concentrated their efforts on holding the *New York* whilst the *Titanic* was passing along, and they succeeded in their task.

It was a narrow squeak. From the quay-side it seemed that there were not more than three or four feet between the two vessels. It was stated that the vessels actually touched, but this was not so. The movement of the *New York* was from the *Oceanic* towards the next berth – No. 37 – and when the *Titanic* finally passed down the Channel the 'nose' of the *New York* was pointing towards the Floating Bridge. Apparently all the tugs endeavoured to do was to hold her, and when the period of danger was past she was brought back to her berth alongside the *Oceanic*. During all this time there was a fear lest the *Oceanic* should also get adrift. There must have been a tremendous strain on her ropes, but they stood the test, much to the relief of the sightseers who had got on board.

(*Southampton Times and Hampshire Express*, 13 April 1912)

VULCAN TO THE RESCUE

The Captain's Story

Captain C. Gale, the captain of the tug *Vulcan*, which by common consent rendered conspicuous service in holding up the *New York* at the moment when an accident seemed imminent, was seen by a representative of the *Southampton Times*, to whom he gave a version of the incident. He said:

I assisted the *Titanic* out of the new dock in the first place, and had hold of her aft. We let go by the starboard quarter and dropped astern in order to go alongside and pick up a number of workmen who were about to leave the *Titanic*. I sung out to the officer of the liner, and he told me to go round to the port side. When I got to the port side we followed up behind the liner, whose port engine was working astern all the time. The *Titanic* was drawing about 35 ft of water. There was a young flood, and she was near the ground. As soon as she got abreast of the *New York* the latter's ropes began to go. It may have been due to the backwash of the liner, or to the pressure of water, but all her ropes gave way, and she began to move. Someone sang out to me to get up and push the *New York* back, but such a thing was impossible. Had I got between the two ships we would almost certainly have been jammed, and goodness knows what might have happened, but, instead of that, I turned the *Vulcan* round and got a wire rope on the port quarter of the *New York*.

Unfortunately, that rope parted, but our men immediately got a second wire on board, and we got hold of the *New York* when she was within four feet of the *Titanic*. Had the *New York* touched the outward-bound liner, she would have hit her abreast of the after funnel. The *Titanic* stood a chance of fouling the starboard screw of the *New York* and of knocking in the latter's starboard quarter, but the American Line steamer was checked just in time, and we got her clear of the *Titanic*.

Captain Gale added that it was one of the closest things he had seen for a long time. The movements of the *Vulcan* were rendered all the more trying because the broken ropes of the *New York* were lying in the water, and the tug might easily have picked them up on her propeller and been rendered helpless. Captain Gale added that the statement that the *New York* was held by her bow ropes was untrue. Every rope on the vessel was snapped, the stern ropes being the first to give out. It was a wonderful thing that nothing of a serious nature happened – only once in a hundred times would three ocean liners escape from such a perilous situation without sustaining damage.

(*Southampton Times and Hampshire Express*, 13 April 1912)

AS SEEN FROM THE NEW YORK

Experience of Sightseers

A correspondent, who happened to be among a number of people on board the *New York* at the time of the incident, sent us the following: 'The sailing of the *Titanic* was accompanied by a most untoward incident. An unusual number of sightseers had assembled on the quays to watch the gigantic liner commence her outward voyage to New York, and some who were anxious to get a better view climbed the gangway of the *Oceanic*, whence they gained the decks of the American Liner *New York*, which was moored alongside. As the *Titanic* emerged from the new dock and was being slowly piloted past the two liners mentioned, the effect produced by her passage was so strong as to cause the *New York* to break from her moorings – much to the consternation of the sightseers on board. At once, all was in a state of commotion, and it seemed inevitable that a collision must occur. Fortunately, this was averted by the prompt action of the Dock officials, working in conjunction with the officers on the liners. Meanwhile, vast crowds of people, including many photographers and police officers, could be seen on the quay sides. Some five or six tugs, already at hand, were immediately employed in preventing what might have been a serious collision. Aided by some of these tugs, the *Titanic* went back on her course, while others arrested the further drifting of the *New York*. Not until the latter vessel had been safely moored at the Dock head was the *Titanic* able to proceed on her voyage. The over-ambitious sightseers were, however, unable to land until the *New York* was again moored alongside the *Oceanic*. A hastily constructed gangway was then thrown across, and the "enforced voyagers" were glad to regain "terra firma". They will doubtless retain for years vivid recollections of the first sailing of the *Titanic* from Southampton Docks.'

*　　*　　*

The *Titanic* arrived at Queenstown on Thursday. She had a good passage from Southampton and Cherbourg, and arrived at the Irish port shortly before noon. On her departure at 1.30 she had on board 350 saloon, 300 second, and 740 third class passengers, 903 crew and 3,814 sacks of mail.

(*Southampton Times and Hampshire Express*, 13 April 1912)

When the *Titanic* left on her maiden voyage on Wednesday there was an unrehearsed incident which might have had serious consequences. On her way from the deep water dock the big ship passed the *Oceanic* and *New York*, which were moored side by side at the Test Quay. The wash from the great liner caused the *New York* to break from her moorings, and she drifted into the channel. The *Titanic* was going dead slow, and she was stopped without any difficulty. Handy tug-boats were immediately in attendance upon the *New York*, and there was a great deal of excitement until the state of affairs was realized.

We are not going to express any opinion why the mooring ropes of the *New York* snapped like twine when the bigger vessel passed her, but we would point out that had the deep channel been wider at this spot no accident would have happened. It would have been impossible for the *Titanic* to have got further away from the *New York* without incurring a grave risk of running aground, and her navigators were in consequence placed in a helpless position. There is a general agreement that the channel should be widened and deepened in the vicinity of the docks, but because the dock proprietors of the Harbour Board agree only in repudiating responsibility the work remains undone.

(*Southampton Times and Hampshire Express*, 13 April 1912)

Roberta Maioni was the young maid to one of the heroines of the *Titanic* story, the Countess of Rothes. Like her employer, Miss Maioni survived the disaster. She later described the launch of the great ship at Southampton.

On the day the *Titanic* set out on her first and only voyage, I was just a girl in my teens looking forward with a schoolgirl's anticipation to a voyage in the world's latest and finest liner on a tour through North America.

The weather was brilliant and the docks at Southampton were crowded with bustling people. For this was no ordinary boat departure; it was the departure of a wonder ship – a floating palace that far excelled all others in size and magnificence, and men said that she could not sink.

We passengers were crushed and pushed about by excited crowds as we struggled to reach the gangway, but once across we were swallowed up in that great vessel.

The noise made in getting the luggage aboard was deafening, but when the *Titanic* started on its journey an even greater pandemonium broke loose – the cheering of thousands of people and the shrieking of many sirens.

Then, as if some unseen hand had silenced them, a hush suddenly fell upon the people. I went to the side to see what was the matter and found that the passing of the mighty *Titanic* had drawn another liner – the *New York* – from her moorings into the fairway.

Tugs soon took the *New York* back to her place and the majority of us went on our way without giving further thought to this incident, but some passengers took it as a bad omen of ill-fortune and were further discomforted by the fact that large numbers of seagulls followed the ship to the sea. This, they said, was a sign of impending disaster. I had no time for such forebodings, for I had entered a fairy city and spent the first few days of the voyage in exploration and in making friends.

THE WHITE STAR LINER *TITANIC*

Mammoth liner at Queenstown

Yesterday the 46,000 ton White Star liner *Titanic*, which is now the largest vessel in the world, arrived at Queenstown at 11.55 a.m.

from Southampton via Cherbourg on her maiden voyage to New York. The *Titanic* left Southampton on Wednesday with 1,380 passengers, and was given an enthusiastic send off from there by hundreds of spectators on the quay side. As she steamed slowly up to Queenstown Harbour yesterday the huge vessel presented an imposing sight, and her commander dropped anchor about two miles off Roche's Point.

Long before the vessel was sighted the local agents, Messrs James Scott and Co., Queenstown, had everything in readiness and a huge staff was engaged in transporting the mails and passengers' luggage to the tenders in waiting. This occupied a very short time, considering the huge consignments, and at 12.40 the first tender left the White Star Jetty. On arrival by the side of the large liner, the gangways were quickly attached and an equally fast delivery of passengers, mails and luggage took place. One hundred and thirty passengers of all classes embarked at Queenstown, and when the transfers had been completed the *Titanic* had on board a total of 1,450 passengers all told, made up of 350 first-class, 300 second-class, and 800 third-class. Her complement of mails amounted to 3,418 sacks, of which 1,388 sacks were embarked at Queenstown. In addition to her huge passenger freight of 1,450 souls, the *Titanic* carries a crew of 903 hands of all ranks from the commander down to the most juvenile pantry boy, making in all a ship's company of 2,353 persons. Another example of the vast size of this modern leviathan of the deep is the fact that she has passenger accommodation – exclusive of that for her crew of 903 – for 2,350, or for 750 first-class, 500 second-class, and 1,100 third-class passengers, so that it will be seen that her Commander, Captain E. J. Smith, R.D.R.N.R., has tremendous responsibility placed on his shoulders. It being the maiden voyage, Commander Smith did not put his vessel to her full test from Southampton to Queenstown, but kept at the pace of 20 knots per hour. In an interview, the genial Commander said that the machinery of the huge vessel worked splendidly, and there was not the slightest hitch on the way across. The luxurious manner in which the vessel has been fitted up has already been dealt with in these columns, but it might be interesting to know that there is one suite of apartments, including a private promenade deck, the charge for which from Southampton to New York is £850. It might also be mentioned that amongst the many distinguished passengers travelling by the liner are Mr Bruce Ismay, one of the principal owners of the White Star Line Company, who takes a particular interest in his line of vessels and generally makes the maiden voyage on each, and the Hon. Thomas Andrews, the managing director of the great ship building firm of Messrs Harland & Wolff, Belfast, which built the *Titanic*. Amongst the other distinguished passengers on board are Colonel J. J. Astor and Mrs Astor, Mr and Mrs H. J. Allison, Major Archibald W. Butt, Mr and Mrs T. W. Cavendish, Mr W. D. and Mrs W. D. Douglas, Colonel Archibald Gracie, Mr Henry Sleeper Harper and Mrs Henry Sleeper Harper, Mr Fletcher-Fellows Lambert Williams, Mr Clarence Moore, Major Arthur Peuchen, The Countess of Rothes and Party, Mr and Mrs Arthur Ryerson, Miss Ryerson and Master Ryerson, Mr and Mrs Frederick O. Speddon and Master Speddon, Mr and Mrs Isidor Straus and family, Mrs J. Stuart White and family, Mr Richard F. and Percival W. White, Mr Wyckoff Vanderhoef, Mr and Mrs G. D. Widener and family. While the necessary work of transferring etc. was being gone through, Messrs James Scott & Co., the local agents, showed the Press representatives round the vessel and afterwards hospitably entertained them. No detail was left out, and every part of the vessel from the lower gangway to the upper boat deck was shown to the visitors. Needless to say, both the Pressmen and the other visitors were much impressed with all they saw, and all were of opinion that the latest addition to the White Star fleet was one of the finest afloat at the present time, and is likely to hold the claim for many years to come.

Commander E. J. Smith is a sailor of the most genial type, and does all that is humanly possible to make things pleasant for the ship's company. Formerly of the *Olympic*, a sister ship of the

Titanic, Captain Smith has always been a conscientious worker in the interests of his profession. He was a member of the Executive Council of the Mercantile Marine Service Association, prior to his removal to Southampton to take over the command of the *Oceanic*. His connection with the White Star is a long and extensive one, and his abilities will fit him for the command of the world's greatest ship.

He is a native of Staffordshire, and was born in 1850, and served his apprenticeship to the sea with the firm of Messrs A. Gibson and Co., the well-known Liverpool shipowners. He joined the White Star Line as Fourth Officer, and secured his first command in 1887. Since then he has commanded most of the large vessels of the fleet.

All arrangements having been completed, the last tender cast off at 1.25pm, and in a few minutes afterwards the *Titanic* weighed anchor and proceeded on her westward voyage, taking with her the best wishes of all who had the privilege of being entertained on board.

(*Cork Free Press*, 12 April 1912)

Miss Nellie Walcroft, a thirty-one-year-old cook from Berkshire, was visiting her sister in New York. She and her travelling companion, Miss Clear Cameron, had been due to travel on another ship but were transferred to the *Titanic* because of a coal strike in Britain. They shared a second-class cabin on E deck. Miss Walcroft recounted her story in a letter to her local paper, dated 23 April 1912.

I left Maidenhead on April 9, stayed in London and caught the special train to Southampton at 8.30 on the morning of April 10. My sister and a friend saw me off. After a splendid quick run we arrived at Southampton Dock Station at 10.15.

Looking through the window, I saw the largest ship I had ever seen. The sun was shining on it, and it was magnificent. Everyone was going over the ship and it was greatly admired.

The bell rang and all the visitors left the ship. Then we started, to the hand waving of thousands of people. We left the docks. We did not know about the near collision we had until we arrived this side. We arrived at Cherbourg at 5 o'clock and at Queenstown on Thursday morning. We had a perfect trip.

(*Maidenhead Advertiser*)

British passenger **Charlotte Collyer** was travelling second-class on the *Titanic* with her husband Harvey and their eight-year-old daughter Marjorie. They had left their home in Bishopstoke, Hampshire, where they ran a small grocery store, to start a new life in Payette, Idaho. There Harvey Collyer planned to buy a half share in an apple orchard. The Collyers had originally booked their passage on the steamer *New York* but that vessel was delayed because of the coal strike in Britain and they transferred to the *Titanic*. All their worldly goods travelled with them, Harvey Collyer having sewn his money and valuables into the lining of his clothes. He never made it to the United States, but Charlotte lived to tell her tale.

From our deck which was situated well forward, we saw the great send off that was given to the boat. I do not think that there had ever been so large a crowd in Southampton and I am not surprised that it should have come together.

The *Titanic* was wonderful, far more splendid and huge than I had dreamed of. The other crafts in the harbour were like cockle shells beside her and they, mind you, were the boats of the American and other lines that a few years ago were thought enormous. I remember a friend said to me, 'Aren't you afraid to venture on the sea?', but now it was I who was confident. 'What, on this boat!' I answered. 'Even the worst storm could not harm her.' Before we left the harbour I saw the accident to the *New York*, the liner that was dragged from her moorings and swept against us in the Channel. It did not frighten anyone, as it only seemed to prove how powerful the *Titanic* was.

I don't remember very much about the first few days of the voyage. I was a bit seasick and kept to my cabin most of the time. But on Sunday April 14th I was up and about. At dinner time I was at my place in the saloon and enjoyed the meal, though I thought it too heavy and rich. No effort had been spared to give even the second cabin passengers on that Sunday the best dinner that money could buy. After I had eaten, I listened to the orchestra for a little while, then at nine o'clock or half past nine I went to my cabin. I had just climbed into my berth when a stewardess came in. She was a sweet woman who had been very kind to me. I take this opportunity to thank her for I shall never see her again. She went down with the *Titanic*.

'Do you know where we are?' she said pleasantly. 'We are in what is called the Devil's Hole.' 'What does that mean?' I asked. 'That is a dangerous part of the ocean,' she answered. 'Many accidents have happened near there. They say that icebergs drift down as far as this. It's getting to be very cold on deck so perhaps there is ice around us now.' She left the cabin and I soon dropped off to sleep. Her talk about icebergs had not frightened me, but it shows that the crew were awake to the danger. As far as I can tell we had not slackened our speed in the least.

(*Semi-Monthly Magazine*, May 1912)

Cornishman **Percy Bailey**, aged eighteen, sailed second class on the *Titanic* bound for Akron, Ohio, where he was to start work as an apprentice butcher. He was originally set to travel on the *Oceanic* but transferred to the *Titanic* on learning that a number of friends were booked on the new flagship of the White Star Line. Percy Bailey went down with the *Titanic*. His last known correspondence was a letter sent to his parents shortly after boarding the ship on 10 April.

Dear Father and Mother, We arrived on board this morning after a night's rest at Southampton. We put up at an Hotel named Berrimans. The lady who owns it is a Cornish lady. We had a good supper and a good breakfast of ham and eggs, we were doing it fine. I slept with a young man named Wills – a brother to the man who married Mrs Trevask's daughter. He came to Southampton to see his sister-in-law. We had several people joined us at St Erth bound for the same place as we are going so we are a big family altogether. Well dear Mother, I suppose you are missing me but don't be downhearted, old dear Percy will be behaved to you as a son ought to treat his Mother and Father. The going away from home will make me a better man and try and lead a good life. The *Titanic* is a marvel, I can tell you. I have never seen such a sight in all my life, she is like a floating palace, everything up to date. I hope you are all well as it leaves me at present. Father I shall never forget your kindness, you have done more for me than many Fathers have done for their sons. Well dear parents I don't think there is any more news I can tell you now. Kiss Grandma for me and tell her I am sorry for all my wicked thoughts which I said to her, but never again, will I cheek her. Give my best love to all who ask for me. I will draw my letter to a close hoping you one and all are quite well. I remain your loving son.

John Lovell, a twenty-year-old steerage passenger from Devon, was visiting his brother Leonard in the United States. He died in the sinking although his body was never identified. He sent two postcards. The first – to his uncle, William Wivell – was posted in Southampton. It read:

Dear Uncle, Just writing a few lines to let you know that I have got to Southampton all right. We got to Southampton about 7.30 in the evening and we all lodge at the Alliance Hotel. I could not sleep that night. I am not downhearted yet, I am happy. J. Lovell.

The second – to his aunt, Beatrice Wivell – was posted from Queenstown.

I am sending you a postcard of the *Titanic*. We started from Southampton about 12 o'clock last Wednesday. Slept well the first night. I been on ship one and a half days. I am not sea sick yet. I am enjoying myself fine. Good bye. J. H. Lovell.

Kate Buss, aged thirty-six, from Sittingbourne in Kent, was travelling second-class on the *Titanic*. She was on her way to meet her fiancé in the United States and broke the first stage of the journey by sending a letter to her brother Percy – on *Titanic* headed paper, dated 10 April 1912. She survived the sinking.

The first class apartments are really magnificent and unless you had first seen them you would think the second class were the same. We were due to reach Cherbourg at 5 p.m., but not there yet although mail is cleared. I think I'd best try and get some postcards of the vessel. My fellow passenger hasn't turned up yet, so if she is coming it will be from Cherbourg or Queenstown. I was advised to eat well so had a good lunch – two clergymen opposite me at table. No sign of sea sickness yet – I mustn't crow . . . The only thing I object to is new paint so far. Must clear and have a wash now. Will pop this in the post in case I'm sea sick tomorrow . . . Much love Kate.

First-class passenger **Mrs Mahala Douglas** of Minneapolis was to lose her husband Walter in the disaster.

We left Cherbourg late on account of the trouble at Southampton, but once off, everything seemed to go perfectly. The boat was so luxurious, so steady, so immense, and such a marvel of mechanism that one could not believe he was on a boat – and there the danger lay. We had smooth seas, clear, starlit nights, fresh favouring winds; nothing to mar our pleasure.

On Saturday, as Mr Douglas and I were walking forward, we saw a seaman taking the temperature of the water. The deck seemed so high above the sea I was interested to know if the tiny pail could reach it. There was quite a breeze, and, although the pail was weighted, it did not. This I watched from the open window of the covered deck. Drawing up the pail, the seaman filled it with water from the stand pipe, placed the thermometer in it, and went with it to the officer in charge.

On Sunday we had a delightful day; everyone in the best of spirits. The time the boat was making was considered very good, and all were interested in getting into New York early.

(US Inquiry, 9 May 1912)

Belfast-born **John Edward Simpson**, an assistant surgeon on board the *Titanic*, wrote a letter to his mother from the ship, dated 11 April 1912. It was posted at Queenstown. It was the last correspondence he would have with her, as he died in the sinking.

Dear Mother, I travelled from Liverpool on Monday by the 12 o'clock train – arrived on Ward at 10 p.m. feeling pretty tired. I am very well and am gradually settled in my new cabin which is larger than my last. This seems all the time as if it were the *Olympic* and I like it very much. I am a member of the Club now which is an advantage. Be sure to let me know how father gets on with his club. I was glad to get away from Liverpool as usual and don't intend to go up for a month or two. I found my two trunks unlocked and five or six dollars stolen out of my pocket-book. I hope none of my stamps have been stolen. Did I have my old portmanteau when I borrowed the kit bag? I think not. With fondest love, John.

Twenty-year-old **Alfred Nourney** from Cologne purchased a second-class ticket but, dissatisfied with his cabin, asked to be upgraded to first-class. He sent a jubilant postcard to his mother from Queenstown:

Dear Mother, I'm so happy being first class! I already know some nice people! A diamond king! Mr Astor, one of the wealthiest Americans, is on board! Thousand kisses, Alfred.

Alfred Nourney was one of the lucky survivors.

Edith Brown was just fifteen when she sailed on the *Titanic* with her sister and father, both of whom died in the sinking. The family, from South Africa, were planning to open a hotel in Seattle. On the journey Edith wrote a postcard to her stepsister. It read:

We are just sailing today by this boat for New York – 4000 tons – all well. With love to all. Your loving Sis E. B.

Unable to post the card, she still had it in her pocket as she jumped into lifeboat No. 14 after the collision. The last she saw of her father was as he stood on the deck of the listing liner with a cigar in one hand and a brandy in the other. When she had recovered from her ordeal, Edith hand-delivered the card to her stepsister in Johannesburg.

Stephen Curnow Jenkin, aged thirty-two, lived in the United States but had been visiting his family in St Ives, Cornwall. He was planning to sail on a different ship, but the coal strike in Britain forced him to transfer to the *Titanic*. He was uneasy about travelling on the *Titanic* and took the precaution of leaving his watch and other valuables with his parents in case anything happened to him. After sending a series of postcards to his family, he went down with the ship.

Dear Father and Mother and Sisters. I am sending another photo of the same ship. This is the third one I sent you. This goes from Queenstown and the last one I sent from Cherbourg, the first one from Southampton. They are three different views of the same ship. I am not sick yet. She is a nice ship to ride on. I'll write from New York next time. From your loving son Stephen.

CHAPTER 3

THE MOMENT OF IMPACT

William Thompson Sloper, aged twenty-eight, a stockbroker from New Britain, Connecticut, returned home on the *Titanic* following a three-month holiday in Europe. He subsequently told how he was persuaded to sail on the liner by a group of new-found friends.

I walked into the palm court of the Carleton Hotel on Pall Mall in the middle of the afternoon. The streets around the hotel and the hotel itself were deserted except for one group of people gathered under the shade of a sheltering palm whom I recognized as a family from Winnipeg, Manitoba, by the name of Fortune who had been passengers to Egypt in January on the same steamer as myself. At once the young people started calling me to join them for tea.

During the trip from New York I became very well acquainted with the second daughter, Alice, who was a very pretty girl and an excellent dancing partner. Soon after I joined them that afternoon, one of the first questions Alice asked me was, 'When are you going home?' I explained I had only the day before paid for a state room on the *Mauretania* for the following Saturday. Before tea was over I promised Alice to drop in at the Cunard Line office the next morning and see if the company would refund my passage money.

If Alice herself was not enough inducement, her assurance that she knew of twenty people who would be passengers on the *Titanic* who had been on our steamer in January certainly was.

I remember I chummed around those first four days with a young, unmarried man about my age by the name of William Dulles who had been on the steamer going over in the winter. He was a gentleman, a trotting horse breeder from Goshen, New York. I saw him early Sunday evening, but I never saw him again.

Sunday night we all enjoyed the glorious sunset from the decks of the *Titanic* as the sun sank like a ball of fire into the sea.

I returned to the library of the ship and sat down at one of the desks to write thank you letters to some of my London friends with whom I had visited during the two weeks I was there. A very pretty young woman approached my desk and introduced herself as Miss Dorothy Gibson. She explained that she and her mother were seated across the room hoping that they would be able to find another card player to make a fourth at bridge. Although I was not then and never have been a good bridge player I accepted to join her as soon as I finished my letter.

At 11.30 we were still playing bridge when the library steward came over to our table and asked us to finish up our game so that he could put out the lights and retire.

At the top of the stairs Dorothy announced that she would like to take a brisk walk around the promenade deck before going to bed. After saying good night to Mrs Gibson I hastily ran to my cabin to don a hat and overcoat.

Suddenly the ship gave a lurch and seemed to slightly keel over to the left. At the same moment Dorothy came hastily up the stairs and we ran together onto the promenade deck on the starboard side. Peering off into the starlit night, we could both of us see something white looming up out of the water and rapidly disappearing off the stern. As we came amidship we seemed to be walking down hill.

We found that in the few moments we had been walking around the deck thirty or forty passengers had gathered, most of them dressed in night clothes and dressing gowns. At this moment the designer of the ship, at whose table in the dining saloon Mrs Gibson and Dorothy had been sitting at mealtimes during the voyage, came bouncing up the stairs three at a time. Dorothy rushed over to him, put her hands on his arm and demanded to know what had happened. Without answering and with a worried look on his face, he brushed Dorothy aside and continued on up the next flight of steps, presumably on his way to the captain's bridge.

Helmsman **Robert Hichens** was at the wheel of the *Titanic* when the giant iceberg suddenly loomed up ahead.

I went on watch at 8 o'clock Sunday night and stood by the men at the wheel until 10. At 10 I took the wheel for two hours.

On the bridge from 10 o'clock were First Officer Murdoch, Fourth Officer Boxhall and Sixth Officer Moody. In the crow's nest were Fleet and another man whose name I don't know.

Second Officer Lightoller, who was on watch while I stood by, carrying messages and the like, from 8 to 10, sent me soon after 8 to tell the carpenter to look out for the fresh water supply, as it might be in danger of freezing. The temperature was then 31 degrees. He gave the crow's nest a strict order to look out for small icebergs.

Second Officer Lightoller was relieved by First Officer Murdoch at 10 and I took the wheel then. At 11.40 three gongs sounded from the crow's nest, the signal for 'something right ahead'.

At the same time one of the men in the nest telephoned to the bridge that there was a large iceberg right ahead. As Officer Murdoch's hand was on the lever to stop the engines the crash came. He stopped the engines, then immediately by another lever closed the watertight doors.

The skipper came from the chart room onto the bridge. His first words were: 'Close the emergency doors.'

'They're already closed, sir,' Mr Murdoch replied.

'Send to the carpenter and tell him to sound the ship,' was the skipper's next order. The message was sent to the carpenter. The carpenter never came up to report. He was probably the first man on that ship to lose his life.

The skipper looked at the commutator, which shows in what direction the ship is listing. He saw that she carried five degrees list to starboard.

The ship was then rapidly settling forward. All the steam sirens were blowing. By the skipper's orders, given in the next few minutes, the engines were put to work at pumping out the ship, distress signals were sent by Marconi and rockets were sent up from the bridge by Quartermaster Rowe. All hands were ordered on deck.

(*New York World*, 19 April 1912)

Mrs Frank M. Warren, aged sixty, of Portland, Oregon, lost her husband when the *Titanic* went down. She remarked how, immediately after the collision, someone had handed him a piece of ice as a souvenir.

We started from Cherbourg on the evening of the tenth, proceeding to Queenstown, at which port we arrived about noon of the eleventh, and, after a delay of about 45 minutes, continued on our voyage. From the time of leaving Queenstown until the time of the accident, the trip was remarkably smooth and it was very bright and sunny except for about half an hour of fog on one occasion.

The vessel on the first day out from Queenstown, that is from noon of the eleventh to noon of the twelfth, made, it was reported, 494 miles. On the second day, from noon of the twelfth to noon of the thirteenth, about 519 miles, and on the third day, from noon of the thirteenth to noon of the fourteenth, 546 miles.

The general impression prevailing aboard the vessel was that the speed on the fourth day would be better than that shown on any preceding day and that we would arrive in New York sometime on Tuesday afternoon. The impression also prevailed among the passengers that the course of the vessel was more southwest than due west, the supposition being that this was to avoid fog. On Sunday, the day of the accident, the weather was particularly beautiful; there were no clouds, the sea was smooth and the temperature very moderate throughout the day.

After dinner in the evening and until about 10 p.m. we were seated in the lounge on the dining room saloon deck listening to the music. About the time stated we went to one of the upper decks, where Mr Warren wanted to take a walk, as was his custom before retiring. He did not, however, as the temperature had fallen very considerably and the air was almost frosty, although the night was perfect, clear and starlit.

We retired about 10.30, ship's time, and we went to sleep immediately. About 11.45, ship's time, we were awakened by a grinding noise and the stoppage of the vessel. Our room was on the starboard side of deck D, about 30ft above the water and in line with the point of impact.

I arose immediately, turned the lights on and asked Mr Warren what terrible thing had happened. He said, 'Nothing at all,' but just at that moment I heard a man across the corridor say, 'We have certainly struck an iceberg.'

I then asked Mr Warren to go and see what was the matter. He first started out partly dressed, but decided to dress fully before going out, after doing which he went to one of the corridors and returned in a very few minutes with a piece of ice, saying it had been handed him as a souvenir.

By that time, I had dressed and had laid out the lifebelts but Mr Warren said there was absolutely no danger and that with her watertight compartments the vessel could not possibly sink and that in all probability the only effect of the accident would be the delaying of our arrival in New York three or four days.

We felt, however, too restless to remain in our room, so went out in the corridor again and talked with both the employees of the vessel and passengers. The general opinion prevailing was that there was no danger except for the expression on the part of one man who stated that the water was coming in below forward.

Following this, we then went to our rooms, put on all our heavy wraps and went to the foot of the grand staircase on D deck, again interviewing passengers and crew as to the danger. While standing there one of the designers of the vessel rushed by, going up the stairs. He was asked if there was any danger but made no reply.

But a passenger who was afterwards saved told me that his face had on it a look of terror. Immediately after this the report became general that water was in the squash courts, which were on the deck below where we were standing, and that the baggage had already been submerged. Just at this point a steward passed, ordering all to don life belts and warm clothing and go to the boat deck at once, saying that this move was simply a precautionary measure.

According to my impression, the time was about 45 minutes after the accident. We went back to our room for a third time, seized the life belts and hastened to a point two decks above, where an officer assisted in adjusting our life belts.

We saw in front of the purser's office ship's papers and valuables laid out, and I asked if we could take anything with us, but was told not.

Continuing up to the boat deck we tried to get out to the port side, but we were unable to open the door. Noticing the starboard door standing open we went out that way. The boat deck was the top deck of the vessel, uncovered and only a few houses on it, such as contained the gymnasium.

At the time we reached this deck there were very few passengers there, apparently, but it was dark and we could not estimate the number. There was a deafening roar of escaping steam, of which we had not been conscious while inside.

The only people we remembered seeing, except a young woman by the name of Miss Ostby, who had become separated from her father and was with us, were Mr Astor, his wife and servants, who were standing near one of the boats which was being cleared preparatory to being lowered. The Astors did not get into this boat. They all went back inside and I saw nothing of them again until Mrs Astor was taken onto the *Carpathia*.

We discovered that the boat next to the one the Astors' boat had been near had been lowered to the level of the deck, so we went towards it and were told by the officer to get in. I supposed Mr Warren had followed, but saw when I turned that he was standing back assisting the women.

People came in so rapidly in the darkness that it was impossible to distinguish them, and while I did not see him again, I thought that he also was in, as there seemed to be still room for more when the boat was lowered.

There were, according to my recollections, either 35 or 36 people in the boat, and I was not aware that Mr Warren was not with us until we were afloat and his name was called with no response.

(*Portland Oregonian*, 27 April 1912)

Sixty-five-year-old **Catherine Crosby** was travelling first-class back to her Milwaukee home with husband Edward and daughter Harriette. In her statement to the Senate Investigation into the disaster she revealed that on the afternoon of Sunday, 14 April, she noticed seamen on the *Titanic* checking the water temperature. The seamen in question said that the temperature of the water was lower than usual, thus indicating that the ship was in the vicinity of ice fields.

At that time my husband and I were walking up and down the promenade deck, which as I recollect it, was the deck below the hurricane deck, and it was while we were walking up and down this deck that we first noticed these seamen taking the temperature of the water. My husband was a sailor all his lifetime, and he told me all about it, and it was from that that I knew what they were doing. I could see what they were doing.

My husband retired at about nine o'clock that evening, and I retired about 10.30. Elmer Taylor, one of the passengers who went over with us on the steamer, told me afterwards, when we were on the *Carpathia*, that at the time I retired that night he noticed the boat was going full speed. I had not retired long when I was suddenly awakened by the thumping of the boat. The engines stopped suddenly. This was about 11.30. Captain Crosby got up, dressed, and went out. He came back again and said to me, 'You will lie there and drown,' and went out again. He said to my daughter: 'The boat is badly damaged, but I think the watertight compartments will hold her up.'

I then got up and dressed, and my daughter dressed, and followed my husband on deck. When she got up on deck, the officer told her to go back and get on her life preserver and come back on deck as soon as possible. She reported that to me, and we both went out on deck where the officer told us to come. I think it was the first or second boat that we got into. I do not recollect other boats being lowered at that time. This was on the left-hand side where the officer told us to come, and it was the deck above the one on which our state rooms were located: our state rooms were located on the B deck, and we went to the A deck where the officer and lifeboat were.

(US Inquiry, 17 May 1912)

Young English schoolmaster **Lawrence Beesley** was travelling second-class in cabin D56. In company with most of the passengers, he was unaware that there had even been a collision.

The voyage from Queenstown was quiet and successful. We had met with very fine weather. The sea was calm and the wind was westerly to south-westerly the whole way. The temperature was very cold, particularly on the last day. In fact, after dinner on Sunday evening it was almost too cold to be on the deck at all. I had been in my berth for about ten minutes when at about 11.40 p.m. I felt a slight jar. Then soon afterwards there was a second shock, but it was not sufficiently large to cause any anxiety to anyone however nervous they may have been. The engines, however, stopped immediately afterwards. At first I thought that the ship had lost a propeller. I went up on deck in my dressing gown, and found only a few people there, who had come up in the same way to inquire why we had stopped, but there was no sort of anxiety in the mind of anyone. We saw through the smoking-room window that a game of cards was going on and I went in to ask if the players knew anything. They had noticed the jar a little more and looking through the window had seen a huge iceberg go by close to the side of the boat. They thought we had just grazed it with a glancing blow, and the engines had been stopped to see if any damage had been done.

None of us, of course, had any conception that she had been pierced below by part of the submerged iceberg. The game of cards was resumed and, without any thought of disaster, I retired to my cabin to read until we went on again. I never saw any of the players or the onlookers again.

A little later, hearing people going upstairs, I went out again and found that everybody wanted to know why the engines had stopped. No doubt many of them had been awakened from their sleep by the sudden stopping of a vibration to which they had become accustomed during the four days we had been on board. Naturally, with such powerful engines as the *Titanic* carried, the vibration was very noticeable all the time, and the sudden stopping had something of the same effect as the stopping of a loud-ticking grandfather's clock in a room. On going on deck again I saw that there was an undoubted list downward from stern to bow, but knowing of what had happened concluded some of the front compartments had filled and weighed her down. I went down again to put on warmer clothing, and as I dressed heard an order shouted: 'All passengers on deck with life belts on.' We walked slowly up with them tied on over our clothing, but even then presumed this was a wise precaution the captain was taking,

63

and that we should return in a short time and retire to bed. There was a total absence of any panic or any expressions of alarm, and I suppose this can be accounted for by the exceedingly calm night and the absence of any signs of the accident.

The ship was absolutely still and except for a gentle tilt downward, which I do not think one person in ten would have noticed at that time, no signs of the approaching disaster were visible. She lay just as if she were waiting the order to go again when some trifling matter had been adjusted. But in a few moments we saw the covers lifted from the boats and the crews allotted to them standing by and curling up the ropes which were to lower them by the pulley blocks into the water.

We then began to realize it was more serious than had been supposed, and my first thought was to go down and get more clothing and some money, but seeing people pouring up the stairs decided it was better to cause no confusion to people coming up by doing so.

Presently we heard the order: 'All men stand back away from the boats and all ladies retire to next deck below' – the smoking deck or B deck. The men all stood away and remained in absolute silence, leaning against the end railings of the deck or pacing slowly up and down.

The boats were swung out and lowered from A deck. When they were to the level of B deck, where all the ladies were collected, the ladies got in quietly, with the exception of some who refused to leave their husbands. In some cases they were torn from them and pushed into the boats, but in many instances they were allowed to remain because there was no one to insist they should go.

Looking over the side, one saw boats from aft already in the water, slipping quietly away into the darkness, and presently the boats near to me were lowered and with much creaking as the new ropes slipped through the pulley blocks down the ninety feet which separated them from the water. An officer in uniform came up as one boat went down and shouted: 'When you are afloat, row round to the companion ladder and stand by with the other boats for orders.'

'Aye, aye, sir,' came up the reply, but I do not think any boat was able to obey the order. When they were afloat and had the oars at work the condition of the rapidly settling boat was so much more of a sight for alarm for those in the boats than those on board that in common prudence the sailors saw they could do nothing but row from the sinking ship to save at any rate some lives. They no doubt anticipated that suction from such an enormous vessel would be more than usually dangerous to a crowded boat mostly filled with women.

(*New York World*, 19 April 1912)

May Futrelle lost her husband – novelist Jacques Futrelle – in the disaster. She described the scene on board ship prior to the collision.

In the elegantly furnished drawing room, no premonitory shadow of death was present to cast cold fear over the gaiety of the evening. It was a brilliant scene; women beautifully gowned, laughing and talking – the odour of flowers. Why, it was just like being at some beautiful summer resort.

All that afternoon and in the evening, everybody was discussing the probability of arriving in New York on Wednesday. It was regarded as certain that the *Titanic* would make her trip in record time. We were not afraid of going too fast. We only knew of the speed by looking at the indicator. The sea was so calm, and the motion of the boat so slight that it was hardly noticeable.

The night was beautiful. The sea was placid and wonderful to look upon. Countless stars were reflected in all their glory in watery depths which gave no hint of the treachery lurking in them. Phosphorus gleamed upon the surface of the sea and reflected back its radiance from giant icebergs which were scattered over the face of the waters. There was not the slightest thought of danger in the minds of those who sat around the tables in the luxurious dining saloon of the *Titanic*. It was a brilliant crowd. Jewels flashed from the gowns of the women. And, oh, the dear women, how fondly they wore their latest Parisian gowns! It was the first time that most of them had an opportunity to display their newly acquired finery. The soft, sweet odour of rare flowers pervaded the atmosphere. I remember at our table there was a great bunch of American beauty roses. The orchestra played popular music. It was a buoyant, oh, such a jolly crowd. It was a rare gathering of beautiful women and splendid men.

There was that atmosphere of fellowship and delightful sociability which makes dinner on the Sabbath on board ship a delightful occasion. I thought, as I glanced over the saloon, that it would be hard to find gathered in one place a crowd which would better typify the highest type of American manhood and womankind.

I remember Jacques and Mr Harris discussing at our table the latest plays on the American stage. Everybody was so merry. We were all filled with the joy of living. We sat over dinner late that night.

I remember we discussed among ourselves a man sitting at a table across the cabin who was suspected of cheating at cards the night before. Card-playing had been permitted on the boat for the first time. The men warned one another against this man, who they said was a professional gambler, who made a practice of fleecing ocean travellers. The men were sure that he had cheated – so sure, in fact, that they had agreed to keep him at a safe distance in the future. He sat in that great dining room, with a cold-blooded smile playing over his features as he gazed over the crowd. It struck me as the one discordant and harsh note in the jollity.

It was suggested that we take a bit of fresh air after dinner and before retiring many of the passengers ventured out on the deck. I stepped out into the open to get one breath of fresh air, as I told Jacques, and to look upon the night before I retired. There was a death chill in the air which sent a shudder through me and caused me to hurry back into the cheer and warmth of the cabin. The terrible chillness affected all alike and a number of the men commented that we must be in the vicinity of icebergs. No one had the slightest fear, however; for Mr Andrews, who had some part in the construction of the vessel (he called it his baby), had laughingly assured us that at last man had constructed an unsinkable craft.

Before retiring, my husband complained of a slight headache. We had both gone to our state room. Nearly everyone on board had retired except the men who chatted over their cigars in the magnificent lounging room. There was the stillness which only comes with the sea. A faint tremor of the boat was the only thing which served to remind one that he was on the sea. Apart from this, one might well have imagined himself to be in one of the magnificent hotels of New York City.

(*Boston Sunday Post*, 21 April 1912)

First-class passenger **Major Arthur Peuchen**, of Toronto, Canada, described how he left $200,000 worth of stocks behind in his cabin when making a hasty evacuation.

It was Sunday evening, a starry night and calm. There was an exceptional bill of fare on the evening dinner. We were all in evening dress and the ladies wore many a jewel. Music went on as usual. I dined with Mrs Markland Molson, Mr and Mrs Allison and their little girl. Everything was exceptionally bright. Then I went to the smoking room and met Mr Beattie, a partner of Hugo Ross, of Winnipeg, formerly of Toronto. I also met Mr McCarthy of the Union Bank of Vancouver, and a financial man from Toronto. Talk was unusually bright. That was about 11 o'clock. Then I said, 'Good night, I am going to turn in.'

I had just reached my berth, when I heard a dull thud. It was like a collision and I didn't think it serious. That's extraordinary, I thought, and went up to see. I ran upstairs and on the way met a friend who laughingly said that we had struck an iceberg and we went up on deck. There we found that we had struck aft of the bow about 75 feet from the point and had scraped along the starboard side. We saw ice falling on us. The berg was about 70 feet high. As the berg passed the portholes it alarmed the women in the berths.

The passengers came on deck one by one, some in pyjamas, some in evening gowns. They were not yet much alarmed. I went inside and spoke with my friend Molson. Mr Hugo Ross was sick in bed. Then I got in touch with Charles M. Hays and Thornton Davidson, a son-in-law of Mr Hays. Then four of us, Mr Hays, Mr Molson and Mr Davidson, went up to see the ice.

I then for the first time saw she was listing. This was about fifteen minutes after the strike. Then I noticed that all the people were putting on lifebelts, and for the first time it looked serious. I went inside, threw off my dress suit, put on my warmest clothes and my steward, a very nice fellow, helped me to put on my life preserver. I never saw him again.

I took three oranges and a pearl pin. There was $200,000 of stocks and bonds, all my jewellery and presents for my daughter Jessie and family in the berth, but I did not touch them.

It was rather sad to turn and leave the cheery room I had occupied – cosy, large and comfortable as it was.

(*Halifax (Nova Scotia) Evening Mail*, 19 April 1912)

Liverpool-born leading fireman **Frederick Barrett** was stationed below in No. 6 boiler room, on the starboard side of the ship, when the crash occurred. He described a sound like roaring thunder, followed by a cascade of water through the gash in the ship's side.

There is a clock face in the stokehole and the red light goes up for 'Stop' . I was talking to Mr Hesketh, one of the engineers, when the red light came up, and I shouted, 'Shut all the dampers.' That order was obeyed, but the crash came before we had them all shut.

There was a rush of water into my stokehole. We were standing on plates about six feet above the tank tops, and the water came in about two feet above the plates. Together with Mr Hesketh, I jumped through the doorway into No. 5 section. The watertight door between the sections was then open, but it shut just as we jumped through. This door is worked from the bridge. I do not know whether any more men in my stokehole were saved. The water was coming in fast enough through the side of the ship to flood the place.

Shortly afterwards the order came from the engine room to send all the stokers up. Most of them went up, but I was told to remain with the engineers to do any errands. Mr Harvey, Mr Wilson, Mr Shepherd (of the engineers' staff) and I waited in No. 5 section.

Mr Harvey told me to send some firemen for some lamps. Just as we got the lamps the electric light came on again. They must have been changing the dynamos over. Mr Harvey told me to fetch some firemen to draw the furnaces. I fetched about fifteen firemen, and they drew the thirty furnaces in the section. That occupied about twenty minutes. I looked at the gauge and found there was no water in the boilers. The ship, in blowing off steam, had blown it out.

Mr Harvey told me to lift the manhole plate, which I did, and then Mr Shepherd, hurrying across to do something and not noticing the plate had been moved, fell down and broke his leg. We lifted him up and laid him in the pump-room. About a quarter of an hour after the fires were drawn there was a rush of water. Mr Shepherd ordered me up the ladder.

(British Inquiry, 7 May 1912)

Able Seaman **Samuel Hemming** claimed that Thomas Andrews of shipbuilders Harland & Wolff had confided shortly after the collision that the *Titanic* was doomed.

I opened the forepeak storeroom. Me and the storekeeper went down as far as the top of the tank and found everything dry. I came up to ascertain where a hissing sound was coming from. I found it was the air escaping out of the exhaust of the tank. At that time the Chief Officer, Mr Wilde, put his head around the hawse pipe and says: 'What is that, Hemming?' I said: 'The air is escaping from the forepeak tank. She is making water in the forepeak tank, but the storeroom is quite dry.' He said, 'All right,' and went away.

Me and the storekeeper went back and turned into our bunks a few minutes. Then the joiner came in and he said: 'If I were you, I would turn out, you fellows. She is making water, one-two-three, and the racket court is getting filled up.'

Just as he went, the boatswain came, and he says: 'Turn out, you fellows, you haven't half an hour to live.' He said: 'That is from Mr Andrews. Keep it to yourselves, and let no one know.' That would be a quarter of an hour from the time the ship struck.

(US Inquiry, 25 April 1912)

The *Titanic*'s Third Officer, **Herbert Pitman**, was asleep in his quarters.

The collision woke me up. It was a sound that I thought seemed like the ship coming to an anchor. It gave just a little vibration. I was about half awake and half asleep. I had a look around and I could not see anything and could not hear any noise, so I went back to the room and sat down and lit my pipe. I thought that nothing had really happened, that perhaps it might have been a dream, or something like that.

A few minutes afterwards I thought I had better start dressing, as it was near my watch, so I started dressing, and when I was partly dressed Mr Boxhall (the Fourth Officer) came in and said there was water in the mail room.

I said: 'What happened?'

He said: 'We struck an iceberg.'

So I put a coat on and went on deck, and saw the men uncovering the boats and clearing them away. I walked along to the after end of the boat deck and met Mr Moody, the Sixth Officer. I asked him if he had seen the iceberg. He said no. But he said: 'There is some ice on the forward well deck.' So to satisfy my curiosity I went down there myself.

I saw a little ice there. Then I went further, to the forecastle head, to see if there was any damage there. I could not see any at all. On my return, before emerging from under the forecastle head, I saw a crowd of firemen coming out with their bags of clothing.

I said: 'What is the matter?'

They said: 'Water is coming in our place.'

I said: 'That is funny.' I looked down No. 1 hatch and saw the water flowing over the hatch. I immediately went to the boat deck and assisted in getting boats uncovered and ready for swinging out.

(US Inquiry, 23 April 1912)

First-class passenger **Mrs Lucian P. Smith** from Huntington, West Virginia, had enjoyed a pleasant evening in the *Titanic*'s splendid Café Parisien.

At 7.30 p.m., as usual, my husband and I went to dinner in the café. There was a dinner party going on, given by Mr Ismay to the captain and various other people on board ship. This was a usual occurrence of the evening, so we paid no attention to it. The dinner did not seem to be particularly gay. While they had various wines to drink, I am positive none were intoxicated at a quarter of nine o'clock when we left the dining room. There was a coffee room directly outside of the café in which people sat and listened to the music and drank coffee and cordials after dinner. My husband was with some friends just outside of what I know as the Parisian Café. I stayed up until 10.30, and then went to bed. I passed through the coffee room, and Mr Ismay and his party were still there. The reason I am positive about the different time is because I asked my husband at the three intervals what time it was. I went to bed, and my husband joined his friends.

I was asleep when the crash came. It did not awaken me enough to frighten me. In fact, I went back to sleep again. Then I awakened again because it seemed that the boat had stopped. About that time my husband came into the room. Still I was not frightened, but thought he had come in to go to bed. I asked him why the boat had stopped, and, in a leisurely manner, he said: 'We are in the north and have struck an iceberg. It does not amount to anything, but will probably delay us a day getting into New York. However, as a matter of form, the captain has ordered all ladies on deck.'

That frightened me a little but, after being reassured there was no danger, I took plenty of time in dressing, putting on all my heavy clothing, high shoes, and two coats, as well as a warm knit hood. While I dressed, my husband and I talked of landing, not mentioning the iceberg.

I started out, putting on my life preserver, when we met a steward who was on his way to tell us to put on life preservers and come on deck. However I returned to the room with the intention of bringing my jewellery, but my husband said not to delay with such trifles. However I picked up two rings and went on deck.

After getting to the top deck, the ladies were ordered on Deck A without our husbands. I refused to go, but, after being told by three or four officers, my husband insisted and, along with another lady, we went down. After staying there some time with nothing seemingly going on, someone called saying they could not be lowered from that deck for the reason it was enclosed in glass. That seemed to be the first time the officers and captain had thought of that, and hastened to order us all on the top deck again. There was some delay in getting lifeboats down – in fact, we had plenty of time to sit in the gymnasium and chat with another gentleman and his wife. I kept asking my husband if I could remain with him rather than go in a lifeboat. He promised me I could. There was no commotion, no panic, and no one seemed to be particularly frightened. In fact, most of the people seemed interested in the unusual occurrence, many having crossed fifty and sixty times. However I noticed my husband was busy talking to an officer he came in contact with. Still I had not the least suspicion of the scarcity of lifeboats, or I never should have left my husband.

(US Inquiry, 20 May 1912)

Saloon steward **William Ward**, a man with twenty years' experience at sea, was in his quarters on E deck.

When I felt the shock I got up. I went to the port and opened it. It was bitterly cold. I looked out and saw nothing. It was very dark. I got back into my bunk again. Presently two or three people came along and said she had struck an iceberg, and some of them went and brought pieces of ice along in their hands. I thought at first it was the propeller gone, the way she went. I lay there for about twenty minutes, and in the meantime the steerage passengers were coming from forward, coming aft, carrying life belts with them. Some of them were wet. Still I did not think it was anything serious, and I lay there for a little while longer when the head waiter came down – Moss, his name was – and said we were all to go on deck and to put on some warm clothing before we went up, as we were liable to be there some time. With that, I think almost everybody in the 'glory hole', as we call it, got dressed and went on deck. I just put on things to keep me warm, because I did not think it was anything serious.

We went up the midship companionway, up to the top deck, and met Mr Dodd (the chief second steward) on D deck. He told us to go forward to the saloon and see if there was anyone about. If there was, we were to order them up on deck and collect the lifebelts and bring them up to the deck cloakroom.

I went forward but did not see anyone around there. So I came back and got seven life belts on my way up. When I got on deck, I adjusted preservers on people that hadn't got one. I put one on myself. Everybody was moving around in a most orderly manner. There did not seem to be any excitement. In fact, a lot of ladies and gentlemen there were just treating it as a kind of joke.

(US Inquiry, 25 April 1912)

When celebrated Broadway producer Henry B. Harris cabled home that he and his wife René had booked to travel on the *Titanic*, his business associate William Klein immediately feared the worst. Indeed Klein was so alarmed by the prospect that he promptly cabled Harris and begged him not to sail on the new liner. Harris replied that it was too late to change his plans and he and his wife duly boarded the ship. As the *Titanic* went down, Harris kissed his wife goodbye and helped her into one of the collapsible boats. He then went down with the ship. **Mrs Henry B. Harris** told her story to American newsmen.

We were in our state room when the word was passed for all passengers to put on life preservers and go on deck. This order followed within a few seconds after the ship struck. We did not realize the seriousness of the crash, thinking some slight trouble had happened to the engines. Even when the order was brought to us to put on life preservers and come on deck we still failed to realize the situation.

As we went on deck we passed groups of men and women who were laughing and joking. When we reached the main deck, forward, and saw the lifeboats being swung overboard the seriousness of the matter began to dawn on us. Then came the command: 'Women and children first.'

When the passengers saw the seriousness with which the officers and crew went about their business they began to realize that something terrible had happened and began to make their way towards the lifeboats.

Colonel Astor and Mrs Astor were standing near us. When the men of the *Titanic* came to her and told her to get into a lifeboat she refused to leave her husband's side. Then I was asked to enter one of the boats. My husband told me to go but I did not want to leave him. He reassured me, saying the danger was not serious and that he would follow after me in a short time. Still I could not believe that everything was as he said. I felt that if I left him something terrible would happen. The officers told me I would have to get into a lifeboat. My husband told me to and finally I was led to the side and lowered into a boat. They put me in a collapsible boat. I was one of three women in the first cabin in the thing; the rest were steerage people. Major Butt helped those poor, frightened steerage people so wonderfully, tenderly and yet with such cool and manly firmness. He was a major to the last.

When the order came to take to the boats he became as one in supreme command. He was a man to be feared. In one of the earlier boats fifty women, it seemed, were about to be lowered, when a man, suddenly panic-stricken, ran to the stern of it. Major Butt shot one arm out, caught him by the neck, and jerked him backward. His head cracked against a rail and he was stunned.

'Sorry,' said Major Butt, 'but women will be attended to first or I'll break every damned bone in your body.'

Mrs Astor had left her husband and had been placed in another boat. As I was being lowered over the side, I saw my husband and Colonel Astor standing together. Jacques Futrelle was standing near them. My husband waved his hand. That was the last I saw of him.

Mrs Emily Richards, aged twenty-four, from Penzance in Cornwall was travelling with her two children and her mother to join her husband in Akron, Ohio.

I had put the children in bed and had gone to bed myself. We had been making good time all day, the ship rushing through the sea at a tremendous rate, and the air on deck was cold and crisp. I didn't hear the collision, for I was asleep. But my mother came and shook me.

'There is surely danger,' said Mamma. 'Something has gone wrong.''

So we put on our slippers and outside coats and got the children into theirs and went on deck. We had on our nightgowns under our coats. As we went up the stairway someone was shouting down in a calm voice: 'Everybody put on their life preservers before coming on deck!'

We went back and put them on, assuring each other that it was nothing.

(*New York World*, 20 April 1912)

American passenger **Mahala Douglas** was travelling with her husband Walter. She survived, but he was lost in the sinking.

We both remarked that the boat was going faster than she ever had. The vibration as one passed the stairway in the centre was very noticeable.

The shock of the collision was not great to us. The engines stopped, then went on for a few moments, then stopped again. We waited some little time, Mr Douglas reassuring me that there was no danger before going out of the cabin. But later Mr Douglas went out to see what had happened, and I put on my heavy boots and fur coat to go up on deck later. I waited in the corridor to see or hear what I could. We received no orders. No one knocked at our door. We saw no officers nor stewards – no one to give an order or answer our questions. As I waited for Mr Douglas to return I went back to speak to my maid who was in the same cabin as Mrs Carter's maid. Now people commenced to appear with life preservers, and I heard from someone that the order had been given to put them on. I took three from our cabin, gave one to the maid, telling her to get off in the small boat when her turn came. Mr Douglas met me as I was going up to find him and asked, jestingly, what I was doing with those life preservers. He did not think even then that the accident was serious. We both put them on, however, and went up on the boat deck. Mr Douglas told me if I waited we might both go together and we stood there waiting. We heard that the boat was in communication with three other boats by wireless. We watched the distress rockets sent off. They rose high in the air and burst. No one seemed excited. Finally, as we stood by a collapsible boat lying on the deck and an emergency boat swinging from the davits was being filled, it was decided I should go. Mr Boxhall was trying to get the boat off and called to the captain on the bridge: 'There's a boat coming up over there.' The captain said, 'I want a megaphone.' Just before we got into the boat the captain called: 'How many of the crew are in that boat? Get out of there, every man of you!' I can see a solid row of men, from bow to stern, crawl over on to the deck. We women then got in. I asked Mr Douglas to come with me, but, turning away, he replied: 'No, I must be a gentleman.' I said: 'Try and get off with Mr Moore and Major Butt. They will surely make it.'

(US Inquiry, 9 May 1912)

Miss Caroline Bonnell of Youngstown, Ohio, was travelling with her aunt Lily and George D. Wick, a steel manufacturer from Youngstown, and his wife and daughter. The women were all saved, but George Wick died.

Miss Wick and I occupied a state room together. We were awakened shortly before midnight by a sudden shock, a grinding concussion. Miss Wick arose and looked out of the state room window. She saw some men playfully throwing particles of ice at one another, and realized that we had struck an iceberg.

She and I dressed, not hastily, for we were not greatly alarmed, and went on deck.

There we found a number of passengers. Naturally they were all somewhat nervous, but there was nothing approaching a panic. The other members of our party also had come on deck, and we formed a little group by ourselves.

We were told to put on life belts and obeyed. Then the sailors began to launch the lifeboats. Still we were not alarmed. We had no doubt that all on board would be saved. In fact we had no idea that the ship was sinking and believed that the resort to the lifeboats was merely a precaution.

Mr Wick kissed his wife goodbye and our boat, the first on that side of the ship, was lowered to the sea. There were about twenty-five women in the boat with two sailors and a steward to row. These were the only men. The boat would have held many more.

(*New York World*, 20 April 1912)

International dress designer **Lucy, Lady Duff Gordon**, and her Eton-educated husband, Sir Cosmo Duff Gordon, booked on the *Titanic* under the names of 'Mr and Mrs Morgan', possibly a joke at the expense of the ship's owner, American businessman John Pierpont Morgan. Their party also included Lady Duff Gordon's secretary, Laura Francatelli. All three survived. Lady Duff Gordon was preparing for bed in cabin A20 when the *Titanic* struck the iceberg.

I was awakened by a long grinding shock as though someone had drawn a giant finger all along the side of the boat. I awakened my husband and told him that I thought we had struck something. There was no excitement that I could hear, but Sir Cosmo went up on deck. He returned and told me that we had hit some ice, apparently a big berg, but there seemed to be no danger. We were not assured of this, however, and Sir Cosmo went upstairs again. He came back to me and said: 'You had better put your clothes on because I heard them give orders to strip the boats.'

We each put on a life preserver, and over mine I threw some heavy furs. I took a few trinkets and we went up to the deck. The ship had listed slightly to starboard and was down a little at the head. As we stood there, one of the officers ran to us and said: 'The women and children are to go into the boats.'

We watched a number of women and children and some men go into the lifeboats. At last one of the officers came to me and said: 'Lady Gordon, you had better go in one of the boats.'

I said to my husband: 'Well, we might as well take the boat, although I think it will be only a little pleasure excursion until morning. Five stokers got in and two Americans, A.L. Solomon of New York and Mr Stengel of Newark. A number of other passengers, mostly men, were standing near by and they joked with us because we were going out on the ocean. 'The ship can't sink,' said one. 'You'll get your death of cold out there in the ice.'

Edward N. Kimball of Boston, Massachusetts, travelled first-class with his wife.

On Sunday evening I had just gone down from the smoke room to my state room and removed my coat and was standing in the middle of the room when the ship struck the iceberg. It seemed to me like scraping and tearing more than a shock. It was on the starboard side of the ship under where our room was located, and the ice from the iceberg poured in our porthole.

After assuring Mrs Kimball that it was nothing, simply an iceberg, and that we had probably scraped it, and as the ship did not seem to slacken her speed, everything was probably all right. I stepped into the companion-way and spoke to some friends who were located in the same section.

I then went on deck to see if I could see the iceberg. There were very few people out around the ship and the stewards and officers were assuring everybody that everything was all right and to return to bed, which many of them probably did.

I came back to our state room, which was located near the stairway, which went down to the deck below, to the squash courts and mail rooms. At that time I saw a mail clerk go down and when he came up he had one mail bag in his hands and was wet to the knees.

I asked him about how bad it was and he seemed very serious and said it was pretty bad, and that he would advise the women to dress as they might have to go on deck and it would be cold. We instructed the rest of the women in our party to dress and also everyone in our corridor, including a number of women who were travelling alone.

Mrs Kimball had already started dressing, and I told her to dress warmly, as we would probably be on deck for some time and put on a sweater and a heavy ulster (a long overcoat).

We then started out feeling that everything was all right. After we had gone a few steps a young lady of our party came back from the upper deck, and I asked her what was going on up there. She said the order had been given out to put on the lifebelts. We returned to our state rooms, which were only a few feet away, got our lifebelts and notified all the women in the corridor to do the same and to come with us.

None of us knew how to put on the lifebelts, but I saw an officer in the companionway and he showed us how to put them on, and also told us that there was no danger and that everything would be all right.

He suggested, however, that we go up on the boat deck. When we arrived, only a few people were there, and as it was about 75 feet from the boat deck to the water, the officers were having great difficulty in getting the people to go into the lifeboats, assuring them at the same time that it would not be a long while before they would probably be back on the big boat.

(*Boston Post*, 20 April 1912)

Charlotte Collyer and her daughter Marjorie had been asleep for half an hour when husband Harvey returned to their second-class cabin. He too was about to retire to bed when the collision occurred. Charlotte later recounted her experiences to an American magazine.

The sensation to me was as if the ship had been seized by a giant hand and shaken once, twice then stopped dead in its course. That is to say there was a long, backward jerk, followed by a shorter one. I was not thrown out of my berth and my husband staggered on his feet only slightly. We heard no strange sounds, no rending of plates and woodwork, but we noticed that the engines had stopped running. They tried to start the engines a few minutes later but after some coughing and rumbling there was silence once more.

Our cabin was so situated that we could follow this clearly. My husband and I were not alarmed. He said that there must have been some slight accident in the engine room and at first he did not intend to go on deck. Then he changed his mind, put on his coat and left me. I lay quietly in my berth with my little girl and almost fell asleep again. In what seemed a very few moments my husband returned. He was a bit excited then. 'What do you think,' he exclaimed. 'We have struck an iceberg, a big one, but there is no danger – an officer just told me so.' I could hear the footsteps of people on the deck above my head. There was some stamping and queer noises as if ships' tackle was being pulled about. 'Are the people frightened?' I asked quietly. 'No,' he replied. 'I don't think the shock woke up many in the second cabin, and few of those in the saloons have troubled to go on deck. I saw the professional gamblers playing with some of the passengers as I went by. Their cards had been jerked off the table when the boat struck, but they were gathering them up and had started their game again before I left the saloon.' The story reassured me. If these people at their cards were not worried, why should I be?

I think my husband would have retired to his berth but suddenly we heard hundreds of people running along the passageway in front of our door. They did not cry out, but the patter of their feet reminded me of rats scurrying through an empty room. I could see my face in the mirror opposite and it had grown very white. My husband too was pale and he stammered when he spoke to me. 'We had better go on deck and see what's wrong,' he said. I jumped out of bed and put a dressing gown over my night-dress. I hurriedly tied my hair back with a ribbon. By this time although the boat had not made any progress, it seemed to have tilted forward a little. I caught up my daughter just as she was in her nightgown, wrapped a White Star cabin blanket around her and started out of the door. My husband followed immediately behind. Neither of us took any belongings from the cabin and I remember that he even left his watch lying on his pillow. We did not doubt for an instant that we would return. When we reached the second cabin promenade deck we found a great many people there. Some officers were walking up and down. My husband stepped over to an officer – it was either Fifth Officer Harold Lowe or First Officer Murdoch – and asked him a question. I heard him shout back: 'No, we have no searchlight but we have a few rockets on board. Keep calm! There is no danger.'

Our party of three stood close together. Suddenly there was a commotion near one of the gangways and we saw a stoker come climbing up from below. He stopped a few feet away from us. All the fingers of one hand had been cut off. Blood was running from the stumps and blood was spattered over his face and over his clothes. The red marks showed very clearly against the coal dust with which he was covered. I went over and spoke to him. I asked him if there was any danger. 'Danger?' he screamed at the top of his voice. 'I should just say so! It's hell down below. This boat will sink like a stone in ten minutes.'

He staggered away and lay down fainting with his head on a coil of rope. At this moment I got my first grip of fear – awful sickening fear. That poor man with his bleeding hand and his speckled face brought up a picture of smashed engines and mangled human bodies. I hung on to my husband's arm and although he was very brave, and not trembling, I saw that his face was as white as paper. We realized that the accident was much worse than we had supposed, but even then I and all the others about me of whom I have any knowledge did not believe that the *Titanic* would go down.

The officers were running to and fro shouting orders. I saw First Officer Murdoch place guards by the gangways to prevent others like the wounded stoker from coming on deck. How many unhappy men were shut off in that way from their chance of safety I do not know, but Mr Murdoch was probably right. He was a masterful man, astoundingly brave and cool. I had met him the day before when he was inspecting the second cabin quarters, and thought him a bull-dog of a man who would not be afraid of anything. This proved to be true. He kept order to the last, and died at his post. They say he shot himself. I do not know.

Those in charge must have herded us towards the nearest boat deck for that is where I presently found myself, still clinging to my husband's arm, and with little Marjorie beside me. Many women were standing with their husbands and there was no confusion. Then above the clamour of the people asking questions of each other, there came the terrible cry, 'Lower the boats! Women and children first.' Someone was shouting these last few words over and over again. 'Women and children first! Women and children first!' They struck utter terror into my heart and now they will ring in my ears until the day I die. They meant my own safety but they also meant the greatest loss I have ever suffered – the life of my husband.

(*Semi-Monthly Magazine*, May 1912)

Young **Marjorie Collyer**, Charlotte's daughter, later gave her version of events to her local paper in England.

The night the *Titanic* hit the iceberg I was asleep. I didn't feel the bump and the ship started to back like a train, and I heard my mother say to my father that she guessed the works had stopped. I could hear feet on the decks. Then mother dressed me, took me by the hand and led me upstairs. I had a big dollie that I got two Christmases before, and we were in such a hurry that I left it behind. I cried for my dollie, but we couldn't go back.

The decks were full of people. Some of them were crying. An

officer said we should all put on life preservers, and my mother put one on me, and then fastened one around herself. Papa put one on too.

I was crying for my doll, but nobody could go back and get her. Then someone said we should get into a boat and two men lifted me up and put me in a boat. My father raised me in his arms and kissed me, and then he kissed my mother. She followed me into the boat.

(*Leatherhead Advertiser*, 18 May 1912)

New Jersey leather manufacturer **Charles Emil Henry Stengel**, who was travelling in a first-class cabin with his wife, was one of the first to sense that a tragedy might be about to unfold before his eyes.

We retired about 10 o'clock. We had attended a concert and we knew that the captain was entertaining and dining his friends, among whom was Bruce Ismay, until 10 o'clock. Please say for me, in justice to Captain Smith, that he had not been drinking. He smoked cigarettes, but he did not drink.

I had been sleeping but a short time and was having a terrible dream, which I cannot fully remember, when I felt a shock. This was no greater than one caused by the propeller coming above the surface of the water. I thought, nevertheless, that I would go on deck and ascertain if there was any trouble. There I found but few persons. No one seemed to fear danger.

The first inkling that I had of danger was when I saw the serious face of Captain Smith as he talked to George Widener, of Philadelphia. I wouldn't have thought anything of it if I hadn't seen Captain Smith's face. Then I knew we were in danger.

(*Newark Star*, 19 April 1912)

As she recounted in a letter to her local paper, English passenger **Nellie Walcroft** was startled by the collision in her second-class cabin.

On the Sunday night we went to our state room about 10.30. We had not been asleep long when suddenly a crash came and I was nearly thrown out of my berth. I woke my friend, Miss Cameron, who did not hear anything unusual, and then I heard the noise of footsteps along the corridor.

I waited very anxiously to hear what was the matter because the engines had stopped. Immediately the steward came down and said, 'Go back to your beds. No danger!' But I heard whisperings of icebergs and then suddenly we heard very loud hammering as if they were closing heavy iron doors. Five minutes later the steward came in and said: 'Will you dress and go on deck with your lifebelts on as quickly as possible. It's only a precaution.'

My friend and I dressed. There were full instructions how to put the lifebelts on in the state room, but we were too nervous to read them. People were going up on deck so we both went, carrying our belts from E deck. A man took the lifebelts from us and put them over our heads, and tied them on.

The order was for women and children to go on the lower deck but there was such a lot he told some to go up on the boat deck, so we went. We walked round, thinking there was no hurry, when suddenly rockets went up! We then began to realize the danger we were in.

(Maidenhead Advertiser)

Bertha Mulvihill, aged twenty-four, was travelling third-class from her native Ireland to meet up with her fiancé, Henry Noon, of Providence, Rhode Island. She lost her trousseau in the sinking.

It was about 11.45. I was in bed and was just getting to sleep.

Then came a heavy jar. I lay still for several minutes, not knowing what was the matter. Then I slipped on a heavy coat over my nightgown, pulled on my shoes and went out into the passage.

The people were rushing up the stairways and way down in the steerage. I could hear the women and men shrieking and screaming. The women called for their children. The men cursed. I knew they were fighting.

Then I hurried back into my room, stood up on the wash stand and took down a lifebelt. This I adjusted about me, and hurried out into the passage.

At the top of the passage I met a sailor with whom I had become acquainted on my passage across. I asked him what the matter was.

'There is no danger, little girl,' he replied to me. 'We have hit an iceberg.'

'We're lost, we're lost,' I cried, but he took me by the arm and told me to follow him. The people already were running to the sides of the boat to get into the lifeboats.

Some of the Italian men from way down in the steerage were screaming and fighting to get into the lifeboats. Captain Smith stood at the head of the passageway. He had a gun in his hand.

'Boys,' he said, 'you've got to do your duty here. It's the women and children first, and I'll shoot the first man who jumps into a boat.'

But this didn't seem to have much effect on them, for they still fought to get into the boats. But the captain – oh, he was a good captain and a brave man – stood guard and wouldn't let the men get in before the women.

There were two Catholic priests aboard. They were coming to America from Ireland. After we got off, I was talking with Eugene Ryan, a boy from my home town in Athlone, and he told me the priests went among the men on the *Titanic* as the vessel was sinking and administered the last rites of the church. And they stuck to it, too, until the water was up to about their knees.

My sailor friend told me to follow him and he would try to get me into a lifeboat. We climbed up bolts and cleats until we got to the next deck. Nearly every woman had left the ship then, I guess, and only two boats remained.

Beside me there was a family named Rice consisting of the father and mother and six children. The father was not permitted to leave the ship, but the mother and her six children could leave if they wished. She was crying and weeping. She wouldn't go into the lifeboat and leave her husband to perish. 'I can't go and leave my husband,' she cried to the officers. 'Let him come with me. Oh, please let him come with me,' she pleaded. 'I don't want to live if he can't come. There will be nobody to earn bread for my little children,' she wailed.

But the officers wouldn't let the father go.

'I'll stay with my husband then,' the woman cried. I saw her clinging to her husband and children just before I left the vessel. That was the last I ever saw of her. The whole family went down together.

(*Boston Post*, 20 April 1912)

American industrialist's wife **Mrs William T. Graham** shared a state room with her daughter Margaret, aged nineteen. Both paid tribute to the quiet heroism of forty-eight-year-old Howard Case, the American-born managing director of the Vacuum Oil Company of London, and thirty-one-year-old Washington A. Roebling II from New Jersey whose uncle was one of the builders of the Brooklyn Bridge. Both men died in the sinking.

My daughter and I had a state room on the port side, near the stern, and we were awake, although in bed, when the iceberg was struck. It was a grinding, tearing sound. We didn't regard it as serious. I dressed lightly, but my daughter tried to go to sleep.

With us, in an adjoining bedroom, was my daughter's companion, Miss E. W. Shutes, a teacher. She was the only other member in our party and was later saved with us. She got up, too, but my daughter insisted that the danger was imaginary and told us to go to sleep.

Shortly after there was a rap at the door. It was a passenger we had met – Washington A. Roebling II. He told us that it would be best to be prepared for an emergency. I looked out of my window and saw a big iceberg. We lost no time in getting into the saloon. In one of the passages I met an officer of the ship. 'What is the matter?' I asked him. 'We've only busted two pipes,' he said. 'Everything is all right. Don't worry.' 'But what makes the ship list so?' I asked. 'Oh, that's nothing,' he replied, and walked away.

On the deck we met Howard Case. We had been introduced to him. We had had many pleasant talks with Mr Case and I asked his advice, because I had already seen one boatload of passengers lowered and I wanted to know if it would be safer to stay on board. Mr Case advised us to get into a boat. 'And what are you going to do?' we asked him. 'Oh,' he replied, 'I'll take a chance and stay here.'

Just at that time they were filling up the third lifeboat on the port side. Then Mr Roebling came up too. He told us to hurry and get into the boat. Mr Roebling and Mr Case bustled our party of three into the boat in less time than it takes to tell it. They were both working hard to help the women and children. The boat was fairly crowded when we three were pushed into it. A few more men jumped in at the last moment, but Mr Roebling and Mr Case stood at the rail and made no attempt to get into the boat.

They shouted goodbye to us, and – what do you think Mr Case did then? He just calmly lighted a cigarette and waved us good-bye with his hand. Mr Roebling stood there too – I can see him now. I am sure that he knew that the ship would go to the bottom. But both just stood there.

(*Trenton Evening Times*, 20 April 1912)

Swedish steerage passenger **Carl Jonsson** described the impact on the third-class quarters.

There was no crash, only a slight jar and creaking, which particularly awakened me. There was no excitement in the steerage, and I paid no attention to the occurrence. I was asleep again when two of the ship's officers passed through the steerage, awakening the passengers. They told us to dress and come on deck – that there had been an accident, but that there was no danger.

When I started to dress I noticed that there was water creeping up about my feet. At first it came very slowly, but after a time it was around my ankles. In the compartment where I was sleeping the water was at an even depth everywhere, and the boat did not seem to have the slightest pitch to starboard or port, indicating that she was settling slowly and steadily and that the bottom had been ripped out. The upper air compartments kept the water from coming in very fast at first and no one seemed to think that she was going to sink.

When I got on deck I saw the first sign of panic among the passengers. Women were screaming with terror and men were rushing this way and that. Then I noticed that the boat had begun to settle in the bow, where I was standing. All the lights on the vessel were still going, however, and were still lighted when they began to lower the first lifeboats. As the second boat swung from the davits, the water reached the dynamos in the engine room, and we were suddenly plunged into darkness save for the cold, clear light of the heavens.

(US press, 19 April 1912)

Gunnar Isidor Tenglin, aged twenty-five, was another Swede travelling third-class.

It was not a hard shock, but my friend and myself, finding the engines stopped thought we would go up and investigate. I put on all my clothes but my shoes, and we went to the forward deck. The deck was covered with particles of ice. We asked an officer if there was any danger and he said: 'No. Go back to your berths and go to sleep.'

We did not go back, however, but walked to the rear deck. There a scene of panic prevailed. The English, Swedish, Irish and German passengers were the most composed, but the Italians were greatly excited. They were swarming up on deck, in all stages of undress, carrying baggage of every description. They were crying, praying and wringing their hands. As we were perfectly sure the boat would not sink, their antics seemed amusing to us. In fact we stood around about an hour or more watching them.

Seeing that everybody was donning lifebelts, we thought we would go to our state room and procure one. We descended to the gangway, but were met with a rush of water that compelled us to retreat to the upper deck again. We could feel the boat gradually sinking and as they had commenced to launch the lifeboats, we set about thinking of our own safety.

(*Burlington Daily Gazette*, 25 April 1912)

Mariana Assaf was travelling from her native Syria to Canada. Her two sons had wanted to go with her, but she insisted that they stay at home. She told of the terrifying scenes in the steerage section.

Although it did not seem to be much at first and we did not feel very much except a jar, some of us wanted to go on deck to see what happened. We were told that everything was all right, and we did not think there was a danger. But when the ship did not go on, some of us began to think they were not telling us the truth and that we might be sinking. I think somebody must have said the boat was going to go down for suddenly there was great confusion and everybody tried to rush the deck. There were many in steerage who tried to rush the boats and at those some of the officers fired revolvers and some of them were shot dead. The rest were driven back. They were not given a chance to escape. As for me, when I thought the ship might sink, I forgot everything and rushed away from the steerage and up to the deck where the first-class passengers were. I could not think of anything. I never saw any of my relations so I do not know what became of them. The last I saw of them was when we were all in the steerage.

When I ran up to first-class, I saw that the ship must be going to sink and I lost my head. But a man, I think he was one of the sailors, when he saw that I was there, he pushed me into one of the boats.

(Canadian press, 24 April 1912)

Russian steerage passenger **Berk Pickard** described his ordeal at the subsequent Senate hearings.

My cabin was No. 10 in the steerage, at the stern. I first knew of the collision when it happened, about ten minutes to twelve. We had all been asleep, and all of a sudden we perceived a shock. We knew something was wrong, and we jumped out of bed and we dressed ourselves and went out, and we could not get back again. I wanted to go back to get my things but I could not. The stewards would not allow us to go back. They made us all go forward on the deck. There were no doors locked to prevent us from going back. I did not take much notice of it, and I went to the deck. The other passengers started arguing. One said that it was dangerous and the other said that it was not; one said white and the other said black. Instead of arguing with those people, I instantly went to the highest spot. I said to myself that if the ship had to sink, I should be one of the last. That was my first idea, which was the best. I went and I found the door. There are always a few steps from the third class, with a moveable door, and it is marked there that second-class passengers have no right to penetrate there. I found this door open so that I could go into the second class, where I did not find many people, only a few that climbed on the ladder and went into the first class, which I did. I found there only a few men and about two ladies. They had been putting them into lifeboats and as no women were there, we men sprang in the boat.

The steerage passengers, so far as I could see, were not prevented from getting up to the upper decks by anybody, or by closed doors, or anything else. While I was on the ship no one realized the real danger, not even the stewards. If the stewards knew, they were calm. It was their duty to try to make us believe there was nothing serious.

(US Inquiry, 4 May 1912)

John Hardy, aged thirty-six, chief steward, second class, had the task of rousing his passengers on decks D, E and F.

I did not retire until twenty-five minutes after eleven. I went down to my room after going around the ship and seeing that all the unnecessary lights were out. I went to my room, and stripped and turned in. I had not been in more than five minutes before I heard this slight shock. I got up, and slipped on my pants and coat over my pyjamas, and went on deck to see what the trouble was. I got on deck and could not see anything. I went below and turned in again within about ten minutes after I had gone on deck.

I was reading a few minutes when the chief first-class steward came to my room and asked me to get up, as he thought it was pretty serious, that she was making water forward. I went with him forward to see what water she was making, and on my return to my end of the ship I met Purser Barker.

He advised me or told me to get the people on deck with their lifebelts on as a precaution. Immediately I sent down for all hands to come up. We assisted the ladies with their belts – those that hadn't their husbands with them – and we assisted in getting the children out of bed. We commenced to close the watertight doors on F deck. I assisted the bedroom stewards also in sending the people up through the companionways to the upper decks.

(US Inquiry, 25 April 1912)

Thomas Whiteley, aged twenty-one, was a waiter in the first-class saloon.

My quarters were on E deck, which is five decks down. I did not feel any shock, but a shipmate of mine took me by the shoulder and said to get out. I said: 'Is it 5.30 already?' He said: 'No, we've hit a berg.'

I looked out of the port, the sea was like glass and I did not believe him. I looked on deck and found it covered with ice. Stokehole No. 2 began to fill with water at once. All the watertight doors were closed. They had to be opened again to let the men go down and draw the fires to prevent an explosion. Then the order came: 'All hands above decks with lifebelts!'

(US press, 19 April 1912)

Eight-year-old **Marshall Drew** was travelling second-class with his aunt and uncle. He later recounted his experiences.

When the *Titanic* struck the iceberg at 11.40 p.m., I was in bed. However, for whatever reason, I was awake and remember the jolt and cessation of motion. A steward knocked on the state room door and directed us to get dressed, put on life preservers and go to the boat deck, which we did. There was a watertight compartment next to our state room. As we left, it was closed. I remember the steward as we passed was trying to arouse passengers who had locked themselves in for the night. Elevators were not running. We walked up to the boat deck.

Fireman **Robert Williams** revealed how some of the crew danced on deck while waiting for women to fill the lifeboats.

I was in my bunk at the time of the collision, and was awakened, but lots of my mates were never disturbed. I ran aft, and a storekeeper told me how the water was rising below, and I hurried back to my quarters to tell my mates. Some of them laughed at me, and wouldn't get up.

They were taking the covers off the boats, and I helped them, and after that I went down below into the steerage to help to get the women and children up. They wouldn't believe there was any danger, and we had to fairly punch some of them up. A lot who were left below couldn't be persuaded at any cost to leave their quarters.

On deck I heard them shouting repeatedly for the women, but none appeared. The band was playing, and while we were waiting for the women several of us were waltzing round with one another, and smoking cigarettes.

Out of a watch of about a hundred firemen, trimmers and greasers, only ten were saved. The men drew the fires in the fore stoke-hold to prevent the boilers exploding, and before they got out the water was above their waists.

(*Daily Sketch*, 29 April 1912)

James R. McGough, a thirty-six-year-old buyer from Philadelphia, submitted an affidavit to the Senate Investigation into the disaster.

I was awakened at 11.40 p.m., ship time. My state room was on the starboard side – deck E – and was shared with me by Mr Flynn, a buyer for Gimbel Bros, New York. Soon after leaving our state room we came in contact with the second dining-room steward, Mr Dodd, in the companionway, of whom we asked the question, 'Is there any danger?' He answered, 'Not in the least' and suggested that we go back to bed, which we did not, however, do.

It was our intention to go up to the promenade deck, but before doing so I rapped on the door of the state room opposite mine, which was occupied by a lady, and suggested to her that she had better get up at once and dress as there was apparently something wrong.

Mr Flynn and I then ascended to promenade deck A, and, after being up there about ten minutes, were notified to put on life preservers as a matter of precaution. We then had to go all the way from promenade deck back to our state room which was on E deck. After procuring our life preservers we went back again to the top deck, and after reaching there, discovered that orders had been given to launch the lifeboats, and that they were already being launched at that time.

(US Inquiry, 1 May 1912)

Charles H. Romaine, 45, from Georgetown, Kentucky, survived by jumping into the sea, from where he was picked up by a lifeboat.

At the time of the smash I was in the smoking room with a Mr Case, an auditor for the Standard Oil Company. The band had just finished playing. There was a decided quiver of the *Titanic*. No one in the smoking room seemed to think anything unusual had occurred, but when we went on deck there was some excitement.

The officers of the *Titanic* were making the lifeboats ready and were ordering the passengers to get into them. None wanted to leave the *Titanic*. They believed she was perfectly safe.

It was a very bright night and I could not see any icebergs. It was my opinion the officers were making a mountain out of a mole hill and I had no intention of getting into any of the boats. So I stayed on deck and watched the other passengers crowding into the lifeboats and on the life-rafts.

Then I saw that the *Titanic* was sinking and decided I would take my chances swimming. I knew if I stayed too long I would be drawn down by the suction.

(*New York World*, 19 April 1912)

Seventeen-year-old **Jack Thayer** was travelling first-class with his parents, John B. Thayer, Second Vice-President of the Pennsylvania Railroad, and Marion Longstreth Thayer, and Mrs Thayer's maid, Margaret Fleming. After dinner on the fourteenth, he was befriended by Milton C. Long, son of Judge Charles M. Long of Springfield, Massachusetts. They met up again in the wake of the collision.

We all went out onto 'A' deck, trying to find where we were supposed to go. They were then uncovering the boats and making preparations to swing them out. Everything was fairly orderly and the crew at least seemed to know what they were doing.

It was now about 12.45 a.m. The noise was terrific. The deep vibrating roar of the exhaust steam blowing off through the safety valves was deafening, in addition to which they had commenced to send up rockets. There was more and more action. After standing there for some minutes talking above the din, trying to determine what we should do next, we finally decided to go back into the crowded hallway where it was warm. Shortly we heard the stewards passing the word around: 'all women to the port side.' We then said good-bye to my Mother at the head of the stairs on 'A' deck and she and the maid went out onto the port side of that deck, supposedly to get into a lifeboat. Father and I went out on the starboard side, watching what was going on about us. It seemed we were always waiting for orders and no orders ever came. No one knew his boat position, as no lifeboat drill had been held. The men had not yet commenced to lower any of the forward starboard lifeboats, of which there were four. The noise kept up. The deck seemed to be well lighted. People like ourselves were just standing around, out of the way. The stokers, dining-room stewards, and some others of the crew were lined up, waiting for orders. The second- and third-class passengers were pouring up onto the deck from the stern, augmenting the already large crowd.

Finally we thought we had better inquire whether or not Mother had been able to get into a boat. We went into the hall and happened to meet the Chief Dining Room Steward. He told us that he had just seen my mother, and that she had not yet been put into a boat. We found her, and were told that they were loading the forward boats on the port side from the deck below. The ship had a substantial list to port, which made quite a space between the side of the ship and the lifeboats, swinging out over the water, so the crew stretched folded steamer chairs across the space, over which the people were helped into the boats.

We proceeded to the deck below. Father, Mother and the maid went ahead of Long and myself. The lounge on 'B' deck was filled with a milling crowd, and as we went through the doorway out onto the deck, people pushed between my father and mother, and Long and me. Long and I could not catch up, and were entirely separated from them. I never saw my father again.

(*New York World*, 21 April 1912)

Honeymoon couple **Mrs Helen W. Bishop** and her husband Dickinson were returning to their home in Dowagiac, Michigan.

We had been in Europe since January and had visited Egypt, Italy, France and Algiers. We sailed on the *Titanic* on the tenth and had had a most enjoyable voyage until the night of the disaster.

I had retired when our ship struck the iceberg, but Mr Bishop was sitting in our state room, reading. I didn't hear the shock, and it was several minutes before someone came to our door and told us to come on deck. I got up and dressed, then we went above. Officers told us we might as well go below and retire; that there was no danger. We did not do so for some time, however. Finally we did, and soon afterwards we were again summoned. We dressed quietly and had plenty of time.

It broke my heart to leave my little dog, Freu Freu, in my state room. I had purchased her in Florence, Italy, and she was the pet of the ship. The steward wouldn't let me take her to the butcher. He said she was too pretty, and she was the only one allowed to stay in the cabin. I made a little den for her in our room behind two of my suitcases, but when I started to leave her she tore my dress to bits, tugging at it. I realized, however, that there would be little sympathy for a woman carrying a dog in her arms when there were lives of women and children to be saved.

The girl who occupied a state room across from us refused to get up and the stewards pulled her out of bed. She got back in and sank with the ship.

(*Dowagiac Daily News*, 20 April 1912)

In the wake of the launch incident at Southampton, **Roberta Maioni**, maid to the Countess of Rothes, had already heard a number of passengers remark that the ship was fated.

On the Sunday evening I went into the music saloon to listen to the band, and found myself in the company of a man who had previously taken a fatherly interest in me. He was travelling alone, and seemed to suffer from his loneliness, for he had been one of the passengers most affected by forebodings.

When 10 o'clock came and I was called away to bed, he begged me to remain with him a little longer, saying he was sure something awful was about to happen. Perhaps he was influenced by the fact that the band was playing such pieces as 'Ave Maria' and 'Nearer, My God, To Thee'.

His seriousness and pessimism frightened me, so for once in my life I was quite glad to be sent to bed. I bade him 'Goodnight' and never saw him again.

After I had been in bed for about an hour and a half, I was awakened by a terrific crash, followed by the rending of metal, the rushing of water and the shouting of men.

I was about to get up when a steward came and said: 'Miss, we have struck an iceberg, but I don't think there's any danger. Should there be, I'll come back and let you know.'

I prepared myself for sleep once more, but in a few minutes the steward was back again, telling me not to be afraid, but to dress quickly, put on my life belt and go on deck. I put on the first clothes that came to hand and found my life belt. I could not fix this, but the steward came and did it for me.

Still realizing nothing of the danger I was in, I joked with him about the funny way in which it was fixed. He did not answer, but smiled very sadly, and shook his head. Then I knew that something serious had happened.

I was carried by a swarm of other passengers to the boat deck, and shall never forget the strange sight that met my eyes. There were pieces of ice all over the deck and groups of men and women, looking gaunt and fearful in their night attire or in odd garments hastily donned. Some of them were talking calmly, firmly believing that her watertight compartments would save the *Titanic* from sinking. Others were frantic with excitement or dumb with terror, huddled closely together in silence as though they knew they were about to be parted by death.

There were men swearing horribly and women quietly sobbing, and I knew that many of them were praying as they never prayed before.

But there was no panic and I, with the fortitude of youth, looked on in wonder. It was bitterly cold.

I watched them preparing to lower the lifeboats. I heard the order, 'Women and children first'. I saw women parting from their husbands and fathers. Some women clung to their husbands and refused to leave them, but the ship's officers pulled them apart – the women to live and the men to die.

Dr Washington Dodge, assessor for the port of San Francisco, travelled first-class with his wife and four-year-old son Washington Jnr.

At 10 p.m. Sunday while my wife and I went out for a stroll along the *Titanic*'s promenade deck, we found the air icy cold – so cold, in fact, that we were driven inside although we had on heavy wraps. This change of temperature had occurred in the previous two hours. We went to bed and were awakened about 11.40 by a jar which gave me the impression that a blow on the side had moved the entire vessel laterally to a considerable angle. With only my overcoat and slippers, I went through the companionway, but, to my surprise, found no one seriously considering the shock.

Men in evening clothes stood about chatting and laughing, and when an officer – I did not know his name – hurried by I asked, 'What is the trouble?'

He replied: 'Something is wrong with the propeller; nothing serious.'

I went back to my state room, where my wife had already arisen to dress herself, and I dissuaded her from dressing herself or our four-year-old son.

A little while later, still feeling nervous, I went up to the promenade deck and there saw a great mass of ice close to the starboard rail. Going back to my cabin again, I met my bedroom steward, with whom I had crossed the ocean before, who whispered to me that, 'Word has come from down below for everyone to put on life preservers.'

I rushed back to my state room and told my wife the news and made her come up on deck with the baby, even half clothed. The boats on the starboard side were then suspended from the davits, but no passengers wanted to get in.

It was a drop of fifty feet to the surface of the sea and apparently everybody considered that they were safer on the 'unsinkable' *Titanic* than in a small boat whose only propelling power was four oars. The first boat was only half filled for the simple reason that no one would get aboard.

Personally, I waited for the lifeboat to become filled, and then, seeing there was plenty of room, I asked the officer at the rail why I also could not get in. His only reply was, 'Women and children first,' and the half-filled boat sheered off.

Before the next boats were lowered passengers who had become excited were calmed by the utterances of the officers that the injury was trivial and that, in case it proved serious, at least four steamships had been summoned by wireless and would be on hand within an hour.

(*San Francisco Bulletin*, 20 April 1912)

Edward Dorking, a nineteen-year-old steerage passenger from Liss in Hampshire, was travelling to America to start a new life working for his uncle, an Illinois cement manufacturer. At the moment of impact, he was in the music room playing cards with several of his fellow travellers.

When the boat collided with the berg, we were thrown from the bench on which we were sitting. The shock was accompanied by a grinding noise, which we took to be the result of an accident to the machinery that suddenly halted the ship.

I went on deck to see what had happened and saw several persons running to the forward part of the ship. I followed and found that the port side was strewn with particles of ice. Someone said we had struck an iceberg and that a huge hole had been torn in the port side below the waterline.

I obtained a good glimpse of the iceberg as it floated by. It was off some distance then, but in the clear night, I could see it rising out of the water like a great white spectre, towering above the funnels of the ship. To me it seemed that the iceberg was at least four or five times as large as the *Titanic*.

At that time there was no sign of panic. The passengers and crew seemed to feel assured that the collision was not serious and that there was no grave danger to the ship. I returned to the music room and resumed our card game. After a while some of the foreigners in the steerage became excited and the women began to weep, and before long there was a stream of them pouring out of the steerage dragging their luggage with them. They were driven out by the water which was rushing into the hold in a huge stream, in spite of the pumps which were working furiously.

In a little while longer, the nose of the boat began to dip forward. As the ship began to list, the excitement of the lower decks increased and there was a scramble for the lifeboats. Men and women, stricken with fright, huddled around the crew, shouting and crying and sending up prayers to heaven for aid.

I was on deck when the first boat was lowered away. The women and children were taken off first. An officer stood beside the lifeboats as they were being manned and, with a pistol in hand, threatened to kill the first man who got into a boat without orders.

The rule of 'women first' was rigidly enforced. Two stewards hustled into a lifeboat that was being launched. They were commanded to get out by the officers and, on refusing to obey the command, were shot down and thrown into the sea. A Chinaman was also shot for the same cause. Afterwards, aboard the *Carpathia*, I saw six Chinamen who had escaped in the lifeboats, disguised as women.

(*Bureau County Republican*, 2 May 1912)

Daisy Minahan from Fond du Lac, Wisconsin, was travelling first-class with her doctor brother and his wife. She escaped via boat No. 14, one of the last – but, contrary to her account, not *the* last – to leave the ship.

We were sitting on the *Titanic*'s deck in the evening enjoying the crisp air and the starlit night. Old sailors told us the sea had never seemed so calm and glassy. About 9.30 the atmosphere took a sudden drop, which drove everybody inside their cabins. We must have been going at a terrific rate in the direction of the icebergs, for the air became so chilly in a few minutes that we found it impossible to keep warm even when we put wraps and blankets around us.

We had retired when there was a dull shaking of the *Titanic*, which was not so much like a shake as it was a slowing down of the massive craft. I noticed that our boat had come to a standstill and then we heard the orders of the captain and went on deck to see what it all meant. I never saw such composure and cool bravery in my life as the men of the first and second cabins displayed. Colonel Astor seemed to be the controlling figure. He, Major Butt, Mr Guggenheim, Mr Widener and Mr Thayer clustered in a group as if they were holding a quick consultation as to what steps should be taken next. Then Colonel Astor came forward with the cry, 'Not a man until every woman and child is safe in the boats.'

Many of the women did not seem to want to leave the vessel. Mrs Astor clung to her husband, begging him to let her remain on the *Titanic* with him. When he insisted that she save herself, she threw her arms around him and begged him with tears to permit her to share his fate. Colonel Astor picked her up bodily and carried her to a boat, which was the one just ahead of ours, and placed her in it.

I lingered with my brother and his wife, loath to leave them, although we all knew the ship was sinking and that the ocean would soon swallow up all that remained of the steamer. We both begged my brother to come with us, but he said: 'No, I will remain with the others, no matter what happens.'

Then, when it was time to go, when the last boat was being lowered to the water line, we were hurried into it by my brother, who bade us goodbye and said calmly but with feeling: 'Be brave; no matter what happens, be brave.'

Senior stewardess **Sarah Stap** had been transferred from the *Titanic*'s sister ship, the *Olympic*. She described the crew as being 'so radiantly happy together' on leaving Southampton and enthused about how well everything was going until the fatal night of the fourteenth.

I was in bed and was awakened by a slight bump. It would then have been about a quarter to twelve at night. I did not take very much heed of the noise at first, because I had been used to a ship's bumping before. In fact I thought that something or other had gone wrong in the engine room.

Presently I heard the night-watchman pass my door and I called out to him, 'What's the matter?'

He replied: 'Oh, we have only touched a bit of ice. I think it is all right. I don't think it is anything.'

It was three-quarters of an hour after I felt the ship bump that I got up and when I reached the deck the lifeboats had been ordered out. I was not in the least frightened; I was simply stunned.

Perfect order prevailed, and everybody seemed calm and collected. The passengers would not believe that we had struck an iceberg, but I myself knew what had happened. The officers and crew behaved magnificently, as did also the dear old captain. Mr Ismay was on deck in his pyjamas and a coat, vainly endeavouring to get the passengers into the boats. He worked might and main all the time, and I did not think he actually realized that the ship was sinking.

(*Birkenhead News*, 4 May 1912)

Hilda Slayter, a doctor's daughter from Halifax, Nova Scotia, had been in England shopping for her trousseau for her impending wedding in Canada. The trousseau was lost at sea, but Miss Slayter survived. She too told of the parting of the Astors.

I was standing right near by when Mrs Astor was helped into one of the boats. He asked the officer who was at the rail whether he might go also, and permission was refused. With the calmest smile in the world, Col. Astor said: 'Goodbye, dearie,' and waved his hand to Mrs Astor. It was plain she did not realize that their parting was anything but momentary, but I'm sure he suspected it, for as though to conceal his emotion he hastily pulled out his cigarette case and started smoking. Then he leant over the rail, and as the boat Mrs Astor was in swung out and was lowered he cried again: 'Goodbye, dearie, I'll join you later.'

I never saw the Colonel again, but a moment later my attention was caught by a Frenchman who approached one of the lowering boats with two beautiful little boys in his arms. An officer waved him back, and he replied:'Bless you, man, I don't want to go, but for God's sake take these boys. Their mother is waiting for them at home.'

So the boys were tossed into the boat and the Frenchman turned away, seemingly quite satisfied. Poor fellow, I did not see him on the *Carpathia* either.

(*New York World*, 19 April 1912)

Miss Constance Willard of Duluth, Minnesota, was in one of the last boats to leave the *Titanic*.

When I reached the deck after the collision the crew were getting the boats ready to lower, and many of the women were running about looking for their husbands and children. The women were being placed in the boats, and two men took hold of me and almost pushed me into a boat. I did not appreciate the danger and I struggled until they released me. 'Do not waste time. Let her go if she will not get in,' said an officer.

I hurried back to my cabin again and went from cabin to cabin looking for my friends, but could not find them. A little English girl about fifteen years old ran up to me and threw her arms about me. 'I am all alone,' she sobbed. 'Won't you let me go with you?'

I then began to realize the real danger and saw that all but two of the boats had been lowered. Some men called to us and we hurried to where they were loading a boat. All the women had been provided with life belts. As the men lifted us into the boat they smiled at us and told us to be brave.

I will never forget an incident that occurred just as we were about to be lowered into the water. I had just been lifted into the boat and was still standing when a foreigner rushed up to the side of the vessel and, holding out a bundle in his arms, cried with tears running down his face: 'Please, kind lady, won't you save my little girl, my baby? For myself it is no difference, but please, please take the little one.' Of course, I took the child.

The newly widowed **Mrs May Futrelle** concluded her narrative to American newsmen.

Jacques died like a hero. He was in the smoking room when the crash came and I was going to bed. I was hurled from my feet by the impact. I hardly found myself when Jacques came rushing into the state room. 'The boat is going down! Get dressed at once,' he shouted.

When we reached the deck everything was in the wildest confusion. The screams of women and the shrill orders of the officers were drowned intermittently by the tremendous vibrations of the *Titanic*'s deep bass fog horn. The behaviour of the men was magnificent. They stood back without murmuring and urged the women and children into the lifeboats. A few cowards tried to scramble into the boats, but they were quickly thrown back by the others. The only men who were saved were those who sneaked into the lifeboats or were picked up after the *Titanic* sunk.

I did not want to leave Jacques, but he assured me that there were boats enough for all and that he would be rescued later. 'Hurry up, May – you're keeping the others waiting.' They were his last words as he lifted me into a lifeboat and kissed me good-bye. I was in one of the last lifeboats to leave the ship. We had not put out many minutes when the *Titanic* disappeared. I almost thought, as I saw her sink beneath the water, that I could see Jacques, standing where I had left him and waving at me.

Twenty-two-year-old Londoner **Harold Bride** was the junior wireless operator on the *Titanic*. Both he and the senior operator, twenty-four-year-old Jack Phillips, were Marconi employees but were classified as junior officers on board the ship. Bride took over from his colleague at midnight each night and was kept busy by a stream of requests from passengers eager to impress friends and family back home by relaying a message from the *Titanic*. Bride and Phillips remained at their posts until the bitter end on that fateful night and Bride's subsequent account of the tragedy was one of the most graphic to emerge. As such, it was printed in newspapers across the world.

There were three rooms in the wireless cabin. One was a sleeping room, one a dynamo room, and one an operating room. I took off my clothes and went to sleep in the bed. Then I was conscious of waking up and hearing Phillips sending to Cape Race. I read what he was sending. It was only routine matter. I remembered how tired he was, and got out of bed without my clothes on to relieve him. I didn't even feel the shock. I hardly knew it had happened until after the captain had come to us. There was no jolt whatever.

I was standing by Phillips, telling him to go to bed, when the captain put his head in the cabin. 'We've struck an iceberg,' the captain said, 'and I'm having an inspection made to tell what it has done for us. You had better get ready to send out a call for assistance, but don't send it until I tell you.' The captain went away, and in ten minutes, I should estimate, he came back. We could hear terrible confusion outside, but not the least thing to indicate any trouble. The wireless was working perfectly. 'Send a call for assistance,' ordered the captain, barely putting his head in the door. 'What call should I send?' Phillips asked. 'The regulation call for help, just that.' Then the captain was gone.

Phillips began to send 'C.Q.D.' He flashed away at it, and we joked while he did so. All of us made light of the disaster. We joked that way while we flashed the signals for about five minutes. Then the captain came back. 'What are you sending?' he asked. 'C.Q.D.,' Phillips replied.

The humour of the situation appealed to me, and I cut in with a little remark that made us all laugh, including the captain. 'Send S.O.S.,' I said. 'It's the new call, and it may be your last chance to send it.' Phillips, with a laugh, changed the signal to 'S.O.S.' The captain told us we had been struck amidships, or just aft of amidships. It was ten minutes, Phillips told me, after he noticed the iceberg, but the slight jolt was the only signal to us that a collision had occurred. We thought we were a good distance away. We said lots of funny things to each other in the next few minutes. We picked up the first steamship *Frankfurt*, gave her our position, and said we had struck an iceberg, and needed assistance. The *Frankfurt* operator went away to tell his captain. He came back, and we told him we were sinking by the head, and that we could observe a distinct list forward.

The *Carpathia* answered our signal, and we told her our position, and said we were sinking by the head. The operator went to tell the captain, and in five minutes returned, and told us the *Carpathia* was putting about and heading for us.

Our captain had left us at this time, and Phillips told me to run and tell him what the *Carpathia* had answered. I did so, and I went through an awful mass of people to his cabin. The decks were full of scrambling men and women. I came back and heard Phillips giving the *Carpathia* further directions. Phillips told me to put on my clothes. Until that moment I forgot I wasn't dressed. I went to my cabin and dressed. I brought an overcoat to Phillips, and as it was very cold I slipped the overcoat upon him while he worked. Every few minutes Phillips would send me to the captain with little messages. They were merely telling how the *Carpathia* was coming our way, and giving her speed.

I noticed as I came back from one trip that they were putting off the women and children in lifeboats, and that the list forward was increasing. Phillips told me the wireless was growing weaker. The captain came and told us our engine rooms were taking water, and that the dynamos might not last much longer. We sent that word to the *Carpathia*.

I went out on deck and looked around. The water was pretty close up to the boat deck. There was a great scramble aft, and how poor Phillips worked through it I don't know. He was a brave man. I learnt to love him that night, and I suddenly felt for him a great reverence to see him standing there sticking to his work while everybody else was raging about. I will never live to forget the work Phillips did for the last awful fifteen minutes.

Phillips clung on, sending and sending. He clung on for about ten minutes, or maybe fifteen minutes, after the captain released him. The water was then coming into our cabin. From aft came the tunes of the band. It was a ragtime tune. I don't know what. Then there was 'Autumn'. Phillips ran aft, and that was the last I ever saw of him alive.

CHAPTER 4

WATCHING AND WAITING

There were some 2,228 passengers on board the *Titanic* but the twenty lifeboats had a total capacity of just 1,178. Even-numbered boats were launched from the port side; odd-numbered from the starboard side. The first lifeboat, No. 7, was lowered at 12.45 a.m. – over an hour after the collision. Its capacity was sixty-five yet it left with only twenty-eight passengers.

BOAT NO. 7

Among the passengers on this boat were newlyweds **Mrs Helen Bishop** and husband Dickinson.

When we got on deck there were few people there. We were in the first lifeboat to be lowered over the side. Someone said: 'Put the brides and grooms in first.'

There were three newly married couples who went in that boat. Altogether, there were twenty-eight in our boat. There might as well have been forty or so, but the half hundred men on deck refused to leave, even though there was room for them.

John Jacob Astor was standing at the foot of the stairway as I started to go back the second time. He told us to get on our life-belts and we did. Before our boat was lowered into the water, Mr and Mrs Astor were on the deck. She didn't want to go, saying that she thought we were all silly, that the *Titanic* couldn't sink.

Because the Astors' state room was close to ours, we had had considerable to do with them on the voyage and I disliked to leave them on deck. As a matter of fact I believed, much as they did, that there was little chance of being picked up in the lifeboats.

The water was like glass. There wasn't even the ripple usually found on a small lake. By the time we had pulled 100 yards, the lower row of portholes had disappeared. When we were a mile away the second row had gone, but there was still no confusion. Indeed everything seemed to be quiet on the ship until her stern was raised out of the water by the list forward. Then a veritable wave of humanity surged up out of the steerage and shut the lights from our view. We were too far away to see the passengers individually, but we could see the black masses of human forms and hear their death cries and groans.

For a moment the ship seemed to be pointing straight down, looking like a gigantic whale submerging itself, head-first.

One dining room steward, who was in our boat, was thoughtful enough to bring green lights – the kind you burn on the Fourth of July. They cast a ghostly light over the boat, but you know we had no light of any kind. Whenever we would light one of these diminutive torches, we would hear cries from the people perishing aboard. They thought it was help coming.

We were afloat in the lifeboat from about 12.30 Sunday night until five o'clock Monday morning. Although we were the first boat to leave the *Titanic*, we were about the fourth picked up by the *Carpathia*. The scenes on that little craft adrift in mid-ocean with little hope of rescue were most heartrending. Still the characters of the individuals appealed to me.

For instance, there was a German baron aboard who smoked an obnoxious pipe incessantly and refused to pull an oar. The men were worn out with the work, and I rowed for considerable time myself. There was a little French aviator in our boat, Pierre Maréchal, who never took his monocle from his eye all the time we were on the water, but he did assist in the rowing.

Whenever a light, however small, was flashed in a lifeboat,

those in the other drifting crafts were given false hopes of rescue. After we had been afloat for several hours without food or water and with everyone suffering from the cold, I felt certain we should all perish. I took off my stockings and gave them to a little girl who hadn't as much time to dress as I had.

When the day broke and the *Carpathia* was sighted, there were indescribable scenes of joy. After we had pulled alongside the rescue ship, many of the women were lifted aboard in chairs, tied to a rope. I was sufficiently composed to climb the ladder alongside to the deck.

Those on board the *Carpathia* did everything in their power for our comfort. They shared everything with us and the captain of that boat was not like Captain Smith of the *Titanic*. You didn't see him at fashionable dinners. He was always on duty.

Mrs Lucian Smith of Huntington, West Virginia, a dear little woman who lost her husband in the disaster, said that before they parted on the deck he told her he had seen Captain Smith at a dinner at 11 p.m. that night. When he left the dining room, the captain was still there, although he may have gone to the bridge before the collision, but it doesn't seem likely. For some reason, for which we will probably never know, the bulkhead doors refused to work. I watched the men for several minutes endeavouring to turn the screws that would lower them and make the compartments watertight, but they were unsuccessful. It may be that the impact so wrenched them as to throw them out of line.

(*Dowagiac Daily News*, 20 April 1912)

American stockbroker **William Thompson Sloper** revealed how he owed his salvation to actress Dorothy Gibson, whom he had met that evening over a game of bridge with her mother and Frederick Seward. One American newspaper alleged that Sloper had dressed in women's clothing to escape the sinking ship, an accusation which he spent the remaining forty-three years of his life denying.

Standing in the shelter of the ship's superstructure we helped each other adjust our life preservers while the terrific racket overhead caused by the steam from the ship's boilers made it almost impossible for us to hear anything we said to each other. Shortly afterwards the First Officer said to the fifty or sixty passengers who in the meantime had collected on the deck, speaking through a megaphone held to his mouth: 'Any passengers who would like to do so may get into this lifeboat.' After a few of the passengers standing between us and the First Officer had been handed into the lifeboat by him and his assistants or had balked at getting into it and stepped aside, our time came to decide whether to get into the boat or pull back.

Every passenger seemed to have taken a firm grip on his nerves. Dorothy Gibson was the only one who seemed to realize the desperate situation we were in because she had become quite hysterical and kept repeating over and over so that people standing near us could hear, 'I'll never ride in my little grey car again.' There was no doubt in Dorothy's mind what she wanted to do and her mother was satisfied to go along with Dorothy. So with the help of the First Officer, I handed Dorothy down into the bow of the lifeboat. Mr Seward and the junior officer handed Mrs Gibson down after her daughter. Luckily for both Seward and me, Dorothy held onto my hand and demanded that we get into the boat with them. 'We don't go unless you do,' she said. 'What do you say?' I asked Seward. 'What's the difference? We may as well go along with them.' Finding seats for ourselves, we sat in the lifeboat designed for sixty-five persons for about ten minutes looking up into the faces of the passengers looking down at us, trying to make up their minds to get in with us. After nineteen people had finally made up their minds and had been lowered into the boat, the First Officer asked for the last time through his megaphone: 'Are there any more who would like to get into this boat before we lower away?' When no one else made the move towards him, he gave the signal to lower away. Then began a jerky descent to the surface of the ocean sixty feet below.

Fortunately for us the three sailors knew their business, for in a few minutes they skilfully launched our boat without accident.

The sea was perfectly calm – not even a ripple on the surface. For the next hour and a half we just sat there and drifted farther and farther away. Two hours after our lifeboat was launched, the sailors estimated that we had drifted more than two miles from where the *Titanic* was sinking. The ship remained until two or three minutes before she sank as brilliantly lighted as she was directly after the accident occurred and all the lights had been turned on. Then suddenly (like the house lights in a brilliantly lighted theatre just before the curtain goes up) all the lights dipped simultaneously to a pale glow. A moment or two later everyone watching in the lifeboats saw silhouetted against the starlit sky the stern of the ship rise perpendicularly into the air from about midship. Then with a prolonged rush and a roar like 10,000 tons of coal sliding down a metal chute several hundred feet long, the great ship went down out of sight and disappeared beneath the surface of the ocean. Then a great cry arose on the air from the surface of the calm sea where the ship had been.

One of the sailors divided the rugs among the women, some of whom were not too warmly dressed. The night air was very cold and Dorothy felt the cold very much. I used Sunday night as an excuse for not changing at dinner time into my evening clothes. I had been wearing a brand new suit of heavy woollen material. When I went down to get my life preserver I had pulled on a heavy Shetland wool sweater and my winter overcoat. With my life preserver I was cumbersomely dressed so that a few minutes of pulling an oar in the lifeboat threw me into a dripping perspiration. So I was glad to take off my winter coat and put it on Dorothy.

It took us an hour to awkwardly row our boat to the side of the *Carpathia*. During the hour we had been rowing the sun came out of the ocean like a ball of fire. Its rays reflected on the numerous icebergs sticking up out of the sea around us.

Sculptor **Paul Chevré** made his escape from the *Titanic* in the company of two other Frenchmen, aviator Pierre Maréchal and cotton dealer Alfred Omont.

When I got on deck, after the boat seemed to tremble from stem to stern, there was some excitement, but it was among the officers and not among the passengers. The officers were running about the deck insisting that persons get into the lifeboats. I didn't want to get into a boat, but when the third one [sic] was launched I simply was made to get in. I much preferred staying on the *Titanic*. In fact, when the officers of the ship insisted on the boats being filled many of the persons drew back and positively refused to obey.

We were some distance from the *Titanic* when we discovered in the bright night that she was sinking. Then there was evidently a panic on board. I saw one of the petty officers draw his revolver and fire three shots. It is my impression that he did this to attract attention and also to get the passengers from their state rooms.

The discipline on the lifeboats and rafts was as good as could be expected. I was off the *Titanic* before there was any real panic. I will take off my hat to the English seamen who went down with their ship and to the men who manned the lifeboats. Every man of them was a man.

(*New York World*, 19 April 1912)

John Snyder, aged twenty-four, of Minneapolis was travelling first-class with his new wife Nelle. They too left on boat No. 7.

We were told to get into a boat and we did, although at the time I much preferred staying on the *Titanic*. It looked safe on the *Titanic* and far from safe in the lifeboat. Before we knew what was being done with us we were swung from the *Titanic* into the sea and then the boat was so crowded that the women lay on the bottom to give the crew a chance to row.

We went about 200 yards from the *Titanic*. We could see nothing wrong except that the big boat seemed to be settling at the bow. Still we could not make ourselves believe that the *Titanic* would sink. But the *Titanic* continued to settle, and we could see the passengers plunging about the decks and hear their cries. We moved farther away. Suddenly there came two sharp explosions as the water rushed into the boiler room and the boilers exploded. The explosions counteracted the effect of the suction made when the big boat went to the bottom and it is more than probable that this saved some of the lifeboats from being drawn to the bottom. Following the explosion we could see persons hanging to the side railings of the sinking boat. It is my opinion that many persons were killed by these explosions and not drowned.

Other passengers were tossed into the water. For an hour after the explosions we could see them swimming about in the water or floating on the lifebelts. We could hear their groans and their cries for help, but we did not go to them. To have done this would have swamped our own boat and everybody would have been lost. Several persons did float up to our boat and we took them on board.

After we had got aboard the *Carpathia*, we did not see J. Bruce Ismay until today, when he came on deck for a short time. He seemed badly broken up. You would hardly have known him.

(US press, 19 April 1912)

Michigan-born **Mrs Lily Potter**, a fifty-six-year-old widow, was returning from a European holiday with her daughter Olive and the latter's old school friend, Margaret Hays. The ladies were due to travel home on board a different ship but, on hearing about the splendour of the *Titanic*, they switched bookings even though it meant sailing a week later than they had planned. The three first-class passengers climbed into boat No. 7, Miss Hays carrying her pet Pomeranian wrapped in a blanket. Mrs Potter recounted:

The men took to the oars. The sea was absolutely calm and the stars were out. We kept rowing and suddenly someone cried out, 'I feel water on my feet!' We checked and found that the drainage plug was not in. It was quickly put back. I asked, 'Are there any provisions aboard?' The men looked and could find none whatsoever.

After rowing for a quarter of a mile, we stood off and watched the mammoth ship. About fifteen minutes after we left the *Titanic*, we were drifting in water filled with cakes of floating ice with our eyes on the great vessel we had deserted. Within a short time, we saw the *Titanic* begin to settle and then we knew that we had been wise to take to the small boats.

On the *Titanic*, the crew kept sending up the distress signals. The rockets would roar upward and light the water for miles around. The orchestra kept playing and their music helped to calm us.

I kept my eyes on the liner and could see six rows of portholes. I looked again and there were five rows, then only four and then I knew she was going down. We who were watching knew that many persons were going to their death when the upper deck neared the level of the water. It was the most tragic sight anyone will ever witness. Scores of men were standing on the decks. All the lights on the *Titanic* suddenly went out, and she slowly began to disappear from sight. Then came the screams, too horrible for words.

First-class passenger **James R. McGough** of Philadelphia related his experiences on boat No. 7.

They called for the women and children to board the boats first. Both women and men, however, hesitated, and did not feel inclined to get into the small boats, thinking the larger boat was the safer. I had my back turned looking in the opposite direction at that time and was caught by the shoulder by one of the officers who gave me a push, saying: 'Here, you are a big fellow. Get into the boat.'

Our boat was launched with twenty-eight people. We, however, transferred five from one of the other boats after we were out in the ocean, which was some time after the ship went down.

When our lifeboats left the vessel, we were directed to row away a short distance from the large boat, feeling it would be but a short time until we would be taken back on the *Titanic*. We then rested our oars. But after realizing that the *Titanic* was really sinking, we rowed away for about half a mile, being afraid that the suction would draw us down.

Although there were several of us wanting drinking water, it was unknown to us that there was a tank of water and also some crackers in our boat. Having no light on our boat, we did not discover this fact until after reaching the *Carpathia*.

(US Inquiry, 1 May 1912)

BOAT NO. 5

This was the second boat to be lowered (again from the starboard side) with forty-one on board. The loading of passengers was done by the ship's Third Officer **Herbert Pitman** with a little help from the *Titanic*'s most controversial figure, White Star Line chairman J. Bruce Ismay.

I stood by No. 5 boat. They would not allow the sailors to get anything, as they thought we should get it again in the morning. In the act of clearing away this boat a man dressed in a dressing gown with slippers on said to me very quietly: 'There is no time to waste.' I thought he did not know anything about it at all, so we carried on our work in the usual way.

It struck me at the time the easy way the boat went out, the great improvement the modern davits were on the old-fashioned davits. I had about five or six men there, and the boat was out in about two minutes.

I got her overboard, and lowered level with the rail of the boat deck. Then this man in the dressing gown said we had better get her loaded with women and children. So I said, 'I await the commander's orders,' to which he replied, 'Very well,' or something like that.

It then dawned on me that it might be Mr Ismay, judging by the description I had had given me. So I went along to the bridge and saw Captain Smith, and I told him that I thought it was Mr Ismay that wished me to get the boat away with women and children on it. So he said: 'Go ahead. Carry on.'

I came along and brought in my boat. I stood on it and said: 'Come along, ladies.' There was a big crowd. Mr Ismay helped to get them along, assisted in every way. We got the boat nearly full, and I shouted for any more ladies. None were to be seen, so I allowed a few men to get into it.

Mr Murdoch said: 'You go in charge of this boat and hang around the after gangway.' I did not like the idea of going away at all because I thought I was better off on the ship.

(US Inquiry, 23 April 1912)

Passengers included **Mrs Catherine Crosby** of Milwaukee.

We got into the lifeboat that was hanging over the rail alongside the deck. Men and women, with their families, got in the boat with us. There was no discrimination between men and women. About thirty-six persons got in the boat with us. There were only two officers in the boat, the rest were all first-class passengers. My husband did not come back again after he left me, and I don't know what became of him except that his body was found and brought to Milwaukee and buried.

There were absolutely no lights in the lifeboats, and they did not even know whether the plug was in the bottom of the boat to prevent the boat from sinking. There were no lanterns, no provisions, no lights, nothing at all in these boats but the oars. One of the officers asked one of the passengers for a watch with which to light up the bottom of the boat to see if the plug was in place. The officers rowed the boat a short distance from the *Titanic*, and

I was unable to see the lowering of any other boats. We must have rowed quite a distance, but could see the steamer very plainly. I saw them firing rockets, and heard a gun fired as distress signals to indicate that the steamer was in danger.

We continued a safe distance away from the steamer, probably a quarter of a mile at least, and finally saw the steamer go down very distinctly. I heard the terrible cries of the people that were on board when the boat went down, and heard repeated explosions, as though the boilers had exploded.

Our boat drifted around in that vicinity until about daybreak when the *Carpathia* was sighted and we were taken on board. We had to row quite a long time and quite a distance before we were taken on board the *Carpathia*. I was suffering from the cold while I was drifting around, and one of the officers put a sail around me and over my head to keep me warm.

We received very good treatment on the *Carpathia*. It was reported on the *Carpathia* by passengers that the lookout who was on duty at the time the *Titanic* struck the iceberg had said: 'I know they will blame me for it because I was on duty, but it was not my fault. I had warned the officers three or four times before striking the iceberg that we were in the vicinity of icebergs, but the officer on the bridge paid no attention to my signals.' I can not give the name of any passenger who made that statement, but it was common talk on the *Carpathia* that that is what the lookout said.

(US Inquiry, 17 May 1912)

Mrs Annie Stengel of Newark, New Jersey, a first-class passenger travelling with her husband Henry, suffered two broken ribs and was knocked unconscious when Dr Henry Frauenthal and his brother Isaac, spotting empty places, jumped from the deck into the boat as it was being lowered away.

As I stepped into the boat an officer in charge said: 'No more; the boat is full.' My husband stepped back, obeying the order. As the boat was being lowered, four men deliberately jumped into it. One of them was a Hebrew doctor – another was his brother. This was done at the risk of the lives of all of us in the boat. The two companions of this man who did this were later transferred to boat No. 7, to which we were tied. He weighed about 250 pounds and wore two life preservers. These men who jumped in struck me and a little child. I was rendered unconscious and two of my ribs were badly dislocated.

Sixty-one-year-old **Max Frolicher-Stehli**, from Zurich, Switzerland, was rescued along with his wife Margaretha and daughter Hedwig.

The lifeboats were lowered. My wife and two women entered one of the first boats. Twelve men, including myself, were standing near. As there were no other women passengers waiting to get into the boats at that time, we were asked to accompany the women.

While we got into the boats for safety's sake, all of us thought we would be able to return to the *Titanic*. The sea was calm. We were rowed by four members of the crew about 300 yards from the steamer.

The steamer's lights were still burning brightly and the picture, with the iceberg as a background, was most beautiful. The steamer slowly sank, the bow sinking first. The water was covered with small boats and rafts. Then there was a loud crash. The lights went out. Other people who left the boat later say that she broke in two.

After the boat had sunk, we began to search for food or other provisions. There was nothing edible on the lifeboats. We could not even find fresh water. Fortunately one man had some stimulants with him, which were given to the women.

After drifting around for what seemed weeks, the *Carpathia* was sighted coming towards us. We had no matches or lanterns, and were not put aboard the rescuing ship until daylight.

(*Brooklyn Daily Eagle*, 19 April 1912)

Unknowingly separated from her husband, **Mrs Frank Warren** left on boat No. 5.

The lowering of the craft was accomplished with great difficulty. First one end and then the other was dropped at apparently dangerous angles, and we feared that we would swamp as soon as we struck the water.

After the lifeboat was safely afloat, great difficulty was experienced in finding a knife with which to cut the lashings. When we reached the water the ship had settled so that my impression was that I was looking through the portholes into state rooms on deck D, which we had formerly occupied, and as we pulled away we could see that the *Titanic* was settling by the head with a heavy list to starboard.

Mr Pitman's orders were to pull far enough away to avoid suction if the ship sank. The sea was like glass, so smooth that the stars were clearly reflected. We were pulled quite a distance away and then rested, watching the rockets in terrible anxiety and realizing that the vessel was rapidly sinking, bow first. She went lower and lower, until the lower lights were extinguished, and then suddenly rose by the stern and slipped from our sight. We had no light in our boat and were left in intense darkness save for an occasional glimmer of light from other lifeboats and one steady green light on one of the ship's boats which the officers on the *Carpathia* afterwards said was of material assistance in aiding them to come direct to the spot.

Later in the night we thought we saw lights in the distance, indicating a vessel, and these afterwards proved to be the *Carpathia*, but at the time we had not expected to be picked up until the arrival of the *Olympic*, which we knew would be on hand some time in the afternoon and was the only ship of which we had any knowledge.

With daylight, the wind increased and the sea became choppy, and we saw icebergs in every direction, some lying low in the water and others tall, like ships, and some of us thought they were. Our boat was picked up about 4.10 a.m. by the *Carpathia* and too much cannot be said of the courtesy, kindness and unceasing care of the officers, crew and passengers of this vessel, who worked from morning until night and almost from night until morning in the relief of the survivors.

I was in the second boat picked up. Others were adrift many hours longer and consequently suffered more. The captain of the *Carpathia* stayed until there were no more boats to pick up and he felt he must get out of the ice before sundown. We left the scene of the disaster about noon with the *Californian* still standing by, and as we turned back, as far as I could see in all directions, was a continuous floe of ice, marked by detached icebergs.

(*Portland Oregonian*, 27 April 1912)

Bostonian **Edward N. Kimball** was spared thanks to the intervention of one of the officers.

The first boat that went off was not more than two-thirds full, and the officers said they would have to do something to get the people started.

When the second boat was being loaded we decided that we would certainly put all the women in this boat. We not only put all the women in our party and those that we had advised to come to the boat deck, but also put in two stewardesses, which were all the women on the boat deck at that time.

Mrs Kimball absolutely refused to leave without me, and one of the officers and myself had to pick her up bodily and put her into the boat, together with all the other women and the two stewardesses.

The boat was then swung off, and the officers ordered it to be lowered. I remained behind on the *Titanic* after having helped to load all the women in the boat. After it had been lowered ten or twelve feet one of the officers of the *Titanic* said to me: 'There are no women on the deck, and there is more room in that lifeboat.

You had better go,' and gave me a push and I jumped and landed in the lifeboat. I feel that I owe my life to that fact.

After we were in the lifeboat the men manned the oars and we rowed away for some distance from the big ship. Even at this time a couple of sailors in our boat stated that they would rather be on the *Titanic* than in the lifeboat, because she was absolutely unsinkable.

After we knew that the *Titanic* was doomed, however, we decided to conserve our strength, as we did not know how soon there would be help. We understood that the *Olympic* would not be along until probably two o'clock the next afternoon, so we tried to row so as to keep near some of the other lifeboats.

Just before daybreak we saw the signal rockets of a boat and rowed towards them. After we had rowed a short time one of the officers in our lifeboat saw the lights but did not know whether it was a ship or only one of our own lifeboats which had a light.

It turned out to be the *Carpathia* and we continued rowing towards it until we came up alongside. We cannot speak too highly of the treatment and kindness shown us by the officers, passengers and stewards of the *Carpathia*.

(*Boston Post*, 20 April 1912)

George A. Harder, a twenty-five-year-old manufacturer from Brooklyn, was travelling first-class with his wife Dorothy.

We saw the crew manning the lifeboats, getting them ready, swinging them out. So we waited around there on the top deck and we were finally told, 'Go over this way. Go over this way.' So we followed and went over towards the first lifeboat, where Mr and Mrs Bishop were. That boat was filled, so they told us to move to the next one. We got to the second one, and we were told to go right in there. I have been told that Mr Ismay took hold of my wife's arm and pushed her right in. Then I followed. When I jumped in, one foot went in between the oars, and I could not move until somebody pulled me over.

As we were being lowered, they lowered one side quicker than the other, but we finally reached the water safely after a few scares. When we got down into the water, somebody said the plug was not in. So they fished around to see if that was in, and I guess it was in. Then they could not get the boat detached from the tackle, so they fussed around there for a while. Finally they asked if anybody had a knife. One of the passengers did, and the rope was cut.

We had about forty-two people in the boat, of whom roughly thirty were women. There was also an officer, a sailor and three other seamen. We rowed out there some distance from the ship – maybe a quarter of a mile – because we were afraid of the suction. The passengers said: 'Let us row out a little further.' So they rowed out further, perhaps about half a mile. It may have been three-quarters of a mile. There we waited, and after waiting around a while, there was this other boat that came alongside, that Officer Pitman hailed alongside. It was the boat in which Mr and Mrs Bishop were. We tied alongside of that, and they had twenty-nine people in their boat. We counted the number of people in our boat, and at the time we only counted, I think it was 36. So we gave them four or five of our people in order to make it even, as we were kind of crowded. They say those boats hold sixty people, but we had only the number of people I have mentioned and, believe me, we did not have room to spare.

Then we waited out there until the ship went down. After it went down, we heard a lot of cries and yells. You could not hear any shouts for help, or anything like that. It was a sort of continuous yelling or moaning. You could not distinguish any sounds. I thought it was the steerage in rafts that were all hysterical. That is the way it sounded in the distance.

Our boat was managed very well. Officer Pitman did want to go back to the ship, but all the passengers held out and said: 'Do not do that. It would only be foolish if we went back there. There will be so many around they will only swamp the boat.' And at that time, I do not think those people appreciated that there were not enough lifeboats to go around. I never paid any attention to how many lifeboats there were. I did not know.

(US Inquiry, 8 May 1912)

BOAT NO. 6

This was the first to be lowered from the port side, which came under the jurisdiction of Second Officer Charles Herbert Lightoller. Throughout the night, Lightoller adhered strictly to the 'women and children first' rule to the extent that on the port side, it was invariably 'women and children only' – this, despite the fact that many of the boats left half full. Boat No. 6 left with some twenty-eight people, the only male passenger being an Italian stowaway with a broken arm. Canadian yachtsman Major Arthur Peuchen was included at the last minute as an additional sailor – a wise move, as it transpired, since quartermaster Robert Hichens stead-fastly refused to row. It was on this boat that the legend of the unsinkable Molly Brown was born, Mrs J.J. Brown removing her life jacket and seizing an oar to compensate for Hichens' inactivity.

Passenger **Mrs Lucian P. Smith** was one of many to criticize the idleness of quartermaster Robert Hichens.

When the first boat was lowered from the left-hand side I refused to get in, and they did not urge me particularly. In the second boat they kept calling for one more lady to fill it, and my husband insisted that I get in it, my friend having gotten in. I refused unless he would go with me. In the meantime Captain Smith was standing with a megaphone on deck. I approached him and told him I was alone, and asked if my husband might be allowed to go in the boat with me. He ignored me personally, but shouted again through his megaphone, 'Women and children first.' My husband said: 'Never mind about that, captain – I will see that she gets in the boat.' He then said: 'I never expected to ask you to obey, but this is one time you must. It is only a matter of form to have women and children first. The boat is thoroughly equipped, and everyone on her will be saved.' I asked him if that was absolutely honest, and he said: 'Yes.' I felt better then because I had absolute confidence in what he said. He kissed me goodbye and placed me in the lifeboat with the assistance of an officer. As the boat was being lowered he yelled from the deck: 'Keep your hands in your pockets, it is very cold weather.'

That was the last I saw of him, and now I remember the many husbands that turned their backs as the small boat was lowered, the women blissfully innocent of their husbands' peril, and said goodbye with the expectation of seeing them within the next hour or two.

By that time our interest was centred on the lowering of the lifeboat, which occurred to me – although I know very little about it – to be a very poor way to lower one. The end I was in was almost straight up, while the lower end came near touching the water. One seaman said at the time that he did not know how to get the rope down, and asked for a knife. Some person in the boat happened to have a knife – a lady, I think – who gave it to him. He cut the rope, and we were about to hit the bottom when someone spoke of the plug. After a few minutes' excitement to find something to stop the hole in the bottom of the boat where the plug is, we reached the water all right. The captain looked over to see us, I suppose, or something of the kind, and noticed there was only one man in the boat. Major Peuchen, of Canada, was then swung out to us as an experienced seaman.

There was a small light on the horizon that we were told to row towards. Some people seemed to think it was a fishing smack or small boat of some description. However we seemed to get no nearer the longer we rowed, and I am of the opinion that it was a star. Many people in our boat said they saw two lights. I could not until I had looked a long time. I think it was the way our eyes focused, and probably the hope for another boat. I do not believe it was anything but a star.

There were twenty-four people in our boat – they are supposed to hold fifty. During the night they looked for water and crackers and a compass, but they found none that night.

We were some distance away when the *Titanic* went down. We watched with sorrow and heard the many cries for help and pitied the captain because we knew he would have to stay with his ship. The cries we heard I thought were seamen, or possibly steerage, who had overslept, it not occurring to me for a moment that my husband and my friends were not saved.

It was bitterly cold, but I did not seem to mind it particularly. I was trying to locate my husband in all the boats that were near us. The night was beautiful – everything seemed to be with us in that respect – and a very calm sea. The icebergs on the horizon were all watched with interest. Some seemed to be as tall as mountains, and reminded me of the pictures I had studied in geography. Then there were flat ones, round ones also.

I am not exactly sure what time, but think it was between 5 and 5.30, when we sighted the *Carpathia*. Our seaman suggested we drift and let them pick us up. However the women refused and rowed towards it. Our seaman was Hichens, who refused to row but sat in the end of the boat wrapped in a blanket that one of the women had given him. I am not of the opinion that he was intoxicated, but a lazy, uncouth man who had no respect for the ladies and who was a thorough coward.

We made no attempt to return to the sinking *Titanic* because we supposed it was thoroughly equipped. Such a thought never entered my head. Nothing of the sort was mentioned in the boat. Having left the ship so early, we were innocent of the poor equipment that we now know of.

The sea had started to get fairly rough by the time we were taken on the *Carpathia*, and we were quite cold and glad for the shelter and protection. I have every praise for the *Carpathia*'s captain and its crew, as well as the passengers aboard. They were kindness itself to each and every one of us, regardless of position we occupied on boat. One lady very kindly gave me her berth, and I was as comfortable as can be expected under the circumstances until we arrived in New York. The ship's doctors were particularly nice to us. I know many women who slept on the floor in the smoking room while Mr Ismay occupied the best room on the *Carpathia*, being in the centre of the boat, with every attention, and a sign on the door: 'Please do not knock.' There were other men who were miraculously saved, and barely injured, sleeping on the engine-room floor and such places as that, as the ship was very crowded.

The discipline coming into New York was excellent. We were carefully looked after in every way with the exception of a Marconigram I sent from the *Carpathia* on Monday morning, April 15, to my friends. Knowing of their anxiety, I borrowed money from a gentleman and took this Marconigram myself and asked the operator to send it for me, and he promised he would. However it was not received. Had it been sent, it would have spared my family, as well as Mr Smith's, the terrible anxiety which they went through for four days. This is the only complaint I have to make against the *Carpathia*. They did tell me they were near enough to land to send it, but would send it through other steamers, as they were cabling the list of the rescued that way. He also said it was not necessary to pay him, because the White Star Line was responsible. I insisted, however, because I thought that probably the money might have some weight with them, as the whole thing seemed to have been a monied accident.

(US Inquiry, 20 May 1912)

In company with other first-class passengers, **Mrs Edgar J. Meyer** of New York had been assured that the accident was a trivial affair and would merely delay the *Titanic*'s arrival in New York. But she was by no means convinced.

I was afraid and made my husband promise if there was trouble he would not make me leave him. We walked around the deck a while.

An officer came up and cried, 'All women into the lifeboats.' My husband and I discussed it, and the officer said, 'You must obey orders.' We went down into the cabin and we decided on account of our baby to part. He helped me put on warm things.

I got into a boat, but there were no sailors aboard. We called to the ship that there were no men in the boat. They sent a sailor down.

An English girl and I rowed for four hours and a half. We were well away from the steamer when it went down, but we heard the screams of the people left on the boat. There were about seventy of us widows on the *Carpathia*, and all were wonderfully brave. The Captain of the *Carpathia* and the passengers did all they could for us. Mrs Harris says my husband and Mr Harris and Mr Douglas lowered the last boatload of women. All three were perfectly calm.

(US press, 19 April 1912)

Chicago-born **Mrs Julia Cavendish** lost her husband Tyrell but was saved along with her two-year-old daughter and maid Nellie Barber. Her account of J. Bruce Ismay's manic behaviour on the *Carpathia* was not substantiated by any other witnesses, raising doubts about its accuracy.

My husband told me to put on some clothes and follow him to the deck. I rushed up the stairways with the hundreds of others. The stewards told us the ship was absolutely unsinkable.

Twenty minutes later came that awful cry, 'Save your lives!' Then there was a mad rush for the boats. My husband told me to get into a lifeboat with the little girl, saying he would wait a little while. I kissed him and said 'Goodbye'. I was put into the boat, together with twenty-two other women. Soon we were a good distance away from the *Titanic*'s side.

Most of the women were in their bare feet and nightgowns, and there was no food except two pocketfuls of crackers I had stuffed into my coat. These I divided among the others.

Later we saw the great ship pitch forward and we heard two explosions and screams. A little later she dove to the bottom. We heard the sucking noise she made. Many had jumped and were sucked into the vortex. With them went my husband.

We were too excited to feel cold. Many wept all night. When the *Carpathia* came we were taken on board, given breakfast and clothed. When we were eating, a man who looked like a human derelict and acted like one half mad came into the room crying: 'I'm Ismay! I'm Ismay!'

(*New York World*, 19 April 1912)

BOAT NO. 3

This was lowered on the starboard side at 1 a.m. and contained somewhere between forty and fifty people, including ten male passengers and an abnormally high number of crew members – fifteen. In charge of the boat was Able Seaman **George Moore** from Southampton.

I went on the starboard side of the boat deck and helped clear the boats. I swung three of the boats out and helped to lower No. 5 and No. 7. When we started lowering the boats all I saw was first-class ladies and gentlemen all lined up with their lifebelts on and coming out of the saloon. When we swung No. 3 out, I was told to jump in the boat and pass the ladies in. I was told that by the First Officer, Mr Murdoch. After we got so many ladies in, and there were no more about, we took in men passengers. We had thirty-two in the boat, all told, and then we lowered away. Two seamen were in the boat. There were a few men passengers and five or six firemen. They got in after all the ladies and children. Mr Murdoch got all the women and children in, and the men started to jump in. When we thought we had a boat full, we lowered away.

I took charge of the boat at the tiller. The passengers were not anxious to get in the first lot of boats and I myself thought that there was nothing serious the matter until we got away from the ship and she started settling down. You could see her head gradually going down. We were about a quarter of a mile away and I saw the forward part of her go down. It appeared to me as if she broke in half, and then the after part went. I can remember two explosions.

I made no effort to go back. All the people in the boat wanted to get clear of the ship. They did not want to go near her. They kept urging me to keep away, to pull away from her. In fact, they wanted to get farther away. I heard the cries of the people in the water – everybody did – but they did not last long. I do not think anybody could live much more than ten minutes in that cold water. If we had gone back, we would only have had the boat swamped. Just five or six pulling on that boat's gunwales would no doubt have capsized the boat.

We rowed for a bright light, two or three miles away on the starboard bow. It was just one single light. I thought it was a fisherman. We kept pulling for it until daylight, but we could not see a thing of it then.

At dawn we were surrounded by ice. There were lots of bergs around, and there was a great field of ice, I should say between twenty and thirty miles long.

(US Inquiry, 25 April 1912)

Mrs William T. Graham and her daughter Margaret were among the passengers rescued on boat No. 3.

I counted our fellow passengers. We were thirty-four, including two sailors, two ship's boys and a half a dozen or more other men. The men didn't say a word. The women quarrelled a little because some of them didn't have room to sit down. There was a long argument as to how far we should go out. Some seemed to think that we ought to stay very near, because, they said, the ship wouldn't sink anyway. Others were in favour of going a way out.

The trouble was that there was no one in command, and the two sailors couldn't do much. The men were silent, and that is why the women did most of the talking. There were sixteen oarlocks in our boat, but we lost three oars right off because those who handled them didn't know anything about rowing. Then I took the oar myself. I don't think I helped very much. I was cold, and I was dressed very lightly. Everybody seemed rather dazed, but not so very excited. That came later.

We went out about three-quarters of a mile, I think, following another boat which carried some green lanterns. That was the only thing we had to go by. Behind us the lights on the *Titanic* went out, and in an hour and a half the big ship went down. It was in that hour and a half that the passengers got their fright. We couldn't tell what was going on, on the ship – but those shrieks and cries! I'll never forget them. And there were many shots. I saw many dead. That was frightful.

(*Trenton Evening Times*, 20 April 1912)

EMERGENCY CUTTER NO. 1

This was launched on the starboard side at 1.10 a.m. Despite having a capacity of forty, it was allowed to leave with just twelve people on board – seven crew and five passengers.

Lady Duff Gordon and her husband, Sir Cosmo, left the *Titanic* on this boat. After the *Titanic* had gone down, it was suggested that emergency boat No. 1 should return to the scene to pick up survivors but it failed to do so. Sir Cosmo's behaviour on the night was strongly criticized after the British inquiry into the tragedy heard that he had offered each of the seven crewmen £5. This was widely interpreted as a bribe to ensure that they did not turn back and risk the boat being capsized by taking on more people. Sir Cosmo maintained that the money was simply an act of generosity to replace their lost kit. Lady Duff Gordon told US reporters:

For two hours we cruised around. We were probably a thousand feet away from the *Titanic*. Suddenly I clutched the sides of the lifeboat. I had seen the *Titanic* give a curious shiver. Almost immediately we heard several pistol shots and a great screaming arise from the decks. Then the boat's stern lifted in the air and there was a tremendous explosion. After this the *Titanic* dropped back again. The awful screaming continued. Two minutes later there was another great explosion.

The whole forward part of the great liner dropped down under the waves. The stern rose a hundred feet, almost perpendicularly. The boat stood up like an enormous black finger against the sky. Little figures hung to the point of the finger and dropped into the water. The screaming was agonizing. I never heard such a continued chorus of utter despair and agony.

The great prow of the *Titanic* slowly sank as though a great hand was pushing it gently down under the waves. As it went, the screaming of the poor souls left on board seemed to grow louder. It took the *Titanic* perhaps two minutes to sink after that last explosion. It went down slowly without a ripple.

Then began the real agonies of the night. Up to that time no one in our boat – nor I imagine in any of the other boats – had really thought that the *Titanic* was going to sink. For a moment an awful silence seemed to hang over all, and then from the water all about arose a bedlam of shrieks and cries. There were women and men clinging to the bits of wreckage in the icy waters. It was at least an hour before the last shrieks died out. I remember the very last cry was of a man who had been calling: 'My God! My God!' He cried monotonously, in a dull, hopeless way. For an entire hour there had been an awful chorus of shrieks, gradually dying into a hopeless moan, until this last cry that I speak of. Then all was silent.

Having seen his wife leave on an earlier boat, **C. E. Henry Stengel** joined the Duff Gordons in the emergency cutter.

After the boats as far as I could see on the starboard side were loaded, I turned towards the bow. There was a small boat that they called an emergency boat, in which there were three people, Sir Duff Gordon and his wife and Miss Francatelli. I asked the officer if I could get into that boat. There was no one else around that I could see except the people working at the boats. The officer said: 'Jump in.' The railing was rather high. I jumped onto it and rolled into the boat. The officer then said: 'That is the funniest thing I've seen tonight,' and he laughed quite heartily. That rather gave me some encouragement. I thought perhaps it was not so dangerous as I imagined. After getting down part of the way, the boat began to tip and somebody hollered to stop lowering. Somebody cut the line and we went on down.

I think between Sir Duff Gordon and myself we decided which way to go. We followed a light that was to the bow of the boat. Most of the boats rowed towards that light, and after the green lights began to burn I suggested it was better to turn around and go towards the green lights because I presumed there was an officer of the ship in that boat.

I saw the first row of port lights of the *Titanic* go under the water. I saw the next port lights go under the water, and finally the bow was all dark. When the last lights on the bow went under, I said: 'There is danger here, we had better row away from here. This is a light boat, and there may be suction when the ship goes down. Let us pull away.' The other passengers agreed, and we pulled away from the *Titanic*, and after that we stopped rowing for a while. She was going down by the bow and all of a sudden there were four sharp explosions. Then she dipped and the stern stood up in the air, and then the cries began for help. I should think that the people who were left on the boat began to jump over. There was an awful wail.

(US Inquiry, 30 April 1912)

Fireman **Robert Pusey** told the Board of Trade inquiry into the disaster:

I heard one of the men say, 'We have lost our kit,' and then someone said: 'Never mind, we will give you enough to get a new kit.' I was surprised that no one suggested going back. I was surprised that I did not do so, but we were all half dazed.

It does occur to me now that we might have gone back and rescued some of the strugglers. I heard Lady Duff Gordon say to Miss Francatelli, 'You have lost your beautiful nightdress,' and I said, 'Never mind, you have saved your lives; but we have lost our kit.' Then Sir Cosmo offered to provide us with new ones.

(British Inquiry, 20 May 1912)

BOAT NO. 8

This boat was launched at around 1.10 (although some sources state that it was the first to be lowered on the port side) and was the setting for one of the most touching moments in the whole drama when elderly New York department store owners Isidor and Ida Straus refused to be separated. Instead they both stayed on the doomed liner where they died together.

Philadelphia banker **Robert W. Daniel** witnessed the scene before making his own escape.

I was dictating some letters to my stenographer when a steward came to my door and said that the ship was in danger. The idea of the big *Titanic* sinking seemed to me ridiculous. I simply went back to my state room and to bed. All the while I could hear running and scampering on the upper decks.

Soon a steward came to my door and yelled at me the ship was sinking. Then I did put on a lifebelt and went to deck B. On the rear of the deck I met Mr and Mrs Straus. I heard him say to her: 'Now, dear, I want you to do as I say and get on that next lifeboat.'

Mrs Straus replied: 'I have been begging you to get into one of the small boats since the first one was lowered and you have refused. I will get into this one if you will.'

Mr Straus shook his head. It was very plain he had made up his mind to drown rather than take a place in the lifeboat and there were not enough boats to go round.

He had an arm about Mrs Straus and hers was about him. They were in plain view of everyone in that part of the ship.

The last lifeboat had gone and the *Titanic* was sinking fast. When the boat began sinking everybody seemed to have gone insane. Men and women fought, bit and scratched to be in line for the lifeboats. Look at my black eye and cut chin. I got them in the fight.

I dived into the water. Keeping afloat, I came upon a lifeboat. There were thirty-seven persons on this boat and I had no right to ask to be picked up, but I was picked up.

Every one of the persons rescued was on the open sea for hours. We had not a bite to eat. The wind, coming over the sea of ice and the great bergs, chilled us to the marrow. Several persons in the boats were frozen to death.

(*New York World*, 19 April 1912)

The **Countess of Rothes** was on her way to Canada to join her fruit-farmer husband. She virtually took command of lifeboat No. 8 when the seamen placed in charge proved inadequate rowers, and was one of the passengers who spotted a mystery ship on the horizon.

It was pitiful, our rowing towards the lights of a ship that disappeared. We in boat number eight saw some tramp steamer's mast headlights and then saw a glow of red as it swung toward us for a few minutes, then darkness and despair.

There were two stewards in boat number eight with us and thirty-one women. The name of one of the stewards was Crawford. We were lowered quietly to the water and when we had pushed off from the *Titanic*'s side I asked the seaman if he would care to have me take the tiller, as I knew something about boats. He said, 'Certainly, lady.' I climbed aft into the stern and asked my cousin to help me.

The first impression I had as we left the ship was that, above all things, we mustn't lose our self-possession; we had no officer to take command of our boat and the little seaman had to assume all responsibility. He did it nobly, alternately cheering us with words of encouragement, then rowing doggedly. Then Signora de Satode Penasco began to scream for her husband. It was too horrible. I left the tiller to my cousin and slipped down beside her, to be of what comfort I could. Poor woman, her sobs tore our hearts and her moans were unspeakable in their sadness. Miss Cherry stayed at the tiller of our boat until the *Carpathia* picked us up.

The most terrible part of the whole thing was seeing the rows of portholes vanishing one by one. Several of us wanted to row back and see if there was not some chance of rescuing anyone that had possibly survived, but the majority in the boat argued that we had no right to risk their lives on the bare chance of finding anyone alive after the final plunge.

Indeed I saw – we all saw – a ship's lights not more than three miles away. For three hours we pulled steadily for the two masthead lights that showed brilliantly in the darkness. For a few minutes we saw the ship's port light, then it vanished, and the masthead lights got dimmer on the horizon until they too disappeared.

Roberta Maioni was maid to the Countess of Rothes.

An elderly officer, with tears streaming down his cheeks, helped us into one of the lifeboats. He was Captain Smith – the master of that ill-fated vessel. As the lifeboat began to descend, I heard him say: 'Goodbye, remember you are British.'

We dropped over sixty feet down the side of that huge vessel and it seemed an eternity before the lifeboat reached the water. There were about thirty-five of us in the boat including three of the crew – a seaman, a steward, and a cook. These men had been told to get away from the *Titanic* as quickly as they could, lest the lifeboat be drawn under by the suction of the sinking vessel.

When we were at a safe distance they stopped rowing and we watched the *Titanic* sink rapidly into the black depths. She was ablaze with electric light until the last minute.

Then I heard the terrible last cries of the twelve hundred men, women, and children left aboard her, rising above the din of the explosion of the boilers. For a moment the sky was lighted up, with black masses thrown up into the air, and we saw that dreadful iceberg towering above us, like some grim monster about to devour its prey. Then came the awful silence – more terrible than the sounds that had gone before.

The sea was calm, otherwise no one would have been saved, but by now it was studded with the wreckage and with bodies of the dead and dying. Some poor souls reached the lifeboats, only to be pushed back into the relentless ice-cold sea, for the boats were full and in grave danger of swamping.

We had one loaf of bread in our lifeboat and this had been trampled upon. There was neither drinking water, compass nor clock and our single lamp would not light. Because of this, we drifted away from other lifeboats.

We rowed all through the night, taking turns at the sweep. I took my place and remember that my long hair was very much in the way for it often caught between my hands and the oar and caused me terrible pain. They steered our boat towards the lights of a tramp steamer in the distance, but we had no means of attracting attention and the steamer's lights slowly passed out of sight. The disappearance of the tramp steamer seemed to leave us alone on the ocean – a handful of people in an open boat – and we were faced with a worse fate than drowning. To add to our misery, the sea became rough and our boat was pitching and tossing helplessly.

At last the morning came and we saw several icebergs around us, grim spectres that would crush our frail craft like an eggshell. As our eyes became accustomed to the light, however, we saw that one of the objects that we had taken for an iceberg was a ship – the Cunard liner *Carpathia* – called to our rescue by the heroic wireless operator of the *Titanic*, Mr Phillips, whom we left behind to perish. He stayed in his cabin to the very last, directing vessels to the scene of the disaster.

We soon reached the *Carpathia* and were taken up her great side one more time in a kind of cradle – just a piece of board, strong hands, and willing hands at the top. This was no easy operation, for the lifeboat was being dashed along the *Carpathia*'s side and, while waiting to be taken up, we were jerked backwards and forwards by the fury of the waves.

As soon as I reached the deck, kindly hands put a rug around my shoulders and pressed brandy to my trembling lips. I was safe, thank God, and little the worse for my adventure.

Caroline Bonnell of Youngstown, Ohio, took a turn at the oars.

As the boat was being loaded, the officer in charge pointed out a light that glowed dimly in the distance on the surface of the sea, and directed our sailors to row to that, land their passengers and return to the *Titanic* for more. As we were rowed away we saw that the great liner was settling. We kept our boat pointed towards the light to which we were to row. As a matter of fact there were two lights, one red and the other white. Sailormen on the *Carpathia* told us subsequently that the lights might have been those of a fishing boat caught in the ice and drifting with it – but who can tell?

After a while our sailors ceased rowing, saying it was of no use to keep on. Then we women tried to row, with the double light our objective. We rowed and rowed, but did not seem to gain on the light, which, like a will-o'-the-wisp, seemed ever to evade us. Finally we gave up and sat huddled in the lifeboat.

Some of the women complained of the cold, but the members of our own party did not suffer, being provided with plenty of wraps.

From the distance of a mile or more we heard the explosion and saw the *Titanic* go down. The lights did not go out all at once. As the ship slowly settled, the rows of lights one after another winked out, disappearing beneath the surface. Finally the ship plunged down bow first and the stern slipped beneath the waves.

Even then we had hoped that all on board might be saved. It was only after we had been taken aboard the *Carpathia*, and saw how few of us there were compared with the great company aboard the *Titanic*, that we got the first glimmer of the appalling reality.

(*New York World*, 20 April 1912)

Mrs J. Stuart White from New York sailed first-class. She left the *Titanic* in boat No. 8, where her cane, fitted with an electric light, provided much-needed illumination. She was highly critical of the male crew members.

We were the second boat pushed away from the ship, and we saw nothing that happened after that. We were not near enough. We heard the yells of the steerage passengers as they went down, but we saw none of the harrowing part of it all. The men in our boat were anything but seamen, with the exception of one man. The women all rowed, every one of them. Miss Young rowed every minute. The men could not row. They did not know the first thing about it. Miss Swift, from Brooklyn, rowed every minute, from the steamer to the *Carpathia*. Miss Young rowed every minute also, except when she was throwing up, which she did six or seven times. Countess Rothes stood at the tiller. Where would we have been if it had not been for our women, with such men as that put in charge of the boat? Our head seaman would give an order and those men who knew nothing about the handling of a boat would say, 'If you don't stop talking through that hole in your face there will be one less in the boat.' We were in the hands of men of that kind. I settled two or three fights between them, and quieted them down. Imagine getting right out there and taking out a pipe and filling it and standing there smoking, with the women rowing.

(US Inquiry, 2 May 1912)

BOAT NO. 9

This was launched on the starboard side at 1.20 a.m. with fifty-six people on board, the increased number reflecting the growing concern on board the sinking *Titanic*. Among the crew on this boat was saloon steward **William Ward**.

I was stationed at No. 7, but they did not want me for that boat. They had sufficient men to man the boat. Then I went aft to No. 9 boat and assisted to take the canvas cover off her. Then we lowered her down to level with the boat deck, and a sailor came along with a bag and threw it in the boat. This man said he had been sent down to take charge of the boat by the captain. The boatswain's mate, Haines, was there, and he ordered this man out of the boat, and the man got out again.

A few minutes later, either Purser McElroy or Mr Murdoch said: 'Pass the women and children that are here into that boat.' There were several men standing around, and they fell back. There was quite a quantity of women and children helped into the boat. One old lady made a great fuss about it and absolutely refused to get into the boat. She went back to the companionway and would not get into the boat.

There were several men in the boat then to assist in getting the women in. One woman – a French lady – had already fallen and hurt herself a little. The purser told two more men to get in and assist these women down into the boat. From the rail of the boat it is quite a step down to the bottom of the boat, and in the dark they could not see where they were stepping. Then the purser told me to get into the boat and take an oar. I did so, and we still waited there and asked if there were any more women. There were none coming along.

Then they took about three or four men into the boat, and the officers that were standing there thought there was quite suffi-cient in it to lower away with safety, and we lowered down to the water, everything running very smoothly.

141

When we lowered boat No. 9 the *Titanic* was not listing at all. She was down by the head, but not listing. She went very gradually for a while. We could just see the ports as she dipped. We could see the light in the ports, and the water seemed to come very slowly up to them. She did not appear to be going fast, and I was of the opinion then that she would not go. I thought we were only out there as a matter of precaution and would certainly go back to the ship. I was still of the opinion she would float.

Then she gave a kind of sudden lurch forward, and I heard a couple of reports, more like a volley of musketry than anything else. It did not seem to me like an explosion at all.

There were four of us rowed all night. There were more men in the boat, but some of them had not been to sea before and did not know the first thing about an oar, or know the bow from the stern. The boat was pretty well packed. We had not room to pull the oars. The women had to move their bodies with us when we were rowing.

We partially rowed to the *Carpathia* and she partially came some of the way. We saw her at a distance. She was headed our way. She stopped and slewed around a little, and we surmised that she was then picking up a boat. It was hardly light enough to see at the time. It was just breaking day, but we could see her lights. Then we started to pull towards her. I think we were about the fourth or fifth boat to be picked up.

(US Inquiry, 25 April 1912)

BOAT NO. 10

This was launched from the port side at 1.20 a.m. with fifty-five people on board. Its crew included Able Seaman **Frank Evans**.

Mr Murdoch was standing there, and I lowered the boat with the assistance of a steward. The Chief Officer said, 'What are you, Evans?' I said, 'A seaman, sir.' He said: 'All right. Get into that boat with the other seamen.'

I got into the bows of this boat, and a young ship's baker was getting the children and chucking them into the boat, and the women were jumping. Mr Murdoch made them jump across into the boat. It was about two and a half feet. He was making the women jump across, and the children he was chucking across, along with this baker. He threw them onto the women, and he was catching the children by their dresses and chucking them in. One or two women refused in the first place to jump but, after he told them, they finally went.

One woman in a black dress slipped and fell. She seemed nervous and did not like to jump at first. When she did jump, she did not go far enough. Her heel must have caught on the rail of the deck, and she fell down and someone on the deck below caught her and pulled her up. Back on the boat deck, she took another jump and landed safely in the boat.

As this boat was being lowered, this foreigner must have jumped from A deck into the boat. He deliberately jumped across into the boat and saved himself.

Later we tied up to No. 12. We gave the man our painter and made fast, and we stopped there. The Fifth Officer, Mr Lowe, came over in No. 14 and said: 'Are there any seamen there?' We said, 'Yes, sir.' He said: 'You will have to distribute these passengers among these boats. Tie them all together and come into my boat to go over into the wreckage and pick up anyone that is alive there.' We picked up four persons alive, one of whom died on the way back. There were plenty of dead bodies about us, mostly men.

We picked up a collapsible boat that had some women and children in it and we sailed to the *Carpathia* with this collapsible boat in tow. One of the ladies there passed over a flask of whisky to the people who were all wet through.

(US Inquiry, 25 April 1912)

Mrs Imanita Shelley, a second-class passenger from Montana, was travelling with her mother, Mrs Lutle Davis Parrish, of Woodford County, Kentucky. Her affidavit read:

A steward brought Mrs Parrish and Mrs Shelley each a lifebelt and showed them how to tie them on. They were told to go to the top deck, the boat deck. As Mrs Shelley was very weak, it took several minutes to reach the upper deck. Mr and Mrs Isidor Straus, who had known of Mrs Shelley being so ill, met them on the way and helped them to the upper deck, where they found a chair for her and made her sit down.

After sitting in the chair for about five minutes one of the sailors ran to Mrs Shelley and implored her to get in the lifeboat that was then being launched. He informed Mrs Shelley that it was the last boat on the ship, and that unless she got into this one she would have to take her chances on the steamer, and that as she had been so sick she ought to take to the boat and make sure.

Mrs Straus advised taking to the boats, and, pushing her mother towards the sailor, Mrs Shelley made for the davits where the boat hung. It was found impossible to swing the davits in, which left a space of between four and five feet between the edge of the deck and the suspended boat. The sailor picked up Mrs Parrish and threw her bodily into the boat. Mrs Shelley jumped and landed safely.

On trying to lower the boat, the tackle refused to work and it took considerable time, about fifteen minutes, to reach the water. On reaching the water, the casting-off apparatus would not work and the ropes had to be cut.

Just as they reached the water a crazed Italian jumped from the deck into the lifeboat, landing on Mrs Parrish, severely bruising her right side and leg.

(US Inquiry, 25 May 1912)

Mrs Daniel Marvin of New York became a widow at eighteen. Married for just five weeks, she and her husband were returning from their honeymoon on the *Titanic*. Her father-in-law, Henry Norton Marvin, was the president of 'a moving picture concern' and had arranged for films to be taken of the wedding which the bride and groom were hoping to keep as souvenirs. Alas the groom never got to see them.

Dan grabbed me in his arms and knocked down men to get me in the boats. As I was put in the boat, he cried, 'It's all right, little girl. You go and I'll stay a little while. I'll put on a life preserver and jump off and follow your boat.' As our boat started off he threw a kiss at me.

When we reached the deck after the accident we were in darkness. While on the deck I heard at least ten revolver shots. See, one bullet was fired at my cheek. Here are the powder marks.

The men whom I saw were brave, for they pushed aside others when the cowards made for the boats before the women.

When we pulled away from the *Titanic* I think I saw Maj. Butt, whom I knew slightly, standing near where they were loading the boats, with an iron bar or stick in his hand beating back the frenzied crowd who were attempting to overcrowd the lifeboats.

(US press, 19 April 1912)

Travelling second-class, **Marshall Drew**, aged eight, got into the boat with his aunt.

All was calm and orderly. An officer was in charge. 'Women and children first,' he said as he directed the lifeboat to be filled. There were many tearful farewells. We and Uncle Jim said 'good-bye'. Waiting on deck before this I could hear the ship's orchestra playing somewhere off to first class.

The lifeboat was near the stern. I will never forget that as I looked over my right shoulder, steerage was blacked out. It made an impression I never forgot. The lowering of the lifeboat 70ft to the sea was perilous. Davits, ropes, nothing worked properly, so that first one end of the lifeboat was tilted up and then far down. I think it was the only time I was scared.

Lifeboats pulled some distance away from the sinking *Titanic*, afraid of what the suction might do. I am always annoyed at artists' depictions of the sinking of *Titanic*. I've never seen one that came anywhere near the truth. There might have been the slightest ocean swell but it was dead calm. Stars there may have been, but the blackness of the night was so intense one could not see anything like a horizon. As row by row of the porthole lights of the *Titanic* sank into the sea this was about all one could see. When the *Titanic* upended to sink, all was blacked out until the tons of machinery crashed to the bow. This sounded like an explosion which of course it was not. As this happened hundreds of people were thrown into the sea. It isn't likely I shall ever forget the screams of those people as they perished in the water said to be 28 degrees.

The reader will have to understand that at this point in my life I was being brought up as a typical British kid. You were not allowed to cry. You were a 'little man'. So as a cool kid I lay down in the bottom of the lifeboat and went to sleep. When I awoke it was broad daylight as we approached the *Carpathia*. Looking around over the gunwale it seemed to me like the Arctic. Icebergs of huge size ringed the horizon for 360 degrees.

Passenger **Miss Kornelia Andrews**, aged sixty-three, from New York State, told reporters of her harrowing experience:

When we finally did get into a boat we found that our miserable men companions could not row and had only said they could because they wanted to save themselves. Finally I had to take an oar with one of the able seamen in the boat.

Alongside of us was a sailor, who lighted a cigarette and flung the match carelessly among us women. Several women in the boat screamed, fearing they would be set on fire. The sailor replied: 'We are going to hell anyway and we might as well be cremated now as then.'

The most pathetic thing I heard was that on one of the boats, a collapsible lifeboat, holding sixteen to twenty persons, the party were up to their knees in water for six hours, so that one man had his legs frozen and eight died.

The eight were thrown overboard to lighten the boat and keep it from being swamped.

(*New York World*, 20 April 1912)

Kornelia Andrews' fifty-one-year-old sister, **Mrs Anna Hogeboom**, got away in the same boat.

A little after twelve we heard commotion in the corridor and we made inquiries and they told us we had better put on life preservers. We had only five minutes to get ready. We put our fur coats right on over our night dresses and rushed on deck.

Our lifeboat was already full, but there was no panic. The discipline in a way was good. No one hurried and no one crowded. We waited for the fourth boat and were slowly lowered 75ft to the water. The men made no effort to get into the boat. As we pulled away we saw them all standing in an unbroken line on the deck.

There they stood – Major Butt, Colonel Astor, waving a farewell to his wife; Mr Thayer, Mr Case, Mr Clarence Moore, Mr Widener, all multi-millionaires, and hundreds of other men bravely smiling at us all. Never have I seen such chivalry and fortitude.

Before our boat was lowered they called to some miserable specimens of humanity and said, 'Can you row?' and for the purpose of getting in they answered 'Yes.' But upon pulling out we found we had a Chinese and an Armenian, neither of whom knew how to row. So there we were in mid-ocean with one ablebodied seaman.

Then my niece took one oar and assisted the seaman and some of the other women rowed on the other side.

Scarcely any of the lifeboats were properly manned. Two, filled with women and children, capsized before our eyes. The collapsible boats were only temporarily useful. They soon partially filled with water. In one boat eighteen or twenty persons sat in water above their knees for six hours.

Eight men in this boat were overcome, died and were thrown overboard. Two women were in this boat. One succumbed after a few hours and one was saved.

About dawn we saw a ship in the dim distance, seemingly many miles away. This gave us our first hope, but at the same time the wind began to rise and the waves grew large. Our oarsmen and oarswomen were nearly exhausted. Had the wind increased, as it did a few hours afterwards, we would never have escaped. Shortly after eight o'clock the *Carpathia* reached near enough for us to row to it, we having rowed about nine miles, and being the last lifeboat to reach the rescue ship.

With our frozen fingers and feet it was difficult to climb up the wet, slippery rope ladder, but a rope fastened around our waists protected us from slipping into the sea.

(*New York World*, 20 April 1912)

Miss Susie Webber from Devon was on her way to Hartford, Connecticut.

I rushed on deck and saw them lowering the boats. A gentleman standing by kindly handed me into a lifeboat [No. 10], which contained women and children. After it was launched, full of women, accompanied by one sailor, a foreigner jumped from the boat deck and landed in the boat just before it struck the water.

Our English people were very brave. I am sure they realized the *Titanic* was going down.

We rowed away from her with only two men. I was facing the *Titanic* and could see her going down. I saw the lights go out deck after deck. When the water got into the engine room there was an explosion, and then I saw the leviathan part in the middle. The stern rose high in the air; the bow less high. Then she went down slowly, amid heartrending cries for help of hundreds of doomed men and women.

We were floating in mid-ocean among the icebergs for six hours. The night was bitterly cold but very calm. At last we saw the lights of the *Carpathia* coming to our aid; this was a welcome sight. We were taken on her and treated with every kindness, both passengers and crew doing everything they could for the survivors.

(Western Morning News, April 1912)

BOAT NO. 11

This went off from the starboard side at 1.25 a.m. with seventy aboard. There were only three first-class passengers, the rest being second or third. Among the crew was saloon steward **Edward Wheelton**.

There were at least a thousand in the water at one time, and most of them died of exposure, but a large number perished when the boilers exploded.

At one time while we were waiting for rescue in the boats every time we moved the oars they would strike a corpse. Two women died from exposure in our boat while we were floating about waiting for the *Carpathia*. We buried them over the side of the boat then and there.

The women in the lifeboats were remarkably calm during the time we were on the water, and the children were very brave. Some women rescued babies which were very small, and a few women voluntarily gave up their lives to protect them.

Luckily the women in our boat did not see the sinking of the *Titanic*. It was too dark, and when the day dawned they saw a few sticks and timber floating on the water, and only then did they realize that something terrible had happened.

The *Titanic* was no longer visible above water, and all around us we could see dead bodies floating.

For the first time the women became terrified, and many wept bitterly, while others seemed dazed. Fortunately we soon sighted the *Carpathia*, and the survivors were quickly taken aboard.

(*Daily Chronicle*, 20 April 1912)

Senior stewardess **Sarah Stap** owed her life to a young cabin boy. On being told to get into boat 11, she heroically suggested that the cabin boy go instead as he was younger and had his whole life ahead of him. The boy responded by simply picking her up and putting her in the boat.

I was helped into the boat and had charge of a baby, whose father and mother were lost. I nursed the little mite for several hours.

Although the night was starry, it was bitterly cold and everyone was nearly starved. We were all huddled up together. It was awful. We could see the lights of the ship slowly disappearing beneath the waves, one by one, until there alone remained the masthead light. Then suddenly the great ship gave a lurch and disappeared gracefully out of sight.

All this time the people on board were shrieking in their death agonies, and the passengers were under the impression that it was the other people in the boats cheering. Only the members of the crew knew what it was and we dared not say.

After the ship had gone an explosion rent the air. The shrieks of the dying were positively awful. During the time we were in the lifeboat we passed about six or seven icebergs. We could hear the music of the band all the time. They were heroes if you like. They were not asked to play, but did it absolutely on their own initiative.

(*Birkenhead News*, 4 May 1912)

Mrs Paul Schabert from Derby, Connecticut, saved her brother's life.

As I heard the cry 'Lifeboats are ready! The ladies will go first!' a bedroom steward rushed by me. 'Steward,' I asked, 'are we sinking?' He stopped, and with perfect coolness said, 'We are.' The way he said it left no room for doubt.

When the women were assembled for the boats I was urged to get in with the other women in one of the first boats. My brother Philip was with me, and I wanted him to go along, too, but they said that was out of the question. 'Very well, then, I will wait until the last boat,' I said. I wanted to be near him as long as I could. Then they called me for the last boat. They told me it was my last chance, so I then decided to go. Fortunately there were no more women left, and they let my brother go with me. I assure you, I am mighty glad I did not go away on the first invitation.

(US press, 19 April 1912)

Mrs Allen Becker was the wife of a missionary based in India. She and her three young children were sailing to America for specialist treatment for an illness which one-year-old Richard had contracted in India.

I stood at the lifeboat helping my babies in. When I got them all in the boat the officer said the boat was filled. I begged him to let me go with my children. He said it was impossible, that there were too many. I pleaded with him. Finally, just as the boat was being lowered, he pushed me, and I landed face down. For a long time I didn't see my children. People told me they were in the other end of the boat. Still I was afraid. And then I saw Richard in a sailor's arms, and the others near him. At that moment I was almost overwhelmed by the gladness. My babies are safe.

I do not know how far away we were from the *Titanic* when she sank. I did not look back. We could see drowning men struggling all around us after the boat went down. Some could not have been very far off. There was no more room in our boat and we had to sit and watch men perish. We were afraid to move for fear of sinking the boat, and the ice grinding against it added to our fright.

It seemed ages and ages before we were picked up by the *Carpathia* – the ship of widows. There were 160 women left husbandless by the wreck, where I was quartered in the second cabin of the *Carpathia*. The scenes of grief were terrible.

But once aboard the *Carpathia* we were in the midst of the most lavish kindness. The ship's company and the passengers were most kind. We were given comfortable quarters and good food while passengers supplied us with clothing. But oh it was so ghastly.

(US press, 20 April 1912)

Swiss-born **Mrs Amin Jerwan**, aged twenty-three, was travelling second-class. She told how mothers and children were separated by the officers and how she herself was handed a baby as she left in boat 11.

Everything was done without the slightest disorder. No one got hysterical and there was no confusion except when a child would be put in a boat and the mother told to wait for another one. I saw several instances of this. The crew and the men passengers all behaved as if everything would turn out all right, and we women thought it would.

When I got in one of the boats I found a baby in my possession without the least idea whom it belonged to. I never found out. When we were picked up by the *Carpathia* the baby was taken on board in a net and I never saw it again. I suppose it was found by the mother.

Before we had been in the boat very long we saw the *Titanic* go down. Then we knew that all the people we had left behind were lost. We saw it go plainly, although it was night. The stars were bright and we could see the lights of the ship. Suddenly those in the bow seemed to go out, and then quickly the same thing happened to those in the stern. The band was in the stern and went down playing. We could hear the screams of those on board and cries of 'Save us!' But of course we could do nothing.

Everybody on the ship blamed the captain. The sailor who rowed our boat told me that he had followed the sea for 45 years and had never been in any kind of an accident before, except on the *Olympic* when she rammed the *Hawke*. 'That was under the same captain,' he said, 'and now I am having my second experience under him.'

(US press, 19 April 1912)

BOAT NO. 12

With boats now being launched in rapid succession as the severity of the situation became apparent, No. 12 was allowed to leave with just forty-two on board, owing to an apparent lack of women and children. When a crowd of men from second-and third-class tried to clamber aboard, the officers held them at bay. The only male passenger to leave on this boat was a Frenchman who leapt in as it was being lowered past B deck. Later, No. 12 picked up passengers from the overturned Englehardt collapsible boat B. Able Seaman **Frederick Clench** described the scene.

There was only one male passenger in our boat, and that was a Frenchman who jumped in, and we could not find him. He got under the thwart and mixed with the women.

We rowed away from the ship about a quarter of a mile, then we rested on our oars according to orders. After the ship was gone down, Officer Lowe came up with us with his boat, and transferred some of his people into ours so that he would have a clear boat to go around to look for the people who were floating in the water. We had close on sixty then. Mr Lowe told us to lie on our oars and keep together until he came back to us.

While Mr Lowe was gone I heard shouts. Of course I looked around, and I saw a boat in the way that appeared to be like a funnel. We started to back away then. We thought it was the top of the funnel. I put my head over the gunwale and looked along the water's edge and saw some men on a raft. Then I heard two whistles blown.

I sang out, 'Aye, aye. I am coming over,' and we pulled over and found it was not a raft exactly, but an overturned boat. Mr Lightoller was there on that boat and I think the wireless operator (Harold Bride) was on there too. We took them on board the boat and we shared the amount of room that was there. They were all wet through. They had been in the water.

Mr Lightoller took charge of us and sighted the *Carpathia*'s lights. Then we started heading for that. We had to row a tidy distance to the *Carpathia* because there were boats ahead of us and we had a boat in tow, besides all the people we had aboard.

(US Inquiry, 25 April 1912)

Lillian Bentham, aged seventeen, from Rochester, New York, was one of a party of eleven on their way home from a trip to Europe.

Although the passengers were being taken off in the lifeboats, I did not think the *Titanic* was going to sink. It was so big, so magnificent, that I did not think it possible. I had gone to my state room and it was just before the last of twelve lifeboats put off that one of the young men in my party rushed to my state room and told me to hurry on deck, that the ship was going down.

I reached the deck with him just in time to get into the boat before it was lowered from the davits. I recall that the officer on deck shouted to the seaman in charge of the lifeboat to pull away quickly, that the *Titanic* was going down, and the suction would pull us under. A man jumped from an upper deck and landed in our boat just as we pulled away.

We had just moved a few yards from the giant ship when she was broken by the explosion of her boilers and sank in two sections. The suction did pull us back towards the great hole in the water the ship left as she plunged. But we kept afloat, a frail craft loaded with women and children, with the exception of the seaman in charge and the man who had jumped.

The greatest horror of the experience was the eight hours we spent floating about until we were picked up by the *Carpathia*. At first the sea was smooth as glass but it was literally dotted with human forms swimming, clinging to wreckage, fighting to climb into the lifeboats. Most of them were lost.

Towards morning the wind freshened, and the boats, which had been lashed together, tossed dangerously and crashed against one another, so they were cut apart. Then the lifeboats separated and drifted in all directions.

For my part, I began to realize that I had lost nothing compared to others, who had been compelled to see their relatives and friends go down with the *Titanic*. There was a Frenchwoman there, too, who was very much possessed. I helped the seaman with the oars and did what I could to comfort the others.

Towards morning we came upon one of the collapsible canvas boats, in a sinking condition, with about twenty men on it. They were huddled together, stiff and cold, absolutely helpless. In their midst was an apparent millionaire, dressed in evening clothes and a fur coat and wearing a life preserver. He had been to a gay party in the first cabin the night before and was gloriously intoxicated. He did not seem to realize the situation and was having the time of his life.

I helped the seamen pull those twenty men into our boat, which already had more than 30 in it. We had to pile them on the bottom of the boat, like so many sacks of flour, because they were unable to do anything to help themselves. The boat was very much overloaded when the task was finished. I took off my coat and gave it to one man – I had two coats and could spare one. One of those men was virtually dead when we pulled him into our boat. Seven of them died from exposure.

It was the most beautiful sunrise I have ever seen. The sun came up like a great ball of fire, casting its rays on a large iceberg behind us, causing the berg to glisten like gold. And then, far off in the distance, we saw smoke, thin and indistinct at first, but gradually coming nearer. Then we made out what it was. It was a ship, answering the SOS call. It was the *Carpathia*. To me, and I guess to all of the others in that boat, that was the most wonderful ship in the world.

Then our hearts sank with terrible fear as the ship disappeared. We were sure we were lost. But it came into view again and hope revived. Several times it did that. We did not know at that time that the *Carpathia* was steaming about the ocean, picking up the survivors from the different lifeboats that had been so widely scattered.

It finally came to our boat and we were lifted on deck. They used ropes with a seat on it for the adults. The children were pulled up in rope baskets. We were given every care on the *Carpathia*, and it must have been a task for that ship to get us all back to New York, for the *Carpathia* is a small boat and was greatly overcrowded.

BOAT NO. 13

First-class steward **Frederick Ray** described the lowering of boat No. 13 on the starboard side.

I got to A deck and went through the door. I went out on to the open deck and along to No. 9 boat. It was just being filled with women and children, and I assisted. I saw that lowered away and went along to No. 11 boat. After that was lowered away with women and children, I went to No. 13 boat. I saw that about half filled with women and children. They said: 'A few of you men get in here.' There were about nine to a dozen men there, passengers and crew. I saw Mr Washington Dodge there, asking where his wife and child were. He said they had gone away in one of the boats. He was standing well back from the boat, and I said: 'You had better get in here, then.' I got behind him and pushed him, and I followed.

After I got in, there was a rather big woman came along, and we helped her in the boat. She was crying all the time, saying: 'Don't put me in the boat – I've never been in an open boat in my life.' I said: 'You've got to go, so you may as well keep quiet.' Then a small child rolled in a blanket was thrown into the boat to me, and I caught it. The woman that brought it along got into the boat afterwards. We left about three or four men on the deck, at the rail, and they went along to No. 15 boat.

The boat was lowered away until we got nearly to the water. Then two or three of us noticed a large discharge of water coming from the ship's side. The hole was about two feet wide and about a foot deep, a solid mass of water coming out from the hole. I realized that if the boat was lowered down straight away the boat would be swamped and we would all be thrown into the water. We shouted for the boat to be stopped from being lowered, and it was.

We got oars and pushed it off from the side of the ship and the next I knew we were in the water free from this discharge. In the meantime we were drifting a little aft and another boat was being lowered immediately upon us, about two feet over our heads. We all shouted again, and again they stopped lowering the other boat.

(US Inquiry, 27 April 1912)

English schoolteacher **Lawrence Beesley**, whose name was not on the original list of survivors sent by the *Carpathia*, lived to give a detailed account of the evacuation. Whilst Beesley's narrative is viewed as one of the most reliable, even he, in the heat of the moment, became confused by the lifeboat numbers, mistaking No. 15 for No. 14.

All this time there was no trace of any disorder, panic or rush to the boats, and no scenes of women sobbing hysterically, such as one generally pictures as happening at such times; every one seemed to realize so slowly that there was imminent danger. When it was realized that we might all be presently in the sea, with nothing but our life belts to support us until we were picked up by passing steamers, it was extraordinary how calm every one was and how completely self-controlled.

One by one the boats were filled with women and children, lowered and rowed away into the night. Presently the word went round among the men, 'the men are to be put into the boats on the starboard side.' I was on the port side, and most of the men walked across the deck to see if this was so. I remained where I was, and presently heard the call: 'Any more ladies?' Looking over the side of the ship, I saw the boat, No. 13, swinging level with B deck, half full of ladies. Again the call was repeated: 'Any more ladies?' I saw none come on and then one of the crew looked up and said: 'Any ladies on your deck, sir?' 'No,' I replied. 'Then you had better jump.'

I dropped in and fell in the bottom, as they cried 'lower away'. As the boat began to descend, two ladies were pushed hurriedly through the crowd on B deck and heaved over into the boat, and a baby of ten months passed down after them. Down we went, the crew calling to those lowering which end to keep level. 'Aft,' 'stern', 'both together', until we were some ten feet from the water, and here occurred the only anxious moment we had during the whole of our experience from leaving the deck to reaching the *Carpathia*. Immediately below our boat was the exhaust of the condensers, a huge stream of water pouring all the time from the ship's side just above the water line. It was plain we ought to be quite a way from this not to be swamped by it when we touched water. We had no officer aboard, nor petty officer or member of the crew to take charge. So one of the stokers shouted: 'Someone find the pin which releases the boat from the ropes and pull it up.' No one knew where it was. We felt as well as we could on the floor and sides, but found nothing, and it was hard to move among so many people – we had sixty or seventy on board.

Down we went and presently floated with our ropes still holding us, the exhaust washing us away from the side of the vessel and the swell of the sea urging us back against the side again. The result of all these forces was an impetus which carried us parallel to the ship's side and directly under boat No. 14, which had filled rapidly with men and was coming down on us in a way that threatened to submerge our boat. 'Stop lowering 14,' our crew shouted, and the crew of No. 14, now only twenty feet above, shouted the same. But the distance to the top was some seventy feet and the creaking pulleys must have deadened all sound to those above, for down it came – fifteen feet, ten feet, five feet, and a stoker and I reached up and touched her swinging above our heads. The next drop would have brought it on to our heads, but just before it dropped another stoker sprang to the ropes with his knife. 'One,' I heard him say; 'two' as his knife cut through the pulley ropes, and the next moment the exhaust steam had carried us clear, while boat 14 dropped into the space we had the moment before occupied, our gunwales almost touching.

We drifted away easily as the oars were got out and headed directly away from the ship. The crew seemed to me to be mostly cooks in white jackets, two to an oar, with a stoker at the tiller. The captain-stoker told us that he had been on the sea twenty-six years and had never seen such a calm night on the Atlantic. As we rowed away from the *Titanic* we looked back from time to time to watch it, and a more striking spectacle it was not possible for anyone to see. In the distance it looked an enormous length, its great bulk outlined in black against the starry sky, every port-hole and saloon blazing with light. It was impossible to think anything could be wrong with such a leviathan were it not for that ominous tilt downward in the bow, where the water was by now up to the lowest row of portholes. Presently about 2 a.m., as near as I can remember, we observed it settling very rapidly, with the bow and bridge completely under water, and concluded it was now only a question of minutes before it went; and so it proved.

It slowly tilted straight on end, with the stern vertically upward, and as it did, the lights in the cabins and saloons, which had not flickered for a moment since we left, died out, came on again for a single flash, and finally went altogether. To our amazement the *Titanic* remained in that upright position, bow down, for a time which I estimate as five minutes, while we watched at least 150 feet of the *Titanic* towering above the level of the sea and looming black against the sky. Then the ship dived beneath the waters.

And then, with all these, there fell on the ear the most appalling noise that human being ever listened to – the cries of hundreds of our fellow beings struggling in the icy cold water, crying for help with a cry that we knew could not be answered. We longed to return and pick up some of those swimming, but this would have meant swamping our boat and loss of life to all of us.

Our rescuer showed up in a few hours, and as it swung round we saw its cabins all alight and knew it must be a large steamer. It was now motionless, and we had to row to it. Just then day broke, a beautiful quiet dawn with faint pink clouds just above the horizon, and a new moon whose crescent just touched the waters. The passengers, officers and crew gave up gladly their state rooms, clothing and comforts for our benefit, all honour to them.

(*New York World*, 19 April 1912)

After seeing his wife and son off in boat No. 5, **Dr Washington Dodge** chanced his luck in No. 13.

I watched the lowering of the boat in which my wife and child were until it was safely launched on an even keel, and I remained on the starboard side of the ship where the boats with the odd numbers from one to fifteen were being prepared for dropping over the side.

The thing that impressed me was that there was not sufficient men to launch the boats and, as a matter of fact, when the ship went down there was still one boat on the davits and one on the deck.

The peculiar part of the whole rescue question was that the first boats had no more than thirty passengers, with four seamen to row, while the latter boats averaged from forty to fifty, with hardly one person aboard who knew how to move an oar.

At this time the *Titanic* had a slight list to port, but just after the collision Captain Smith, coming hurriedly up and inquiring what the list was and finding it 18 degrees to starboard, said, 'My God!'

I waited until what I thought was the end. I certainly saw no signs of any women or children on deck when I was told to take a seat in boat No. 13. When lowered we nearly came abreast of the three-foot stream that the condenser pumps were still sending out from the ship's side. We cried out and the flow halted. I cannot imagine how that was done.

In my boat when we found ourselves afloat, we also found that the four oars were secured with strands of tarred rope. No man in the crowd had a pocket knife, but one had sufficient strength in his fingers to tear open one of the strands. That was the only way in which we got our boat far enough away from the *Titanic*'s side to escape the volume of the condenser pumps.

Here is another thing that I want to emphasize; only one of the boats set adrift from the vessel's side had a lantern. We had to follow the only boat that had one, and if it had not been for that solitary lantern possibly many other boats might have drifted away and gone down.

To show how lightly even the executive officers of the ship took the matter of the collision is proven by the fact that the officer in charge of the boat in which my wife was saved refused to let his men row more than half a mile from the *Titanic* because he would soon have orders to come back.

We saw the sinking of the vessel. The lights continued burning all along its starboard side until the moment of its downward plunge. After that a series of terrific explosions occurred, I suppose either from the boilers or weakened bulkheads.

And then we just rowed about until dawn when we caught sight of the port light of the *Carpathia*, and knew that we were saved.

If a sea had been running I do not see how many of the small boats would have lived. For instance, on my boat there were neither one officer or a seaman. The only men at the oars were stewards who could no more row than I could serve a dinner.

While order prevailed until the last lifeboat had been lowered, hell prevailed when the steerage passengers, who had been kept below by the officers with their revolvers pointed at them to prevent them from making their way to the upper deck, came up. Many of them had knives, revolvers and clubs and sought to fight their way to the two unlaunched, collapsible boats. Many of these were shot by the officers.

Only one of the rafts floated, and even that did not float above the water's edge. From forty to fifty persons who had jumped overboard, clambered aboard it and stood upon it, locked arm and arm together until it was submerged to a depth of at least eighteen inches. They all tried to hold together, but when the *Carpathia*'s boat reached them, there were only sixteen left.

The most horrible part of the story is that statement that several persons in the lifeboats saw, when the *Titanic* took her final plunge, that her four great smokestacks sucked up and carried down in their giant maws dozens of the third-class passengers, then huddled together on the forward upper deck.

(*San Francisco Bulletin*, 20 April 1912)

BOAT NO. 15

With a passenger load composed almost entirely of women and children from steerage, boat 15 was launched with seventy people on board. Among the crew members was long-serving chief bathroom steward **Samuel Rule**, a Cornishman from Hayle.

I was asleep when the cessation of the engines woke me. I heard no crash, but the engines were going full speed astern, and I knew something was wrong. I got up and went upstairs, but as there was no commotion I went back and dressed. A few minutes later a messenger came down and said we all had to leave our cabins, that all had to be served with lifebelts, and the cabins were to be locked. I assisted in getting up some provisions and when I got on deck I saw they were preparing to lower the boats. Though placed on the boat deck, the provisions were never used.

Mr Murdoch was in charge of my side of the ship – the starboard – and he directed the getting away of the boats without confusion. I helped to lower the boats – all the odd numbers were on my side – and I was told to get in No. 15 as one of the crew. She was the last of the starboard boats to go down from the davits. The other fellows who were not wanted to man the boats watched us. They were standing by with lifebelts on.

Before we left the ship there were several appeals as to whether there were more women and children, but none came. I saw women refuse to leave their husbands, and some decided to stand by the ship, evidently under the impression that she would not sink.

We loaded down to the gunwales and we could pull just about half a stroke. When we were being lowered away we nearly came down on No. 13 boat, which was in some difficulty in consequence of coming in front of an aperture through which water was being pumped. We shouted to the men above, 'Hold on,' and they did. I tell you, there were cool heads above, although they knew the last boats were leaving them.

We were five or six hundred yards away from her when she went. Her propellers were far above water. Just before she was lost sight of, there was a rumbling, and I believe the boilers and engines must have broken away and crashed through the forward bulkheads. In my opinion every one of the engine room staff and firemen of the watch on duty must have been lost. There were some brave men down there that night. They kept the lights going until the vessel was under water abaft the bridge. We watched the lights go out section by section as she went down by the bows.

The worst part of the disaster was just after the ship went down. The groans were awful, and of course we could do nothing. I shall never forget it.

Some of my greatest friends have gone down. Many of us have been a lifetime together, and I feel the pick of the White Star fleet has been lost. During most of my service I have been on ships with Captain Smith, starting when he was a junior officer. A better man never walked a deck. His crew knew him to be a good, kind-hearted man, and we looked upon him as a sort of father.

(*St Ives Times*, 3 May 1912)

Mrs Selma Asplund from Sweden was a steerage passenger on board the *Titanic*. She and two of her children – Lillian, aged six, and baby Felix – were saved but her husband Carl and her three boys (aged eight, ten and fourteen) all drowned. Of the crash, she said:

My husband was by my side in an instant, and all in our night-dresses made our way to the deck to see what had happened. There was no panic, no cries, just orderly procession to learn the cause of the shock and see if there was any danger – none of us believed there really was.

With a mother's instinct, I clasped my sleeping baby to my breast and took him with me. Little Lillian followed, while my three older boys clung to their father. On deck, we found them lowering the boats and as we were near where one was being manned, with others I was told to get in. I did not want to leave my husband and children, but he said it was all right. He would come down with the boys after me, that it was only for a few minutes till they shifted the ship and then we would all be back again.

I had no clothing on to speak of and the night was bitter cold. A man from the steerage took off his coat and wrapped it around little Felix, my baby. Looking far up, I saw my husband with six-year-old Lillian in his arms. He cried out to a man in the boat with me and dropped Lillian over to him. He caught her and placed her by my side.

'Now you come,' I cried, 'with the boys.' But he shook his head. We pulled away. As the water came between us and the *Titanic* I still saw him standing there by the rail. Farther and farther we moved away and soon he was blotted out – but there at the rail I shall always see him, as I did in the last few minutes. There at the rail with my three grown boys, hand in hand, smiling sweetly at me to the last.

Oh, the long hours before we were taken aboard the *Carpathia*. Thinly clad as we were, we suffered from the cold. Only the baby, wrapped in a passenger's coat, was warm. Lillian cried with the pain. She was nearly frozen when we set foot upon the steamer that picked us up, but thank God they are both well now and I still have them to live for.

I expected to find my husband and the boys on the *Carpathia*, but they were not there. Throughout the day I lived in hope that he would be picked up, and even when we docked I expected to see him standing on the pier to meet me.

There was a boy saved just the age of one of mine, who was as gallant as any man. He was Cervine Swensen, a lad of fourteen. He was all alone on the *Titanic*, travelling to his father who lives somewhere in the west. He made his way by himself to the upper decks soon after the crash came and climbed into one of the boats.

When we were on the *Carpathia* he told us that he had no one to look out for him, and he thought he had better look out for himself. His mother, he said, had told him when he kissed her goodbye in Sweden that if anything happened to run to the boats, so he did.

Then he added that he hoped he didn't prevent some woman from being saved for he knew his mother would want to do that first in spite of what she had told him.

(*Boston Post*, 20 April 1912)

Irish steerage passenger **Bertha Mulvihill**, travelling to meet her sister, Mrs Norton, in America, and her fiancé, took her chances in No. 15 although there were a few more boats left than she thought at the time. She had just witnessed a mother with six children refuse to get into a lifeboat because it meant the woman being parted from her husband.

Only two boats remained. One of these pushed off. I stood directly over the other. 'Jump,' said the sailor. I jumped and landed in the boat. Then a big Italian jumped and landed on me, knocking the wind out of me.

The *Titanic* was going down slowly, yet surely. I had marked in my mind's eye the two portholes on the vessel. I watched the water come to them, pass them and swallow them from sight. I was fascinated.

Then the lights on the *Titanic* began to glimmer and go out. A few minutes later there were two heavy explosions.

The big vessel quivered and seemed to settle. Then she leaned over on the other side a little and slowly sank to her grave. I think I heard the band playing.

The sailors rowed hard, thinking the suction from the big vessel would pull us down. But the explosions threw the water away from the vessel, so the small boats were able to get away all right.

Then began the long vigil for the rescuing ship. All night we bumped among the ice cakes out there on the Atlantic. From midnight till dawn of the morning we wept and moaned on the face of the ocean.

All the boats that had left the port side of the vessel had clustered together and all the boats that left the starboard side clustered in another little bunch a little distance away.

At 11 o'clock the *Carpathia* took us aboard. Everybody was kind to us. They had hot whisky and brandy for all of us. They wrapped us up in blankets and gave us food. A physician came and visited all of us. Then the passengers let us sleep in their beds.

The first-class passengers aboard the *Titanic* had first-class accommodations on the *Carpathia*, as near as possible. I was in the third class because I decided on the spur of the moment to visit my sister here and it was impossible to get anything else until June, so far ahead were the passengers booked.

So we herded in the steerage until we crept up New York harbour. I sent a wireless message off to my mother in Ireland to reassure her.

I am afraid I always will see that mother clinging to her husband and six children.

(*Boston Post*, 20 April 1912)

BOAT NO. 14

This was launched on the port side five minutes after boat 12. Among the sixty passengers was an Italian stowaway.

Fifth Officer **Harold Lowe** was the officer in charge. His decision to tie five boats together in a flotilla undoubtedly saved many lives that night.

I herded five boats together. I was in No. 14, then I had 10, 12, collapsible D and one other boat (No. 4), and made them tie up. I waited until the yells and shrieks had subsided for the people to thin out, and then I deemed it safe for me to go amongst the wreckage. So I transferred all my passengers, somewhere about fifty-three, from my boat and equally distributed them among my other four boats. Then I asked for volunteers to go with me to the wreck, and it was at this time that I found the Italian. He came aft and had a shawl over his head, and I suppose he had skirts. Anyhow, I pulled the shawl off his face and saw he was a man. He was in a great hurry to get into the other boat and I got hold of him and pitched him in the boat because he was not worth being handled better.

Then I went off and rowed to the wreckage and around the wreckage, and picked up four people alive. But one died, and that was a Mr Hoyt, of New York. It took all the boat's crew to pull this gentleman into the boat, because he was an enormous man, and I suppose he had been soaked fairly well with water, and when we picked him up he was bleeding from the mouth and from the nose. So we did get him on board and I propped him up at the stern of the boat. We took his collar off and loosened his shirt so as to give him every chance to breathe, but unfortunately he died. I suppose he was too far gone when we picked him up. But the other three survived.

(US Inquiry, 24 April 1912)

Able Seaman **Joseph Scarrott** recounted how Fifth Officer Harold Lowe fired warning shots to deter unwelcome foreign boarders from steerage.

The port side boats were got ready first and then the starboard ones. As the work proceeded passengers were coming on deck with lifebelts on. Then we realized the situation. Every man went to his station. There was no panic, everybody was cool, and when the boats were ready the usual order was given, 'Women and children first.' That order was carried out without any class distinction whatever. In some cases we had to force the women into the boats as they would not leave their husbands.

The men stood back to allow the women to pass, except in one or two cases where men tried to rush, but they were very soon stopped. This occurred at the boat I was in charge of, No. 14. About half a dozen foreigners tried to jump in before I had my complement of women and children, but I drove them back with the boat's tiller. Shortly afterwards the Fifth Officer, Mr Lowe, came and took charge of the boat. I told him what had happened. He drew his revolver and fired two shots between the boat and ship's side into the water as a warning to any further attempts of that sort.

The sight of that grand ship going down will never be forgotten. She slowly went down bow first with a slight list to starboard until the water reached the bridge, then she went quicker. When the third funnel had nearly disappeared I heard four explosions, which I took to be the bursting of the boilers. The ship was right up on end then. Suddenly she broke in two between the third and fourth funnel. The after part of the ship came down on the water in its normal position and seemed as if it was going to remain afloat, but it only remained a minute or two and then sank. The lights were burning right up till she broke in two. The cries from the poor souls struggling in the water sounded terrible in the stillness of the night. It seemed to go through you like a knife. Our officer then ordered all the boats under his charge to see if we could pick up anybody. Some of our boats picked up a few.

I cannot say how many. After that we tied all our boats together so as to form a large object on the water which would be seen quicker than a single boat by a passing vessel. We divided the passengers of our boat amongst the other four, and then taking one man from each boat so as to make a crew we rowed away amongst the wreckage as we heard cries for help coming from that direction. When we got to it the sight we saw was awful. We were amongst hundreds of dead bodies floating in lifebelts. We could only see four alive. The first one we picked up was a male passenger. He died shortly after we got him in the boat. After a hard struggle we managed to get the other three.

One of these we saw kneeling as if in prayer upon what appeared to be part of a staircase. He was only about twenty yards away from us but it took us half an hour to push our boat through the wreckage and bodies to get to him; even then we could not get very close so we put out an oar for him to get hold of and so pulled him to the boat.

All the bodies we saw seemed as if they had perished with the cold as their limbs were all cramped up. As we left that awful scene we gave way to tears. It was enough to break the stoutest heart. Just then we sighted the lights of a steamer, which proved to be the steamship *Carpathia* of the Cunard line. What a relief that was.

We then made sail and went back to our other boats. By this time day was just beginning to dawn. We then saw we were surrounded with icebergs and field ice. Some of the fields of ice were from 16 to 20 miles long. On our way back we saw one of our collapsible boats waterlogged; there were about eighteen persons on it, so we went and took them off. We left two dead bodies on it, and we were told two others had died and fallen off.

(*The Sphere*, 1912)

Charlotte Collyer, an English passenger travelling to America, lost her husband in the *Titanic* disaster. She and her young daughter Marjorie survived.

The first lifeboat was quickly filled and lowered away. Very few men went in her, only five or six members of the crew. The male passengers made no attempt to save themselves. I have never seen such courage, or believed it possible. How the people in the first cabin and the steerage may have acted I do not know, but our second cabin men were heroes. The lowering of the second boat took more time. I think all those women who were really afraid and eager to go had got into the boat. Those who remained were wives who did not want to leave their husbands or daughters who would not leave their parents. The officer in charge was Harold Lowe. Mr Lowe was very young and boyish looking, but somehow he compelled people to obey him. He rushed among the passengers and ordered the women into the boat. Many of them followed him in a dazed kind of way, but others stayed with their men. I should have had a seat in that second boat but I refused to go. It was filled at last and disappeared over the side with a rush. There were two more lifeboats at that part of the deck. A man in plain clothes was fussing about them and screaming instructions. I saw Fifth Officer Lowe order him away. I did not recognize him but from what I have read in the newspapers it must have been Mr Bruce Ismay, the Managing Director of the Line.

The third boat was about half full when a sailor caught Marjorie in his arms and tore her away from me and threw her into the boat. She was not even given a chance to tell her father goodbye! 'You too!' a man yelled close to my ear. 'You're a woman, take a seat in that boat or it will be too late.' The deck seemed to be slipping under my feet. It was leaning at a sharp angle for the ship was then sinking fast, bows down. I clung desperately to my husband. I do not know what I said but I shall always be glad to think that I did not want to leave him. A man seized me by the arm then another threw both his arms about my waist and dragged me away. I heard my husband say: 'Go, Lotty, for God's sake be brave and go! I'll get a seat in another boat.'

The men who held me rushed me across the deck and hurled me bodily into the lifeboat. I landed on one shoulder and bruised it badly. Other women were crowding behind me, but I stumbled to my feet and saw over their heads my husband's back as he walked steadily down the deck and disappeared among the men. His face was turned away so that I never saw it again, but I know that he went unafraid to his death. His last words when he said he would get a seat in another boat buoyed me up until every vestige of hope was gone. Many women were strengthened by the same promise or they must have gone mad and leapt into the sea. I let myself be saved because I believed that he too would escape, but I sometimes envy those whom no earthly power could tear them from their husbands' arms. There were several such among those brave second cabin passengers. I saw them standing beside their loved ones to the last, and when the roll was called the next day on board the *Carpathia* they did not answer.

The boat was practically full and no more women were anywhere near it when Fifth Officer Lowe jumped in and ordered it lowered. The sailors on deck had started to obey him when a very sad thing happened. A young lad hardly more than a schoolboy, a pink-cheeked lad, almost small enough to be counted as a child, was standing close to the rail. He had made no attempt to force his way into the boat though his eyes had been fixed piteously on the officer. Now when he realized that he was really to be left behind his courage failed him. With a cry he climbed upon the rail and leapt down into the boat. He fell among us women and crawled under a seat. I and another woman covered him up with our skirts. We wanted to give the poor lad a chance, but the officer dragged him to his feet and ordered him back onto the ship. We begged for his life. I remember him saying that he would not take up too much room but the officer drew his revolver and thrust it into his face. 'I give you just ten seconds to get back onto that ship before I blow your brains out,' he shouted. The lad only begged the harder and I thought I should see him shot where he stood. But the officer suddenly changed his tone. He lowered his revolver and looked the boy squarely in the eyes. 'For God's sake be a man,' he said gently. 'We have got women and children.' The little lad turned round-eyed and climbed back over the rail without a word. He was not saved.

All the women about me were sobbing and I saw my little Marjorie take the officer's hand. 'Oh, Mr Man, don't shoot, please don't shoot the poor man,' she was saying and he spared the time to shake his head and smile. He screamed another order for the boat to be lowered, but just as we were getting away, a steerage passenger, an Italian I think, came running the whole length of the deck and hurled himself into the boat. He fell upon a young child and injured her internally. The officer seized him by the collar and by sheer brute strength pushed him back onto the *Titanic*. As we shot down towards the sea I caught a last glimpse of this coward. He was in the hands of about a dozen men of the second cabin. They were driving their fists into his face and he was bleeding from the nose and mouth. We did not stop at any other decks to take on other women and children. It would have been impossible I suppose. The bottom of our boat slapped the ocean as we came down with a force that I thought must shock us all overboard. We were drenched with ice cold spray but we hung on and the men at the oars rowed us rapidly away from the wreck.

It was then that I saw for the first time the iceberg that had done such terrible damage. It loomed up in the clear starlight, a bluish white mountain, quite near to us. Two other icebergs lay quite close together, like twin peaks. Later I thought I saw three or four more, but I cannot be sure. Loose ice was floating in the water. It was very cold. We had gone perhaps half a mile when the officer ordered the men to cease rowing. No other boats were in sight and we did not even have a lantern to signal with. We lay there in silence and darkness in that utterly calm sea. I shall never forget the terrible beauty of the *Titanic* at that moment. She was tilted forward head down with her first funnel partly under the water. To me she looked like an enormous glow worm for she was alight from the rising waterline to her stern – electric light blazing in every cabin, lights on all her decks and lights to her mast head. No sound reached us except the music of the band which I was aware of for the first time. Oh those brave musicians! How wonderful they were! They were playing lively tunes, Ragtime, and they kept it up to the very end. Only the engulfing ocean had power to drown them into silence. The band was playing 'Nearer My God to Thee'. I could hear it distinctly. The end was very close. It came with a deafening roar that stunned me. Something in the very bowels of the *Titanic* exploded and millions of sparks shot up to the sky.

I saw hundreds of human bodies clinging to the wreck or jumping into the water. Cries more terrible than I have ever heard rung in my ears. We went in search of other lifeboats that had escaped. We found four or five and Mr Lowe took command of the little fleet. He ordered that the boats should be linked together with ropes so as to prevent any of them drifting away and losing itself in the darkness. This proved to be a very good plan and made our rescue all the more certain when the *Carpathia* came. He then, with great difficulty, distributed most of the women in our boat among the other craft. This took perhaps half an hour. It gave him an almost empty boat and as soon as possible he cut loose and we went in search of survivors.

I have no idea of the passage of time during the balance of that awful night. Someone gave me a ship's blanket which seemed to protect me from the bitter cold and Marjorie had the cabin blanket that I had wrapped around her but we were sitting with our feet in several inches of icy water. The salt spray had made us terribly thirsty and there was no fresh water and certainly no food of any kind on the boat. The suffering of most of the women from these various causes was beyond belief. The worst thing that happened to me was when I fell, half fainting against one of the men at the oars, my loose hair was caught in the row-locks and half of it was torn out by the roots.

I know that we rescued a large number of men from the wreck, but I can recall only two incidents. Not far away from where the *Titanic* went down we found a lifeboat floating bottom-up. Along the keel were lying about twenty men. They were packed closely together and were hanging on desperately but we saw even the strongest amongst them were so badly frozen that in a few more moments they must have slipped into the ocean. We took them on board one by one, and found that of the number four were already corpses.

The dead men were cast into the sea. The living grovelled in the bottom of our boat, some of them babbling like maniacs. A little further on we saw a floating door that must have torn loose when the ship went down. Lying upon it face down was a small Japanese. He had lashed himself with a rope to his frail craft using the broken hinges to make his knots secure. As far as we could see he was dead. The sea washed over him every time the door bobbled up and down and he was frozen stiff. He did not answer when he was hailed and the officer hesitated about trying to save him. He had actually turned the boat round, but he changed his mind and went back. The Japanese was hauled on board and one of the women rubbed his chest while others rubbed his hands and feet. In less time than it takes to tell, he opened his eyes. He spoke to us in his own tongue; then, seeing that we did not understand, he struggled to his feet, stretched his arms above his head, stamped his feet and in five minutes or so had almost recovered his strength. One of the sailors near to him was so tired he could hardly pull his oar. The Japanese bustled over, pushed him from his seat, took the oar and worked like a hero until we were finally picked up. I saw Mr Lowe watching him in open-mouthed surprise.

After this rescue, all my memories are hazy until the *Carpathia* arrived at dawn. She stopped maybe four miles away from us, and the task of rowing over to her was one of the hardest things that our poor frozen men, and women too, had to face. Many women helped at the oars, and one by one the boats crawled over the ocean to the side of the waiting liner. They let down rope ladders to us, but the women were so weak that it was a marvel that some of them did not lose their hold and drop back into the water. When it came to saving the babies and young children, the difficulty was even greater, as no one was strong enough to risk carrying a living burden. One of the mail clerks on the *Carpathia* solved the problem. He let down empty United States mail bags. The little ones were tumbled in, the bags locked and so they were hauled up to safety. We all stood at last upon the deck of the *Carpathia*. More than six hundred and seventy of us, and the tragedy of the scene that followed is too deep for words. There was scarcely anyone who had not been separated from husband, child or friend. Was the last one among the handful saved? We could only rush frantically from group to group, searching the haggard faces, crying out names, and endless questions. No survivor knows better than I the bitter cruelty of disappointment and despair. I had a husband to search for, a husband whom in the greatness of my faith, I had believed would be found in one of the boats. He was not there.

(Semi-Monthly Magazine, May 1912)

First-class passenger **Daisy Minahan**, who lost her brother in the disaster, sent a sworn affidavit detailing her escape in lifeboat No. 14 commanded by Fifth Officer Lowe.

The crowd surging around the boats was getting unruly. Officers were yelling and cursing at men to stand back and let the women get into the boats. In going from one lifeboat to another we stumbled over huge piles of bread lying on the deck. When the lifeboat was filled there were no seamen to man it. The officer in command of No. 14 called for volunteers in the crowd who could row. Six men offered to go. At times when we were being lowered we were at an angle of 45 degrees and expected to be thrown into the sea. As we reached the level of each deck men jumped into the boat until the officer threatened to shoot the next man who jumped.

We landed in the sea and rowed to a safe distance from the sinking ship. The officer counted our number and found us to be forty-eight. The officer commanded everyone to feel in the bottom of the boat for a light. We found none. Nor was there bread or water in the boat.

The *Titanic* was fast sinking. After she went down the cries were horrible. This was at 2.20 a.m. by a man's watch who stood next to me. At this time three other boats and ours kept together by being tied to each other. The cries continued to come over the water. Some of the women implored Officer Lowe, of No. 14, to divide his passengers among the other three boats and go back to rescue. His first answer to those requests was, 'You ought to be damn glad you are here and have got your own life.' After some time he was persuaded to do as he was asked. As I came up to him to be transferred to the other boat he said, 'Jump, God damn you, jump!' I had showed no hesitancy and was waiting only my turn. He had been so blasphemous during the two hours we were in his boat that the women at my end of the boat all thought he was under the influence of liquor. Then he took all of the men who had rowed No. 14, together with the men from the other boats, and went back to the scene of the wreck. We were left with a steward and a stoker to row our boat, which was crowded. The steward did his best, but the stoker refused at first to row, but finally helped two women who were the only ones pulling on that side.

(US Inquiry, 10 May 1912)

Born in Newlyn, Cornwall, twenty-nine-year-old **Mrs Addie Wells** was travelling second-class with her two young children – Joan, aged four, and Ralph aged two – to join her railway conductor husband Arthur in Akron, Ohio. They were originally due to travel on the *Oceanic* but the coal strike necessitated a switch to the *Titanic*. Mrs Wells escaped in boat 14 and nestled her children in her skirts to keep them warm through the bitter night.

> When the crash came I took the children and went on deck. I hadn't more than got there when someone grabbed me, saying, 'This way,' and hustled me and the children up to the lifeboat.
>
> An officer was shouting, 'Come on here, lively now, this way, women and children,' and before I knew what was happening we were in a lifeboat, and the boat was going down the side while the men stood back serious and sober, watching us.
>
> I thought even then it was some sort of a drill or something, except that just as we went down I saw a revolver in an officer's hand.
>
> A Mrs Davis and a little boy were in the boat with us, and she asked me what it was all about.
>
> As soon as the boat struck water, the seamen began pulling away with all their might. As we got away, we saw a lot of wild-eyed men come rushing up from steerage, but they were met by a man with a gun who pushed them back into a crowd of men and said: 'Stand back there now, the first word out of you and I'll . . .' I didn't catch the rest. Some of the men from the first and second-class cabins were standing beside the officer.
>
> There were forty or fifty in our boat and I couldn't get a chance to sit down, but stood up keeping the babies warm and dry in my skirts. The sailors pulled at the oars for all they were worth, but the boat kept drifting back against the ship. Finally we got away a hundred feet and we didn't have any more trouble. We spent the night in the boat and were picked up at daybreak.
>
> (*Akron Beacon Journal*, 20 April 1912)

Passenger **Nellie Walcroft**, accompanied on the journey by her friend Miss Clear Cameron, detailed the events of the night in a letter to her local paper in Berkshire.

There was room for two more in boat 14 which, I think, was the last but three to leave the ship. Immediately the order was given to lower the boats, we began to descend. There were fifty-eight women and children but only about three to row when going down. There was no man in charge and Fifth Officer Harold Lowe jumped on our boat and gave the orders. Some men in the steerage were going to spring in and he threatened them with his revolver to shoot the first, knowing that another one would buckle up the lifeboat. He shot twice, but only at the side, so that the men who were panic-stricken in the steerage should know it was loaded and that he meant what he said.

The men lowered our boat. One side worked better than the other and the ropes on one side did not act so the officer gave the order to cut the ropes and the boat fell some distance. Then we got away safely from the ship's side. It was a lovely starlight night, but not light enough for us to see who were in the boats.

The officer told the men to lay on their oars so as to be handy later on. We did not seem to be long on the water. We could see the ship gradually going down, but all the lights were on, when suddenly two terrible explosions took place. The ship seemed to go forward and then split in the middle, and then there were two more explosions that seemed from underneath the water. No more could be seen of that grand ship. All was silent for a moment and then the cries of 1600 men. All were crying for help: it was terrible. I should think the cries must have lasted two hours, or even more, and then the day dawned and we could see six large icebergs. Each looked as large as a house and all the time the cries of the drowning were getting fainter.

Then Officer Lowe wanted to go back to the rescue, but the women begged him not to go. He got about four boats together and distributed his passengers amongst them as many as he possibly could and then went back to the rescue. I believe they rescued six alive from that raft. The others had all died from exposure as it was intensely cold. The boat I got in was No. 10. There had been six picked up but one man was mad. He shook the boat and we were afraid it would capsize. Two men revived but they were terribly frozen, and two were dead and fell into the water at the bottom of the boat.

Several times we thought we saw the lights of a ship, but no. Then we saw the lights of the *Carpathia*. We tried to shout for joy but it was a poor noise. My friend, Miss Clear Cameron, took an oar and the sea was getting much rougher and several of the passengers were very sick. By this time the cries of the drowning had ceased and the men rowed as quickly as possible. We wondered if we would ever get to it. Our boat had about two feet of water in it although we baled out all the time. Every wave we thought would swamp us, and the wreckage was sailing down right in our course. We got safely over that, but when the boat was so deep in the water we were pulled back to lie at the end of the boat. Oh, that last hour's row with hope in sight!

When we got to the *Carpathia*, we were helped up with ropes. The kindness of the officers and crew we shall never forget. They took us along to the saloon and gave us neat brandy. The women were brought in screaming on account of children they had lost. Some of the children got separated from their parents and others looked after them. Those we had said goodnight to on the *Titanic* on the Sunday evening we shook hands with on the Monday at a quarter to seven. That was the time we were picked up by the *Carpathia*, thanking God for our safety.

All the boats were not in, so we went up on deck and watched the others coming up. Quite near the *Carpathia* were quite large icebergs and ice about 12 miles long, broken ice, it was a most imposing sight. I went to the wireless operator who was very kind and promised, if possible, to get a wireless through to tell Mother I was saved, but he was unable to do so, having so much to do.

We tried to sleep that night on the tables in the saloon, but it thundered and lightened all night. How thankful we were that it was not the previous night!

(*Maidenhead Advertiser*)

BOAT NO. 16

Boat 16 was lowered at 1.35 a.m. with fifty-six people on board, mainly women and children from second and third class. One of the crew members was thirty-six-year-old Able Seaman **Ernest Archer**.

I went to the starboard side and assisted in lowering about three boats. Then an officer came along and he sang out that they wanted some seamen on the other side, on the port side, to assist over there. I assisted in getting Nos. 12, 14 and 16 out. When I got to No. 16 boat, the officer told me to get into the boat and see that the plug was in. So I got in the boat. I saw that the plug was in tight, then they started to put passengers in. I never saw any men get in – only my mate. We lowered the boat, and my mate pulled at the releasing bar for both falls, and that cleared the boat, and we started to pull away. There were about fifty passengers and only my mate and myself until the master-at-arms came down the fall to be coxswain of the boat. He took charge.

We rowed, I should say, a quarter of a mile from the ship, and we remained there. I did not think the ship would go down. I thought we might go back to her again afterwards. I heard a couple of explosions. I should say there was about twenty minutes between each explosion. I assumed that water had got into the boiler room.

After the ship went down, one of the lady passengers asked to go back and see if there was anyone in the water we could pick up, but I never heard any more of it. Another lady – a stewardess – tried to assist with the rowing. I told her it was not necessary for her to do it, but she said she would like to do it to keep herself warm.

(US Inquiry, 25 April 1912)

ENGLEHARDT COLLAPSIBLE BOAT 'C'

The first of the four collapsible boats to leave was lowered on the starboard side at 1.40 a.m.. There were thirty-nine people on board including four oriental stowaways. But the most controversial occupant was White Star Line chairman J. Bruce Ismay who crept in unnoticed at the last minute along with another first-class passenger, wealthy American Billy Carter. Ismay later claimed that he only stepped in because there were no more women or children in the vicinity but he was widely condemned for saving his own skin while all around him perished. The man in charge of this boat was thirty-two-year-old Quartermaster **George Rowe**.

I felt a slight jar and looked at my watch. It was a fine night, and it was then twenty minutes to twelve. I looked towards the starboard side of the ship and saw a mass of ice. I then remained on the after bridge to await orders through the telephone. No orders came down, and I remained until twenty-five minutes after twelve, when I saw a boat on the starboard beam. I telephoned to the fore bridge to know if they knew there was a boat lowered. They replied, asking me if I was the third officer. I replied: 'No, I am the quartermaster.' They told me to bring over detonators, which are used in firing distress signals.

I took them to the fore bridge and turned them over to the fourth officer. I assisted the officer to fire them, and was firing the distress signals until about five-and-twenty minutes after.

At that time they were getting out the starboard collapsible boats. The chief officer, Wilde, wanted a sailor. I asked Captain Smith if I should fire any more, and he said: 'No, get into that boat.' I went to the boat. Women and children were being passed in. I assisted six – three women and three children. The order was then given to lower the boat. The chief officer wanted to know if there were more women and children. There were none in the vicinity. Two gentlemen passengers got in. The boat was then lowered. When we reached the water we steered for a light in sight, roughly five miles. We pulled through the night, but seemed to get no nearer to the lights. So we altered our course back to a boat that was carrying a green light. During that time daylight broke and the *Carpathia* was in sight. When daylight broke, we found four men – Chinamen, I think they were, or Filipinos. They came up between the seats.

(US Inquiry, 25 April 1912)

Londoner **Hugh Woolner** was a first-class passenger on the *Titanic*. He described how Chief Officer William Murdoch fired warning shots while the first collapsible boat was being loaded on the starboard side.

There was a scramble on the starboard side. I looked around and saw two flashes of a pistol in the air. I heard Mr Murdoch shouting: 'Get out of this, clear out of this,' and that sort of thing to a lot of men who were swarming into the boat. Lt Steffanson and I went to help clear the boat of the men who were climbing in because there was a bunch of women – I think Italians and foreigners – who were standing on the outside of the crowd, unable to make their way towards the side of the boat. So we helped the officer to pull these men out, by their legs and anything we could get hold of. We pulled out five or six. I think they were probably third-class passengers. When the men cleared out, we lifted these Italian women and put them into the boat. They were very limp.

(US Inquiry, 29 April 1912)

Amy Stanley, aged twenty-four, from Oxfordshire was travelling third-class to the US to start a job there as a children's maid. She later described her ordeal in a letter to her parents, which was printed in their local paper.

I was writing a postcard the night that the boat struck the iceberg. It was about 11.30 p.m. I got out of bed and put my coat on and went out on deck and asked the steward what was the matter. He told me it was only the engines stopped, and ordered all the women back to bed. But I did not go. I shared a cabin with an American lady and child. I assisted them to dress, and then we went up on deck. We tried to reach the boats. Then

I saw two fellows (whom we met at meals, the only men we made real friends of) coming towards us, who assisted us over the railings into the lifeboat. As we were being lowered a man about 16 stone jumped into the boat almost on top of me. I heard a pistol fired – I believe it was done to frighten the men from rushing the boat. This man's excuse was that he came because of his baby. When we rowed off, the child must have died had I not attended to it.

We were rowing for several hours. I seemed to have extra strength that night to keep up my nerves, for I even made them laugh when I told them we had escaped vaccination, for we were all to have been vaccinated that day [Monday]. I will say no more of that awful row, except that I was able to fix the rope around the women for them to be pulled up on the *Carpathia* while then men steadied the boat. The women seemed quite stupefied yet when I was safe myself, I was the first to break down.

The sight on board was awful, with raving women. Barely six women were saved who could say they had not lost a relative. Oh! the widows the *Titanic* has made!

(Oxford Times, 18 May 1912)

EMERGENCY CUTTER NO. 2

The second emergency boat was launched from the port side at 1.45 a.m. with twenty-five people on board under the command of Fourth Officer Joseph Boxhall. As the boat was lowered, Walter Douglas bade farewell to his wife **Mahala Douglas** and her maid, Miss Le Roy. It was the last time they would see him alive.

I got into the boat and sat under the seats on the bottom, just under the tiller. Mr Boxhall had difficulty getting the boat loose and called for a knife.

The rowing was very difficult, for no one knew how. I tried to steer, under Mr Boxhall's orders, and he put the lantern – an old one, with very little light on it – on a pole which I held up for some time. Mr Boxhall got away from the ship and we stopped for a time. Several times we stopped rowing to listen for the lapping of the water against the icebergs.

In an incredibly short space of time, it seemed to me, the boat sank. I heard no explosion. I watched the boat go down, and the last picture in my mind is the immense mass of black against the starlit sky, and then . . . nothingness.

Mrs Appleton and some of the other women had been rowing, and did row all the time. Mr Boxhall had charge of the signal lights on the *Titanic*, and he put in the emergency boat a tin box of green lights, like rockets. These he commenced to send off at intervals, and very quickly we saw the lights of the *Carpathia*, the captain of which stated he saw our green lights ten miles away, and, of course, steered directly to us, so we were the first boat to arrive at the *Carpathia*.

When we pulled alongside, Mr Boxhall called out: 'Shut down your engines and take us aboard. I have only one sailor.' At this point I called out, 'The *Titanic* has gone down with everyone on board,' and Mr Boxhall told me to 'shut up'. This is not told in criticism; I think he was perfectly right. We climbed a rope ladder to the upper deck of the *Carpathia*. I at once asked the chief steward, who met us, to take the news to the captain. He said the officer was already with him.

In the afternoon I sent a brief Marconigram with the news that Mr Douglas was among the missing. I went myself to the purser several times every day, and others also made inquiries for me in regard to it, but it was not sent.

(US Inquiry, 9 May 1912)

Able Seaman **Frank Osman**, aged thirty-eight, was one of the sailors on board Boat No. 2.

All of us went up and cleared away the boats. After that we loaded all the boats there were. I went away in No. 2, the fourth from the last to leave the ship. Mr Boxhall was in command; Mr Murdoch directed the loading. All passengers were women and children except one man, a third-class passenger.

After I got in the boat the officer found a bunch of rockets which was put in the boat by mistake for a box of biscuits. The officer fired some off, and the *Carpathia* came to us first and picked us up half an hour before anybody else. Not until morning did we see an iceberg about 100 feet out of the water with one big point sticking on one side of it, apparently dark, like dirty ice, 100 yards away. I knew that was the one we struck because we could see it was the biggest berg there, and the other ones would not have done so much damage, I think. It looked as if there was a piece broken off after she struck.

When we were in the boat we shoved off from the ship, and I said to the officer, 'See if you can get alongside to see if you can get any more hands – squeeze some more hands in.' So the women then started to get nervous after I said that, and the officer said: 'All right.' The women disagreed to that. We pulled around to the starboard side of the ship and found we could not get to the starboard side because it was listing too far. We pulled astern that way again, and after we got astern we lay on our oars and saw the ship go down. After she got to a certain angle she exploded, broke in halves, and it seemed to me as if all the engines and everything that was in the after part slid out into the forward part, and the after part came up right again.

We did not go back to the place where the ship had sunk because the women were all nervous. We pulled around as far as we could get to her, so that the women would not see, and it would not cause a panic. We got as close as we would dare to. We could not have taken any more hands into the boat – it was impossible. We might have got one in, that is about all.

(US Inquiry, 25 April 1912)

St Louis judge's widow **Elisabeth Robert**, aged forty-three, was travelling first-class with her daughter Georgette Madill, niece

Elisabeth Allen and maid Emilie Kreuchen. Mrs Robert claimed to shed light on the fate of Captain Smith.

> I was lying in my cabin awake when the crash came. I arose and called to my daughter and niece to dress, and we all went up on deck, but even then they were beginning to load the lifeboats. We got seats in one, thanks to the men who stood back to make room for us.
>
> We soon cleared the *Titanic* and were rowing aimlessly about when I heard a fearful shrieking. I sounded as if hundreds of throats were calling for help. Then, quite clearly, I saw Colonel Astor and Captain Smith standing side by side. The explosion threw them into the water. Colonel Astor I did not see reappear, but Captain Smith was blown into the water with a couple of officers and swam quite near our boat.
>
> The officers we dragged aboard, but when we offered to help Captain Smith he shook his head and swam back towards where the *Titanic* had sunk.

(New York World, 20 April 1912)

BOAT NO. 4

With lifeboats being launched in rapid succession, Second Officer Lightoller appeared to have completely forgotten about Boat No. 4 – the first to be uncovered – with its passenger list of wealthy women, including Mesdames Astor, Carter, Ryerson, Thayer and Widener. It was finally launched – almost an hour and a half later – at 1.55 a.m. after these eminent socialites had suffered the ignominy of having to clamber out of the cranked-open windows on A deck. Colonel Astor helped load the women and children, including his pregnant wife Madeleine. As the boat was barely two-thirds full, he asked whether he might be allowed to join her, but Lightoller refused to shift from his 'women and children only' policy. Colonel Astor's final act was to rush down to the dog kennels on F deck, where he managed to free his pet

Airedale, Kitty, as well as the other dogs. Madeleine Astor later said that her final memory of the *Titanic* was seeing Kitty running about on the sloping deck.

Second Officer **Charles Herbert Lightoller** admitted his mistake to the Senate Investigation.

> We had previously lowered a boat from A deck, one deck down below. That was through my fault. It was the first boat I had lowered. I was intending to put the passengers in from A deck. On lowering the boat I found that the windows were closed. So I sent someone down to open the windows and carried on with the other boats, but decided it was not worth while lowering them down, that I could manage just as well from the boat deck.
>
> When I came forward from the other boats, I loaded that boat from A deck by getting the women out through the windows. My idea in filling the boats there was because there was a wire hawser running along the side of the ship for coaling purposes and it was handy to tie the boat in to hold it so that nobody could drop between the side of the boat and the ship.
>
> (US Inquiry, 19 April 1912)

Walter Perkis, aged thirty-nine, was the quartermaster placed in command of lifeboat No. 4.

> I lowered No. 4 into the water, and left that boat, and walked aft. I came back and one of the seamen that was in the boat at the time sung out to me: 'We need another hand down here.' So I slid down the life line there from the davit into the boat. It was a drop of 70-odd feet.
>
> I took charge of the boat after I got in. We left the ship with three sailormen and about forty-two passengers. We were the last big boat on the port side to leave the ship. Later we picked up eight men that were swimming with life preservers. Two died afterwards in the boat. One was a fireman and one was a steward. After we had picked up the men, I could not hear any more cries

anywhere. Everything was over. We stopped picking up. The last man we picked up, we heard a cry, and we did not hear any more cries after that. I waited then until daylight, or just before daylight, when we saw the lights of the *Carpathia*.

(US Inquiry, 25 April 1912)

Mrs Emily Ryerson of Philadelphia was the wife of steel magnate Arthur Ryerson. The latter famously finished a game of cards with Archie Butt, Frank Millet and Clarence Moore in the first-class smoking room before finally heading for the boat deck at 2 a.m. All four men perished.

At the time of collision I was awake and heard the engines stop, but felt no jar. My husband was asleep, so I rang and asked the steward, Bishop, what was the matter. He said: 'There is talk of an iceberg, ma'am, and they have stopped not to run into it.' I told him to keep me informed if there were any orders.

After about ten minutes I went out in the corridor and saw far-off people hurrying on deck. A passenger ran by and called out: 'Put on your lifebelts and come up on the boat deck.' I said: 'Where did you get those orders?' He said: 'From the captain.'

I went back then and told Miss Bowen and my daughter, who were in the next room, to dress immediately, roused my husband and the two younger children, who were in a room on the other side, and then remembered my maid who had a room near us. Her door was locked and I had some difficulty in waking her.

By this time my husband was fully dressed and we could hear the noise of feet tramping on the deck overhead. He was quite calm and cheerful and helped me put the lifebelts on the children and on my maid. I was paralyzed with fear of not all getting on deck together in time as there were seven of us. I would not let my younger daughter dress, but she put on a fur coat over her nightgown. My husband cautioned us all to keep together, and we went up to A deck where we found quite a group of people we knew. Everyone had on a lifebelt, and they all were very quiet and self-possessed.

We stood about there for quite a long time – fully half an hour, I should say. I know my maid ran down to the cabin and got some of my clothes. Then we were ordered to the boat deck. I only remember the second steward at the head of the stairs who told us where to go. My chief thought and that of everyone else was not to make a fuss and to do as we were told. My husband joked with some of the women he knew and I heard him say: 'Don't you hear the band playing?' I begged him to let me stay with him but he said: 'You must obey orders. When they say, "Women and children to the boats", you must go when your turn comes. I'll stay with John Thayer. We will be all right. You take a boat going to New York.' This referred to the belief that there was a circle of ships around waiting – the *Olympic*, the *Baltic* were some of the names I heard.

All this time we could hear the rockets going up – signals of distress. Again we were ordered down to A deck, which was partly enclosed. We saw people getting into boats, but waited our turn. There was a rough sort of steps constructed to get up to the window. My boy, Jack, was with me. An officer at the window said: 'That boy can't go.' My husband stepped forward and said: 'Of course that boy goes with his mother. He is only thirteen.' So they let him pass. They also said: 'No more boys.'

I turned and kissed my husband, and as we left he and the other men I knew – Mr Thayer, Mr Widener and others – were all standing there together very quietly. The decks were lighted, and as you went through the window, it was as if you stepped out into the dark. We were flung into the boats. There were two men – an officer inside and a sailor outside – to help us. I fell on top of the women who were already in the boat, and scrambled to the bow with my eldest daughter. Miss Bowen and my boy were in the stern and my second daughter was in the middle of the boat with my maid. Mrs Thayer, Mrs Widener, Mrs Astor and Miss Eustis were the only others I knew in our boat. Presently an officer called out from the upper deck: 'How many women are there in that boat?' Someone answered: 'Twenty-four.' 'That's enough,' said the officer. 'Lower away.'

The ropes seemed to stick at one end and the boat tipped. Someone called for a knife but it was not needed until we got into the water, as it was but a short distance, and I then realized for the first time how far the ship had sunk. The deck we left was only about 20ft from the sea. I could see all the portholes open and water washing in.

Then they called out: 'How many seamen have you?' We answered, 'One.' 'That is not enough,' said the officer. 'I will send you another.' And he sent a sailor down the rope. In a few minutes several other men – not sailors – came down the ropes and dropped into our boat.

The order was given to pull away, but we made little progress. There was a confusion of orders. We rowed towards the stern, someone shouted something about a gangway, but no one seemed to know what to do. Barrels and chairs were being thrown overboard. Then suddenly, when we still seemed very near, we saw the ship was sinking rapidly. I turned to see the great ship take a plunge towards the bow, the two forward funnels seemed to lean and then she seemed to break in half as if cut with a knife. As the bow went under, the lights went out. The stern stood up for several minutes, black against the stars, and then that too plunged down. There was no sound for what seemed like hours, and then began the cries for help of people drowning all around us.

Someone called out, 'Pull for your lives or you'll be sucked under,' and everyone that could rowed like mad. I could see my younger daughter and Mrs Thayer and Mrs Astor rowing, but there seemed to be no suction. Then we turned to pick up some of those in the water. Some of the women protested, but others persisted and we dragged in six or seven men. They were so chilled and frozen already they could hardly move. Two of them died in the stern later, and many were raving and moaning and delirious most of the time.

We had no lights or compass. There were several babies in the boat, but there was no milk or water. I believe these were all stowed away somewhere but no one knew where, and as the bottom of the boat was full of water and the boat full of people, it was very difficult to find anything.

After the *Titanic* sank we saw no lights, and no one seemed to know what direction to take. Lowe, the officer in charge of the boat, had called out earlier for all to tie together, so we now heard his whistle. As soon as we could make out the other boats in the dark, five of us were tied together, and we drifted about without rowing, as the sea was calm, waiting for the dawn. It was very cold and soon a breeze sprang up, and it was hard to keep our heavy boat bow on, but as the cries died down we could see dimly what seemed to be a raft with about twenty men standing on it back to back. It was the overturned boat. As the sailors on our boat said we could still carry eight or ten more people, we called for another boat to volunteer and go to rescue them. So we two cut loose our painters and between us got all the men off. They were nearly gone and could not have held out much longer.

Then when the sun rose, we saw the *Carpathia* standing up about five miles away, and for the first time we saw the icebergs all around us.

(US Inquiry, 10 May 1912)

Young Cornish wife **Emily Richards** told of the desperate scene on board lifeboat No. 4.

When we got on deck we were told to pass through the dining room to a ladder that was placed against the side of the cabins and led to the upper deck.

We were put through the portholes into the boats, and the boat that I was in had a foot of water in it. As soon as we were in we were told to sit down on the bottom. In that position we were so low that we could not see over the gunwale.

Once the boat had started away, some of the women stood up, and the seamen, with their hands full with the oars, simply put their feet on them and forced them back into the sitting position.

We had not got far away by the time the ship went down, and after that there were men floating in the water all around, and seven of these were picked up by us in the hours that followed, between that and daybreak. Some of these seven were already mad with exposure, and babbled gibberish and kept trying to get up and overturn the boat. The other men had to sit upon them to hold them down.

Two of the women picked up were so overcome with the cold of the water that they died before we reached the *Carpathia* and their dead bodies were taken aboard. One woman, who spoke a tongue none of us could understand, was picked up by the boat and believed that her children were lost. She was entirely mad. When her children were brought to her on the *Carpathia* she was wild with joy and lay down on the children on the floor trying to cover them with her body like a wild beast protecting its young, and they had to take her children away from her for the time to save them from being suffocated.

(New York World, 20 April 1912)

Sixteen-year-old **Jean Gertrude Hippach** was returning to Chicago after spending three months abroad to improve her health. She and her mother Ida had intended to travel back by the *Olympic* but, because they wanted to visit Paris, they switched to the *Titanic* instead. They boarded Boat No. 4.

Mrs Astor, too, was in our boat. We already knew her, that is, we knew who she was. She was crying and her face was bleeding from a cut. One of the oars struck her somehow. There was a little bride in our boat with her husband. She clung to him and cried that she would not go and leave him, so the officers finally pushed them both in together. There were about thirty-five in all in our boat, mainly from the steerage.

We had gone back for our lifebelts before we got in, as the officers told us to do. I got mine on wrong side before and the officer changed it. That was the reason, perhaps, why some people couldn't sit down with them on. And we went back still another time and got some heavy steamer rugs, two of them, as the officers said it was going to be very cold on the water and we might have to stay out several hours. Even then we didn't expect the *Titanic* to go down, you see. The rugs were more than we needed, and we gave them to a poor woman who had on only a nightgown and a waterproof coat and her baby was in a nightgown only. That poor little baby! It slept through everything!

After we had pushed away a little we looked at the steamer and I said to mother, 'It surely is sinking. See, the water is up to those portholes!' And very soon it went under. To the last those poor musicians stood there, playing 'Nearer, My God, to Thee'.

We had only one or two in the boat who knew anything about rowing and they kept turning it this way and that and again and again it seemed as if we might be capsized. But we did get away from the *Titanic* a little distance before it went down.

We picked up eight men from the water, all third-class passengers, I think. The water was very still and the sky – so many stars! Nothing but the sea and the sky. You can't think how it felt out there alone by ourselves in the Atlantic. And there were so many shooting stars; I never saw so many in all my life. You know they say when you see a shooting star someone is dying. We thought of that, for there were so many dying, not far from us.

It was so long, such a long, long night. At last there was a little faint light. The first thing we saw we thought was one of the *Titanic*'s funnels sticking out of the water. But it wasn't; it was the raft, the collapsible boat that didn't open, with twelve men on it, standing close together. They came up to us and demanded that we take them. But we thought they ought to say who they were; we were already pretty full and the water was getting rough. But they said they would jump in anyhow, so we let them come aboard, as we knew that jumping would surely capsize us. They were all stewards and waiters, men of the service of the *Titanic*. After we took them in it got still rougher, so that we sometimes shipped water. In fact, there was nearly a foot of water in the bottom of the boat and we hadn't a basin, or dipper, not so much as a cup to dip it out with. Meanwhile the waves were rising and if we hadn't been picked up when we were, another half hour would surely have been the end of us.

Able Seaman **Samuel Hemming** swam 200 yards to reach Boat No. 4.

I went to the bridge and looked over and saw the water climbing upon the bridge. I went and looked over the starboard side, and everything was black. I went over to the port side and saw a boat off the port quarter, and I went along the port side and got up the after boat davits and slid down the fall and swam to the boat about 200 yards. When I reached the boat I tried to get hold of the grab-line on the bows. I pulled my head above the gunwale, and I said, 'Give us a hand in, Jack.' Foley (a storekeeper) was in the boat. He said, 'Is that you, Sam?' I said, 'Yes,' and him and the women and children pulled me in the boat.

After the ship sank we pulled back and picked up seven of the crew. We made for the light of another lifeboat and kept in company with her. Then day broke and we saw two more lifeboats. We pulled towards them and we all made fast by the painter. Then we helped with Boat No. 12 to take off the people on an overturned boat.

(US Inquiry, 25 April 1912)

ENGLEHARDT COLLAPSIBLE BOAT 'D'

This was the last lifeboat to be launched from the *Titanic*, at 2.05 a.m., with forty-four of its forty-seven places filled, but only after Second Officer Lightoller had drawn his revolver and got crewmen to form a human barrier to hold back a sudden surge of men from steerage who had just arrived on the deck. Amid the crush of bodies, second-class passenger Michel Navratil, a native of Slovakia, managed to pass his two young sons through the human chain and on to the boat. Navratil was travelling under an assumed name, Michel Hoffman, having snatched the children from their mother. He died in the sinking and a revolver was found in his pocket.

Steward **John Hardy** helped with loading the boat before making up the crew numbers.

I went to my station, which was Boat No. 1, on the starboard side. I saw that lowered before I myself got there – I did not get into it as there was no room. I went over to the port side and assisted the ladies and children in getting into the boats and finally I was working on deck until the last collapsible boat was launched.

We launched the boat parallel with the ship's side, and Mr Lightoller and myself loaded the boat. When the boat was full, Mr Lightoller was in the boat with me. He said he would step out himself and make room for somebody else, and he stepped back on board the ship and asked if I could row. I told him I could, and I went away in that boat. We could not get the boat lowered from one end. The forward part of the boat was lowered, but there was nobody there to lower the after end. Mr Lightoller stepped from the boat aboard the ship and did it himself.

We lowered away and got to the water, and the ship was then at a heavy list to port. We got clear of the ship and rowed out some little distance from her, and finally we all got together, about seven boats of us, and I remember quite distinctly Officer Lowe telling us to tie up to each other, as we would be better seen and could keep better together. Then Officer Lowe, having a full complement of passengers in his boat, distributed among us what he had, our boat taking ten. We had twenty-five already, and that number made thirty-five.

Officer Lowe then returned with his crew to back to the ship to pick up all he could. We hung around then until dawn, until we sighted the *Carpathia*, pulling now and again. We were towed up by Mr Lowe with a sail to the *Carpathia*, not having enough men in the boat to pull. There was only the quartermaster Bright and myself, two firemen, and about four gentlemen passengers, and the balance were women and children. Bright took the tiller. He was using an oar to steer by. I myself pulled with all my might. The passengers were all strangers to me. There were a number of third-class passengers, that were Syrians, in the bottom of the boat, chattering the whole night in their strange language.

Greatly to my surprise, when I got on the *Carpathia* I saw Officer Lightoller coming in the following afternoon. When he stepped from the collapsible boat, I was sure he had gone down on the ship.

There was no panic on board the ship because everybody had full confidence that the ship would float. I had great respect and great regard for Chief Officer Murdoch, and I was walking along the deck forward with him, and he said, 'I believe she is gone, Hardy.' That is the only time I thought she might sink – when he said that. That was a good half hour before my boat was lowered.

(US Inquiry, 25 April 1912)

Lt Mauritz Hakan Bjornstrom-Steffanson of the Swedish army was travelling to the US on business. He and another first-class passenger, Englishman Hugh Woolner, had been sitting talking in the Café Parisien at the moment of impact. They saved their skins by dramatically jumping from the flooded promenade deck into collapsible boat 'D' as it was being lowered past them.

Mr Woolner and I went to a lower deck. It was deserted, but as we wished to find out what had happened we went down a deck lower. Then for the first time we realized the seriousness of that twisting which had rent the ship nearly asunder. We saw the water pouring into the hull and where we finally stood water rose to our knees. Woolner and I decided to get out as quickly as we could and as we turned to rush upward we saw sliding down the portside of the drowning ship a collapsible lifeboat. Most of those it contained were from the steerage.

'Let's not take any chances,' I shouted to Woolner, and as it came nearly opposite us, swinging in and out slowly, we jumped and fortunately landed in it. I should say we jumped at least ten feet clear of the boat. The boat teetered a bit and then swiftly shot down to the water. A second later a fat man bobbed up in the water in front of the boat, and he was also dragged in. Woolner and I took oars and started to pull with all our might to get from the ship before she sank. We could see some gathered in the steerage, huddled together, as we pulled away, and then cries of fear came to us.

We hardly reached a point 100 yards away from the *Titanic* when we saw all the lights go out in a flash. Thirty seconds later there was a roar, and we saw the big boat settle a second and then plunge straight down head foremost. It was quiet for a moment, and then we saw the people who had been on the decks bob up, and there was the most terrible cry that I have ever heard in my life. It was so terribly sudden, and then there was a vast quiet, during which we shivered over the oars and the women cried hysterically. Some of them tried to jump overboard and we had to struggle in the shaky boat to hold them until they quieted down.

For about two hours we just rowed around. We rolled badly at times, but it didn't seem dangerous. Some of the people didn't have any clothes. There were women from the first and second cabins and from the steerage in our boat. About 4 o'clock in the morning we saw the lights of a big boat coming. It was the *Carpathia*. The wind was rising then and it was very cold. For a time it looked as if they wouldn't see us, but they finally did and we were taken aboard.

(US press, 19 April 1912)

Hugh Woolner told his account to the Senate investigation.

I said to Steffanson: 'There is nothing more for us to do. Let us go down to A deck again.' And we went down again, but there was nobody there that time at all. It was perfectly empty the whole length. It was absolutely deserted, and the electric lights along the ceiling of A deck were beginning to turn red, just a glow, a red sort of glow. So I said to Steffanson: 'This is getting rather a tight corner. I do not like being inside these closed windows. Let us go out through the door at the end.' And as we went out through the door, the sea came onto the deck at our feet.

We hopped up onto the gunwale, preparing to jump out into the sea, because if we had waited a minute longer we should have been boxed in against the ceiling. And as we looked out we saw this collapsible, the last boat on the port side, being lowered right in front of our faces. It was about nine feet out. It was full up to the bow, and I said to Steffanson: 'There is nobody in the bows. Let us make a jump for it. You go first.' He jumped out and tumbled head over heels into the bow, and I jumped too, and hit the gunwale with my chest, which had on this life preserver, of course, and I sort of bounced off the gunwale and caught the gunwale with my fingers, and slipped off backwards. As my legs dropped down, I felt that they were in the sea.

I pulled myself up out of the water and then I hooked my right heel over the gunwale. By this time Steffanson was standing up, and he caught hold of me and lifted me in. Then we looked over into the sea and saw a man swimming in the sea just beneath us, and pulled him in.

At dawn, Officer Lowe transferred five or six from his boat, No. 14, to ours, which brought us down very close to the water. At daylight we saw a great many icebergs of different colours, as the sun struck them. Some looked white, some looked blue, some looked mauve and others were dark grey. There was one double-toothed one that looked to be of good size; it must have been about 100ft high.

(US Inquiry, 29 April 1912)

ENGLEHARDT COLLAPSIBLE BOAT 'B'

In the desperate race to launch the remaining two lifeboats before the *Titanic* went down, there was no time to release collapsible boats 'A' and 'B', which had been tethered to the roof of the officers' quarters above the boat deck, and both were swept away as the sea rushed over the decks. Officers Wilde and Murdoch were last seen trying to free boat 'B' but, after it had fallen into the water upside down, neither man was able to scramble aboard. The upturned collapsible 'B' provided a precarious perch for as many as forty people that night.

Junior wireless operator **Harold Bride** had remained at his post with senior operator Jack Phillips until the very last minute. After being washed overboard, Bride was trapped in an air pocket beneath boat 'B' for some forty-five minutes. He finally managed to extricate himself and spent at least another half-hour in the freezing water before being picked up by the upturned collapsible. His ankles were gashed and bruised and his feet riddled with frostbite, but he survived.

I went to the place where I had seen the collapsible boat on the boat deck, and to my surprise I saw the boat, and the men still trying to push it off. I guess there wasn't a sailor in the crowd. They couldn't do it. I went up to them, and was just lending a hand when a large wave came awash of the deck. The big wave carried the boat off. I had hold of an oar-lock and I went with it. The next I knew I was in the boat. But that was not all. I was in the boat, and the boat was upside down, and I was under it. I remember realizing I was wet through, and that whatever happened I must not breathe, for I was under water. I knew I had to fight for it, and I did. How I got out from under the boat I do not know but I felt a breath of air at last. There were men all around me – hundreds of them. The sea was dotted with them, all depending on their lifebelts. I felt I simply had to get away from the ship. She was a beautiful sight then. Smoke and sparks were rushing out of her funnel. There must have been an explosion, but we heard none. We only saw a big stream of sparks. The ship was gradually turning on her nose – just like a duck that goes for a dive. I had only one thing on my mind – to get away from the suction. The band was still playing. I guess all of them went down. They were heroes. They were playing 'Autumn' then. I swam with all my might. I suppose I was 150 feet away when the *Titanic*, on her nose, with her afterquarter sticking straight up in the air, began to settle slowly. When at last the waves washed over her rudder there wasn't the least bit of suction I could feel. She must have kept going just as slowly as she had been.

I felt after a little while like sinking. I was very cold. I saw a boat of some kind near me, and put all my strength into an effort to swim to it. It was hard work. I was all done when a hand reached out from the boat and pulled me aboard. It was our same collapsible. The same crowd was on it. There was just room for me to roll on the edge. I lay there not caring what happened. Somebody sat on my legs. They were wedged in between the slats, and were being wrenched. I had not the heart to ask the man to move. It was a terrible sight all around – men swimming and sinking.

I lay where I was, letting the man wrench my feet out of shape. Others came near. Nobody gave them a hand. The bottom-up boat already had more men than it would hold, and it was sinking. At first the larger waves splashed over my clothing. Then they began to splash over my head, and I had to breathe when I could. As we floated around on our capsized boat and I kept straining my eyes for a ship's lights, somebody said, 'Don't the rest of you think we ought to pray?' The man who made the suggestion asked what the religion of the others was. Each man called out his religion. One was a Catholic, one a Methodist, one a Presbyterian. It was decided the most appropriate prayer for all was the Lord's Prayer. We spoke it over in chorus with the man who first suggested that we pray as the leader. Some splendid people saved us. They had a right-side-up boat and it was full to capacity. Yet they came to us and loaded us all into it. I saw some lights off in the distance and knew a steamship was coming to our aid. I didn't care what happened. I just lay and gasped when I could, and felt the pain in my feet. I feel it still. At last the *Carpathia* was alongside, and the people were being taken up a rope ladder. Our boat drew near, and one by one the men were taken off it. One man was dead. I passed him, and went to a ladder, although my feet pained me terribly.

The dead man was Phillips. He died on the raft from exposure and cold. I guess he had been all in from work before the wreck came. He stood his ground until the crisis passed and then collapsed.

Waiter **Thomas Whiteley** managed to clamber aboard Collapsible 'B'.

The deck was crowded. The Second Officer was getting boat No. 1 ready. He asked me to give him a hand. I helped fill the boats. They were crowded with women and children. There were two collapsible boats on each side in addition to the regular lifeboats. At the order of the Second Officer we got the collapsible boat on the port side ready and No. 1 on the starboard followed. The collapsible boat No. 2 on the starboard jammed. I got my leg caught in one of the ropes. The Second Officer was hacking at the rope with a knife. I was being dragged around the deck by that rope when I looked up and saw the boat filled with people turning end up on the boats. The boat overturned.

In some way I got overboard and found something to hold on to – an oak dresser. I wasn't more than sixty feet from the *Titanic* when she went down. I saw all the machinery drop out of her.

I was in the water about half an hour and could hear the cries of thousands of people, it seemed. Then I drifted near a boat wrong side up. About thirty men were clinging to it. They refused to let me get on. Someone tried to hit me with an oar, but I scrambled on to her.

(US press, 19 April 1912)

201

After supervising the evacuation of the passengers, Second Officer **Charles Herbert Lightoller** told of his own escape from the jaws of death.

I was on top of the officers' quarters and there was nothing more to be done. The ship then took a dive and I turned face forward and also took a dive from on top, practically amidships a little to the starboard. I was driven back against the blower, which faces forward to the wind and which then goes down to the stoke-hole. But there is a grating there and it was against this grating that I was sucked by the water, and held there under water.

There was a terrific blast of air and water, and I was blown out clear. I came up above the water, which barely threw me away at all, because I went down again against these fiddly gratings immediately abreast of the funnel over the stoke-hole. Colonel Gracie, I believe, was sucked down in identically the same manner, caused by the water rushing down below as the ship was going down.

I next found myself alongside the overturned boat. This was before the *Titanic* sank. The funnel then fell down and if there was anybody on that side of the Englehardt boat, it fell on them. I hardly had any opportunity to swim. It was the action of the funnel falling that threw us out a considerable distance away from the ship. We had no oars or other effective means for propelling the overturned boat. We had little bits of wood, but they were practically ineffective.

(US Inquiry, 19 April 1912)

The chief baker on the *Titanic* was **John Joughin**. When told to provision the boats, he sent thirteen men up with four loaves of bread each. As the ship reeled, he took a last swig of alcohol to prepare himself for the ordeal ahead.

As we could not find sufficient women to fill the boat, two or three others went with me and forcibly brought the women to the boats. As there was not sufficient room, I remained on the ship when the boat was lowered away. Then I went to my room again and had a drop of liquor. When I went upstairs again all the boats seemed to have gone, and I threw about fifty deckchairs overboard because I was looking out for something to cling to.

I went into the pantry for some water, and while there I heard a crash and a noise as though people were rushing along the deck. I looked out on deck and saw people rushing aft to the poop. There was a buckling and crackling as if the vessel was breaking. I kept out of the crush of people as long as I could. I went down to the well deck and just as I got there she gave a great list to port and threw everybody in a bunch. The people were piled up, many hundreds of them. I eventually got to the starboard side of the poop.

Just as I was wondering what to do next she went. I was not dragged under water, but I was in the water about two hours. I did not try to get anything to hold on to. Instead I was just paddling until daylight came. Then I saw what I thought was some wreckage and started to swim towards it slowly. I then found it was a collapsible not properly afloat, but on its side, with an officer and, I think, about twenty-five men standing on the top, or rather the side of it. The officer was Mr Lightoller.

I tried to get on it, but I was pushed off, and I, what you would call, hung around. I eventually got round to the opposite side, and a cook on the collapsible recognized me and held out his hand, and I got the edge of my lifebelt hitched on to the side of the boat. Eventually a lifeboat came in sight. They got within fifty yards of us, and then they sung out that they could only take ten people on board. Then I said to the cook who was holding me: 'Let go my hand, and I will swim to that boat. I am going to be one of the ten.'

(British Inquiry, 10 May 1912)

Eminent historian **Colonel Archibald Gracie**, an authority on the American Civil War, was returning first-class to his home in

Washington, having been conducting research in England. As the *Titanic* sank, he bumped into the ship's professional squash player, Frederick Wright, and had the presence of mind to cancel his Monday morning half-hour on the court, which was by then flooded to the ceiling. He jumped from the top deck of the *Titanic* and was sucked down with her.

After sinking with the ship it appeared to me as if I was propelled by some great force through the water. This might have been occasioned by explosions under the water, and I remembered fearful stories of people being boiled to death. The Second Officer has told me that he has had a similar experience. I thought of those at home as if my spirit might go to them to say 'Goodbye' for ever. Again and again I prayed for deliverance, although I felt sure that the end had come. I had the greatest difficulty in holding my breath until I came to the surface. I knew that once I inhaled, the water would suffocate me. When I got under water I struck out with all my strength for the surface. I got to the air again after a time which seemed to me to be unending. There was nothing in sight save the ocean, dotted with ice and strewn with large masses of wreckage. Dying men and women all about me were groaning and crying piteously.

The Second Officer and Mr J. B. Thayer, Jun., who were swimming near me, told me that just before my head appeared above the water one of the *Titanic*'s funnels separated and fell apart near me, scattering bodies in the water. I saw wreckage everywhere and all that came within reach I clung to. At last by moving from one piece of wreckage to another, I reached a raft. Soon the raft became so full that it seemed as if she would sink if more came on board her. The crew, for self-preservation, had, therefore, to refuse to permit any others to climb on board. This was the most pathetic and horrible scene of all. The piteous cries of those around us ring in my ears, and I shall remember them to my dying day. 'Hold on to what you have, old boy,' we shouted to each man who tried to get on board. 'One more of you would sink us all.' Many of those whom we refused answered, as they went to their death, 'Good luck, God bless you!' All the time we were buoyed up and sustained by the hope of rescue. We saw lights in all directions. Particularly frequent were some green lights which, as we learned later, were rockets fired in the air by one of the *Titanic*'s boats. So we passed the night with the waves washing over and burying the raft deep in water.

We prayed through all the weary night and there never was a moment when our prayers did not rise above the waves. Men who seemed long ago to have forgotten how to address their Creator recalled the prayers of their childhood and murmured them over and over again. Together we said the Lord's Prayer again and again.

Seventeen-year-old **Jack Thayer** had befriended judge's son Milton C. Long on the voyage. After dramatically diving together from the sinking ship, Thayer eventually found refuge on the upturned boat, but Long was less fortunate and perished.

Long and I stood by the rail just a little aft of the captain's bridge. The list to port had been growing greater all the time. About this time people began jumping from the stern. I thought of jumping myself, but was afraid of being stunned on hitting the water. Three times I made up my mind to jump out and slide down the davit ropes and try to make the boats that were lying off from the ship, but each time Long got hold of me and told me to wait a while. He then sat down and I stood up waiting to see what would happen. Even then we thought she might possibly stay afloat.

I got a sight on a rope between the davits and a star and noticed that she was gradually sinking. About this time she straightened up on an even keel and started to go down fairly fast at an angle of about 30 degrees. As she started to sink we left the davits and went back and stood by the rail about even with the second funnel.

Long and myself said goodbye to each other and jumped up on the rail. He put his legs over and held on a minute and asked me if I was coming. I told him I would be with him in a minute. He did not jump clear, but slid down the side of the ship. I never saw him again.

About five seconds after he jumped, I jumped out, feet first. I was clear of the ship, went down, and as I came up I was pushed away from the ship by some force. I came up facing the ship, and one of the funnels seemed to be lifted off and fell towards me about fifteen yards away, with a mass of sparks and steam coming out of it. I saw the ship in a sort of red glare, and it seemed to me that she broke in two just in front of the third funnel.

This time I was sucked down, and as I came up I was pushed out again and twisted around by a large wave, coming up in the midst of a great deal of small wreckage. As I pushed my hand from my head it touched the cork fender of an overturned lifeboat. I looked up and saw some men on the top, and asked them to give me a hand. One of them, a stoker, helped me up. In a short time the bottom was covered with about twenty-five or thirty men. When I got on this I was facing the ship.

The stern then seemed to rise in the air and stopped at about an angle of 60 degrees. It seemed to hold there for a time and then with a hissing sound it shot right down out of sight with people jumping from the stern. The stern either pivoted around towards our boat, or we were sucked towards it, and as we only had one oar we could not keep away. There did not seem to be very much suction and most of us managed to stay on the bottom of our boat.

We were then right in the midst of fairly large wreckage, with people swimming all around us. The sea was very calm and we kept the boat pretty steady, but every now and then a wave would wash over it.

The assistant wireless operator [Harold Bride] was right next to me, holding on to me and kneeling in the water. We all sang a hymn and said the Lord's Prayer, and then waited for dawn to come. As often as we saw the other boats in the distance we would yell, 'Ship ahoy!' But they could not distinguish our cries from any of the others, so we all gave it up, thinking it useless. It was very cold and none of us were able to move around to keep warm, the water washing over her almost all the time.

Towards dawn the wind sprang up, roughening up the water and making it difficult to keep the boat balanced. The wireless man raised our hopes a great deal by telling us that the *Carpathia* would be up in about three hours. About 3.30 or 4.00 some men on our boat on the bow sighted her mast lights. I could not see them as I was sitting down with a man kneeling on my leg. He finally got up and I stood up. We had the Second Officer, Mr Lightoller, on board. We had an officer's whistle and whistled for the boats in the distance to come and take us off.

It took about an hour and a half for the boats to draw near. Two boats came up. The first took half and the other took the balance, including myself. We had great difficulty about this time in balancing the boat, as the men would lean too far, but we were all taken aboard the already crowded boat, and in about a half or three-quarters of an hour later we were picked up by the *Carpathia*.

(*New York World*, 21 April 1912)

Seventeen-year-old **John Collins**, Irish assistant cook in the first-class galley, told how a child was swept from his arms by a huge wave.

The word came that we were to get out of our beds and get the lifebelts on and get up to the upper deck. This was half an hour after the collision. I met a steward and I asked him what number my boat was, and he said No. 16. So I went up to No. 16 boat, and I saw sailors with their bags ready for No. 16 boat. I said to myself, 'There is no chance there,' and so I ran back to the port side on the saloon deck with another steward and a woman and two children. The steward had one of the children in his arms, and the woman was crying. I took the child off the woman and made for one of the boats. Then the word came around from the starboard side there was a collapsible boat being launched there and that all women and children were to make for it. But when we got there we saw that it was forward. We saw the collapsible boat taken off the saloon deck, and then the sailors and the firemen that were forward saw the ship's bow in the water and saw that she was intending to sink her bow. So they shouted that we were to go aft. Word came there was a boat getting launched. We were just turning round and making for the stern end when a wave washed us off the deck, and the child was washed out of my arms.

(US Inquiry, 25 April 1912)

Edward Dorking, a nineteen-year-old Englishman travelling third-class, baled out of the sinking ship as she prepared to plunge beneath the waves.

As the last boat departed I turned to go below to get my life-belt, which was under my bunk. As I passed the engine room, I saw Captain Smith, standing in the doorway, giving orders to the crew. The perspiration was pouring down his face in streams, but he was calm and collected, and as I recollect him now, he appeared like a marble statue after a rain.

I never reached the life preserver. The water by that time was above my bunk and I had to retreat on deck. All the time the forward part of the boat, where the side had been jammed by the iceberg, was dropping lower and lower into the water, until it became necessary for those remaining on board to grasp something stationary to keep erect.

How long it was after the last boat left the ship until the *Titanic* went down, I have no distinct recollection. It seemed like an age to me. As I clung to the ship rail, turning the situation over in my mind, I finally concluded that I would take a chance of jumping into the water and risk being picked up by some of the boats.

It seemed certain doom to remain. I sat down on the deck and, removing my shoes and outer garments, I plunged over the rail and shot into the water forty feet below.

As I struck the chilly water, I received a shock that took my breath away, but as soon as I rose to the surface, I struck out from the ship, with no idea in mind except to get beyond the suction line when the *Titanic* should go down. I was perhaps twenty yards off when the grand liner suddenly tipped up on its nose, the rear end lifted out of the water exposing the propeller blades, and slid gently forward to its watery grave. The sinking of the ship caused scarcely a ripple on the ocean's surface.

It seemed to me that a half hour elapsed from the time I left the ship until an upturned lifeboat with about thirty men and one woman on it passed the spot where I was swimming. There were many others in the same predicament as myself and it was a constant fight to prevent those whose strength was almost spent from grasping me about the neck or by the limbs in a desperate effort to keep from drowning.

I was fortunate enough to grasp the side of the upturned lifeboat as it floated past me. I clung on with both hands, at the same time warding off two men who had given up their hold on the lifeboat and had grasped me by the legs. When my strength was about giving out, the men on the raft gave me assistance and dragged me over the side to a place of safety.

We drifted about during the remainder of the night, suffering intensely from cold and exposure. Three of our number died and were thrown overboard, and two others slipped off and failed to get back again.

It was just about daybreak that our sinking spirits were cheered by the sight of a rocket, which announced that succour was near. An hour later, as the morning light was dawning, we were picked up by a rescue boat. I guess I must have become unconscious then, for when I woke up, my companions were feebly cheering at the sight of the *Carpathia* standing off about a mile distant.

One of my companions at the hospital was a lookout, who had been saved from the *Titanic*. He told me that before the ship struck the iceberg, he had been warning three times of the impending danger. The first time, he said, no attention was paid to the warning; the second time, the result was the same; and the third warning came too late.

(*Bureau County Republican*, 2 May 1912)

Burly Swedish emigrant **Ernst Persson** was plucked from the freezing waters by collapsible boat 'B'.

After the boats had all gone and we were still on the *Titanic*, a calm settled over everyone. The lights had gone out and only the stars indicated what was going on. When the last boats put away there was some panic among a few to get aboard, but the majority were calm and everyone prepared to meet his fate in his own way.

The band was playing and kept playing while the vessel sank lower and lower into the water. Suddenly there was a rush of water and the deck slipped away from under me like a bullet and I went down, down, down. It seemed as if I would never stop. I must have gone down a mile, then the progress stopped it and I came to the surface just as I was giving up all hope.

The ocean was very calm but how cold. Fortunately I always did a great deal of swimming at home and did not mind the frightful chill as much as I might have otherwise. As long as I had come to the surface I felt there must be some hope, and I began to swim with others swimming all around me. But I was fast going and several times I was almost ready to give up when my hand struck something.

I found it would float and just had strength enough to climb aboard. It appeared to me to be a door. I lay on it for a moment to get back my strength. Then I felt something tugging at my back. It was a boat hook that one of the men in the lifeboat had thrown at me. Another threw an oar and between them they managed to get me on board. How I was ever able to get there I do not know. When they pulled me in a chill came over me and I must have fainted. I knew nothing more until they brought me to on the *Carpathia*.

(*Boston Post*, 22 April 1912)

Irishman **Eugene Daly** told the world of his thrilling escape on collapsible boat 'B'. What it may have lacked in accuracy, it more than made up for in colour.

After the accident, we were all held down in steerage, which seemed to be a lifetime. All this time, we knew that the water was coming up and up rapidly. Finally some of the women and children were let up, but we had quite a number of hot-headed Italians and other peoples who got crazy and made for the stairs. These men tried to rush the stairway, pushing and crowding and pulling the women down – some of them with weapons in their hands. I saw two dagos shot and some that took punishment from the officers.

After a bit, I got up on one of the decks and threw a big door over the side. I caught hold of some ropes that had been used setting free a lifeboat. Up this I climbed to the next deck because the stairs were so crowded that I could not get through. I finally got up to the top deck and made for the front. The water was just covering the upper deck at the bridge and it was easy to slide because she had such a tip. I reached a collapsible boat that was fastened to the deck by two rings. It could not be moved.

During that brief time that I worked on cutting one of those ropes, the collapsible was crowded with people hanging upon the edges. The *Titanic* gave a lurch downward and we were in the water up to our hips. She rose again slightly, and I succeeded in cutting the second rope which held her stern.

Another lurch threw this boat and myself off and away from the ship into the water. I fell upon one of the oars and into a mass of people. Everything I touched seemed to be women's hair.

As I looked over my shoulder, as I was still hanging to this oar, I could see the enormous funnels of the *Titanic* being submerged in the water. The poor people that covered the water were sucked down in those funnels, each of which was 25ft in diameter, like flies. I managed to get away and succeeded in reaching the same boat I had tried to set free from the deck of the *Titanic*. I climbed upon this, and with the other men, balanced ourselves in water to our hips until we were rescued. People who came up beside us begged to get on this upturned boat. As a matter of saving ourselves we were obliged to push them off. One man was alongside and asked if he could get upon it. We told him that if he did, we would all go down. His reply was: 'God bless you. Goodbye.'

Another steerage passenger, **Carl Jonsson**, a thirty-two-year-old Swedish/American, recounted his escape from the stricken ship.

People began to run by me towards the stern of the ship, and as I started to run I realized that the boat was beginning to go down very rapidly, and there was quite a decline noticeable in the deck, showing that her nose was being buried. A wave struck me and I went overboard.

As I rose to the surface I saw a board floating to the top of the water and I seized it. A wave threw me away from the ship and I began to swim, clutching to the board to keep me afloat. The shock seemed to restore my senses, and I began to see objects in the water quite clearly. The air was rent with screams and curses, and there were a lot of men and women in the water trying to get away from the ship to escape the awful suction when she went down.

There was an overturned lifeboat riding a big wave near me. I was swept towards it, and managed to catch hold of its edge. There were seven or eight of its original passengers clinging to its sides. By this time we were almost half a mile from the ship and we could still see it clearly. It was quite low in the bow and was settling rapidly. Suddenly it seemed to give a great lurch forward.

The stern seemed to rise from the water, and the ship plunged head-first beneath the waves.

For fully a minute as she was going down there was an awful silence everywhere. Not a sound was heard from the life-boats, which we could now see clustered in a semi-circle a few hundred yards ahead of us, nor was there any sound from the waters behind us, where even then we could see hundreds of dark forms struggling in the water with bits of wreckage and debris.

At the second that the ship took her final dive there was an awful shriek carried to us from the waters behind, as though all of the poor, drowning wretches had joined in a final death cry of agony.

(US press, 19 April 1912)

Yorkshire-born fireman **Harry Senior** painted a heroic picture of Captain Smith's final moments.

When I was awakened by the noise of the collision I thought I was dreaming that I was on a train which had run off the lines, and that I was being jolted about. I jumped out and went on deck. There was a lot of ice about the decks, and I said: 'Why, we have struck an iceberg. That's nothing, we'll go back and turn in.' About an hour afterwards an order came to man the boats and put lifebelts on. I went on deck again.

We got up to the hurricane deck to lower some of the collaps-ible boats, but there was no tackle or anything to lower them by. We had to throw them down to the boat deck and run the risk of their breaking. The ship was pretty near sinking then, and the captain shouted: 'Each man for himself.' I had noticed him on the bridge before that. He was pacing up and down, sending up rockets and giving orders.

I dived over the side, and got on the keel of a boat which floated off overturned. There were thirty-five of us on the keel of that boat. The other boats picked us up.

While I was swimming I saw the captain in the water. He was swimming with a baby in his arms, raising it out of the water as he swam back to the ship. I also had picked up a baby, but it died from the cold before I could reach the boat.

(Daily Graphic, 29 April 1912)

ENGLEHARDT COLLAPSIBLE BOAT 'A'

The last collapsible floated off the deck before it could be properly launched. It nevertheless provided a welcome refuge for over a dozen survivors. First-class steward **Edward Brown** told of the vain attempt to launch the boat and how he – a non-swimmer – had survived in the water with the aid of his lifebelt.

We got two planks on the bow end of the boat, and we slid it down on to the boat deck. We tried to get it to the davits, and we got it about halfway and then the ship got a list to port, and we had great difficulty. We could not get it up the incline right up to the davits. We made it fast by slackening the falls, but we could not haul it away any further. There were four or five women that I could see there waiting to get into this boat if we got it under the davits. The captain came past us while we were trying to get this boat away with a megaphone in his hand. He said to us: 'Well, boys, do your best for the women and children, and look out for yourselves.' He walked on the bridge.

While we were trying to get the boat up to the davits, the bridge went right under water. I found the water come right up my legs. I jumped into the collapsible boat. When the sea came onto the deck they all scrambled into the boat. Then I cut the fall, and I called out to the men on the forward end of the boat to cut her loose. She would float if we got the falls loose. I cut the rope and then I was washed right out of her. The boat was practically full when the sea came into it and washed everybody out of the boat. The last I saw of the women they were in the water.

When I got in the water, I was in a whirlpool going round. I

had my lifebelt on and I came up to the top. There was no wreckage around then, but a lot of people in the water. They tore my
clothing away from me with struggling in the water. I saw a
black object. I never swam in my life, but I kept myself up with
the lifebelt and made my way the best I could towards it. The
black object proved to be a collapsible boat. There were sixteen
or seventeen on it, and it was half submerged with its weight
of men. I got on the boat, and later we picked up a woman and
a very big gentleman. Eventually we were picked up by No. 14
boat and taken to the *Carpathia*.

(British Inquiry, 16 May 1912)

Swedish steerage passenger **Gunnar Isidor Tenglin** and his friend
desperately searched for a lifeboat as the ship started to sink.

We walked along from one lifeboat to another, but officers and
crew were keeping the men back and loading the women and
children. I noticed a number of boats that had been loaded on the
upper deck stop at the second deck to take on women there. In
many of these boats were men, but the officers made them get out
and give place to the women.

The lifeboats all gone, it looked to us as if we were doomed to
perish with the ship, when a collapsible lifeboat was discovered.
This boat would hold about fifty people and we had considerable
trouble getting it loose from its fastenings. The boat was on the
second deck and the ship settled the question of its launching as
the water suddenly came up over the deck and the boat floated.

There must have been fully 150 people swimming around or
clinging to the boat and we feared it would capsize or sink. We
had no oars, or anything else to handle the boat with and were at
the mercy of the waves, but the sea was calm. There was no way
to sit down in the boat and we stood up knee-deep in ice-cold
water while those on the edges pushed the frantic people in the
water back to their fates, it being feared that they would doom
us all.

The shock of the cold water and the fright caused many to succumb. I do not know how many died on that lifeboat. One big Swede was kept busy throwing the corpses overboard as we desired to make the boat as light as possible to increase its buoyancy. One woman was stark crazy, her mania taking the form of embracing the men. There were three men insane, but they made no attempt to jump overboard. It seemed to us as if we had been standing up in that boat for a week, when it was in reality only about six hours. I was numbed with the cold. I had no feeling in my hands or feet, as I did not put on my shoes when I left my room, although I had on my overcoat. It could not have been twenty minutes after we launched our life raft from the deck of the *Titanic* that the big liner sank.

When we were picked up by the *Carpathia* there were only twelve of us left. The lifeboats got pretty well separated during the night, as some left from the port side and some from the starboard side of the ship, pulling away in different directions.

The *Carpathia* remained on the scene for about two hours, picking up the lifeboats and moving slowly about among the wreckage and the ice. It appeared to us as if the ocean was carpeted with dead.

I saw Captain Smith only once during the voyage and that was the day before the accident. He came into the third cabin quarters and told some of the crew who had been loafing there to keep out, and threatened to impose a fine of $5 on each member of crew who was found among the passengers.

While I was still on the ship I saw two Swede girls who were in a lifeboat jump overboard when they observed some of their friends who had been left behind. One old man named Lindahl, when he became convinced the boat was sure to sink, said: 'It's no use trying to get away. I'm an old man and I will not be missed. I will go down to my berth and wait the end.' I guess he did as he disappeared in the direction of the sleeping apartments. One big fellow, also a Swede, became literally paralyzed with fright. He stood with one arm extended like a statue, unable to move a muscle. I know of one Swedish woman who, with her four children, was lost. Another woman lost her husband, brother, son and uncle. These folks were all steerage passengers. I think there were more of the crew saved than the steerage people.

We in the steerage did not know anything about being among icebergs until the *Titanic* hit one. I lost everything I had. I had about $30 in a suitcase, concealed well, as there had been several robberies among passengers the day before the accident. When we got to New York we got $25 from some relief committee, $5 from a man who was giving away money right and left, and $10 from the Salvation Army. We were also fitted out with clothing. I got a suit of clothes, overcoat and other attire, and a first-class ticket to Burlington, which had been my destination, my ticket having been lost with my other effects.

It was a terrible experience and when I look back at it, I can scarcely believe my good luck in getting away as there were so many chances against me.

(*Burlington Daily Gazette*, 25 April 1912)

Norwegian steerage passenger **Olaus Abelseth** related how he dived from the stern of the *Titanic* moments before she went under.

I asked my brother-in-law if he could swim and he said no. I asked my cousin if he could swim and he said no. We could see the water coming up, the bow of the ship was going down, and there was a kind of explosion. We could hear the popping and cracking, and the deck raised up and got so steep that the people could not stand on their feet on the deck. So they fell down and slid on the deck into the water right on the ship. We hung on to a rope in one of the davits.

My brother-in-law said to me, 'We had better jump off or the suction will take us down.' I said, 'No. We won't jump yet. We might as well stay as long as we can.' It was only about five feet down to the water when we jumped off. It was not much of a jump. My brother-in-law took my hand just as we jumped off, and my cousin jumped at the same time. When we came into the water, we went under and I swallowed some water. I got a rope tangled around me, and I let loose of my brother-in-law's hand to get away from the rope. I thought then, 'I am a goner.' But I came on top again, and I was trying to swim. There was a man – lots of them were floating around – and he got me on the neck and pressed me under, trying to get on top of me. I said to him, 'Let go.' Of course, he did not pay any attention to that, but I got away from him. Then there was another man and he hung on to me for a while, but he let go. Then I swam for about fifteen or twenty minutes. I saw something dark ahead of me. I did not know what it was, but I swam towards that, and it was one of those rafts or collapsible boats. When I got on they did not try to push me off, and they did not do anything for me to get on. All they said was, 'Don't capsize the boat.' So I hung on to the raft for a little while before I got on. Some of them were trying to get up on their feet. They were sitting down or lying down on the raft. Some of them fell into the water again. Some of them were frozen, and there were two dead that they threw overboard.

(US Inquiry, 3 May 1912)

One of the ship's barbers, fifty-one-year-old Philadelphia-born **Augustus H. Weikman**, was blown off deck by the explosion and spent over two hours in the water before finding refuge on collapsible boat 'A'.

The crew and passengers had faith in the bulkhead system to save the ship and we were lowering a collapsible boat, all confident the ship would get through, when she took a terrible dip forward and the water rushed up and swept over the deck and into the engine rooms.

The explosions were caused by the rushing-in of the icy water on the boilers. A bundle of deck chairs, roped together, was blown off the deck with me, and struck my back, injuring my spine, but it served as a temporary raft.

The bow went down and I caught the pile of chairs as I was washed up against the rail. Then came the explosions and blew me 15ft.

After the water had filled the forward compartments the ones at the stern could not save her. They did delay the ship's going down. If it wasn't for the compartments hardly anyone would have got away.

The water was too cold for me to swim, and I was hardly more than 100ft away when the ship went down. The suction was not what one would expect and only rocked the water around me. I was picked up after two hours. I have done with the sea.

(*New York World*, 19 April 1912)

Los Angeles cement manufacturer **George Brayton** saw Henry B. Harris bid farewell to his wife. He also shed some light into the possible fate of Captain Smith.

Shortly after the lifeboats left, a man jumped overboard. Other men followed. It was like sheep following a leader. I saw one of the stewards shoot a foreigner who tried to press past a number of women and enter a lifeboat.

Captain Smith was washed from the bridge into the ocean. He swam to where a baby was drowning and carried it in his arms while he swam to a lifeboat which was manned by officers of the *Titanic*. He surrendered the baby to them and swam back to the steamer. About the time Captain Smith got back, there was an explosion. The entire ship trembled. I had secured a life preserver and jumped over. I struck a piece of ice and was not injured. I swam about sixty yards from the steamer when there was a series of explosions. I looked back and saw the *Titanic* go down bow first. I was in the water two hours, clinging to a piece of wreckage when I was picked up by a lifeboat.

Miss Mary Lowell of Boston, Massachusetts, was a passenger on the *Carpathia*. After watching the rescue, she shared her cabin with one of the survivors, actress Dorothy Gibson, who was brought aboard wearing a low-necked ball gown of white satin. Miss Lowell described her experiences:

I was awakened by a strange thumping and pounding from the interior of the steamer, and I didn't know what to make of it. I lit the light and looked at my watch, and saw that the hands pointed to 3.30. Then I heard some people talking outside and saying something about a sinking steamer and icebergs, so I got up and dressed.

At four o'clock I came on deck. Dawn had not begun to break, and the air was terribly cold. The steamer was tearing through the water at a great rate. Up in the bow there was a little crowd of people, and just as I started towards them, two or three of them shouted and pointed straight ahead. When I joined them I saw a little flickering light in the distance. It was that at which they were pointing.

As soon as this light was sighted the *Carpathia* slowed down. Her regular speed is 13 knots an hour, but when our wireless operator learned that the *Titanic* was sinking, her speed was increased by more than one third so that she was making 17 knots an hour. The speed at which she was running was responsible for the thumping and pounding which had awakened me.

Ahead of us, and on every side of us, the water was filled with ice cakes and icebergs. It was so dark at first that I could not see how far away this ice extended. The ship's surgeon who came down and stood beside me just after the light was sighted, said that he had been on the bridge for two hours with the captain and that for every minute of that time, we had been running through ice fields.

As we got nearer and nearer to the little flickering light, the sky began to grow very grey, and we were able to see a little.

The sky got greyer and greyer and finally the east showed a tinge of pink and yellow. Then all of a sudden we saw two little boats among the ice cakes. We looked and looked, and then away beyond the first two we saw two more. As the day grew brighter and brighter we kept discovering more and more boats, until we had located all of them, scattered ahead of us over two or three square miles of ocean.

The first boat seemed to creep to us and we thought it would never reach us. We didn't know what had happened or how many had been saved or anything at all about the accident; but when the little boat was close up against our side and we could look down into her we knew that the accident had been a terrible one.

The men and women who were huddled into the boat's bottom were only half dressed. Until I saw their faces I never knew what the word 'haggard' meant. They had been exposed to the biting cold for so many hours that they could scarcely move. Some of them were so frozen that they couldn't even look up or move from the bottom of the boat when it came their turn to come aboard the *Carpathia*.

Our captain had made the sailors get chairs on the ends of ropes and big bags on the ends of ropes and fix them around the rails so that they could be used in unloading the boats. It was lucky that he did, for the poor women were so frozen that when they were helped up from the positions that they had been cramped in for so many hours, they could do nothing except fall back into the bottom of the boat. So the chairs were used to get the women up on deck, and the bags were used for the children.

It was really terrible to see the poor women stagger out of their chairs, and fall into the arms of the people who were so anxious to help them. The experience they had been through was such a horrible one that they were completely dazed by it. I was helping one girl when she was hoisted out of a boat, and she turned her face towards me with a smile, and said in a perfectly unemotional, conversational tone: 'My husband's drowned, isn't it awful?' There was as much expression in her face and voice as if she had said: 'I've forgotten my handkerchief. Isn't that terrible?'

The children could not appreciate what they had been through, of course. When the first sack was hoisted on deck we all crowded around it while it was being opened. When the mouth was finally undone, a little four-year-old boy was blinking at me. We pushed the bag down around his feet, and then we saw that he had a wooden soldier in his hand. He put the head of the wooden soldier in his mouth and sucked it, and didn't make a sound. Poor little boy. He'd lost his father and mother.

Nobody could watch those poor people come aboard without crying. Everyone was crying. I cried fearfully. In fact, I simply howled. Men were crying, too, and they weren't ashamed of it. I saw one sailor carrying deck chairs away from one part of the deck and stacking them up in another. He had seen the women coming aboard and heard them asking for their husbands and fathers and as he carried the chairs down the deck, the great big tears rolled out of his eyes and dropped down on his jersey.

For four hours those little boats were creeping up to our side, and survivors were coming aboard. In one of the boats there was only one man, and he was afraid. He steered the boat and the women rowed. While they rowed the man kept telling them that they would never get away alive. He was a steward. When these women got aboard, their hands were blistered fearfully from swinging the heavy oars for so many hours.

All of us aboard the *Carpathia* either gave our state rooms to the survivors or took them into our cabins. I took in Miss Dorothy Gibson of New York.

I asked her what had happened. In common with almost every survivor she said the shock of hitting the iceberg was so light as to be almost imperceptible. She had just gone down from the deck to her cabin to get an overcoat when it occurred so she went right back on deck again.

Not only Miss Gibson, but many other survivors, told me that many more persons could have been put into the boats. I saw every one of them come up to the side of the *Carpathia* and there were only one or two of them that were really crowded.

(*Boston Post*, 20 April 1912)

Mr J. W. Barker, a member of the victualling department on board the *Carpathia*, recounted the rescue.

At midnight on Sunday, April 14, I was promenading the deck of the *Carpathia* when, hearing eight bells strike, I went below to retire for the night. I had just turned in when an urgent summons came from the chief steward, and I learned that an urgent distress message had been received from the *Titanic*.

We were then about 58 miles to the south-east of her, and Captain A. H. Rostron had already given orders for the *Carpathia* to be turned around and proceed at utmost speed in her direction. The heads of all departments were aroused and every precaution was quietly and quickly made to receive 2000 passengers.

Blankets were placed in readiness, tables laid up, hot soups and consommes, coffee and tea prepared, and the surgeries stocked and staffed. Men were mustered at the boats and given instruction to be in immediate readiness to launch and row to the *Titanic* and bring off all passengers and crew.

Within an hour every possible preparation had been made by the stewards' department, and, to their great credit be it recorded, not a single passenger of the 1000 we were carrying had been aroused. It was now only possible to wait and look for any signals from the distressed vessel. Their wireless had failed some time. We were then forging ahead at the utmost speed that could be got out of our engines, making us about 18 knots per hour as against our usual 13 to 14. No words of praise can be too great for the unsparing efforts of the engineering department and the firemen.

At about a quarter to three we got the first signal, a blue flare on our port bow. Shortly after we sighted our first iceberg, undoubtedly the cause of the disaster, a huge ghostly mass of white looming up through the darkness a few miles distant. A little later we found ourselves in a field of icebergs, large and small, and it became frequently necessary to alter our course.

It was a little before 4 o'clock when we came near enough to discern the first lifeboat, which came alongside at 4.10 a.m. She was not much more than half-filled with women and children, and was in the charge of an officer, who reported that the 'unsinkable' *Titanic* had foundered a little more than an hour after striking the iceberg. The survivors were taken aboard and handed over to the care of the medical staff and the stewards, under the perfect control of Chief Steward Hughes.

Day was breaking, and over an area of four miles we were able to see the other boats. We were surrounded by icebergs of all sizes, and three miles to the north was a big field of drift ice dotted with bergs. During the next two or three hours we endured the most heartrending experiences we have ever known. Some of the incidents were almost too pathetic for description.

One woman was heartbroken and uncontrollable. She cried hysterically for her husband, and it was only with the greatest difficulty that she could be restrained from jumping into the sea to look for him. It was necessary to resort to the subterfuge of a lie, and tell her that her husband was safe before she could be calmed.

A Colonel was brought aboard unconscious. He had been swimming in the icy water for over two hours. His mother was placed in a collapsible boat which was launched only to capsize on reaching the water. Immediately he dived from the ship to his mother's rescue.

He was unable in the darkness to find her, and commenced a frantic search among the bodies and wreckage. One after another the lifeboats endeavoured to take him aboard, but he resisted until the coldness of the water overcame him. He was hauled into a boat just as he was about to sink and join his mother in death. It is doubtful if he will recover. He has spoken to no one. His mother was about to pay a visit to three other of her sons.

Another young woman went down with the *Titanic* rather than desert her dog – a huge St Bernard, and a great favourite on board. When the lifeboats were being launched a seat was prepared for her, but she demanded that the dog be taken also.

This was impossible, human lives being the first considera-tion, and she was urged to sacrifice the dog and save herself. She refused, and was last seen on the deck of the vessel, clasping her pet to her bosom. Her dead body was afterwards found floating by the side of her dog.

An old lady was bewailing to a steward that she had lost 'every-thing'. Indignantly he told her she should thank God that her life was spared, and not at such a time regret the loss of her property. Her reply was pathetic – steward, I have lost everything – my dear husband – and she burst into tears.

About 8 o'clock we had picked up the last boat, and got all the survivors aboard. Two were so exhausted from exposure that they died whilst being brought aboard. These, together with a sailor and steward who had perished at the oars, were buried at 4 o'clock.

The *Carpathia*'s passengers behaved splendidly, giving up their cabins voluntarily, and supplying the distressed women with clothes. The captain, officers and crew also gave up their quar-ters, and did their utmost to alleviate the sufferings of the survi-vors. The saloons, library, and smoke-rooms were also utilized for sleeping quarters.

(*Daily Sketch*, 6 May 1912)

An unnamed passenger on the *Carpathia* gave her version of the rescue.

I was awakened at about half past twelve at night by a commo-tion on the decks which seemed unusual, but there was no excite-ment. As the boat was moving I paid little attention to it, and went to sleep again. About three o'clock I again awakened. I noticed that the boat had stopped. I went to the deck. The *Carpathia* had changed its course.

Lifeboats were sighted and began to arrive – and soon, one by one, they drew up to our side. There were sixteen in all, and the transferring of the passengers was most pitiable. The adults were assisted in climbing the rope ladder by ropes adjusted to their waists. Little children and babies were hoisted to the deck in bags. Some of the boats were crowded, a few were not half full. This I could not understand. Some people were in full evening dress. Others were in their night clothes and were wrapped in blankets. These, with immigrants in all sorts of shapes, were hurried into the saloon indiscriminately for a hot breakfast. They had been in the open boats four and five hours in the most biting air I ever experienced. There were husbands without wives, wives without husbands, parents without children and children without parents. But there was no demonstration. No sobs – scarcely a word spoken. They seemed to be stunned. Immediately after breakfast, divine service was held in the saloon. One woman died in the lifeboat; three others died soon after reaching our deck. Their bodies were buried in the sea at five o'clock that afternoon. None of the rescued had any clothing except what they had on, and a relief committee was formed and our passengers contributed enough for their immediate needs.

When its lifeboats pushed away from the *Titanic*, the steamer was brilliantly lighted, the band was playing and the captain was standing on the bridge giving directions. The bow was well submerged and the keel rose high above the water. The next moment everything disappeared. The survivors were so close to the sinking steamer that they feared the lifeboats would be drawn into the vortex.

On our way back to New York we steamed along the edge of a field of ice which seemed limitless. As far as the eye could see to the north there was no blue water. At one time I counted thirteen icebergs.

(British press, 20 April 1912)

John Kuhl of Nebraska was a passenger on board the *Carpathia*.

It was almost four o'clock in the morning, dawn was just breaking, when the *Carpathia*'s passengers were awakened by the excitement occasioned by coming upon a fleet of life-saving boats. At that hour the whole sea was one mass of whitened ice. The work of getting the passengers over the side of the *Carpathia* was attended by the most heart-rending scenes. The babies were crying. Many of the women were hysterical, while the men were stolid and speechless. Some of the women were barefooted and without any headgear. The impression of those saved was that the *Titanic* had run across the projecting shelf of the iceberg, which was probably buried in the water, and that the entire bottom of the *Titanic* had been torn off. Shortly afterwards she doubled up in the middle and went down. Most of the passengers did not believe that the boat was going to sink. According to their stories it was fully half an hour before a lifeboat was launched from the vessel. In fact, some of the passengers keenly questioned the wisdom of Captain Smith's orders that they should leave the big ship.

(US press, 20 April 1912)

Miss Sue Eva Rule, sister of Judge Virgil Rule of St Louis, Missouri, was a passenger on the *Carpathia*.

Just as day broke a tiny craft was sighted rowing towards us and as it came closer we saw women huddled together, the stronger ones manning the oars. The first to come aboard was a nurse maid who had wrapped in a coat an eleven-months-old baby, the only one of a family of five persons to be rescued. The men and women both seemed dazed. Most of them had almost perished with the cold, and some of them who had been literally thrown into the lifeboats perished from exposure.

One of the most harrowing scenes I ever saw was the service of thanksgiving, followed by the prayers for the dead, which took place in the dining saloon of the *Carpathia*. The moans of the women and the cries of little children as their loss was brought home to them were heartrending.

How those who were saved survived the exposure is a miracle. One woman came aboard devoid of underwear, a Turkish towel wrapped about her waist served as a corset, while an evening wrap was her only protection. Women in evening frocks and white satin slippers and children wrapped in steamer rugs became common sights. Soon the passengers were almost in as bad a plight as the rescued. Trunks were unpacked and clothing distributed right and left. Finally the steamer rugs were ripped apart and sewn into impromptu garments.

Shooting was heard by many in the lifeboats just before the ship took its final plunge, and the opinion of many was that, rather than drown, the men shot themselves.

Mrs Astor was one of the first to come aboard. She was taken at once to the captain's room. Others were distributed among the cabins, the *Carpathia*'s passengers sleeping on the floors of the saloons, in the bathrooms, and on the tables throughout the ship in order to let the survivors have as much comfort as the ship afforded. One woman came aboard with a six-month-old baby she had never seen until the moment it was thrust into her arms as she swung into the lifeboat.

Mrs Regina Steiner of New York was also a passenger on the *Carpathia*. She described the harrowing scene to American pressmen.

I saw sixteen of the *Titanic* boats picked up. The poor women were in a frightful state from exposure and anxiety and all of them were holding to the hope that their male relatives whom they had left behind had been rescued by some miracle after the small boats drew clear of the sinking *Titanic*.

In one of the *Titanic* boats a sailor, one of the *Titanic* crew that was manning one of the boats, was dead from exposure before we picked them up. Later seven of those rescued died aboard the *Carpathia*. Oh, it was terrible! Four of them, I was told, were sailors, overcome by the exposure of that terrible night, and three were passengers. They were all buried at sea. There was no ceremony for any of them that I saw and we knew of their burial only because we saw the unmistakable canvas sacks dropped into the sea.

(*New York World*, 19 April 1912)

A steward on board the *Carpathia* gave his version of events.

Just as it was about half day we came upon a boat with eighteen men in it but no women. It was not more than a third filled. All the men were able to climb up a Jacob's ladder which we threw over the port side. Between 8.15 and 8.30 we got the last two boats, crowded to the gunwale, almost all the occupants of which were women. After we had got the last load on board the *Californian* came alongside. The captains arranged that we should make straight for New York, while the *Californian* looked around for more boats. We circled round and round and saw all kinds of wreckage. While we were pulling in the boatloads the women were quiet enough, but when it seemed sure that we should not find any more persons alive, then bedlam came. I hope never to go through it again. The way those women took on for the folk they had lost was awful. We could not do anything to quiet them until they cried themselves out.

(British press, 20 April 1912)

Dr Stanton Coit, President of the West London Ethical Society, was a passenger aboard the *Carpathia* on the fateful night. Before re-sailing from New York to Europe aboard the same vessel, he gave his impressions of the rescue to a periodical.

At 5.30 Monday morning last our bedroom steward reported that the ship had stopped to rescue the passengers from the *Titanic*, which had sunk the night before. I hurried on deck, saw great icebergs about, and looking over the railing, saw some fifteen rowboats approaching us, full chiefly of women. These were drawn up on board and passed us by, most of them so stiff with cold and wet that they could not walk without being supported.

Soon the tragic news spread among us that some 1,500 people had been drowned, and for the most part only women had been saved.

My first and lasting impression was the inward calm and self-poise – not self-control, for there was no effort or self-consciousness – on the part of those who had been saved. I said to one woman, whose dress, but not her face, betrayed that she was one of those who had undergone tragic experiences: 'You were on the *Titanic*?' She answered: 'Yes, and I saw my husband go down.' The only hysteria displayed was after the physician had administered brandy to the half-frozen sufferers. The people struck me not as being stunned and crushed, but as lifted into an atmosphere of vision where self-centred suffering merges into some mystic meaning. Everyone reported a magnificent self-possession of the husbands when parted from their wives. Many related the cases of women who had to be forced from their husbands. Touching beyond words was the gratitude towards those of us who gave clothes and our state rooms. More magnificent than the calm of the clear dawn was the unconsciousness of any personal horror, or need to pity, on the part of those who related how they had met their fate.

One youth of seventeen told, as if it had been an incident of everyday life, that he was hurled from the deck and that as he found himself sinking he took a deep breath. When he came up and found that he was again to be drawn under, he thought it would be well again to breathe deep. Upon rising the second time, he said, he saw the upturned bottom of a canvas boat. To this he clung until he was rescued. One woman in one boat insisted that they should row back and rescue eight men clinging to wreckage, although the oarsmen feared the suction of the great steamer might endanger their lives, and the eight were thus rescued.

My feeling is that in the midst of all this horror, human nature never manifested itself as greater or tenderer. We were all one, not only with one another, but with the cosmic being that for all time had seemed so cruel.

On board the *Carpathia* there was much discussion as to the possible culpability of the captain of the *Titanic*, but there was no judgement offered. But I return again to what I say was my first and abiding impression – the self-poise that is so because the human soul is not self-centred. One young woman with whom I talked was so calm and full of the stories of the heroism and the suffering of others that I said: 'How fortunate that you lost no friend!' Then for the first time her face changed and, with tears streaming down her cheeks, she said: 'My brother, who was my only living relative, went down before my eyes. He scorned to disobey the discipline, so now I am alone.'

(*Outlook*, 27 April 1912)

Maude Sincock, aged twenty-one, was on her way from her Cornish home to see her father who had emigrated to Hancock, Michigan. She travelled second-class on the *Titanic* with Mrs Agnes Davis, a friend of her mother's, and Mrs Davis's two sons, John and Joseph. After being picked up the *Carpathia*, Miss Sincock wrote to her mother, the letter being published in their local paper.

I am saved but I have lost everything. I must however be thankful for my life. I have not a penny and no clothes. I was thrown on board a little boat in my nightdress and boots. I had no stockings on. We were in this little boat in the middle of the ocean for six hours, and I was nearly frozen when we were picked up. I shall be a pretty sight when I land. We were rescued by a passing ship, the *Carpathia*. The *Titanic* struck just before midnight and was underwater about two o'clock. There were over 1,000 persons on board when she foundered. Mrs Davis and her son John are saved, but we have seen nothing of Joe. We think he is drowned. We have not seen anything of the other 'boys' who left St Ives. We could hear the screams from the men as the *Titanic* was sinking. I think there are hundreds drowned.

I don't know what I shall do when I get to New York. I am frightened to death nearly, and I am afraid I shall catch my death of cold by the time I get to Hancock. I will write again as soon as possible and tell you more news. I don't know where they are going to put us when we get to New York.

Your loving daughter, Maude.

(*St Ives Times*, 3 May 1912)

Rescued *Titanic* passenger **Elizabeth Nye**, aged twenty-nine, sent a letter to her parents in Folkestone, Kent, from the *Carpathia*. It was dated Tuesday, 16 April, and was published in their local paper three weeks later.

My dear mother and dad, I expect you have been wondering whether you would ever hear from me again. You have seen by the papers the wreck of the *Titanic*, but after the most terrible time of my life, I am safe. My nerves are very shattered, I look and feel about ten years older, but I will get over it again after a time.

You will like to hear the truth of the wreck from me, for the papers never tell the right news. We were all in bed on Sunday night at about 11.30 when we felt an awful jerk, and the boat grazed something along its side, and the sea seemed to splash right over the deck. The men in the next cabin slipped on their coats and ran up to see what it was, and came and told us the ship had run into an iceberg nearly as large as herself.

Most of the people went back to bed again, but then came an order to 'get up and put something warm on, put on a lifebelt and come on deck.' So I got one underskirt on and a skirt, and stockings, and shoes and coat, and ran up to find a lifebelt, because there were only three in our berth for four of us. A boy from the next cabin stole one from ours, but he went down with it – poor boy. We did not have time to go back to our cabins again to get anything, and we did not dream it was serious. I thought I should get back to get more clothes on and get a few other things, but we were put into the lifeboats, and pushed off at once. They put all ladies and children in first. I guess there were thirty or forty in our boat. It seemed to be the last one lowered with women in it.

When we got away from the ship we could understand the hurry and the order to get half a mile away as soon as possible. For the *Titanic* was half in the water. We watched the portholes go under until half the ship, only the back half, stuck up. Then the lights went out, and the boilers burst and blew up. There was a sickening roar like hundreds of lions, and we heard no more but the moaning and shouting for help from the hundreds of men and a few women who went down with her.

There were not enough boats for so many people. Twenty lifeboats were lowered, and only fourteen boats were picked up. Several men were on a raft that was thrown out, and their cries for help were so pitiful for so long. Only one fellow, about twenty-one years old, is alive from the raft. He says the men were pushed off to make it lighter. This man was on it for six hours and then saved.

Just before the ship went down the captain, the same Captain Smith of the twin ship *Olympic*, jumped into the sea and picked up a little girl who was hanging to the ship, and put her on the raft. They pulled him on, too, but he would not stay. He said: 'Goodbye boys, I must go with the ship.' He swam back through the icy waters and died at his post.

We had no drink or provisions. The only thing in our favour was the clear starlight night and fairly smooth sea.

This boat, the *Carpathia*, of the Cunard line, was going from Halifax to Berlin. She was the only ship near enough to catch the wireless message for help from the *Titanic*, and then the operator says he was just leaving and closing the door when he heard the clicking of the wireless. So it was taken just in time, for they never sent another message, and it was an hour and a quarter after that before the first lifeboat got to the ship. Of course, she stood still, and waited for us all to come up. They were all in but two when we got in.

We were in the little boat for just five hours and a half before being rescued. They lowered bags for the babies to pull them up, and we sat on a kind of swing and were drawn up by a rope to safety. They have been most kind to us. They led us one by one to the dining room, and gave us brandy. I drank half a glass of brandy down without water. We were all perished, and it put life into us. The ship is, of course, filled with its own passengers. But they found places for us all to sleep, but none of us slept well after going through such a horrible nightmare. This ship stood right over the place where the *Titanic* went down, and picked us up. Two small boats were picked up later. They were floating. One had seven dead bodies in it, and the other just a dead boatman. They sewed them up in canvas here, weighted them, and gave them a Christian burial at sea. Two small boats filled with passengers capsized. They all went down but two or three who clung to the upturned boat and were saved.

We are told that the SS *Baltic* picked up about fifty men, and the poor women here are hoping their husbands are among the fifty. It is supposed there are 160 more widows through this wreck, and most of them have children. It was so heartbreaking to see and hear them crying for their husbands.

We were all gathered together, and our names taken for the newspapers. Of course, they cannot tell how many are dead, but we have on this ship only 200 hundred crew out of 910 and 500 passengers out of 2000. I am amongst the fortunate, for God has spared my life when I was so near death again. I have lost everything I had on board. The only thing I saved was my watch Dad gave me eleven years ago. But all my treasures and clothes and some money have gone. I have only the scanty clothes that I stand up in, including my big coat, which has been a blessing.

We expect to land on Wednesday night, or the next morning. I shall be so thankful, for I feel so ill on this boat. The boat is not so nice, and we have to sleep in the bottom of the boat. But still, I thank God I am alive.

I could tell you much more of the horrors of Sunday night, but will write again later on land. I can't bear to think of it all now.

Will you let Auntie and Edie see this letter, and tell my friends I am safe. You must have all been anxious.

. With fondest love to all, from Lizzie.

The previous narrow escape to which Mrs Nye (who is well known in Folkestone) refers, was a serious illness from appendicitis. Her life has been full of sad and trying experiences. Her first sweetheart was washed off the Harbour Pier and drowned. She married a few years later, but had the misfortune to lose her two children by death, and also her husband.

(*Folkestone Herald*, 4 May 1912)

Steerage passenger **Daniel Buckley**, of Kingwilliamstown, Ireland, wrote a letter to his mother from the *Carpathia*, dated 18 April. He appeared remarkably well informed although details of his escape did differ slightly when he subsequently gave his evidence to the Senate Inquiry.

Dear Mother, I am writing these few lines on board the *Carpathia*, the ship that saved our lives. As I might not have much time when I get to New York I mean to give you an account of the terrible shipwreck we had. At 11.40 p.m. on the fourteenth our ship *Titanic* struck an iceberg, and sank to the deep at 2.22 a.m. on the fifteenth. The present estimation is 1,500 lost, 710 saved. Thank God some of us are amongst the number saved. Hannah Riordan, Bridgie Bradley, Nonie O'Leary, and the Shine girl from Lisrobin are alright. There is no account of Patie O'Connell, Michael Linehan, from Freeholds, or Jim O'Connor, Hugh's son from Tureeavonscane. However, I hope they were taken into some other ship. There were four of us sleeping in the same apartment. We had a bed of our own, and in every apartment there were four lifebelts, one for each person. At the time when the ship struck I heard a terrible noise. I jumped out of bed and told my comrades there was something wrong, but they only laughed. I turned on the gas, and to my surprise there was a small stream of water running along the floor. I had only just dressed myself when the sailors came along shouting: 'All up on deck unless you want to get drowned.' We all ran up on deck. I thought to go down again to my room for a lifebelt and my little bag. When I was going down the last flight of stairs the water was up three steps on the stairs, so I did not go any further. I just thought of Den. Ring's saying: 'Stick to your lifebelts, and face a tearing ocean.' We were not long on deck when the lifeboats were prepared. There were only sixteen boats, and that amount was only enough to carry a tenth of the passengers. The third boat that was let down I went on it. There were about forty men in it. An officer came along and said half the men should come out of the boat and let some ladies in. When I heard this I hid in the lower part of the boat. We were only fifteen minutes in the boat when the big ship went down. It was a terrible sight. It would make the stones cry to hear those on board shrieking. It made a terrible noise like thunder when it was sinking. There were a great many Irish boys and girls drowned. I got out without any wound. There were a lot of men and women got wounded getting off the steamer. There did a good many die coming out on the lifeboats and after getting on the *Carpathia*. It was a great change to us to get on this strange steamer as we had a grand time on the *Titanic*. We got very good diet and we had a very jolly time dancing and singing. We had every kind of instrument on board to amuse us, but all the amusement sank in the deep. I have no more to say at present. I will write a lot when I get to New York. Goodbye at present. – Dannie.

(*Cork Free Press*, 13 May 1912)

CHAPTER 5

THE NEWS BREAKS

TITANIC STRIKES AN ICEBERG, BEGINS TO SINK AT HEAD

Greatest Liner Afloat on Maiden Voyage Sends Wireless Calls for Help Off Newfoundland – Women Being Taken Off in Boats – Virginian, Olympic *and* Baltic *Racing to the Rescue – Last Messages Faint and Blurred*

Cape Race, N.F., April 14. At 10.25 tonight the White Star steamship *Titanic* called 'C.Q.D.' and reported having struck an iceberg. The steamer said that immediate assistance was required.

Half an hour afterwards another message came reporting that they were sinking by the head and that women were being put off in the lifeboats.

The weather was calm and clear, the *Titanic*'s wireless operator reported, and gave the position of the vessel 41.46 north latitude and 50.14 west longitude.

The Marconi station at Cape Race notified the Allan Liner *Virginian*, the captain of which immediately advised that he was proceeding for the scene of the disaster.

Cape Race, April 15, 2 a.m. The *Virginian* at midnight was about 170 miles distant from the *Titanic* and expected to reach that vessel about 10 a.m. Monday.

The *Olympic* at an early hour Monday morning was in latitude

40.32 and longitude 61.18 west. She was in direct communication with the *Titanic* and was making all haste towards her.

The steamship *Baltic* also reported herself as about 200 miles east of the *Titanic* and was making all possible speed towards her.

The last signals from the *Titanic* were heard by the *Virginian* at 12.27 a.m.

The wireless operator on the *Virginian* says these signals were blurred and ended abruptly.

VIRGINIAN GETS FIRST CALL FOR HELP AND SPEEDS TO GIVE NEEDED ASSISTANCE

Montreal, April 14. – The news of the *Titanic* disaster was received at the Allan Line offices here in a wireless message from the captain of the steamer *Virginian* of that line.

The *Virginian* sailed from Halifax this morning and at the time the wireless was sent she is reckoned to have been about abeam of Cape Race. She was 900 passengers on board, but can accommodate all of the *Titanic's* passengers.

The message from the *Virginian's* captain was sent by wireless to Cape Race, thence by cable to Halifax and then by wire to Montreal.

The Allan Line officials here expect to hear further news at any moment.

The *Titanic* was 1,284 miles east of Sandy Hook at 2.15 Sunday morning.

This is the giant *Titanic's* maiden voyage, and a disaster was narrowly averted when she sailed from Southampton Wednesday last. It was similar to that which befell her sister ship, the *Olympic*. Capt. E.J. Smith was commander of the *Olympic* at that time and he is charge of the *Titanic*.

The *Titanic*, with about 1200 passengers aboard, 350 of whom are in the first cabin, was leaving her pier when there was a sound as of a mountain battery being discharged. There was a rush of passengers to the port rail to see what the trouble was.

It then developed that as she passed out into the stream the 45,000-ton steamship had sucked the water between herself and the quay to so great an extent that the seven huge hawsers which the American liner *New York* was moored to the pier had been snapped like threads.

The *New York* began drifting helplessly, stern first, towards the *Titanic*, which seemed to act like a magnet. Slowly the *New York* bore down on the *Titanic*, which reversed her engines. In a few minutes her headway was stopped and she began to move slowly astern. The tugs *Neptune* and *Vulcan* sped to the helpless American liner, caught her with hawsers bow and stern and towed her back to her berth. The tugs' timely arrival and quick work probably prevented a bad smash between the two liners.

One assuring feature of the accident to the *Titanic* is that a large number of ships appear to be within the big liner's call. Besides the *Virginian* of the Allan Line, which appears to be the first to have heard the *Titanic*'s distress, and the White Star liners *Baltic* and *Olympic*, both of which were reported on the way to the scene, there is also the *Cincinnati* of the Hamburg-American Line and the Cunarder *Mauretania*, the Hamburg-American liner *Prinz Adelbert*, and the *Amerika* of the same line, and the North German Lloyd liner *Prinz Friedrich Wilhelm*, bound from this port to Plymouth, all of which and many smaller liners are shown on today's steamship chart as in the vicinity of Cape Race.

TITANIC A MARVEL IN SIZE AND LUXURY

The *Titanic* and her sister ship, the *Olympic*, of the White Star Line are the largest ships afloat in the world, being 100ft longer than their next rival. These sea monsters are at the same time floating mansions of luxury, each capable of holding a townful of people. They are 882½ft long, 92ft in the beam and 94ft in depth, with 45,000 tons register and 66,000 tons displacement.

With officers and crew numbering 860, the *Titanic* is capable of carrying 3,000 to 3,500 passengers – cabin and steerage. She was built to be the last word in size, speed, power, and sea luxury, and it would take a powerful imagination to conceive the magnificence and detail for comfort and luxury and pastime on the great ship. Its interior more closely resembles a huge hotel, with heavy balustraded wide stairways, elevators running up and down for nine storeys; its great saloons and restaurants, its miniature theatre, squash and tennis courts, swimming pools and Turkish bath rooms; its great smoking room, card rooms and beautiful music rooms, and even on the top of its 12 decks a miniature golf links.

Captain Smith, her commander, the admiral of the White Star fleet, was in command of her sister ship, the *Olympic*, when she made her maiden voyage to New York and also when she collided with the British cruiser *Hawke* in the Solent last September.

(*New York World*, 15 April 1912)

THE BIGGEST SHIPWRECK IN THE WORLD THE *TITANIC* COLLIDES WITH AN ICEBERG NEAR CAPE RACE LINERS TO THE RESCUE ALL PASSENGERS SAFELY TAKEN OFF BY LIFEBOATS CRIPPLED VESSEL STEAMING TO HALIFAX

The biggest ship in the world, the *Titanic*, has met with disaster on her maiden voyage.

She collided with an iceberg last evening, 270 miles from Cape Race, and was reported in a sinking condition.

Not till after two o'clock this afternoon was the tense anxiety in London relieved by the news that all the passengers had been put off in lifeboats, and that the liner *Virginian* was standing by her. The sea was calm.

Later, it was reported that the *Titanic* was still afloat, and making her way to Halifax.

Only last Wednesday the *Titanic*, the pride of the White Star Line and the very last word in shipbuilding, sailed majestically from Southampton to New York, crowds of people watching her stately progress. 'A floating island', 'a gorgeous hotel on the waves', 'a town in motion', were some of the admiring phrases bestowed on her.

This mighty vessel dwarfed the *Oceanic* and the *New York*, both huge liners in their day. The very suction caused by her screws caused the seven mooring ropes of the *New York* to snap like threads.

So the *Titanic* proudly left port. But disaster was to come, and that from an unexpected cause. There is a phenomenal amount of ice in the track of westward-bound vessels this spring, and several liners have had narrow escapes.

Last evening, apparently a little after 10 o'clock American time (three o'clock this morning, English time), the *Titanic* collided with an iceberg. She was then about 270 miles south-east of Cape Race, Newfoundland.

The details up to the time of writing are meagre in the extreme. All that is known definitely is that the indispensable wireless apparatus was set in motion, and the terrible signal 'S.O.S.' was flashed out in every direction.

The biggest ship in the world was sinking, and in urgent need of help!

Thirty minutes after the first wireless message, a second communication reported that the *Titanic* was sinking bow first, and that the women were being put into the lifeboats.

(*London Evening News*, 15 April 1912)

A COINCIDENCE

The Olympic's *Collision with the* Hawke *Recalled*

In design and construction the *Titanic* is similar to her sister ship the *Olympic* and it is a tragic coincidence that both vessels have met with misfortune.

The *Titanic* has a tonnage of 46,382, or 1,004 more than the *Olympic*. Her length is 582ft with a 92ft beam; and she is luxuriously fitted up with especial regard to the requirements of wealthy Americans.

The *Olympic*, it will be remembered, was in collision with the cruiser *Hawke* soon after leaving port, and sustained such damage that she had to be placed again in the hands of her builders.

The misfortune that has now befallen the *Titanic* will cause widespread regret, for the vessel, in the estimation of those who were privileged to view her, was another triumph in British shipping and shipbuilding.

(*Nottingham Evening News*, 15 April 1912)

1500 PERSONS HURLED TO DEATH AS MONSTER LINER *TITANIC* IS SUNK BY COLLISION WITH MOUNTAIN OF ICE

Enormous Mass Fatal to World's Greatest Steamship on Maiden Voyage, Despite Aid by Sister Ships

WIRELESS CALLS BRING AID TOO LATE

The greatest marine disaster in the history of the world occurred last Sunday night when the *Titanic*, of the White Star Line, the biggest and finest of steamships, shattered herself against an iceberg and sank, with 1500 of her passengers and crew in less than four hours.

Out of nearly 2200 people that she carried only 675 were saved, and most of these were women and children. They were picked up from small boats by the Cunarder *Carpathia*, which found, when she ended her desperate race against time, a sea strewn with wreckage of the lost ship and the bodies of drowned men and women.

Among the 1320 passengers of the giant liner were Col. John Jacob Astor and his wife; Isidor Straus; Maj. Archibald W. Butt, aide to President Taft; George W. Widener and Mrs Widener of Philadelphia; Mr and Mrs Henry S. Harper; William T. Stead, the London journalist, and many more whose names are known on both sides of the Atlantic. The news that few besides women and children were saved has caused the greatest apprehension as to the fate of these.

When the *Titanic* plunged headlong against a wall of ice at 10.40 p.m. (New York time) on Sunday night, her fate established that no modern steamship is unsinkable, and that all of a large passenger list cannot be saved in a liner's small boats. The White Star Line believed that the *Titanic* was practically invulnerable and insisted, until there was no doubting the full extent of the catastrophe, that she could not sink. The great ship was the last word in modern scientific construction, but she found the ocean floor almost as quickly as a wooden ship.

On her maiden trip, the *Titanic*, built and equipped at a cost of $10,000,000, a floating palace, found her graveyard. Swinging from the westerly steamship lane at the south of the Grand Banks of Newfoundland to take the direct run to this port she hurled her giant bulk against an iceberg that rose from an immense field drifted unseasonably from the Arctic. Running at high speed into that grim and silent enemy of seafarers, the shock crushed her bow. From a happy, comfortable vessel she was converted in a few minutes into a ship of misery and dreadful suffering.

Through rent plates and timbers water rushed so swiftly that her captain, E. J. Smith, the admiral of the White Star fleet, knew there was no hope of saving her. That much the faltering wireless has told us.

It has been many years since the world was left in such suspense and dread as followed the first faltering calls for help from the crushed *Titanic*. At 10.30 p.m. on Sunday night, the *Virginian*, speeding on her way to Glasgow, picked up the White Star steamship's insistent, frantic C.Q.D., the Marconi signal of distress and peril that clears the air of all lesser messages and stops ships at sea full in their tracks.

Dash by dash and dot by dot, the wireless operator of the *Virginian* caught the cry for help.

'Have struck an iceberg. Badly damaged. Rush aid.'

Seaward and landward, J. G. Phillips, the *Titanic*'s wireless man, was hurling the appeal for help. By fits and starts – for the wireless was working unevenly and blurringly – Phillips reached out to the world, crying the *Titanic*'s peril. A word or two, scattered phrases, now and then a connected sentence, made up the messages that sent a thrill of apprehension for a thousand miles east, west and south of the doomed liner.

(*New York Call*, 16 April 1912)

LINE'S OFFICIALS BELITTLED DISASTER, REASSURED ALL INQUIRERS UNTIL 7 P.M.

All day long the most hopeful spirit seemed to prevail in the officers of the White Star Line at No. 9 Broadway. Inquiring friends were reassured, intending passengers on other steamers were booked with smiles and laughter by the clerks, who spoke of the 'little difficulty of the *Titanic*'.

This feeling of confidence, which extended from Vice-President P. S. Franklin down to the door porters, ran high until exactly 7 o'clock.

Just after seven had struck one of the waiting newspaper men 'sensed' that something had occurred. Gloom seemed to have settled over the offices where all had been cheerful before. In an instant there was a rush to the office of Mr Franklin. Instead of being away to dinner, as had been expected, he was at his desk showing great depression.

'What's the matter?' he was asked by a score of reporters. In reply he only shook his head and looked out of the window into the murky street below.

'Gentlemen,' he muttered, after what seemed an hour of seconds, 'I regret to say that the *Titanic* sank at 2.20 this morning.'

He was alone the next moment, for every one of his callers had rushed to a telephone. When they returned the reporters were armed with additional information obtained from the Marconi Wireless Company. But it was some time before Mr Franklin could be induced to talk for publication.

Through a representative he sent out, piecemeal, the news that had reached him in the telegram from Capt. Haddock of the

Olympic, which had already been reported by the Marconi Press Agency.

At first Mr Franklin would only admit that the *Titanic* had sunk and that the *Carpathia* was bound for New York with the 'survivors'. Then he was forced to say that so far as he knew but 675 of the 2200, or thereabouts, aboard had been saved. Finally he sent for the newspaper men and made this statement.

'As far as we know the rumours from Halifax that three steamers had passengers on board from the *Titanic* – the *Virginian*, the *Parisian* and the *Carpathia*, are true.'

(*New York World*, 16 April 1912)

ANXIOUS CROWD CLAMOURS AT OFFICES HERE FOR NEWS

Crowds of distraught inquirers after news besieged the offices of the White Star Line at No. 9 Broadway until early this morning. Each answer that the officers of the I.M.M. had less information by far than the newspapers added another to the company of those that waited, hoping against hope that news might come. From 9 o'clock on all the officers of the company were present in Vice-President Franklin's office. There were many weeping and hysterical women in the throng.

Vincent Astor, accompanied by N. Biddle and W. A. Dobbyns, Col. Astor's secretary, drove to the offices in an automobile at 9.30.

He was asked if he had received any word from his father and Mrs Astor.

'Nothing, except what I have read in the newspapers,' he replied.

As he entered the offices of the company he heard a rumour that was current, but which was not confirmed, to the effect that his father, John Jacob Astor, had been drowned, but that Mrs Astor had been saved.

Young Astor hurried to the private office of Vice-President Franklin, where he remained for fifteen minutes in conference with that official. When he left the offices and entered his automobile he was weeping.

Mr Astor and Col. Astor's secretary were asked if they had received any news relative to Col. Astor and Mrs Astor. They declined to answer.

Sylvester Byrnes, secretary to Isidor Straus, reached the offices of the steamship company shortly before 10 o'clock and made inquiry relative to Mr and Mrs Isidor Straus, who were on the *Titanic*. He was informed by the officials of the company that no detailed report had been received relative to the identity of the passengers reported saved.

Mr Byrnes said Jesse Straus left New York late yesterday afternoon for Halifax in the hope of meeting his parents.

Another who made inquiry was Miss Wheelock, of No. 317 Riverside Drive, who requested information relative to the safety of her brother-in-law and sister, Dr and Mrs D. W. Marvin, whom, she said, were returning from a honeymoon trip.

Vice-President Franklin last night said that knowing Capt. Smith as he has for many years, and being familiar with his record as a seaman, he is certain that if any passengers in the *Titanic* were drowned Capt. Smith remained on board assisting in the rescues and went down with the ship while at his post of duty.

(*New York World*, 16 April 1912)

WEALTH OF PASSENGERS IN SALOON $500,000,000

The combined wealth of the first cabin passengers totals more than $500,000,000. Among those on board and their estimated wealth are the following:

Mr and Mrs John Jacob Astor	$150,000,000
Mr and Mrs G. D. Widener	$50,000,000
Benjamin Guggenheim	$95,000,000

C. M. Hays, president of the Grand Trunk railway	$1,000,000
Henry B. Harris of New York and Boston	$3,000,000
Frederick M. Hoyt	$1,000,000
Bruce Ismay, chairman and managing director of the White Star Steamship Company	$40,000,000
Mrs Isidor Straus, wife of Isidor Straus, the New York merchant	$50,000,000
Washington A. Roebling	$25,000,000

VALUE OF A NATION REPRESENTED BY TRAVELLERS OF THE *TITANIC* – MANY MULTI-MILLIONAIRES

Untold wealth was represented among the passengers of the *Titanic*, there being on board at least six men, each of whose fortunes might be reckoned in tens of millions of dollars. A rough estimate of the total wealth represented in the first-class passenger list would each over half a billion dollars.

The wealthiest of the list is Col. John Jacob Astor, head of the famous house whose name he bears, and who is reputed to be worth $150 million. He is connected with most of the large corporations of the country and for years has had direct control of the vast estate left by his father, the late William Astor. Mr Astor was returning on the *Titanic* from a tour of Egypt with his bride, who was Miss Madeline Force, the 19-year-old daughter of Mr and Mrs William H. Force. They were married in Providence on September 9.

Mr and Mrs Astor occupied a bridal suite on the doomed liner.

Two years ago Col. Astor and his son Vincent figured in a sea scare when their yacht, the *Noma*, having both on board, could not be traced after a storm in the Caribbean Sea. While government and other vessels were searching for the yacht she steamed safely into Jacksonville, Florida.

Benjamin Guggenheim, probably next in financial importance, is the fifth of the seven sons of Meyer Guggenheim, who founded the American Smelting and Refining Co., the great mining corporation, and is a director of many corporations including the International Steam Pump Co., of which he is now president. His fortune is estimated at $95 million. His wife, whose name does not appear on the passenger list, is the daughter of James Seligman, the New York banker.

George D. Widener is the son of P. A. B. Widener, the Philadelphia 'traction king', whose fortune is estimated at $50 million. Isidor Straus, one of New York's most prominent dry goods merchants, and notable for his philanthropies, has a fortune also estimated to be worth $50 million. He is a director in various banks, trust companies and charitable institutions and with his brother, Nathan Straus, is the owner of three of New York's largest department stores.

J. Bruce Ismay, president and one of the founders of the International Mercantile Marine, who has always made it a custom to be a passenger on the maiden trip of every new ship built by the company, is said to be worth $40 million. It was Mr Ismay who, with J. P. Morgan, consolidated American and British steamship lines under the International Mercantile Marine's control.

Col. Washington Roebling, builder of the Brooklyn bridge and president and director of John A. Roebling & Sons Co., is credited with a fortune of $25 million.

Among others of reputed wealth who were on board are J. P. Thayer, vice-president of the Pennsylvania railroad; the Countess of Rothes, daughter of an English plush manufacturer, who expected to visit Newport; Clarence Moore, a well-known sportsman, whose wife was Miss Mabel Swift, daughter of E. C. Swift, the Chicago meat packer; Col. Alfonso Simonius, president of the Swiss Bankverein, and Charles M. Hays, president of the Grand Trunk Pacific and vice-president and general manager of the Grand Trunk of Canada.

(*Boston Post*, 16 April 1912)

THOUGHT STEAMER COULD NOT SINK CAPTAIN OF *TITANIC* SAID FIVE YEARS AGO THAT DAY OF MARINE DISASTERS HAD PASSED

Bad luck has come to Capt. E. J. Smith, commander of the *Titanic* and commodore of the White Star Line, after forty years on the sea, during which time he worked up from apprentice to commander of the largest steamship in the world.

During all this time, up to last September, when his steamer, the *Olympic*, then, as now, with the sinking of the *Titanic*, the queen steamship of the world, crashed into the British cruiser *Hawke*, he did not figure in a single disaster.

Since then, however, misfortune has come thick and fast, for in February the *Olympic* struck what is believed to have been a submerged wreck and lost a blade from one of her propellers, which made it necessary to put her in dry dock, and last Wednesday the *Titanic*, in leaving Southampton on her maiden voyage, narrowly missed colliding with the *New York* of the American line, which had been pulled from her anchorage by suction from the new ocean giant.

It was undoubtedly because of Capt. Smith's previous fine career that the officers of the White Star Line retained him in its service after the mishaps to the *Olympic*, thus violating a deep sea tradition that has been more rigorously maintained by the British merchant marine than by any other nation. The rule has been almost invariable among steamship companies to dispense with the services of officers in command of vessels that have met with disaster.

One reason for this is the insistence of the insurance companies. Lloyds keeps in its London office the records of all marine officers so that when a man is put in command of a vessel his whole career can be immediately inspected.

Much interest attaches to the fate that now awaits Capt. Smith, if he has survived. If proved at fault in the collision of the *Titanic* with an iceberg – and this will depend in great measure on the degree of vigilance used after the delicate instruments all vessels now carry warned of the vessel's proximity to ice – he may not only be deprived of his command, but also of his certificate, which will force him to give up the sea.

Capt. Smith began his sea career in 1869, when he shipped as apprentice on the *Senator Weber*, an American clipper purchased by Gibson & Co. of Liverpool. In 1878 he got a commission as fourth officer of the square-rigger *Lizzie Fennel*, and in 1880 was appointed fourth officer of the old steamship *Celtic* of the White Star Line. He attained the rank of captain in 1887, when he took command of the old *Republic*.

It was in 1892 that the White Star Line bestowed its first great honour on Capt. Smith, when it made him commander of its best steamship, the *Majestic*, on Mediterranean voyages. Since that time he has commanded every large steamship of the White Star Line. When he was put in command of the *Titanic*, it was reported that he would retire after he had conducted her across the Atlantic and back, but the White Star officials afterwards announced that he would have charge of the *Titanic* until the company built a larger and finer steamship.

Thought Sinking Impossible

Capt. Smith had the utmost confidence in the safety of the ocean giants that are now being constructed. In 1907 when he came to New York in command of the *Adriatic* on her maiden trip, he said: 'Shipbuilding is such a perfect art nowadays that absolute disaster, involving the passengers, is inconceivable. Whatever happens, there will be time enough before the vessel sinks to save the life of every person on board. I will go a bit further. I will say that I cannot imagine any condition that would cause the vessel to founder. Modern shipbuilding has gone beyond that.

'When anyone asks me how I can best describe my experiences

of nearly 40 years at sea I merely say, uneventful. In all my experience I have never been in an accident worth speaking of.'

(*Boston Post*, 16 April 1912)

The grim truth was broken to the British public in a special late
edition of the *Daily Graphic*.

APPALLING DISASTER *TITANIC* FOUNDERS ON MAIDEN VOYAGE TO NEW YORK TERRIBLE LOSS OF LIFE RESCUERS ARRIVE TOO LATE

An appalling disaster has overtaken the White Star liner *Titanic* on
her maiden voyage to New York.

The huge vessel, which left Southampton on Wednesday, was
in collision on Sunday night with an iceberg while still some 400
or 500 miles from land.

She sank at 2.20 on Monday morning – four hours after the
collision.

Her wireless messages were picked up by other liners, which
hastened to her assistance; but the *Carpathia*, which reached the spot
where she foundered at daybreak, found only boats and wreckage.

The full extent of the disaster is not yet known, but it is stated
that 675 souls – mostly women and children – have been saved.

If all the others have gone down with the vessel the loss of life
will be appalling as the *Titanic* had 2,358 persons on board.

There may still be some hope that vessels other than the
Carpathia have picked up some survivors.

The *Titanic*'s survivors on board the *Carpathia* are stated at the
White Star offices in New York to include all first-class passengers. She is expected to reach New York on Friday morning.

A message sent out by Reuter from New York at 9pm states that
the White Star officials now admit that probably only 675 out of
the 2,358 persons on board the *Titanic* have been saved.

(*Daily Graphic*, 16 April 1912)

THE *TITANIC* SUNK
COLLISION WITH ICEBERG
HORRIBLE LOSS OF LIFE
ONLY 675 SOULS SAVED

The latest information with regard to the wreck of the *Titanic*, in consequence of collision with an iceberg, leaves little room for doubt that the most awful shipping disaster in the history of the world has occurred. And this on the maiden voyage of the largest and most luxurious liner the world has ever known.

Messages from New York to hand early this morning, containing the expressed opinion of a prominent White Star Line official, state that the *Titanic* has sunk, and that probably only 675 of the 2,490 souls aboard the doomed ship have been saved. Thus there is the most terrible loss of 1,825 [sic] lives.

Another estimate of the number of passengers and crew on board is 2,358, but whatever the exact figure, the awful news will stagger humanity.

The *Carpathia*, with the 675 survivors, who include most, if not all, of the first-class passengers, is on her way to New York.

Many west country passengers were on board the vessel.

The earlier news gave hope that the passengers and crew had all been saved, but in the light of the more authentic accounts, many of the telegrams must be discounted.

The main facts stand out plainly. The *Titanic* sank soon after striking the iceberg, and when the *Virginian* arrived on the scene there were nothing but boats and wreckage visible. Some of the passengers picked up by the *Virginian* were afterwards transferred to the *Carpathia*, and it is to be feared that all the souls saved are the 675 on the *Carpathia*, which is now on her way to New York.

The abrupt stoppage of the *Titanic*'s wireless message and the absence of definite news during the greater part of yesterday are only circumstantial confirmations of the frightful catastrophe. If the *Titanic* had remained afloat full details of her condition would have been made known by her wireless operators.

THIS MORNING'S TERRIBLE NEWS

Appended are the latest messages received through Reuter's Agency, this morning:

NEW YORK, April 15 – The *Titanic* sank at 2.20 this morning. No lives were lost.

NEW YORK, April 15, 8.20 p.m. – The following statement has been given out by the White Star officials:

'Captain Haddock, of the *Olympic*, sends a wireless message that the *Titanic* sank at 2.20 a.m., Monday, after all the passengers and the crew had been lowered into the lifeboats and transferred to the *Virginian*. The steamer *Carpathia*, with several hundred passengers from the *Titanic*, is now on her way to New York.'

NEW YORK, April 15, 8.40 p.m. – The White Star officials now admit that some lives have been lost.

8.45 p.m. – A despatch from Cape Race says that all the *Titanic*'s boats are accounted for. About 675 souls have been saved of crew and passengers – the latter nearly all women and children. The *Carpathia* is returning to New York with survivors.

NEW YORK, 8.45 p.m. – The following despatch has been received from Cape Race: The steamer *Olympic* reports that the steamer *Carpathia* reached the *Titanic* position at daybreak, but found boats and wreckage only.

She reports that the *Titanic* foundered about 2.20 a.m. in latitude 41 deg. 16 min., longitude 50 deg. 14 min.

The Leyland liner *California* is searching in the vicinity of the disaster.

NEW YORK, 9 p.m. – The *Titanic* survivors on board the *Carpathia* are stated by the White Star offices to include all first-class passengers. She is expected to reach New York on Friday morning.

NEW YORK, 9.50 p.m. – The White Star officials now admit that probably only 675 out of 2,200 passengers on board the *Titanic* have been saved.

The White Star clerks state that the *Carpathia* is proceeding to New York with the survivors.

HORRIBLE LOSS OF LIFE

NEW YORK, April 15, Later – At the White Star offices it is believed that many of the *Titanic*'s passengers are aboard the *Parisian* or *Virginian*.

Mr Franklin now admits there has been a horrible loss of life. He says he has no information to disprove the Press despatch from Cape Race that only 675 passengers and crew had been saved.

The monetary loss could not be estimated tonight, but he intimated that it would run into millions.

MONTREAL, April 15 – It is announced at the Allan Line offices that the *Virginian* retransferred the passengers she took from the *Titanic* to the *Carpathia* shortly after she received them, and that the change was made because the *Carpathia* was bound for New York, while the *Virginian* was east bound with mails.

THE CALL FOR ASSISTANCE HOW IT WAS RECEIVED

NEW YORK, April 15 – A telegram received here from Montreal says the liner *Virginian* reports herself in wireless communication with the liner *Titanic*, which is reported to have been in collision with an iceberg and to have requested assistance. The *Virginian* is hastening to her aid.

MONTREAL, April 15 – A wireless message was received late last night from the Allan liner *Virginian*, which sailed from Halifax yesterday morning, and which reports that the huge White Star liner *Titanic* has struck an iceberg off Cape Race.

It is understood that the *Virginian* is now on the way to answer the wireless call for assistance which was given by the liner, and is prepared if necessary to take off the *Titanic*'s passengers.

The Allan Line officials have received no further news, but are expecting a message at any moment.

NEW YORK, April 15, 3.45 a.m. – A telegram from Cape Race at 10.25 Sunday evening says: The *Titanic* reported she had struck an iceberg.

The steamer said that immediate assistance was required.

Half an hour afterwards another message was received saying that the *Titanic* was sinking by the head, and that the women were being taken off in lifeboats.

NEW YORK, April 15, Later – A Cape Race telegram says the wireless telegraph operator on the *Titanic* reported the weather calm and clear.

The *Virginian* at midnight was 170 miles west of the *Titanic* and is expected to reach her at 10 a.m. today.

The *Olympic* is also hastening to the *Titanic*.

The liner *Baltic* has reported herself within 200 miles of the *Titanic*, and is speeding to her help.

The *Virginian*'s operator says the last signals from the *Titanic* were blurred and ended abruptly.

MANY LINERS WITHIN CALL

NEW YORK, April 15 – Messages which are arriving here from Newfoundland are reassuring in so far as they show that a number of vessels are within call of the *Virginian*. The *Mauretania* is responding to the signal, as well as the German liners *Prince Adelbert*, *Amerika*, *Prinz Friedrich Wilhelm*, and other smaller ships.

A wireless message which was sent to the *Virginian* and other vessels in the vicinity of the disaster has failed up to the present to bring any response.

A CURIOUS OMISSION

NO NEWS TRANSMITTED TO WHITE STAR LINE

NEW YORK, April 15 – Up to 8 a.m. the officials of the White Star Line had not received a word regarding the reported accident to the *Titanic*.

The company in a statement say, 'It is very strange that the *Titanic*'s sister ship *Olympic*, which has a wireless installation of sufficient strength to send a message across the Atlantic, should have sent us nothing. The *Olympic* should be alongside the *Titanic* at two o'clock this afternoon.'

The Central News was informed at the head offices of the White Star Line in London yesterday morning that no official information has been received there regarding the disaster which had overtaken the *Titanic*.

On learning of the accident from the papers the managers immediately telephoned to the firm's offices at Liverpool, but no information was to hand there.

'WE ARE NOT WORRIED'

STATEMENT BY INTERNATIONAL MERCANTILE MARINE OFFICIAL

NEW YORK, April 15 – Mr Franklin, vice-president of the International Mercantile Marine, has issued the following statement: 'We have nothing direct from the *Titanic*, but are perfectly satisfied that the vessel is unsinkable.

'The fact that the Marconi messages have ceased means nothing. It may be due to atmospherical conditions, the coming up of the ships, or something of that sort.

'We are not worried over the possible loss of the ship, as she will not go down, but we are sorry for the inconvenience caused to the travelling public.

'We are absolutely certain that the *Titanic* is able to withstand any damage. She may be down by the head, but would float indefinitely in that condition.

'We figure that the *Virginian* will be alongside the *Titanic* at 10 o'clock this morning, the *Olympic* by three this afternoon, and the *Baltic* by four o'clock.'

ENORMOUS QUANTITIES OF ICE

The Canadian Pacific liner, *Empress of Britain*, which arrived at Liverpool from Halifax on Sunday, reports the presence of an immense quantity of ice in the Atlantic.

Last Tuesday, when three days out from Halifax, she encountered an ice field 100 miles in extent with enormous bergs, and she steered a wide course.

The *Empress of Britain* had previously received a wireless message from the Allan liner *Virginian* warning her of the presence of ice.

The extent of the ice was regarded as phenomenal, and the bergs seemed to be joined to the ice field, which appeared as an enormous white line on the horizon.

CONFLICTING STATEMENTS

The following messages were also received yesterday but, in view of the latest cablegrams giving the awful news of the loss of life, they are obviously of a contradictory character:

HALIFAX, NOVA SCOTIA, April 15 – A message just received here states that the *Titanic* was still afloat at half past eight and her engines were working. She was crawling slowly in the direction of Halifax, and towards the *Virginian*.

It is further reported that the women and children aboard are in the lifeboats, which are ready to be lowered in a moment's notice, but this will not be done until it is certain that the vessel is actually sinking.

The weather continues to be clear and calm.

The *Titanic*'s pumps are working at their utmost power.

The forward holds are full, but the watertight compartments are holding. There is good hope of the vessel making port.

NEW YORK, April 15 – A message from Montreal timed 8.30 a.m. says the *Titanic* is still afloat and heading towards Halifax with her own engines.

The women and children have not been taken off though the lifeboats are ready in case of emergency.

It is thought the bulkheads will prevent her sinking.

A later message says wireless telegraphy brings word that two vessels are standing by the *Titanic* and all the passengers have been taken off.

NEW YORK, April 15 – A despatch from Halifax states that all the passengers of the *Titanic* had left the ship by 8.30 this morning – Reuter.

NEW YORK, April 15 – The *Montreal Star* reports from Halifax that the *Titanic* is still afloat, and is making her way slowly to Halifax..

NEW YORK, April 15, 10.40 – A wireless message has just come through from the *Virginian* stating that the *Titanic* is sinking.

The *Olympic*, which sent a wireless message to the *Titanic* direct at 24 minutes past four, was informed in a reply that great damage had been done.

The captain reported he would tranship the passengers to the first steamer which came alongside. The *Virginian*, which will in all probability be the vessel, will it is believed, go back to Halifax, Nova Scotia.

THE TITANIC *IN TOW*

NEW YORK, April 15, 11.30 a.m. – A wireless message says 24 boat loads of passengers have already been taken aboard the *Carpathia* from the *Titanic*. The *Olympic* is nearing the *Titanic*, as also is the *Baltic*, while the *Parisian* and *Carpathia* are in attendance. An unofficial message says the *Virginian* has taken the *Titanic* in tow. – Reuter.

NEW YORK, April 15 – An official message, via the cable ship *Minia*, off Cape Race, says steamers are towing the *Titanic* and endeavouring to get her into shoal water near Cape Race for the purpose of beaching her.

A Halifax message states that the Government Marine Agency has received a wireless message that the *Titanic* is sinking.

The vice-president of the International Mercantile Marine today gave out the following, received from the White Star Line's Boston office: 'Allan Line, Montreal, confirm report *Virginian, Parisian, Carpathia* in attendance, standing by *Titanic*.'

ALL PASSENGERS TRANSFERRED

NEW YORK, April 15 – The transfer of the *Titanic*'s passengers was made safely in calm weather to the *Carpathia* and the *Parisian*. The *Baltic* was reported at three o'clock hurrying to get to these vessels for the purpose of taking over the *Titanic*'s passengers who should reach Halifax tomorrow. Most of the *Titanic*'s crew remained aboard. It was reported at 4 o'clock that all the passengers had been transferred from the *Titanic*. – Reuter.

The following cablegram was received last night at the White Star Line offices, Liverpool:

'Captain Haddock of the *Olympic* wires: The *Parisian* reports the *Carpathia* to be in attendance on the *Titanic*, and has picked up twenty boats of passengers. The *Baltic* is returning to give assistance. Position not given. It is reported that all the passengers are saved, and that the *Virginian* is towing the *Titanic* towards Halifax, Nova Scotia. The report is also confirmed that the *Virginian, Parisian* and *Carpathia* are in attendance on the *Titanic*.'

WIRELESS OPERATOR'S MESSAGE

The Press Association's Godalming correspondent telegraphs: Mr and Mrs Phillips, of Farncombe, Godalming, parents of a wireless telegraphy operator on the *Titanic*, last night received the following message from their son: 'Making slowly for Halifax; practically unsinkable. Don't worry.'

(*Western Daily Mercury*, 16 April 1912)

ANXIOUS FATHER'S MISTAKE

A Godalming correspondent telegraphs that the message stated to have been received last night by Mr and Mrs Phillips from their son, the wireless operator aboard the *Titanic*, turns out not to have been from him at all, but from another son in London. On receiving the message the father came to the conclusion that it was from his son on the *Titanic*, but this morning he stated that he felt he was mistaken.

(*Liverpool Evening Express*, 16 April 1912)

TERROR TO CAPTAINS

Death Lurking from Floating Ice Monsters

With the movement of the ice southwards each year the perils of the Atlantic passages are increased. Ships' captains warn each other of the presence of these great floating islands, but they are often hidden by fog – even in broad daylight there may be only a few feet of a monster floe visible above the surface – and there is little warning of their presence.

Monster bergs have been reported in the month of May. The French liner *Lorraine* saw one in a recent May which was 675ft high and 1,500ft long. The steamer *American* sighted another in June 1905, in the very neighbourhood from which the urgent calls came from the *Titanic*, and that berg was 300ft high and 900ft long.

Generally the portion of the berg visible above water is only one-eighth or one-tenth of the total depth.

Many ships have been wrecked by these floating monsters. In 1903, 23 steamers met with serious accidents through contact with ice near the Banks, and two were totally lost.

In 1879 the liner *Arizona* drove her stern against a berg almost to the foremast, but floated owing largely to the fact that 300 tons of ice were jammed in her forepeak. She had 650 people on board, but got them all to port.

The *City of Berlin*, with a company of 700, had a similar

experience. In the spring of 1899 ten large tramp steamers were all put on the list of missing, and each of them was in the neighbourhood of the Newfoundland Banks when last heard of. Another bad ice year was 1909, when the ice peril was exceptionally severe.

It is generally believed that the two missing liners of the sixties, the *City of Washington* and the *City of Boston*, which disappeared with all hands, were lost by collision with icebergs.

PREVIOUS DISASTERS

	Lives lost
HMS Victoria, sunk after collision with HMS Camperdown, June 22, 1893	359
Elbe, sunk off Lowestoft, January 30, 1895	334
Reina Regence, Spanish cruiser, wrecked off Cape Trafalgar March 10, 1895	400
Colinia, wrecked off coast of Mexico, May 27, 1895	108
Drummond Castle, wrecked off Ushant, June 16, 1896	247
Saliar, wrecked off north coast of Spain, December 7, 1896	139
Aden, wrecked off Socotra, June 9, 1897	32
La Bourgogne, sunk after collision in Atlantic, July 4, 1898	546
Mohegan, wrecked on Manacles, October 14, 1898	107
Stella, wrecked off Casquets, March 30, 1899	105
City of Rio de Janeiro, wrecked off San Francisco, February 22, 1901	122
Cobra torpedo boat destroyer, sunk in a gale on the Outer Downing Shoal, Lincolnshire, 1901	67
Asian, Turkish transport, wrecked in Red Sea, April 1, 1901	180
Govermoria, lost in cyclone, Bay of Bengal, May 6, 1902	739
General Slocum, burnt, Long Island Sound, June 15, 1904	1020

Norge, emigrant ship, wrecked on Rocan Reef,
June 28, 1904   654
Mikasa, Admiral Togo's flagship, sunk by explosion
in her magazine, September 10, 1905   599
Hilda, wrecked off St Malo, November 19, 1905   125
Berlin, Great Eastern Harwich boat, driven by a
violent gale on to a pier at the Hook of Holland
and totally lost, February 21, 1907   141

(*Nottingham Evening News,* 16 April 1912)

FEARED LOSS OF ALL STEERAGE OCCUPANTS

But Relatives, for Lack of Money, Were Denied Tidings

That all the 800 steerage passengers of the *Titanic* went down with the liner after the collision with the iceberg was feared at first. While fortunes were spent by relatives of wealthy surviving and missing passengers for news incoming by wireless, there was no money to facilitate the obtaining of tiding anent the third-class passengers.

In the pitiful crowd of sad-faced men and women who remained on the pavement outside of the White Star offices were many who will not know the fate of relatives and friends for several days. The penalty of poverty will keep thousands in ignorance until the ships that searched for survivors over the *Titanic's* grave have made some port. For the names of steerage passengers are not being forwarded by wireless.

(*New York Call,* 17 April 1912)

THE FOUNDERING OF THE *TITANIC*

Details of the great ocean disaster are still lacking, but it seems clear that only some 868 persons were saved when the *Titanic* foundered in the early hours of Monday morning after collision with an iceberg.

The following message from the King was received last night by the White Star Company:

The Queen and I are horrified at the appalling disaster which has happened to the *Titanic* and at the terrible loss of life. We deeply sympathize with the bereaved relations, and feel for them in their great sorrow with all our hearts.

George R. and I.

Queen Alexandra telegraphed: 'It is with feelings of the deepest sorrow that I hear of the terrible disaster to the *Titanic* and of the awful loss of life. My heart is full of grief and sympathy for the bereaved families of those who have perished.'

All the circumstances combine to invest the loss of the mammoth liner with the sense of supreme tragedy.

She was on her maiden voyage; she was the last word in mechanical skill and daring as applied to shipbuilding; she was, it was fondly thought, all but danger-proof.

The floating township of more than 2300 souls left the Old World amid rejoicings; the New World was awaiting to welcome her.

And then, after four brief days, when the voyage should have been nearing its triumphal end, came the wireless cry out of the night. The great steamer had struck an iceberg and was in deadly peril.

Even then the belief in her power to reach port, crippled but not vanquished, was slow to die. Throughout Monday the world listened for the wireless messages that came from over the Atlantic. They were sadly conflicting, but they did not wholly extinguish the hope that the *Titanic*'s first voyage would not be her last. And they did suggest that the greater number of the passengers and crew would be safe.

Then, just after midnight yesterday, came the dread news that the *Titanic* had sunk. At first it was reported that the vessel had gone down without loss of life, but soon the extent of the disaster began to be revealed.

In special editions of the *Daily Graphic* the terrible story was briefly told. At that time the loss of life was thought to be some 1600, the number of the saved being returned as 675.

Now there is reason to hope that almost 200 more have been rescued by the Cunarder *Carpathia*, which reached the scene of the foundering some hours after it took place and picked the survivors up from the lifeboats to which they had committed themselves.

Beyond this there is nothing to minimize the remorseless extent of the disaster. Among the 1400 victims are believed to be scores of those whose names are familiar on both sides of the Atlantic – men such as the veteran journalist Mr W. T. Stead.

But in a disaster which overtakes the Anglo-Saxon race it is the men who wait behind to die, and the race will for long be proud to remember that it was the women and children on the *Titanic* who were saved, while the men went down with her. Of 248 names of the saved which have been reported only 79 are those of men.

Of the many liners that raced to the *Titanic*'s rescue the *Carpathia* was the only one, as far as is known, to be rewarded by the rescue of survivors. She is steaming to New York, and by President Taft's orders is to be met by a fast United States scout cruiser which, equipped with a powerful wireless installation, will transmit to the American Government the full list of the saved.

It was at first thought that liners like the *Virginian* and the *Parisian* might have survivors on board. This hope, however, is now abandoned, and to the *Carpathia*, and the *Carpathia* alone, the anxious eyes of friends and relatives are turning.

(*Daily Graphic*, 17 April 1912)

SAD SOUTHAMPTON

– From Our Special Correspondent

Southampton is a stricken town. More than 700 of the *Titanic's* crew were Southampton men, and there is scarcely a street in the town which has not given toll.

Eager crowds last night besieged the White Star offices, and anxiously packed Canute Road. They went home at midnight happy in the belief that the report, 'All saved' was correct.

But this morning brought a terrible awakening, and wives, mothers, sisters and sweethearts thronged the road outside the company's office from eight o'clock, and diminished and grew again throughout the whole of the day.

The message which was posted up soon after midday that 200 of the crew were on the *Carpathia* brought a gleam of hope, but with it a terrible nerve-racking suspense.

I stood by one woman for a few moments this afternoon. She had brought a sympathetic neighbour with her.

'Bill's sure to be all right, ain't he?' she suggested pathetically to her friend. 'He was always one of the lucky ones; look how he got out before.' The friend agreed eagerly.

The next moment a clerk made his appearance for a moment on the office steps. The crowd surged towards him with one tumultuous impulse, and fifty voices pleaded for news.

The boy looked abashed. 'We haven't any,' he said slowly and sorrowfully. 'As soon as we have we'll tell you.'

From time to time women with dragging steps and backward glances detached themselves from the crowd and went home to get tea for the children or – forlorn hope! – to see if by chance there were a telegram; for every wife knows that the company will not keep her in suspense a moment longer than can be helped.

At six o'clock a notice was posted on the west gate of the docks. Two constables stood guard by the few words upon a piece of foolscap telling that the names of the survivors among the crew would be posted there as soon as they were received. They would be received by wireless, and there might be delay, ran the words significantly; but from then onwards an ever-swelling crowd clustered about the gates and spread over the green.

The two stalwart Hampshire policemen were full of patience and tact. To every inquiry throughout the long evening (and they came at the rate of about ten to every sixty seconds) they replied kindly and sympathetically. They reiterated the same sad story, 'No news.'

One woman stood dry-eyed and haggard for hours. A baby was in her arms; two mites clung to her skirts. The children grew fretful, and wanted supper and bed. She soothed them in a whisper, and when at last the baby awoke with a whimper she fed it. It was like waiting at a pit mouth after some terrible mine disaster.

As I left to write this I heard a girl sobbingly say, 'And they were so proud to be on *Titanic* too.' It is the greatest tragedy Southampton has ever known.

(*Daily Graphic*, 17 April 1912)

THE TRAGEDY OF THE *TITANIC*

No element of tragedy seems to have failed to contribute its share to the overwhelming catastrophe of the *Titanic*. Not the least bitter aspect of this, perhaps, the greatest disaster in the grim record of the sea, was the confident news of the safety of every soul involved that came immediately with the announcement of the wreck and prevailed, and continued, indeed, to be strengthened, for many hours thereafter. In our earlier issues of yesterday there was every reason to believe with a great thankfulness that a mishap, pregnant with dread possibilities, had miraculously been spared loss of life. Most bitterly, and wringing with a dreadful poignancy hearts that had been bound up with relief and gratitude, this confidence has been falsified. The miracle was too great for man's endeavours to encompass. The forces of nature shook themselves free from the chains with which he would bind them, burst in all their power from the limits in which he has sought to confine them, and dealt him a blow that has sent mourning through two nations. His last word in ship construction, equipped with every last device making for safety, or for aid in case of need, met at her maiden issue with the sea a challenge that broke her utterly and took her in toll with over 1200 of the lives she carried.

The magnitude of such a disaster leaves the mind as incapable of expressing the emotions aroused in it as its agencies were powerless to avert the catastrophe. For years we take our eager, heedless way, demanding more and more of life, increasingly impatient of its hindrances to our pleasure and our business, increasingly bold and cunning in overcoming them, and never pausing but to congratulate ourselves upon our triumphs. Every now and then comes some cataclysmic reminder that, if it is not possible to go too far and too fast, it is very possible to congratulate ourselves too well. For a brief moment we are brought to a full stop. We are at such a full stop now; and the lightest among us can scarcely reflect upon its cause without bowed head and thoughts too deep for words. It is in that atmosphere that we trust the relatives of those who have perished may find some solace. They have been called upon to suffer a grief almost unendurable to bear; but at least they suffer it amidst that deepest sympathy which only when we are brought to face the realities of life can be aroused. For us, as for them, moreover, there is heartening thought in one thing that already can be read into the disaster from the facts that have come to light. It is now clear that the rescuing liners did not reach the *Titanic* until too late. It is terribly clear that scenes of most dreadful horror must have taken place in the few hours between her striking and her disappearance. And it is clear, finally, from the fact that women and children form by far the greater majority of the saved, that in this dire emergency the imperilled rose to supreme heights of courage and devotion. Millionaire and steerage emigrant alike were called upon: alike they have presented us with that most inspiring of all spectacles – the inherent nobility of mankind.

(*Daily Graphic*, 17 April 1912)

On 17 April most daily newspapers published a preliminary list of passengers rescued from the *Titanic* by the *Carpathia*, as sent from New York. The list contained numerous omissions and inaccuracies. For example railroad boss Charles M. Hays was listed as among those saved when it subsequently emerged that he had gone down with the ship. On the other hand, a quantity of passengers not included on this list – and who were therefore presumed lost – emerged safe and well when the *Carpathia* docked in New York. This initial round-up of names made grim reading for many that morning.

Abelsom, Anna	Angle, Wm.
Abbott, Rose	Allen, Miss E. W.
Allison, Master and nurse	Amadill, Miss Giorgetta
Andrews, Miss K. T.	Anderson, Mr H.
Appleton, Mrs E. D.	Appleton, Mrs Edward W.
Astor, Mrs John Jacob	Bailey, Mr and Mrs D. H.
Bassina, Miss A.	Brayton, Mr Geo.
Baxter, Mrs James	Beathem, Miss Lillian
Beckwith, Mr and Mrs R. L.	Blank, Mr H.
Bowen, Miss G. C.	Braham, Mrs
Bishop, Mr and Mrs D.	Brown, Mrs J. M.
Burns, Miss G. M.	Behr, Mr K. H.
Buchell, Mrs William	Barkworth, Mr A. H.
Bowerman, Mrs Eric	Brown, Edith
Brown, T. W. S.	Beale, E. D.
Beane, Mrs Ethel	Buyhl, Miss Dagran
Bystrom, Caroline	Balls, Mrs Ada E.
Bonnell, Miss C.	Buss, Miss Kate
Chiver, Paul	Cherry, Gladys
Chambers, Mr and Mrs V. C.	Carter, Mr and Mrs W. E.
Carter, Master	Cardell, Mrs Churchill
Calderhead, E. P.	Chandison, Mrs Victorine
Cornell, Mrs R. C.	Cavendish, Mrs Turrell and maid
Chafee, Mrs H. F.	Cardeza, Thomas
Cardeza, Mrs J. W.	Cummings, Mrs J. B.
Carter, Miss Lucille	Carter, William
Casselbere, Miss D. D.	Chibenaco, Mrs B.
Chibnall, Mrs E. M. B.	Clark, Mrs W. M.

Clarke, Mrs William

Crosbie, Mrs E. G.

Crosbie, Miss H. E.

Collyer, Mrs Charlotte

Christy, Miss Lulu

Cameron, Miss Clear

Caldwell, Mr Albert F.

Caldwell, Master Aiden G.

Charles, William

Duff-Gordon, Sir Cosmo and Lady

Daniel, Robert W.

Douglas, Miss Walter

Drachensted, Alfred

Durante, Leonora Asuncion

Doling, Mrs Ada

Drew, Mrs Lulu

Davis, Miss Agnes

Duran, Miss Fiorentina

Ellis, Miss

Emock, Philip

Fortune, Mrs

Frauenthal, Mrs

Francatelli, Miss

Erohliche, Margaret

Flynn, Mr J.

Faunthorpe, Miss Lizzie

Googht, James

Graham, Mrs Wm.

Graham, Mr

Goldenburg, Mrs Samuel

Greenfield, Mrs D.

Gibson, Mrs Leonard

Garside, Miss Ethel

Harris, Mrs L. Y. B.

Connell, Miss C.

Crosbie, Miss E. G.

Cummings, Miss

Christy, Mrs Alice

Clarke, Mrs Ada M.

Collett, Mrs Stuart

Caldwell, Mrs Sylvia

Carmacion, Benardom

Dessett, Miss

Dodge, Mrs Washington and son

Dick, Mr and Mrs

Davidson, Mr and Mrs Thornton

Daniel, Sarah

Douglas, Mrs Fred C.

Douglas, Mrs Robert

Doling, Miss Elsie

Driscoll, Miss B.

Davis, Master John M.

Davis, Miss Mary

Earnshaw, Miss Boulton

Fortune, Mabel

Frauenthal, Henry W.

Frauenthal, Mr and Mrs T. G.

Flegenheim, Miss Antoinetta

Futrelle, Mrs Jacques

Fortune, Miss Alice

Formerly, Miss Elein

Gracie, Colonel Archibald

Graham, Margaret

Gibson, Dorothy

Goldenburg, Ella

Greenfield, Wm.

Genivez, Mr Argene

Gerrcai, Mrs Marcy

Hays, Mr C. M.

Hays, Mrs C. M.

Hogeboom, Mrs J. C.

Haren, H.

Hewlett, Mrs Mary D.

Herman, Mrs Jane

Herman, Miss Alice

Hart, Mrs Asther

Harper, Miss

Hamalainer, Master

Hocking, Miss Nellie

Homer, H.

Harder, Mrs

Halverson, Mrs Alex

Henry, Mr and Mrs L.

Hanson, Miss Jennie

Hippach, Miss Jane

Ismay, Mr Bruce

Keane, Miss Nora

Kenyman (query Kenyon), F. A.

Keuchen, Emile

Laroche, Miss Louisa

Lamore, Mrs

Lehman, Miss Bertha

Leader, Mrs A. F.

Lesueur, Mr Gustave J.

Lindstroem, Mrs

Lines, Miss Mary C.

Longley, Miss G. F.

McGowan, Miss Annie

Mellinger, Mrs Elizabeth
    and child

Mallett, Master Andrero

Minahan, Miss

Maréchal, Pierre

Marvin, Mrs D. W.

Hays, Miss Margaret

Hawksford, W. J.

Hoyt, Mr and Mrs Fred M.

Harris, George

Herman, Miss Kate

Hold, Miss Annie

Hart, Miss Eva

Hamalainer, Anna

Hocking, Mrs Elizabeth

Holverson, Mrs A. O.

Harder, George

Hippach, Mrs Ida

Harris, Mrs H. B.

Healy, Miss Norah

Hososons, Miss E. Fame

Hooper, Mrs W. A.

Jacobsohn, Mrs Amy

Kelly, Miss Fannie

Kenehen, Miss Emile

Kimberley, Mr Ed

Leitch, Miss Jessie W.

Louch, Miss Alice

Lavory, Bertha

Leader, Mrs F. A.

Lindstroni, Mrs Sigfrid

Lines, Mrs Ernest H.

Longley, Miss G. R.

Mare, Mrs Florence

McDearmont, Miss Letitia

Mallett, Mrs A.

Mellicard, Madam

Mile, Mr

Maimy, Ruberia

Minahan, Mrs W. O.

Newell, Miss Madeleine

Newell, Mrs	Newson, Mrs Helen
Nye, Mrs Elizabeth	Omond, Mr Fiennad
Ostby, Mr E. C.	Ostby, Miss Helen R.
Panhard, Ninette	Peasry, Miss Kossi
Potter, Mrs T., Jun.	Potter, Mrs Thomas
Peachen, Major Arthur	Phillips, Miss Alice
Pailas, Emilio	Padro, Julian
Parish, Mrs L.	Portaluppi, Mrs Emilio
Quick, Mr Janeo	Quick, Miss Wennie
Quick, Miss Phyllis	Redone, Mrs Lillie
Ridsdale, Mrs Lucy	Rugg, Mrs Emily
Richard, Mr and Mrs Emile	Richard, Master
Rothschild, Mrs M.	Ranelt, Miss Appio
Renago, Mrs Maman J.	Rosenbaum, Edith
Rheims, Mrs George	Roberts, Miss
Robert, Mrs Edna S.	Rolmane, Mr C.
Ryerson, Miss Susan R.	Ryerson, Miss Emily
Ryerson, Mrs Arthur	Ryerson, John
Rothes, Countess of	Slayter, Miss Hilda
Smith, Mrs H.	Stewart, Mrs J.
Sharper, H. S. and manservant	Simonius, Col. Alfonso
Sincock, Miss Maude	Smith, Mrs Marion
Steffason, Mr W. B.	Stone, Mrs George M.
Segesser, Emma	Seward, Frederick
Shutter, Miss	Sloper, William T.
Swift, Mrs Frederick J.	Schabert, Mrs Pauline
Speddin, Mr and Mrs J. O.	Stahelin, Max
Smith, Mrs Lucien	Stephenson, Mrs Walter P.
Salomon, Abraham	Silvey, William B.
Skeliery, Mrs William	Stengel, Mr and Mrs
Spencer, Mrs W. A. and maid	Sheddell, Robert D.
Snyder, Mr and Mrs John	Saalfield, Adolph
Silverthorn, R. S.	Serepeca, Augusta
Tauusig, Ruth	Thor, Ella
Taylor, Mr and Mrs E. Z.	Tucker, Gilbert M.

Thayer, Mrs J. B.	Thayer, Mr J. B., Jun.
Trout, Mrs Jessie	Trout, Miss Edina
Tucker, Mrs and maid	Taussig, Emil
Villiers, Mme de	Ward, Mr and Mrs A.
Ward, Anna	Warren, Mrs F. M.
White, Mrs J. Stewart	Widener, Mrs Geo D. and maid
Willard, Miss C.	Wick, Miss Mary
Wilson, Helen A.	Woolner, Mr H.
Walter, Mrs	Washington, Mr
Weisse, Mrs Matilde	Webber, Miss Susan
Wright, Miss Marion	Watt, Miss Bessie
Watt, Miss Bertha	West, Mrs and two children
Wells, Mrs Addie	Wells, Miss J.
Wells, Ralph	Williams, Charles
Williams, Mr Richard M., Jun.	Young, Miss M.

SCENES IN LONDON

Inquiries of Distressed Relatives

The disaster of the *Titanic* made a profound sensation in the Metropolis yesterday, where folk had been reassured overnight by the reported rescue of all the passengers and crew only to be shocked again by the tragic news of the early morning.

From an early hour the officials were inundated by frantic inquiries by telegram and telephone, while as soon as the offices of the White Star Line in Leadenhall Street were open relatives and friends of passengers poured in and begged for news.

The flags of all the big shipping houses in Cockspur Street (where the West End offices of the line are situated) were flying at half-mast, and outside the offices of the White Star Line a crowd of continually increasing proportion gathered.

Many fashionably dressed women called at the office, and the red eyes of some betrayed that they had been weeping. All came with the hope that the names of their relatives were included with the lists issued, and when they learnt that this was not so, their emotions were touching to witness. One young lady burst into tears and had to be led outside.

The distress of the ladies was pitiful to see, and formed a striking contrast to the quiet way in which the men, with tight lips, received the news.

A dramatic incident was brought under the notice of a Press representative who was seated near a lady waiting at the office. She asked the reporter if there was any later information, and received a reply in the negative. He inquired if she had any relatives on board the *Titanic* and the reply was, 'Yes, my three children were going out to join their dad, and I was following next week.' On being informed that the name was 'Davis', the journalist scanned the list, and amongst the survivors found the names of Miss Agnes Davis, Miss Mary Davis and Master John Davis. He drew the lady's attention to the fact, when she almost collapsed with joy and exclaimed, 'Thank God, thank God.'

An athletic girl in a Harris tweed costume had her hopes dashed, but was told there might be better news if she came back in an hour and a half.

'How can I wait all that time?' she asked in agonized tones. 'It's an eternity.' Nevertheless she returned two hours later and when the name, which meant so much to her was not on the lists again, her composure gave way and she left sobbing.

(Daily News, 17 April 1912)

PATHETIC SCENES

INQUIRIES AT THE WHITE STAR OFFICES

Yesterday there was a constant stream of callers at the White Star offices in Leadenhall Street, City.

Unfortunately the London offices of the company seemed to be getting very little information, and little was known except that which was being received from the principal news agencies.

Information concerning seventy passengers had been received, and this was quickly typewritten and distributed.

Among those who called for news concerning relatives or friends, several were French people who had relatives who had embarked on the *Titanic* at Cherbourg.

Some pathetic scenes were witnessed. One elderly lady for some time walked up and down disconsolately in the offices, her eyes red with tears. Two nurses in uniform, after inspecting the list of those known to have been saved went away very agitatedly, one remarking to the other, 'I told you so. He is gone.'

Several shipping offices in the vicinity of the White Star premises are flying their flags at half mast.

A large crowd of people assembled outside the White Star offices in Cockspur Street yesterday, having been gathering since an early hour. Many of them had tear-stained eyes as they waited for news.

(*Western Daily Mercury*, 17 April 1912)

LONDON OFFICES BESIEGED

Scores of anxious inquirers paraded the front office of the White Star Company's premises up to a late hour last night. Many had waited from the early hours of the morning nursing the hope that the particular friend or relative in whom they were concerned might appear in the lists of the survivors. Some were doomed to disappointment, and as each additional list of saved passengers was posted their concern was tragically evident. Hopes which had been sustained during the long anxious day could be kept up no longer, and as the night hours advanced, and the cabled reports became fewer, optimism gave way to the worst fears.

One elderly woman, who with quiet fortitude and calm had waited for hours in the precincts of the offices, was almost overcome with joy after the sustained agony of the day, when late in the evening she found in one of the lists the name for which she had so long sought in vain.

Many who waited anxiously during the evening seemed prepared to maintain their vigil throughout the night, and every facility and comfort was given by the sympathetic and kindly disposed officials who sought as best they could to ease their anxiety.

(*Western Daily Mercury*, 17 April 1912)

CROWDS STAND ALL DAY IN RAIN, ANXIOUS FOR NEWS; MANY RUSH HERE FROM FAR-OFF CITIES

The crowds of anxious relatives and friends thronging the offices at the White Star Line at No. 9 Broadway in search of the latest tidings grew bigger yesterday and last night. The first contingent of out-of-town people, rushing frantically here to get information at first hand, reached Bowling Green Park, opposite the doors of the White Star Line, early yesterday morning.

New Yorkers who had inquired vainly the day before were there, but the poignancy of their grief had turned to settled gloom and hopelessness of manner.

The newcomers from the West, from New England and the South – white-haired mothers and fathers, young wives striving to suppress the outward signs of their mental torment, young children seeking information of parents, and now and then a young man anxiously asking concerning his sweetheart who was on her way to marry him in the new land where he had started a little home – renewed the scenes of unutterable sadness that had shattered the nerves of the White Star clerks and officials the day before.

A drizzling rain turned all outdoors to a grey and depressing nightmare, but the people kept coming in automobiles, carriages, on street cars and afoot and after inquiring in the offices and getting scant information, because there was little news to be had, joined the crowds outside in the rain, seemingly unable to leave the neighbourhood. From time to time they came back, asking over and over for further details. To the credit of the clerks be it said that those repeated questions were answered over and over with never failing courtesy and kindness.

In the early grey dawn Henry W. Taft, brother of President Taft, made his way up to the steps of the building and waited his turn to speak to the clerks. He was about to hand in his card when a young woman with tear-stained face hurried in and rushed up to the desk. Mr Taft drew back deferentially and waited while she volleyed hysterical questions about a brother who had been a passenger.

Finally he gave his card to the clerk and asked to see Vice-President Franklin. No one recognized the President's brother till then. He was instantly taken to Mr Franklin's offices, where he remained a short time and came down looking very sober.

He said that among other persons he had asked for information of Frank D. Millet, the artist, whom he had known well, and K. H. Behr, the tennis player, the latter reported as saved. Especially he had wished for information concerning the fate of Maj. A. W. Butt, the President's military aide. He shook his head sadly over the probable fate of Maj. Butt.

Mrs Benjamin Guggenheim, and her brother De Witt J. Saligman, who had spent most of the day previous at the offices waiting for information, were there again early yesterday, Mrs Guggenheim wearing the look of one who had not slept, but who was determined not to give up hope till the last.

Having assured themselves that there was no news from her husband, Mrs Guggenheim spoke sympathetically to several other waiting women and then went away. She returned during the day several times.

Though the crowd in the offices sat silent and wrapped in gloom between times, it took but the least rustle of excitement to throw it into a fever of expectancy. So when a clerk came out to say that word had been received that the *Mackay-Bennett* cable boat had left Halifax at 11 o'clock to go to the scene of the wreck and cruise about to pick up bodies, there was a rush in his direction that nearly took him off his feet.

One woman who had been told again and again as gently as

possible that her husband was not on the list of those saved, over-heard that the boat was 'to cruise and pick up bodies' and seeming for the first time to realize the awfulness of the reality, dropped suddenly in a pathetic little heap upon a bench.

Her head dropped to one side, and for a minute or two she was fanned strongly with a newspaper while a glass of water was pressed to her white lips. Then she came to, smiled faintly and whispered, 'How terrible it all is.' In a little while she was trying to encourage an old lady who had tottered in to ask about her daughter.

There was a note of rejoicing when a white-faced young man pressed about the bulletin board looking for the names of Mr and Mrs John Snyder of No. 61 Snyder avenue, Flatbush, Brooklyn, who had been passengers. Finally he found their names among those saved and rushed pell-mell out of the office crying to some-one outside: 'They are safe! They are safe!'

A pathetic atmosphere, suggestive of the friendliness of the immigrant in a strange land, hung over the steerage class offices on the floor below. Though the list of steerage passengers had been printed in the morning papers only two persons called to ask after relatives before noon.

(New York World, 18 April 1912)

THINK FIVE CARD SHARPS LOST

New York, April 17

Three and possibly five of a band of seven professional card sharps and confidence men who were aboard the *Titanic* when she struck an iceberg last Sunday night are known to be among those who went to the bottom of the ocean with the ship.

News of the drowning of 'Tom' McAuliffe, William Day and 'Peaches' Van Camp was received from George Homer and Ralph Bradley, two other members of the band, who sent wireless messages to friends in this city today informing them that they were aboard the *Carpathia*, but that McAuliffe, Day and Van Camp had gone down with the *Titanic*.

Another wireless message, which was received from the gamblers on the *Carpathia* by a well-known New York sporting man early this evening, said that the remaining members of the band, 'Buffalo' Murphy and James Gordon, had not been seen aboard the *Carpathia*, and that they, too, must have been drowned.

That the messages are authentic has not been doubted by those who received them as it is known to the recipients that the gamblers were aboard the *Titanic* when she left Southampton on April 10. Just before sailing one of the band cabled a friend in New York that they were about to sail and asked the friend to meet the band at the White Star Line pier with two taxicabs.

When the White Star Line officials made known the initial sailing date of the *Titanic* more than a score of New York confidence men and gamblers, who are known to the police of Scotland Yard, as well as New York, made a hurried trip to England.

Friends of the men in New York declare that at least three bands of card sharps were aboard the *Titanic* when she sailed. None of them sailed under his real name as that is not the custom with ocean gamblers.

(*Boston Post*, 18 April 1912)

CARPATHIA IN ROUGH WEATHER

Only Five Officers of the Titanic *Saved*

Official messages received yesterday hold out no hope that there are any survivors of the *Titanic* disaster beyond those on board the *Carpathia*.

According to the latest compilations there were on board:

316 first-class passengers
279 second-class
698 steerage
850 crew
2,143 total

It is stated that there are 705 survivors, so that the death toll is 1,438.

The following cablegram was received by the White Star Line last evening from their New York office: '*Carpathia* now in communication with Siasconset reports 705 survivors aboard.'

It is reported that the *Carpathia* has encountered rough weather, which put her out of wireless touch with other vessels for a long time.

She is expected to arrive at New York this evening, and until then full details of the disaster will not be available.

The principal officers of the *Titanic* went down with the ship, and only five of them (including a wireless operator) are reported to be among the saved.

The steamer *Mackay Bennett* has been sent from Halifax to search the scene of the disaster for bodies. Just prior to sailing she took on board 600 roughly constructed pine-wood coffins, and her passengers include an undertaker and a clergyman. It is believed that bodies will be given proper sea-burial as they are recovered.

(*Daily Sketch*, 18 April 1912)

TITANIC'S LAST MESSAGES

Liners which reached British shores yesterday report having received wireless messages from the *Titanic*. These messages, which must have been among the last the ill-fated liner sent, have a tragic significance now.

The most pathetic of the messages was received by the Cunarder *Caronia*, which arrived at Queenstown yesterday from New York with 697 passengers.

On Monday morning, at 4.39, the *Caronia* received from the *Titanic* a message stating that the White Star liner had been in collision with an iceberg, was in a sinking condition, and required immediate assistance.

Being about 700 miles distant from the *Titanic* Captain Barr knew that the *Caronia* could not reach the White Star liner in time to render help.

The Allan liner *Tunisian* on arriving at Liverpool yesterday from Canada reported that on Saturday midnight she spoke to the *Titanic* by wireless, sending the message: 'Good luck!'

To this the reply came: 'Many thanks, goodbye.'

The *Tunisian*, when 887 miles east of St John's, entered a huge icefield, through which she carefully picked her way for 24 hours, then stopped all night, and eventually turned 60 miles south. No fewer than 200 icebergs were seen.

The commander was on the bridge for a 36 hours' spell.

Still another wireless message from the *Titanic* was received on Sunday at 9pm by the United States Hydrographic Office at Baltimore. This read:

'German steamer *Amerika* reports passing two large icebergs, latitude 41.27, longitude 50.8.'

RUMOUR AND THE BALTIC

The wireless operator of the cable steamer *Minia* reports having received a message announcing that 250 of the *Titanic*'s passengers are on board the *Baltic*.

The message did not come from the *Baltic* direct, and the name of the steamer through which this news was re-transmitted is not known, but the same message states that the *Carpathia* had 760 survivors on board.

Captain De Carteret, of the *Minia*, confirms the operator's report about the picking up of the message, but does not vouch for its authenticity.

It should be added that it is not credited in New York.

A cablegram from Montreal received in London last night by the Allan Line says that the *Parisian* is delayed by fog. The captain reports that no *Titanic* passengers are on board, and he thinks that all the survivors are on board the *Carpathia*.

Captain Haddock, the commander of the *Olympic*, has sent to New York the following wireless message:

'Please allay rumours that the *Virginian* has any of the *Titanic*'s passengers. The *Tunisian* also has none, and I believe the only survivors are those on board the *Carpathia*.

'The Second, Third, Fourth and Fifth Officers and the second Marconi operator are the only officers reported to have been saved.'

(*Daily Graphic*, 18 April 1912)

THE SAILORS' WIVES
WOMEN'S WEARY VIGIL IN THE STREET
AT SOUTHAMPTON
PITEOUS SCENES

Southampton, Wednesday night

The shadow of death has hung over Southampton today like a black thunder cloud.

As the hours passed from dawn to midday-gloom of the eclipse, and soon to sunset and night, it ever became lower and blacker. In Canute Road, that street of tragedy, a common grief has made us all friends. Those who come and go from the White Star offices are questioned with pathetic eagerness. Four times today one woman, who has kept vigil with two tiny children for eight hours, asked me for news.

'Is there any hope?' she pleaded a few minutes ago. 'They must know something, those gentlemen in the office.'

'They know nothing,' I said. 'The moment they do they will tell you.'

She gave a pitiful little moan and turned away.

Early this afternoon the White Star Company, to obviate any danger of a crush when the names arrived, put up a great board outside the offices, and the centre of interest was immediately transferred here. From the dock gates a great crowd of men, women, and children hurried eagerly down the road. Something was being done. There must be news. But still the hours passed and the board remained bare. As afternoon grew to dusk an electric light was attached, and a shudder went round. 'It isn't coming till tonight, that message,' cried an elderly woman, and suddenly fell fainting.

Canute Road is dark now. The boys selling papers disturb a tragic stillness. No one speaks aloud near the fateful board. The looming shadow of death awes everyone to a whisper, but the tragedy is not over yet. We still wait. We still hope.

SISTERS IN SORROW

At the White Star offices in Cockspur Street there was again a steady stream of inquirers yesterday. Women in furs and velvet rubbed shoulders with others whose clothes were almost thread-bare. They were united in the common anxiety.

The clerks at the counter were seldom appealed to. The callers simply walked up to the notice board, and when they saw that no fresh news had come through they sat down to wait. Outside in Cockspur Street the police kept a large crowd on the move.

As soon as the City offices of the line were opened yesterday the telephone bell began ringing, and the clerks' voices were heard repeating again and again the sad and by now monotonous phrase, 'His name is not on the list.'

On the desks were to be seen prepaid telegraph forms, already filled in, which the officials, who throughout have shown the utmost sympathy with inquirers, had undertaken to dispatch directly the required name was received as that of a survivor.

(Daily Graphic, 18 April 1912)

TRAGIC HONEYMOONS

A Pathetic Phase of the Disaster

A peculiarly sad phase of the *Titanic* disaster is the number of honeymoon couples or newly married people on board. Among these were:

Col. and Mrs J. J. Astor, who were returning from their honeymoon tour in Egypt. Mrs Astor is reported to have been saved, while her husband is among the missing.

Mr and Mrs D. W. Marvin, returning to America after a three months' honeymoon tour in England. Mrs Marvin was rescued, but her husband, the son of the head of a large cinematograph firm, is believed to have drowned.

Mr and Mrs Beane, married at Norwich three days before *Titanic* sailed. Both saved.

Mr Sedgwick, an engineer, of St Helens, Lancs, married a week before leaving England to take up an appointment in South America. His bride was to have followed later. Not in the list of survivors.

Mr and Mrs McNamee, married a month ago, and neither in the list of survivors. Mr McNamee, one of the branch managers of Liptons, was on his way to take up a post in New York.

Mr and Mrs Marshall, on a honeymoon trip to California. Mr Marshall was a partner in a big boot business in Scotland.

Mr Alfred Davis [sic], of West Bromwich, married two days before the boat left. He was accompanied by his brother and his brother-in-law.

The Rev T. R. D. Byles, of Leeds, sailed in the *Titanic* for the purpose of officiating at the wedding of his brother which had been arranged to take place in New York on Sunday.

(Nottingham Evening News, 18 April 1912)

A SHIP OF SORROW

New York, 18 April

'The *Carpathia* is a ship of sorrow, with a company almost mad with grief,' said Mr Franklin, Vice-President of White Star Line today at noon, after having received messages from the Cunarder which is bringing to this city the survivors of the *Titanic*.

'Definite information,' said Mr Franklin, 'concerning the sinking of the vessel is absolutely unavailable. Many messages have been sent to the *Carpathia*, but we could get no response to our inquiries.

'I have received absolutely no details of the actual loss of the vessel, and we know nothing about what has happened, except such scrappy information as has been contained in the few authentic wireless messages received and already made public.

'Everyone on board the *Carpathia* is so overcome that no connected story can be obtained. I have had a code message from Mr Bruce Ismay but it relates to business and throws no light whatever on the tragedy.

'It has been stated that Mr Ismay would probably return by the *Cedric*, which now will sail tomorrow, instead of today, but I have no reason to believe that he intends to sail on the *Cedric*.'

(*Daily Chronicle*, 19 April 1912)

CHAPTER 6

TEARFUL REUNIONS

CARPATHIA LANDS 705 *TITANIC* SURVIVORS

Pathetic Scenes When Ship Docks

Lifted from the gates of death, the 705 survivors of the *Titanic* were landed last night by the *Carpathia*, which rescued them two hours and a half after the great White Star liner hurled itself against an iceberg last Sunday night. Disfigured by calamity and misery and oppressed by awful sorrow the women and children and the few men who escaped from the world's greatest marine disaster were in better physical condition than the most optimistic had hoped for.

Out of the great company that waited for hours in bitter cold among the grinding bergs, many of them thinly clad, many bruised and hurt by the collision which destroyed their ship, few needed the ministrations of physicians when they came out in sight of the vast crowd that had been waiting in almost unbearable uncertainty. Many, it is true, were weak and nervous and hysterical from an experience that had left the world cold and empty for them. But – and thousands thanked God for it as they watched – the majority of the saddened, bereaved company were well in body.

The unhappy company so marvellously torn from the grip of the sea was received solemnly and with remarkable quiet by the enormous crowd which gathered near the Cunard piers and by the few hundreds that penetrated by right of relation or friendship of merciful business to the interior of the pier. There was no cheering, no upraising of voices in salute of the living, for the thought of the dead was in their minds.

Only one of the *Titanic*'s survivors died while the *Carpathia* was driving through fogs and storms to this port.

The tragedy of the *Titanic* was written on the faces of nearly all of her survivors. Some, it is true, who were saved with their families, could not repress the joy and thankfulness that filled their hearts, but they were very few compared to the number of the rescued. These others bore the impress of their time of darkness when their people passed in an accident that seemed like an insane vision of the night. Their faces were swollen with weeping. They had drunk as deeply of sorrow as is ever given to humankind. But many, whose spirits were fainting from despair, walked firmly enough down the gangplank.

It was with difficulty that the tongues of many were loosened to speak of the scenes of agony and fear that fell over the *Titanic*'s peaceful company when it became swiftly known that the ship must go down. Some told haltingly, with dread still frozen in their eyes, of men who strove and struggled against women for the lifeboats and of officers shooting them down.

One woman saw an officer shoot two men, she said, and other passengers recalled how officers had stood with drawn pistols while the women and children were being guided into the boats. No one seemed to know of the exact fate of the *Titanic*'s captain, E.J. Smith. There was a story that he had committed suicide, but the *Carpathia*'s passengers did not know that was true.

(*New York Call*, 19 April 1912)

New York
At 8.20 p.m. last night the *Carpathia* had arrived opposite her dock. It was a wild night outside the harbour and a heavy fog hung over the bay as the rescue ship hurried up the channel. It

was raining drearily, and at intervals lightning lit up the big vessel with vivid flashes.

The crowd began to gather in the vicinity of the Cunard docks before dark, and as the hours wore on it became larger and larger.

Police Insp. McCluskey was in command, and he had at his disposal 300 men. Ropes were stretched across all the streets leading to the pier and the crowd was halted at Eleventh Avenue. Eleventh, Twelfth, Thirteenth and Fourteenth streets were blocked off.

Inside of the lines were grouped many automobiles, ambulances, and patrol wagons in readiness for use.

Relatives of the survivors gathered on the pier early. By direction of the Customs men, they arranged themselves in alphabetical sections so that there would be no confusion.

It was a sorrowful assembly. There was little talking and the only noise was the beating of the rain on the covered roof and the swishing of the tide as it ran strongly into the great slips on each side.

In one corner was a little knot of embalmers, sent under orders. White-uniformed ambulance surgeons were scattered here and there, their cases of instruments in their hands, prepared to minister to any sufferer.

When the news came that the *Carpathia* had passed the Battery, there was an air of tense expectancy, but no one moved from the place assigned to them.

Half a hundred black-garbed Sisters of Mercy were in the forefront of the crowd. There were a score of priests.

At 9.55 the first passenger walked down the gang plank. Three women were first off *Carpathia*. They did not wait for the boat to stop, but climbed down ladders and went through the freight elevator.

After the women came a sailor. He was followed by a man in a big brown raincoat and a soft hat. Next came a woman, who looked around as if startled. Then she screamed several times: 'Helen, Helen.'

Then followed other survivors. It was plain from the appearance of the survivors that they had lost all their clothing and had been fitted by the *Carpathia*'s passengers. Clothes did not fit and in many instances women wore sweaters. One wore an opera hat on her head and an old skirt that had several rents in it. She was immediately surrounded by several fashionably dressed women who assisted her from the dock.

Two women apparently violently insane were carried from the steamer, while there were scores of women in a state of coma and plainly mentally unsettled.

People on the dock surged forward as soon as the plank was made fast and the police were forced literally to fight them back. Most of the passengers who came now were plainly hysterical.

When Mrs John Jacob Astor left the ship she was at once taken in charge by the family physician, members of her family and the Astor family. She was assisted into an automobile and driven to the Astor home on Fifth Avenue. Mrs Astor left the automobile and walked into the house, unassisted. Once within the house, it was reported at midnight by members of the family that she collapsed, but rallied in a few moments.

Mrs Astor, because of her delicate condition, was allowed the captain's cabin for the trip home and was given the best care possible.

Bound for a farm in Manitoba, Mrs Esther Hart and her five-year-old daughter were among others that landed from the dreary *Carpathia*, having left her husband to his death on the sinking *Titanic*.

'My husband and I started for Manitoba to buy a farm,' said the little woman with quivering smile that was more pathetic than weeping. 'He sold all his property in London and we left on the *Titanic*. When the accident happened my husband had a place in the boat. He gave it up to a woman who came along. He kissed me and our little girl goodbye and said he would see us in New

York. He expected to be saved by another ship soon. But I guess he won't come now.'

(*Montreal Daily Star*, 19 April 1912)

Titanic survivor **Nellie Walcroft** described the scene that awaited her and her fellow passengers at New York.

When we arrived at New York it was about 8 o'clock and the steamers all round were making flash-light photographs of the *Carpathia* and passengers, and the reporters kept shouting at us for news. When we arrived at the pier we did not know that we should be allowed off the ship, but the gangway was put up and, having no customs to go through, having lost everything, we were allowed ashore. There were gentlemen from the Stock Exchange, Sisters-of-Mercy and ladies to meet us. We felt very dazed and strange. They took us and gave us necessary clothes and then I met my brother, and very glad I was.

They took us to a cab and we were 'flash-lighted' going along. 70,000 people were waiting, roped off, to see us. How glad we were to get to my sister and have a wash and go to bed again.

There were thirty-six women saved whose husbands were left on the *Titanic*. It was fearfully sad when they knew their husbands had gone. They had hoped to meet them in New York. When they were told that no more had been picked up they were in a terrible state. How much more fortunate were my friend and I than so many other poor things!

(*Maidenhead Advertiser*, 29 April 1912)

WANTED TO DIE WITH HER HUSBAND AND FIVE TIMES LEFT BOAT IN WHICH HE PLACED HER

By Post Correspondent
New York, April 18
When I met Mrs Jacques Futrelle here tonight after landing from

the *Carpathia* she was in a hysterical condition racked with grief because of the loss of her husband.

Friends and relatives from Boston met Mrs Futrelle. She had hoped to the last that on arriving in New York there would be news that her husband had survived the frightful disaster.

The grief of Mrs Futrelle was pitiful in the extreme when she learnt of the probable death of Mr Futrelle.

Not one of the survivors from the *Titanic* had a more heart-breaking tale. Surrounded by loving friends she told part of the terrible story.

Five times Mrs Futrelle was thrust into the lifeboat by her husband. Each time she returned crying that she wanted to die with him. Mr Futrelle finally induced her to remain in a lifeboat after explaining to her that he had on a life saving jacket and would take a chance of being rescued from the icy water.

Alone, he told her, he would be able to keep himself afloat but that with her in his arms both would surely be drowned.

The scene which took place as I sat in the room with Mrs Futrelle was most pathetic. There was not a dry eye in the room.

In the arms of her woman friends who sought to console her, Mrs Futrelle between hysterical sobs gasped out parts of the story of that horrible night. This is the story that Mrs Futrelle told me:

When the smash came Jack had retired. I was taking a bath. There was a frightful concussion. There was a rush of feet from every part of the boat.

There were screams of fright from the women. The terrible crashing sound as the ship struck the iceberg cannot be portrayed in words.

Jack sprung from his bed. I think it was about 10.30 when we struck the iceberg. He told me to dress as quick as possible and that he would go out on deck and find out what had happened. He was only half dressed when he left the state room.

When he returned within a few moments, I saw in his eyes that something terrible had happened. He was white and trembling a little, but cool.

'Come, dear,' he said. 'Come with me.'

With his arm around me we went out on deck. The scene was terrible. Women were screaming and clinging to the men. At this time the lights had not gone out.

The officers and crew were at their posts with drawn revolvers. Every effort was made to quiet the panic-stricken thousands. The officers shouted above the din that there was nothing to fear.

The half light showed the shadow of an iceberg. It seemed to me that the great ship had broken in two.

I don't know how long a time elapsed before the lifeboats were lowered, but it could have been but a short while after the boat struck.

The men in the first cabin, following the instructions of the officers, stood back and made way for the women and children. Oh, but they were brave! Knowing that they were going to their death, they smiled and assured their women, who were clinging to them in an agony of fear, that all would turn out right and urged them to get into the lifeboats.

The crew of the ship were urging all the men to put on life jackets.

When the rush of the men from the steerage came it was different. The men in the steerage poured up on the deck and fought like demons to get in the lifeboats. Oh, it was awful.

I will not attempt to quote Mrs Futrelle's description of her parting with her husband. It was a story of heroism, sacrifice and love for woman that deserves to go down in history.

Mrs Futrelle broke down completely when telling of her separation from Jack. She said that all about her, women were clinging to their husbands.

Mrs Futrelle was mercifully saved for a few hours from the terrible scenes which took place about her. The sea was alive with human beings crying for assistance. Great cakes of ice floated on the water and the intense cold killed many. 'When the dawn broke,' said Mrs Futrelle, 'I noticed that there were four women aboard and some men from steerage.'

Then came one of the most horrible experiences which could befall a human being. Mrs Futrelle told of seeing a man floating near the boat whom she thought was her husband. The man was encased in a life jacket. Urged by Mrs Futrelle the crew of the boat moved in the direction of the floating body.

She called out to the man, 'Jack, Jack,' and stretched out imploring hands. For an instant she was possessed of the wild hope that it might be her husband. Even to have secured his dead body would have been consolatory.

The boat pulled alongside of the man. It was not Jacques Futrelle.

To what depth of agonized disappointment Mrs Futrelle was plunged can only be imagined by one who heard her tell her heartbreaking story. The man was pulled aboard. Life was not extinct and an effort was made to resuscitate him. The effort was fruitless. The man died and his body remained in the boat with the terrified woman.

(*Boston Post*, 19 April 1912)

Returning to America on the *Titanic* following his wedding in France, forty-nine-year-old **Dr Henry W. Frauenthal** and his new bride, Clara, were two of the lucky ones. But the suffering he had witnessed would continue to haunt him.

When the ship first struck, none of us dreamed of the danger we faced. All who had been asleep after the first rush to the decks returned to their cabins to dress.

When the word came that we were sinking and the lifeboats were ordered over the side, the panic was fearful. From all sides came shrieks and groans and cries, and it seemed as if all the devils of hell had been let loose.

Just now I am so thankful to be alive that my appreciation of the horror is dulled. I am only afraid that when I recover from the first shock it will all come back to me again, and I would rather have gone down with the boat, I think, than have to live over again, even in my imagination, the last few minutes of that fearful night.

I would rather have stayed, too, than know that women went down with the *Titanic,* but I swear we thought every woman on the ship had been placed safely in the boats. It was 'women first' with all of the men, and at least it seemed as if the decks had been cleared of them, for not one was to be seen save those already lowered. Then the officers ordered the men to leave the sinking vessel and we left for the boats, not knowing, any one of us, I think, how many of our fellow men we were leaving behind as prey to death.

(US press, 19 April 1912)

Parisian passenger **George Rheims** had travelled first-class on the *Titanic* from Southampton to New York with his brother-in-law Joseph Loring. Rheims relived the sinking in a letter to his wife, dated 19 April 1912, in which he claimed to have witnessed the suicide of First Officer William Murdoch.

I dined with Joe Sunday evening and went up to my cabin to go to sleep around 11 p.m. I felt, being in the front part of the ship, a strong shock and heard a noise that sounded like steam escaping, it was dreadful. I thought we had an accident in the engine. After one fourth of an hour there was an announcement informing us that we had collided with an iceberg but that there was no danger and we should all go back to sleep!!! Since I noticed that the ship wasn't listing I thought nothing of it. Soon after Joe came to join me and we stayed together until the end. Around 11.30 all passengers left their cabins. The ship tilted more and more. An officer came to tell us to put on our life jackets. You can well imagine how this news affected me!

I went down to my cabin to put on some warm clothing and my life jacket. Joe did the same and rejoined me on the boat deck, where by now a crowd of people gathered. We started lowering the lifeboats down in the ocean – sixteen lifeboats for 3,000 people. The men were forbidden to use the lifeboats. A few men – traitors – did not hesitate to jump into the lifeboats just the same. In general the people's attitude was admirable. It took one and a half hours for all sixteen lifeboats to be lowered. A few of them were only half full. While the last boat was leaving, I saw an officer with a revolver fire a shot and kill a man who was trying to climb into it. As there remained nothing more to do, the officer told us, 'Gentlemen, each man for himself, goodbye.' He gave a military salute and then fired a bullet into his head. That's what I call a man!!!

We were about 1,500 people left on board without any means of escape. It was death for us all. I can not convey how calm everyone was. We said goodbye to all our friends and everyone prepared himself to die properly. Joe took both my hands and said, 'George, if you survive, look after my babies. If I live you will not have to worry about Mary.' I did not lose one second of composure and had decided to jump overboard to save myself by swimming. I can not describe the unbelievable things I saw at that moment. Suddenly the ship started nosediving and I was thrown to the deck by an explosion. I found myself entangled in chairs and ropes. I was able to free myself. Joe wanted to go back in the rear of the ship. I told him it would mean death and that he should follow me. He told me that he could not swim well enough. Then I took my momentum and jumped overboard. The fall seemed endless, then suddenly icy cold and a long plunge down into the ocean. When I came up again I started swimming vigorously to get away from the ship fearing that I would be dragged down with it. It was frightfully cold. Suddenly I saw the *Titanic* going straight down with horrible explosions and piercing screams. All the passengers were pressed against the railing like flies. There was a big whirlpool swirling movement, then silence. Suddenly there were pitiful pleas that I will never forget. It was all those who were able to float crying for help. It was atrociously grim, mysterious – supernatural. This lasted for half an hour, then all was quiet. The poor people went down.

I swam alone in the night, when at a distance I noticed a raft, half sunk and filled with men. It took me I suppose fifteen minutes to reach it. At first they refused to let me come aboard, but I was able to persuade them after all. I stood up on the raft. We were about twenty men and women, with icy water up to our thighs. We had to balance ourselves to avoid capsizing. I stayed six hours in my underwear, shaking with cold. Twice I thought of throwing myself into the ocean and each time the thought of you held me back. I regained courage and resumed – I don't know how – my efforts to stay on the raft. What a horrible night! We had to push back about ten poor people who wanted to climb aboard. We were filled to the limit. During the night eight people died from cold or desperation. I am sparing you the details for they are too frightful. I had the pleasure to be able to save a poor man, father of nine children, who asked me to give him a picture of myself with a dedication fit for the King of England. At 8.00 in the morning a lifeboat from the *Titanic* came to pick us up and took us aboard the *Carpathia*. They took marvellous care of us.

I had some trouble walking, my feet being frostbitten. I think that a little rest of a few days will do me a lot of good.

I affirm that I am a little tired. You must not hold it against me for ending this letter so abruptly.

WHITE STAR LINE WELCOMES INQUIRY, SAYS MR FRANKLIN

A tense feeling of expectancy pervaded the city, especially downtown all morning yesterday, and the officials of the White Star Line showed the great strain under which they are suffering in their every word and motion. From earliest dawn till the actual word came that the *Carpathia* had been sighted at Sandy Hook rumours ran rife that she would be delayed possibly till this morning, because of the rain and the fog that had settled over the harbour in the forenoon.

Vice-President Franklin of the White Star Line declared all day that he had no direct communication from the *Carpathia*, but through the Cunard Line he received one or two messages indicating that the ship was making her way right along and that he expected her to reach Sandy Hook by seven o'clock and her dock some time between nine and ten. The event proved that he was right and that the prognosticators of delay were wrong.

Mr Franklin admitted that he had received during the day personal messages from J. Bruce Ismay, managing director of White Star Line. It was learnt that one of these messages dealt with the engaging of rooms at the Ritz-Carlton for Mr and Mrs Ismay. Mr Franklin said that he was sure Mr Ismay was under the deepest distress because of the disaster, but he denied a rumour that Mr Ismay was mentally unbalanced.

'We will know nothing till the ship docks,' said Mr Franklin, 'concerning the condition of her passengers. As a precautionary measure we have ordered several ambulances and we have also retained physicians and taken all other measures for the relief of any sick, injured or destitute aboard the *Carpathia*. There must be some, but we have no specific news of any.

'The White Star Line,' added Mr Franklin, 'finds itself in a very unpleasant situation owing to what we consider unfair and unjust criticism. We have given the Press every atom of information we have been able to get just as soon as we could get it. Yet we are constantly accused of holding back important news. We are doing all we can to relieve the situation. Yet one would think to read the papers, that we are acting in a cruel and high-handed manner towards the survivors.

'I wish to say that the White Star Line, so far from trying to escape any government inquiry, courts and solicits such an inquiry by both the US and British governments. These inquiries cannot be too broad for us, and if they result in the adoption of any measures calculated to prevent the recurrence of such a disaster as the *Titanic*'s loss the White Star Line will be only too thankful that such has been the outcome.

'Mr Ismay will not shirk his duty, nor will any other officer at the company. All the information the Senate committee seeks will be cheerfully afforded and we will co-operate in every way with the committee.'

A report was current that J. P. Morgan had intended to return to New York on the *Titanic*'s maiden trip, but had changed his mind some weeks ago. Henry C. Frick and Mrs Frick had engaged state rooms but owing to an accident to Mrs Frick in Europe the state rooms were transferred to Mr Morgan, who later cancelled the engagement, so ran the report. The story could not be verified at the White Star offices.

(*New York World*, 19 April 1912)

BOATS FOR 1,178
MR BUXTON'S STATEMENT IN THE COMMONS

A clear statement on the number of boats and life-saving appliances carried by the *Titanic* was made yesterday in the House of Commons by the President of the Board of Trade in answer to questions.

'Coming to the actual facts of the case,' said Mr Buxton, 'the present rule of the Board of Trade with regard to shipping of 10,000 tons and upwards requires a minimum boat accommodation of 9,625 cubic feet (that is, sixteen boats under davits with a capacity of 5,500 cubic feet and an addition of 75 per cent, in the shape of other boats, rafts, etc). This would provide for about 960 persons.

'The *Titanic* actually carried sixteen boats under davits, with accommodation for 990 persons, and four Engelhardt boats accommodating 188 persons in addition. That is, altogether, accommodation for 1,178 persons. Besides these, there were 48 lifebuoys and 3,560 lifebelts.

'The total number of passengers and crew which the vessel was certified to carry was 3,547, and on the recent voyage the actual number on board when the vessel left Queenstown was 2,208.'

Mr Buxton began his statement by explaining that the Board of Trade were empowered by Sec. 427 of the Merchant Shipping Act, 1894, to make rules for life-saving appliances on British ships, and Sec. 428 required owner and master to give effect to the rules.

The rules now in force were originally drawn up in 1890, and revised in 1894 and subsequently, and prescribed a scale indicating the minimum number of boats to be provided in accordance with the gross tonnage of the ship.

The highest provision made in this scale was for vessels of 10,000 tons and upwards. In view of the increased size of modern passenger steamers the Board of Trade early last year referred to the Advisory Committee on Merchant Shipping the question of the revision of the rules, and in particular the provision to be made in the case of steamers of very large size.

After considering this report, together with the views of their expert advisers, the Board of Trade were not satisfied that the increased provision recommended by the Advisory Committee was altogether adequate. After additional investigations and tests in regard to the best type and proportions of lifeboats, the Board within the last few days referred the question back to the Committee for further examination.

Boats For All Unnecessary

He did not desire to forecast in any way the result of the inquiry which would be held into the loss of the *Titanic*, or any modification of policy that might be necessitated by the finding of that inquiry or by the new situation created by the present disaster. He wished the House, however, to understand quite clearly that up to the present it had never been the intention of the Board of Trade regulations, and so far as he knew it had not been suggested by any responsible expert authority, that every vessel, however large and however well equipped as regarded watertight compartments, should necessarily carry lifeboats adequate to accommodate all on board.

(*Daily Graphic*, 19 April 1912)

'TO MY FELLOW SUFFERERS'

Touching Message From The Wife Of The Captain

The following message from Mrs E. J. Smith, widow of Captain Smith, was posted at Southampton yesterday afternoon.

'To my poor fellow sufferers: My heart overflows with grief for you all, and is laden with sorrow that you are weighed down with this terrible burden that has been thrust upon us.

'May God be with us and comfort us all. – Yours in deep sympathy, Eleanor Smith.'

(*Daily Graphic*, 19 April 1912)

WEEPING CROWDS BESIEGE PIERS

Friends of Steerage Survivors Learn Record Was Not Kept

Another drama of sorrow, rage and despair was enacted around the Cunard dock yesterday, where Thursday night the pier groaned beneath the weight of grief and joy when the rescue ship *Carpathia* brought *Titanic* survivors to land.

It was the relatives and friends of the steerage passengers of the wrecked liner who haunted the pier yesterday. The night previous while loved ones of those on the first and second cabin list of the *Titanic* were given passes to the pier and permitted to strain their hearts for those succoured from the leviathan that was, a pitiful crowd of poorly dressed men, women and children from the East Side pleaded and stormed behind police lines for the same privilege. They were denied access to the pier. Those whom they sought to see were hurried off to hospitals, Salvation Army homes, the Municipal Lodging House, and missions. Not a glimpse did they get of anxious loved ones.

When the last of the survivors had been taken off and the pier was cleared, this crowd of the disappointed invaded the dock. Then it was that officials remembered that in the hurry and excitement of the landing no record had been kept of where the steerage passengers were sent. Grief-stricken men and women poured out their hearts in protestation and appeal, but officials could give them no news of their loved ones.

The arrival of the *Carpathia* with the survivors of the *Titanic* disaster did not diminish the crowds of anxious-faced persons at the White Star offices in Bowling Green yesterday.

Many went there refusing to believe that the published lists of survivors were complete and hoping to find that relatives and friends might by chance have been on the rescue ship.

(*New York Call*, 20 April 1912)

ACUTEST MISERY INFLICTED UPON SURVIVORS OF *TITANIC'S* STEERAGE

While great physical suffering was endured by all of the survivors of the *Titanic*, the most acute privation fell to the lot of the steerage passengers, many of whom lost not only husbands, fathers, children and relatives but all their worldly belongings, to be thrust penniless upon a foreign shore. That much of the misery inflicted upon the poor third-class passengers was preventable was made apparent by the stories told by the steerage survivors landed by the *Carpathia*.

Of the thrilling stories of the disaster one had a happy ending. It was told by Mrs Leah Aks, who is on her way to Norfolk, Virginia, with her eight-month-old baby, Philip, to join her husband, Samuel Aks, a tailor. The father has never seen the baby.

Mrs Aks says that when the alarm was given she ran into her room to arouse other women sleeping there and to get her baby. Carrying her child wrapped in a shawl, she tried to make her way up the stairs leading to the boat deck, but the jam of struggling humanity was too great for her to get past. Four sailors who saw her told her they would lift her and the baby to the boat deck from the outside. One of the sailors climbed the rail and swung himself to the deck above, and the other three formed a human ladder, passing the woman and her child from one level to another.

Nadji Narsani, an Armenian peasant, died with the *Titanic*. Maria Narsani, his widow, is about to become a mother.

No greater in death was John Jacob Astor than Nadji Narsani, who kissed his wife, placed her in the small boat and said: 'Maria, perhaps we may never meet again: but some day you tell our child how I died.'

Perhaps the master of millions and the peasant stood together at the rail as the sea carried off their hopes and loves, but that chapter in the *Titanic* tragedy will never be written, the story of just what happened when the small boats floated off and left millionaire and peasant, savant and deckhand to wait for death.

When Maria Narsani stepped off the steerage gangway of the *Carpathia* she was at once the ward of charity.

The jewels, a king's ransom, of Madeline Force Astor, went down with the ship, but Maria Narsani lost everything she had in the world, the linens she had made against the day of her marriage, and Nadji had saved up $100 in addition to the price of the steamship tickets, and this, too, was lost.

C. M. Hays, president of the Grand Trunk Line, and Jim Hawkins perished. Six months ago old man Hawkins died in Ireland and left his son and widow a little farm and a home. They sold these and mother and son started for America. They were going to the northwest. Jim was to work as a farmhand.

'And we were going to have a farm ourselves some day,' said his mother. 'Jim was a strapping boy. He could have been saved, but he gave his place to a lady.'

(*New York Call*, 20 April 1912)

Some of the survivors' accounts as reported in the jingoistic American press were wildly inaccurate. Blaming Britain for the loss of so many American passengers, newspapers revelled in the opportunity to depict the British officers as little more than callous murderers. A typical story was that attributed to **Ellen Shine**, a twenty-year-old steerage passenger from Cork in Ireland who had been on her way to visit her brother in New York.

> Those who were able to get out of bed went to the upper decks, where they were met by the members of the crew, and first and second class passengers, who endeavoured to keep them in the steerage quarters. However, the women rushed by the officers and crew, knocking them down, and finally reached the upper decks. There the women, when they saw the excitement and when informed that the boat was sinking, got down on their knees and started to pray.
>
> I saw one of the lifeboats and made for it. In it were four men from steerage. They were ordered out by an officer and they refused to leave. Then one of the officers jumped into the boat and, drawing a revolver, shot them dead. Their bodies were picked out from the bottom of the boat and thrown into the water. In this boat there were about forty women and men, and we were drifting about for more than four hours before we were picked up.
>
> (*New York Call*, 20 April 1912)

The 'Unsinkable' **Molly Brown**'s reported story also had a number of holes in it.

A story shockingly brutal in contrast with the tales of heroism and sacrifice that have come from the *Titanic* disaster was told by

Mrs J. J. Brown of Denver, Colorado, one of the survivors who is stopping at the Ritz-Carlton.

Col. Astor and Isidor Straus and Mrs Straus would have been saved had it not been for the officers in command of the first lifeboat, Mrs Brown declares. In addition to this, she accused the officer of having made Mrs Astor row the lifeboat for two hours and also says she was compelled to handle the oars for four hours herself.

'We'll teach these rich Yankee wives we're running things,' the officer sneered, she says, when the women in the boat pleaded with him to save a man who was drowning close to the boat, and he refused. Mrs Brown's story follows:

I was in one of the lifeboats – the first to be made ready – when Col. Astor and his wife came out. The colonel helped Mrs Astor in the boat, then got in himself, as there was plenty of room. 'Get out!' shouted the officer. 'All right, sir,' Col. Astor replied politely. And he got out of the boat.

Col. Astor was very nice about it. He told the officer there was plenty of room in the boat, and he would like to be with his wife, if possible, because she was ill. Then he lit a cigarette he had taken from his pocket and walked into the saloon. That was the last I saw of him.

It was only a minute or so later when almost the same scene was repeated, Mrs Brown said:

Mr and Mrs Straus came out of the saloon, and both took seats in the boat, in which there was still plenty of room. 'Get out of this boat: it's for the women,' the officer said. All the ladies in the boat protested that Mr Straus should remain. They pointed to the empty seats.

Mr Straus, however, said of course he would get out and did so. It was then that Mrs Straus, saying that she would not leave his side, started to follow him out of the boat, despite his protests. He begged her to retain her seat, saying he would get in another boat.

'No, if you get out I will follow you,' Mrs Straus said, and clambered out of the boat. The ladies again protested to the officer, who was firm in his refusal to allow Mr Straus in the boat. Mrs Straus walked away with her husband clinging to her. After the *Titanic* had sunk, the officer started to bulldoze the women, Mrs Brown says, and commanded them to man the oars.

'I rowed until my arms ached as though they would fall off,' she continued. 'It must have been fully four hours. Mrs Astor was compelled to row, too. She was rowing about half as long as I was.'

There was ample room in the lifeboats for all the first and second cabin passengers, Mrs Brown declares. She saw several leave the ship with plenty of room in them.

(*New York Call*, 20 April 1912)

Stoker **William Jones** was quoted as claiming that many passengers and crew were killed on impact.

I was on watch in the steerage with about 100 other members of the crew when the first crash came. It was almost immediately followed by the explosion of the forward boiler, which controlled the turbines.

I rushed on deck and was told with two firemen to man lifeboat no. 8. About sixty women were crowded into the little craft with us, and we put off immediately, pulling with all the strength that we could muster because we knew that the ship was doomed, and that if we did not get far enough away from her we would be pulled down by the suction.

Of the 300 members of the crew that were in the quarters forward but 47 that I know of managed to get away. They were crushed when she struck. The same death came to the first cabin passengers that were quartered forward. Practically none of those that were in that section of the ship managed to get out of the wreckage in the crash. Those that were not killed outright remained where they were pinned and went down with the ship.

(*New York Call*, 20 April 1912)

LITTLE BOY'S STORY OF LOSS OF *TITANIC*

Little Arthur Olsen, eight years old, the only *Titanic* child left unclaimed after the *Carpathia*'s arrival Thursday night, said yesterday that America was a pretty good place, and that he was going to like it.

Arthur came to that conclusion because so many people had been good to him. First there was Fritzjof Madsen, one of the survivors, who took care of him in the lifeboat. Then Miss Jean Campbell gave him hot coffee and sandwiches and propped him comfortably against some clothing while she busied herself with others.

Mrs William K. Vanderbilt Jnr next appeared with two nice big men, put him in a taxi with Miss Campbell and sent him to a hot bath and bed at the Lisa Day Nursery, No. 458 West 20th Street. And the next morning Miss Florence Hayden taught him kinder-garten songs and dances with her class.

Later Arthur's stepmother, Mrs Esther Olsen, of No. 978 Hart Street, Brooklyn, appeared and clasped him in her arms. Her husband, Arthur's father, Charlie Olsen, perished in the wreck.

Mrs Olsen had never seen Arthur, because after Charlie Olsen's first wife died in Trondhjem, Norway, leaving the little baby Arthur, he had come to America, where he married again. A while ago Olsen crossed to see about the settlement of his estate and to bring his son home. He and the boy were in the steerage of the *Titanic*.

Arthur is a sturdy, quiet-faced little chap with red hair, freck-les and a ready smile. He speaks only Norwegian, but Mrs Olsen translated for him when he told his story.

I was with papa on the boat, said the youngster timidly, and then something was the matter. Papa said I should hurry up and go into the boat and be a good boy. We had a friend, Fritzjof Madsen, with us from our town, and he told me to go too.

The ship was kind of shivering and everybody was running around. We kept getting quite close down to the water, and the water was quiet, like a lake. Then I got into a boat and that was all I saw of papa. I saw a lot of people floating around drowning or trying to snatch at our boat. Then all of a sudden I saw Mr Madsen swimming next to the boat and he was pulled in. He took good care of me.

In our boat everybody was crying and sighing. I kept very quiet. One man got very crazy, then cried just like a little baby. Another man jumped right into the sea and he was gone.

It was awful cold in the boat but I was dressed warm, like we dress in Norway. I had to put on my clothes when my papa told me to on the big ship. I couldn't talk to anybody, because I don't understand the language. Only Mr Madsen talked to me and told me not to be afraid, and I wasn't afraid.

(*New York World*, 20 April 1912)

LOST LINER'S TRAGEDY

The largest ship in the world went to sea from Southampton harbour on the tenth of April, 1912. People spoke of the tenth of April as a great day in the history of Southampton, for many fathers of families had found employment on the *Titanic*, many women's faces were lightened because the shadow of need and poverty had been banished from their homes.

It was a day that no one who stood upon the quayside will ever forget. We who saw it saw a sight that will be unforgettable until our eyes are turned to dust. We saw the sight of the mightiest vessel in the world upon her solitary and uncompleted voyage. She was named *Titanic* and she has been *Titanic* in her sorrow. We saw her, the mightiest, finest product of human brains in the matter of ships to sail the sea, a gigantic vessel that realized in her being a floating city of treasured glories, riches, and luxury, as she first ploughed the grey fields of the ocean.

And her displacement of water, the foam, and the rush of her passage was so tremendous that the stern ropes of another mighty liner parted and the *New York*, but for the ready aid of holding tugs, would have swung out aimlessly into the fairway.

We paused in our cheering then, chilled to a sudden silence at this first evidence of the great ship's untested powers for evil as for good. And our cheering now is hushed into sobbing, for within a week of her majestic passage from Southampton harbour, the displacement of the *Titanic* has been so tremendous that she has drenched the bosom of the world in an ocean of tears.

Those of us who had come to wish the vessel 'Good speed' – in the dark wisdom of Providence to wish 'Good speed' and 'a fair journey' to those loved ones who were going out upon the longest and loneliest voyage in Eternity – were up 'by times' on that pleasant Wednesday morning, long before the stroke of noon when we knew Captain Smith would climb into his lofty perch on the navigating bridge and give the order to 'let go' from the Trafalgar landing stage.

The air was busy with chatter, with 'goodbye for the present' and good wishes. We lived that morning in an atmosphere of pride. All these happy-faced Southampton women were proud that their men had entered into service on the greatest vessel ever built by man. They prattled of the *Titanic* with a sort of suggestion of proprietorship.

Rumours and legends and tales of her glories and luxuries and powers were bandied about in every street in Southampton. She was a caravanserai of marvels; a mighty treasure house of beauty and luxurious ease. In the phrase of the people, she was 'the last word'. The phrases of the people are often true, because they are double edged.

Another phrase sticks now in the puzzle of a darkening mind: 'They're breaking all records this time.' And so they were. It had been determined that the *Titanic* should excel in luxury and equipment her sister vessel, the *Olympic*, which had sailed for New York a week before.

And in a sort of desperate endeavour to achieve this we who had come to take temporary parting from dear ones and friends were shown a new and latest marvel on the promenade deck of the *Titanic*. It was called the Café Parisien. Its walls were covered with a delicate trellis work around which trailed cool foliage. We looked at the soft-cushioned chairs, we regarded the comfort of the whole scene, and, feeling the suggestive atmosphere of the place, thought of those who would be taking coffee there after dinner with music lulling every sense, melting into the gentle roll and rhythm of the open sea. What a place in which to dream! – perhaps if one were young to hold a little romantic dalliance – what a place in which to forget the trials and harass of the world! What a place in which to sleep!

Some of us looked into the private suites that were to cost a mere trifle of £870 a voyage, and here we found snug dining rooms, bedrooms that looked in themselves like little enchanted palaces of slumberous rest, and private promenade decks.

Let us note that everyone spoke of 'dining rooms' and 'bedrooms'. The word 'cabin' would have been an anachronism in this floating citadel of luxurious beauty. We examined the delicate glass and napery, the flowers and the fruit, the baths and the playing-courts, and the innumerable mechanical appliances that seemed to make personal effort or discomfort the only human impossibility on board.

There was one thing that no one looking even for a brief half-hour on this cushioned lap of luxury ever thought of giving a cursory glance or a thought. No one looked at the boats.

Punctually at noon Captain E. J. Smith, a typical figure of an English sailor as we knew him and imagined him in pre-*Titanic* days, took up his post of captainship on the navigating bridge. And as the bells sounded, the cheers of the multitudes went upward and hands and handkerchiefs were waved from quay and ship's side, and kisses were blown across and last familiar greetings exchanged.

So she went away with her human freight of 2,208 souls. We cheered to the last and waved our salutations, and that night I think there was not an unhappy woman in all Southampton. And tonight – who is to count the tear-stained faces or to cast a reckoning over the travail of these broken hearts, some here, some 2,000 miles away, but all united beyond the cleavage of the pitiless seas, by the sacred companionship of sorrow!

So the *Titanic* went her way, and we went ours, and thought perhaps little about her, save thoughts of remembered joy in her strength and beauty, until on Tuesday morning came the news that smote our hearts with the thunder of doom. These were, of course, the first indefinite rumblings that woke fear in every human breast.

She had struck an iceberg; she had been rent; but she was unsinkable. She was heading slowly for shore, a great giant wounded thing in the wake of the *Virginian*. How our hopes died down until it seemed that the heart was burnt into a heap of dead cold ashes, only to rise, Phoenix-like, in jubilant and hopeful expectancy. Human lips have sobbed out strange prayers before today, but what volume of prayer went up to heaven in thankfulness to the Lord of Hosts who had brought the new wonder of wireless telegraphy out of the slow womb of time.

We thought of that unforgettable message speeding through the viewless air that is marked upon the chart sheets SOS. We picked up the common phrase of the operator and repeated to ourselves: 'Save Our Souls', and thanked Providence for their salvation.

We pictured the scene. The lonely operator, composed with that old English valiance that has turned the blood of history into wine, calmly tapping out the cry of help. We saw the realization of that message in the operator's cabin on other vessels. We saw the wonderful chain composed of those three words, stronger than wind or sea, suddenly dragging all the vessels within the sphere of hearing away from their allotted course, and sending them on the great adventure of succour and mercy. We pictured them racing along the railless roads of the open sea, rushing with insensate speed towards the spot of the catastrophe. We had leisure to imagine the scene, because we were told there had been a great deliverance; because we felt that man had fought his battle with the ocean and had won.

Then we knew that we had lost.

All the world knows how slowly those confessions of defeat came in upon us, how slowly the last flicker of an expiring hope was beaten down within our breasts, with what dilatory hands the veils were drawn from the implacable face of doom. Gradually the hush laid hold upon us, gradually a realisation of what had happened sank into our souls.

We knew that nothing but a miserable residue of the great human freightage had been saved to us. We knew that the enchanted floating palace, conceived by the brain of man and wrought by his hands, with all its mighty scheme of luxurious ease, health, and comfort, lay somewhere tangled in an old sea forest, two miles beneath the quiet surface of the sea. Little more do we know as I write. We can only hear the sobbing of the women at the street corners of Southampton, and find in them an eternal echo of the cheers with which we sent the *Titanic* out on her first, her last, her only voyage.

(*Daily Graphic*, 20 April 1912)

SURVIVORS' THRILLING STORIES

'Nearer My God To Thee' Played By
Orchestra As Titanic *Settled*

Mr W. C. Chambers, one of the *Titanic*'s survivors, interviewed by a Central News reporter, said the *Titanic* struck the iceberg head on. The passengers came running out on deck, but believing that the ship could not sink, and being assured that this was so by the liner's officers, they went back to their state rooms again.

After about two hours, however, the alarm was sent round, and the passengers started to enter the lifeboats. There was nothing in the way of a panic at first, as everybody believed there were plenty of lifeboats to go around.

After the lifeboat in which he was seated had gone about four hundred yards from the ship they saw the *Titanic* begin to settle down very quickly. It was then that there was a rush for the remaining boats, and one was swamped.

So far as his own boat was concerned, she created no suction. No shots were fired. There was nothing of that kind. Of those who were rescued from the *Titanic*, seven were subsequently buried at sea, four being sailors and three passengers. Two rescued women had gone insane.

As the liner continued to gradually recede into the trough of the sea the passengers marched towards the stern. The orchestra belonging to the first cabin assembled on deck as the liner was going down and played 'Nearer My God to Thee'.

Mr and Mrs Isidor Straus were drowned together, Mrs Straus refusing to leave her husband's side. They went to their deaths together, standing arm in arm on the first cabin deck of the *Titanic*.

Mr C. H. Stengel, a first class passenger, said that when the *Titanic* struck the iceberg the impact was terrific, and great blocks of ice were thrown on the deck, killing a number of people. The stern of the vessel rose in the air, and people ran shrieking from their berths below.

Women and children, some of the former naturally hysterical, having been rapidly separated from husbands, brothers, and fathers, were quickly placed in boats by the sailors who, like their officers, it was stated, were heard by some survivors to threaten that they would shoot if male passengers attempted to get into the boats ahead of the women.

Mr Stengel added that a number of men threw themselves into the sea when they saw that there was no chance of their reaching the boats. He himself dropped overboard, caught hold of the gunwale of a boat, and was pulled in because there were not enough sailors to handle her. In some of the boats women were shrieking for their husbands, others were weeping, but many bravely took a turn with the oars.

Mrs Dickinson Bishop, of Detroit, Michigan, said: 'I was in my bed when the crash came. I got up and dressed quickly, but being assured that there was no danger I went back to bed. There were few people on deck when I got there, and there was little or no panic.'

Mr Robert Daniel, of Richmond, Virginia, said: 'I jumped overboard, and I reckon that over a thousand did likewise. I swam about in the icy water for an hour before being picked up by a boat. At that moment I saw the *Titanic* take her final plunge. It was awful.

'Colonel Astor has gone down. So has Major Butt and Mr W. T. Stead. I believe they jumped into the sea. I was in a state of collapse when picked up, and there are scores of survivors seriously ill. Captain Smith stuck to the bridge and behaved like a hero.'

William Jones, a fireman, of Southampton, who was making his first trip, said that when the *Titanic* sank four of her lifeboats were swamped. He also declared that her boilers exploded, and that ice from the berg falling on her decks killed many people.

(*Daily Graphic,* 20 April 1912)

An extremely pathetic instance of the disaster is the separation of families and fathers and mothers from their children. Seven babies, who may never be identified and whose parents, or mothers at least, perished in the *Titanic* horror, were brought ashore last night from the *Carpathia* by the nurses sent aboard from hospitals.

They are now being tenderly cared for in one of the New York foundling asylums. No one has claimed them, nor can it yet be ascertained to whom they belong. These babies were thrown into the lifeboats by their parents.

No one knows their names, and their clothing gives no clue to identity. They are all under the age of two years.

In addition to these seven infants, who are well and supremely contented under the tender ministrations of Roman Catholic nuns, are two other children, respectively five and four years of age.

They are nameless as far as the other survivors know. The poor children are both insane. One has scarlet fever, and the other has cerebral meningitis. The doctors do not believe that either will live.

In the frenzy of the departure from the sinking *Titanic* nobody remembers what parents hurled their beloved babies into the water, hoping that they might be saved, and all efforts by the authorities to have the survivors on the *Carpathia* identify them have failed.

A little one-year-old baby boy, Travers Allison, cried himself to sleep at the Manhattan Hotel in the early hours of this morning. He was attended by his nursemaid, who is ill herself.

This little lad is the sole survivor of a family of four, Mr H. J. Allison, a banker of Montreal, his wife and their three-year-old daughter, Lorraine.

This family of four, with Mrs Allison's maid and Travers's nursemaid, embarked on the fated liner, and when the time came to get into the lifeboats, there being no room for Mr Allison, his wife refused to leave him, and the little daughter, Lorraine, clung to her mother.

The three were left to go to their death in the icy sea when the women and children were sent off, but Mr Allison sent the servant with the baby boy in one of the first of the boats to get away. Relatives are coming on from Montreal to claim the child, who is the heir to a large fortune.

(*Daily Chronicle*, 20 April 1912)

HALF-EMPTY BOATS

Three French-speaking survivors, M. Pierre Maréchal, aviator; M. Omont, a Havre manufacturer; and M. Chevré, the Canadian sculptor, have sent *Le Matin* a graphic description of their experiences.

We were quietly playing auction bridge with a Mr Smith of Philadelphia, they say, when we heard a violent noise similar to that produced by the screw racing. Through the portholes we saw ice rubbing against the ship's sides. We rushed on deck, and saw that the *Titanic* had a tremendous list. There was everywhere a momentary panic, but it speedily subsided, all being convinced that the *Titanic* could not founder.

Captain Smith nevertheless appeared nervous; he came down on deck chewing a toothpick. 'Let everyone,' he said, 'put on a lifebelt, it is more prudent.' He then ordered the boats to be put out. The band continued. Nobody wanted to go into the boats, everyone saying 'What's the use?' and firmly believing there was no risk in remaining on board. Then some of the boats went away with very few passengers; we saw boats with only about fifteen persons in them. Disregarding the advice of the officers, many passengers continued to cling to the ship.

A particularly painful episode occurred on board the *Titanic* after all the boats had left. Some of the passengers who had remained on the ship, realizing too late that she was lost, tried to launch a collapsible boat which they had great difficulty in getting into shape. They succeeded in lowering it, and some fifty got in. It was soon half full of water and many occupants were drowned or perished with cold, the bodies of those who died being thrown out. Of the original fifty, only fifteen were picked up by the *Carpathia*.

Much useless sacrifice of life, they add, would have been avoided but for the blind faith in the unsinkableness of the ship and if all the places in the boats had been taken in time.

(*Daily News*, 20 April 1912)

SURVIVORS' STORY

Criticisms and Recommendations

A committee of passengers on the *Titanic* rescued on the *Carpathia*, gave out, on the arrival of that vessel at New York on Thursday evening, the following narrative, which had been prepared for the Press:

> We, the undersigned surviving passengers of the *Titanic*, in order to forestall any sensational and exaggerated statements, deem it our duty to give the Press a statement of the facts which have come to our knowledge and which we believe to be true.
>
> On Sunday, 14 April 1912, at about 11.40 on a cold, starlit night, the ship struck an iceberg which had been reported to the bridge by the lookout, but not early enough to avoid collision. Steps were taken to ascertain the damage and save the passengers and the ship. Orders were given to put on lifebelts. The boats were lowered, and the usual distress signals were sent out by wireless telegraphy, and rockets were fired at intervals. Fortunately a wireless message was received by the *Carpathia* about midnight. She arrived on the scene of the disaster about 4 a.m. on Monday.
>
> The officers and crew of the *Carpathia* had been preparing all night for the rescue work and for the comfort of the survivors. They were received on board with the most touching care and kindness. Every attention was given to all, irrespective of class. Passengers, officers, and crew gladly gave up their state rooms, clothing, and comforts for our benefit. All honour to them.
>
> The English Board of Trade passengers' certificate on board the *Titanic* allowed for a total of approximately 3,500. The same certificate called for lifeboat accommodation for approximately 950 in the following boats: – 14 large lifeboats, two smaller boats, four collapsible boats. Life preservers were accessible in apparently

sufficient number for all on board. The approximate number of passengers carried at the time of the collision was: first-class, 330; second-class, 320; third-class, 750; total, 1,400. Officers and crew, 940; total 2,340. Of the foregoing about the following number were rescued by the *Carpathia*: first-class, 210; second, 125; third, 200; officers, 4; seamen, 39; stewards, 96; firemen, 71; total of crew, 210; passengers and crew (about), 775; total of missing (about) 1,565. The number saved was about eighty per cent of the maximum capacity of the lifeboats.

We feel it our duty to call the attention of the public to what we consider the inadequate supply of life-saving appliances provided for modern passenger steamships, and recommend that immediate steps be taken to compel passenger steamers to carry sufficient boats to accommodate the maximum number of people carried on board. The following facts were observed and should be considered in this connection. In addition to the insufficiency of the lifeboats, rafts, etc. there was a lack of trained seamen to man the same. Stokers, stewards, etc., are not efficient boat-handlers. There were not enough officers to carry out the emergency orders on the bridge and to superintend the launching and control of the lifeboats, and there was an absence of searchlights. The Board of Trade rules allow for entirely too many people in each boat to permit that to be properly handled. On the *Titanic* the boat deck was about 75ft above water; and subsequently the passengers were required to embark before the lowering of the boats, thus endangering the operation and preventing the taking on of the maximum number that the boats would hold. The boats at all times to be properly equipped with provisions, water lamps, compasses, light, etc. Life-saving boat drills should be more frequent and thoroughly carried out, and officers should be armed at boat drill. A great reduction in speed in fog and ice – as the damage if a collision actually occurs is liable to be less.

In conclusion we suggest that an international conference should be called, and we recommend the passage of identical laws providing for the safety of all at sea. We urge the United States Government to take the initiative as soon as possible.

This statement was signed by Mr Samuel Goldenburg, chairman of the Passengers' Committee, and 25 others.

(*Southampton Times and Hampshire Express*, 20 April 1912)

AMONG THE MOURNERS

Some Heart-rending Stories

That there will very soon be urgent necessity for bringing into operation the fund for the relief of sufferers by the disaster is evident from the result of inquiries which have been made in parts of the town from which members of the *Titanic's* crew were drawn in a conspicuous measure. To take St Mary's Parish, for instance. The Rev. Arthur Cuming, called upon on Thursday evening as being likely to be informed of the amount of distress to be relieved among a class typical of the seafaring population of the town, said that cases of dire necessity called for immediate assistance. An indication of the extent to which the clergy of St Mary's systemacize their work, though no show was made of it, was found in the fact that the rev. gentleman had by him a list of 61 'cases' in the parish arising out of the disaster. Commenting upon the particulars of these which had already been obtained, Mr Cuming said that the majority of the 61 were young men who had been wholly or partially supporting their parents. The disaster had intensified the distress which had been felt most acutely in the poorest districts as the effect of the coal strike and consequent lack of employment, and many of the St Mary's men had sailed on the *Titanic* after having been out of work for weeks.

The worst case that Mr Cuming had yet heard of was that of Mrs Wardner, of Endle Street, and her eight children (referred to below). This he recommended, and he next mentioned the case of Mr and Mrs Perry, of Ryde Street, who had two sons on board, upon whom they were dependent. As particularly good examples of sons who helped their mothers, he named young Evans, of Deal Street, and Binstead, of Endle Street, without, of course, wishing to detract from any other similar cases. (The list of saved includes the names of Perry, Evans and Binstead). Mrs Hurst, of Chapel Road, had been left a widow with three quite young children, and two or three orphans had been left by Mrs Wallis, a stewardess on the vessel, who was a widow.

The Rev E. G. Wells, another of St Mary's curates, was also seen, and he said that several sad cases had come under his notice. In Coleman Street a fireman had left a widow and four children, and in the same thoroughfare at least two other family circles had been broken. In another case where the breadwinner had been taken away, the mother had recently had her family increased by the arrival of a twin.

In the course of some personal inquiries at the homes of men whose names were to be found in the list of the crew, our reporters ascertained that College Street seems to have been hit somewhat heavily, eight men from this thoroughfare having joined the ship. One or two of them were single, but others had been the sole support of families. A young fireman named Blackman had been the mainstay of his mother, who was left a widow some years ago with nine children. The landlady of a young man named Jewell said her lodger had looked after his old father down in Cornwall, from whom she had received pitiful messages appealing to her to send news of his son.

(Yesterday she was able to send glad news to the aged parent.)

Married Three Days Before Sailing

In Richmond Street there was a widow of a steward named Whitford at 33, and next door was given as the address of another steward named Brookman who had, in fact, been living there with his aunt, but had set up a home of his own at the Polygon having been married on the Sunday previous to his sailing on the *Titanic*.

At No. 10 a third steward had been the sole support of his mother, and on the opposite side of the road had lived Frederick Dall, who shipped on the ill-fated liner as fireman.

(His name appears among the saved.)

A curious incident was related at 38, Anderson's Road. In one list of the crew which had been published, the name of A. Burrows was given in connection with that address, while in another list Oliver was printed. It turned out that neither a Burrows nor an Oliver had shipped from that address. Mrs Burrows was to be seen there, however, and she said: 'My son Harry goes to sea, and he had stayed home for a month on the expectation of getting engaged on the *Titanic*. He went down to the Docks to sign on, but at the last moment changed his mind and came away, for which we are very thankful. I can't explain why he changed his mind; some sort of feeling came over him, he told me.'

Mrs Saunders, of Albert Road, mourns the loss of a son who had been a 'good boy' to her. He had followed the sea for some years, having been transferred from the *Adriatic* to the *Olympic*. Lately he had been unwell, and dropped out of the *Olympic*. When he recovered, he was transferred to the *Titanic*. Mrs Saunders said she had suffered terribly from anxiety. 'I have bought two and three papers a day in the hope of seeing his name among the saved, but it seems that I shall never see him again.'

In the case of C. Mills (saved), of the same thoroughfare, it appeared that his only son sailed in the R.M.S.P. *Tagus* on the same day that the father left in the *Titanic*. The lad was just beginning his sea career, and he left his father on Wednesday in high spirits. Mills was on the *Olympic* at the time of the collision in the Solent with the cruiser *Hawke*. Another butcher, H. G. Hensford, living in Malmesbury Road, would have reached his twenty-seventh birthday on Wednesday. He was married about three months ago.

Three consecutive houses in Threefield Lane were keenly concerned. In one, a fireman named McRae has left a wife and two children; next door, a young man named Dilley had been a lodger; and in the third house had lived a young man named

King, who perished in the disaster. A little lower down an able seaman, named Bradley, resided, and he has left a widow, and there were other cases in the street.

Four Trimmers Who Missed the Ship

Inquiries in Chantry Road led to the discovery that in one house there resided four men, all of whom signed to sail in the *Titanic*, but arrived at the quay-side too late to get on board. They were the three brothers Slade and another trimmer named Penney. They left home together to go to the ship, but when they arrived the gangway had been removed, and they were told they could go home again. Mrs Slade was seen by our representative, and her first words were, 'What a good job they missed their ship! I have thanked God for it ever since.' 'How did they miss the boat?' was asked. 'I can't tell you exactly, but they left home in good time. Somehow or other my boys did not seem very keen on going in the ship. You may not believe in dreams, but I am telling you the truth when I say that one of my boys had a dream about the boat the night before sailing-day, and he afterwards said that he had a dread of her. I knew they were not very keen on going, but nevertheless they went down. The engineer called to them to get on board, but for some reason they didn't go. The boys had had a great deal of unemployment lately. Mr Penney has been out of work since just before Christmas, and my eldest boy has only earned £2 10s in four months.'

In other houses in Chantry Road there was keen sorrow for lost ones. A greaser named Kearl has left a wife and one young son, and two men named Clench and Edwards, residing at No. 10, have perished. The most distressing case in the district, however, was discovered in Endle Street, where the wife of a fireman named F. Wardner has been left with a family of eight young children. The youngest was but a few months old, and Wardner had lately been out of a ship. He was in the *Olympic* when she and the *Hawke* collided, but during the last six weeks he has been out of work.

He took the job on the *Titanic* somewhat eagerly in consequence, and has lost his life. Another fireman, named Bennett, who went down on the *Titanic*, also served on the *Olympic* at the time of the collision. He helped to support his father and mother, and has a brother on the *Armadale Castle*.

There are two or three cases in which brothers have died together. In Cawte Road an old sea captain has to mourn the loss of two sons, whilst of two step-brothers, Fredk. Dall, of Richmond Street, and Charles Olive, of College Street – the latter is believed to have perished. In Ryde Terrace, an aged couple named Perry feared that they had lost their two sons, who were their sole source of support, but the name of one appears in the list of survivors.

No doubt there are many distressing cases in other parts of the town, but the foregoing will serve to indicate the severity of the blow which has fallen on Southampton.

(*Southampton Times and Hampshire Express*, 20 April 1912)

BANDSMEN HEROES WENT DOWN PLAYING BEAUTIFUL HYMN

Not since the wreck of the *Birkenhead*, when brave troops lined up on the side of the deck of the sinking ship, and went down at the salute to a watery grave, has there been so stirring an exhibition of sublime heroism as that shown by the bandsmen of the *Titanic*.

From narratives of survivors it is clear that after the liner crashed into the iceberg, and it was deemed advisable to transfer the women to the boats. the band lined up on deck and began to play operatic and other lively airs in order to allay any excitement among the passengers.

Few among those on board at that time realized that the ship was doomed, but when the worst became known, and lifeboats were making away for safety, the spirit of the music was changed, and the beautiful hymn, 'Nearer, my God, to Thee', was played with deep religious feeling by the bandsmen as the ship was fast sinking. It was a fitting end to a solemn and terrible tragedy.

The leader of the orchestra, Mr Wallace Hartley, of Dewsbury, whose aged parents, though terribly distressed by the loss of their son, are proud to think that he faced the end with such courage.

He toured for three years with the Carl Rosa Opera Co. and for three years with the Moody-Manners Co.

Attracted by the possibilities and the pay on board an ocean liner, he secured the post of bandmaster with the Cunard Co., and was on the *Mauretania* and the *Lusitania*.

When he arrived back in Liverpool on Tuesday week Mr Black, the musical director for the Cunard and White Star Companies, asked him to direct the orchestra of eight for the *Titanic*'s first voyage.

Mr Hartley was not anxious, according to the father, to accept the offer, but finally agreed to go, and proceeded to Southampton only a day after his arrival in Liverpool.

After every voyage his sweetheart, Miss Robinson, eldest daughter of the late Mr Robinson, a well-known Holbech manufacturer, was in the habit of meeting him at Liverpool, and Mr Hartley invariably paid a visit to his parents at Dewsbury. He had resolved to leave the sea and to marry in about three months' time.

(*Liverpool Evening Express*, 20 April 1912)

TITANIC SURVIVOR WEDS OREGON MAN

Fiancé Missed Her at the Pier and Did
Not Locate Her Until Friday

Miss Marion Wright, a young Englishwoman, one of the rescued *Titanic*'s passengers, was married at 11 o'clock yesterday morning in St Christopher's Chapel at No. 211 Fulton Street, to Arthur Woolcott, a fruit grower of Cottage Grove, Oregon. There is romance for you.

Engaged to Mr Woolcott for the past year, Miss Wright came from her home in Yeovil, Somerset, England, to marry him here.

He, to meet her when the *Titanic* arrived, came from Oregon to this city last Monday.

Imagination is not capable of drawing the picture of last Monday morning – Mr Woolcott starting white-faced from his breakfast at the Grand Union Hotel, and Miss Wright looking hopelessly from her seat in a lifeboat upon a sea of ice cakes, that did not promise even the faintest hope of rescue. Neither then expected to meet the other again.

Mr Woolcott is 32; his bride 26. When the young man learnt that the *Titanic* had sunk he sought to learn the names of the saved, but the list was slow in coming, and when it was flashed by wireless there were so many errors it was imprudent to even hope that his sweetheart, who was in the second cabin, had escaped. At length the tension lessened with authoritative news.

Among the first to stand watch at the Cunard pier on Thursday night was Woolcott. His fiancée had been unable to get through to him a wireless message saying that her health was unimpaired. He heard all of the wild rumours flying about the pier that scores of survivors were dying on the *Carpathia*, and that others were hopelessly maimed.

Keen-eyed though he was, Woolcott did not see the young woman leave the ship. Frantically he rushed onto the vessel. He was told that Miss Wright had landed. He did not believe it. He believed then that she had been lost and that this fact had been concealed through an error in the wireless.

Miss Wright, on failing to see her sweetheart, roamed around the pier, but she could not find Woolcott. Then she went to No. 204 West 128th Street with Mrs Bessie Watt of Edinburgh, and the latter's daughter, Bertha, 14, both of whom had been saved from the *Titanic*.

This was not known to Woolcott. From the Grand Union Hotel he called up all of the hospitals and vainly asked for his fiancée. Miss Wright, unable to explain his failure to find her, called up all of the hotels. On Friday afternoon, while he was still searching anxiously for her, she learnt that he was stopping at the Grand

Union. She left her address. When he returned, practically heart-broken, to the hotel in the evening, the information was given to him. He went to No. 204 West 128th Street and his fiancée answered the ring at the door.

Yesterday morning they secured a marriage licence at the City Hall. Mrs Watt and her brother, Harry Milne, went with them. The Rev. J. Wilson Sutton accompanied them to St Christopher's Chapel and performed the ceremony.

'She was very cool,' said Mr Sutton in speaking about it after-wards. 'She could not have been less frightened at the prospect of matrimony than if she had to experience another *Titanic* wreck.'

(*New York World*, 21 April 1912)

FIRST OFFICER KNEW OF ICEBERG AHEAD 15 MINUTES BEFORE THE *TITANIC* STRUCK

That First Officer Murdoch of the *Titanic* committed suicide because he had known a quarter of an hour before she struck that the liner was headed for an iceberg was only one detail of the story told by Thomas Whiteley, first saloon steward, to a *World* reporter last night. Whiteley is at St Vincent's Hospital receiving treatment for feet and legs frostbitten and bruised by the falls of a boat tackle on the night of the disaster.

People lingered long over their dinners Sunday night, he said. Just before the doors closed at 9.30 Chief Surgeon O'Laughlin got up in his chair at the head of his table, which was next to the one I served. In his hand was a glass of champagne.

'Here's to the mighty *Titanic*!' he said. 'Long may she defy the seas!'

Captain Smith dined as usual at the head of his own table, Mr Andrews on his right, on his left a very beautiful woman who always wore white furs of great richness, but whose name I did not know. Mr Ismay during the whole trip sat at one of the small tables for two persons. Throughout the voyage he was always served by the head waiter; always he ate alone.

When the alarm was rung we began rounding up people and started the boats off, beginning forward on the port side and working around to the starboard, from aft to forward. John Jacob Astor could not have helped anyone into boats after Mrs Astor was put into the lifeboat, for no one was allowed to do that but the people of the ship. But I saw him just outside the smoking room. I knew him well, for he sat at the next table to mine in the saloon.

'Steward,' he said to me, 'are we going to pull through?'

'Don't you doubt it, sir,' I answered, 'she's good for seven or eight hours yet.' We all believed she was practically unsinkable.

He took out his cigarette case and handed me a cigarette. Then he lit one himself. I saw him go into the smoking room and sit down. It was only a few minutes later that the end came. I believe Mr Astor met his death there.

The last boat was just pulling off. The order had come to slash the falls and all but one was cut. I was told to leap for it. My foot, as I went over the side, caught in the fall and I was badly burnt, though I never found it out till I reached the *Carpathia*. Of course I went down. Somehow I cut myself loose from that rope and arose amidst a lot of wreckage as the *Titanic* was sinking. Four Italians and I clung to a state room wardrobe that floated up from the wreck. One by one, the others dropped off, overcome by the cold.

Then I drifted near the overturned boat of Second Officer Lightoller. There was no room for me. By and by one of the men died and I took his place. As we stood there, each man holding on to his neighbour's shoulders, fearful every moment that some lurch would send me off again into that icy water, two of the men I knew had been on watch in the crow's nest that night spoke up.

'It's no wonder Mr Murdoch shot himself,' said one to the other. I asked them why.

'From the crow's nest we sighted the iceberg that hit us at 11.15,' he replied. 'I at once reported it to Mr Murdoch. It was not white, but a sort of bluish colour, plainly distinguishable against the clear sky. Twice afterwards I reported the berg to Mr Murdoch. I could not see that he at all varied the *Titanic*'s course. He knew he should have changed his course. He shot himself because he knew it.'

Now, I carry an old gold watch of my father's that has always kept fair time, and that I was in the habit of setting every day by the ship's time. My watch showed 11.30 when the ship struck. The time I read here in the newspapers must be wrong. I believe from that that Mr Murdoch must have known about the iceberg a quarter of an hour before we struck.

(New York World, 21 April 1912)

TITANIC'S ENGINES RACING TOP SPEED WHEN SHE HIT

Two injured members of the *Titanic*'s crew in the infirmary of St Vincent's Hospital believe they hold between them the key to the two vital facts of her disaster. John Thompson, fireman, with a broken arm, occupies the cot next to Thomas Whiteley, first saloon steward, who in yesterday's *World* testified that First Officer Murdoch shot himself because he had known a quarter of an hour before she struck that the *Titanic* was headed for an iceberg. Whiteley told the *World* reporter yesterday that he had not a word to add or take away from that statement or any other in his narrative.

Thompson's faith in the accuracy of New York reporters grew after he had read the exact presentation of his shipmate's story in *The World* and he broke the silence, which he had stolidly maintained, as to events in the *Titanic*'s stokehole and engine room to tell *The World* man.

That top speed was maintained from the beginning to the end of the *Titanic*'s fatal course. That she was speeded uniformly as close to 77 revolutions as could be. That she was racing at the utmost capacity of her engines when she ripped off her plates on the iceberg.

John Thompson is forty-two years old and hails from Liverpool.

From Queenstown out, he said, all the firemen had been talking of the orders we had to fire her up as hard as we possibly could. We were to make as quick a passage as possible, the orders ran, and we were to beat all records on our maiden trip. I heard that these orders came from the engineering department. But, bless you, we men didn't have time to talk about where those orders came from. There was no spare time whatever for any of us firemen.

We were carrying full pressure. From the time we left Queenstown until the moment of the shock we never ceased to make from 74 to 77 revolutions. It never went below 74 and as during that whole Sunday we had been keeping up to 77, surely she must have been making that speed then.

At 11 we were called to be ready to go on watch at 12. Our quarters were in the forecastle. We felt the crash with all its force up there in the eyes of the ship and my mates and I were all thrown sprawling from our bunks. It was a harsh, grinding sound, as if everything were being torn out of her. I judge it must have lasted at least five minutes, until she came to a standstill. I ran on deck and found the forward well-deck covered with masses of ice torn from the berg. We went below to grab some clothes. Our leading fireman, William Small, rushes in, and shouts, 'All hands below!' But we had no chance to go down the tunnels to the fireroom, for the water was rising and plainly to be seen. So we had to go up on the main deck. Next the leading fireman rushes up there and orders us back to get lifebelts and go on the boat-deck.

We put out again for the forecastle, got our lifebelts on and then up to the boat-deck. The chief officer wanted to know what in hell we were doing up there and sent us down to the sun-deck. We walked about there, watching her sink.

About one o'clock the chief officer called us all up again to hoist up a pair of lifeboats. The first we launched was No. 16 from starboard. On the port-side we put off the rest, with two collapsibles on the boat-deck. Two other collapsibles were on a platform alongside the funnels, 12ft at least above the boat-deck, and we had to slide them down to the deck on planks, for launching. By that time the water was rising right onto the boat-deck, and Captain Smith sings out:

'Every man for himself!'

Next thing she parted in two. I managed to get into the collapsible boat we had on the planks, in which there were twenty-seven altogether, with one woman from the steerage. We were washed over the side. The boat went right under water with the weight of us as we rowed away from the *Titanic*.

Captain Smith was standing within five feet of me at the time our lifeboat went over the side, with nobody between us. He was swept away with the rush of water. He had two lifebelts on, one on his stomach and another over his neck and chest. As he went overboard he shouted, 'Every man for himself!' That was the last I saw of him.

On the collapsible we drifted out from the *Titanic*'s side. We could not have been more than twenty or thirty yards away when we saw the stern end coming right up in the air. On it there were hundreds of human beings. Next came the explosion. It was like a waterspout, filled with black things that must have been bits of iron. Then she glided down, headed straight for the bottom.

We had no oars or other means of moving our boat and there we stuck, standing knee-deep in water, till the Fourth Officer came up in one of the sail lifeboats and picked us up. I was told to get up the ladder when we reached the *Carpathia*'s side. But I found I could not use my right arm. So they lowered a boat-swain's chair and hoisted me up. I remembered then that my arm must have been broken by the forward one of a broken set of davits as the collapsible was washed against it when we went off the deck. The cold of that night was so intense that when we got to the *Carpathia* my jaws were tight locked together as if with lockjaw.

It was common talk on the *Carpathia* about the 'money boat' Mr Whiteley told you of yesterday. I think another reason why First Officer Murdoch shot himself may perhaps be found in the story of that boat, for the story runs among the men that he was there when the millionaire's boat was loaded.

(*New York World*, 22 April 1912)

HEROIC PRIESTS GAVE UP LIVES TO QUIET CROWDS

Two priests of the Roman Catholic Church went down on the *Titanic* with men and women grouped about them responding to prayers. Not only Catholics, but Protestants and Jews, realizing that their last hour was at hand, took part in the final religious service on the sloping deck of the *Titanic* as she was heading downward for the depths.

One of the clergymen was Rev. Thomas R. Byles of Westminster Parish, London, who was on his way to this city to officiate at the marriage of his brother in Brooklyn. The other was a German priest who spoke the Hungarian language in addition to his own. Father Byles was in the first cabin. The German priest was in the third cabin. The name of the German priest has not been ascertained.

Both priests celebrated mass for the steerage passengers Sunday morning. Father Byles delivered a sermon in English and French, the other in German and Hungarian. Strangely enough each of the priests spoke of the necessity of man having a lifeboat in the shape of religious consolation at hand in case of spiritual shipwreck.

After the *Titanic* struck, Father Byles made his way to the steerage. He was active in getting the steerage passengers up to the boat deck and assisting women and children to the lifeboats. Of the two clergymen he was the leader, not only in rendering material aid to the frightened emigrants, but in keeping the religious aspect of the terrible occasion to the fore.

Three of the survivors who vividly remember the last hours of the heroic English priest are Miss Ellen Mocklare, a pretty dark-haired young girl from Galway, now at her sister's home at No. 412 17th Street; Miss Bertha Moran, who has gone to Troy, N.Y., and Miss McCoy, who is in St Vincent's Hospital. These told their story in concert at the hospital today.

'When the crash came we were thrown from our berths,' said Miss Mocklare. 'Slightly dressed, we prepared to find out what had happened. We saw before us, coming down the passageway, with his hand uplifted, Father Byles. We knew him because he had visited us several times on board and celebrated mass for us that very morning.

' "Be calm, my good people," he said, and then he went about the steerage giving absolution and blessings.'

'Meanwhile the stewards ordered us back to bed,' spoke up Miss McCoy, 'but we would not go.'

'A few around us became very excited,' Miss Mocklare continued, 'and then it was that the priest again raised his hand and instantly they were calm once more. The passengers were immediately impressed by the absolute self-control of the priest. He began the recitation of the rosary. The prayers of all, regardless of creed, were mingled and the responses, "Holy Mary," were loud and strong.'

'Continuing the prayers,' said Miss Bertha Moran, 'he led us to where the boats were being lowered. Helping the women and children in, he whispered to them words of comfort and encouragement.'

'One sailor,' said Miss Mocklare, 'warned the priest of his danger and begged him to board a boat. Father Byles refused. The same seaman spoke to him again and he seemed anxious to help him, but he refused again. Father Byles could have been saved, but he would not leave while one was left and the sailor's entreaties were not heeded.

'After I got in the boat, which was the last one to leave, and we were slowly going further away from the ship, I could hear distinctly the voice of the priest and the responses to his prayers. Then they became fainter and fainter, until I could only hear the strains of "Nearer, My God, To Thee" and the screams of the people left behind. We were told by the man who rowed our boat that we were mistaken as to the screams and that it was the people singing, but we knew otherwise.'

'Did all the steerage get a chance to get on deck?' she was asked.

'I don't think so, because a great many were there when our boat went out, but there were no more boats, and I saw Father Byles among them.

'A young man who was in the steerage with us helped me into the boat. It was cold and I had no wrap. Taking off the shirt he was wearing, he put it around my shoulders, used the suspenders to keep it from blowing undone and then stepped back in the crowd.'

Wedding bells, quickly followed by a funeral march, changed on Saturday what was to have been the happiest day in the lives of Miss Isabel Katherine Russell and W. E. Byles. More than 2000 people were expected to be present.

The ceremony was to have been performed in St Augustine's Church and the Rev. Thomas R. D. Byles of Ongar, Essex County, England, brother of the groom, was asked to officiate.

Miss Russell and Mr Byles did not give up hope that Father Byles had been saved until every passenger had arrived from the *Carpathia*. They returned to the Russell residence, No. 119 Pacific Street, and, by telephone and telegram, recalled the numerous invitations.

Believing in the superstition, however, that it is bad luck to postpone a wedding, the ceremony was performed Saturday by a life-long friend of the bride, in St Paul's Church. The bride wore her white satin gown which had been imported from Paris, and was attended by her sister. Only relatives and a few friends were present.

Instead of the usual reception following, the party hastened home, and, donning garments of mourning, returned to the church where the Rev. Father Flannery, rector, performed a requiem mass for the late father.

(*New York World*, 22 April 1912)

NO LIGHT ON THE MYSTERY HIDING THE IDENTITY OF TWO WAIFS OF THE SEA

Of all the survivors of the *Titanic* those two whose impressions would be most worth gathering remain resolutely silent. The two little waifs whose father perished in the disaster and who gained a temporary home with Miss Margaret Hays, a fellow passenger on the ill-fated steamer, are still at Miss Hays' home at No. 304 West 83rd Street, and not a word have they vouchsafed to anyone as to their names, their relatives or any other matter which might shed a ray of light on their antecedents or identity.

Under the shadow of a giant azalea they sat yesterday afternoon, each with a brand new boat in hand with which they entertained themselves while the French Consul to New York strove vainly to extract some enlightening word from the elder boy, whose age has been given as three and a half.

To every question the little curly-haired chap replied with a polite and baffling, 'Oui' and said nothing more.

'Do you like to play with your boat?' asked the Consul, taking the little fellow on his knee.

'Oui,' came the monotonous reply.

'What city do you come from?'

'Oui.'

'Do you remember the big boat that brought you away from France?'

'Oui.'

This time the child's assent was rather bored as though he wished to add: 'Why do you bother me with questions about that old boat when I have this new shiny, painted, wonderful boat of tin in my hands?'

Probably I am the only person to whom it seemed in the least incongruous that these two babies should be playing with brand new tin boats. The boats obviously delight them and bring back no memory of the night of horror which saw the younger boy tossed naked from the *Titanic* into a lifeboat while the older boy followed later, clad in a flannel shirt . . .

We have no intention of keeping them, remarked Miss Hays's father, beyond the time when their relatives are found or the search for them is given up. A Montreal family who were passengers on the *Titanic* are anxious to adopt them, and my daughter says they shall have the preference. Of course, many persons here in New York have also offered to take them.

The published story that the children were in the same boat with my daughter and clung to her instinctively, is a misstatement. My daughter left in the first lifeboat and the two children followed on in later boats. The smaller boy was tossed from the deck of the *Titanic* into a lifeboat without a stitch of clothing. The older child wore only a shirt when he was taken aboard the *Carpathia*. The survivors of the *Titanic* on board formed a ladies' committee, and as my daughter was the only one among them who had not suffered some personal loss through the disaster, she was asked to care for the two children, and gladly did so. She was told that the two children had been in the second cabin of the *Titanic* in the care of a man named Hoffman, but we have been unable to get any clue to their whereabouts from the White Star Line or anywhere else.

(*New York World*, 22 April 1912)

TWO SURVIVORS CALL ON
MAYOR TO ASK RELIEF

Two survivors of the *Titanic* called on Mayor Gaynor today. One is a sailor who was assigned to help man a lifeboat, the other a steerage passenger who, wearing a lifebelt, leapt overboard from the sinking ship, was picked up by passengers aboard an already over-burdened life-raft, again to be hurled back into the ocean and again to be saved by the occupants of a lifeboat. They sought immediate assistance, having lost every possession when the *Titanic* sank.

Eugene P. Daly, the rescued steerage passenger, was playing the bagpipes in the third cabin to the amusement of his fellow passengers shortly before the iceberg was struck. Daly says he was just about to retire when the impact startled him. He grabbed some clothing and started for the deck. Stewards went through the steerage and reassured the passengers, saying there was no danger.

Most of the women believed these statements, said Daly, until it was too late. That is why so many of the women in the steerage were drowned. When they finally realized that the ship was sinking they tried to reach the boats, but could not get through the crowd of other frightened passengers.

I managed to don a life preserver and, failing to get a seat on a lifeboat or on a raft, jumped overboard and struck out just before the ship sank. The water was icy and for the first few minutes I thought I could not survive the cold shock. I do not know how long I was in the water when I caught the edge of a life-raft or collapsible boat already crowded. It upset, but the people in it did not drown. Some of them scrambled back while others, including myself, were dragged into a lifeboat containing women and a few men. My sufferings in the lifeboat were intense until we reached the *Carpathia* where we were made comfortable.

Here I am now, stripped of every worldly possession, including my beloved bagpipes, my baggage and £98 sterling which I saved in fourteen years in anticipation of spending the rest of my days in the United States.

Daly is living with friends at No. 901 Dean Street, Brooklyn. Secretary Adamson gave Daly a note to those in charge of the mayor's relief fund at the headquarters of the American Red Cross Society at No. 1 Madison Avenue.

Robert Hopkins, the sailor of the *Titanic*, was also referred to the fund managers. He was assigned by a superior officer to get into one of the boats whose occupants all were women and to help handle the boat. He says that when he put off from the sinking *Titanic* he was under orders to steer a course towards lights which were burning on the distant horizon.

'We all believed that those lights came from the *Frankfurt* but she was steaming away. We found out when we tried to row towards her,' said Hopkins.

Hopkins is one of the White Star crew who refused to sail back to England by company's orders. He said he had to quit the company and expected therefore no relief from that quarter. Hopkins threw some additional light on the so-called 'millionaires special' lifeboat, which was one of the first boats to leave the *Titanic*. This boat, Hopkins said, contained Sir Cosmo Duff Gordon, Lady Duff Gordon, a man who was indicated as a millionaire and only ten others, including a few women. The millionaire, according to Hopkins, who received the story afterwards from fellow crew members, offered to do handsomely by the crew in the boat if they 'put right away from the *Titanic*', although there was plenty of room for others.

The crew did as requested by the millionaire, continued Hopkins, and after they had boarded the *Carpathia* the millionaire gave each of the *Titanic*'s crew who had handled his boat a cheque for five pounds upon Coutts's Bank. If anybody can get hold of one of these cheques the identity of the millionaire will be established.

(*New York World*, 22 April 1912)

'NEARER, MY GOD, TO THEE'

Band Conductor's Favourite Hymn

Mr Wallace Hartley, the conductor of the *Titanic*'s orchestra, was well known in Leeds, where for several years he was connected with local orchestras.

'A splendid musician he was,' said one of his former colleagues to the *Daily Sketch*, 'and a better fellow you could not meet in a day's march. He was one of the best.'

Apparently Mr Hartley had a presentiment that one day he would meet his end at sea, and it may have been no sudden inspiration that led him at the last moment to direct his orchestra to play 'Nearer, My God, To Thee.'

On one occasion he discussed the subject with Mr E. Moody, of Leeds, who played in the orchestra conducted by Mr Hartley on the *Mauretania*.

I do not know what made me say it, said Mr Moody, but one night when Hartley and I were walking round the *Mauretania*'s deck together I suddenly asked, 'What would you do, old chap, if you were on board a liner that was rapidly sinking?'

'I'd get my men together and play,' he replied without hesitation.

'What would you play?' I asked.

'Well,' he said, 'I don't think I could do better than play 'O God our help in ages past' or 'Nearer, My God, To Thee'. They are both favourite hymns of mine, and they would be very suitable to the occasion.'

(*Daily Sketch*, 22 April 1912)

OCEAN HIGHWAY
WHY ATLANTIC ROUTES ARE CHANGED
ARE THEY SAFE NOW?

The shortest ocean route from Northern Europe to North American ports lies past Cape Race, the extreme point which Newfoundland pushes in southerly direction into the sea. This route lies across the Grand Banks. Cape Race is a terrible danger to navigation. It makes the current tricky, it creates fogs to entrap the unwary mariner into its deadly embrace. Past Cape Race there come from the north in the spring the wandering icebergs, and the great floes which sweep in fog or darkness across the ocean routes sending the big liner and the small tramp with relentless impartiality to their doom.

From August 15 to January 14, before the ice begins to break off from the Greenland ice cap and float across the high roads of the Atlantic, the big steamers are able to cut the corner of Cape Race pretty closely, and shorten their distance from Queenstown to New York or Montreal by several hundred miles. They make almost a straight line from the south of the Cape, across the Grand Bank to New York; or rounding the Cape to the north-west make the Gulf of St Lawrence between Newfoundland and Nova Scotia.

When the northern sun gains strength and begins to send the ice down, then the big steamers have to look out, and instead of steering within 300 miles of Cape Race they clear the Grand Banks altogether, and take a course more southerly by 250 miles or so.

In fifty years something like a hundred ocean-going vessels have been lost in the dangerous seas off Cape Race. The Newfoundlander, wrote Mr P. McGrath in an article in *Pearson's Magazine* some time ago, 'counts on a few wrecks every year to help him to maintain his family.' The tramp steamers, which often run risks to make a short and economic passage and pass the Cape and its 500 miles of ice-infested seas too closely, have suffered tremendously in risking too short a course across that part of the North Atlantic.

The recognized 'safety' highways of the sea more than 300 miles south of Cape Race were fixed by the shipping companies in consultation many years ago, and have been found in ordinary practice to be safe enough. But Nature is unreliable. Though the average limit of the field ice is north of the summer course, an early spring, or an unusually warm season now and then carries the bergs further to the south before they dissolve in the warm currents of the Gulf Stream and across the summer course. The captain of the *Titanic* had evidently recognized that this is a bad season for ice, for he was apparently steering some 30 miles south of his normal course, though he dared not steam so far south as to get on the eastward route. (The westward route is nearly 60 miles north of the eastward route, the object being to avoid the danger of collision between vessels steaming in opposite directions.) That the allowance was not enough is proved by the terrible disaster which has just shocked the civilized world.

It is a profound misfortune that, knowing that the ice had appeared earlier this year, the Atlantic lines did not immediately change the ocean routes, as they have decided to do since the *Titanic* went down. The new routes agreed upon will take the steamers about 200 miles further south of the old summer routes, and quite out of the danger zone, even allowing for early and exceptional ice seasons in the North Atlantic. The new course, it is confidently predicted, will be quite outside the extreme limit of drift ice, and at no part of the journey across the ocean will any ship be within sight of ice.

It is obvious that the lengthening of the journey from Great Britain to North America means an additional expense to the shipping companies. This is the price which will be paid, necessarily and cheerfully, for absolute safety from ice.

(*Liverpool Evening Express*, 22 April 1912)

FRANK KORUN REACHES HOME

Titanic *Survivor, Daughter and Austrian*
Friend Saved From Ocean Grave

When Frank Korun, one of the *Titanic* survivors, stepped from the Burlington train at 10 o'clock, Monday night, with his little daughter, Amie, clasping his hand, there were awaiting him a happy family group of his wife and four other children, and the moment that he reached the platform they surrounded him and the little girl and an affectionate reunion ensued, warming all that saw it. The stalwart Austrian was deeply affected by the warm greeting and as for little Amie, she knew how much better it was to be in her mother's arms than on the crowded boat in the Atlantic, dodging ice floes and freezing in Christmas temperature.

With Mr Korun was a fellow Austrian who was with the party that came over on the *Titanic* and who was also saved from the wreck. These wended their way to the Korun home a happy group, once more reunited after an experience that comes to but few.

When Mr Korun was seen this forenoon by a representative of the *Republican Register*, he was still suffering from the effects of his experiences, and evidently had sustained an attack of delirium from which, however, he is recovering. 'I feel it in my head,' he said, in broken English, and he put his hand on his forehead. He was just out of the hospital in New York where, with his daughter, he spent over two days. A number crowded around to hear his story which was all the more dramatic as, owing to his scanty knowledge of English, it had to be told in fragments.

With only the suit of clothes he now has on, he made his escape. The $700 that he received from the rent of his land near Krom, Austria, all in cash, and all his belongings in his trunk valued at $150 are at the bottom of the Atlantic. The company paid his fare to Galesburg for the misfortune left him without a cent.

I was a third class passenger and sleeping in a room at the rear of the boat, he remarked. With me were my little girl, and also my brother-in-law, John Markum [sic], who was coming to this country to get work, and who left his wife and five children in Austria.

The man's voice grew soft and tremulous as he thought of the wife and five children across the waters. He then produced a rude drawing of the big ship, to show where his room was, not far from the rear of the boat. The damage he indicated to the front end and side of the vessel.

I was fast asleep when the ship hit the iceberg, he continued. So were the rest in my room. I got up and dressed in the suit I have on and my little girl put on her dress. I put on a life preserver and the rest of our party did the same. It was about 11 o'clock when someone woke us up. When we got to the top I could see that the forward end of the boat was sinking down and that there was quite a decline that way. There was a lifeboat lowered and I think that was the last one put down. They put my little girl down first, letting her down with a rope. Then they let me down. I do not know why they did this – perhaps it was because it was the last boat and there was still room for somebody. When I got into the boat I found that I was the only man there. All the rest were women and children. Of course the sailors were in the boat to pull it. I think that I was the last man to get off the ship. There were fifty-two people in the boat. There were seven babies in the company. Thirty passengers were on it.

At a quarter to one o'clock, when we were about 300 feet from the steamship, it sank. Its forward end went down and it seemed to raise right in the air and dive.

At this point Mr Korun took his drawing and lifted it up straight to indicate the position of the ship when it took the plunge.

I heard two big booms, he continued. I think it was the boilers exploding. I did not see the ship break in two. An awful scene followed, people drowning and crying for help. I shall never forget the sight. I did not feel the suction from the ship when it went down.

Then for four and a half hours we were in the boat. The sea was smooth but it was full of chunks of ice, some small and some large. It was cold like Christmas and we shivered from it. My little girl was in the same boat and was very brave. I tried to keep her warm.

What became of my brother-in-law? I do not know. He went on top too, but I lost sight of him. You could not see much there. He went down with the ship.

(Galesburg Republican Register, 23 April 1912)

OVER £150,000 FOR WRECK VICTIMS

'Money is pouring in.' This announcement, made at the Mansion House last night, supplements the news that the Lord Mayor's fund for sufferers by the *Titanic* disaster has now reached over £100,000.

This huge total is an effective illustration of the full realization by the charitable public of the effect of the disaster. But more is required to meet the needs of the widows and fatherless and other sufferers by the wreck, and there is no doubt that it will be forthcoming.

Elsewhere the relief funds are being liberally supported. At Southampton last night the Mayor's fund had reached £12,380. Liverpool, New York and other cities in the United Kingdom, the United States and Canada are raising funds for the same noble purpose. Altogether it is estimated that over £150,000 has already been willingly subscribed.

(Daily News, 23 April 1912)

THE LAST PARTING

Mrs Astor has told her experiences, bit by bit – because she is not yet strong enough to speak for any length of time – to her relatives in New York.

She said that when Colonel Astor awakened her and told her that something was wrong with the ship he assured her that the *Titanic* could not sink. She dressed hurriedly, put on some jewellery, went with her husband to the boat deck, and they put on lifebelts. Noticing that she was lightly dressed, her husband sent to their state room for a heavier dress and helped her to change and wrapped a fur coat around her.

Mrs Astor added that she got into the last boat but one.

Colonel Astor said to me, she continued: 'The sea's calm. You'll be all right. You're in good hands. I'll meet you in the morning.' Then he kissed me affectionately and stood smiling down at me as the lifeboat was lowered. I noticed that the ship was settling as we rowed away, and I could make out the figure of Kitty, my favourite terrier, running about the deck.

Then I saw the *Titanic* go down. We floated seven hours. It was very cold and the icy water was sweeping through the bottom of the boat up to my knees when the *Carpathia*'s men rescued us. I rowed part of the time, as I knew how to handle an oar, and so did Mrs G. D. Widener. We picked up eight or ten drowning men during the night.

(Daily Graphic, 24 April 1912)

LADY SURVIVOR

Married in the Hospital at New York

Miss Sarah Roths [sic], one of the *Titanic* survivors, who had been taken to St Vincent's Hospital, New York, suffering from shock, was married in the hospital on Monday to Mr Daniel Michael Iles, a clerk in New York. Both were born in sight of the Tower of London, and had been companions in childhood. The bride's trousseau and money are at the bottom of the Atlantic. She told her story to Mrs Frederick Vanderbilt and other charity workers at the hospital, and Father Grogan, of the Church of Our Lady of the Rosary, was consulted.

The bridegroom was speedily found, and the Women's Relief Committee saw that the necessary trousseau for the bride was forthcoming. The news of the impending wedding spread quickly through the hospital, and nurses, doctors, charity workers, patients, and survivors begged to be allowed to witness the ceremony. Some were wheeled to the door of the hall in invalid chairs, while others watched from the stairways. The hall was decorated with pink roses.

Miss Teresa E. O'Donoghue, a member of the Women's Relief Committee, stepped to the piano and played the Wedding March from 'Lohengrin'. The bride was given away by Mr Gerald Redman, whose sister was saved with Miss Roths. Miss Redman, of course, was the bridesmaid. Mrs Vanderbilt was one of the first to wish the bridal pair a long and prosperous life.

Mr and Mrs Iles will start housekeeping at the bridegroom's address, in 24th Street.

(*Nottingham Evening News*, 24 April 1912

TITANIC'S SURVIVOR COMES TO ROCKFORD

Having lost her brother and sweetheart and herself barely escaped death, Miss Dagmar Bryhl [sic], the Rockford-bound survivor from the mid-ocean tragedy of the *Titanic*, reached this city at 6.30 o'clock this morning in company with her uncle, Oscar R. Lustig, and is now rested at his home at 502 Pearl Street.

Thus is ended what was to have been a summer visit of Miss Bryhl [sic], her brother, Kurt Bryhl [sic] and her affianced sweetheart Ingvar Enander, to Rockford relatives, and gloom has been cast over a number of families in this city to whom the brother and sister are related.

The arrival of Mr Lustig and his niece has been anxiously awaited. They reached here much later than was expected but this was due to Miss Bryhl's [sic] condition. Although she is reported to be gaining composure, she still is said to be feeble, and her uncle positively refused everyone permission to see her this morning.

'Poor Dagmar!' exclaimed Mr Lustig, the tears welling into his eyes as he spoke to a *Republic* reporter. 'You cannot see her now. Nobody knows what the poor girl went through. Her nerves are all a-tremble, and I am afraid it will be some time before those awful hours will be effaced from her mind. I have not asked her a thing about it myself, but sometimes she would sit with her chin on her hand, brooding, and then she would tell me snatches of her terrible experiences.'

Mr Lustig and his niece left New York Tuesday evening about 6 o'clock and arrived in Chicago last night. He was anxious to get back to Rockford and went to Rochelle hoping to get an early accommodation train out of there. They passed the night in Rochelle and the constant travelling so wore out Miss Bryhl's [sic] strength that she was put to bed as soon as she reached her uncle's home here.

While the reporters were not permitted to talk with Miss Bryhl [sic] today, her uncle, who is a well educated man, told the account that his niece had given him from time to time since he met her in New York last Saturday.

Dagmar and her brother, Kurt, and her sweetheart, Ingvar Enander, left their home in Skara, in Sweden, April 3. They all sailed second class, and none of them had any intentions of remaining in Rockford. It was simply to be a visit, although it might have happened that Kurt would have remained. Enander had taken a course in agriculture and expected to continue his studies and observations here.

Dagmar told me that on the Sunday evening when the *Titanic* hit the iceberg the weather was quite balmy. Several hours before the crash came Dagmar says that she was on deck wearing a light summer dress. She says it was a wonderfully bright night. About 9 o'clock or so, however, the air was recommended to be chilly and soon it was positively cold.

'It was so cold,' said Dagmar, 'that I went after my coat and everybody else did. Finally it became almost too cold for the deck. The coldness, of course, indicated we were in the region of the icebergs and that warning it seems the ship's officers should have taken.'

The story of the crash and the subsequent happenings Mr Lustig says his niece has told him substantially as follows:

I was in my berth when the *Titanic* hit the berg. I noticed the jar and soon I heard Ingvar knocking on the door of my cabin. 'Get up, Dagmar,' he said. 'The ship has hit something.' I put on a skirt and a coat as quickly as possible and hurried up to the deck. But the officers said: 'Go back, there is no danger; you go to your cabins.'

I returned to my berth and went back to bed. I had not laid very long before there was more knocking on my door and Ingvar was yelling: 'Get up, Dagmar, we are in danger. I don't care what the ship's officers say, I tell you we are in danger of our lives. The boat is sinking.'

Again I flung on my skirt and coat and ran up. Someone said we had hit an iceberg. The screaming and yelling was awful. They were putting women and children into the boats and lowered them into the sea. Men and women were kissing each other farewells. Ingvar and Kurt led me to a boat and Ingvar lifted me into it. I seized his hands and wouldn't let go. 'Come with me!' I screamed as loud as I could and still holding his hands tight. There was room in the boat. It was only half-filled, but an officer ran forward and clubbed back Ingvar. This officer tore our hands apart and the lifeboat was let down. As it went down I looked up. There, leaning over the rail, stood Kurt and Ingvar side by side. I screamed to them again, but it was no use. They waved their hands and smiled. That was the last glimpse I had of them.

The men that rowed our boat pushed away from the *Titanic*. The air was very cold and we all shivered. They rowed us around and we saw the great ship sink. Then came more dreadful screams.

The water filled with crying people. Some of them climbed in our boat and so saved their lives.

We were out in the lifeboat from 11 o'clock Sunday night until 6 o'clock Sunday morning, when the *Carpathia* came. Seven hours without any clothing thick enough to protect me from the cold benumbed my limbs. Oh, I can't ever tell the thoughts that came to me out there. The sea was so still and clear as a mirror, it seemed, and over us was a clear and cloudless sky.

When Miss Bryhl [sic] was taken aboard the *Carpathia* with the other survivors, her plight attracted the sympathy of a wealthy Jewish woman from New York. This kind-hearted woman's generosity, however, gave Mr Lustig some hours of anxiety when he reached New York. Miss Bryhl's [sic] benefactor took her in charge and, instead of registering her with the relief committee in New York, walked her down the gang-plank, placed her in an automobile and hurried her to the Hospital for Deformities and Joint Diseases, a charitable institution at 1915 Madison Ave., which is supported by Jewish philanthropists. The result was, although the *Carpathia*'s survival list included Miss Bryhl's [sic] name, no one could tell her uncle where he would find his niece. Miss Bryhl [sic] wrote to Mr Lustig the morning after reaching the hospital, supposing that he was still in Rockford, but it was not until his relatives here telegraphed him the address at which the girl was stopping that he came in communication with her.

The uncle had left Rockford as soon as the full details of the wreck and the rescue of his niece were reported. He intended to be on hand when she arrived and to take her in charge, and does not feel in the least satisfied with the treatment accorded him by some of the White Star Line officials.

He says he was met with icy looks and chilly courtesy at the steamship office. No one seemed to know anything. The manager refused to talk with him. Then Mr Lustig threatened to go to the newspaper offices and tell the press about the treatment he was receiving, and he says that the effect of this threat was electrical. Even the manager then had time to see him.

Miss Bryhl [sic], according to her uncle, has again and again declared between hysterical sobs, that if she had thought that her brother and her sweetheart would be lost that she would never have allowed them to put her in the lifeboat. She says that she would rather have died with them when the great ship settled into the deep than to live with the memory of all that took place graven into her mind for all the subsequent days to come.

(Rockford (Illinois) Republic, 25 April 1912)

MEN, WOMEN AND CHILDREN

Mr Chiozza Money, M.P., has received from the President of the Board of Trade the following particulars showing the numbers saved and percentage of each class and sex of passengers on the *Titanic*.

First-class passengers

Men carried 173; saved 58; per cent saved 34.
Women carried 143; saved 139; per cent saved 97.
Children carried 5; saved 5; per cent saved 100.
Total carried 321; saved 202; per cent saved 63.

Second-class passengers

Men carried 160; saved 13; per cent saved 8.
Women carried 93; saved 78; per cent saved 84.
Children carried 24; saved 24; per cent saved 100.
Total carried 277; saved 115; per cent saved 42.

Third-class passengers

Men carried 454; saved 55; per cent saved 12.
Women carried 179; saved 98; per cent saved 55.

Children carried 76; saved 23; per cent saved 30.
Total carried 799; saved 176; per cent saved 25.

Crew

Men carried 875; saved 189; per cent saved 22.
Women carried 23; saved 21; per cent saved 91.
Total carried 898; saved 210; per cent saved 23.

Total passengers and crew

Men carried 1,662; saved 315; per cent saved 19.
Women carried 439; saved 336; per cent saved 77.
Children carried 105; saved 52; per cent saved 49.
Total passengers and crew carried 2,206; saved 703; per cent
   saved 32.

(*Cork Free Press*, 25 April 1912)

CAPTAIN SMITH DIED HERO'S DEATH

Taking refuge on the bridge of the ill-fated *Titanic*, two little children remained by the side of Capt. Smith until that portion of the big ship had been swept by water. Survivors of the crew who went down with the *Titanic* but were saved by clinging to an overturned lifeboat, told of their gallant commander's efforts to save the life of one of the children. He died a sailor's death, and the little girl who had entrusted her life to his care died with him.

He held the little girl under one arm, said James McGann, a fireman, jumped into the sea and endeavoured to reach the nearest lifeboat with the child. I took the other child into my arms as I was swept away from the bridge deck. Then I was plunged into the cold water. I was compelled to release my hold on the child, and I am satisfied that the same thing happened to Captain Smith.

I had gone to the bridge deck to assist in lowering a collapsible boat. The water was then coming over the bridge and we were unable to launch the boat properly. It was overturned and was used as a life-raft, some thirty or more of us, mostly firemen, clinging to it. Captain Smith looked as though he was trying to keep back the tears as he thought of the doomed ship.

He turned to the men lowering the boat and shouted: 'Well, boys, It's every man for himself.' He then took one of the children standing by him on the bridge and jumped into the sea. He endeavoured to reach the overturned boat but did not succeed. This was the last seen of Captain Smith.

(Nova Scotian, 26 April 1912)

A BUSINESS DELAY PREVENTED TRIP ON THE *TITANIC*

What I considered at the time a vexatious and unlooked-for delay in closing up some business affairs in London prevented me from embarking on the ill-fated *Titanic*, and I sailed the following day on the White Star *Celtic* from Liverpool instead.

This was the statement to a *Star* representative today by Mr John McDowell, general manager of the Frederick King and Co., Ltd, Belfast and London, and one of the prominent citizens of the former city.

It was partly for the sentimental reason that they both belonged to the same city which made Mr McDowell anxious to be a passenger on the maiden trip of the *Titanic*.

Up to the last minute there was doubt whether Capt. Smith would arrive in Belfast in time to take command of the *Titanic*. All the big steamship men in Belfast regarded him as one of the finest and most careful navigators on the high seas.

The wireless operator on board the *Celtic* received the death call from the *Titanic* and informed the captain. We were far behind her, but full speed was kept up for some hours until word was received that the other vessels were much nearer and were hastening to aid the doomed steamer. Our course was then changed southward to escape the icefield, and we met no ice all the way into New York.

(*Montreal Daily Star*, 26 April 1912)

'DRESSED AS A SAILOR'

Mme. Cardéza, whose husband and mother-in-law were among the survivors of the *Titanic* disaster, will go to New York today in order to accompany her husband on the homeward voyage.

She has received, it is stated, a letter from her husband in which he says that he bribed two sailors to give him sailor's clothing.

He and his secretary, dressed in these clothes, with his mother and her companion, succeeded in gaining the lifeboat, as they were supposed to be sailors.

(*Daily Sketch*, 26 April 1912)

BELFAST VICTIMS

News About Local People on Board Liner

Nowhere did the grim details of the *Titanic*'s last moments create a more profound effect than in Belfast. The closer one approaches to the tragedy, the greater becomes its terrible significance and the narratives of the survivors have driven the awful truth home to the public consciousness.

Friday's news supply from across the Atlantic had much that is of special interest to Belfast, which for the time being is a city of mourning, not merely in the outward display of half-masted flags, but in the feeling amongst all classes and sections of the citizens, as evidenced in the tone of everyday conversation. There were not a few families in the city and district who had a peculiarly intimate connection with the event by reason of personal relationship with passengers on board the lost liner; and the whole community of workers on the Queen's Island had, in addition to the fact of the result of their handicraft being lost in the deeps of the Atlantic, to face the wiping away of some of their most capable leaders, and popular colleagues. Mr Thomas Andrews, Jun., is one of those regarding whom the keenest anxiety was felt, and it will be recalled that only a short time ago – on the occasion of the trial trip of the *Patriotic* – he delivered a speech which had great interest and importance for Belfast people. In it he declared the intention of Messrs Harland & Wolff, with regard to Belfast and subsidiary yards. It is not without interest to recall the actual words of Mr Andrews on that occasion. He said he was glad to be able to say that the prosperity of Harland & Wolff's was never greater than at the present time, and so great were the demands of the firm's business that they were finding it necessary to make extensions in other cities and other countries. He could not say that that had met with entire approval, but no matter how their business might develop he felt sure that in Belfast they would always have their headquarters. It was sufficient for him to say that today they employed in Belfast over 15,000 men, and the total wages bill on last Friday evening reached the record figure of £27,500. A good deal of that had been involved in the completion of two first-class passenger ships, the *Patriotic* and *Titanic*.

Another member of the Queen's Island staff about whom special feeling exists is Mr Frost, who has a hereditary connection with the firm.

On Friday morning, however, reassuring news of one Belfast representative on board the ill-fated liner was forthcoming. Mr William Brown, of Kersland Crescent, Newtownards Road, being apprised by cablegram of the safety of Miss Sloan, one of the stewardesses. The formal list of survivors issued up to the present includes also Robert Hopkins, able seaman, of Belfast, and persons named Couts [sic], who are stated to belong to this neighbourhood, but who have not yet been definitely traced.

The fact that the survivor lists published so far are not exhaustive is indicated by a telegram received on Friday by Mr Pears, of Messrs Combe, Barbour and Combe, Belfast, stating that his daughter-in-law was amongst the saved, although her name did not appear on the official list.

Mr A. Irvine [sic], rate collector, on Friday received a message from the White Star Line Offices, Southampton, regarding his son, who sailed on the *Titanic* as assistant electrician.

Deeply regret your son's name is not in the list of those who were saved. Please accept our deepest sympathy.

A HERO'S DEATH

How Mr Thos. Andrews, Jun., Met His Fate

The keen anxiety felt in Belfast regarding the fate of Mr Thomas Andrews, Jun., managing director of Harland & Wolff, was tempered by the knowledge, shared in by all his acquaintances, that if he met his end he would do so in a manner worthy of his race and name. Too plainly it was seen by the later messages that he was amongst those who sank with the giant vessel, in the construction of which he had such a prominent and all-important part. But the deep shadow cast upon the community by the disaster was relieved by the gleam of glory reflected from the high courage and grand self-sacrifice which he conspicuously displayed in the awful last hours of the *Titanic*.

How he gave his life away for others was barely indicated in the brief messages already published, but on Sunday a prominent official of Messrs Harland & Wolff received from the White Star Company's offices, New York, a cablegram which condenses into half a dozen jerky phrases a narrative of heroism calculated to stir the feelings of the most stolid, and to mingle with the deep, heartfelt regret of those who knew Mr Andrews, a sensation of pride that he should have faced his fate so grandly. No more remarkable sidelight has been thrown on the disaster than by this message, dramatic in its brevity:

> After accident Andrews ascertained damage. Advised passengers put heavy clothing, prepare leave vessel. Many sceptical about serious damage, but impressed by Andrews's knowledge, personality, followed his advice, saved their lives. He assisted many women children to lifeboats. When last seen officers say was throwing overboard deck chairs other objects to people in water. His chief concern safety of everyone but himself.

The news of Mr Andrews's tragic end will be received with feelings of the most profound sorrow by his large circle of acquaintances, and the deepest sympathy will be extended to his bereaved widow, who was a Miss Barbour, his father and mother, and his other relatives in their affliction. He was beloved and respected by all who had the pleasure of his acquaintance, and by none will the news of his sad but heroic death be more regretfully read than by the thousands of men at the Queen's Island over whose labours he superintended with such rare ability and with such conspicuous success.

The late Mr Andrews was a nephew of Lord Pirrie and the Right Hon. W. Drennan Andrews, an ex-judge of the King's Bench Division in Ireland.

RIGHT HON. A. M. CARLISLE

A memorial service was held in St Paul's Cathedral, London, on Friday, for those who perished in the *Titanic*. The congregation numbered over 5,000, and included members of the Cabinet, Government officials, Ambassadors, among the latter being Mr Whitelaw Reid, the Lord Mayor, and representatives of the great shipping companies.

Right Hon. A. M. Carlisle fainted during the service, and had to be removed. He subsequently recovered.

(Irish Weekly and Ulster Examiner, 27 April 1912)

OLYMPIC'S RACE

Passengers Alarmed at Grim Preparations

Some 300 passengers of the *Olympic* arrived at Waterloo Station on Sunday (twenty-first) morning. In interviews it was stated that, although they learnt on the ship by means of Marconi messages of the loss of the *Titanic*, it was not until they obtained the English newspapers at Plymouth that the full shock of the disaster was brought to their minds. Many of the passengers had friends on board the ill-fated sister ship; and there was hardly a member of the crew who was not wearing mourning for some relative or shipmate of long standing. The musicians in particular were most of them intimately associated with the members of the *Titanic*'s orchestra, and they were overcome with emotion when they heard of the magnificent heroism of their old comrades. Although it was understood that Captain Haddock had received a message about midnight on Sunday (fourteenth) that the *Titanic* had struck an iceberg it was considerably later that the news found its way to the passengers. The first intimation that anything was amiss was given by the altered course and accelerated speed of the vessel. The *Olympic* 500 miles away was going to the rescue of her disabled sister ship, travelling at a rate she had never attempted before. The stokers and engineers were working like trojans to get the last fraction of speed out of the ship's engines, and for 400 miles she tore along at a rate of 24 knots an hour. In the meantime the lifeboats were all prepared for lowering the moment she reached the wreck. The tension was relieved by another wireless message stating that all on board the *Titanic* had been saved. The *Olympic*, however, kept on her way, and it was only when she was within 100 miles of the scene of the disaster that she received the message from the *Carpathia* stating that the Cunard liner had picked up some 800 of the *Titanic*'s survivors, and that pieces of wreckage was all she could find of the mammoth ship.

One of the saloon passengers said that when the ship's course was altered, and the lifeboats were got ready, the *Olympic*'s passengers were filled with alarm. Until that time they had received no communication whatever as to anything untoward, and such an air of mystery was maintained that it was decided to approach the captain of the ship for an explanation. A committee of saloon passengers was formed, and two of their number waited on Captain Haddock, who then told them of a message that he had received that the *Titanic* had struck an iceberg. The greatest anxiety prevailed, and although later on they were informed that the *Titanic* had gone down, and that the *Carpathia* had picked up a large number of survivors, it was not until Plymouth was reached that those on the *Olympic* knew the full extent of the disaster. The passenger added that as the *Olympic* was tearing her way to bring succour to the *Titanic* they passed by a great iceberg, although their vessel was never in any danger from it. He said he had twice crossed the Atlantic in a steamer commanded by Captain Smith, than whom he believed no finer skipper ever sailed a ship, and to whose sterling worth, both as a man and a seaman, he paid a high tribute.

Gloom on Board

All night long the wireless operator was frantically endeavouring to get fuller news of the catastrophe, but his efforts were unavailing. Meanwhile excitement was hourly growing on board, and with the failure of the *Titanic*'s signals, followed a feeling of intense depression among the ship's company. The *Olympic* raced on her errand of mercy, and it was not until six o'clock on Monday evening that she learnt by wireless from the *Carpathia* that all the boats had been picked up, and those on board heard with dismay that the *Olympic* could be of no further service. The extent of the disaster was not then known, but it was feared that there must have been serious loss of life, for the lifeboat capacity of the *Titanic* was known to the *Olympic* crew. An atmosphere of gloom pervaded all grades of passengers and crew. For the remainder of the voyage the ship's band ceased playing, and there was no more music on board. Concerts and dances which had been arranged for seamen's charities and other diversions usually indulged in on ocean trips, were at once cancelled, and in their place committees were formed to raise subscriptions for the dependants of those whose lives had been lost. The first-class passengers subscribed something like £700 in very quick time. The ship's officials all contributed handsome amounts, and the firemen and stewards and other ratings of the crew forfeited several days' pay for the wives and families of their dead comrades. In all a sum of £1,500 was raised.

The news of the full extent of the loss of life was received with blank amazement, when it became known, and the passengers as they stepped ashore at Southampton to entrain for London, eagerly bought up the Sunday papers to learn the full details of the catastrophe.

No sooner were the passengers cleared than preparations commenced for the *Olympic* to sail again during the week, and coaling operations continued all through the day. To allay any anxiety the White Star Line have arranged for a large number of additional boats of the collapsible type to be placed on the *Olympic* for her next voyage, and it is understood provision will be made for all on board.

(*Irish Weekly and Ulster Examiner*, 27 April 1912)

TAFT'S EULOGY OF MAJOR BUTT

Of Major Butt, President Taft's eulogy, perhaps, best covers the situation. When the details of his aide-de-camp's end were conveyed to him, Mr Taft said:

I never really had any hope of seeing him again. Archie was a soldier, and was always where he was wanted. When I heard that 1,200 people had gone down in the *Titanic* I knew Archie would be among them. He would be on deck doing his duty to the end.

SERVICES IN ENGLAND

In most places of worship in the United Kingdom on Sunday special pulpit references were made, or prayers read, with reference to the *Titanic* disaster. The services in the large cities partook largely of a memorial character. The 'dead march in Saul' was generally played, and the hymns chosen frequently included 'Nearer, My God, to Thee'. In London moving scenes were witnessed as during the singing of hymns or rendering of the dead march men and women broke down, and grief for lost relatives and friends found expression in tears.

SAFETY BEFORE SPEED

The White Star and Cunard Companies issued an announcement at Liverpool on Monday that they have standing instructions to their captains to ensure safety before speed. The Cunard rule reads:

Captains are to remember that whilst they are expected to use every diligence to secure a speedy voyage, they must run no risks which by any possibility might result in accident to their ships. They will ever bear in mind that the safety of the lives and property entrusted to their care is the ruling principle which shall govern them in the navigation of their ships, and that the supposed gain in expedition or saving of time on a voyage is not to be purchased at the risk of accident.

(*Irish Weekly and Ulster Examiner*, 27 April 1912)

OUR LADIES' COLUMN BY MRS HUMPHRY 'MADGE'
TITANIC REFLECTIONS

The sympathy of every true woman must go out to the unhappy women and girls who have lost husbands and fathers in this heartrending accident to the *Titanic*. It must have made the catastrophe even more afflicting that every one of the passengers went on board with the conviction that the vessel was practically unsinkable. No one reckoned for a single instance on collision with an iceberg. The imagination vainly tries to picture the terrible scene when the women and children were handed first to the boats. The men were interrogated, 'Married or unmarried?' The married men were given the first chance, but comparatively few of these could be saved, while the unmarried had to stand back with no smallest hope of rescue. Many of them were in the prime of life, others were youths seeking a livelihood and hoping to build a home in the great continent. What could their thoughts have been as they awaited the final sinking of the vessel? It completely beggars fancy when one tries to realize the scene and attempts to guess the feelings of husband and wife, mother and daughter, father and son, parting in the unspeakably harrowing circumstances.

(*Southampton Times and Hampshire Express*, 27 April 1912)

THE *TITANIC'S* CREW ARRIVAL OF THE *LAPLAND* AT PLYMOUTH

A hundred and sixty-seven survivors of the crew of the *Titanic* landed at Plymouth yesterday from the Red Star liner *Lapland*.

They told a large number of full and graphic stories of the disaster.

One of the chief facts brought to light is that Mr Murdoch, the Chief Officer, after working assiduously at getting the women and children into the boats and launching them, shot himself.

Captain Smith was on the bridge practically to the last. He was seen swimming in the water after the ship went down, with a child in his arms, which he vainly attempted to rescue. He afterwards disappeared.

Practically all the survivors agree that the band played hymns and not 'ragtime tunes'. After all his fellow musicians had been washed away the solo violinist continued playing 'Nearer, My God, to Thee', until he went under with the ship.

The *Titanic* broke in two between the funnels. There were explosions. The men believe that the machinery fell out of the hull when she split and the bow went down. The stern rose straight up in the air before the final plunge.

A great many of the passengers and crew lost their lives by the falling of one of the funnels when the ship broke. Others, when she dipped, were killed by being thrown violently into the well of the forecastle.

More lives might have been saved but for over-confidence in the unsinkability of the vessel.

Having varied her normal course to the extent of about 130 miles so as to keep more safely south, the Red Star liner *Lapland* arrived in Plymouth Sound yesterday morning almost on the stroke of eight o'clock. She was met by three G.W. tenders, one of which was entirely set apart for a party of 167 survivors of the crew of the ill-fated *Titanic*. This was the *Sir Richard Grenville* and on her were Messrs Harold and T. Wolferstan (Board of Trade solicitors), W. Woollven (collector of Customs and receiver of wreck), with other officials, who were present to collect the evidence of the survivors and sort it with a view to securing any vital statements for submission to the Royal Commission which opens its inquiry on Thursday.

It was generally known that unusual steps were contemplated to keep the survivors together so long as the Board of Trade officials needed them, and to prevent them being tampered with by unauthorized people, but the little army of journalists, who had assembled from all parts, were unprepared for the rigorous exclusion from even the dock premises to which they were subjected.

A number of them chartered boats, but were unable to get on board the liner. They had as colleagues two members of the British Seamen's Union, who called out and shouted to the men not to say anything 'until you have seen us.' The immediate result of this was really to upset the plans of the authorities, and quite early in the afternoon the men were at liberty. There were thus plenty of opportunities for interviews, and some new light was thrown on the disaster. The men spoke with the utmost frankness and earnestness, though almost without exception they declined to consent to the publication of their names, fearing unpleasant consequences. In the main, however, the story secured from them may be accepted as quite authentic, even though it naturally concerns phases of the disaster rather than one entire memory.

The precautions taken to exclude Pressmen and visitors from the Docks and the tenders were elaborate to an extreme degree. Not only were the officials suspicious of everybody, but regular servants were kept out unless armed with a pass. Then at about ten minutes to six, a score of postal employees, mostly in uniform, and the rest comprising telegraph and postal clerks regularly in the docks and quite well known to the officials, were 'held up' because they had not first called at the G.P.O. for a permit! When the tender which they used returned to the jetty members of the Dock staff were detailed to watch and 'see if anything is thrown or passed overboard to a boat.' The brilliance of this order is revealed by the fact that half an hour later the postal gentlemen were all outside the docks, and had in no way been searched. As a matter of fact, few had ever left the tender for the *Lapland*, and none had caught more than a glimpse of the survivors as they transferred to the *Sir Richard Grenville*.

This special tender was fastened to a gangway in the fore part of the liner, while the other two were aft, one on either side. A flotilla of boats cruised about, but the London journalists who had chartered most of them were ill rewarded for their enterprise. The best off were the cinematograph operators, who succeeded in getting a clear, continuous view of the men of the *Titanic* passing from the liner to the *Grenville*, carrying their kit-bags with them. Ordinary cameras were numerous, and were 'snapping' fairly continuously.

To revert to the earlier hours, a large crowd had gathered at the Millbay end of the docks by six o'clock, though most of them were dock porters. They were rigidly excluded until eight o'clock, much to their indignation, and threats to refuse to work were general, but after the last tender had cleared away badges were distributed, and a sufficiency of men accepted them readily enough. There were many in the crowd who had friends on board, and who chafed under the restrictions but the police on the gate were adamant. One petty officer came down from Dartmouth to meet his brother, but was not allowed to go off, although two other brothers were. For the rest the gathering was chiefly composed of journalists, bathers, and a number of townspeople, drawn together by the unusual occurrence and anxious to get a glimpse of those who had been saved from the disaster. They waited patiently enough in the broiling sun, and seemed to take great interest in the progress of the tenders, some of which were freely photographed from a terrace above Rusty Anchor.

There were some inevitable scenes of pathos at the dock gates during the morning, one of the most affecting being the distress of Mr Jewell and his wife, who were kept without. They had two sons on the *Titanic*. One was lost; the other was on the *Lapland*. Their reunion, which took place inside the waiting-room, was a saddening one, tragic in the extreme. Other relatives of survivors were present but the majority had their emotions well under control.

The *Grenville* had been watched for some hours very eagerly from the back of West Hoe Terrace, by several hundred people, and when she was seen to be steaming back to the dock, after an apparently aimless cruise around Jennycliffe Bay, there was a general move to the dock entry, but there was no relaxing of the restrictions keeping the public out. The *Grenville* was berthed about noon, and the men proceeded at once to the waiting-room for the meal which had been prepared. Many of them quickly found the windows which overlooked the thoroughfare, and had brief, jerky conversations with some of the assembled journalists. The stewardesses were accommodated in a long restaurant car on the railway siding.

It was at once apparent that many of the men resented the restrictions placed upon their freedom. As soon as they reached the rooms prepared for them several of them opened windows facing the road approach, and spoke to friends who were included in the hundreds of interested spectators assembled outside the premises.

'They won't let me pass the gates,' announced a man, one of whose two brothers serving on the *Titanic* was drowned.

'And we can't get out,' answered one of the crew from the window, 'but we intend to do so even if we have to get out of this window.'

What happened afterwards was not apparent to those outside, but about half-past one Chief Constable Sowerby announced that those men who would obtain a pass might leave the docks till four o'clock. Naturally there was a rush for the necessary permission, and soon the men were free to have a stroll. It was then possible to interview many, the result being that some thrilling stories of heroism and hairbreadth escapes were obtained.

SOME HAIRBREADTH ESCAPES

On the *Lapland* the survivors were kept very much to themselves, and only came in touch with a few of the ordinary passengers who were peculiarly interested, having crossed the Atlantic with some of them on previous trips, and become acquainted. There was no questioning, or endeavour to secure news, yet some of these passengers called attention to the haggard faces and wan condition of several of the men, as eloquent testimony of the horror and severity of their awful experience. Most of them wore ill-fitting clothes, their new 'kits' having been hastily got together by warm-hearted Americans, for the bulk were saved in just their bare working attire.

Another member of the *Titanic*'s crew had an experience almost as remarkable. He was carried down by the suction following the sinking of the vessel but struck a grating so violently as to secure a rebound, which sent him to the surface. He was able at once to secure a hold on floating wreckage and was one of the earliest to be picked up. Several members of the crew declared that just before the ship made her fatal dive, the foremost funnel broke off and fell into the sea, killing and injuring a number of men who were already in the water struggling and swimming towards the boats.

A *Lapland* passenger who knew one of the *Titanic*'s crew and had talked with him, but who, like all the others, declined to give permission for the use of his name, said the crew were so confident that the ship was unsinkable that, even when they went about calling the passengers by the captain's orders, they had pipes in their mouths, and were quite unconcerned. Some of them, just before the vessel went down, had such faith in her stability that they 'had a few bouts' in the ship's gymnasium! This fact was vouched for by several of the survivors.

THE LAST BOAT TO LEAVE
PEOPLE WHO PREFERRED TO REMAIN ON THE LINER

One of our representatives, who was able to interview several of the firemen of the *Titanic* who were awaiting transference from Plymouth to Southampton, found that, according to their story, the news from America has not been unduly exaggerated.

Frank Dymond, fireman, of King's Lane, Southampton, said he was in charge of the last boat that left the ship. He gave a graphic account of what happened. He said that the day preceding the disaster was beautifully fine and a brilliant starlit night gave place to a day of warm sunshine. There was hardly a breath of air, and the water was as still as a miniature lake.

They were proceeding at 22½ knots, or about 29 miles an hour, and had entered the iceberg zone. Small clumps of ice could be seen in all directions, but there was no indication of large floes, or bergs.

The crew and passengers were calculating on a most enjoyable trip in probably record time. This fact was gathered by the general tone of the conversations carried on on all hands. Most of the passengers had retired by 11.30, and there were only a few moving about the vessel, enjoying the quietness of the scene which was of an inspiring character.

Mr Dymond had just looked at his watch, which indicated twenty minutes to midnight, when he suddenly heard a rasping sound. To give it in his own words, he said it was 'like a knife being drawn over a rasp'. He ran up on deck to see what was the matter. No harm seemed to have been done, so he went back to the stokehold again.

It was not long, however, before water began to pour in, and it had reached his ankles when he saw that something serious must have happened. He was then about to come off duty.

When he came on deck again he saw the boats being taken off. In fact, they had all except one left the side of the vessel. He was told to man this boat, but just as he was getting into her something happened, and he was swept on one side. There was no eagerness to get into the boat, however, the difficulty really was to get sufficient persons to go away in her.

He was again warned off to man the boat, and this time he took his place. Eventually there were sixty-eight souls on board this boat. There were no sailors. So far as he could see there was a deal of confusion, and scores who had first chance to get into the boats preferred to remain on the ship.

He took charge of the boat, in which there were twenty-two women and five children (one a Dago – Italian – woman and child), and one or two stewards. He was ordered to stand by a time, and an officer shouted: 'Are there any more women to go?'

There was no answer to this. The women appealed to refused to leave their husbands and relatives. Mr Dymond sat anxiously in the boat awaiting orders, and when no women came forward to take their places the officer shouted: 'Very well, fill up with passengers and crew.' Altogether he had sixty-eight souls in his boat and, except for the women and children, they were nearly all stewards.

He had not got more than 400 yards from the *Titanic* when he heard the first explosion. This happened at a quarter to two o'clock in the morning. The great vessel then dipped at the head and remained in that position for a considerable time. He thought it was nearly half an hour. Then suddenly there was another great explosion, and the bow gave a sort of jump and then seemed to wrench away from the middle portion. A few seconds later the whole fabric dived head foremost and was gone, leaving hundreds of souls floating on the water. From the time of striking to the end was not more than two hours and a half, if so long.

His boat was but slightly affected by the suction of the sinking leviathan. He had a tank of biscuits on board, and these were distributed to the children, and anyone else who wanted them, but most of them were too excited to think about eating. It was bitterly cold, but fortunately there was no wind, and the sea was smooth. The women and children lay huddled together for warmth, and the men took it in turns to row the boat. It was six hours before they were picked up, by which time many of them were in a prostrate condition. Kind attention on board the *Carpathia* soon brought them round, but even then most of them seemed to be unable to realize the full character of the experience that had befallen them.

Thomas Patrick Dillon told our representative that he was the last to leave the ship and be saved. He also is a fireman, and lives at 12, Oriental Terrace, Southampton. He remained down in the stokehold until the water was awash with his knees. He had been assured that the vessel was unsinkable, and did not trouble very much at the time.

When he came on deck the bow of the *Titanic* was pointing downwards as though it had been broken off from the main part of the bulk, 12 or 14 feet in from the cutwater. He stood on the poop which was at a slope of about 60 degrees, and was in time to see a second explosion. The bow seemed to bob up and then break down off like a piece of carrot.

HEROIC SOLOIST MUSICIAN

Musicians had been playing on the poop, but they and the captain had slid off into the sea, which was strewn with bodies. There was one musician left. He was a violinist, and was playing the air of the hymn: 'Nearer, My God, to Thee.'

Mr Dillon said the notes of this music were the last thing he heard before he went off the poop and felt himself going into the icy water headlong, with the engines and machinery buzzing in his ears. He was drawn down, he should think, about a couple of fathoms. Of that, however, he had no positive knowledge.

The next thing he could remember was waking up in one of the boats in terrible pain. The cold had numbed his limbs, and he had severe cramp in his stomach. He found that he was in No. 4 boat.

Frederick Harris, 57, Melville Road, Mill Lane, Gosport, had also a graphic story to tell. When the last moment came, and it was found that all the boats were gone and the vessel was going to sink, there was wild confusion. Deck chairs, and anything that would float were seized as the men jumped overboard.

He saw the captain jump into the water and grasp a child, which he placed on one of the rafts, of which there were all too few. He did not see the captain afterwards. He thought the First Officer, Mr Murdoch, shot himself. He himself got on to a small raft, but was afterwards taken into a boat. He was half-dead with the cold.

William Nutbean, 5 Horsman's Buildings, High Street, Southampton, said he was ordered away in No. 4 boat. They stood off some distance whilst the other boats were loading. At first there was no hurry, the difficulty being to get people to enter the boats. The women especially were courageous. They preferred to remain with their husbands when the latter were ordered to stand back. This caused some delay.

So far as he could remember, the first explosion took place about a quarter to two, and the second almost a quarter past two, the vessel disappearing within two hours of first striking. It seemed that her plates were ripped open from a dozen feet in from the bow to the second funnel. That accounted for the bow breaking off first and the ship making her final dip as described.

Chairs, small rafts, and other gear were floating about amongst a crowd of agonized strugglers in the water. The bitter cold soon put an end to most of these battles. His boat put back and picked up several persons, but the majority of the people they found floating were dead. It was an awesome sight, and one he had dreamed about ever since. The boat looked so small, in the great expanse of dark grey water, relieved here and there by clumps of ice, which only served to make sea and sky appear greyer.

He had many sufferers in his boat, and others were heartbroken at the loss of relatives and friends. The long, dreary hours spun out without much thought of eating and drinking until they were mercifully picked up by the liner.

A graphic description was given by a young fellow who served on the *Titanic* as a third-class steward.

I was asleep when the collision occurred, he observed, and the impact was not sufficient to disturb me. The first moment I knew anything was wrong was when I and others were ordered to man the boat-deck by the boats with our lifebelts on. I thought an emergency drill was being held, but, on reaching the deck, was told the ship had struck an iceberg.

The officers were endeavouring to get the women and children who were quartered aft into the boats, but they experienced some little difficulty at first, because a number of foreigners attempted to rush into the boats. They were soon forced back, however. These men were arrant cowards. When I started to go on deck I saw two of them crying bitterly in the companion-way.

We filled the boats with women and children, and got them away safely. I stayed on deck, not thinking the ship was going down, but when she gradually became submerged, and the water came up over the boat deck and the bows, I knew there was no hope, so jumped overboard. I swam about for four or five minutes, till I reached an upturned collapsible boat, to which twenty-seven others were clinging, including a saloon passenger and two third-class passengers (an Irishman and a Swede) and the Second Officer. We clung to this boat for five hours until picked up by the *Carpathia*.

I saw the *Titanic* go down. Two of her funnels fell off and after an explosion, which I distinctly heard, being only a short distance away at the time, she smashed in the middle. Her bows went down, and then her stern, which was almost upright when it sank. Fortunately there was very little suction; had there been as much as I had anticipated, none of us would have been saved. As it was, the Second Officer fell off the boat to which we clung, and was not seen afterwards.

Asked how long it took him to get over the shock of his experience, the steward said that it was hardly possible for him yet to realize what had really happened. 'I cannot fully comprehend that so many of my comrades of the ship have been drowned,' he added.

The band on the *Titanic*, composed of six Englishmen, a German, and a Frenchman, displayed conspicuous bravery. In order to prevent a panic Capt. Smith instructed them to play. As the musicians ran after their instruments they were laughed at by several of the crew, who did not realize how serious matters were; but they began to render hymn tunes, and continued to do so to the last. While playing 'Nearer, My God, to Thee', the water was washing over their feet, and in a very short time they disappeared beneath the waves.

Several of the crew testified to this yesterday, and spoke in highest commendation of the bandsmen.

I shall never forget hearing the strains of that beautiful hymn as I was leaving the sinking ship, one observed. It was always a favourite hymn of mine, but at such a time, and under such tragic circumstances, it had for me a solemnity too deep for words. No praise could be sufficient for those courageous musicians whom we left behind; they were heroes to a man.

But the contrast was too awful to be described. At one moment it was music, at the next moanings and groanings of the ill-fated men who were left behind as they struggled in the water. We could not see them, neither were we able to render any assistance, for our boat was full; but for along while they harrowed our feelings as, in their agony, they gave full vent to their suffering. I shall never forget that night as long as I live.

Another seaman intimated that he was asleep in his bunk at the time of the collision. He and some of his comrades went on deck and then returned to their bunks, one of them remarking: 'We have glanced an iceberg. Let us turn in again.' A quarter of an hour later they were ordered on deck with their lifebelts on.

The captain would not allow me on the boat deck for some time, he proceeded, but after a while he told me to assist in launching the boats. The women and children were put in first.

After the last boat had gone I was standing on the deck and just before the ship went down the captain shouted, 'Everyone for himself.' An Italian woman with two children was standing near me. She gave me one of the babies and kept the other herself. We both jumped into the sea. No small boats could be seen, and the last I saw of those on the liner was a crowd standing on the poop, which was rising.

The intensely cold water killed the baby in my arms and I let it go. I swam about for some minutes, and then caught hold of some wreckage. After about an hour I saw the upturned boat to which the Second Officer and others were clinging. I joined them. The Second Officer said, 'Now all keep calm, and we shall be picked up.'

This proved to be true, for we were rescued by a boat which was already pretty full.

The seaman added that he saw the Chief Officer shoot at two Italians who were pushing women aside on the steamer in a frantic endeavour to reach the lifeboats. As the first shot fired above their heads did not serve as a warning, the officer shot one of them.

The only one of twenty-six greasers saved jumped overboard shortly before the liner disappeared, and was picked up by one of the small boats. He spoke in high terms of the gallantry of the engineers, and stated that the *Titanic* had been steaming very smoothly, thus making the voyage for the passengers thoroughly enjoyable.

When the accident happened a fireman with one or two others were on deck procuring some refreshment. They should have been relieved in about ten minutes. The starboard deck was covered with ice, and one of his comrades expressed the opinion that it was 'pretty serious, Bill!' An officer came along and ordered them to go below to their work, but they stopped where they were, and were shortly afterwards mistaken for the relief watch, which, for some reason or another, did not turn up as usual. The men were accordingly told to help with the boats. He was sitting in one of the boats attending to the gear when he felt somebody underneath the thwarts, and on making a search found two Chinamen concealed.

This man did not leave in a boat, but swam towards an upturned collapsible.

CAPTAIN COULD HAVE SAVED HIMSELF

I was just a short distance from the ship, and I knew that Captain Smith could have saved himself if he liked. He could have jumped into the water and been rescued as others were, but up to the last he walked up and down the deck, giving through a megaphone to those trying to save their lives.

Another fireman assisted to free a collapsible boat in the officers' quarters, and got it over the side just in time. It overturned, but he clung to it, and one of the liner's funnels falling into the water created a swell which carried the boat away from the ship. He was so affected by the cold water that he had to receive attention in a New York hospital.

Another version was given by a second-class steward of the conduct of Mr Lowe, the Fifth Officer. He stood on the bulkhead of the top deck and heard Mr Murdoch giving directions as to lowering the boats. The steward was called upon to assist, after which he was lowered into a boat with Mr Lowe in charge. When the boat was within four feet of the water there was not sufficient rope to lower her further, so that she had to be dropped into the water. The steward was jerked overboard, picked up by another boat, and transferred to his original position. They rowed away, and Mr Lowe, who had done more than anyone else, this steward said, to keep people afloat, got the other lifeboats which had preceded his together, and by transferring passengers practically emptied one boat, which was manned by seven men, including the speaker.

They proceeded to row towards the wreck with the object of saving as many lives as possible. In this they were successful. On getting within a hundred yards of her the liner sank. Mr Lowe said, 'Well, boys, I am prepared to row nearer and take my chance. I don't think there's any fear of being sucked down. Are the rest prepared to go? At the same time it practically means certain death because if we go among all these people we shall probably be lost.'

They proceeded to draw nearer, but those in the boat demurred. They spent all night rowing round, however, and picked up several more people.

One of these was a stalwart German. They tried several times to get him into the boat, but failed; and then Mr Lowe expressed the opinion that the cause was due to the poor man's legs being doubled up by the cold. The steward went into the water to try and straighten the limbs, and after many difficulties the German was hauled into the frail craft only to die within five minutes.

'I saw Mr Bruce Ismay run on deck in his pyjamas,' the steward went on. 'He rendered most valuable assistance, being cool and collected all the time. He only went into the last boat at the pathetic request of the women as there was no other man who understood handling a boat available.'

Asked what the crew generally thought of Mr Ismay, the steward emphatically declared that they held him in the highest respect, and thought he had been shabbily treated in America. This opinion was further confirmed by a fireman who worked in the electrical engine-room.

MR ISMAY'S EXAMPLE
'DON'T FORGET YOU ARE ENGLISH'

Percy Keene, who was one of the waiters of the *Titanic*, testified to the discipline that prevailed on the ship when the emergency arose. He said the boats were got out as smartly as possible, but no one seemed to realize what was about to happen. It was treated as a joke even among the sailors, and this over-confidence in the unsinkability of the *Titanic* accounted for the death roll being so heavy. Some people even got out of the boats again to secure warmer clothing, and they found too late that they were unable to get back again to the deck as the end came with amazing suddenness.

All through the anxious time Mr Bruce Ismay set an example which stirred the crew to great exertions. He was wonderfully calm, and went from boat to boat assisting in the lowering of them and in placing women and children in them. Once he was not recognized by the officer in charge, who ordered him away, but it was generally felt among the crew that he had struggled hard, and in no way deserved the unkind things said of him in the American Press.

'Once I heard Mr Ismay say,' continued Mr Keene, ' "Don't forget you are English." This was just before the last boat was sent away. Mr Ismay took his place in it because there were no passengers, women or children, on the deck or in sight anywhere.'

Continuing, Keene bore testimony to the devotion to duty of the bedroom stewards. He had seen for himself how valiantly they had driven back the men who had attempted to reach the boats before all the women and children had been accommodated. They had given their lives willingly for others.

He described in detail how he saw the *Titanic* break into two or three parts, but after the middle section, with the machinery, gave out the end quickly followed.

Walter Hurst, fireman, stated that when he reached the boat deck, after the collision, he assisted into getting the passengers into the boats. About five minutes before the *Titanic* went down he thought the time had come to look out for himself, and fearing the suction that was expected, he leapt into the sea. For three hours he battled for his life, being eventually picked up at daylight, when he was almost done for.

'I could not have lasted very much longer,' he said. 'I was numbed to the bone with the cold, and I still feel the effects, and shall do so for a long time.'

He mentioned that the engine-room staff died practically at their posts. He pointed out that a watch comprised fifty-three firemen, twenty-four trimmers, twenty greasers, five leading firemen, and ten engineers.

Of the watch on duty only six men, and these of the lower ratings, were saved. How they got out he could not explain, but said that the others remained raking out the fires probably to the very last. The fact that so many firemen were saved was due to the fact that they had been sent away to assist in the boats, whilst many were picked up after jumping into the sea as a last chance.

MR MURDOCH'S FATE
'ONE LEFT FOR YOU AND ANOTHER FOR MYSELF'

One of the crew told our representative that Mr Murdoch, the First Officer, who was in charge of the ship when the collision occurred, played a hero's part. He it was who personally superintended the lowering of practically every boat that was put into the water. He moved from one boat to another urging and cheering the men at their task. When the end came, and as the last boat was being handled, the water rose above his knees, and it was obvious that the boat could not survive.

'Mr Murdoch calmly pulled out his revolver and blew out his brains.'

Previously he had used it to threaten the excited steerage passengers and a group of firemen who he feared were likely to rush the boats. He drove them back, as one man said, like a flock of sheep, remarking significantly as he patted the barrel of his revolver: 'There is one left for you and one for myself.'

A number of men declared yesterday that they saw Mr Murdoch fire the fatal shot shortly before the *Titanic* plunged into the darkness of the ocean depths.

Another stirring story concerns the closing chapter of the career of Chief Purser McElroy, who has a relative at Bodmin. From the outset McElroy was kept busily employed rousing the passengers and then encouraging them to face the ordeal that awaited them. From one to the other he went with characteristic sang-froid and coolness, his cheery manner giving heart to many. Here he stopped to fasten a lifebelt a little more securely; there it was to persuade a passenger to put on warmer clothing.

Then he conducted them to the boats, and as the last one drew away from the side of the *Titanic* sailors saw the popular purser standing calmly on the topmost deck sucking a lemon. By his side stood Mr Wm. Gwynne [sic], one of the United States postal clerks, and together they awaited with complacency the end. Three American and two English postal clerks were lost, the latter being Messrs Williamson and Jago Smith (a Cornishman). They were endeavouring to save the registered mail when last seen, being under the impression that the ship would float for eight to ten hours.

Equally heroic was the manner in which Drs O'Loughlin and Simpson, with Chief Steward Latimer, faced the end. After they had done all they could to help the passengers, they gathered in the lounge, a beautiful apartment, and then seated in chairs, calmly smoked cigarettes as if nothing was about to happen.

THE 'MONEY BOAT' STORY
INDIGNANT DENIAL THAT REWARDS
WERE PROMISED BY RICH FOLK

Probably the most interesting description of the calamity was given by J. Horswell, who hails from Ugborough, near Ivybridge. His father was in the Metropolitan Police at Devonport. Horswell, who served as a sailor, was one of the men who went away in an emergency boat. This boat contained only thirteen people, including Sir Cosmo and Lady Duff Gordon, five firemen, two sailors (Horswell and a man named Symons, who has been detained in New York to give evidence at the inquiry), and two Americans.

Horswell indignantly repudiated the suggestion that the boat was the 'millionaires' boat', and that the crew had been bribed to take her passengers away, but admitted having in his possession an order on Coutts's Bank, Ltd, dated April 15, 1912, for 'the payment of £5 to J. Horswell', the document bearing the signature of 'Cosmo Duff Gordon'.

He stated that nothing was said about money at any time in the boat, either before or after she left the *Titanic*, but on reaching the *Carpathia*, Sir Cosmo spontaneously expressed a wish to present each of the boat's crew with £5 to help them replace the clothes and effects they had lost.

Horswell explained further that the boat went from the side of the liner with such a small number through the instrumentality of

Mr Murdoch, who hustled Sir Cosmo and his wife in and ordered them to get away. It was not thought at the time that the ship would sink, or that it would be long before they were back again.

The small boat was wanted out of the way because the davits were required for the purpose of lowering other boats.

Horswell said he saw Captain Smith in the water swimming, with a baby in his arms, towards a raft. The captain afterwards disappeared.

Before the *Titanic* went down Horswell saw the light of a vessel about one point or one and a half points on the port bow. The liner had been sending up rockets, but they apparently did not attract the attention of the vessel for no answer came. After the boat was lowered they started to pull in the direction of the light, which, it transpired, was but one of a number of lights, thus indicating that the ship was a large one. Unfortunately, the lights seemed to get further away.

FATAL OVER-CONFIDENCE

Horswell attributed a great deal of loss of life to the over-confidence of the people, who apparently relied too much on the unsinkability of the *Titanic*. He instanced cases where people who had been placed in the boats got out of them again and returned to the liner, feeling assured that they were safer there than in the small craft.

So far as the effect of the collision was concerned, Horswell was of opinion that the starboard side of the liner was torn away from the forecastle to the bridge – a distance of about 80 feet. 'I was in my bunk asleep at the time, and I was jerked out on the floor.'

The lights of the *Titanic* were visible practically to the last minute, 'and it appeared to me,' he proceeded, 'that as she plunged beneath the surface there was a momentary reflection below water.'

When he left his bunk and reached the deck he saw a quantity of ice there, and also had his attention directed to the fact that water was coming out of the hatches of the lower decks. As the liner began to take a dangerous list he was engaged with others in preparing the boats, prior to being ordered away by Mr Murdoch.

Just before the end the *Titanic* separated between the third and fourth funnels. The foremost funnel had previously fallen into the water on the starboard side with a terrific splash, unquestionably doing a great deal of injury to people struggling in the water.

Afterwards the ship broke in two, and the after part came up on a level keel for a brief space, the bow having already disappeared. Then the stern rose, and an instant later plunged below. He felt four distinct explosions after that, and regarded it as particularly fortunate that the boilers burst below water rather than above, as otherwise few would have lived to tell the ghastly story.

Horswell did not pick up anybody. The temperature of the water, together with the consequent shock and excitement, was such that the death of hundreds must have been almost instantaneous. No bodies were seen floating about by Horswell, although he made a search.

He further urged that the suggestion that a number of bodies were found on the ice floe was impossible, unless they had been washed there, for before the *Carpathia* left she carefully searched the vicinity of the fatality.

'The *Titanic* was a wonderful ship,' added Horswell. He regarded her as a much finer ship than the *Olympic*, being more speedy and far more easy for the crew to work. At the time of the accident she was steaming at a speed of nearly 23 knots an hour, her previous day's run being 546 miles. Instructions had been given for the following day for a full test of her power. Two other boilers which had not been used were to have been worked.

TRYING TO RUSH THE BOATS

One of the stewards last evening described how there were many instances among the steerage passengers of attempting to rush the boats. The officers behaved with great resource and cowed them by a display of revolvers.

Continuing his story, however, he said that he would have been afraid to have jumped into a lifeboat even if he had felt inclined to do so, as he saw seven men shot for attempting to do so. One had his chin blown off.

Another of the arrivals spoke of the devotion of Capt. Smith, who stuck to his post until the bridge disappeared beneath the waves. Once he leapt overboard, clutched an infant, swam with it to a lifeboat, and then returned to the sinking ship.

Harry Oliver, of Southampton, a fireman, told our representative that he had turned in when a crash aroused him, and he went on deck to see what had happened. Then he saw a quantity of ice on deck, and was told that the ship had struck an iceberg. Satisfied with the information, he returned to his bunk and turned in again, confident that nothing serious had happened.

He was just dropping off to sleep again when one of the other firemen rushed into the room and said, 'Turn out quickly; she is making water in the winding staircase.'

On going to have a look around, Oliver realized that his previous confidence was misplaced and went back to pack his bag, which he took up to the mess-room. Then a leading fireman said, 'Put on your stokehold gear, and get ready for watch.' This he did and then orders were given to put on lifebelts and get to the boats.

On reaching the boat-deck, he found that most of the boats had already been launched except number nine. One of the officers ordered him into the boat, and it was then lowered away, having on board a number of women and children. Recognizing that the *Titanic* was fast settling down, the crew pulled vigorously to get beyond the region of a possible vortex.

Suddenly there was a terrible crash, and the great ship appeared to split in 'twain, if not in three distinct sections, the rending of her timbers and steel plates making a noise that carried terror into the hearts of all.

The end came swiftly. One of the huge funnels toppled over the side, and then the bow parted just in a line with the bridge.

Tilting forward, the *Titanic* appeared to be going down slowly by the head, when there was a rush and a roar which led the horrified onlookers to come to the conclusion that the machinery had burst through the bulkhead and had fallen out of the ship.

Then for a moment or two the after portion of the vessel looked to be righting herself, and she came up on an even keel, yet with a lurch that raised her stern high in the air. For a brief period she remained in this position, and then vanished from view, whilst at that moment the air was rent with cries of 'Mercy!' and 'Help!'

It was a pitiable scene, and I can scarcely get the cries out of my ears now. It was too awful to realize that near us were our shipmates doomed to a dreadful death in the icy seas over which but a few brief hours before the *Titanic* had been driving in all the pride of a maiden voyage.

STEWARD'S STORY
SOLE SURVIVOR OF THE ENGINEERS' DEPARTMENT

An intensely thrilling story was told to our representative last evening by Cecil William Fitzpatrick, engineer's room steward, and the sole survivor of the engineering staff.

On the fateful Sunday evening he was aroused from sleep by a sudden lurch of the vessel and the stopping of the engines. One of his mates inquired the cause, but was told it was nothing serious. A little later Fitzpatrick was again awakened by a fireman, who was in the act of taking a lifebelt belonging to the engineers' stewards. They refused to let him have it, and he then told them the Chief Engineer wanted them to muster.

FOREIGNER SHOT DEAD

When I was on deck, proceeded Fitzpatrick, the ship was listing to port, and I went to help lower away one of the lifeboats. Women and children were put in, and as she was being lowered a Dago (Italian) tried to jump from the taffrail to the edge of the boat. The officer in charge pointed a revolver at him, and told him to get back on deck. The Dago refused, the officer fired, and I saw the man fall back dead on the deck. There were crews of foreigners hanging around the lifeboat ready to leap, but they cowered when they saw one of their number shot dead.

As the lifeboat was lowered away the officer kept continually firing his revolver, from deck to deck until he got below deck level.

Similar instances of firing occurred on the port side. A man whom I took to be a saloon passenger tried to claim a seat in one of the boats. The officer told him to leave, and as the man hesitated, the revolver rang out and his body fell into the sea.

I then went for's'd on the port side, and I was passing through the bridge when I saw Capt. Smith speaking to Mr Andrews, the designer of the *Titanic*. I stopped to listen. I was still confident that the ship was unsinkable, but when I heard Capt. Smith say: 'We cannot stay any longer; she is going!' I fainted against the starboard side of the bridge entrance.

After some minutes I recovered sufficiently to realize that unless I got into a boat or swam for it, there would be no chance of being saved.

I then went to launch one of the collapsible boats which had been eased down off the top decks on the starboard side. We found, when we tried to swing her in the davits, that she was wedged between the winch of the davits and the spar – which helped to ease her down from the lower deck, which is the deck below the boat deck.

The next thing I remember was the ship suddenly dipping, and the waves rushing up and engulfing me. After ten seconds the *Titanic* again righted herself, but then I saw that everyone who a minute before had been attempting to lower away, except myself, had been swept into the fo'castle head. I saved myself by clinging on to the davit winch.

I looked down the fo'castle, and saw the most horrible, heartrending scenes I have ever witnessed. There were women and children and firemen and stewards all fighting, shrieking for help in their death struggles. I got on the other side of the winch which was towards the after-part of the vessel, and levered myself up on to the deck.

Then I went to the edge of the ship and jumped into the icy water. In order to escape the suction which I surmised would be caused by the sinking of the gigantic liner, I struck out for very life. I swam from the ship as the for's'd was sinking. I did not feel any suction.

I am a strong swimmer, and I had managed to keep afloat quite twenty minutes, when I got on to an overturned lifeboat, on which was Officer Lightoller and a number of other people. We drifted about until daybreak, when we were sighted by No. 12 lifeboat of the *Titanic*. Then we rowed towards the *Carpathia*, which loomed into sight, and were taken on board at 7.30 a.m.

Questioned as to other details of the disaster, Fitzpatrick said he heard the band playing a hymn at the last moment, but as he was a Catholic he failed to recognize the tune.

'I was the next to the last man to leave the doomed ship,' he remarked. The last man climbed up the poop.

When Fitzpatrick was in the water he saw the *Titanic* stick her screws and propellers high into the air, and he heard her go down with a swish – 'as clean a dive as ever was made by a fish.'

As to the engineers, he said: 'Every man Jack stuck to his post to the end. I am the only one of that section of the ship's crew saved out of forty-one.'

(*Western Daily Mercury*, 29 April 1912)

SOME LOCAL INCIDENTS
POLICE OFFICERS WITH A WARRANT FOR A MISSING MAN

There were many incidents of note during the day, and one very exciting escape from drowning in the Sound. While the mails were being transferred to the *Sir Francis Drake* in Cawsand Bay, one of the bags fell overboard. A seaman from the *Lapland* was slung over the side by a rope in an attempt to recover it, but the rope was short, and the man, who could not swim, fell into the sea. Instantly a lifeline was thrown him from the *Drake*, and he clambered inboard, none the worse for his ducking.

The Chief Constable of Plymouth (Mr J. D. Sowerby) and Detective Inspector Hitchcock visited the docks for the purpose of performing an unpleasant task. They had a warrant for the arrest of one of the crew, issued by his wife, for failing to keep up payments in respect of a maintenance order. Mr Sowerby and Mr Hitchcock interviewed a man of the same name, but the description did not correspond with the man who is wanted, and there is little doubt that the unfortunate fellow is among those who were drowned.

Each of the crew received 7s 6d or 6s 6d yesterday from the Board of Trade, according to their rating. A sum of £300 sent from America by a lady will be divided among the crew on the way to their homes.

(*Western Daily Mercury*, 29 April 1912)

TITANIC SURVIVORS ARRIVE

A large number of the survivors of the *Titanic*'s crew were landed at Plymouth yesterday by the *Lapland*.

Some of them had amazing stories to tell. One of them spoke of a millionaire who offered 5000 dollars if he could be saved.

Another described the escape of a wealthy man and his wife in the emergency boat, and added that there was a distribution of cheques on the *Carpathia*.

It appears that great difficulty was experienced in getting some of the third-class passengers and crew to believe that the liner was in peril, and the survivors say that many perished through disregarding the warnings given.

Of the 'black squad' on duty at the time of the disaster only very few were saved. They drew the fires to prevent the boilers exploding, and before they got out the water was above their waists.

On being put ashore the men whose depositions had been taken were free to roam about the dockyard, and many of them made for the gates outside which friends and townspeople were congregated. Many affectionate reunions took place in spite of the barrier between.

Comedy and tragedy went hand in hand. A pale youth from the stokehold leaning against the gates told his friends of the loss of his brother. 'He was in the watch down below at the time we struck,' he said. 'I was in the watch which was to relieve him at midnight. As I started to go down I found the water rising in the stoke-hold. It being impossible for me to get below, I went on deck. I never saw my brother again.'

A young steward said his chief memory of the disaster was the nonchalance that prevailed. 'Lots of us who turned out when we felt the first shock of the collision went back to our bunks again, thinking nothing had happened,' he said. 'For some of them the sleep to which they returned proved to be the last sleep, I think.'

Many of the New York stories that have been regarded as inventions found corroboration among the crew.

'I heard one millionaire who was offering 5000 dollars if he could be saved,' one man told me. 'I didn't hear him myself, but it was all the talk among our gang. Some of them heard it. Today the American papers are printing the man's name in letters a foot long as a national hero.'

Another man, one of the firemen, spoke of a wealthy man who escaped in what is called the emergency boat – that is a boat which is kept ready for prompt lowering in case of 'man overboard'.

'He got his wife and family and some friends into that boat and got it lowered, promising the men who were rowing £5 apiece. The morning after we were picked up by the *Carpathia* the boat's crew was summoned to the saloon deck, and there received the money, in cheques.'

(*Daily Sketch*, 29 April 1912)

On landing at Plymouth, an unnamed steward in the first-class saloon tried to separate fact from fiction.

The millionaires certainly did not run the ship and all talk of Maj. Butt and Mr Astor introducing a system and seeing after the boats is entirely wrong. I saw them all the time, and they were just standing by and doing what they were told like anyone else. They did not, however, show any sign of panic.

Until the very end no one had any idea how serious the affair was. The only panic was among the Dagoes, one of whom I did see shot through the chin. As for the ladies, they behaved splendidly during the disaster, but told some terrible falsehoods after. The stories of their having helped in the rowing are much exaggerated. In my own boat, a dinghy, a lady put her arm on my shoulder, and I dare say she thought she was helping me. The difficulty all through was to get them into the boats, and several of them I had personally to throw head foremost in.

If you ask me who were the real heroes of the disaster I should say certainly Colonel Gracie, the best American there. Then there was Mr Andrews, one of the designers of the ship, who was here, there and everywhere, helping always and never troubling about his own life. He did not even put on a lifebelt nor, of course, did Captain Smith, who behaved splendidly. Captain Smith's last words were not 'Be British' although by sentiment they might have been: they were, 'I'm finished. Look after yourselves.'

Murdoch was splendid too, but I fear it is true that he did shoot himself. He did not do so, however, till the very end, when he had done everything he could for others.

Another hero was old Freeman, the deck steward, who to the very last was tying deck chairs together as hard as he could and throwing them overboard to serve as rafts for the people who had dived. He could easily have saved his own life, but did not seem to think of it.

(*Daily Chronicle*, 29 April 1912)

THE WRONG NAME

Tragic Disappointment of a Waiting Woman

From dawn this morning till darkness Southampton has been anxiously awaiting the return of the *Titanic* survivors. Among those on the steamer *Lapland* were 150 Southampton people.

The most pathetic incident of the day was a terrible misunderstanding. A Mrs F. W. Barrett, whose husband was on the *Titanic*, had received a message from New York saying that her husband was saved and was on his way home.

She had prepared to meet him, and was even informed that he was travelling in the train from Plymouth.

This afternoon, however, Mrs Barrett received a telegram stating that the traveller was not her husband, but another man with the same name. Mrs Barrett gave birth to twins two days after the wreck of the *Titanic*.

(*Daily Graphic*, 29 April 1912)

HEROES AND VICTIMS

Inquiries among other survivors brought to light several instances of heroic self-sacrifice. When the vessel took her last terrible plunge, two young stewards, who had been awaiting the event together, found themselves still companions in the icy water. They had been chums on board, and they determined to make their bid for life together. One, stronger than his friend and a good swimmer, set out in the darkness, helping his shipmate with his strength and encouraging words. Though not seen he was heard to say: 'Keep your pecker up, old man, or you'll never see Southampton.' The next minute they were hauled into a boat, one at each end. Both were exhausted, and for one the ordeal had been too much. The man of weaker frame had succumbed when his body was lifted on to the *Carpathia*.

Another grim tragedy, more tragic, because it happened hidden away in the depths of the *Titanic*, amidst the din of the reversed engines. One of the engineers hurrying to a point of duty, and observing that a plate had been removed, stepped into an opening and broke his leg – according to some, both legs. He lay groaning and helpless, when a leading hand and a greaser, putting aside all thoughts of their own safety, carried him to the power-room, where he remained.

With the greaser, the poor fellow went down with the ship, unable to help himself even if opportunity had offered. The leading hand was more fortunate.

When the full story of the *Titanic* is unfolded, these displays of magnificent pluck will be found unsurpassed. For instance, nothing could be finer than the resolute nobility of the engineer who swam up to an already fully laden boat just at the moment that the last cries of the victims were ringing in the ears of the survivors. He came up to the side of the boat.

'Don't come to us, or we shall all go,' the occupants yelled.

With a display of self-possession that nothing could exceed, he shouted back, 'Don't mind me; go on.' Though the alternative was death, he made no attempt to grasp the gunwale, and he was lost to view.

THE CHILD SAVES THE FATHER

A brighter incident may be recorded here. A boat was about to be lowered away. 'More women and children,' had been shouted. The only response was that of a father who stepped forward with his child in his arms. He wished to place the little one in the boat and remain on board, but the child clung to him frantically. The occupants of the boat exhorted him to come as well, and he yielded. A few moments sufficed, and the child had saved his father.

One of the crew, who has crossed the Atlantic many times, was openly incredulous regarding the story that some well-known ocean gamblers escaped in women's clothing, which they had bought from stewards, but he admitted that men of that class were on board the *Titanic*, and expressed surprise to find them afterwards on the *Carpathia*.

A *Mercury* reporter had a chat with Mr B. Thomas, one of the stewards, who was allotted to No. 15 boat, on the starboard side – the last of the odd numbers. 'I was lying awake in my bunk,' he said, 'when the ship struck. She struck gently, and I thought so little of it that I was going to sleep again.'

He declared that, although he had spent many years in the Atlantic service, he had never seen so much ice as he did on that morning when daylight came. He laughingly described an incident in his boat. A lady – a second-class passenger – complained of the lack of room, and grumbled almost all the way to the *Carpathia*. If she realized her good fortune in being saved, she did not show it.

He endorsed the statement made by others that some of the officers made sure of order by firing their revolvers over the heads of the people. Just after one of the boats was launched, the officer in charge said: 'If anyone disobeys me I will shoot.'

A HUNDRED SWIMMERS
NUMBER QUICKLY REDUCED BY THE EXTREME COLD

Mr Frank Prentice, assistant storekeeper of the *Titanic*, seen yesterday, admitted that he had had a really miraculous escape. With nine of his companion storekeepers, he clambered in the poop after having done everything possible to assist the passengers. Some he supplied with lifebelts, and a number he handed into the lifeboats. Among them was Mrs Clarke, who expressed a hope that she would meet him again. Little did either anticipate the startling circumstances in which her wish was to be gratified.

When once the lifeboats were away, Mr Prentice proceeded right aft, and clambered on to the stern, which already was lifting out of the water preliminary to the final plunge. He described the scene as being awe-inspiring, all the people on deck clambering one after another away from the advancing waves.

When at length he realized that there was no hope of safety from the fast sinking vessel, he decided to plunge into the sea, and he calculated that he must have jumped over 100 feet, the three propellers of the ship being then well out of the water. He had a lifebelt around him, and being a powerful swimmer quickly came to the surface and found in his vicinity nearly 100 of the crew and passengers swimming for their lives. He shouted to them, inquiring for a close companion called Ricks, who he knew was not a good swimmer. Ricks eventually came to his side and he encouraged him for some time to swim with him, but like many others he disappeared, being overcome by the extreme cold and exhaustion, following a long exposure to the water.

Mr Prentice explained that, during the time he was in company with the swimmers, they encouraged one another by shouts, and advised each other to keep in close company. So swiftly was the number reduced, however, that he decided to swim away on his own, and he advised Ricks to follow his example. Had the latter done so, he would probably have been saved, as very soon he came in contact with a quantity of wreckage. Then, with deck chairs and cushions, he made a sort of frail raft, and on this he supported himself, swimming whenever it was necessary to keep himself warm, as the icy waters were even more terrible than the cries of his drowning friends, harrowing as they were to his feelings.

After being over four hours in the sea, he was picked up and taken aboard one of the lifeboats, in which, strangely enough, Mrs Clarke was seated. This lady took off her coat and wrapped him in it, while others assisted to restore him to animation.

Mr Prentice emphasizes the wonderful presence of mind that prevailed amongst the ship's officers, mentioning that just before he left Mr McElroy, the purser, to go on deck to see about the boats he had been engaged in provisioning, Mr McElroy inquired if anything had been locked up below, meaning the store rooms, thus indicating that he had no idea how seriously the ship had been injured.

One of the stewards, Mr A. J. Littlejohn, who lives at Cheshunt, Herts, was one of those who escaped in a lifeboat in which there were about fifty people, and in the course of a conversation about the accident he expressed the opinion that if it had not been a fine night with a smooth sea not a single soul would have survived. He explained that the boats were lowered from a tremendous height, and only in smooth seas would it have been possible to do such good work as was done on the *Titanic*.

Before any of the crew more than necessary for the management of the boats clambered in, all the passengers on A deck, on the starboard side, where No. 13 lifeboat was situated, had been accounted for. The women and children were at first dealt with, and then several male passengers were taken on board. It was after this, when there was no one present but members of the crew, that one of the officers directed them to take their seats and to row away.

PANIC AMONG THE STEERAGE PASSENGERS

At this stage she had not listed, but she was beginning to go down by the head. The B deck ports forward were underwater, the result being that the third-class passengers in the steerage, who were accommodated under, were hurrying up, carrying with them their boxes, baggage, and lifebelts. They had not stopped to put on the last-mentioned. Many of the stewards, Mr Littlejohn admitted, looked on amused at the scenes, being firmly under the impression that the ship was unsinkable, and some regarded the whole procedure and the launching of the boats as a huge joke. Many of the crew were convinced that it was only an emergency boat drill, and it was some time after that they recognized that the responsible officers had come to the conclusion that the *Titanic* was doomed.

Amongst the steerage passengers there was a state of affairs bordering on panic. Moaning and weeping piteously, they hurried through the alleyways that led to the third-class promenade deck, and it was a long time before the water got there; not, in fact, until the poop had risen in the air.

Once the water touched the boilers the end of the *Titanic* was not long delayed. Immediately after the collision with the iceberg – within two or three minutes – the engines were stopped, and there arose the sound of the escaping steam. But what was more alarming was the inrush of water, which caused the hissing in the machinery. There was an early explosion, which led to the fracture of the main fabric of the vessel, and a few minutes after the bow portion disappeared. Then the machinery took charge, and within another twenty minutes the great vessel had passed from view.

Mr Littlejohn mentioned that when he came up on deck the first time he found broken ice to the depth of two feet in the forward well-deck, this showing that the berg was above the surface of the water. He added that on the arrival of the *Carpathia* the stewards resumed their normal occupation and assisted in looking after the passengers who had been rescued.

With reference to the experiences on the *Carpathia*, it was generally agreed amongst the stewards that Mr Bruce Ismay did not appear during the voyage and that he kept himself in the cabin and was under medical treatment. It is asserted that he refused to take food, and that the only thing he consumed until he reached New York was water.

In the course of conversations yesterday morning our representatives gained some additional information of interest. One of those, a waiter named Percy Keene on the ill-starred ship, described the collision as being violent enough to awaken everyone in the *Titanic* who was asleep, though it partook of the nature of a prolonged trembling such as he had before experienced at sea when a vessel had shed a propeller. That that was the case was generally believed in the 'glory hole', a central suite used by the stewards' mess, in which is a winding staircase leading to the top deck.

Presently, he said, the engines, which had at once slowed down, entirely stopped and they were never restarted.

Capt. Smith went to the bridge, closed the watertight doors and sent for Mr Andrews, designer of the vessel. Together they went below to the scene of the damage and found many of the fore-holds full of water. The extent of the ripping of plates was such as to convince the captain of the seriousness of the damage, and he communicated this to Mr Bruce Ismay, whom he joined on the bridge.

Steps to secure safety were quietly proceeded with from that moment, though the stewards had the greatest difficulty to persuade many of the souls on board to leave their state rooms, the women being especially loath to get up.

Mr Keene said he had come to the conclusion that the high loss of life among the female passengers of the third class was due to their lack of knowledge as to how to reach the boat deck. Many of them must have become hopelessly lost in the hull of the levia-than when her doom became obvious. Fright and hopelessness doubtless accounted for many.

There were no end of small rafts secured, he added, but in the darkness it was very difficult to make effective use of them. The handling of the collapsible boats was also hampered by the night. 'Many, many more would have been saved if daylight had come soon after the accident. We should have been able to open the lower gangways and pass the people down by rope ladders, but that was impossible in the prevailing blackness.'

Shortly before the special train steamed out of the docks, two of the stewardesses who are returning to their homes – Mrs Gold and Mrs Martin – granted a brief interview, in which they narrated their experiences. They were first-class stewardesses on the *Titanic*, and were both saved in No. 11 boat. They had been old 'shipmates', having sailed together in the *Olympic* and the *Adriatic* whilst earlier in their careers they were both on the *Cedric*, of the same line.

When the alarm, or the first idea of alarm, came to us, said one, we were sleeping. We received the notification with much amusement, and quite ignored what we thought was a joke. We were advised to get up and put our lifebelts on, but we did not stir. It was only when Mr Andrews, one of the principals of Messrs Harland & Wolff, the builders of the ship, came to us and told us to hurry up on deck that we began to realize the urgency of the situation.

On deck, they continued, the bandsmen were playing 'ragtime' music as the crew were getting out the boats, and it was a noteworthy fact that so interested and engrossed in their duty were these gallant musicians that they would not stop playing to put on the lifebelts which were brought to them. The ladies put on their own belts, yet were laughing and joking all the time, considering they were obeying orders which were part of drill. When ordered to the boats, though, they began to realize otherwise.

GERMANS HIDE IN A BOAT

In No. 11 boat there were seventy-five people, sixty-two being women. After pulling away from the side of the *Titanic* it was found two German males had concealed themselves in the boat before she was lowered. They were found under the seats, and one of them refused to come out, wrapping Mrs Gold's skirts around him for warmth. One of the crew prodded him several times with an oar yet failed to induce him to budge an inch. His compatriot did take his share of work at the oars, but the skulking fellow was permanently idle – except when he was once heard counting out his money!

The first boat to leave the ship was full of firemen, but that was because few ladies were willing to go, and it was imperative to fill the boats. The other members of the crew saved were those required to man the boats and those who saved themselves at the last moment by jumping overboard to chance being able to float until picked up. Many more could have been saved if the imminence of the danger had been realized at the time of the first alarm.

Why so many ladies hung back at first, said one of the stewardesses, was because the experience presenting itself was an awesome one, the mere act of getting into the boats being a difficult one, and the long lowering in the water presenting terrifying prospects.

She confirmed the statement that it was a brilliant, starlit night, and Mrs Martin said she was almost the only woman insufficiently robed. At first she was little inconvenienced, but when the breeze sprang up they had the greatest difficulty in keeping up the circulation in the icy cold.

Mr Bruce Ismay helped all he could to get the women into the boats. He implored one group of stewardesses to take their place with the others. The reply was: 'But we are only stewardesses, sir!' when he said: 'You are women; please get in at once,' and he insisted on their doing so. 'We saw him later on when he was sitting on the gunwale of one of the last boats to leave. He had nothing on but his pyjamas and an overcoat and was blue with the cold.'

Mrs Gold said they did not sight the *Carpathia* until just before the sun was rising. One of the sailors caused the only laugh that was heard in the boat when, as a bird rose from the water, he facetiously said: 'I like a bird that sings in the morning.'

We didn't talk very much, she added, and almost the only sounds we had to attract our attention were the cries of the babies in the boat. This was, of course, after we had heard the last of the despairing shrieks of those who went down in the liner and those were left swimming in the water when she disappeared.

Mrs Gold said the behaviour of the older children in the lifeboat was splendid, and they were a great consolation to the women. Other people, she continued, were Mrs A. Ryerson, of

Philadelphia, and her two daughters. Mr Ryerson was a victim and went down with the ship. They had been coming over from Europe in consequence of a cablegram received announcing that one of the sons of Mr Ryerson had been killed in a motor accident.

PORTUGUESE BRIDE'S GRIEF

Another of the women passengers in this lifeboat was a Portuguese bride on her honeymoon, whose husband was lost. A pathetic scene was witnessed in the early morning when the *Carpathia* appeared in sight. The bride was full of joy in the belief that it was still the *Titanic*, and that the husband, consequently, was yet safe. When she was disillusioned her grief was something terrible to witness. She broke down and cried piteously, being quite inconsolable.

'The steerage matron, Mrs Wallis,' continued one of the stewardesses, 'refused to leave her room when summoned to do so. She disregarded all warnings, and said, "I am not going on deck. I am quite safe here." '

Another person who refused to leave her bedroom was the second cabin stewardess, Mrs Snape, a young widow, of Southampton, twenty-one years of age. She leaves a little girl. She was seen busy tying on lifebelts on her passengers, and as she did so she wished them all 'Goodbye'. She refused suggestions that she should hurry to deck herself, telling some of the passengers and the stewardesses that she did not expect to see them again.

CAPTAIN'S LAST WORDS

C. Maynard, aged thirty, who was a cook on the *Titanic*, was picked up from the bottom of a collapsible boat, to which he had clung for several hours, with many other survivors of the tragedy.

I was asleep at the time of the disaster, said Maynard, but the shock which aroused me was not a serious one. The engines stopped suddenly, but they never went astern. Aroused from my sleep, I went to the top deck, and was told off with others to No. 4 boat. Then I was ordered to one of the lower decks to open the windows to let the passengers get in. After this had been done I went back on the boat deck to find all the lifeboats had been launched, only a few collapsible boats being left.

By this time the *Titanic* was down by the stern and was rapidly sinking. Then I saw Captain Smith on the bridge. A rush of water washed me overboard, and as I went I clung on to one of our upturned boats. There were some six other men clinging to the woodwork when we were in the water. I saw Captain Smith washed from the bridge, and afterwards saw him swimming in the water. He was still fully dressed, with his cap on his head. One of the men clinging to the raft tried to save him by reaching out a hand, but he would not let him, and called out, 'Look after yourselves, boys.' I do not know what became of the captain, but I suppose he sank.

We were clinging to the upturned boat for two or three hours before we were picked up by one of the lifeboats just before daybreak.

Thomas Threlfall, a leading stoker, states that he was off duty at the time of the collision and in his bunk. When he got on deck about midnight Second Engineer Everitt told him to get all the men below. He went below to section No. 4, and took on with the stoking.

I had ten firemen and four trimmers under me, he continued, and we had to look after five double boilers with thirty fires; that is, fifteen fires in each stokehold. I don't mind telling you that it did not feel nice going down below because we knew that a bad accident had happened, but every man Jack of my gang went on with his work and never murmured. The engineers were running about a lot, and this made things look black, but my men went on with the stoking until about 1.30 a.m.

Then we were warned that the end was close at hand, and we were ordered to come on deck. All the fires had been drawn, and what trouble there was with the boilers must have been caused when steam had been largely reduced.

The fourth funnel of the *Titanic* was chiefly a ventilating shaft, and was used to carry off the vapours and steam from the kitchens of the ship. It contained a winding staircase, by which there was communication between the stokehold and the topmost deck.

CHIEF CONSTABLE'S TRIBUTE

Presiding at a meeting in Ebenezer Church last evening, the Chief Constable of Plymouth (Mr J. D. Sowerby) paid a warm tribute to the survivors who came to England on the *Lapland*.

On Sunday he said he spent eight hours in the Great Western Docks assisting others to make as comfortable as possible the rescued members of the *Titanic*'s crew. He conversed with many, and was impressed by the different views expressed. One of the seamen told him that he was in the sea for two and a half hours. His hands had swollen in the icy water to three times their ordinary size, and just before he was picked up he had almost abandoned hope. The survivor added that he trembled at the thought of going to sea again; whilst another man, taking quite a different view, said, 'Well, you know, a thing like this only happens once in a thousand years.'

(*Western Daily Mercury*, 30 April 1912)

THE ENGINEERS
STOKER'S THRILLING STORY

One of the most interesting of survivors, a leading stoker, or 'captain stoker', who was on duty in the stokehold in the very bowels of the ship at the time she struck the iceberg, and who stayed there facing death until driven out by the inrush of water, tells a graphic story. He is a fine, stalwart North of England man, says the *Manchester Guardian*, who has stoked many of the White Star liners across the Atlantic. He is Mr H. G. Harvey, son of the late Mr J. Thompson Harvey, of Belfast. This is the first account from the stokehold to be published. He said:

I am a leading fireman, and I was on the eight to twelve o'clock watch, so I was on duty when the collision with the iceberg occurred. There were three stokeholds in the *Titanic* built athwart ship, and there would be 83 men in that watch – namely 54 stokers, 23 coal trimmers, and six leading firemen. Eight of us out of the 83 are now alive. Two of them were detained to give evidence in New York; the others are here. The rest of the 83 were drowned. There were thirteen men working in my section; two of those thirteen were saved. We were working away, and thinking our watch was nearly up, when all of a sudden the starboard side of the ship came in on us. It burst in like big guns going off, and the water came pouring in. It swilled our legs, and we made a dash into the next section and slammed the watertight door to, quick. There was no time to waste. My section was about one-third of the ship's length from the bows, and we found that the whole of the starboard side was smashed in as far aft as our section. Well, we got into the next section aft, and there we stayed, for being on the watch it was our business to stay. I did not think, and nobody thought at the time, that the *Titanic* could sink.

Not a Man Saved

There was a poor fellow named Shepherd, an engineer, who joined at Southampton, whose leg was broken. When the side was stove in we carried him into the pump-room near our section, and there he lay with his broken leg, cursing because he was unable to be of any further assistance. There would have been time at first to carry him up if we had thought the ship would sink. I don't know whether he was carried up afterwards, but at any rate we know he was not saved, for there were thirty-six engineers aboard, and not a man of them was saved. They talked in America of millionaire heroes, but what of the engineers? They stuck to their work to the last, and went down with the ship. They kept the engines going until three minutes before the *Titanic* went out of sight. They were the heroes, I think. Those who in the ordinary way would have gone off duty stayed on the couple of extra hours, and they died like men.

Some time after I and my chaps got into the next section most of the stokers were sent up on deck, but I went up and brought twenty of them down again to keep the boilers going. Afterwards they were sent up again, and three engineers and I had orders to stop where we were. The engineers were there to work the section pumps to try to pump the water out of the section from which we had been driven. Harvey was the engineer in charge of us. Wilson was the second, and Shepherd was the third. While we were there the electric lights went out, and I was sent creeping along the alleyway to fetch some lamps. When I got back the lights were on again, and we found they had been switching from the main dynamos to the emergency dynamos, which were situated in the fourth funnel, which was a dummy funnel. So we had light again, and we stuck to the job. Then all of a sudden the water came with a rush into where we were.

How it came in I don't know, but in it came and Harvey, the engineer, said to me, 'Get up on deck.' I was nearly swilled off my feet, but I managed to get out, and I reached the deck beneath the boat deck. I knew then that the ship must sink, for the forecastle head was under water, but men were leaning up against the saloon walls smoking cigarettes, and no one seemed alarmed. I dared not say what I believed for fear of causing panic. When I got on the deck a lifeboat was hanging from the davits, and the boatswain, who knew me, as I had sailed with him in other ships before, said to me, 'You go in this boat and pull an oar.' I took his orders, and got in as she swung from the davits. When they had lowered us I had to cut the ropes, as she was so crowded I could not free her otherwise. It was No. 13 lifeboat, and we had in her sixty women, eight other men, and two little babies, one two months and the other ten months old. One of the men was one of the lookout men. He is now in New York. The women were of all kinds – Irish emigrants, Scandinavians, and others. I had to take charge of the boat and steer, as most of the men were stewards, and knew little about boat work. It was bitterly cold, and one of the women, seeing how cold I was at the tiller, wrapped her cloak round me. I should have been glad to pull an oar.

Bravery of Women

The two babies were wrapped in blankets, and they both survived, poor little things. Those women were brave, if you like. They never cried, although most of them had husbands in the ship, and man, I tell you, when the ship sank and the moans of the drowning came over the water, one of those women began right away to sing a hymn. It was this: 'Eternal Father, Strong to Save.' She sang it out so that the other women should not listen to those pitiful moans, and we all joined in and sang. It was only the moaning of the hundreds who were being chilled to death in the icy water. It was too cold for them to be able to shout. Well, it was ten minutes past one when I entered the boat, and we had to row away for fear the boat might be sucked down. We rowed away, and we watched the *Titanic* until she sank. She looked like a great lighted theatre floating on the sea. We saw her head sink until her stern was right out of the water with the propellers in the air. Then she broke in half, the weight of the half out of the water being too great a strain, I suppose. The after end sunk down level with the water for a few moments, and then as the water rushed in it went down at an angle again and slid down gently beneath the waves. We were too far off to see any of those who jumped into the water, and our boat was too full for us to dare to go back. Most of those who jumped into the sea died within a quarter of an hour, for the awful moaning ceased after that. We saw nothing but ice and dead bodies.

Need for More Boats

There were thirty-five men who clung to an upturned boat all night and were taken up next morning. One was Mr Lightoller, one of the best officers that ever sailed. Two out of every three of the crew who have been saved were picked up out of the water after the ship went down. It is said the bandsmen were not so brave as has been made out, but some of the chaps who have come in the *Lapland* saw them playing when the water was over their feet. There were some brave people, but not all those who have got the credit. Let me tell you, there was a boat ahead of us all night, and we hailed her time after time, for we could see she was high out of the water and we were nearly to the water's edge. They never stopped nor answered us. We found next day that there were only thirteen people in that boat.

The captain stoker said, about the shooting that is said to have taken place on board: 'Just as she was going down we heard some shots fired. I think there were people who preferred to put an end to it themselves. There are men here who saw Captain Smith swimming in the water with a child under his arm after the ship sank. He gave the child to the boat and then swam away. He refused to get into the boat himself.' As to the number of boats the captain stoker said: 'Opinions differ, but my opinion is that if the *Titanic* had carried twenty more boats twice as many lives could have been saved.'

A Demented Survivor

A Southampton man who was doing his usual shift at the electric light machinery when the ship struck the ice said:

We scarcely noticed the shock in our part of the ship and did not know there was any danger for a good while. We just went on at our work. There were four of us on the electric engine, and I am the only one of the four who was saved. We were working until within twenty minutes of the time she broke up; then when we knew she must sink we threw overboard everything we could that would float – 800 chairs from one of the saloons and chests of drawers and anything we could move. At the finish I climbed up the davits and slid down the ropes into the water and struck out. I was swimming for twenty minutes before I was picked up by No. 4 boat. Two persons in the boat died, and one of the two went raving mad before he died and wanted to jump into the water again. Both of them were blue in the face, real blue, when we picked them up.

(Ulster Echo, 30 April 1912)

Irish stewardess **Mary Sloan** wrote to her sister Maggie from the *SS Lapland* carrying *Titanic* survivors from New York to Plymouth. Her letter pays tribute to the noble courage of the doomed liner's designer Thomas Andrews.

SS *Lapland*, April 27, 1912. My Dear Maggie, I expect you will be glad to hear from me once more and to know I am still in the land of the living. Did you manage to keep the news from Mother? I hope you got the cablegram all right. I never lost my head that dreadful night. When she struck at a quarter to twelve and the engines stopped I knew very well something was wrong. Dr Simpson came and told me the mails were afloat. Things were pretty bad. He brought Miss Marsden and me into his room and gave us a little whiskey and water. He asked me if I was afraid, I replied I was not. He said, 'Well spoken like a true Ulster girl.' He had to hurry away to see if there was anyone hurt. I never saw him again. I got a lifebelt and I went round my rooms to see if my passengers were all up and if they had lifebelts on. Poor Mr Andrews came along; I read in his face all I wanted to know. He was a brave man. Mr Andrews met his fate like a true hero realizing the great danger, and gave up his life to save the women and children of the *Titanic*. They will find it hard to replace him. I got away from all the others

VOICES FROM THE TITANIC

and intended to go back to my room for some of my jewellery, but I had no time. I went on deck. I saw Captain Smith getting excited; passengers would not have noticed but I did. I knew then we were soon going. The distress signals were going every second. Then there was a big crush from behind me; at last they realized the danger, so I was pushed into a boat. I believe it was the last one to leave. We had scarcely got clear when she began sinking rapidly. We were in the boats all night until the *Carpathia* picked us up, about seven in the morning. Mr Lightoller paid me the compliment of saying I was a sailor. Your Loving Sister, Mary.

ONLY A SLIGHT SHOCK

Steward's Story of the Sinking of the Titanic
Iceberg Mistaken For a Cloud

A simple but graphic account of the sinking of the *Titanic* was told to the *Daily Sketch* yesterday by Mr Jacob W. Gibbons, a second-class steward.

Mr Gibbons, who is a married man with five children, was on his maiden voyage and had taken the trip to improve his health.

Describing his experiences he said:

I had just turned in to the 'glory hole' – as our sleeping quarters are termed – and was hanging up my watch when I felt a sudden jar.

The shock was very slight, and to this fact I attribute the great loss of life, as many of those aboard must have gone to sleep again under the impression that nothing serious had happened.

When I got up on deck the boats were being lowered away, but many of the passengers seemed to prefer sticking to the ship. I helped some of the passengers into boat No. 11, including two little children. Before doing this I had scanned the deck for others, but could see nobody about.

Mr Gibbons, commented on the obstinate way in which passengers would go back to their cabins for nick-nacks: I saw one lady covered in furs complaining that she had several more left behind. She had a mascot in the shape of a little pig, which played a tune, and she would not leave the ship until she had secured her treasure. We drew away from the *Titanic* in charge of Mr Wheat, another steward, and when about half a mile away we saw her sink. The cries of those on board were terrible, and I doubt if the memory of them will ever leave me during my lifetime.

It has been denied by many that the band was playing, but it was doing so, and the strains of 'Nearer, My God, To Thee' came clearly over the water with a solemnity so awful that words cannot express it.

Mr Gibbons mentioned a curious circumstance in connection with the iceberg that struck the *Titanic*. The berg, he said, was seen in the morning by the passengers, who mistook it for a cloud.

(*Daily Sketch*, 1 May 1912)

THE TRAGEDY OF A WIFE LEFT A WIDOW

New York, May 1

One of the strangest stories that have eddied out from the wake of the ill-fated *Titanic* drifted into this city today when Justice Zeller of the court of special sessions, made public a letter which he received from a friend of a woman survivor.

It is a story of hopeless tragedy that this letter reveals – the story of a widow whose baby was snatched from her and lost on the night the *Titanic* went down and who then, seeking the comforting pressure of a brother's hand upon her arrival here, was denied even that, because the hand she hoped to cling to had committed theft.

The woman whom the grim Nemesis has so relentlessly pursued is Mrs Bertha Moran, of London. Her husband died a few months ago, and after she settled his meagre estate she decided to take her baby and come over to the new world to begin a new life, under the protection and guidance of a beloved brother, who had come here a dozen years previous.

She took passage with her baby in the third cabin of the *Titanic*. The night the big ship struck the iceberg she was asleep and did not know of the danger until a fellow passenger awakened her and warned her.

What followed she only vaguely remembers. She remembers seizing her baby and running towards one of the boats. Then, it seems, someone snatched her baby from her and pushed her into a boat that was being lowered.

Crazed with grief, the frantic woman was taken aboard the *Carpathia* and brought on to New York. She had written her brother that he might expect her on the *Titanic*, and her anguish increased when he was not on the pier to meet the rescue ship. She did not know that he was serving a term in the penitentiary here for shoplifting.

This knowledge was kept from her when she looked up his only friend here, Edward Walsh, whose wife received her into their home tenderly and who wept when she heard of the baby's loss.

It is difficult to hold back bad news, and the Walshes knew it. So after telling Mrs Moran a diplomatic story of how her brother had gone west on a business trip without leaving any address where he could be reached, Mr Walsh wrote a letter to Justice Zeller who had sentenced the brother.

'What I want to ask you,' the letter said, 'is this: Can you arrange some way to have this man released, providing the sum is paid to cover the balance of his term? I am not rich. But if you can arrange to release him on these conditions, you will have not only my deepest gratitude, but that of this woman, who, God knows, has pretty near all the trouble she can bear.'

Through the chief clerk of the court Justice Zeller sent word back to Walsh that he does not see any way clear to help him release the brother. 'This is only another instance of offenders against the law

visiting punishment upon their relatives by their own misdoings,'
he said sadly. 'I can do nothing.'

(*Halifax Evening Mail*, 3 May)

PANIC IN THEATRE AT SHOWING
OF *TITANIC*'S PICTURES

During a performance at an electric theatre at Cardiff on Saturday
night, when it was crowded on the occasion of the display of the
Titanic pictures, a film fired. There was momentary alarm, many
women shrieking, and some disposition to stampede was manifested. The operator promptly closed shutters, and dashed water
over the burning film, and the audience ultimately reached the
exits without mishap.

(*Cork Free Press*, 6 May 1912)

BRISTOL WOMAN'S TERRIBLE EXPERIENCE

The *New York World* publishes an interview with Mrs Florence
Ware, the Bristol lady who was one of the *Titanic* survivors. Mrs
Ware formerly resided at Grosvenor Road, St Paul's. Her husband
was drowned in the disaster.

Mrs Ware in telling her story said:

I sailed with my husband, J. J. Ware. He was a builder in Bristol
and expected to take up the same business with Charles Ware
of number 186, South Main Street, New Britain, Connecticut. We
had $250 for our expenses, and he carried $1000 cash in a belt.
Everything is gone.

We sailed second cabin. My husband who is lost was always
talking about our chances in America and I was happy.

I heard the noise when the steamer hit the iceberg, but did not
pay any attention to it. The next I knew a man was pounding
on the door of our state room and saying, 'Men and women put
on lifebelts and get upon deck.' We did not put on our lifebelts,

but ran on deck. As soon as we arrived there some men led me towards a boat. I did not wish to leave my husband, but the men said I must.

My husband just shook my hand and said I should go, and that he would see me soon.

In our boat there were a lot of women, and one steward and a fireman. None of the men knew anything about managing a small boat, so some of the women who were used to it took charge.

I had nothing on but a nightgown and was very cold and I worked as hard as I could at an oar until we were picked up. There was nothing to eat or drink in our boat.

(Bristol Times and Mirror, 11 May 1912)

MR ISMAY ARRIVES AT LIVERPOOL ON THE *ADRIATIC*

Enthusiastic Reception

The White Star liner *Adriatic* arrived at the Liverpool Landing Stage this morning shortly after 7.30 having on board Mr Bruce Ismay and some of the survivors of the *Titanic* disaster.

It was early announced that Mr Ismay had by wireless last night expressed his desire that pressmen would spare him the ordeal of an interview. The reporters pressed for at least a few words, and this statement was made on his behalf:

Mr Ismay asks the gentlemen of the press to extend their courtesy to him by not pressing for any statement from him. First, because he is still suffering from the very great strain of the *Titanic* disaster and subsequent events; again because he gave before the American commission a plain and unvarnished statement of facts which have been fully reported; and also because his evidence before the British court of inquiry should not be anticipated in any way. He would, however, like to take this opportunity of acknowledging with a full heart the large number of telegraphic messages and letters from public concerns and business and private friends conveying sympathy with him and confidence in him, which he very much appreciates in the greatest trial of his life.

Later, when Mr Ismay appeared on the gangway leading to the Landing Stage he met with a splendid reception. Hats were raised, walking-sticks and handkerchiefs waved, and three rousing cheers were given. Mr Ismay, looking pale and haggard, was evidently much touched by this expression of sympathy and confidence, but he confined himself to quietly raising his hat in acknowledgement.

(*Liverpool Evening Express*, 11 May 1912)

CHAPTER 7

THE OFFICIAL INQUIRIES

On 19 April 1912, just four days after the sinking of the *Titanic*, the United States Senate began its investigation into the disaster. Over a period of 17 days the committee, under the chairmanship of Senator William Alden Smith, a Republican lawyer from Michigan, heard testimony and affidavits from witnesses amounting to 1,145 pages.

The first witness at New York's Waldorf-Astoria Hotel was White Star Line chairman **J. Bruce Ismay**, who had to be flanked by bodyguards after being vilified by the American press for not going down with his ship. Despite intense probing from Senator Smith, Ismay remained firm in his view that the *Titanic* had not been going too fast.

'Did you have occasion to consult with the captain about the movement of the ship?' – 'Never.'

'Did he consult you about it?' – 'Never. Perhaps I am wrong in saying that. I should like to say this: I do not know that it was quite a matter of consulting him about it, or of his consulting me about it, but what we had arranged to do was that we would not attempt to arrive in New York at the lightship before 5 o'clock on Wednesday morning.'

'That was the understanding?' – 'Yes. But that was arranged before we left Queenstown.'

'Was it supposed that you could reach New York at that time without putting the ship to its full running capacity?' – 'Yes. There was nothing to be gained by arriving at New York any earlier than that.'

'During the voyage, do you know, of your own knowledge, of your proximity to icebergs?' – 'I did not know that we were near icebergs. I know ice had been reported.'

'Do you know anything about a wireless message from the *Amerika* to the *Titanic* saying that the *Amerika* had encountered ice in that latitude?' – 'No, sir.'

'Were you aware of the proximity of icebergs on Sunday?' – 'On Sunday? No, I did not know on Sunday. I knew that we would be in the ice region that night sometime.'

'That you would be or were?' – 'That we would be in the ice region on Sunday night.'

'Did you have any consultation with the captain regarding the matter?' – 'Absolutely none.'

'Or with any other officer of the ship?' – 'With no officer at all. I was absolutely out of my province. I am not a navigator. I was simply a passenger on board the ship.'

'What were the circumstances of your departure from the ship?' – 'The boat was there. There was a certain number of men in the boat, and the officer called out asking if there were any more women, and there was no response, and there were no passengers left on the deck. As the boat was in the act of being lowered away, I got into it.'

'What can you say about the sinking and disappearance of the ship? Can you describe the manner in which she went down?' – 'I did not see her go down.'

'You did not see her go down?' – 'No, sir.'

'How far were you from the ship?' – 'I do not know how far we were away. I was sitting with my back to the ship. I was rowing all the time I was in the boat. We were pulling away.'

'You were rowing?' – 'Yes. I did not wish to see her go down.'

(US Inquiry, 19 April 1912)

Arthur Henry Rostron, captain of the *Carpathia*, testified that his ship, three and a half days out of New York en route for Gibraltar, was 58 miles from the *Titanic* when receiving her distress signal.

Immediately on getting the message, I gave the order to turn the ship around. I asked the operator if he was absolutely sure it was a distress signal from the *Titanic*. He assured me he was. In the meantime I was dressing, and I picked up our position on my chart, and set a course to pick up the *Titanic*. I then sent for the chief engineer and told him to call another watch of stokers and make all possible speed to the *Titanic*, as she was in trouble. Immediately I had done that I sent for the heads of the different departments and issued my orders. Knowing that the *Titanic* had struck ice, I had to take extra care and every precaution to keep clear of anything that might look like ice. Between 2.45 and four o'clock, the time I stopped my engines, we were passing icebergs on every side and making them out ahead. We had to alter our course several times to clear the bergs.

We picked up the first boat – it was in the charge of an officer. I saw that he was not under full control of this boat, and he called out that he had only one seaman on board, so I had to manoeuvre the ship to get as close to the boat as possible since I knew it would be difficult to do the pulling. However they got alongside, and they got them up all right. By the time we had the first boat's people it was breaking day, and then I could see the remaining boats all around within an area of about four miles. I also saw icebergs all around me. There were about twenty icebergs that would be anywhere from 150 to 200ft high and numerous smaller bergs. There were also numerous what we call 'growlers'. You could not call them bergs. They were anywhere from 10 to 12ft high and 10 to 15ft long above the water.

I manoeuvred the ship and we gradually got all the boats together. We got all the boats alongside and all the people aboard by 8.30. I was then very close to where the *Titanic* must have gone down, as there was a lot of small pieces of broken-up stuff. I asked for the purser and told him that I wanted to hold a service, a short prayer of thankfulness for those rescued and a short burial service for those who were lost. I consulted with Mr Ismay. While they were holding the service, I was on the bridge, and I manoeuvred around the scene of the wreckage. We saw nothing except one body. It appeared to me to be one of the crew. He was only about 100 yards from the ship. We could see him quite distinctly and saw that he was absolutely dead. He was lying on his side and his head was awash. I did not take him aboard because the *Titanic*'s passengers were then knocking about the deck and I did not want to cause any unnecessary excitement or any more hysteria among them so I steamed past, trying to get them not to see it.

(US Inquiry, 19 April 1912)

Second Officer **Charles Herbert Lightoller** was asked to explain why so many of the early lifeboats were allowed to leave only half-full.

'Who determined the number of people who should go into the lifeboats?' – 'I did.'

'How did you reach a conclusion as to the number that should be permitted to go in?' – 'My own judgement about the strength of the tackle.'

'How many did you put in each boat?' – 'In the first boat I put about twenty or twenty-five.'

'How many men?' – 'No men.'

'How many seamen?' – 'Two.'

'It was not much more than half loaded, was it?' – 'Its floating capacity; no.'

'How did it happen you did not put more people into that boat?' – 'Because I did not consider it safe.'

'In a great emergency like that, where there were limited facilities, could you not have afforded to try to put more people into that boat?' – 'I did not know it was urgent then. I had no idea it was urgent.'

'Supposing you had known it was urgent, what would you have done?' – 'I would have acted to the best of my judgement then.'

'Tell me what you would have thought wise.' – 'I would have taken more risks. I should not have considered it wise to put more in, but I might have taken risks.'

'As a matter of fact are not these lifeboats so constructed as to accommodate forty people?' – 'Sixty-five in the water.'

'Sixty-five in the water, and about forty as they are being put into the water?' – 'No, sir. It all depends on your gears. If it were an old ship, you would barely dare to put twenty-five in.'

'But this was a new one?' – 'And therefore I took chances with her afterwards.'

'You put twenty-five in?' – 'In the first.'

'Were the people ready to go?' – 'Perfectly quiet and ready.'

'Any jostling or pushing or crowding?' – 'None whatever.'

'The men all refrained from asserting their strength and crowding back the women and children?' – 'They could not have stood quieter if they had been in church.'

(US Inquiry, 19 April 1912)

Twenty-one-year-old **Harold Thomas Cottam**, the sole wireless operator on the *Carpathia*, told Senator Smith that it was only by pure chance that he came to hear the *Titanic*'s distress call as he was just about to retire to bed for the night. After two successive late nights and having been on duty since 7 a.m., Cottam had planned to go to bed early and would have shut down his station half an hour earlier had he not been waiting for confirmation of receipt of a transmission he had sent to the liner *Parisian*. He had been passing the time listening to the land station at Cape Cod.

'How did you happen to catch this communication from the *Titanic*?' – 'I was looking out for the *Parisian*, to confirm a previous communication. I was about to retire.'

'Had you disrobed?' – 'No, sir.'

'Had you taken off your shoes?' – 'No, sir.'

'Had you taken off any of your clothing?' – 'I had my coat off.'

'When you took your coat off, did you have any instruments attached to your head?' – 'Yes, sir. Telephones.'

'How did you happen to leave that on?' – 'I was waiting for the *Parisian*.'

'How long would you have waited; just long enough to undress?' – 'I would have waited a couple of minutes. I had just called the *Parisian* and was waiting for a reply, if there was one.'

'What did you hear at that time?' – 'I heard nothing, sir. I went back on to Cape Cod which was sending messages for the *Titanic*. I was taking the messages down with the hope of retransmitting them the following morning. Then I called the *Titanic* and asked him if he was aware that Cape Cod was sending a batch of messages for him.'

'And did they reply?' – 'Yes, sir.'

'What did they say?' – ' 'Come at once. It is a distress message; C.Q.D.' '

'What did you do?' – 'I confirmed it by asking him if I was to report it to the captain. The reply said "Yes".'

'How much time elapsed between the time when you received that distress call and the time you communicated it to the captain?' – 'A matter of a couple of minutes.'

'Did you send any messages after that to the *Titanic*?' – 'Yes, sir. I sent our position.'

'Did you get any reply to that?' – 'Yes, sir; immediately. It simply said, "Received".'

'When did you next hear from the *Titanic*?' – 'About four minutes afterwards. We both confirmed our positions. I then heard the *Frankfurt* calling the *Titanic*. Then I heard the *Olympic* calling the *Titanic*. For about half a minute everything was quiet. I asked the *Titanic* if he was aware that the *Olympic* was calling him. He said he was not – he told me he could not read him because of the rush of air and escape of steam. I told the *Titanic* to call the *Baltic*, but the communication was apparently unsatisfactory.'

'When did you hear anything again?' – 'I heard the *Baltic* calling Cape Race.'

'You were in regular communication with the *Titanic* until the last communication was heard?' – 'Yes; until the last communication was heard.'

'What was the last one?' – ' "Come quick; our engine room is filling up to the boilers." '

'Did you make any reply to it?' – 'I acknowledged the message and reported it to the captain.'

'So that in response to this last call the only reply they got was "received"?' – 'Yes, sir.'

'But the position of your boat was not stated?' – 'No, sir. I also called him with a message, but I got no acknowledgement.'

'Tell us what that message was.' – 'The captain told me to tell the *Titanic* that all our boats were ready and we were coming as hard as we could come, with a double watch on in the engine room, and to be prepared, when we got there, with lifeboats. I got no acknowledgement of that message.'

'Whether it was received or not, you don't know?' – 'No, sir.'

(US Inquiry, 19 April 1912)

Alfred Crawford, a bedroom steward in first class who hailed from Southampton, retold the story of Isidor and Ida Straus who refused to be separated, and died together on the *Titanic*. But first they oversaw the safe departure of Mrs Straus's maid, Ellen Bird, who tearfully accepted her mistress's fur stole as a farewell gift.

'Did you know Mr and Mrs Straus?' – 'I stood at the boat where they refused to get in.'

'Did Mrs Straus get into the boat?' – 'She attempted to get into the boat first and she got back again. Her maid got into the boat.'

'What do you mean by "she attempted" to get in?' – 'She went to get over from the deck to the boat, but then went back to her husband.'

'Did she step on the boat?' – 'She stepped on to the boat, on to the gunwales, sir; then she went back.'

'What followed?' – 'She said, "We have been living together for many years, and where you go I go." '

'To whom did she speak?' – 'To her husband.'

'Was he beside her?' – 'Yes, he was standing a way back when she went from the boat.'

'You say there was a maid there also?' – 'A maid got in the boat and was saved.'

'Did the maid precede Mrs Straus into the boat?' – 'Mrs Straus told the maid to get into the boat and she would follow her. Then she altered her mind and went back to her husband.'

(US Inquiry, 19 April 1912)

Sitting in a wheelchair, his left foot bandaged, the *Titanic*'s assistant wireless operator, **Harold Bride**, recounted how the senior operator, Jack Phillips, had effectively told his counterpart on the nearby German ship, the *Frankfurt*, to keep out of the way as the *Titanic* went to her watery grave.

'I understand that the first response to the C.Q.D. call of distress was from the *Frankfurt*?' – 'Yes, sir. He told us to stand by. That means to wait.'

'Did anyone say in your hearing that they thought the *Frankfurt* was in closer proximity to the *Titanic* than any other ship?' – 'Yes, sir. Mr Phillips told me so.'

'Did Mr Phillips tell you that he was trying to establish such communication with the *Frankfurt* as would bring that ship to your relief?' – 'Well, Mr Phillips was under the impression that when the *Frankfurt* had heard the C.Q.D. and got our position, he would immediately make it known to his commander and take further steps. Apparently he did not.'

'Did you have any other communication with the *Frankfurt* after that ship responded to the distress call?' – 'Yes. He called us up at a considerably long period afterwards and asked us what was the matter.'

'How long after?' – 'I should say it would be considerably over twenty minutes afterwards.'

'To that message what did you say?' – 'I think Mr Phillips responded rather hurriedly.'

'What did he say? I would like to know.' – 'He told him he was a fool.'

'Did Mr Phillips then tell him what was the matter?' – 'No, sir.'

'Did he have any further communication with the *Frankfurt*?' – 'No, sir. He told him to stand by, to keep out of it.'

'Keep out of what?' – 'Not to interfere with his instrument, because we were in communication with the *Carpathia*, and we knew that the *Carpathia* was the best thing doing.'

(US Inquiry, 20 April 1912)

EVIDENCE GROWS THAT WHITE STAR LINE KNEW *TITANIC'S* FATE HOURS BEFORE IT MADE IT PUBLIC

Cumulative evidence was adduced yesterday before the Senate Committee investigating the loss of the *Titanic* to show that the White Star Line was in full possession of the facts concerning the disaster to the *Titanic* long before the news was made public.

Through the testimony of the Marconi operators on both the *Titanic* and the *Carpathia* it developed the White Star liner *Baltic* was in communication with both the *Titanic* and the *Carpathia* on the fateful Sunday night and Monday morning when the *Titanic* struck the iceberg that sent her to destruction.

The *Baltic* was notified by wireless first that the *Titanic* was sinking fast and that those aboard were getting ready to leave the ship. That was between one and two o'clock in the morning – less than an hour before the *Titanic* vanished under the waves.

A few hours later the *Baltic* received word from the *Carpathia* that the *Titanic* had sunk and that the *Carpathia* had picked up survivors from lifeboats, but that it was certain there had been a considerable loss of life. In a word, the *Carpathia*'s wireless operator told the whole tragic story to the *Baltic* so far as it was then known. The time of that message was about 10.40 Monday morning, which would be about half-past nine New York time. The *Baltic*, which had gone out of her course to come to the assistance of the *Titanic*, then proceeded on her easterly way. Practically the same news was communicated at the same time to the *Olympic*, sister ship of the *Titanic*.

There can be no doubt that the commander of the *Baltic* took all possible steps to notify the owners of his line, the White Star, of the information he had received both from the *Titanic* herself and from the *Carpathia*.

Yet at the offices of the White Star Line it was insisted upon all day Monday till seven o'clock in the evening that no word had been received there concerning the *Titanic's* troubles. The Press associations, the Wall Street offices and scores of other mediums of news were filled all day with reports that the *Titanic* was in a bad way or that she had sunk. At the very time that this information, springing from nobody knew where, was ringing in the streets of the city the White Star Line, with the very best sources of original information, was not only denying to the newspaper men that it had any information whatsoever concerning the *Titanic*, but it was sending out telegrams to a few anxious inquirers whose prominence and position made it impossible to ignore their requests for information concerning their relatives on board the *Titanic*. These telegrams were of the most encouraging nature, and one of them sent to Congressman Hughes at Huntington, West Virginia, Monday afternoon was read in evidence yesterday at the Senate Committee's hearing. That telegram said: '*Titanic* proceeding to Halifax. All on board safe. White Star Line.'

(*New York World*, 21 April 1912)

A STATEMENT FROM J. BRUCE ISMAY

When I appeared before the Senate Committee on Friday morning I supposed the purpose of the inquiry was to ascertain the cause of the sinking of the *Titanic* with a view to determining whether additional legislation was required to prevent the recurrence of so horrible a disaster.

I welcomed such an inquiry and appeared voluntarily without subpoena, and answered all questions put to me by the members of the Committee to the best of my ability, with complete frankness and without reserve. I did not suppose the question of my personal conduct was the subject of the inquiry, although I was ready to tell everything I did on the night of the collision. As I have been subpoenaed to attend before the Committee in Washington tomorrow I should prefer to make no public statement out of respect for the Committee, but I do not think that courtesy requires me to be silent in the face of the untrue statements made in some of the newspapers.

When I went on board the *Titanic* at Southampton on April 10 it was my intention to return by her. I had no intention of remaining in the United States at that time. I came merely to observe the new vessel as I had done in the case of other vessels of our lines. During the voyage I was a passenger and exercized no greater right or privileges than any other passenger. I was not consulted by the commander about the ship, her course, speed, navigation, or her conduct at sea. All these matters were under the exclusive control of the captain.

I saw Captain Smith casually, as other passengers did. I was never in his room; I was never on the bridge until after the accident. I did not sit at his table in the saloon. I had not visited the engine-room, nor gone through the ship, and did not go, or attempt to go, to any part of the ship to which any other first-cabin passenger did not have access. It is absolutely and unqualifiedly false that I ever said that I wished that the *Titanic* should make a speed record or should increase her daily runs. I deny absolutely having said to any person that we would increase our speed in order to get out of the ice zone, or any words to that effect. As I have already testified, at no time did the *Titanic* during the voyage attain her full speed. It was not expected that she would reach New York before Wednesday morning. If she had been pressed she could probably have arrived on Tuesday evening.

The statement that the White Star Line would receive an additional sum by way of bounty, or otherwise, for attaining a certain speed is absolutely untrue. The White Star Line received from the British Government a fixed compensation of £70,000 per annum for carrying mails without regard to the speed of any of its vessels, and no additional sum is paid on account of any increase in speed.

I was never consulted by Captain Smith, nor by any other person. Nor did I ever make any suggestion whatsoever to any human being about the course of the ship. The *Titanic*, as I am informed, was on the southernmost westbound track. The transatlantic steamship tracks or lanes were designated many years ago by agreement on the part of all the important steamship lines and all the captains of the White Star Line are required to navigate their vessels as closely as possible on these tracks, subject to the following standing instructions:

'Commanders must remember that they must run no risks which might by any possibility result in accident to their ships, and that no supposed gain in expedition or saving time on the voyage is to be purchased at the risk of accident. The company desires to maintain for its vessels a reputation for safety, and only looks for such speed on the various voyages as is consistent with safe and prudent navigation.'

The only information I ever received in the ship that other vessels had sighted ice was a wireless message received from the *Baltic* which I have already testified to. This was handed to me by Captain Smith, without any remarks, as he was passing me on the passenger deck on the afternoon of Sunday, April 14. I read the telegram casually, and put it in my pocket. At about ten minutes past seven, while I was sitting in the smoke-room, Captain Smith came in and asked me to give him the message received from the *Baltic* in order to post it for the information of the officers. I handed it to him, and nothing further was said by either of us. I did not speak to any of the other officers on the subject.

If the information I received had aroused any apprehension in my mind – which it did not – I should not have ventured to make any suggestion to a commander of Captain Smith's experience and responsibility, for the navigation of the ship rested solely with him.

It has been stated that Captain Smith and I were having a dinner party in one of the saloons from 7.30 to 10.30 on Sunday night, and that at the time of the collision Captain Smith was sitting with me in the saloon. Both of these statements are absolutely false. I did not dine with the captain. Nor did I see him during the evening of April 14. The doctor dined with me in the restaurant at 7.30, and I went directly to my state room and went to bed at about 10.30.

I was asleep when the collision occurred. I felt a jar, went out into the passageway without dressing, met a steward, asked him what was the matter, and he said he did not know. I returned to my room. I felt the ship slow down. I put on an overcoat over my pyjamas and went up on the bridge deck, and on the bridge I asked Captain Smith what was the matter, and he said we had struck ice. I asked him whether he thought it serious, and he said he did.

On my way to my room I met the chief engineer, and asked him whether he thought the damage serious, and he said he thought it was.

I then returned to my room and put on a suit of clothes. I had been in my overcoat and pyjamas up to this time. I then went back to the boat deck and heard Captain Smith give the order to clear the boats. I helped in this work for nearly two hours as far as I can judge. I worked at the starboard boats, helping women and children into the boats and lowering them over the side. I did nothing with regard to the boats on the port side. By that time every wooden lifeboat on the starboard side had been lowered away, and I found that they were engaged in getting out the forward collapsible boat on the starboard side. I assisted in this work, and all the women that were on this deck were helped into the boat. They were all, I think, third-class passengers.

As the boat was going over the side Mr Carter, a passenger, and myself got in. At that time there was not a woman on the boat deck, nor any passenger of any class, so far as we could see or hear. The boat had between thirty-five and forty in it, I should think most of them women. There were, perhaps, four or five men, and it was afterwards discovered that there were four Chinamen concealed under the thwarts in the bottom of the boat. The distance that the boat had to be lowered into the water was, I should estimate, about 20ft. Mr Carter and I did not get into the boat until after they had begun to lower it away.

When the boat reached the water I helped to row it, pushing the oar from me as I sat. This is the explanation of the fact that my back was to the sinking steamer. The boat would have accommodated certainly six or more passengers in addition, if there had been any on the boat deck to go.

These facts can be substantiated by Mr W. E. Carter, of Philadelphia, who got in at the time that I did, and was rowing the boat with me. I hope I need not say that neither Mr Carter nor myself would, for one moment, have thought of getting into the boat if there had been any women there to go in it. Nor should I have done so if I had thought that by remaining on the ship I could have been of the slightest further assistance.

Mr William E. Carter, a well-known Philadelphian, gives the following story of his departure and that of Mr Ismay from the *Titanic*. After seeing his wife and children into the boats on the port side of the vessel he went to the starboard side and there found Mr Ismay with several officers filling boats with women. As the last boat was being filled they looked around for more women. The women in the boat were mostly steerage passengers.

Mr Ismay and myself and several officers walked up and down the deck crying, 'Are there any more women here?' We called for several minutes and got no answer. One of the officers then said that if we wanted to, we could get into the boat if we took the place of seamen. He gave us preference because we were among the first-class passengers. Mr Ismay called again, and after we had no reply we got into the lifeboat. We took oars and rowed with two seamen.

(*New York World*, 22 April 1912)

Joseph Boxhall was the *Titanic's* Fourth Officer. He stated that he fired distress rockets and flashed Morse signals to an unidentified steamer whose lights he had seen on the horizon.

'I was around the bridge most of the time, sending off distress signals and endeavouring to signal to a ship that was ahead of us.'

'How far ahead of you?' – 'It is hard to say. I saw her masthead lights and I saw her side light.'

'In what direction?' – 'Almost ahead of us.'

'On the same course, apparently?' – 'No.'

'On the same general course?' – 'By the way she was heading she seemed to be meeting us.'

'Do you know anything about what boat that was?' – 'No, sir.'

'You say you fired these rockets and otherwise attempted to signal her?' – 'Yes, sir. She got close enough, as I thought, to read our electric Morse signal, and I signalled to her. I told her to come at once, we were sinking. I told the captain about this ship. He was with me most of the time when we were signalling.'

'Did he also see it?' – 'Yes, sir.'

'Did you get any reply?' – 'I cannot say I saw any reply. Some people say she replied to our rockets and signals, but I did not see them.'

'In referring to "some people", whom do you mean?' – 'People who were around the bridge, stewards and people waiting in the boats.'

'From what you saw of that vessel, how far would you think she was from the *Titanic*?' – 'Approximately five miles.'

'What lights did you see?' – 'The two masthead lights and the red light.'

'Were the two masthead lights the first lights that you could see?' – 'Yes.'

'And what other lights?' – 'As she got closer, I saw her side lights, and eventually her red light.'

'So you were quite sure she was coming in your direction?' – 'Quite sure.'

'How long was this before the boat sank?' – 'It is hard to tell. I saw them from our ship before I left the ship. I saw the steamer's stern light before I went into my boat, which indicated that the ship had turned around. I saw a white light and I could not see any of the masthead lights that I had seen previously. I do not know when she turned because I was leaving the bridge to go and fire off some more distress rockets. I did not see her after we pulled around to the starboard side of the *Titanic.*'

(US Inquiry, 22 April 1912)

TITANIC INQUIRY

Mr Franklin's Remarkable Evidence
News Withheld Because He Believed It Was Unauthentic

The United States Senate Committee, which is inquiring into the loss of the *Titanic*, resumed its sittings today (Monday).

Mr Franklin, Vice-President of the International Mercantile Marine (the Morgan combine which includes the White Star Line), was the first witness called.

He admitted that the report circulated on Monday to the effect that the *Titanic* was safe might have originated in the White Star Office, but certainly no responsible officer ever made such a statement.

He said that he knew at noon on Monday that the *Carpathia* had picked up twenty boatloads of survivors from the *Titanic*.

This was not made public because he believed that it was unauthentic, although it came by a relayed wireless message via Cape Race.

Mr Franklin produced copies of wireless messages from Mr Ismay, asking for the liner *Cedric* to be held back to enable him and the crew of the *Titanic* to sail immediately for England without landing at New York. A message also asked for clothing to be provided for Mr Ismay. Mr Franklin replied, refusing to hold the *Cedric* back.

Further questioned, Mr Franklin denied sending to Congressman Hughes on Monday a message stating that the *Titanic* was still afloat and was being towed to Halifax. He had been unable to ascertain that any such message had been sent from the White Star offices.

The Chairman: 'When did you first learn that the *Titanic* had gone down?' – 'At twenty minutes past six in the evening. It was relayed from the *Carpathia* by the *Virginian*. We first heard at 2.20 from newspaper men of persistent reports that the *Titanic* had gone down, and we got into telephonic communication with Montreal, but we were unable to get confirmation. The message from the *Virginian* informed us that the *Carpathia* was alongside, and was doing everything that was possible.'

'What did you do after the receipt of that message?' – 'It took us some time to pull ourselves together. There were two directors, Mr Steele and Mr J. P. Morgan, Jun., with me. Then we read the message to the newspaper men, but we had only got as far as the foundering when they all rushed away.

'Messages were received signed "Yamsi" (Ismay backwards) insisting that the crew of the *Titanic* should be returned as quickly as possible.'

The Chairman: 'Has any effort been made by your company to spirit any member of the crew out of the country?' – 'Not to my knowledge. As far as Mr Ismay and myself are concerned, it is our desire that every man needed shall appear in order to give the committee every opportunity to ascertain the facts.'

(*Daily Sketch*, 23 April 1912)

Herbert Pitman was the Third Officer on the *Titanic*. He was in charge of lifeboat No. 5, the second boat to leave, with some forty passengers on board.

'Did you hear any cries of distress?' – 'Oh, yes. Crying, shouting, moaning.'

'From the ship or from the water?' – 'From the water after the ship disappeared.'

'But you were not in close proximity to those who were uttering the cries?' – 'I may have been four or five hundred yards away.'

'Did you attempt to get near them?' – 'As soon as she disappeared, I said: "Now, men, we will pull towards the wreck." Everyone in my boat said it was a mad idea, because we had far better save what few we had in my boat than go back to the scene of the wreck and be swamped by the crowds that were there.'

'Do you not know your boat would have accommodated twenty or twenty-five more people?' – 'My boat would have held more.'

'You say your passengers discouraged you from returning or going in the direction of these cries?' – 'They did. I told my men to get their oars out, and pull towards the wreck. I said, "We may be able to pick up a few more." They commenced pulling towards the ship, but the passengers in my boat said it was a mad idea on my part to pull back to the ship, because if I did, we should be swamped with the crowd that was in the water, and it would add another forty to the list of drowned. So I decided not to pull back.'

'You turned this No. 5 boat around to go in the direction from which these cries came?' – 'I did.'

'And were dissuaded from your purpose?' – 'Certainly.'

'Then did you turn the boat towards the sea again?' – 'No. Just simply took our oars in and lay quiet. We just lay there doing nothing although we may have drifted a little bit.'

'How many of these cries were there? Was it a chorus?' – 'I would rather you did not speak about that.'

'I realize that it is not a pleasant theme, and yet I would like to know whether these cries were general and in chorus, or desultory and occasional?' – 'There was a continual moan for about an hour.'

'And you lay in the vicinity of that scene for about an hour?' – 'Yes, we were in the vicinity of the wreck the whole time.'

'And drifted or lay on your oars during that time?' – 'We drifted towards daylight as a little breeze sprang up.'

'Did those cries of distress die away?' – 'Yes, they died away gradually.'

'Is that all you care to say?' – 'I would rather you would have left that out altogether.'

'I know you would. But I must know what efforts you made to save the lives of passengers and crew under your charge. If that is all the effort you made, say so.' – 'That is all, sir. That is all the effort I made.'

(US Inquiry, 23 April 1912)

First-class passenger **Major Arthur Peuchen**, a chemical manufacturer from Toronto and keen yachtsman, was ordered into lifeboat No. 6 as an oarsman since there were only two other men in the boat at the time. He testified that the women in the boat wanted to turn back for survivors but that the officer in charge, the *Titanic*'s helmsman Robert Hichens, insisted on rowing towards a light he had spotted in the distance.

'The quartermaster who was in charge of our boat told us to row as hard as we could to get away from the suction, and just as we got a short distance away a stowaway made an appearance. He was an Italian, I think, who had a broken wrist or arm and was of no use to us to row. He got an oar out, but he could not do much, so we got him to take the oar in.'

'Where did he make his appearance from, Major?' – 'Underneath. I think he was stowed away underneath the bow of the boat. As we pulled away from the *Titanic*, there was an officer's call of some kind. We stopped rowing.'

'A whistle?' – 'A sort of whistle. Anyway the quartermaster told us to stop rowing so he could hear it, and this was a call to come back to the boat. So we all thought we ought to go back to the boat. But the quartermaster said: "No, we are not going back to the boat. It is our lives now, not theirs." And he insisted upon our rowing farther away.'

'Who made the rebellion against it?' – 'Some of the married women that were leaving their husbands. I did not say anything. I knew I was powerless. He was at the rudder. He was a very talkative man. He had been swearing a good deal, and was very disagreeable. I had already had one row with him. I asked him to come and help with the rowing, and to let one of the women steer the boat, but he refused. He told me he was in command of the boat, and that I was to row. He remained at the tiller, and if we had wanted to go back while he was in possession of the tiller, I do not think we could have. Then he imagined he saw a light. I have done a good deal of yachting in my life, and I could not see these lights. All I saw was a reflection. He thought it was a boat of some kind so we kept on rowing towards this imaginary light. Then we started to hear the *Titanic* breaking up. There were dreadful calls and cries.'

'While these cries of distress were going on, did anyone in the boat urge the quartermaster to return?' – 'Yes, some of the women did but I said to the women: "It is no use you arguing with that man." Later, he said it was no use going back there, there was only a lot of stiffs there, which was very unkind, and the women resented it very much.'

(US Inquiry, 23 April 1912)

LACK OF GLASSES

– Sensational Admission in American Inquiry

Mr Pitman was succeeded in the witness-box by Frederick Fleet, twenty-five years of age, sailor and lookout man on the *Titanic*. His watch was at ten o'clock. He had Sailor Lee in the crow's nest. The men whom Fleet relieved told him to keep a sharp lookout for small ice.

'Did you keep a sharp lookout?' – 'Yes.'

'Did you see any ice?' – 'Yes. At seven bells I reported a black mass ahead.'

'How long before the collision did you report ice ahead?' – 'I have no idea.'

'What did you do when you saw the iceberg?' – 'I sounded three bells, and then telephoned to the bridge. I got prompt response to my ring, and the report was not delayed.'

'Was it five minutes or an hour before the collision that you saw the iceberg?' – 'I don't know.'

'Tell the Committee whether you apprehended danger when you sounded the signals?' – 'I thought the berg was pretty close, but it didn't seem so large when I first saw it.'

'How large was it then?' – 'About the size of two large tables, but it got larger as we went along, and when we struck it was about 50 or 60ft high above the water.'

'After you gave the telephone signal, was the ship stopped?' – 'No, she didn't stop until after she struck the iceberg, but she started to go to port after I telephoned.'

'Where did the iceberg strike the ship?' – 'On the starboard bow about 20ft from the stern.'

'Did it alarm you?' – 'No, I thought it was a narrow shave.'

'Did you have any glasses?' – 'No.'

'Isn't it customary for lookouts to use glasses in their work?' – 'Yes, but they did not give us any on the *Titanic*. We asked for them at Southampton, but they said there were none for us.'

'Whom did you ask?' – 'Mr Lightoller.'

'You expected glasses?' – 'We had them from Belfast to Southampton, but had none from Southampton.'

'What became of the glasses you had from Belfast to Southampton?' – 'I don't know.'

'If you had had glasses could you have seen the iceberg sooner?' – 'We could have seen it a bit sooner.'

'How much sooner?' – 'Enough to get out of the way.'

'Were you and Lee disappointed that you had no glasses?' –
'Yes.'
'Did the officers on the bridge have glasses?' – 'Yes.'

(*Daily Graphic*, 24 April 1912)

The *Titanic*'s helmsman, **Robert Hichens**, gave a more detailed account of the collision than he had delivered previously to the press, and also refuted allegations about his conduct in boat No. 6.

I went on watch at 8 o'clock. The officers on watch were the Second Officer, Mr Lightoller, senior in command; the Fourth Officer, Mr Boxhall; and the Sixth Officer, Mr Moody. My first orders when I got on the bridge was to take the Second Officer's compliments down to the ship's carpenter and inform him to look at his fresh water – that it was about to freeze. I did so. On the return to the bridge, I had been on the bridge about a couple of minutes when the carpenter came back and reported the duty carried out. Standing by waiting for another message – it is the duty of the quartermaster to strike the bell every half hour – I heard the Second Officer repeat to Mr Moody to speak through the telephone, warning the lookout men in the crow's nest to keep a sharp lookout for small ice until daylight and pass the word along to the other lookout men. The next order I received from the Second Officer was to go and find the deck engineer and bring him up with a key to open the heaters up in the corridor of the officers' quarters, also the wheelhouse and the chart room, on account of the intense cold.

At ten o'clock I went to the wheel. Mr Murdoch came up to relieve Mr Lightoller. All went along very well until twenty minutes to 12, when three gongs came from the lookout, and immediately afterwards a report on the telephone: 'Iceberg right ahead.' The Chief Officer rushed from the wing to the bridge. I heard the telegraph bell ring and the order 'Hard astarboard,' with the Sixth Officer standing by me to see the duty carried out. The Sixth Officer repeated the order, 'Hard astarboard. The helm is hard over, sir.'

'Who gave the first order?' – 'Mr Murdoch, the First Officer, the officer in charge. The Sixth Officer repeated the order. But, during the time, she was crushing the ice, or we could hear the grinding noise along the ship's bottom. I heard the telegraph ring. The skipper came rushing out of his room – Captain Smith – and asked: "What is that?" Mr Murdoch said: "An iceberg." Captain Smith said: "Close the emergency doors." Mr Murdoch replied: "The doors are already closed." The captain then sent for the carpenter to sound the ship. He also came back to the wheelhouse and looked at the commutator in front of the compass, which is a little instrument like a clock to tell you how the ship is listing. The ship had a list of five degrees to the starboard.'

'How long after the impact?' – 'About five minutes. I stayed at the wheel until twenty-three minutes past 12. I was relieved by Quartermaster Perkis. One of the officers said: "That will do with the wheel; get the boats out." I got in No. 6 boat, put in charge of her by Mr Lightoller. We lowered away from the ship and were told to, "Pull towards that light," which we started to do. Everybody seemed in a bad condition in the boat. Everybody was quite upset, and I told them somebody would have to pull – there was no use stopping there alongside of the ship, and the ship gradually going by the head. We were in a dangerous place, so I told them to man the oars, ladies and all: "All of you do your best." We got away about a mile, I suppose, from the ship, going after this light, which we expected to be a codbanker – a schooner that comes out on the Banks.'

'A fisherman's boat?' – 'Yes, sir, but we did not get any nearer the light. There were several other boats around us at this time and one boat that had no light came close up to us. He had four to six men in his boat and I borrowed one fireman from him to put in my boat, to enable me to pull. We did not seem to get any nearer the light, so we conversed together, and we tied our boats side by side. We stopped there until we saw the *Carpathia* heave in sight about daybreak. The wind had sprung up a bit then, and it got very choppy. I relieved one of the young ladies with the oar, and told her to take the tiller. She immediately let the boat come athwart, and the ladies in the boat got very nervous. So I took the tiller back again, and told them to manage the best way they could. The lady I refer to, Mrs Meyer, she was rather vexed with me in the boat and I spoke rather straight to her, and she accused me of wrapping myself up in the blankets in the boat, using bad language, and drinking all the whisky, which I deny, sir. I was standing to attention, exposed, steering the boat all night, which is a very cold billet. I would rather be pulling the boat than be steering. But I saw no one there to steer, so I thought, being in charge of the boat, it was the best way to steer myself, especially when I saw the ladies get very nervous with the nasty tumble on. We got down to the *Carpathia* and I saw every lady and everybody out of the boat, and I saw them carefully hoisted on board the *Carpathia*. I was the last man to leave the boat.'

(US Inquiry, 24 April 1912)

CALIFORNIAN 20 MILES AWAY, OPERATOR ASLEEP

Here are some facts, anyone may see just how near we were to the *Titanic* when she struck, said Capt. Stanley Lord of the Leyland liner *Californian* today.

On April 14 at 10.21 p.m. when we were in latitude 42.05, longitude 50.07, the engines were shut off and the *Californian* stopped in the middle of the ice field. There we remained till six the next morning, when we proceeded to the position of the *Titanic* in latitude 41.46, longitude 50.14 given to us by the *Virginian*. This shows the vessels to have been 20 miles apart.

The *Californian* is a 12-knot ship. We started as soon as we got the position of the *Titanic*, at six o'clock, and the ship was driven for all it was worth. We stopped alongside the *Carpathia* at 8.30 and learnt that everyone had been picked up.

We remained in the vicinity four hours, thinking we might find someone on floating wreckage.

The wireless operator on the *Californian* went to bed about 11 o'clock the night before. Up to the moment of shutting down, no message of distress or any signal was received or sighted.

The first thing the *Californian*'s operator got was a confused message from the *Frankfurt*, from which he finally made out that the *Titanic* was in distress.

The captain of the *Californian* did not sight any other ship which might have been the steamer said to have passed so close and refused aid. This is believed to bear certain significance inasmuch as if the vessel which was seen from the *Titanic* while she was sinking was moving it should have at some time during the night passed near enough to the *Californian* to have been sighted by her, and no such ship was seen, according to Capt. Lord.

(New York World, 25 April 1912)

FIFTH OFFICER'S ORDERS

Peremptory Advice to Mr Ismay

'Get to hell out of this' was the peremptory advice given to Mr Bruce Ismay by Mr G. Lowe, the Fifth Officer of the *Titanic*, when the chairman of the White Star Line was repeatedly urging him to lower away the lifeboats before the liner sank.

In stating this in evidence yesterday before the Senatorial Commission at Washington, Mr Lowe admitted that at the time he did not know to whom he was talking, but Mr Ismay walked away and assisted at another boat.

Mr Lowe, questioned as to the speed of the *Titanic*, declared that she could have travelled at 24 or 25 knots had she been required to do so. He was submitted to half an hour's detailed examination regarding the rules in force on the liner, and stated that there was no boat drill after the liner left Southampton.

Mr Lowe indignantly denied that he had been drinking on the

night of the disaster. He was not a drinker. After the collision occurred he got out a revolver.

'Why?' – 'You never know when you will need it.'

He took charge of the launching of lifeboat No. 5, said Mr Lowe. Mr Ismay, whom he did not know at the time, was present, and seemed over-anxious and excited. Mr Ismay kept repeatedly urging him to 'lower away'. He resented Mr Ismay's interference, and in the heat of the moment exclaimed: 'If you will get the hell out of this I shall be able to do so.'

Mr Ismay made no reply, but walked away and assisted at boat No. 3. He believed there were fifty people in the first boat lowered, including ten men. Five men were necessary to man it.

After the *Titanic* sank he transferred some of the passengers from his boat to another, and then returned to where the wreckage was floating. He picked up four persons alive. One of them was Mr Hoyt, of New York, who was bleeding from the nose and mouth and afterwards died. Mr Lowe said he saw no females in the wreckage.

At daybreak he took on board, from an overturned collapsible boat, twenty men and one woman. The woman was Mrs Henry B. Harris, of New York, one of whose arms was broken. Three people found clinging to the boat were dead.

'It would have been suicide,' said Mr Lowe, 'for us to go back into the zone where the 1500 people, whose cries we heard, were drowning. I did my best, and went as near the scene as I dared. I am not ashamed of what I did.'

The Second Officer, Mr Lightoller, said that Mr Ismay, when on board the *Carpathia*, had expressed his regret at having been saved, and added that he should have remained on board and gone down with the *Titanic*.

The Second Officer told the committee that Mr Ismay's words were: 'I ought to have gone down with the ship. Women went down. I should.'

(*Daily Sketch*, 25 April 1912)

Quartermaster **Alfred Olliver**, twenty-seven, was just entering the bridge when the collision occurred.

I had been relieved from the wheel at 10 o'clock, and I was stand-by after 10 o'clock. I was running messages and doing various other duties. I had just performed an errand when I heard three bells rung up in the crow's nest, which I knew meant that it was something ahead. So I looked, but I did not see anything. I happened to be looking at the lights in the standing compass at the time. That was my duty, and I was trimming them so that they would burn properly. When I heard the report, I looked, but could not see anything, and I left that and was just entering the bridge just as the shock came. I knew we had touched something. I found out we had struck an iceberg.

'Did you see that iceberg?' – 'Yes, I did. It was about the height of the boat deck; if anything, just a little higher. The top did not touch the side of the boat, but it was almost alongside of the boat.'

'What kind of a sound was there?' – 'The sound was like she touched something; a long grinding sound, like.'

'What was the length of the iceberg beside the boat?' – 'That I could not say, because I only saw the top. It was impossible to see the length of the iceberg from where I was standing.'

'What was the shape at the top?' – 'The shape was pointed. It was not white, as I expected to see an iceberg. It was a kind of a dark blue.'

'Did you notice the course of the berg as it passed you?' – 'No, sir. It went towards the after part of the ship, but I did not see it afterwards because I did not have time to know where it was going.'

'Do you know whether the wheel was hard aport then?' – 'What I know about the helm is, hard aport.'

'Do you mean hard aport or hard astarboard?' – 'I know the orders I heard when I was on the bridge after we had struck the iceberg. I heard hard aport, and there was Hichens, the man at the wheel, and the Sixth Officer, Mr Moody. The officer was seeing it was carried out right.'

'You do not know whether the helm was put hard astarboard first, or not?' – 'No, sir.'

'But you know it was put hard aport after you got there?' – 'After I got there; yes, sir.'

'Where was the iceberg, do you think, when the helm was shifted?' – 'The iceberg was away up stern.'

'That is when the order "hard aport" was given?' – 'Yes, sir.'

'Who gave the order?' – 'The First Officer.'

'And that order was immediately executed, was it?' – 'Immediately executed, and the Sixth Officer saw that it was carried out.'

(US Inquiry, 25 April 1912)

As the crew member in charge of collapsible boat 'C', quartermaster **George Rowe** witnessed J. Bruce Ismay's controversial escape.

'Tell us the circumstances under which Mr Ismay and that other gentleman (Carter) got into the boat.' – 'When Chief Officer Wilde asked if there was any more women and children, there was no reply. So Mr Ismay came aboard the boat.'

'Was it light enough so that you could see anyone nearby?' – 'Yes, sir.'

'I understand there were firemen and stokers in that neighbourhood?' – 'Yes, sir.'

'But no women and children?' – 'No women or children, sir.'

'Did you see Mr Ismay and Mr Carter get in the boat?' – 'I saw the gentlemen get in; yes, sir.'

'Did you hear anyone ask them to get in?' – 'No, sir.'

'How were you occupied at the time they got in?' – 'I was occupied in attending the after fall, sir.'

'Were you watching Chief Officer Wilde?' – 'Yes, sir.'

'Did you see him speak to them?' – 'No, sir.'

'If he had spoken to them, would you have known it?' – 'I think so, because they got in the afterpart of the boat.'

'Did you see the light of a boat, or anything of that kind?' – 'I saw the light – that was the light we were pulling for when we left the ship.'

'What do you conclude that light was?' – 'A sailing ship.'

'What sort of light was it?' – 'A white light, a stern light.'

'Did you get any nearer to it?' – 'We did not seem to get nearer to it. We kept on pulling for it, because it was the only stationary light. Towards daylight the wind sprung up, and she sort of hauled off from us.'

'What was the bearing of this light with regard to the *Titanic* – forward or aft?' – 'Right forward, sir.'

'Dead ahead?' – 'Not dead ahead, but just a little on the port bow.'

'When did you first see her?' – 'When I was on the bridge firing rockets. I saw it myself, and I worked the Morse lamp at the port side of the ship to draw her attention.'

(US Inquiry, 25 April 1912)

Able Seaman **Edward Buley** described leaving in boat No. 10 and the harrowing search for survivors.

'How many people were in that boat?' – '60 to 70.'

'Were any ladies on the deck when you left?' – 'No. Ours was the last boat up there, and they went around and called to see if there were any, and they threw them in the boat at the finish because they didn't like the idea of coming in.'

'Pushed them in, you mean?' – 'Threw them in. One young lady slipped, and they caught her by the foot on the deck below, and she came up then and jumped in. We got away from the ship, and about an hour afterwards Officer Lowe came alongside, and he had his boat filled up. He distributed them among the other boats, and he said to all the seamen in the boat to jump in his boat until he went back among the wreckage to see if there were any people that had lived.'

'Who had charge of the boat you were in?' – 'I was in charge.'

'But when you left that?' – 'I left that, and I believe he put some more stewards in the boat to look after the women. All the boats were tied together.'

'You were then with Lowe in his boat and went back to where the *Titanic* sank?' – 'Yes, sir, and we picked up the remaining live bodies.'

'How many did you get?' – 'There were not very many there. We got four of them. All the others were dead.'

'Were there many dead?' – 'Yes, there were a good few dead. Of course you could not discern them exactly on account of the wreckage, but we turned over several of them to see if they were alive. It looked as though some were drowned. They looked as though they were frozen. The lifebelts they had on were out of the water and their heads laid back, with their faces on the water.'

'They were head and shoulders out of the water?' – 'Yes, sir.'

'With the head thrown back?' – 'Yes, sir.'

'And the face out of the water?' – 'Yes, sir.'

'They were not, apparently, drowned?' – 'It looked as though they were frozen altogether.'

(US Inquiry, 25 April 1912)

George Crowe, a steward from Southampton, stated that his colleagues initially thought the collision to be little more than a joke. His testimony did little to improve Anglo-Italian relations.

About 11.40 there was a kind of shaking of the ship and a little impact, from which I thought one of the propellers had been broken off. I had been dozing in my berth on 'E' deck. I got out of my bed. I came out of the alleyway and saw quite a number of stewards and steerage passengers carrying their baggage from forward to aft. I inquired of the trouble and was told it was nothing, and to turn in again. The stewards were making quite a joke of it. They did not think of the seriousness of it at the time. I went back to my bunk again, and a saloon steward came down shortly afterwards and told me to come up on the upper deck with as much warm clothes on as I could get. I went up on the boat deck. When I got outside of the companion-way, I saw them working on boat No. 1. After that I went to boat No. 14, the boat allotted to me – that is, in the case of fire or boat drill – and I stood by according to the proceedings of the drill. I assisted in handing the women and children into the boat, and was asked if I could take an oar. I said, 'Yes' and was told to man the boat.

'Was there any shooting that occurred at the time the boat was lowered?' – 'Yes, sir. There were various men passengers, probably Italians or some foreign nationality other than English or American, who attempted to rush the boats. The officers threatened to shoot any man who put his foot into the boat. He fired the revolver, but either downward or upward, not shooting at any of the passengers at all and not injuring anybody. He fired perfectly clear, upward or downward.'

'Did that stop the rush?' – 'Yes, sir.'

'There was no disorder after that?' – 'No disorder.'

(US Inquiry, 25 April 1912)

Yorkshireman **George Hogg** was a *Titanic* lookout on the 12 to 2 watch. He rued the lack of glasses.

'Could anything have been done to save more lives than were saved?' – 'No, sir. The only thing I can suggest is in regard to the glasses. If we had had the glasses, we might have seen the berg before.'

'In an ordinary way, can you not see better with your plain eyes than you can with artificial glasses?' – 'But the idea of the glasses is that if you happen to see something on the horizon you can pick your ship out – if it is a ship, for instance.'

'As soon as you see anything, you signal the officer on the bridge, do you not?' – 'Yes, sir. You would strike the bell. But you would make sure if you had the glasses that it was a vessel and not a piece of cloud on the horizon. On a very nice night, with the stars shining, something you might think it was a ship when it was a star on the horizon. If you had glasses, you could soon find out whether it was a ship or not.'

'As soon as you discover anything unusual, however, you call the attention of the officer on the bridge to it, do you not?' – 'Quite so.'

'And he has glasses, of course?' – 'Yes, sir. He has glasses.'

(US Inquiry, 25 April 1912)

Lookout **George Symons**, twenty-four, from Weymouth, Dorset, was placed in charge of emergency lifeboat No. 1. He was interrogated by Senator Perkins regarding the empty spaces in his boat.

'How many passengers did you have on her?' – 'From fourteen to twenty. First they put in seven of the crew. There were seven men ordered in – two seamen and five firemen. They were ordered in by Mr Murdoch.'

'How many did the boat carry?' – 'I could not say for certain. It was one of the small accident boats.'

'After she got into the water, would she take any more?' – 'She would have taken more.'

'You did not return to the ship again?' – 'Yes, we came back after the ship was gone, and we saw nothing.'

'Did you rescue anyone that was in the water?' – 'No, sir. We saw nothing when we came back.'

'Did you hear any cries of people in the water?' – 'Oh, yes, sir. I heard the cries.'

'Did you say your boat could take more? Did you make any effort to get them?' – 'Yes, we came back. But when we came back we did not see anybody or hear anybody.'

'Then what did you do after that?' – 'We rowed around and picked up with another boat.'

'Did you pass a painter from one boat to another?' – 'No, sir. We went close to her. They did not want any assistance, as the women were pulling. I asked if they wanted my assistance, and they would not take it. They said they could pull through.'

'Your boat could have accommodated more. How many more?' – 'I should say that she could have accommodated, easily, ten more.'

'And you made no effort to fill her, and you were in charge of her?' – 'Yes, sir, I was. I was ordered away by Mr Murdoch, the First Officer. He ordered the boat to be lowered.'

'But you did not pull back to the ship again?' – 'Not until she went down.'

(US Inquiry, 25 April 1912)

THE WIRELESS MYSTERIES
MR MARCONI'S DENIALS AT *TITANIC* INQUIRY

The Senatorial inquiry into the *Titanic* disaster was resumed this morning, when Mr Marconi was placed on the witness stand.

In his evidence Mr Marconi said that the wireless station at Cape Race was capable of communicating with ships having wireless installations similar to that on the *Titanic* and *Olympic* up to a distance of 1200 to 1500 miles.

He was closely questioned regarding the alleged instructions to the *Carpathia*'s operator to hold up news of the disaster. Mr Marconi admitted that a wireless message was sent to Mr Cottam, the operator on the *Carpathia*, which read: 'Hold news story disaster for four figures.'

This telegram, however, was not sent until the *Carpathia* was off Sandy Hook, and it referred not to a general story of the disaster by wireless but to a personal interview. Mr Marconi denied having authorized his wireless operators to sell exclusive stories to newspapers. He said he understood that Mr Bride, the surviving operator of the *Titanic*, was paid £300 by the *New York Times* for his narrative.

'There is an ironclad rule of the company's regulations,' said Mr Marconi, 'prohibiting operators from acting as reporters. Under British law it is a penal offence for operators to send out information on their own initiative.

'This is probably the reason why no reports of the disaster were forthcoming from the *Carpathia* on her way to New York.

'What I meant when I told the operator to take something for the story was that the newspaper reporters would be so interested in what he had to say that, without holding back any general information, they would be willing to pay him for his personal experiences.'

Mr Marconi thought that the operator on the *Carpathia* should have sent an earlier description of the disaster.

(*Daily Graphic*, 26 April 1912)

Ernest Gill, assistant engineer on the *Californian*, fuelled speculation that his ship had seen the *Titanic*'s distress flares and was near enough to have been the mystery ship sighted by various people on the doomed liner.

On the night of April 14 I was on duty from 8 p.m. until 12 in the engine room. At 11.50 I came on deck. The stars were shining brightly. It was very clear and I could see for a long distance. The ship's engines had been stopped since 10.30 and she was drifting amid floe ice. I looked over the rail on the starboard side and saw the lights of a very large steamer about ten miles away. I could see her broadside lights. I watched her for fully a minute. They could not have helped but see her from the bridge and lookout.

It was now 12 o'clock and I went to my cabin. I woke my mate, William Thomas. He heard the ice crunching alongside the ship and asked, 'Are we in ice?' I replied: 'Yes, but it must be clear off to the starboard, for I saw a big vessel going along full speed. She looked as if she might be a big German.'

I turned in, but could not sleep. In half an hour I turned out, thinking to smoke a cigarette. Because of the cargo I could not smoke 'tween decks, so I went on deck again. I had been on deck about ten minutes when I saw a white rocket about ten miles away on the starboard side. I thought it must be a shooting star. In seven or eight minutes I saw distinctly a second rocket in the same place, and I said to myself: 'That must be a vessel in distress.' It was not my business to notify the bridge or the lookouts, but they could not have helped but see them.

I turned in immediately after, supposing that the ship would pay attention to the rockets. I knew no more until I was awakened at 6.40 by the chief engineer who said: 'Turn out to render assistance. The *Titanic* has gone down.'

I went down on watch and heard the second and fourth engineers in conversation. Mr J. O. Evans is the second and Mr Wooten is the fourth. The second was telling the fourth that the third officer had reported rockets had gone up in his watch. I knew then that it must have been the *Titanic* I had seen.

(US Inquiry, 26 April 1912)

Contrary to Ernest Gill's assertions, **Stanley Lord**, Captain of the *Californian*, insisted that his ship was some twenty miles away from the *Titanic* and therefore out of visual range. But Lord did admit to seeing another vessel – which he claimed was not the *Titanic* – which had flashed signals. However, he said, they were definitely not distress signals.

When I came off the bridge at half past ten, I pointed out to the officer that I thought I saw a light coming along, and it was a most peculiar light, and we had been making mistakes all along with the stars, thinking they were signals. We could not distinguish where the sky ended and where the water commenced. You see, it was a flat calm. He said he thought it was a star, and I did not say anything more. I went down below. I was talking with the engineer about keeping the steam ready. We saw these signals coming along and I said, 'There is a steamer coming. Let's go to the wireless and see what the news is.'

On our way down I met the operator. I said: 'Do you know anything?' He said: 'The *Titanic*.' So then I gave him instructions to let the *Titanic* know. I said: 'This is not the *Titanic* – there is no doubt about it.'

She came and lay, at half past eleven, alongside of us until, I suppose, a quarter past one, within four miles of us. We could see everything on her quite distinctly, we could see her lights. We signalled her at half past eleven with the Morse lamp. She did not take the slightest notice of it. That was between 11.30 and 11.40. We signalled her again at 12.10, 12.30, 12.45 and one o'clock. We have a very powerful Morse lamp. I suppose you can see that about ten miles, and she was about four miles off, and she did not take the slightest notice of it.

When the second officer came on the bridge around 12 o'clock, I told him to watch that steamer, which was stopped, and I pointed out the ice to him. At 12.40 I whistled up the speaking tube and asked him if she was getting any nearer. He said: 'No, she is not taking any notice of us.' So I said: 'I will go and lie down a bit.' At a quarter past one he said, 'I think she has fired a rocket.' He said: 'She did not answer the Morse lamp and she has commenced to go away from us.' I said: 'Call her up and let me know at once what her name is.' So he put the whistle back, and, apparently, he was calling. I could hear him ticking over my head. Then I went to sleep.

(US Inquiry, 26 April 1912)

Twenty-year-old **Cyril Furmstone Evans**, a native of Liverpool, was the Marconi wireless operator on the *Californian*. He revealed that he had informed the *Titanic* of ice at around 11 p.m. on the Sunday night but had been told to 'shut up.'

'What time did you communicate with the *Titanic*?' – 'In the afternoon, sir. I was sending a message to the *Antillian*, of our line. I was sending an ice report, handed in by the skipper. The *Titanic* called me up, and we exchanged signals. I said, "Here is a message, an ice report." He said, "It's all right, old man. I heard you send to the *Antillian*." '

'When did you next communicate with the *Titanic*?' – '9.05 New York time, sir, on the fourteenth, the same evening. I went outside of my room just before that, about five minutes before that and we were stopped, and I went to the captain and I asked him if there was anything the matter. The captain told me he was going to stop because of the ice, and he asked me if I had any boats. I said, "The *Titanic*." He said: "Better advise him we are surrounded by ice and stopped." So I went to my cabin, and at 9.05 New York time I called him up. I said: "Say, old man, we are stopped and surrounded by ice." He turned around and said: "Shut up, shut up, I am busy. I am working Cape Race," and at that I jammed him.'

'What do you mean by that?' – 'By jamming we mean when somebody is sending a message to somebody else and you start to send at the same time, you jam him. He does not get his message. I was stronger than Cape Race. Therefore my signals came in with a bang, and he could read me and he could not read Cape Race.'

'What time did you retire that night?' – 'At 11.25 I still had the phones on my ears and heard him still working Cape Race. At 11.35 I put the phones down and took off my clothes and turned in.'

'When you were awakened?' – 'About 3.30 a.m., New York time, by the chief officer, Mr Stewart. He said, "There is a ship that has been firing rockets in the night. Please see if there is anything the matter." I jumped out of bed, slipped on a pair of trousers and a pair of slippers, and I went at once to my key and started my motor and gave "C.Q.". About a second later, I was answered by the *Frankfurt*. He told me the *Titanic* had sunk.'

'Did any officer of the ship or member of the crew tell you about Captain Lord being notified three times that a vessel was sending up rockets?' – 'I think the apprentice did. Gibson.'

'What did he say to you?' – 'I do not know exactly. I know the effect. I think he said that the skipper was being called; called three times. I think that is all he said.'

(US Inquiry, 26 April 1912)

In a hard-hitting editorial, the Socialist *Daily Herald* expressed its outrage at the perceived class distinctions on board the *Titanic*.

SLAUGHTER OF THE STEERAGE

- Driven Back From The Deck
- Half-Empty Boats Rush Past Them
- Steerage Passengers Kept At Bay With Revolver Shots
- 'Five Thousand Dollars For A Place In The Boat'

'With my own eyes I saw an officer shoot two or three third-class passengers.'

'Five thousand dollars for a place in the boat.'

The above paragraphs are quotations from our own reporter's interviews with *Titanic* survivors at Plymouth last night.

The first was an interview with a fireman, and the subject of the second remark was a wealthy American struggling in the icy waters during the great debacle.

Shall we ever know the truth? Will the crime of the *Titanic* ever be made plain? Or is it possible for 399 steerage men, 81 steerage women and 53 steerage children to be done to death and the world to pass on to discussion of straw hats for summer wear?

Are we such a superficial people that we can weep over the damning figures, complain of the hardness of fate, and forget?

We do not believe it. The conscience of England is roused, and justice will be done. But by the people of England! – not by its officials – not by the capitalist press. That great voice of protest which is to be heard in the street finds no echo in the columns of the newspapers. And it is before that final and inexcrable judge – the people – we put the evidence of how the women and children of the steerage died.

This is how it stands.

Major Peuchen said:

The boats were being prepared for lowering at the port side. They would only allow women to pass, and the men had to stand back. No men passengers got into the boat. When I came on deck first at seemed to me that about 100 stokers came up and crowded the deck. One of the officers, a splendid man, *drove these men right off the deck like sheep*. When we got to the next boat a quartermaster and a sailor were put in, and the boat was then filled with women.

The Washington correspondent of the *Daily Telegraph* gives quite another version of this piece of evidence:

One thing I greatly admired was the conduct of *200 stokers who advanced in a body along the boat deck, and drove every man back* so as to give the women a better chance. I do not know that such action was necessary on the part of the stokers, but it was not resented by the men. It seemed to me at the time a brave thing for the stokers to act as a body on behalf of the women and children.

Who were the men driven back under the orders of this magnificent officer? And were they all men? And were they driven off to give the steerage women a better chance? On the lower decks we shall find the answer to our question.

Abraham Hyman, steerage passenger, said that he saw many steerage passengers hurrying up but when they got on the deck they were waved back by an officer, who told them there was no danger. Hyman said he also noticed a rope stretched across the deck guarded by several members of the crew. Women came on deck crying, and were waved back by officers.

One man started a rush and was knocked down. Other men stood their ground, comforting the women. The crowd broke away only when they had seen the water rushing into the steerage. Then there was a scramble for the boats, but he saw men helping women and children and making no attempt to save themselves.

The crowd broke away only when they had seen water rushing into the steerage. They rushed on deck and were driven back like sheep by a magnificent officer! But that is not all.

Mr Lowe was asked:

'Did you hear any pistol shots on that Sunday night?' – 'Yes.'

'Where did you hear them?' – 'I heard them and fired them.'

'At whom?' – 'As lifeboat No. 15 [sic] was going down the ship's side I expected it would double up under our feet as it was. It would not have done for me to have told anyone else, or there would have been trouble. I feared that many would leap into it as we passed the decks. I thought, well, I shall have to see that no one else gets into that boat. *As we were lowering away I saw a lot of Italians at the ship's rail glaring and ready to spring. I yelled "Look out!" to the men, and fired down the ship's side.*'

'How far was your lifeboat from the ship's side?' – 'About 3ft from the rail. I fired the shots with no intention of hurting anyone. I know I did not hurt anyone.'

'How many shots did you fire?' – 'Three times. *I fired at three decks*. I fired horizontally along the boat. Afterwards I locked my revolver. I have never had occasion to use it since.'

Was the boat full from which Mr Lowe so bravely fired his revolver? Was that the only revolver fired? Were the steerage passengers kept in their quarters awash with water at the pistol-point?

Were boats sent down to the water half-full? We know they were. Take this as a sample of the evidence:

Mr Pitman, Third Officer, admitted that forty persons did not tax the capacity of his boat, which, he said, would have carried sixty at a tight fit. He had transferred women and a child from his boat to boat No. 7.

'Then you think that No. 7 could have held more people?' – 'Yes.'

'Both these boats could have held more people then?' – 'Yes.'

'Why were not more taken?' – 'There were no more women about when my boat was lowered. I can't say about No. 7.'

'Were there any men around?' – 'There may have been.'

There were no more women (and children?) about when his boat was lowered! Where were they then? Were they penned in their quarters waiting for the water to rush up and cover them? Had they tried to rush up on deck and been driven back? Were they whimpering helplessly in the dark? And were they only Italian men who stood at the ship side glaring and ready to spring?

Mr Lowe went away with his boat one-third empty, and he did not pull back. Why? The Senatorial Inquiry asked him that.

'Did you hear any cries of distress?' – 'Oh, yes.'

'Crying and shouting? Was it in the water?' – 'Yes, from the water. I heard no cries of distress before the ship went down. The cries were probably several hundred yards away. Then I told my men to get out their oars and pull towards the wreck so that we might be able to save a few more. They demurred,' he continued, 'saying it would be a mad idea,' but he corrected himself at once by saying that it was not the crew who demurred, but the passengers. Even the women did not urge him to go back. He yielded to the importunities of the passengers and let the boat drift aimlessly . . .

Is that true? Did he refrain from going back because of the importunities of his first-class passengers? And was it because of their importunities that they hurried past the lower decks?

Is that the final picture that remains to us – of the boat deck kept clear of steerage passengers, of intruders driven off it like sheep, of men knocked down in ineffectual desperate rushes out of the death trap, of guarded ropes and women and children driven back into the rushing water, of frenzied men (and women?) glaring from the ship's side at the rapidly descending boats, and frightened away with revolver shots? Do we see first-class passengers urging instant escape, clamorous against a stoppage of the lower decks with their 'glaring' occupants, insistent that the half-filled boats should not return?

Is it the fact that not one boat went down empty to the lower decks, that steerage passengers were driven off the upper deck, that what steerage passengers were saved were saved by sheerest accidents?

Were the steerage passengers treated like wild beasts to be kept under? Was the order of the day all thought and consideration for the first-class and second-class passengers? Were those dreadful creatures kept as far as possible out of the way until the first-class was clear?

The people of England shall decide. It has decided already that the course taken by the *Titanic* was unjustifiable, that the speed held by the *Titanic* was unjustifiable, that there was too little boat drill, that there were too few boats. Will it come now to the dreadful conclusion *that there were too few boats because the lives of the steerage passengers were not worth saving*?

(Daily Herald, 29 April 1912)

STORY OF THE *MOUNT TEMPLE* RUSH TO THE RESCUE *TITANIC'S* LAST MESSAGES WRONG POSITION GIVEN

Mr Lightoller, the Second Officer of the *Titanic*, was again recalled when the Senatorial Inquiry into the *Titanic* disaster was resumed at Washington on Saturday. A few questions regarding a ship's barber, who disappeared after making a sensational statement, having been put to him, he was released from further attendance.

Captain Moore, of the liner *Mount Temple*, was then called. He said that he had been at sea for thirty-two years, and for twenty-seven of these in the North Atlantic.

'Are you familiar with ice and icebergs?' asked Senator Smith. 'Yes, sir, very familiar.'

In reply to further questions, the witness said an iceberg was ice broken off from the land in the Arctic regions, and might be composed of land, rocks, or almost anything it would pick up in its course.

Senator Smith explained he made the inquiry because some levity had been caused by a question he asked a few days ago of what is an iceberg composed, and by a witness answering ice.

'Have you seen icebergs both by day and night?' he continued. – 'Yes, sir.'

'How did they look on a starlit night?' – 'White, sir: in fact, luminous.'

'Where was your ship on the night of Sunday, April the fourteenth?' – 'In latitude 41.25, longitude 51.14 at 12.30 in the morning (ship's time).'

'I wish you would tell the Committee in your own words just what happened on that Sunday night and on Monday morning at 12.30?' –'On Monday the fifteenth,' said Captain Moore, 'I was awakened by the steward with a message from the Marconi operator to my ship to the effect that the *Titanic* was sending out a "C.Q.D." call. Here is the message: "Titanic sinking. C.Q.D. Requires assistance. Position 41.44 N 50.24 W. Come at once. Iceberg." This was the message my operator had picked up.'

'What reply did you send?' – 'None whatever, sir. I did not want to stop those distress messages going out. My operator said the *Titanic* could not hear him. I blew the whistle at once, and ordered a course to be laid towards the *Titanic*'s position. I dressed and went to the chart room. We steamed up and sailed east by the compasses, turning right towards the *Titanic*. Then I went to the chief engineer, told him about the *Titanic*, and asked him to push up the fires, to wake all extra firemen, and get them busy. I said: "If necessary, give firemen a tot of rum." '

'A what?' asked Senator Smith. – 'A tot of rum, sir, to wake them up; spur them to action.'

'At the time you got this message from the *Titanic*, how far distant did you figure your vessel?' – 'About 49 miles.'

The Mysterious Lights

'What speed did you make towards the *Titanic*?' – 'A trifle more than 11 knots. About three in the morning we ran into the first ice. I immediately doubled the lookouts. At 4.25 (ship's time) we had to stop. At the time I figured we were about 14 miles distant from where the *Titanic* had signalled. Another delay was occasioned by a small schooner, whose green light stopped us for a moment.'

'Was the schooner between you and the *Titanic*?' – 'Yes, sir.'

'How much nearer the *Titanic* was the schooner than you were?' – 'The schooner could not have been more than 1½ miles from me. I heard the schooner's foghorn, and put the *Mount Temple*'s engines full speed astern to avoid her. After we had stopped a few minutes to avoid her, we proceeded slowly on our course towards the *Titanic*. The schooner was coming from the direction of the *Titanic*, and was moving not more than two knots an hour when we saw her. At three in the morning she would be about 12 miles from the *Titanic*.'

Senator Smith asked the captain if he thought the light on this schooner might have been the light which Mr Boxhall and others on the liner saw when the *Titanic* was firing distress rockets and flashing Morse signals? – 'It might have been the light of a tramp steamer which was on our port bow and passed to starboard of us.'

'How large a ship was it?' – 'About 4,000 tons, sir. I did not get her name, but she was a foreigner. She showed no sign. We tried to raise her by wireless, but I don't believe she had any. At 5.30 in the morning the *Mount Temple* ran into ice so heavy that we were forced to turn. The last we saw of the strange steamer was about nine o'clock on Monday, when we were both trying to avoid the icepack.'

'You have no means of determining that vessel's name or that of its commander?' – 'We had no communication whatever. So far as I recalled she had a black funnel, with some device or band near the top.'

'Did you get any nearer the *Titanic*'s position?' – 'We went slowly after 3.25 and reached very close to that position at 4.30 on Monday morning.'

'Was any other vessel there?' – 'None but a tramp ship that had cut ahead of me earlier, sir. The icepack,' continued witness, 'consisted of field icebergs.' He counted between forty and fifty bergs, the largest of them being between 100 and 200 feet high.

Senator Smith then took up the question of the use of glasses by lookout men, asking whether they were useful for the detection of danger ahead.

Witness: 'I am not sure whether they would be of extraordinary value.'

Senator Smith: 'Well, do you believe in the use of searchlights during a fog and at night? Would they not lessen the danger?' – 'No, sir. The use of a searchlight in a fog would be of no avail. It would be like throwing it against a blank wall. If the light were equipped with a powerful projector it might be some use at night.'

On the Scene of the Disaster

Captain Moore also told of his arrival on the scene of the *Titanic*'s sinking about 4.30 in the morning, two hours after the liner had gone down. He saw no wreckage and no bodies. He saw nothing but ice and a tramp steamer. The ice was so thick he was compelled to hoist men to the mastheads to seek a line out of the field.

Asked whether he had heard that certain of his passengers said they had seen rockets fired from the *Titanic* that night, Captain Moore replied that all his passengers were asleep. He had seen statements in the newspapers to that effect, but there were no passengers on the deck of the *Mount Temple* when she started for the *Titanic*. 'I got all the officers on deck,' he continued; 'got out all the lifeboats – twenty of them – and all the lifebelts. We were ready for any emergency, and I reckoned we could accommodate 1,000 people in the lifeboats. We have only one wireless operator. He had picked up the telephones just before going to bed to see what was on, and it was then he caught the signals from the *Titanic*. He also picked up other messages. One of them said that the *Titanic* had got the *Carpathia*, and had given her her position, which was then 41.46 N, 50.18 W, which was about ten miles eastward of her first position. The second message picked up by the *Mount Temple* was from the *Titanic* to the *Carpathia*. It read: "We struck iceberg. Come at once our assistance." He picked up many other messages. One was from the *Carpathia* asking the *Titanic* if she wanted any special boat to stand by. The *Titanic* answered she wanted all she could get.

'He also got a message from the *Frankfurt* to the *Titanic* on Sunday giving her position. *Titanic* asking, "Are you coming to our assistance?" The *Frankfurt* asked: "What is the matter?" The *Titanic*, according to messages received by the *Mount Temple*, answered: "We struck iceberg: sinking. Tell captain to come."

'My wireless operator, J. Burrant, informed me,' continued Mr Moore, 'that from the sound of the signals he judged the *Frankfurt* to be the nearest to the *Titanic*. The last message from the *Baltic* the operator told me was at 1.30 on Monday morning. A few minutes after that the operator told me that the *Olympic*, *Baltic* and *Frankfurt* were all trying to get the *Titanic*. He said that he had not spoken with her since 1.30 a.m. That was about an hour after I had been given the first "C.Q.D." from the *Titanic*.'

'Did you send any messages from the *Mount Temple*?' – 'No, we kept out. We did not want to interfere with the interchange of messages that was going on all the time between the *Titanic* and other vessels, but steamed ahead, and made ready for rescue, if we could reach the scene in time.'

Appeal to the Frankfurt

After the *Titanic* had advised the *Frankfurt* of her condition the *Titanic* sent out a second appeal to the *Frankfurt*, saying, 'Come quick.' The messages grew weaker and weaker, until the *Titanic*'s operator was undoubtedly using auxiliary or storage batteries. By that time the vessel's dynamos had been rendered useless by the water. The *Titanic* was still calling 'C.Q.D.' and at 1.20 she got the *Olympic* and said, 'Get your boats ready. Going down fast by the head.' The *Frankfurt* replied at 1.35, 'Starting for you.' Six minutes later the *Titanic* flashed, 'C.Q.D. Boilers flooded.' Then came the question, 'Are there any boats around you already?' To that there was no answer. Other ships then began calling, but could get no answer. Later the Russian steamer *Birma* got the *Olympic*, and reported, 'All quiet now.' The *Titanic* had not spoken since the *Carpathia* at 1.20 sent the message, 'Are you still there? We are firing rockets.'

Senator Smith: 'Did you see those rockets?' – 'I saw no rockets at all that night. I thought of sending up rockets myself, but I did not do so, because I feared it might divert other ships hurrying to the *Titanic*.'

Titanic's *Position Not Properly Fixed*

The *Titanic*, undoubtedly, had not fixed her position properly. She must have been eight miles further east than the spot reported. My observations, taken on Monday, indicated that the *Titanic*'s actual position was probably 50½ W.

Senator Smith: 'Does that indicate to you that the *Titanic* drifted?' – 'No. I think she stopped, but that her position was wrong.'

'The fact that you found no evidence of the wreck when you got to the *Titanic*'s position tends to confirm the idea that the ship was eight miles to the east of the position she gave?' – 'Yes, sir. Later I sighted the *Carpathia* on the other side of the field of ice, where she had picked up the *Titanic*'s boats. I heard from the *Carpathia* at 6.30 that she had picked up the *Titanic*'s boats, and that the *Titanic* had sunk. By that I had given up hope of sighting the *Titanic*. I had been steaming about the sea all night. After I got the news I stayed in the neighbourhood, and then steamed on my course.'

'Were there other vessels in sight at the point where the *Titanic* was supposed to have gone down?' – 'I saw a tramp steamer, and at eight o'clock on Monday morning I sighted the *Birma*. I also sighted the *Californian*, but there was ice between us.'

Mr Moore told the Committee he did not see how it was possible there could have been no suction when the *Titanic* went down. He thought the reason why so few bodies had been found was probably due to suction, which would have held the drowning between the decks as the boat sank. He thought the bodies were still in the ship.

The Wireless Records

Witness then read further extracts from the report of his wireless operator, Mr Burrant.

1.40 a.m. *Birma* thinks she hears *Titanic*. She sends: 'We are coming. You are only 50 miles away.' *Carpathia* calls: '*Titanic* all quiet.'

3.10 a.m. We (*Mount Temple*) back out of ice. There are large bergs all around.

3.25 a.m. *Californian* call C.Q.D. I answered to give her *Titanic*'s position. She had it before.

3.30 a.m. The *Californian* is now working with the *Frankfurt*. The *Frankfurt* also gives *Titanic*'s position.

4 a.m. *Californian* is now working with *Virginian*.

4.25 a.m. *Californian* is now working with *Birma*.

5.10 a.m. Signalled *Californian*. She wants my position. We were very close together.

6 a.m. Much jamming in wireless instrument.

6.45 a.m. *Carpathia* reports 20 boatloads rescued from *Titanic*.

7.30 a.m. *Baltic* sends service message to *Californian* as follows: 'Stand by. You have been instructed to do so frequently. This is signalled by the Inspector.'

7.40 a.m. *Californian* gets message saying that there was no need to stand by as nothing more could be done. *Carpathia* and *Olympic* were very busy.

Mr Moore said he did not see or hear of the *Amerika* on Sunday night or Monday.

Driving Through Ice

'What would you do if you met ice at night?' asked Senator Smith abruptly. – 'I would stop and drift. My instructions from the company are not to attempt to pass through any ice, no matter how thin it looks.'

'Do you think it was wise or discreet to run a ship at 21 knots through the night?' – 'It is frequently done. A field of ice is seldom met with at this time of the year.'

'Suppose you had been advised of ice ahead, would you consider it wise to drive a ship at that speed through the night?' – 'It would be very unwise.'

EVIDENCE OF STEWARDS

Andrew Cunningham, state room steward on board the *Titanic*, was called to the witness stand.

Senator Smith: 'Where were you on Sunday evening before the accident?' – 'I was summoned on duty just before the collision. At 12.30 an order was given to arouse all the passengers who were in the state rooms.'

'Not until 12.30? Why, that was 50 minutes after the accident?' – 'Yes, sir.'

'Were you notified of the gravity of the situation?' – 'No, sir. I saw the water in the Post Office and formed my own conclusion.'

'Was there any emergency alarm call for passengers on the *Titanic*?' – 'I do not think so.'

'How were the passengers alarmed then?' – 'In time of distress each state room steward calls his passengers.'

'Then at such time the passengers are dependent upon the vigilance of the steward?' – 'Yes. At 12.20 all my passengers had gone on deck except Mr Cummings [sic], who was in his state room getting his overcoat. After that Mr W. T. Stead asked me to show him how to put on his lifebelt. I put the lifebelt on him. It was the last I put on.'

'Did you ever see Mr Stead again?' – 'No, sir.'

'What did you do then?' – 'I put on a lifebelt myself after the passengers had been taken care of. After all the boats had gone my mate and I jumped to the sea and swam clear of the *Titanic*. We rested on each other while we were swimming, and after we saw the ship go down we struck out for the boats. Finally I was picked up by lifeboat No. 4. She was crowded. There were nine men and many women aboard, and there was no room to row.'

Henry Samuel Etches, Southampton, another steward, was then called. He had charge of the state room occupied by Mr Andrews, representative of Messrs Harland & Wolff.

Senator Smith: 'Did you see Mr Andrews frequently?' – 'Every morning at seven, when I took him his tea and fruit, and every evening when he dressed for dinner.'

'Did you know him before?' – 'Yes, I knew him on the *Olympic*. He built that, too. He was busy all the time of the voyage. His room was full of charts. He was looking out for improvements, and went about the boat with his workmen all day long.'

'When did you last see Mr Andrews?' – 'At 12.30 on Sunday night, when he asked me if I had called all the passengers. Then he told me to go with him and see that all the passengers had opened their doors, and that all of them had lifebelts. Then we walked up to the purser, who was standing, surrounded by a crowd of excited women, the purser telling them to go back to their state rooms and not be frightened. "That is just what I have been trying to get them to do," said Mr Andrews. After that he went down below, and I never saw him again. I saw a man run up on deck with a piece of ice in his hand. He threw it on the deck, and exclaimed to other passengers: "Will you believe it now?" I was also steward to Mr Benjamin Guggenheim. I went to his room, and started to put a lifebelt on him. "This will hurt," said Mr Guggenheim to me. I said to him, "Put on some clothes," and said I would be back in a minute. I went to another room.'

Mr Ismay and the Women

'Did you go back?' – 'Yes, I put a lifebelt on to Mr Guggenheim. I then went on deck, and assisted launching lifeboat No. 7. Mr Pitman and Mr Ismay helped keeping the falls clear. This was on the boat deck. Mr Ismay called out for the men to form a lane so as to let the ladies through. Mr Murdoch also kept calling for ladies, saying, "Are there any other ladies here?" Before this boat was lowered I assisted in loading boat No. 5. A woman came along before it was got off, and Mr Ismay called to her to get in. "I am only a stewardess, sir," she said. Mr Ismay said: "That makes no difference. You are a woman. Take your place." And she came away with us. Mr Murdoch ordered me into boat No. 5. He came to me after the women were in, and said, "Are you the steward regularly assigned to this boat?" I said, "Yes, sir; No. 5 is my boat." "All right," said Mr Murdoch, "get in." As it was about to be lowered Mr Pitman, who was in charge, called out to ask if there was a sailor in the boat. I shouted back there was not, and he called Seaman Oliver, who was ordered in. Then Mr Murdoch shook Mr Pitman's hand, and said, "Goodbye, old man; good luck." Just then a man and woman were standing beside the boat. She had her arms around his neck, and was crying. I heard her say, "I can't leave without you. I can't leave without you." I turned my head away, and next moment I saw the woman with the man sitting behind her in the boat. Just then a voice said, "Throw out that man," but we were already being lowered away, and the man remained. I don't know his name. I never heard it. He was a stoutish man, an American. When the boat hit the water we pulled away about 100 yards from the *Titanic* until she started to go down, when we rowed away a quarter of a mile. When she went down I saw a crowd of people on her afterdeck. Mr Pitman wanted to go back to help those in the water, and gave orders to do so. The women pleaded with him not to, asking him why they should risk their lives in a hopeless effort.'

(*Ulster Echo*, 29 April 1912)

459

THE *TITANIC* INQUIRY
WIRELESS TANGLE
OPERATOR'S STORY

Mr Sammis, the chief engineer of the Marconi Company, was called. He resented bitterly the imputation that he had been the means of suppressing news from the *Carpathia*, which, he said, had resulted in his neighbours pointing the finger of scorn at him. He said that he told the *Carpathia*'s operators to hold their personal stories for sale in order to get a reward for them. He did not send the messages direct, but telephoned to Davidson, in charge of a wireless station, and instructed him to tell the 'boys' that an arrangement had been made to care for them. He thought it would 'brace' them up. He carried out the plan, and went to the Strand Hotel to meet Operator Cottam, but failed to get in touch with him. The operators each got $750 for their stories.

Senator Smith: 'Did you get any part of that?' – 'Absolutely not; and no other official of the company received anything.' He acknowledged that a mistake had been made in the manner in which the stories had been 'placed', saying: 'I think it would have been better to have placed them with the Associated Press. They would then have had general circulation.'

Continuing, he said Bride and Cottam should not be blamed for not sending news from the ship. 'If there is any blame, it should fall upon the captain of the *Carpathia*. The captain of a ship is censor of all wireless messages sent from it. The operators are there to send and receive. They send nothing that the captain does not pass on.'

Mr Sammis said further that the American operators on board the ship receive $45 a month, and English operators £4.

Senator Smith: 'Do you not believe that it would have been more creditable to yourself and your company if you rewarded such heroism as was shown by Bride rather than seal their lips and arrange a pittance for them from private means?' – 'We were all doing the best we could.'

'I dislike to press these questions, but I want to bring out all the facts, in order to end the practice, which is vicious, and which shall be stopped.' Witness said he was in complete accord with Mr Marconi, who frowned upon the custom, but the abolition of the practice would have to be effected with great care, in order to save the feelings of the operators.

WIRELESS OPERATIONS

The Frankfurt's Messages

Mr Bride, the surviving operator of the *Titanic*, was then recalled. He gave evidence at New York the day after the *Carpathia* arrived there. He was first asked how much he received for the story of his experiences on the wreck from a New York newspaper. He said that he got $1,000.

Senator Smith: 'When did you last see Captain Smith?' – 'When he went overboard from the bridge. About three minutes before I left the ship myself.'

'Did he have on a life preserver?' – 'I don't know. He had none on when we were working in the cabin just before the ship sank.'

'You mentioned that your mate, Operator Phillips, and yourself put on life preservers about ten minutes before the boat sank?' – 'Yes, about that.'

'Had everyone else gone when you jumped into the water?' – 'There were several people on deck. I don't know who; some sailors. When the collapsible fell into the water it fell over me. I swam out and grabbed it. We then got away about 150 feet from the side of the *Titanic* just before she sank.'

'Did you not say before that you saw the captain after you got into the water?' – 'No. The captain left from the bridge before Phillips and I did. After the captain told us that we could go we stayed on the boat for a time. Phillips sent another C.Q.D. after that. I don't think he got an answer. If he did he did not tell me.'

'Did you see Phillips after?' – 'I saw him walking down the deck aft as I was helping to get on the collapsible boat.'

'Then you never saw him again?' – 'No. He died later, before he got to the *Carpathia*, in a lifeboat.'

'At what hour did the *Californian* try to get you?' – 'About five o'clock.'

'You did not answer for about half an hour because you were busy with your accounts?' – 'It was about twenty minutes, I think. I picked up the *Californian*'s ice warning while it was being sent to the *Baltic*.'

'Can you recollect the message?' – 'It was to the effect that the *Californian* had just passed three large icebergs, and it gave the ship's latitude and longitude. I took the message to the bridge, and gave it to the officer in charge. I don't remember who the officer was, but it was not the captain. No other warnings of ice, so far as I know, were received that day or night.'

Senator Smith: 'What about the *Frankfurt*'s answer to the *Titanic*'s C.Q.D.?' – 'Phillips told me to write in the log replies as he wrote them. The reply from the *Frankfurt* was first. It was "O.K. Will stand by." That was to our C.Q.D. and position.'

'Did the *Frankfurt* call you later?' – 'Yes, she asked what was the matter. The *Frankfurt* was not heard from again. The next response came from the *Carpathia*. I never got the *Frankfurt*'s position, and have not heard since how near to the *Titanic* she was. The messages were delayed. The *Carpathia* was the first to announce her position, and the first to say that she was on her way to assist us. Phillips also thought that the *Frankfurt* was much nearer, because her signals were much stronger.'

Senator Smith: 'If you had given your position to the *Frankfurt* there might be a different story today?' – 'Yes, sir.' The witness said that Phillips was on at duty at the time when the *Californian* wireless operator said his warnings were refused by the *Titanic*, which was then working with Cape Race.

'Was Phillips working with Cape Race at the time of the collision?' – 'He got through to it about ten minutes before.'

Senator Smith called the attention of witness to Captain Rostron's evidence to the effect that the *Carpathia* did not get the

Titanic's C.Q.D. until 12.35 on Monday morning, which, he said, showed a discrepancy of 51 minutes between the time the message was sent to the *Titanic* and received by the *Carpathia*.

Witness replied that this discrepancy might be due to difference in clocks. He was not sure of the exact time at which the message was sent.

Mr Boxhall, the Fourth Officer, who has been unwell since he last appeared before the Committee on Monday last, explained that the operator's clock had been set forward fully half an hour at midnight.

Bride, continuing his evidence, said that only ten minutes elapsed after the collision before Captain Smith appeared in the wireless room, and ordered the call for aid to be sent.

THE MYSTERY SHIP

Mr Boxhall, Fourth Officer of the *Titanic*, was next examined.

Senator Fletcher asked him if the portholes were closed before or after the collision with the iceberg. Witness replied that he did not know. He heard no orders for portholes to be closed.

He was asked as to the positions of various steamers the *Titanic* heard from on Sunday and as to the position of the icebergs of which the *Titanic* was warned by the *Amerika*. Witness replied, 'I put down no positions which were south of our track.'

Asked again about the steamer's light seen from the deck of the *Titanic* on the night of the disaster Mr Boxhall said: 'I am quite positive that they were steamer's lights. She was coming towards us and was about five miles away. I saw those lights after the order to man the lifeboats was given and when I got into my boat after firing rockets she had turned. I could see her stern light.'

The witness explained to the Committee that all ships' rockets were not distress signals. He pointed out that there was a system of rockets for signalling when passing a ship at night, and that those might have been the rockets which passengers on the *Californian* said they had seen on a ship in the distance on Sunday night.

'Are you sure that the ship you saw from the deck of the *Titanic* was a steamer?' – 'Yes; it was a steamer on account of the arrangement of the lights.' Mr Boxhall saw the lights on the phantom ship near the *Titanic* disappear to the west some time after he left the *Titanic* in the lifeboat.

Senator Smith: 'I have evidence to support the belief that the *Californian* was only 14 miles from the *Titanic*. Do you think that you could have seen the lights of the *Californian*?' – 'I don't know. Five miles is the greatest range that the British Board of Trade requires a ship's lights to show, but we know that they can be seen further on clear nights such as that was. I should think, however, that we could not see the *Californian*'s lights that night.'

'If the *Californian* had fired rocket signals do you think you would have seen them 14 miles away?' – 'I think not.'

Senator Smith asked the witness many questions regarding the *Titanic*'s watertight compartments.

'They were watertight so far as they extended,' said Mr Boxhall. 'Were the compartments watertight at the ceiling?' – 'No, sir.'

'Would it have made any difference?' – 'Not in this particular case, as the *Titanic*'s compartments were damaged in the collision. Moreover, the compartments need not be watertight at the ceiling, because the water never rises to the space above the surface of the sea.'

CARPATHIA'S WIRELESS MAN

Offers of Money

Mr Cottam, wireless operator on board the *Carpathia*, was then called. He said that he had received $750 from a New York newspaper for his story of the disaster. He had received no message instructing him to suppress any message containing an account of the disaster.

'Did you transmit any messages from Mr Ismay to his Liverpool, London, or New York office while you were on the *Carpathia*?' – 'Yes, sir.'

'How did you get a message to Liverpool?' – 'Via an American land station.'

Pressed as to whether he had sent any messages to Liverpool via London direct, the witness said that he remembered despatching one via the *Olympic* on Monday. His recollection as to the contents of the message was hazy, because the rush of work was so great he had little fixed idea as to any individual message.

'At what time on Monday did Mr Ismay send a message to Mr Franklin about the *Titanic*?' – 'I don't believe that any was sent on Monday, because I was in touch with no land station on Monday. Some messages were, however, sent through the *Olympic* on Monday. I remember a message from Mr Marconi several days after the accident asking why no news of the disaster had been sent.'

'Did you answer it?' – 'No, I had too much official business to do. There was no order from the captain to send news. The captain told me to handle nothing but official and passenger traffic.'

Senator Newlands asked Mr Cottam when he and Mr Bride first received news that they would be paid handsomely for their exclusive stories.

Mr Cottam: 'When we were docking. I was preparing to go on shore when Bride took the message.'

'Would it have made any difference if you had received the message earlier?' – 'Not a bit. We were extremely busy. Besides, we were acting on the captain's orders.' Witness added that the weather during the *Carpathia*'s voyage to New York after she had rescued the *Titanic* survivors was most unfavourable for the transmission of wireless messages. It was raining incessantly, and that diffused the current.

On the conclusion of Mr Cottam's examination Senator Smith announced that the examination of the officers and crew of the *Titanic* was practically concluded. He directed the sergeant-at-arms to arrange for all of them to leave for home.

Mr Lightoller, the Second Officer, will be recalled for a short time today at the opening of the hearing. He will be followed by

Mr Ismay whose examination will then be concluded. Then all the *Titanic* official witnesses will be released. The men will proceed to New York, where the White Star Company will send them home to England on the first available boat.

All the *Titanic*'s crew expressed their delight when they heard that they might leave for home.

(*Ulster Echo*, 30 April 1912)

Recalled for further interrogation, **J. Bruce Ismay** admitted receiving a telegram relating to the presence of ice from Captain Smith but rejected press comments from American passenger Emily Ryerson that he had told her the ship would increase speed to get through the ice field.

'Mr Ismay, I believe some passengers state that Captain Smith gave you a telegram reporting ice?' – 'Yes, sir.'

'On Sunday afternoon?' – 'Sunday afternoon, I think it was.'

'What became of that telegram?' – 'I handed it back to Captain Smith, I should think about ten minutes past seven on Sunday evening. I was sitting in the smoking room when Captain Smith happened to come in the room for some reason, and on his way back he happened to see me sitting there and came up and said: "By the way, sir, have you got that telegram which I gave you this afternoon?" I said, "Yes." I put my hand in my pocket and said: "Here it is." He said: "I want to put it up in the officers' chart room." That is the only conversation I had with Captain Smith in regard to the telegram. When he handed it to me, he made no remark at all.'

'Can you tell what time he handed it to you and what its contents were?' – 'It is very difficult to place the time. I do not know whether it was in the afternoon or immediately before lunch. I did not pay any particular attention to the Marconi message – it was sent from the *Baltic* – which gave the position of some ice. It also gave the position of some steamer which was short of coal and wanted to be towed into New York, and I think it ended up by wishing success to the *Titanic*.'

'Would you not regard it as an exercise of proper precaution and care to lessen the speed of a ship crossing the Atlantic when she had been warned of the presence of ice ahead?' – 'I am afraid that question I can not give any opinion on. We employ the very best men we possibly can to take command of these ships, and it is a matter entirely of their discretion.'

'Did you have any conversation with a passenger on the *Titanic* about slackening or increasing speed when you heard of the ice?' – 'No, sir, not that I have any recollection of. I presume you refer to what Mrs Ryerson said. I testified in New York, the day after we arrived, that it was our intention on Monday or Tuesday, assuming the weather conditions to suit, and everything was working satisfactorily down below, to probably run the ship for about four to six hours full speed to see what she could do.'

'You did not have any conversation on that Sunday about increasing the speed, did you?' – 'Not in regard to increasing the speed going through the ice.'

(US Inquiry, 30 April 1912)

Irishman **Daniel Buckley**, twenty-one, was a steerage passenger on board the *Titanic*. He recounted how a female passenger – thought to be Madeleine Astor – wrapped him in a shawl so that he could avoid detection in boat No. 4.

I was sleeping in my room when I heard a terrible noise. I jumped out on the floor, and the first thing I knew my feet were getting wet. Water was coming in slightly. I told the other fellows to get up, that there was something wrong. They just laughed at me. Two sailors came along and shouted: 'All up on deck unless you want to get drowned!'

When I heard this I went for the deck as quick as I could. When I got up on the deck I saw that everyone else had life preservers. I went back again to my room to get one of the preservers but as I was going down the last flight of stairs the water was up four steps and dashing up. I did not go any farther. I got back on the deck again and as I was looking around to see if I could get any of those lifebelts, I met a first-class passenger, and he had two. He gave me one, and fixed it on me.

When the lifeboat was prepared, there was a big crowd of men standing on the deck. They all jumped in, so I said I would take my chance with them. There were no ladies there at the same time. I went into the boat. Then two officers came along with a lot of steerage passengers – ladies and gentlemen – and said all of the men should come out and let the ladies in. But six men were left in the boat. I think they were firemen and sailors. At first they fought and would not get out, but the officers drew their revolvers and fired shots over our heads. Then the men got out. I was crying. There was a woman in the boat, and she had thrown her shawl over me, and she told me to stay in there. I believe she was Mrs Astor. Then they did not see me, and the boat was lowered down into the water.

'Was there any effort on the part of the officers or crew to hold the steerage passengers in the steerage?' – 'I do not think so. They tried to keep us down at first on our steerage deck. They did not want us to go up to the first-class place at all.'

'Who tried to do that?' – 'I think they were sailors. There was one steerage passenger and he was getting up the steps, and just as he was going in a little gate, a fellow came along and chucked him down – threw him down into the steerage place. This fellow got excited and he ran after him, but he could not find him.'

'What gate do you mean?' – 'A little gate just at the top of the stairs going up into the first-class deck. The first-class deck was higher up than the steerage deck, and there were some steps leading up to it, nine or ten.'

'Was the gate locked?' – 'It was not locked at the time we made the attempt to get up there, but the sailor, or whoever he was, locked it.'

'Did these passengers in the steerage have any opportunity

at all of getting out?' – 'Yes, they had. I think they had as much chance as the first and second class passengers.'

(US Inquiry, 3 May 1912)

LOSS OF 1,519 ON *TITANIC* NEEDLESS, REPORT DECLARES

A severe arraignment of the late Capt. Smith of the *Titanic* for what were termed his overconfidence, his indifference to danger and his utter disregard of repeated warnings from other vessels concerning icebergs in his path; a bitter condemnation of Capt. Lord of the *Californian*, who slept while the *Titanic* sank only a few miles away from where the *Californian* lay to all night; an urgent call upon 'the honest judgement of England' for a 'painstaking chastisement' of the British Board of Trade because of its lax regulations and its hasty inspection of the *Titanic*; praise for Capt. Arthur H. Rostron of the *Carpathia*, whose foresight and courage saved the 700 souls that were adrift in unmanned and unequipped lifeboats, and an urgent call upon Congress and the Legislatures of all other nations to pass new and stringent laws that would make such another horror impossible – these are the outstanding features of the report submitted to the Senate today by Senator William Alden Smith.

The principal conclusions of the Senate Committee are these:

That the supposedly watertight compartments of the *Titanic* were not watertight because of the non-watertight condition of the decks where the transverse bulkheads ended.

That the *Californian*, controlled by the same company as the *Titanic*, was nearer the sinking steamer than the 19 miles reported by her captain, and that her officers and crew 'saw the distress signals of the *Titanic* and failed to respond to them in accordance with the dictates of humanity, international usage and the requirements of law.' The committee concludes that the *Californian* might have saved all the lost passengers and crew of the ship that went down.

That the full capacity of the *Titanic*'s lifeboats was not utilized, because, while only 706 persons were saved, the ship's boats could have carried 1,176.

That no general alarm was sounded, no whistle blown and no systematic warning given to the endangered passengers, and it was fifteen or twenty minutes after the collision before Capt. Smith ordered the *Titanic*'s wireless operator to send out a distress message.

That the *Titanic*'s crew was only meagrely acquainted with its positions and duties in an accident and that only one drill was held before the maiden trip and none after the vessel left Southampton though many of the crew joined the ship but a few hours before she sailed.

Warnings Disregarded

That the warnings received on every side by the *Titanic* that ice was in her path, warnings which her captain forwarded to the Hydrographic Bureau in Washington, were disregarded so far as the navigation of the vessel was concerned, and that her speed was not relaxed but increased and her lookout watch not doubled.

That the wireless operator of the *Carpathia* was not 'duly vigilant' in handling messages concerning the *Titanic* disaster, either official or from passengers, and that the practice of allowing wireless operators to send newspaper accounts of their experience in the line of duty should be stopped.

That all ships carrying 100 passengers or more should be equipped with double searchlights; that all ships should carry lifeboats sufficient to hold every soul aboard; that wireless telegraphy should be regulated by law so as to prevent amateur interference and also compel ships to maintain a day and night watch of operators.

Senator Smith's speech began with an explanation of the course of his committee in taking prompt steps to gather at first hand the evidence of the rescued sailors of the *Titanic* before they should sail for England.

'Questions of diverse citizenship,' he said, 'gave way to the universal desire for the simple truth. It was of paramount importance that we should act quickly to avoid jurisdictional confusion and organized opposition at home and abroad.

'Absolute Unpreparedness'

'Though without any pretension to experience or special knowledge in nautical affairs,' continued the Senator, 'nevertheless, I am of the opinion that very few important facts escaped our scrutiny.'

Continuing, the Michigan Senator said in part:

'In the construction of the *Titanic* no limit of cost circumscribed their endeavour, and when this vessel took its place at the head of the line every modern improvement in shipbuilding was supposed to have been realized; so confident were they that both owner and builder were eager to go upon the trial trip; no sufficient tests were made of boilers or bulkheads or gearing or equipment, and no life-saving or signal devices were reviewed; officers and crew were strangers to one another and passengers to both; neither was familiar with the vessel or its implements or tools; no drill or station practice or helpful discipline disturbed the tranquillity of that voyage, and when the crisis came a state of absolute unpreparedness stupefied both passengers and crew and, in their despair, the ship went down, carrying as needless a sacrifice of noble women and brave men as ever clustered about the Judgement Boat in any single moment of passing time.

'Captain's Recklessness'

'We shall leave to the honest judgement of England its painstaking chastisement of the British Board of Trade, to whose laxity of regulation and hasty inspection the world is largely indebted for this awful fatality. Of contributing causes there were very many. In the face of warning signals, speed was increased and messages of danger seemed to stimulate her to action rather than to persuade her to fear.'

Of Capt. Smith, Senator Smith said that 'his indifference to the danger was one of the direct and contributing causes of this unnecessary tragedy, while his own willingness to die was the expiating evidence of his fitness to live.'

The Senator pointed to the reckless disregard even of the falling, chilling temperature that was a matter of comment among all the passengers as they got into the icefield. The blow which the *Titanic* struck the iceberg was severe, yet many of the passengers and crew 'did not even know of the collision until tardily advised of the danger by anxious friends, and even then official statements were clothed in such confident assurances of safety as to arouse no fear.

'No Orderly Routine'

'The awful force of the impact was well known to the master and builder, who, from the first, must have known the ship was doomed and never uttered an encouraging sign to one another, while to the inquiry of President Ismay as to whether it was serious, the captain only replied, "I think it is." ' There is evidence tending to show that even the watertight compartments were not successfully closed either above or below. No general alarm was given, no ship's officers formally assembled, no orderly routine was attempted or organized system of safety begun. Haphazard, they rushed by one another, on staircase and in hallway, while men of self-control gathered here and there about the decks, helplessly staring at one another or giving encouragement to those less courageous than themselves.

'And yet,' exclaimed the Senator, 'it is said by some well-meaning persons that the best of discipline prevailed. If this is discipline, what would have been disorder?'

The 'recklessness and indifference' of many of the crew, the haste of some of the junior officers to ensure their own safety while passengers were still trying to get into the boats, the woeful ignorance of the stewards and others manning the boats of even the rudiments of seafaring knowledge, were all touched upon by Senator Smith.

He paid a tribute to Phillips and Bride, the wireless operators of the *Titanic*, who stayed till the very end was at hand before seeking to rescue themselves, and commented on the lucky fact that the *Carpathia*'s operator, listening for a Cape Race message, kept his telephone over his head while undressing and so was able to receive, just as he was turning in for the night, the distress call of the *Titanic*.

'The spirit of venality' that brought about the 'systematic reign of silence' in the wireless operation of the *Carpathia* was strongly condemned by Senator Smith, and he declared also that the White Star Line officials in New York received information 'containing absolutely the entire story' about 8.30 Monday morning, yet 'battled against the truth all day', and after seven o'clock that night sent a message to Representative Hughes assuring him that the *Titanic* was safe and being towed to Halifax.

'It is little wonder,' said the Senator, 'that we have not been able to fix with definiteness the author of this falsehood.'

Of Capt. Lord's conduct in failing to proceed to the *Titanic*'s rescue when her distress signals had been seen from the *Californian* Senator Smith spoke in scathing terms. He read the English law which makes it a misdemeanour for the master of a vessel to fail to proceed forthwith to the assistance of any person or vessel in danger of being lost at sea.

Senator Smith compared with Lord's the conduct of Capt. Rostron, and concluded with a declaration that 'obsolete and antiquated shipping laws should no longer encumber the parliamentary records of any government,' and that the best way to honour the dead of the *Titanic* was to pass such laws as would serve to prevent the recurrence of such disasters.

(*New York World*, 29 May 1912)

LONDON PAPERS DENOUNCE SMITH

The London morning papers print lengthy extracts from the Senate Committee's report on the *Titanic* disaster and from Senator Smith's speech, but only a few comment upon the matter editorially. The *Daily Mail* says the report is not likely to provoke serious criticism, but thinks it regrettable that Senator Smith was not content to allow it to speak for itself, as it regards his speech as 'a violent, unreasonable diatribe, in which the Senator betrays once more the amazing ignorance that prompted some of his questions during the inquiry.'

The *Daily Express* says: 'Although much of the report sounds sensible, the grotesque oration of Senator Smith deprives it of much value. That extraordinary mass of grandiloquent bosh is probably without a parallel in the history of parliaments. Its mock heroics and ludicrous verbosity relieve it of any taint of sincerity or sense.'

The *Express* thinks that in view of Senator Smith's behaviour at the inquiry the report will not benefit from his association with it, but admits there is some justification for the charge of lack of discipline in loading the boats after the collision. As regards the censure of the *Californian*'s captain, it believes the British people will reserve judgement until after the report of the Mersey Commission.

The *Daily News*, on the contrary, believes Senator Smith has no need to apologize for his committee, which got its witnesses when the facts were too fresh in their memories for art or delusion to colour them and whose questions were a model of rigorous investigation.

'Some, at least, of its conclusions,' it declares, 'are irresistible, and they are very disturbing. We cannot believe the *Titanic* alone of British ships had these defects.'

(*New York World*, 29 May 1912)

The British Board of Trade Inquiry convened for the first time on 2 May under the auspices of Wreck Commissioner Lord Mersey.

The Board of Trade, represented by the Attorney General, Sir Rufus Isaacs, drew up a list of 26 questions to be answered by the court relating to the construction of the *Titanic*, navigation, ice warnings, and the proximity of the *Californian*. To clarify the events on the night of the sinking, Lord Mersey and his team of five assessors were able to refer to a large model of the *Titanic*, specially built for the hearings. By the time the jury retired on 21 June, the testimony of the various witnesses had amounted to 25,622 questions and answers.

Able Seaman **Joseph Scarrott** was the second witness to testify at the Board of Trade Inquiry.

I myself took charge of No. 14 as the only sailorman there. The Chief Officer ordered women and children to be taken in. Some men came and tried to rush the boat. They were foreigners and could not understand the orders I gave them, but I managed to keep them away. I had to use some persuasion with a boat tiller. One man jumped in twice and I had to throw him out the third time. I got all the women and children into the boat. There were fifty-four women and four children – one of them a baby in arms. There were myself, two firemen, three or four stewards and Mr Lowe, who got into the boat. I told him the trouble I had with the men and he brought out his revolver and fired two shots between the boat and the ship's side. He said: 'If there is any more trouble I will fire at them.'

The after fall got twisted and we dropped the boat by the releasing gear and got clear of the ship. There were four men rowing. There was a man in the boat who we thought was a sailor, but he was not. He was a window cleaner. The *Titanic* was then about 50 yards off, and we lay there with the other boats. Mr Lowe was at the helm.

After the ship sank, we heard cries coming from another direction. Mr Lowe decided to transfer our passengers among the other boats, and then make up the full crew of men to go in the direction of the cries. Then we went among the wreckage. When we got where these cries were, we were among hundreds of dead bodies floating in lifebelts. The wreckage and the bodies seemed to be hanging in one cluster. We pushed our way among the wreckage, and as we got towards the centre we saw a man – I have since found out he was a storekeeper – on the top of a stair-case or a large piece of wreckage as if he was praying and at the same time calling for help.

When we saw him we were about 15 yards from him, and the wreckage was so thick – I am sorry to say that there were more bodies than there was wreckage – that it took us quite half an hour to get that distance to that man. We could not row the boat through the bodies. We had to push them out the way, to force our way to the man. We could not get close enough to get him right off, only within reach of an oar. We pulled him off with that and he managed to hang on and get into the boat.

(British Inquiry, 3 May 1912)

AWAY JUST IN TIME

Able Seaman William Lucas, an ex-Navy man, another witness at the *Titanic* inquiry, said he was playing 'nap' when the ship struck.

He got into a collapsible boat and they had only just got clear when the *Titanic* went down.

Lucas said he knew there was some ice 'knocking about'. The shock of the collision nearly knocked him off his feet.

'After the collision what did you do?' – 'I went down and put on an extra jersey.' (Laughter)

Lucas said that as far as he knew the passengers on the boat deck were all of the first class. The boats lowered from that deck were not full by a long way. That was 'because there were no women knocking about'.

He got into the last boat to get away on the port side – a collaps-ible boat – but Mr Lightoller ordered him out.

He then went to the starboard side to see if there were any boats left there, but there were not, so he went back to the collapsible boat. A lady called out that there were 'no sailors or plugs' in the boat, so he got in. The water was then up to the ship's bridge. With the rising of the water and the tilting of the *Titanic* the boat 'floated off'.

Lucas said the women were afraid of the collapsible boat when it had been lowered, and he transferred them to another boat. Afterwards his boat rescued thirty-six people clinging to an over-turned collapsible boat. Two boats rowed back to the scene of the wreck, but they found nobody alive.

He said that after the boat drill at Southampton he went ashore. 'It is a regular thing for the sailors to go ashore and have a final drink.'

'In the lowering of the boats was there sufficient interval to enable the female passengers from the steerage to get on to the boat deck?' – 'They would have been able to if there had been anyone there to direct them to the boat deck.' Lucas did not think there was anyone directing them.

There were two girls on deck when he left with the collapsible boat. 'I said to them, "Wait a minute, there is another collapsible boat being put down from the funnel. You had better get into that." I could not take them because my boat was full.'

Lucas said that he and Mr Lightoller helped one elderly lady into the collapsible boat and then had to help her out again as she would not go without her husband. 'There were several cases like that,' he said.

The inquiry was adjourned.

(*Daily Sketch*, 8 May 1912)

Reginald Lee, forty-two, from Oxfordshire, was on lookout duty with Frederick Fleet in the crow's nest when the iceberg suddenly loomed into view. The Attorney General was greatly concerned by the absence of binoculars on the *Titanic*.

'You have had about 15 or 16 years' experience at sea alto-gether?' – 'Yes.'

'Have you had experience in mail steamers?' – 'Yes.'

'Are glasses usually supplied to the lookout man in mail steamers?' – 'Not that I know.'

'Have you acted as lookout man in other ships before the *Titanic*?' – 'Yes.'

'On mail steamers?' – 'Yes.'

'Have you ever had glasses for use as a lookout man?' – 'Yes, but I do not know whether they were private or supplied by the company.'

'Have you found them of use?' – 'They are better than ordinary eyesight.'

'Are they of use at night at all?' – 'Certainly: night glasses.'

'Do you know whether they are supplied in any other vessels of the White Star Line?' – 'I cannot say they are for certain, but my mate in the crow's nest, Fleet, who was four years in the *Oceanic* as lookout man, told me they had them there.'

'Were there any on the *Titanic*?' – 'No, not for our use anyway.'

'Was there any place in the crow's nest for glasses?' – 'Yes, there was a small box.'

'Did you look for glasses at all in the crow's nest?' – 'We asked for them. I did not personally ask for them, but one of the other fellows did, and they said there were none for us.'

'Did you come on the lookout at 10 o'clock on Sunday night the fourteenth of April?' – 'Yes. We relieved Symons and Jewell.'

'Did one of you take the starboard side and one the port side of the crow's nest on the lookout?' – 'I generally took the starboard side and Fleet took the port side.'

'When you relieved Jewell and Symons, did they pass any word to you?' – 'Yes, they told us to keep a careful lookout for ice – and growlers in particular.'

'What sort of a night was it?' – 'A clear, starry night overhead, but at the time of the accident there was a haze right ahead. In fact it was tending more or less round the horizon. There was no moon. And no wind whatever, barring what the ship made herself. The sea was quite calm, but it was very cold, freezing – the coldest we had had that voyage.'

'Did you notice this haze, which you said extended on the horizon, when you first came on the lookout, or did it come late?' – 'It was not as distinct then, not to be noticed, but we had all our work cut out to pierce through it just after we started. My mate happened to pass the remark to me. He said: "Well, if we can see through that we will be lucky." That was when we began to notice there was a haze on the water.'

'At the time you came on watch, up to the moment just before the collision, can you tell us whether there was any difference in the speed at which the vessel was travelling compared with the rest of the voyage?' – 'She seemed to be going at the same rate all the way.'

'Did you receive any orders from the bridge at all during this watch?' – 'No. The orders were turned over by the people we relieved.'

'Before half past 11 on that watch – that is seven bells – had you reported anything at all?' – 'There was nothing to be reported.'

'What was the first thing you did report?' – 'It was some minutes after seven bells struck, it might have been nine or ten minutes afterwards. Three bells were struck by Fleet, warning, "Right ahead," and immediately he rung the telephone up to the bridge: "Iceberg right ahead." The reply came back from the bridge: "Thank you." As soon as the reply came back, the helm must have been put either hard-a-starboard or very close to it, because she veered to port, and it seemed almost as if she might clear it, but I suppose there was ice under water. As she struck on the starboard bow, there was a certain amount of ice that came on board the ship. That was the forewell deck. It seemed as if she struck just below the fore-mast. The berg was on my starboard side. It was higher than the forecastle, which was about 55 feet out of the water. It was a dark mass that came through that haze and there was no white appearing until it was just alongside the ship, and that was just a fringe at the top. That was the only white about it, until she passed by, and then you could see one side seemed to be black and the other side seemed to be white.'

'When you are at sea in a fog is it usual practice to station a watchman at the bows in addition to the lookout in the crow's nest?' – 'The captain of the ship has to be responsible for that kind of thing.'

'Just tell me in your experience, is it usual to do that?' – 'If the captain of the ship thinks it is necessary.'

'Have you seen it done?' – 'I have, frequently.'

'Is not a haze a kind of fog?' – 'It is a kind of fog, but you could not describe it as a fog.'

'When you are going through a haze at night, is it usual to slow up – slacken speed?' – 'That has nothing to do with me. I am not on the bridge.'

'When your ship is sailing through an ice-field, is it usual to go slow – to slacken speed?' – 'Certainly.'

'And speed on this occasion was not slackened?' – 'I could not tell you.'

'Did Symons tell you that he asked for glasses on the bridge?' – 'I think so. I know that we all spoke about it. Fleet, Hogg, Evans, Symons and myself were all there.'

'And they were all talking about binoculars?' – 'They were asking why they could not have them, because they had been in use from Belfast to Southampton, and they wanted to know what had become of the glasses that we had used in that time.'

'Is your sight good?' – 'I hope so.'

'Is there an examination of the eyes before you are appointed lookout man at Southampton, or elsewhere?' – 'Yes.'

'Were you examined at Southampton by a doctor?' – 'Yes, but not especially for eyesight though.'

'What sort of examination did the doctor make?' – 'I suppose he pleased himself. A medical man generally does. We were falling in on the lounge deck and the doctor came and examined us all. It was a casual kind of examination.'

'He did not ask you anything at all about your eyes?' – 'No.'

Sir Robert Finlay (for the White Star Line): 'About a light you saw after you were in the boat. You saw it before the *Titanic* went down?' – 'Yes.'

'Were there more lights than one?' – 'It seemed like a masthead light, or it might have been one of our own boats with a small light.'

'How far off do you think it was?' – 'Five or six miles.'

'The haze could not have been very bad if you thought it was a masthead light, five or six miles off?' – 'This is after she had passed the berg. As she got clear of the berg, the weather was clearer.'

'Then did this haze come in some time before 12 o'clock, and then lift just at the time the *Titanic* was sinking? Are you sure this haze existed at all?' – 'Yes, sir, quite positive.'

'Was it ever very bad?' – 'It was so bad that you could not see the iceberg.'

(British Inquiry, 8 May 1912)

WATERTIGHT DOORS RAISED
TITANIC TRIMMER'S SENSATIONAL EVIDENCE

The *Titanic* inquiry was resumed at the London Scottish Hall, London, this morning. There was no falling off in public interest, the increased public accommodation at the rear of the hall being fully utilized, while the galleries were crowded with fashionably dressed ladies.

Thomas Patrick Dillon, coal trimmer, who was in the engine room at the time of the collision, examined by Raymond Asquith, spoke of the stopping and reversing of the engines just before the shock. The enginemen at once rushed to the pumps and in the meantime the watertight doors were closed. They were then ordered to go into the stokehold which they reached after forcing up a watertight door. The order came, 'Keep steam up,' and then they were instructed to draw the fires. Other watertight doors were opened in order to let the engineers pass through.

'Who ordered you to open them?' – 'The chief engineer.'

'The doors were closed from the bridge, but opened by order of the chief engineer?' – 'Yes, sir.'

Mr Laing (White Star Co.) explained that the doors could only have been opened by the release of a catch on the bridge, so that the chief engineer must have telephoned to the bridge. Witness said they were ordered on deck an hour and forty minutes later. 'The last boat was just going then,' he said. 'They were singing out, "Any more women aboard?" We saw two and chased them up the ladder.'

'Chased them up?' – 'Yes, drove them up.'

'You were on board the *Titanic* when she went down?' – 'Yes.'

Witness said he went down in the ship and shoved himself away from her in the water. He was sucked down again about two fathoms and then seemed to be lifted up to the surface. He was picked up by No. 4 boat after swimming about twenty minutes.

'Did you see any other people in the water?' – 'About a thousand. That is my estimate.' As soon as he was picked up by the lifeboat he became unconscious. When he recovered consciousness he found a passenger and a sailor lying dead on top of him.

Answering Sir Rufus Isaacs, witness said he and some of his mates were in the stokehold when the watertight doors were closed. He and his companions forced their way through No. 4 boiler-room through three watertight doors. These were raised by two or three men.

(*Liverpool Evening Express*, 9 May 1912)

WHY *TITANIC* SURVIVORS DID NOT HELP THE DROWNING

Remarkable evidence as to why those in the *Titanic* lifeboats did not attempt to rescue those in the water after the disaster was given yesterday at the inquiry at the London Scottish Drill Hall.

In each case where the cries of distress were not heeded witnesses alleged that the reason was the wish of the lady passengers, who feared the boats would be swamped in endeavouring to pick up the drowning.

Charles Hendricksen, a leading fireman, said the boat he was in did not attempt to pick up anybody.

The President: 'When you were picked up by the *Carpathia* there were only twelve people on board?' – 'Yes.'

'Of these twelve how many belonged to the crew?' – 'Seven: there were five passengers.'

'Did the men object?' – 'Yes. We had room for a dozen more.'

'What were the names of the passengers?' – 'I heard the name of one: Duff Gordon. I think his wife was there, Lady Duff Gordon.'

'Did his wife object?' – 'Yes, she was scared to go back in case of being swamped.'

'When Lady Duff Gordon objected did her husband reprove her?' – 'He upheld her.'

'He did not to try to get her courage up to go back?' – 'No.'

'Tell what was said.' – 'Duff Gordon and his wife said it was dangerous, and that we would be swamped.'

'Am I to understand that because two of the passengers said it would be dangerous you all kept your mouths shut and made no attempt to rescue anyone?' – 'That is right, sir.'

'Was any money given to you and the crew of this lifeboat by any of the passengers when you got on the *Carpathia*?' – 'Yes, £5.'

'Who gave this money to you?' – 'Duff Gordon.'

'When did he promise it?' – 'When we got aboard the *Carpathia*.'

(*Daily Graphic*, 10 May 1912)

SHIP APPRENTICE'S STORY
ROCKETS SEEN ON NIGHT OF *TITANIC* DISASTER
DENIALS BY CAPTAIN OF *CALIFORNIAN*

There has been no more remarkable evidence at the *Titanic* Inquiry than that given yesterday by the captain, the Second Officer, and an apprentice of the Leyland liner *Californian*.

Searching questions were asked by the President and the Attorney-General with a view to probing the story told by a donkeyman on board the *Californian* that the *Titanic*'s distress rockets were seen by the *Californian*, but ignored.

Captain Lord, of the *Californian*, yesterday admitted that a vessel was seen about five miles from the *Californian* on the night of the accident, but he denied that the rockets she sent up were distress signals. He also declared she was not the *Titanic* which, he said, must have been over 30 miles distant from his ship.

The apprentice declared that he informed Captain Lord of the signals, but the latter said he was asleep at the time and had no recollection of being informed.

CAPTAIN LORD'S STORY
NO RECOLLECTION OF A VISIT FROM
THE APPRENTICE

Captain S. Lord, master of the Leyland Line S.S. *Californian*, was first examined by Sir Rufus Isaacs.

The Attorney-General: 'Close upon 11 o'clock on the Sunday night did you see a steamer's light?' – 'I did.'

'Did you think that the vessel that approached you was the *Titanic*?' – 'No, I remarked at the time that she was not the *Titanic*.'

'How could you tell that?' – 'You can never mistake those vessels. There is a blaze of light.'

'About what distance did you consider she was from you then?' – 'Six or seven miles.'

'Did you continue to watch the approach of the vessel?' – 'Yes, until 11.30.'

'What size steamer did she appear to be?' – 'Something like ourselves.' (The *Californian*'s gross tonnage is 6,223).

'Did you see your Third Officer attempting to communicate with her?' – 'Yes. I did.'

'How?' – 'By a Morse lamp.'

'Did he get any reply?' – 'No.'

At twenty minutes to one the witness asked the Second Officer if the steamer had changed its course. He replied that she was just the same, and that he had called her up once but she would not reply.

'Did he tell you whether he had seen any signals?' – 'He said he saw a white rocket from the vessel.'

The President: 'Am I right in supposing that this vessel, the name of which you apparently do not know, was at the time that her rocket was sent up in the position in which the *Titanic* probably was?' – 'No, sir.'

The President: 'You know what is in my brain at present is this – that what they saw was the *Titanic*.'

The Attorney-General: 'She was certainly very close. It is a point which your Lordship will probably have to determine on this evidence.'

The witness said he saw one masthead light, but that the Third Officer said he saw two, while the Second Officer said he saw one.

'DID NOTHING FURTHER'

The President: 'This is very important because the *Titanic* would have two masthead lights.'

The Attorney-General: 'If the Third Officer did see two lights it must have been the *Titanic*?' – 'That doesn't follow.'

'Do you know of any other vessel there with two lights?' – 'Any amount.

'At this particular time and at this particular spot – 19 miles from you?' – 'That is not, in my opinion, the spot where the *Titanic* hit the berg. She was 32 miles from me, from where I met the wreckage.'

'Did you know of any other passenger steamer except the *Titanic*?' – 'No.'

'You know the *Titanic* was not very far away?' – 'I did not know where she was.'

'But you had been in communication?' – 'Yes, but I never knew her position.'

'Have you ever thought that the steamer approaching you was the *Titanic*?' – 'I never thought that.'

The Attorney-General: 'You were called by the Chief Officer at 4.30. What did he say?' – 'He told me that the steamer that had fired the rockets was still to the southward.'

'Have you heard from other officers that she fired a number of rockets?' – 'I did afterwards, the next day.'

'Did you hear that this vessel fired altogether eight rockets before the Chief Officer came to you at 4.30?' – 'No.'

'Did you remain in the chart-room when you were told that the vessel was firing rockets?' – 'Yes.'

'You knew, of course, that there was danger in this field of ice for steamers?' – 'To steamers steaming.'

'You knew also that it was desirable to communicate with the *Titanic* to tell her that there was ice?' – 'Yes, I had done that.'

The President: 'You knew that the vessel sending up these rockets was in a position of danger?' – 'No, I did not.'

'Well, danger if she moved?' – 'If she moved, yes.'

'What did you think she was sending up the rocket for?' – 'I thought she was acknowledging our Morse lamp signals.'

'Have you ever said that before?' – 'That has been my story right through.'

'You had heard of the rocket. You wanted to know what the rocket was? You tried to find out by Morsing it?' – 'Yes.'

'And you remained in the chart-room and did nothing further?' – 'I did nothing further.'

'Must it not have been a distress signal?' – 'If it had been a distress signal the officer on watch would have told me.'

'You know perfectly well that the apprentice Gibson went down to you?' – 'I know now.'

'You knew then?' – 'I did not.'

'But you were expecting him to tell you the meaning of the signal?' – 'In the meantime I was asleep.'

The President: 'You were not asleep when you said to the boy, "What is it?"' – 'I was just wakened up by the banging of the door.'

IMPOSSIBLE TO MISTAKE THE TITANIC

The Attorney-General: 'How do you know that the rocket was not a distress signal?' – 'I am under the impression that it was not, because we did not hear the report, as we would have done at that distance.'

'How many miles off?' – 'About four or five miles.'

The Attorney-General questioned witness about a conversation he had had with the Chief Officer at about five o'clock. The Chief Officer asked him if he would look at the steamer. Witness remarked that there were no signals, and the Chief Officer then said that another fireman had stated that several rockets had been fired. Witness sent the Chief Officer to the wireless operator, and he came back and said that a ship had sunk. The Chief Officer went back to the wireless operator and again returned, and said that the *Titanic* had struck a berg and sunk. Witness then left the bridge and went to the wireless-room.

The Attorney-General: 'Did you say anything about the rockets then?' – 'No.'

'On the ship you had seen the night before?' – 'No.'

'Or the possibility of it being the *Titanic*?' – 'No.'

'Were you quite comfortable in your mind with reference to the matter?' – 'I thought we ought to have seen her signals at 19 miles.'

'Does it not strike you now that the ship was the *Titanic*?' – 'No, I am positive it was not.'

'Why are you positive?' – 'Because it is an utter impossibility for anyone to mistake a ship like the *Titanic* at sea?'

Mr Scanlon: 'When did you go to sleep?' – 'I told the Second Officer I was going to be down at 12.50 a.m.'

'When did your wireless operator go off duty?' – 'So far as I was concerned, he went off at 11 o'clock on Sunday night, after he had sent the last message.'

'Would it not have been quite a simple thing for you at that time when you were in doubt as to the name of the ship and the reason of her sending up rockets to have wakened your Marconi operator and asked him to speak this ship?' – 'I would have if it had worried me a great deal, but it did not.'

Mr Scanlon: 'Suppose the *Titanic* was seven or eight miles from you between 11.30 and 12 o'clock, would those on the bridge have been able to see your lights?' – 'Easily.'

'When did you first hear of the wireless message from the *Titanic* that you were to shut up and keep off as they were busy?' – 'Some time on the morning of the fifteenth.'

WHEN THE CAPTAIN WAS ASLEEP

'Did you regard it as an insulting message?' – 'Oh, no.'

Mr Edwards: 'Your message to the *Titanic* was one of courtesy?' – 'A message of advice.'

Answering Sir Robert Finlay, witness said the *Mount Temple* must have been very close to the spot where the *Titanic* was reported to have foundered. After he heard of the wreck he steamed to the spot at full speed and estimated the rate at 13 knots. They were an hour on the journey.

The Attorney-General: 'Mr Stone is your Second Officer. Did he tell you there had been rockets sent up?' – 'He did. That was the message the boy was supposed to have said to me, which I heard the next day.'

'I must put it to you, did not the boy deliver the message to you, and did you not inquire whether they were all white ones?' – 'I do not know. I was asleep.'

'This is a very important matter. It is just as well to tell me exactly what happened.' – 'I have inquired very closely of the boy. He said I opened my eyes when he gave the message, and I said, "What time is it?" and that I asked whether there were any colours in the light.'

The Attorney-General: 'You see what that means. That means that the boy did go to the chart-room to you, that he did tell you about the rockets from the ship, and that you asked whether they were white rockets, and told him he was to report if anything further occurred?' – 'So he said.'

'Have you any reason to doubt that it is true?' – 'No, I was asleep.'

'Do you mean to say that you said this in your sleep to him?' – 'I very likely was half-awake. I have no recollection of this apprentice speaking to me at all.'

The President: 'Is there any reference in your log as to your steamer having seen this rocket or this mysterious ship which was not the *Titanic*?' – 'No.'

'Why was all reference to these rockets kept out of the log?' – 'If we had realized they were distress rockets we should have entered them in the log.'

Further questioned, witness said that even if they had received the distress message he did not think they could have reached the scene of the disaster before the *Carpathia*.

James Gibson, aged 20, an apprentice on board the *Californian* said that he went on duty at 12 o'clock. At five minutes to one, after he had been off the bridge for twenty minutes, Mr Stone told him that the ship had fired five rockets.

The Solicitor-General: 'What else did Mr Stone say?' – 'That he had reported it to the captain.'

'What else?' – 'And that the captain had instructed him to call her on the Morse light.'

'What had been the result?' –'She had not answered him, but fired more rockets.'

'Did you see her fire these further rockets?' – 'I saw three.'

'What colour rockets were they?' – 'White.'

'When you had your glasses on her, could you make out what ship it was?' – 'No, only the lights.'

'SHE LOOKS VERY QUEER'

'What did you notice between one o'clock and 1.20, looking at her through your glasses?' – 'The Second Officer remarked to me, "Look at her now. She looks very queer out of the water. The lights look queer." '

'Did he say what he meant?' – 'I looked at her through the glasses, and the lights did not seem to be natural.'

'What did you see through the glasses?' – 'She seemed as if she had a heavy list to starboard.'

'Did you think yourself when you looked at her through the glasses that something was wrong?' – 'We had been talking about it together.'

The President: 'What were you saying?' – 'The Second Officer remarked to me that the ship was not going to send up the rockets at sea for nothing.'

The President: 'As I understand it, you and the Second Officer came to the conclusion that it was a ship in distress?' – 'Not exactly.'

'What then?' – 'That everything was not all right.'

Answering the Solicitor-General, witness said he thought the vessel he saw was a tramp.

Subsequently, he said, he was ordered by the Second Officer to report to the captain.

'Did you give him the report you were ordered to give?' – 'Yes.'

'What did the captain say?' – 'He asked me whether they were all whites.'

'What did you tell him?' – 'I told him they were all white.'

The President: 'Was he awake?' – 'Yes.'

'Was there anything else?' – 'Yes. I saw three more rockets.'

'When was that?' – 'About twenty minutes to four.'

'What do you mean when you say that later on when you looked at her you thought she had got a list, or that her lighting looked queer?' – 'The side lights seemed to be higher out of the water.'

'What colour are distress signals?' – 'White.'

'Did you not think it curious that so many rockets should be sent up so near?' – 'Yes.'

'Did the Second Officer say this vessel must be in distress?' – 'No; he said there must be something wrong.'

'You thought she was in distress?' – 'Yes.'

'Did you see stars with the rockets?' – 'Yes, white stars.'

'Do you know the regulation distress signal is a rocket throwing white stars?' – 'Yes.'

The President: 'Did you know it then?' – 'Yes.'

A SCENE WITH THE PRESIDENT

The next witness was Herbert Stone, Second Officer on the *Californian*, who said he saw the rockets.

The President asked him several times what he thought the rockets meant, and the witness answered that he did not know.

The President remarked: 'Do be frank. You don't make a good impression.'

Mr Aspinall: 'Did you think they were distress signals?' – 'No, not at the time.'

'Did it occur to you at some later time?' – 'After I had heard about the *Titanic* going down.'

'What did you think then?' – 'That they might possibly have been distress signals.'

The President: 'From the *Titanic*?' – 'Not necessarily.'

At two o'clock the witness said to Gibson, 'Go down to the master, and be sure you wake him up and tell him that we have seen eight of these white lights like white rockets in the direction of this other steamer; that this steamer was disappearing in the south-west; that we had called her up repeatedly on the Morse lamp, and had received no information whatever.' The gradual disappearance of the lights was perfectly natural in a steamer steaming away.

Mr Aspinall: 'Did they not have the appearance of being the lights of a ship which had suddenly foundered?' – 'Not by any means.'

The President: 'Do you mean to tell us that neither you or Gibson expressed the opinion that there was something wrong about that ship?' – 'No, sir, not wrong with the ship, but merely with the changing of her lights.'

'Do you want me to believe that, notwithstanding these rockets, neither you nor Gibson thought there was anything wrong about that ship?' – 'Yes, sir.'

DISTRESS SIGNALS EXAMINATION

In answer to Mr Scanlon, the witness said he obtained his certificate as mate last December twelve months. In the examination he sat for to obtain his certificate he had to answer a question as to distress signals.

'For that question you read something about distress signals?' – 'I learnt it.'

The President: 'And the very thing was happening that you knew indicated distress?' – 'Had the steamer stood on its bearings . . .'

'No, no. Do not answer me like that. Is it not a fact that the very thing was happening which you had been taught indicated distress?' – 'Yes, sir.'

Mr Scanlon: 'You knew, did you not, that these rockets sent up were signals of distress?' – 'No.'

The President: 'Do think what you are talking about. You have just told me that what you saw from that steamer were just what you had been taught to expect as signals of distress. Is that true?' – 'It is true that similar lights are distress signals.'

'And you saw those lights?' – 'When the steamer was steaming away.'

Mr Harbenson: 'Did you notice this ship had a list?' – 'I did not.'

In answer to Mr Dunlop, the witness said that he judged the ship to be a smallish steamer.

'Could she be the *Titanic*?' – 'Not by any means.'

The President: 'Have you heard of any other steamer in the vicinity at that hour?' – 'No, sir.'

'You knew the *Titanic* was there?' – 'Yes.'

(*Daily Graphic*, 15 May 1912)

CONVINCED HE SAW THE *TITANIC*

Californian Officer's Evidence

The first witness at the *Titanic* inquiry yesterday was Charles Victor Groves, the Third Officer of the *Californian*, who was on duty from 8 o'clock until 12 on the Sunday night.

He said he saw a steamer with two white masthead lights. (The *Titanic* had two white masthead lights.) She had 'a lot of lights,' and was a large passenger steamer. About 11.30 he reported what he had seen to the captain, and told him the vessel was a passenger steamer.

As ordered by the captain, Groves tried to call the steamer up with the Morse lamp. Afterwards he saw a light and sent the message, 'What?' That meant, 'What vessel are you?' The light on the steamer still flickered, and Groves concluded definitely that the steamer was not answering.

Captain Lord went on to the bridge and said: 'That does not look like a passenger steamer.' Groves said: 'It is. When she stopped, her lights seemed to go out, and I suppose they put them out for the night.' The lights went out at 11.40.

In the course of their conversation about the steamer the captain said: 'The only passenger steamer near is the *Titanic*.'

The court discussed the question of the apparent going out of the lights that Mr Groves noticed. Lord Mersey pointed out that the *Titanic*'s engines were stopped at 11.40, whereupon he was informed that the order from the bridge to stop the main engines would not result in the stopping of the engine that lighted the ship. It was pointed out that the *Titanic* was stated to have made a turning movement when the iceberg was sighted, and Groves said that the lights might have been shut out by such a movement.

Groves said that when he went off duty he told Stone, the Second Officer, that he had seen a passenger steamer that stopped about 11.40. Between 12.15 and 12.30 Groves went to the Marconi room, woke up the operator, and said, 'What ship have you got, Sparks?' (Sparks is a ship nickname for the Marconi operator.) Sparks replied, 'Only the *Titanic*.' Groves then put the wireless instrument to his ear. He could read a message if it was sent slowly. He heard nothing.

'How long did you listen?' – 'I do not suppose it would be more than fifteen to twenty seconds. I did it almost mechanically.'

(The Marconi operator, who gave evidence later, explained that the 'detector' stopped when he left off working. That being so, any signals that the *Titanic* might have made afterwards would not be recorded.)

Groves then went to his bunk. Next morning the Chief Officer called him and said the *Titanic* had sunk. Groves then went to Stone, the Second Officer (who on Tuesday gave evidence that he saw several white rockets go up.)

Groves said to Stone: 'Is this right about the *Titanic*?' Stone replied: 'Yes, it is right. Hurry up and get dressed; we shall be wanted in the boats. I saw rockets in my watch.'

Lord Mersey: 'That conveys to me the notion that when he said he saw rockets in his watch he was referring to rockets which he believed came from the *Titanic*. Did he give you that impression?' – 'It is rather difficult to say what impression I got. I was rather excited.'

Lord Mersey: 'Knowing what you do now, do you think the steamer that you now know was throwing up rockets, that you thought was a passenger steamer, was the *Titanic*?' – 'Most decidedly I do, sir.'

Groves said that in the morning he saw a steamer whose name he did not know. It was smaller than the ship whose lights he saw the night before.

George Frederick Stewart, the Chief Officer of the *Californian*, was the next witness. Asked why there was no reference to the distress signals in the log, Stewart was understood to reply that it might have been forgotten.

'Do you think a careful man is likely to forget distress signals?' – 'No, my Lord.'

Lord Mersey: 'Then don't talk to me about forgetfulness.'

The Chief Officer added that he never questioned the Second Officer about the absence of any reference to the distress signals in the log. Stewart was questioned about the unknown steamer seen in the morning. He said it had four masts and one funnel. He had been unable to find out her name.

Cyril Evans, the Marconi operator on the *Californian*, said that on the Sunday evening he told the captain that the *Titanic* was near. The captain told him to let the *Titanic* know that the *Californian* was stopped and surrounded by ice.

About 11 o'clock he called up the *Titanic*, but, as the *Titanic* operator was sending private messages to Cape Race, he was told to 'keep out'. The *Californian's* signals, Evans explained, would obliterate those from Cape Race.

Evans said he turned in about 11.30. He remembered Mr Groves visiting the Marconi room after midnight. Evans said he would have sent a call at any time during the night had he been asked.

(*Daily Sketch*, 16 May 1912)

Third-class steward **John Hart**, a thirty-one-year-old Londoner, was responsible for the welfare of around fifty-eight steerage passengers on E deck. Thinking the collision to be a trivial affair, he went to sleep, only to be stirred by the chief third-class steward, Mr Kiernan.

'He said, "Get your people roused up and get lifebelts placed upon them." '

'Did you knock them all up?' – 'Yes.'

'Were most of them up or were they asleep?' – 'The majority were up. They had been aroused before I got there.'

'And what did you do about the lifebelts?' – 'I saw the lifebelts placed on them that were willing to have them put on.'

'Some would not put them on?' – 'Some refused to put them on. They said they saw no occasion for putting them on; they did not believe the ship was hurt in any way. After that there was a large number of men coming from the forward part of the ship with their baggage – those that were berthed third-class up forward. When I saw that my own people had the required number of lifebelts – or those who were willing to have them – I placed the remainder of the lifebelts in one of the alleyways beside which these people would have to pass, in case any came through without lifebelts from the forward part of the boat. I waited about there with my own people, trying to show them that the vessel was not hurt to any extent to my knowledge, and waited for further orders. After some little while the word came down, "Pass your women up on the boat deck." Those that were willing to go to the boat deck were shown the way. Some were not willing, and stayed behind. Some of them went to the boat deck and found it rather cold, and saw the boats being lowered away, and thought themselves more secure on the ship, and consequently returned to their cabin. I heard two or three say they preferred to remain on the ship than be tossed about on the water like a cockle shell.'

'This would be about 12.30?' – 'Yes.'

'How did you take them?' – 'I took them along to the next deck, the C deck, the first saloon deck. I took them along to the first-class main companion from there.'

'At that time, when you took up your people by that route, was there any barrier that had to be opened?' – 'There were barriers that at ordinary times are closed, but they were open.'

'How many people of your lot did you take up the first time you went up this course to the boat deck?' – 'Somewhere about thirty, all women and children of the third-class. I took them to boat No. 8, which at that time was being lowered. I left them there and went back again, but on the way of my getting back other passengers were coming along, third-class passengers. They were also being shown the way to the boats. Amongst them were females – the husbands and fathers were with them.'

'Did you bring up any more?' – 'I had some little trouble in getting back owing to the males wanting to get to the boat deck. After the word was passed around for women and children, I was delayed a little time in getting a little band together that were willing to go to the boats.'

'A band of women and children?' – 'Yes.'

'How many did you gather?' – 'Somewhere about twenty-five.'

'Were those all people from the rooms you were responsible for?' – 'No, also from other sections.'

'Were they all third-class passengers?' – 'Yes. I took them to the only boat that was left then on the starboard side of the ship, boat No. 15. They got in from the boat deck. Mr Murdoch said: "What are you?" I said: "One of the crew. I have just brought these people up." He said: "Go ahead; get into the boat with them." The boat was then lowered to A deck. We there took in about five women, three children, and one man. He had a baby in his arms.'

'When you left the third-class part of the ship the second time, the last time, were there any more third-class passengers down there?' – 'Yes, there were some that would not come to the deck. They would not leave their apartments.'

'By that time you at any rate had realized that this was a very serious accident?' – 'Yes, but they would not be convinced.'

'Did you do your best to convince them?' – 'Everybody did their best.'

'On this second journey of yours, the last journey, did you see other stewards engaged in getting people?' – 'Yes, I met several on the deck directing them the way to the boat deck. There was one man at the foot of the companion leading from the sleeping accommodation to the after-well deck; there was one man at the end of the companion leading from the well-deck to the E deck;

and there were others along the saloon and second cabin deck showing them the way to the boat deck. So there was no difficulty for anybody who wanted to get to the boats to find their way there.'

Mr Harbinson (for the third-class passengers): 'I should like to know what are the means employed to prevent the third-class passengers during the voyage from straying into the first and second-class decks and quarters of the ship. First, are there two collapsible gates?' – 'Yes, gates that can be removed. Dividing the third-class deck there is a companion; dividing the second-class deck and the first-class deck there is a barrier.'

'Are those kept fastened during the course of a voyage – the barrier and the companion?' – 'No.'

'Are they open?' – 'Well, the barrier that lifts over and the gate that fixes in you can just take it out with your hand. It is never locked.'

'So that at any time a third-class passenger, by pushing the gate or raising the barrier, can go to the second-class deck or the first-class deck. Is that right?' – 'That is correct. That is, of course, if there is nobody there on watch. There is usually a quartermaster standing by there or a seaman.'

'Have you ever seen those gates locked?' – 'No.'

'Do I gather rightly from you that it was a considerable time after the chief third-class steward had told you to rouse up your people that you went about reassuring these people and telling them that the vessel was not hurt?' – 'No. Right from the very first we were trying to convince the people that she was not hurt.'

'Why did you, upon your own authority, go round and tell them that the vessel was not hurt?' – 'It was not on my own authority at all.'

'Who told you to do that?' – 'The chief third-class steward told me to get my people about, as quietly as possible.'

'Why did he tell you to get them up?' – 'I cannot answer why he did; I take it, on account of the collision. He must have had word that there had been an accident.'

'And, knowing from him that there must have been an accident, and that he considered the accident was of such a character that these people should be roused, you went round among them, and tried to assure them that the vessel was not hurt?' – 'In the first place.'

'Why did you do that?' – 'Because it was my instructions to.'

'I put it to you that as a result of these assurances given to the people, they refused to leave their berths?' – 'I do not think so.'

'It is a considerable distance, is it not, from the aft part of the ship to the boat deck?' – 'Yes.'

'You have told us that you saw a number of stewards placed at various portions to direct the third-class passengers how they were to go?' – 'Yes. I passed about five or six on the starboard side.'

'Who else besides you were bringing the people from their berths?' – 'Almost eight. A portion of the third-class stewards were room stewards, of whom I am the only survivor.'

'You told us about a rush of men from the front part of the ship coming aft?' – 'Yes.'

'Why do you think they were coming aft?' – 'Because the forward section had already taken water.'

'And that was the only way they could escape?' – 'Not necessarily, no. They could escape from the fore part of the ship.'

'Up the companion ladder would have been the nearest way for them, would it not?' – 'Yes.'

'But they did not do that; they chose the other way. That is rather curious, is it not?' – 'No.'

'That is to say, they go the whole length of the ship and come up from the well deck at the back rather than go up the companion ladder leading from the fore deck to the boat deck?' – 'Perhaps the people did not stop to think where they were going to.'

'If there had been anybody to show them, they would not have had occasion to think?' – 'That may be so.'

'According to you, all the women and children from the aft part of the boat who were taken up and who wanted to escape could have done so?' – 'I do not doubt that for a moment.'

'Can you explain, that being so, how it was that 55 per cent of the women of the third-class were drowned?' – 'I cannot account for it. No, sir.'

(British Inquiry, 16 May 1912)

Sir Cosmo Duff Gordon defended his conduct on the night of the sinking.

No. 7 was the first boat I went to. It was just being filled. There were only women and the boat was lowered away. No. 3 was partially filled with women, and as there were no more, they filled it up with men. My wife would not go without me. Some men on No. 3 tried to force her away, but she would not go.

I heard an officer say: 'Man No. 1 boat.' I said to him: 'May we get in that boat?' He said: 'With pleasure; I wish you would.' He handed the ladies in and then put two Americans in, and after that he said to two or three firemen that they had better get in.

When the boat was lowered I thought the *Titanic* was in a very grave condition. At the time I thought that certainly all the women had got off.

There was a man sitting next to me and about half an hour after the *Titanic* sank he said to me: 'I suppose you have lost everything?' I said: 'Yes.' He said: 'Well, we have lost all our kit, for we shall not get anything out of the Company, and our pay ceases from tonight.' I said: 'Very well, I will give you five pounds each towards your kit.'

(British Inquiry, 17 May 1912)

SIR COSMO DUFF GORDON'S DENIALS

Sir Cosmo said he was asleep at the time of the collision.

'What were your wife and Miss Francatelli [her secretary] doing when the boats were being manned?' – 'Standing on the deck. They refused to go. My wife refused to leave me.'

'Did anyone attempt to place your wife into one of the life-boats?' – 'Yes. Some men got hold of her and tried to pull her away, but she would not go. Later my wife said to me, "Ought we not to do something?" I said, "No. We have got to wait for orders." '

'Then did you hear any orders given with reference to No. 1 boat?' – 'Yes. One of the officers said, "Man the emergency boat," and then he told a number of the crew to get in. I then spoke to him and said, "May we get in that boat?" And he said, "Yes, I wish you would," or "Very glad if you would," or some expression like that. There were no other passengers at all. I think he then told two or three other firemen that they might just as well get in.'

'When the boat was lowered did you think the *Titanic* was in danger?' – 'I thought it was in a very grave condition.'

'When the *Titanic* went down did you hear a cry?' – 'I heard a wail, one confused sound.'

'They were the cries of persons drowning. There is no doubt about that?' – 'Yes, I think so.'

'Did it occur to you that there was room in the boat and that if you could get to the people you could save some?' – 'It is difficult to say what occurred. I was minding my wife, and the conditions were abnormal. It might well have occurred to one that they could have been saved by a boat.'

'And that there was room in your boat?' – 'I think it was possible.'

'Did you hear a suggestion that the boat should go back to where the cries came from?' – 'No, I did not.'

'Did not you think about whether or not your boat would be able to save people in the water?' – 'I do not know. It might have been possible, but it would be very difficult to get back the distance we were away in that darkness.'

'Did you hear one of the ladies say anything about the danger of being swamped?' – 'No, I did not.'

'No thought entered your mind at the time that you ought to

go back and try to save some of those people?' – 'No, I suppose not.'

(*Daily Graphic*, 18 May 1912)

Lady Duff Gordon disowned the contents of various newspaper articles attributed to her, and, when questioned by the Attorney General, gave her version of events in the emergency lifeboat.

After three boats had gone down, my husband, Miss Francatelli and myself were left standing on the deck. There were no other people on the deck at all visible and I had quite made up my mind that I was going to be drowned. Then suddenly we saw this little boat in front of us, and we saw some sailors, and an officer apparently giving them orders.

I said to my husband: 'Ought we not to be doing something?' He said: 'Oh, we must wait for orders.'

We stood there for quite some time while these men were fixing up things, and then my husband went forward and said: 'Might we get into this boat?' And the officer said in a very polite way indeed: 'Oh certainly, do. I will be very pleased.'

Then somebody hitched me up from the deck and pitched me into the boat, and then I think Miss Francatelli was pitched in. It was not a case of getting in at all. We could not have got in – it was quite high. After we had been in a little while, the boat was started to be lowered and one American gentleman got pitched in, and one American gentleman was pitched in while the boat was being lowered down.

'Had you heard any orders given?' – 'As far as I can remember it was to row quickly away from the boat for about 200 yards.'

'And come back if called upon?' – 'No. I did not hear that.'

'Before she sank, did you hear the men saying anything in the boat?' – 'No.'

'Did you hear anything said about suction?' – 'Well, perhaps I may have heard it, but I was terribly sick, and I could not swear to it.'

'I am asking you about something which I understood you have said quite recently, something which I only know from your statement to your solicitor. Did you hear a voice say, "Let us get away"?' – 'Yes, I think so.'

'Did you hear it said, "It is such an enormous boat; none of us know what the suction may be if she is a goner"? ' – 'Yes, I heard them speaking of the enormous boat. It was the word "suction" I was not sure of.'

'Did you hear a proposal made that you should go back to where the *Titanic* was sunk?' – 'No.'

'Did you hear anybody shout out in the boat that you ought to go back?' – 'No.'

'With the object of saving people who were in the *Titanic*?' – 'No.'

'You knew there were people in the *Titanic*, did you not?' – 'No. I did not think so. I did not think I was thinking anything about it.'

'Did you say that it would be dangerous to go back, that you might get swamped?' – 'No.'

(British Inquiry, 20 May 1912)

MR LIGHTOLLER IN THE BOX

Conversation With Captain
Nothing Said About Reducing Speed

Mr Charles Herbert Lightoller, the *Titanic*'s Second Officer, who was on the bridge from 6 o'clock until 10 on the night of the disaster, began his evidence at the inquiry yesterday.

Mr Lightoller, who is the senior surviving officer, dived from the ship as it was sinking. He was twice sucked under the water, and saved himself by clinging to an upturned collapsible boat.

He told the Court that the night was clear, and an extra lookout was not required. Throughout her voyage the ship had been making her normal speed of 21½ knots.

The Solicitor General: 'At 21 knots the ship travelled 700 yards a minute?' – 'Yes.'

'Was it your view you could see a 'growler' at a safe distance?' – 'Yes, I could see a 'growler' at a mile and a half or probably two miles.'

Lord Mersey: 'Is this leading to a suggestion that the lookout men were to blame?' Mr Lightoller: 'Not at all.'

The officer then explained to the Court that with a slight swell (or a slight breeze) there was a phosphorescent line round an iceberg. That night there was no swell to be seen. It was the first time in 24 years' experience that he had seen an absolutely flat sea.

Mr Lightoller said it was not his experience that the temperature fell as large bodies of ice were approached. It might even go up, he said. He then described, as far as he could remember, a conversation he had with Captain Smith on the bridge about 9 o'clock.

'I said something about its being rather a pity a breeze did not get up, as we were going through the ice region. He would know what I meant. I was referring to the breeze making the waves break on the side of the berg.'

Mr Lightoller continued: 'We then discussed the indications of ice. I remember saying there would probably be in any case a certain amount of reflected light from the berg. He said: "Oh, yes, there will be a certain amount of reflected light." He said probably even if the blue side of the berg was turned towards us the white outline would give us sufficient warning. He said: "We shall be able to see it at a good distance." '

Lord Mersey: 'Then you had both made up your minds at this time that you were about to encounter icebergs?' – 'Not necessarily. We discussed it as a natural precaution.'

Mr Lightoller said that Captain Smith was with him on the bridge until nearly 9.30. There was no discussion at all as to reduction of speed. As he left the bridge Captain Smith said: 'If it becomes at all doubtful call me at once. I'll be just inside.' That, the officer said, had reference to the risk of ice. Mr Lightoller said he sent a message to the crow's nest shortly after the captain had left him telling the men to keep a sharp lookout for ice, especially 'growlers'.

Asked what his view was as to the usefulness of glasses at night in detecting ice, he said that it was rather difficult to say. He should naturally think that glasses would be helpful. He himself had never seen ice through his glasses first. As a rule he preferred to rely on the naked eye.

(*Daily Sketch*, 21 May 1912)

WIRELESS MYSTERY

Did Captain Smith Receive All The Warnings?

A mystery of wireless warnings about ice occupied the attention of the Titanic Court of Inquiry yesterday. The question raised was whether the *Titanic* received all the warnings, and, if so, what was done with them.

To assist the Court the positions of ice reported in these messages have been marked on a chart, and an oblong enclosing them has been described on it. It was within the oblong that the ship sank.

The Court's attention was chiefly directed to two messages, sent from the *Amerika* and the *Mesaba* respectively. Both were sent on the Sunday, and the Solicitor General has stated that the *Mesaba*'s message was sent about two hours before the collision.

Second Officer Lightoller, who was on the bridge from 6 o'clock till 10 on the Sunday night, and Fourth Officer Boxhall said they knew nothing of these two messages. Lightoller said that had such a message as that from the *Mesaba* been received by the officers he had no doubt that the *Mesaba* would have been communicated with immediately.

Mr Turnbull, deputy manager of the Marconi Company, gave evidence to show that the message from the *Amerika* was sent to Cape Race through the *Titanic*.

This message, which reported the position of two large icebergs, was addressed to the Hydrographic Office at Washington. Mr Turnbull said that, though in the ordinary course a message passed on was regarded as private, it was the practice that messages important to navigation should be communicated to the captain.

The message from the *Mesaba* reported pack ice and a great number of bergs in latitude 42 to 41.25, longitude 49 to 50.30. (According to Fourth Officer Boxhall, who worked out the position, the *Titanic* struck the iceberg at lat. 41.46 long. 50.14.) At the bottom of the message, said Mr Turnbull, there was an entry to the effect that a reply was received from the *Titanic* operator. It was not the answer of the captain.

At this point Lord Mersey said: 'I am very anxious to know exactly what knowledge can be traced to Captain Smith. That is my anxiety.' Later he remarked: 'This message seems to me to justify the allegation made by the Solicitor General that the *Titanic* must have known of the presence of ice in the oblong.'

Sir Robert Finlay (for the White Star Line): 'It comes to this, of course, that the operator of the *Titanic* who received this message would know of it. I think it must have been Phillips. He has gone, of course, and it does not carry it a step further towards showing that the captain or any of the officers knew of it.'

Lord Mersey: 'It would be a very extraordinary thing if a man in the Marconi room did not communicate a telegram of this kind to the captain.'

Harold Bride, the junior operator on the *Titanic*, said that the only message he took about ice was one from the *Californian*. It was received on the Sunday afternoon, and it stated that the *Californian* had passed three large icebergs.

Bride said he overheard the message as it was being sent to the *Baltic*. Before that the *Californian* had called him up with the same message, but he could not take it then because he was busy making up accounts. Bride delivered the message to an officer on the bridge.

Bride described how Phillips sent out the distress calls after the collision, and said that the last time he went to the wireless room a man who was dressed like a stoker was trying to take off Phillips's lifebelt. 'We stopped him,' said Bride.

Mr Lewis (for the Seafarers' Union): 'You are supposed to have hit him?' – 'Well, I held him and Phillips hit him.'

Mr Lewis: 'That is rather different from what I read. Are you positive of this?' – 'Yes.'

'You are not likely to see him again,' Bride added.

(Daily Sketch, 24 May 1912)

TITANIC'S BOATS

Startling Evidence at the Inquiry
How Board of Trade Was Warned

Some startling evidence was sprung upon the Titanic Commission yesterday by the Right Hon. A. M. Carlisle, who until 1910 was chairman of managing directors and general manager of works for Harland and Wolff, the builders.

He said that plans were worked out and submitted to the White Star Company providing for four boats under each set of davits on the *Titanic* and *Olympic*.

Mr Carlisle said he considered there were not enough boats on the *Titanic*. Before she sailed he told the Merchant Shipping Act Committee (appointed by the Board of Trade), of which he was a member, that she was inefficiently boated. She should have had at least forty-eight lifeboats on board instead of sixteen.

Mr Carlisle said he took the plans with him to the committee meeting at the Board of Trade offices.

Lord Mersey said that the Court would procure the minutes of the committee's meetings.

Mr Carlisle was closely questioned as to two interviews that took place between representatives of the White Star Line.

Asked who was present when plans showing facilities for

increased boat accommodation were submitted, Mr Carlisle named Mr Bruce Ismay and Mr Sanderson, the manager of the White Star Line. He could not say whether Mr Sanderson realized what the plan was, as he did not speak.

Mr Carlisle continued, 'I came especially from Belfast in October 1909, with those plans, and also the decorations, and Mr Ismay and Mr Sanderson, Lord Pirrie, and myself spent about four hours together.

'I showed them the plans,' Mr Carlisle went on, 'and said it would put them to no expense or trouble in case the Board of Trade came on them to do anything at the last minute.'

Mr Carlisle replied that the builders had a very free hand, but he did not think they could possibly have supplied any more boats for the ship without getting the sanction of the White Star Line.

'Did you try?' – 'You must remember I retired before the ship was launched.'

In reply to further questions Mr Carlisle said he was a party to the Board of Trade's Advisory Committee's report last year, the recommendations in which required a less boating capacity than there was on the *Titanic*. He was asked to join the committee two days before it finished its report, and when it had come to certain conclusions he did not consider them satisfactory, and told the committee so. But he signed the report.

Mr Carlisle said, 'I am not usually soft, but I must have been soft when I signed that.'

(*Daily Sketch*, 11 June 1912)

TITANIC VERDICT

There were about 200 people present during the reading of the Titanic Report yesterday by Lord Mersey who occupied two and a half hours in his task. An hour and forty minutes after he had started Lord Mersey touched upon what was one of the most serious phases of the inquiry. Did the *Californian* see the *Titanic* after the latter had struck the iceberg? His voice hardened when, after referring to the rockets seen by the *Californian*, he said in clear, even tones that the ship seen by the *Californian* was the *Titanic*, and that the former could have gone to the rescue without serious risk, and that had she done so she might have saved all the lives. In his speech Lord Mersey gave a history of the action of the Board of Trade in relation to the provision of boat accommodation on emigrant ships and added:

'The outstanding circumstance in it is the omission, during so many years, to revise the rules of 1894, and this, I think, was blameable. I am, however, doubtful whether even if the rules had been revised, the change would have been such as to have required boat accommodation which would have increased the number of lives saved.'

Referring to the first ice message, Lord Mersey recalled that the master handed the message to Mr Ismay almost immediately after it was received. Mr Ismay showed this message to two ladies, and it was therefore probable that many persons on board became aware of its contents. The message ought to have been put in the chart-room as soon as it was received. 'I think it was irregular for the master to part with the document,' said Lord Mersey, 'and improper for Mr Ismay to retain it, but the incident had, in my opinion, no connection with or influence upon the manner in which the vessel was navigated by the master.'

As to the action that should have been taken, the Report stated that for many years the practice of liners using this track when in the vicinity of ice at night had been in clear weather to keep the course, to maintain the speed, and to trust to a sharp lookout. This procedure was probably to be found in competition and in the desire of the public for quick passages rather than in the judgement of navigators, but experience appeared to justify it.

'In these circumstances,' went on Lord Mersey, 'I am not able to blame Captain Smith. He made a mistake, a very grievous mistake, but one in which, in the face of the practice and of past experience, negligence cannot be said to have had any part; and in the absence of negligence, it is, in my opinion, impossible to fix Captain Smith with blame. It is, however, to be hoped that the last has been heard of the practice. What was a mistake in the case of the *Titanic* would, without doubt, be negligence in any similar case in the future.'

With regard to the lowering of the boats after the collision the Report stated that the officers did their work very well and without any thought of themselves. The discipline, both among passengers and crew was good, but the organization could have been better, and if it had been it was possible that more lives could have been saved. If women could not be induced to enter the boats, the boats ought to have been filled with men.

Proceeding, Lord Mersey said: 'I regret to say that in my opinion some of the boats, particularly No. 1, failed to attempt to save lives when they might have done so.

'The very gross charge against Sir Cosmo Duff Gordon that, having got into No. 1 boat, he bribed the men in it to row away from drowning people, is unfounded. At the same time I think that if he had encouraged the men to return they would probably have saved some lives.

'As to the attack on Mr Bruce Ismay, it resolved itself into the suggestion that, occupying the position of managing director of the steamship company, some moral duty was imposed upon him to wait on board until the vessel foundered. I do not agree. Had he not jumped into the boat he would merely have added one more life, namely, his own, to the number of those lost.'

Lord Mersey then went on to deal with the circumstances in connection with the *Californian*. The truth of the matter was plain. The *Titanic* collided with the iceberg at 11.40. The vessel seen by the *Californian* stopped at this time. The rockets sent up from the *Titanic* were distress signals. The *Californian* saw distress signals. The number sent up by the *Titanic* was about eight. The *Californian* saw eight. The time over which the rockets from the *Titanic* were sent up was from 12.45 to 1.45 o'clock. It was about this time that the *Californian* saw the rockets. At 2.40 Mr Stone called to the master that the ship from which he had seen the rockets had disappeared. At 2.20 the *Titanic* had foundered. It was suggested that the rockets seen by the *Californian* were from some other ship, not the *Titanic*. But no other ship to fit that theory had ever been heard of.

These circumstances convinced him that the ship seen by the *Californian* was the *Titanic*, and if so, the two vessels were about eight to ten miles apart at the time of the disaster. The night was clear and the sea was smooth. When she first saw the rockets the *Californian* could have pushed through the ice to the open water without any serious risk, and so have come to the assistance of the *Titanic*. Had she done so, she might have saved many, if not all, of the lives that were lost.

CHIEF RECOMMENDATIONS

Watertight Compartments

Newly appointed Bulkhead Committee should inquire into desirability of longitudinal and vertical watertight bulkheads, of watertight decks above the water line, and of increasing protection given by sub-division.

Boats

Life-saving accommodation should be based on persons carried, not tonnage, sufficient for all on board. One boat should be mechanically propelled. All should have protective fender to lessen risk when launching. More frequent boat, fire, and watertight door drill, and adequate number of men trained and tested in boat work.

Passenger Discipline

A police system to secure proper control, obedience and guidance.

Ice

Moderation of speed or alteration of course when ice reported.

International Conference

Should be called on sub-division of ships, life-saving appliances, wireless, searchlights, speed in vicinity of ice.

(*Daily Graphic*, 31 July 1912)

CHAPTER 8

THE RETURN OF THE DEAD

STEAMER OFF ON HUNT FOR BODIES

Halifax, April 18

The closing scenes of the terrible *Titanic* disaster, the sad aftermath of the world's greatest marine tragedy, will be enacted here within a space of ten days, when the sea shall have given up its dead, and when the cable steamer *Mackay-Bennett* will return from its search for the bodies of the drowned passengers.

With her deck piled high with coffins, the *Mackay-Bennett* was tonight just halfway to the latitude and longitude of the spot where the *Titanic* went down, and by midnight tomorrow the first wireless report from her should be received.

Upon the success of her attempt now rests the last sad hope of the relatives and dear ones of the drowned passengers of the sunken giant of the waters – the hope that they may have the bitter satisfaction of burying the dead.

The *Mackay-Bennett* is equipped with the most powerful wireless apparatus of any vessel in these waters, and will flash back the news at the moment the bodies of any of the passengers of the *Titanic* are discovered.

(*Boston Post*, 19 April 1912)

AN OCEAN GRAVE

Gruesome Sights Witnessed at Scene of Wreck

FLOATING BODIES

A harrowing account was given at New York yesterday by passengers on the German steamer *Bremen* which reported that she had sighted 100 bodies from the *Titanic*.

Mrs Johanna Stunke, a cabin passenger, said: 'It was between four and five o'clock on Saturday afternoon when we sighted an iceberg. The sun glistening upon it was a wonderful picture, but as we drew nearer we could make out small dots floating in the sea, which we knew were bodies of the *Titanic*'s passengers.

'Approaching closer, we passed within 100ft of the southernmost of the drifting wreckage, and, looking down, we distinctly saw a number of bodies so clearly that we could make out their clothing and distinguish the men from the women.

'We saw one woman in a nightdress with a baby clasped closely to her breast. Several of the women passengers screamed at the sight and left the rail in a fainting condition. There was another woman fully dressed, with her arms tightly clutching the body of a shaggy dog.

'We noticed the bodies of three men in a group clinging to a steamer chair, and just beyond were the bodies of a dozen more, all in life preservers, and locked together as they died in the struggle for life. We could see white life preservers dotting the sea all the way to the iceberg.'

Mrs Stunke said that a number of the passengers demanded that the *Bremen* should stop, but the officers assured them that the *Mackay-Bennett* was only two hours away and was coming for the express purpose of attending to the bodies.

(*Nottingham Evening News*, 25 April 1912)

WILL BRING *TITANIC'S* DEAD TO HALIFAX

In the grey of an early spring morning, the Western Union cable steamer *Minia*, transformed into a floating mortuary, stole down Halifax harbour today like a spectre ship and silently headed for the open sea to join in the search for such of the *Titanic's* dead as the sea shall give back to man. On the edge of the Grand Banks, where a week ago human impotence received the most striking exemplification in all the annals of the sea, the *Minia* will take up the work of her sister ship, the *Mackay-Bennett*, whose quest for the dead has been crowned with at least partial success, and which will come to Halifax with half a hundred bodies snatched from the grasp of the waves.

It was not until four o'clock yesterday afternoon that confirmation of the report that the *Mackay-Bennett's* voyage had been successful, reached Halifax. It came from New York in the shape of an order to equip the *Minia* for sea as soon as possible to aid in the search, and within ten hours she had cast off her moorings, and with a gruesome cargo of rough pine coffins in her forehold, was off for the scene.

To outfit the *Mackay-Bennett* a few days ago took every coffin to be procured but, by operating a wood factory until ten o'clock at night, enough receptacles were produced to enclose all the corpses that could be taken back on one trip of the steamer. There were 150 or so of them, mere rough boards knocked together in the crude shape of a human form and destitute of covering. The one touch needed to complete the gruesome spectacle was to be found in the tons of ice stowed away in the cable tan for preservation purposes and the piles of grate bars, pig iron and old cable which, together with bales of canvas, were provided to furnish decent burial at sea for those mutilated bodies which it is feared may be recovered in such numbers.

(*Nova Scotian*, 26 April 1912)

MOURNING CAMP AWAITS HEARSE SHIP THAT BRINGS 205 BODIES TO HALIFAX

Halifax, Nova Scotia, April 25

Mourners seeking to identify the bodies of the *Titanic* dead are gathering at Halifax, and it is expected that 500 will be on hand when the *Mackay-Bennett* arrives, probably on Sunday. Representatives of the Astor, Harris, Guggenheim, Straus and Widener families are among those already at Halifax, and President Taft has detailed an army officer to report there and search for the body of Major Butt.

Wireless despatches from the *Mackay-Bennett* told of the finding of 205 bodies.

Each incoming train adds to the number of those seeking the *Titanic*'s dead to give them a decent burial. The despatch this afternoon from Captain Larnder of the *Mackay-Bennett*, that he had discovered a floating field of bodies caused each of the visitors to hope that the one he sought would be among them. Most of those here are seeking bodies which have not been recognized.

It is believed here the *Mackay-Bennett* will reach the port on Sunday. By then she will have received the wireless instructions to return as well as the supplemental orders carried by Captain de Carteret on the Western Union cable repair ship *Minia*. When she gets in, there will be as many as 500 awaiting her to learn if the relatives they seek are included in her cargo.

The vessel is having great difficulties to overcome in her work of rescue. When she was fitted out the entire town and the vicinity was searched for certain supplies, and as delay was considered unwise she started out without all that she needed. For example, she has embalming fluid for only 70 corpses, the only undertakers who could be spared were the three that went with her, and the city's stock of coffins was exhausted by the 100 that she took.

Today additional coffins reached the city. All afternoon loads of them were driven from the station to the Snow's store, which is ready to be converted into a vast morgue. Four hundred coffins have been sent for, one of the biggest orders ever placed on one occasion. The shipment made 40 wages loads, and as they passed through the streets another touch was added to the solemnity that hangs over Halifax, the city of wrecks.

The undertaker handling the work has arranged to have the bodies exposed for identification in his shop and a big chapel adjoining it. Should these spaces be insufficient, a chapel about a half mile out of town will be pressed into service. It is expected that the *Mackay-Bennett*, which has tonight 207 bodies aboard, will have at least 250 when she gets in, and almost as many are expected through the search of the *Minia*, which is now on the ground, although no report has come in that she has communicated with her sister ship.

A partial list of those brought here in the hope of recovering their dead includes:

George D. Widener Jnr in search of his father, George D. snr, and his brother, Harry Elkins Widener; Morris Rothschild who seeks the bodies of his uncle and aunt, Mr and Mrs Isidor Straus; E. H. Wallach, for the body of his brother-in-law, Henry B. Harris; J. D. Richardson of the Pennsylvania forces is looking for the body of John B. Thayer, Second Vice-President of the road.

H. Bull is here in search of the body of Ahme Fahelstrom [sic], the 20-year-old son of a wealthy Norwegian theatrical manager. The boy did not know a single person in America except Bull, so in response to the appeal of the parents, the latter came on here from the Pacific coast in the hope of making the identification.

The Canadian Express Co. and the Dominion and American have announced that all bodies will be carried free for those families upon whom express charges would be a burden.

(*New York World*, 26 April 1912)

MAJORITY OF BODIES LOST FOREVER, SAYS CABLE SHIP

The cable ship *Mackay-Bennett* bearing many scores of bodies found in the vicinity of the wreck of the *Titanic* may not reach

Halifax till Sunday. A wireless received from the ship yesterday showed that it was the intention of her captain to remain searching for bodies until it should become hopeless to waste any further time there.

Few names of any importance were added to the list of identified dead in the cable despatch, and it is feared that the great majority of the *Titanic's* victims were sucked down to immediate death when the ship foundered and that the terrific pressure to which these bodies were subjected is responsible for their present unembalmable condition.

These are the wireless messages received by the White Star Line offices in this city from the *Mackay-Bennett*, via Cape Race.

Drifting in dense fog since noon yesterday. Total picked up 205. We brought away all embalming fluid to be had in Halifax, enough for 70. With a week's fine weather I think we would pretty well clean up relics of the disaster. It is my opinion that the majority will never come to the surface.

Another despatch from the *Mackay-Bennett* states:

Bodies are in latitude 41.35 north, longitude 48.27 west, extending many miles east and west. Mail ships should give this a wide berth. Medical opinion is death has been instantaneous in all cases, owing to pressure when bodies were drawn down in vortex.

The instructions to the *Mackay-Bennett* are to bring in every body concerning which there seems to be even the feeblest hope of making an identification, but owing to the lack of embalming fluids and the impractability of bringing in unembalmed bodies, it is certain that the funeral ship will have to abandon a great many of the floating corpses.

The *Minia*, which left Halifax a few days ago on a similar errand, is equipped with a much more extensive undertaking outfit, and she will surely bring back many bodies the *Mackay-Bennett* was unable to handle.

In the list of identified dead from the *Mackay-Bennett* there appeared at first the name 'Nikllachig Bhatt'. Subsequent messages have reduced this conglomeration to Nikki Schedig, a steerage passenger, and L. Butt. Considerable hope exists that the L. Butt as named is the body of Maj. Archibald Butt, President Taft's military aide.

Only 43 identifications of recovered bodies have been made thus far and some of these are rather doubtful. Considerable hope has been expressed that the 'W. Vear' mentioned in some despatches from the *Mackay-Bennett* as one of the identified dead might turn out to be W. T. Stead's body.

(*New York World*, 26 April 1912)

'INSTANTANEOUS DEATH'

The following message has been received by wireless from the cable ship *Mackay Bennett*:

Bodies are numerous in latitude 41.35 north, longitude 48.37 west, extending many miles both east and west. Mailships should give this region a wide berth.

The medical opinion is that death has been instantaneous in all the cases, owing to the pressure when the bodies were drawn down in the vortex.

We have been drifting in a dense fog since noon yesterday. The total number of bodies picked up is 205. We brought away all the embalming fluid in Halifax, which is enough for 70. With a week's fine weather we think we should pretty well clear up the relics of the disaster. In my opinion the majority of the bodies will never come to the surface.

The medical opinion (if correctly telegraphed) hardly coincides with the statement of Third Officer Pitman, that moans and cries were heard for an hour after the liner sank.

A Central News message says that the body identified as W. Vear is believed to be that of Mr W. T. Stead, and that reported as R. Butt is believed to be that of Major Butt.

(Daily Sketch, 26 April 1912)

MORGUE SHIP PUTS 190 BODIES ASHORE; 57 OF KNOWN DEAD CAST INTO THE SEA

Halifax, Nova Scotia, 30 April

Slowly the cableship *Mackay-Bennett* steamed up the harbour of Halifax this morning bearing 190 of the *Titanic*'s dead. It was just two weeks from the day that the new queen of the sea was to have crowned herself by landing her passengers in New York after a record maiden trip. At the pier here 500 persons from all quarters of the world had gathered to claim their dead.

To some she brought bitter disappointment; for the *Mackay-Bennett* had been compelled to bury at sea many of the bodies she had wrested from the sea. There were 116 thus recommitted to the waters, 57 of which had been identified aboard the *Mackay-Bennett*.

Despite the shock brought by this announcement, no one expressed any criticism of Capt. Larnder's action, all believing him sincere in his explanation that lack of space on board, shortage of embalming material and the mutilation of bodies were solely responsible for his course.

A shocking incident of the disaster was revealed by the announcement that thirty bodies, many those of women, were found near a lifeboat which had capsized. A woman's skirt was tied to one of the oars, showing that it had been used as a signal.

That no favouritism was shown in the reburial at sea – that is, that the bodies of prominent persons were not kept aboard to the exclusion of the more humble – is shown by the White Star Line's announcement that among those bodies sunk again was that of George D. Widener, the Philadelphia capitalist. Although this appears to be a mistake, in that Mr Widener's son, now here, believes that the body was that of his father's valet, the name

Widener stands on the official list of reburied as issued by the White Star Line late today.

With a flag drooping below the main deck the black-sided *Mackay-Bennett* looked the hearse she was. The roofs and the harbour banks were crowded, but it was a reverent crowd that with bowed heads, heard in silence the tolling of the church bells.

Capt. Larnder got word to the waiting crowd that of the 116 buried most had been members of the crew, for whom, while there is sorrow, there were no claimants on the pier. He authorized the statement that he recovered a total of 306 bodies, of which he was bringing 190 bodies back to port.

At once there was a rush to learn if the bodies that relatives were there to seek had been disposed of. The first to have his distress ended was Vincent Astor, who learnt that the Colonel's body was positively aboard.

Then Maurice Rothschild learnt to his great relief that the body of his uncle, Isidor Straus, was surely among those lifted ashore.

Dr E. G. Tomlin of Philadelphia learnt that his father-in-law, Frederick Sutton, a wealthy and public spirited merchant of the Pennsylvania city, another whose name was put on the list of recovered, had been buried at sea.

There was another first-class passenger, Walter H. Anderson, recovered, whose body was likewise recommitted. In addition there were many from the second cabin, the rest of the 116 buried at sea being made up of the steerage and the crew.

Two little children were picked up. One was a ten-year-old boy who went back to the waters. The second was a little girl, about three years old, with long golden curls that drooped pitifully about her face as she was put into a little coffin this morning. Hers was the first body taken from the ocean when the *Mackay-Bennett* started on her search. She was found floating serenely, looking very much like a big doll. The crew proposes to erect a monument to her in the local cemetery. So far as can be learnt there was nothing on her clothes to identify.

From the pockets of the dead came many things. From the rich there fell a stream of gold and jewels and from the poor rolled pieces of food. At least $30,000 was recovered from clothes of the dead and perhaps $50,000 worth of jewellery. In Colonel Astor's pockets there was found almost $3000 in money.

(*New York World*, 1 May 1912)

MACKAY-BENNETT'S CAPTAIN TELLS OF QUEST FOR BODIES

Halifax, April 30

The *Mackay-Bennett*, her black sides a fitting colour for the work she had been doing, had been tied up in the navy dock for an hour before the master was able to see the newspaper correspondents waiting to hear the details of one of the strangest missions ever a ship was sent on.

Capt. F. H. Larnder is an upstanding, frank-spoken Englishman, 45 years old. His face is bronzed from the 30 years he has spent at sea. Because of that training he has a clear mind and seeks accuracy first, so his story was simply told, and in that quality lay its greatest strength.

The ship was put under charter to put out to the scene of the wreck and to bring in all bodies found, but owing to the number of bodies and other conditions, such as adverse weather, this unfortunately proved impossible. We were unable to carry out the letter of our instructions, and some of the bodies found were buried at sea after appropriate religious service by the chaplain here.

We left Halifax on the afternoon of Wednesday April 17. Fog and bad weather delayed us on our run and we didn't arrive on the scene until Saturday at 8 p.m.

On Saturday at noon, having asked all ships within our wireless range to report to us any evidence of the wreck, we received a communication from the German liner *Rhein* that in latitude

42.1 north, longitude 49.13 west, she had passed much wreckage and had seen several bodies.

Our course was shaped north 34 degrees east, and while we were heading this way, later in the afternoon, we spoke to the steamer *Bremen*, which told us of having passed three big bergs and several bodies in latitude 43 north, longitude 49.2 west. Roughly speaking, these two reports showed that the drift was to the north and east, and so I made up my mind to try to go over the trail that the bodies had taken.

We reached the spot where I thought the *Titanic* had sunk just after the first watch began, and we shut down and let the ship drift with whatever current chose to carry her, on the theory that where the ship would be carried there we would find the bodies.

Four hours after we began floating north by east on the rise of a gentle swell three bodies were sighted. This was in the midwatch and at the same time we saw quantities of lighter wreckage, steamer chairs, hatches and pieces of wood.

We kept a sharp watch on the bodies and at daylight on Sunday two boats were lowered, and though a heavy sea was running we succeeded in recovering 51 bodies. We had to work slowly and carefully and it was well along towards six o'clock that we got the last of the bodies aboard.

They were in pretty fair shape. Now and then some would be found in mutilated condition. We judged this to be due to the seas smashing over the *Titanic* as she settled and throwing the men against the railings and fixtures, breaking their heads and otherwise hurting them. Then, again, some may have been hurt by the screws of passing ships.

The bodies that were in worse shape from these wounds or from being in the water we concluded to bury at sea, so at eight o'clock that night twenty-four of them were recommitted. Canon Hind spoke the service and we helped out as best we could. The bodies were almost all those of the crew. In some cases the undertaker didn't think it was safe to try to keep them. That night we did not bury any bodies that had been identified.

Monday, at daylight, when we resumed work, we found the bodies scarce. After a long, careful search all we got was twenty-five. We followed a line of wreckage for sixteen miles and then a batch of bodies was discovered just at dark.

The ship drifted pretty well on the course the bodies were taking during the night, and at dawn we were not far off. With the findings of the night before we had a good start on Tuesday's work.

Finishing with one pack we ran into another. It was our best day's work. By noon we had 90 aboard.

One pack we sighted at a distance the bodies looked like seagulls swimming on the water, and the flapping in the breeze of the loose ends of the lifebelts made the resemblance to wings almost complete.

When we bore down upon them the bodies looked like swimmers asleep. They were not floating, but bolt upright, with heads up. The arms were outstretching, as if aiding to support the body. All faced one way – the way they were drifting.

We saw a big berg when we made this pack. It might have been the berg that sunk the liner. She was long and low lying, rising perhaps 125ft, or maybe 160 at her highest point, which was well in from a bunch that sloped into the water. It was surrounded by wreckage and several bodies.

The bodies were floating, some near together, some far apart. There seemed no order among them – none hand in hand or embraced. We would come upon them within a few feet of each other in big numbers and then stretched out at great lengths from each other.

Tuesday afternoon the weather came on and so we only got twenty-nine. There was a thick fog all day Wednesday and it was blowing fresh from the south-west, so we headed to wind and sea. All day we saw nothing. At midnight the weather eased and we shaped to where we expected to find them.

At 4.30 Thursday morning one was seen from the bridge through glasses. With so little showing above water the bodies were not easy to pick out against the water, and the job was harder when they were surrounded by bits of wreckage, which aided in concealing them.

As soon as we sighted the body we stopped and drifted. We had got back on the track and that day we picked up thirty-seven more. This was the day that we got word that the *Minia* was on the way to join us in the work. She spoke to us just after midnight by wireless and after getting our position came alongside about a quarter to one Friday morning. At daylight the two ships began the search together. She confirmed to us having the body of Charles M. Hays aboard.

The second burial we had was on Monday night when twelve bodies were sunk. We had the final service on Wednesday morning when the weather kept us from our work, so we used our time to bury 78 bodies. The task was no easy one.

At noon the *Mackay-Bennett* picked up sixteen more bodies. We then left for Halifax, having as many bodies on board as we could look after.

As the bodies were hoisted up to the deck each body was searched, was numbered and all the contents of the pockets and valuables were put into a canvas bag, bearing the same number as the body. Close examination of the contents of the bag led to later identification. Each bag was separately examined at night after the work of the day was finished.

There were doors, chairs and wood from the *Titanic* spread over thirty miles. We found an empty broken lifeboat upside down with a few bodies near it. It was a flat boat of the collapsible type. We saw no sign of shooting on any of the bodies. We found several men dressed in evening clothes, but found no bodies lashed to doors. Those whom we found it necessary to bury were not men of prominence.

Regarding the body found at first and supposed to be that of Mr Widener, it has since been established that it was Mr Widener's valet, with some of Mr Widener's papers on his person. He was buried at sea. The body was badly damaged. The body of Mr

Widener is not on board, and his son is satisfied that the body buried is that of his father's valet.

As to Mr Widener, we were never altogether satisfied as to his identity, because, though his papers were found on the body, his underclothing did not look as though it would be worn by him. It was of a poorer texture than he would be expected to wear.

It is my opinion that the bulk of the bodies are in the ship. I think when she went down the water broke into her with great force and drove them into the hull. Mrs Straus's body was not yet found.

I explain the reason that so many of the bodies picked up were members of the crew because they probably jumped before the ship took the fatal plunge. They were used to the ways of the sea and knew the danger of staying aboard her until the end. The passengers stayed aboard her and went down with her. They were crushed down in her as she sunk, and deep in her body they are finding their graves.

Those aboard her, the doctors think, were killed almost instantly by the terrible pressure in the vortex. Those who got away died later from freezing. I think few were drowned.

I had only one embalmer aboard and he treated something like 100 bodies. We took them in the order they came; no preference was shown. That is, the passengers were given consideration over the crew because the crew must expect such things when they put to sea, and we felt that in cases where great estates and large wills depended upon the body as proof of death it was best for us to do all in our power to have the body in shape to bring back.

I have no doubt that the families of the crew would like to have had their bodies sent to them, too. So far as we could, we did. But I thought it proper to give the preference to the men of affairs and, besides, it is fit and proper for a sailorman to be buried at sea. He lives by the sea and so he should be willing to be buried in the sea.

(*New York World*, 1 May 1912)

RECOVERING THE DEAD

Upturned Boat on Scene of Titanic *Disaster*
Mutilation Caused by a Terrific Explosion

A surprising discovery was made on the scene of the *Titanic* disaster by the cable ship *Mackay-Bennett*, which returned to Halifax yesterday from its search for bodies.

An Exchange telegram received yesterday stated that a group of thirty bodies, including those of several women, was found alongside an upturned lifeboat. A woman's red skirt was attached to an oar, and had apparently been used as a distress signal. There were indications that the boat was afloat some time after the *Titanic* foundered.

It will be remembered that before the *Carpathia* reached New York the White Star Company received a wireless message from the *Olympic* reporting that all the *Titanic's* boats were accounted for. This message was read in the House of Commons by the Prime Minister.

The *Mackay-Bennett* recovered 306 bodies, and 190 of them were taken to Halifax. One hundred and sixteen bodies were mutilated beyond recognition. Arms and legs were fractured, and the features in many cases were so terribly cut and bruised that (it is declared) the injuries could not have been caused by the sea or wreckage, but must have resulted from a terrific explosion.

The body of Colonel Astor, which has been embalmed, is to be conveyed on the journey to New York by special train today. His son, Mr Vincent Astor, will travel with the remains. At the sad landing yesterday the proceedings were conducted with impressive solemnity.

Cash to the extent of 16,000 dollars was found in the pockets of dead people. On Colonel Astor's body was found 2,500 dollars, and he was wearing a wire belt with a gold buckle, which is said to be a family heirloom. Many bodies were identified by papers, letters and cards. Most of the watches found had stopped between

2.10 and 2.15. The bodies of the first-class passengers were found in groups.

The corpses taken to Halifax were landed at Government Dock and were guarded by Canadian bluejackets. All shipping was kept outside the Channel for the time being, and very few people besides Government officials were allowed in the dock premises.

Only one woman was admitted, and she was an undertaker. The rest of the undertakers, together with the mourners, gathered outside.

Captain Larnder, of the *Mackay-Bennett*, reports that the bodies were recovered 60 miles north-east of the scene of the disaster in the waters of the Gulf Stream. The searchers swept a square of 30 miles.

The first body discovered was supposed to be that of Mr Widener, but it was later established as Mr Widener's valet, Edward Keeping, who had some of Mr Widener's papers on him.

The captain believes that all the bodies buried at sea were those of the ship's crew. He is satisfied that the passengers were properly identified. The bodies of eighteen women were found but none of them were those of first-class passengers.

Most of the bodies found were just on the edge of the Gulf Stream, and had they not been rescued at the time they were they would in all probability have floated for many miles in the current. One hundred bodies were in one group.

The White Star officials at New York yesterday morning received a wireless message from the *Minia* expressing the belief that if any more bodies of *Titanic* victims are floating they have been swept by the late northerly gales into the Gulf Stream and carried many miles to the east.

Fourteen bodies have been recovered by the *Minia*, of which two are unidentified, and these have been buried at sea.

(*Daily Sketch*, 1 May 1912)

Frederick Hamilton, a cable engineer on the *Mackay-Bennett*, kept a diary of the ship's sad mission.

April 20. 7 p.m.

A large iceberg, faintly discernible to our north, we are now very near the area where lie the ruins of so many human hopes and prayers. The embalmer becomes more and more cheerful as we approach the scene of his future professional activities. Tomorrow will be a good day for him.

April 21

The ocean is strewn with a litter of woodwork, chairs, and bodies. The cutter lowered, and work commenced and kept up continuously all day, picking up bodies. Hauling the soaked remains in saturated clothing over the side of the cutter is no easy task. Fifty-one we have taken on board today, two children, three women, and 46 men, and still the sea seems strewn. With the exception of ourselves, the bosum bird is the only living creature here.

8 p.m.

The tolling of the bell summoned all hands to the forecastle where 30 bodies are ready to be committed to the deep, each carefully weighed and carefully sewn up in canvas. It is a weird scene, this gathering.

April 24. Noon

Another burial service held, and 70 bodies follow the other. The hoarse tone of the steam whistle reverberating through the mist, the dripping rigging, and the ghostly sea, the heaps of dead, and the hard weather-beaten faces of the crew, whose harsh voices join sympathetically in the hymn tunefully rendered by Canon Hind, all combine to make a strange task stranger. Cold, wet, miserable and comfortless, all hands balance themselves against the heavy rolling of the ship as she lurches to the Atlantic swell, and even the most hardened must reflect on the hopes and fears, the dismay and despair, of those whose nearest and dearest, support and pride, have been wrenched from them by this tragedy.

LOST FIREMAN'S VINDICATION

Among the 'remarkable' stories published by London journals concerning men who had been lost in the *Titanic* disaster was one about a fireman named Hart. It was stated that a Liverpool man named T. Hart had joined the ill-fated ship at Southampton, and when the list of the crew was published his mother claimed compensation, on the assumption that her son had been lost. A few days later, however, the son turned up, and it transpired that he had never seen the *Titanic*. He had, however, lost his discharge book, and it was presumed that 'someone had signed on with her son's name and credentials'. We quote the words of a London paper.

That there was a man named Hart on the *Titanic* there is no doubt. J. Hart, of 51, College Street, attached his signature to the ship's articles, and the inference was that he had sailed under false pretences. The suggestion that he used another man's book has given intense pain to the members of the family, who indignantly deny the statement. Mr Hart has sailed out of Southampton for over twenty years. He served the Union-Castle Company and the R.M.S.P. before transferring to the White Star Line, and we are assured that his discharge book was a good one. There was, therefore, no reason why he should hide behind another man's character, and that he made no attempt to do so is proved by the fact that he gave his College Street address when signing on. Had he assumed the name of the Liverpool man, he must also have given the Liverpool address of that fireman. J. Hart was a member of the British Seafarers' Union, and we have been asked by the members of his family to publish these facts in order that the dead might be vindicated.

(*Southampton Times and Hampshire Express*, 18 May 1912)

FUNERAL OF MR WALLACE HARTLEY

The body of Mr Wallace Hartley – Colne's hero, Britain's hero, the world's hero – picked up on the crest of the ocean, thousands of miles distant on the great rolling Atlantic, was borne to Colne on Friday last, to the town of his nativity, and interred the following day in the family vault in the Public Cemetery. It was an impressive funeral. The coffin bearing his remains passed before the eyes of a multitude, saddened but proud, stricken in heart but of manly bearing, grave, yet secretly grateful that a townsman and a friend should have died so heroically.

> O Death, where is thy sting?
> Grave, where is thy victory?

Colne rose to the highest eminence of its character and traditions on Saturday and girded with warm sincerity and pride and love, paid to the hero a tribute of sympathy, spontaneous, heartfelt, ungrudging, the outpoured sympathy of a people who felt and gloried in the magnificence of a townsman's courage. The keynote of the whole proceedings was Victory, a hero's triumph. Gaunt Death had claimed his poor weak body of clay, but the soul of the man had climbed far above earthly things into the highest thoughts of man, and the splendour of the man's character, the golden worth of the man at heart, had won the plaudits and admiration of two hemispheres.

Probably 40,000 persons did homage to the dead musician. Of these a very large percentage were, of course, people of Colne, and nearly all of these had kinship with the deceased. Many more far-distant sent flowers where they could not attend in person.

All of the 40,000 were fully acquainted with the deathless story of a story of death. The loss of the *Titanic* is an occurrence that can never die or fade from the memory of the men and women of today. The ghastliness of it, the unbelievable horror of it, the scarce-comprehensible significance of it, the awful dread which the picture of the ship taking its last plunge and with it a heavy freight of brave, powerless humans, conjures up, has impressed the event on the human heart beyond eradication. But while we mourn we glory in what we have learnt of the capabilities of the soul, and we are proud of our race and our destiny. For while we shall ever recoil from the horrors of the disaster we shall never fail to feel a glow of pride in the magnificent heroism which inspired men to puff the smoke from cigarettes in the face of Fate while the crew rescued the women and children, which prompted stokers and engineers to battle with the elements unflinchingly, which kept the brave Phillips at his wireless instrument, and which upheld Wallace Hartley and his comrades as they played on, on, into another world.

We know that all aboard answered the captain's command to 'Be British'. And none more faithfully than the orchestra. Can we picture the scene? Indescribable confusion on board in the lowering of boat-loads of people down the mountain-sides of the ship, the cries of the weak, the frantic despair of the coward, the ravings of the bully, and the quiet Christian confidence and equanimity of the true British gentleman wielding his baton or fingering his violin, who snapped his fingers in the face of Death and died a fighting hero, succouring the weak and cheering all – playing the violin soon to be the angel's harp. The bandsmen received word that the ship must go down and they with it lost in the intoxication of light music and around them all the luxury that their profession could desire. They heard of the approach of death, and the tune changed. No longer the merry whirling American ragtime music. Now it was the slow, impressive appeal to God by hymn, 'Nearer, my God, to Thee'. A dumb horror gripped the hearts of the players, yet they never faltered under the firm lead of Wallace Hartley. Outside, men and women were hastening away back to life; the bandsmen were left to cheer those whose doom was sealed. None could help them; theirs was to do and die, and they died.

Wallace Hartley put into practice a resolution he had expressed to a friend, that if ever disaster overtook the ship on which he was aboard he would stick to his violin and play the hymn he loved, 'Nearer, my God, to Thee'. With the water creeping, creeping slowly but surely over his body he played and played – he was nearer to Him – he was with Him.

The heroic band-leader died on April 15, and a fortnight later his body was found attired in the evening dress in which he had played and with his music-case strapped to it.

(Colne & Nelson Times, 24 May 1912)

The following story was typical of accounts which appeared in local newspapers the length and breadth of the British Isles during the months of May and June.

TITANIC VICTIM INTERMENT OF A YOUNG MAN AT ST IVES

The funeral of a *Titanic* victim took place yesterday. The deceased was William Carbines, whose embalmed body had been brought across the Atlantic that it might rest near the old home at Nanjivey on the outskirts of the Cornish borough. When death overtook him, in the worst of all shipping disasters, young Carbines, just entering manhood, was setting out hopefully on a new career. His brothers, John and Robert, were copper mining in Michigan, and the intention of the St Ives boy was to join them. The remains of the deceased were picked up from the ocean by the steamer *Mackay-Bennett* which sailed to the region of the catastrophe for the purpose of recovering bodies, and were landed at Halifax, where the brothers received them. Afterwards the corpse was placed on board the *Oceanic* for conveyance to England, John and Robert Carbines being passengers by the same ship. From Southampton the deceased was taken by rail to St Ives, and removed thence to Nanjivey to await interment. In the cemetery chapel the simple service was read by the Rev. W.A. Chettle (Wesleyan). After the coffin had been committed to the grave, Mr Chettle delivered an address. Every man's life, he said, was like a diary, in which he intended to write one thing, but wrote another. Why? Because he was not his own. Their departed brother planned yonder – should they say a home and a career? – and there intervened that sudden stroke so terrible in its mystery to them.

(*Western Daily Mercury*, 31 May 1912)

HIS THOUGHTFULNESS SAVED GIRL'S LIFE

Dr Pain's Last Act Made Possible The Romance of Titanic

In the midst of all the bitter disappointment and sorrow which have come into the lives of Mr and Mrs Albert Pain, of this city, through the loss of their son, Dr Alfred Pain, by the sinking of the *Titanic* eight weeks ago, there has been a ray of sunshine through the numerous letters of sympathy from friends on two continents. One of those especially discloses a lovely little act of romance which the thoughtfulness of Dr Pain made possible, and a happy young couple in the far Western States will ever bless the memory of Dr Alfred Pain.

While in England, Dr Pain arranged that he should meet Miss Marion Wright of Yeovil, England, who had arranged to come to America on the *Titanic*, to be married on her arrival in New York to a young Englishman who some time ago came to this country and took up fruit farming at Cottage Grove, Oregon. Circumstances prevented Miss Wright from being present at the home of a mutual friend, but he looked her up on board the *Titanic*, and promised that she would be his charge. His last known act was to put her into a lifeboat. She was the last person put into that boat, and unquestionably Dr Pain's thoughtfulness in taking her out of the crowd on one side of the boat and getting her into a lifeboat on the other side saved her life and made possible the marriage which subsequently took place in New York.

Miss Wright lost all her trousseau and wedding gifts but when she arrived in New York her plight became known to the Women's Relief Committee who, seeing the romance in it, quickly procured a new trousseau, and the wedding took place the Saturday after the arrival of the *Carpathia* – in St Christopher's chapel. Mr and Mrs Woolcott went to their home in Oregon and only last week Mrs Albert Pain received a letter from the bride. It was really the first precise news she had had of her son and the fact that it showed that he had been the saviour of the young English girl's life helped to soften the anguish of the loss of her son. Mrs Woolcott wrote as follows:

Cottage Grove, Oregon, U.S.A., May 28.
Dear Mrs Pain, I have been wanting so much to write to you some time, but I didn't know your address until a few days ago, when I got a letter from Miss Richards, written from Devonshire, in which she asked me to write her all I could about your dear son, Dr Alfred Pain. She also gave me your address, so now I feel I must do my duty, painful though it is. How your poor heart must be torn to lose him as you have, in all his prime, and in such perfect health. We did not get acquainted till the Friday after we sailed. So, though I only knew him for three days, yet I felt he was a friend. He said I was the first lady he had spoken to. I had noticed him before. He seemed so good at getting up games for the young fellows on board. We had several meals together and he told me how much he had enjoyed his stay in England. On the Sunday I asked him to come to the service in the second class saloon. He did, and again in the evening came with a number of others to sing hymns in the dining saloon, and himself chose one or two. I believe he especially asked for 'Abide With Me, Fast Falls The Eventide'. Afterwards we had supper with one or two other people who had been singing with us, and then retired to our berths. About 12.30 p.m., when I had been on deck already for some time, your son came up, properly dressed, and with his lifebelt on. I could see he was looking for someone, and after a while he found me and said: 'I have been trying to find you for some time.' I asked him if he thought there was any great danger, and he assured me there could not be. We stood for some time on

the starboard, watching them load boats. There were hundreds of women on that side, and your son suddenly said: 'I think we had better go round the other side; there aren't so many people there.' We did so, and scarcely had we got round when the call came, 'Any more ladies, this way!' Your son said, 'You had better run.' I did so, and he followed and put me in the lifeboat. It is such a grief to me that I didn't say goodbye to him, but I thought, as everyone else did, that we would go back to the *Titanic* before very long. When we got out on the sea we could see the boat gradually sinking, deck after deck, and oh! how much we hoped all would be saved ere she went down. But when the awful news came to us that only 700 were saved, and those were with us on the *Carpathia*, how grieved I felt and how I wished your son had been among that 700. It all seems so sad and overwhelming, and I will never forget it, as long as I live. I trust just these few lines may comfort the heart of Dr Pain's sorrow stricken mother, is the prayer of yours, with much sympathy, Marion Woolcott.

(*Hamilton (Canada) Spectator*, June 1912)

Able Seaman Thomas Jones from Anglesey, Wales, had been placed in command of lifeboat No. 8. He had so admired the conduct of the Countess of Rothes that he subsequently presented her with the boat's brass number plate. It would seem that the feeling was mutual for the Countess's cousin, **Gladys Cherry**, who had also been a passenger in boat 8, wrote to Jones to express her gratitude for his gallantry that night. The letter was published in several newspapers.

I feel I must write and tell you how splendidly you took charge of our boat on the fatal night. There were only four English people in it – my cousin, Lady Rothes, her maid, you and myself – and I think you were wonderful.

The dreadful regret I shall always have, and I know you share with me, is that we ought to have gone back to see whom we could pick up; but if you remember, there was only an American

536

lady, my cousin, self and you who wanted to return. I could not hear the discussion very clearly, as I was at the tiller; but everyone forward and the three men refused; but I shall always remember your words: 'Ladies, if any of us are saved, remember, I wanted to go back. I would rather drown with them than leave them.' You did all you could, and being my own countryman, I wanted to tell you this.

Yours very truly, Gladys Cherry.

Miss Marie Grice Young, thirty-six, a former music teacher at the White House, shared a first-class state room on the *Titanic* with Mrs J. Stuart White. Both women escaped in lifeboat No. 8 where Miss Young assisted manfully with the rowing. She later wrote a personal account of the wreck for an American magazine.

Six months have elapsed since the *Titanic* – the most splendid of all passenger ships – sank in the North Atlantic Ocean, in sight of fifteen boatloads of survivors, numbering less than a third of the passengers and crew who had embarked at her three ports of call.

Perhaps no two survivors would answer alike the question: 'What is your most poignant memory of the fatal voyage, and of its fifth and final night?'

A panorama of incidents passes before the mind – trivial events ordinarily, but rendered tragic because of the death of many who sailed on the *Titanic*, but who never heard the eager roll call of the *Carpathia*. What became of the merry group of boys who were beside me, in the telegraph office at the dock at Cherbourg, hurrying off last messages to friends on shore?

Who can forget the cruel change in the faces of those who waved gay farewells as the tender left the French harbour, and ere they again sighted land, had yielded up all that made life beautiful to them?

Figures, faces and even varying facial expressions are remembered of those, who though strangers, were fellow passengers, beloved of many ashore to whom even our fading impressions

VOICES FROM THE TITANIC

and slight knowledge would be a consolation, should the paths of our lives ever cross.

In my thoughts I often lie again in my steamer chair, and watch the passing throng on the *Titanic*'s promenade deck. After the usual excitement of buying lace from the Irish girls who came aboard at Queenstown was over, the routine of life on deck was established. Two famous men passed many times every day in a vigorous constitutional, one talking always – as rapidly as he walked – the other a good and smiling listener.

Babies and nurses, dear old couples, solitary men, passed sunlit hours of those spring days on deck, while the *Titanic* swept on to the scene of the disaster; approaching what might not have been so much a sinister fate awaiting her, as it was an opportunity for her commander and the President of the White Star Line to prove true seamanship and their great discretion in the presence of reported and recognized peril.

It so happened that I took an unusual interest in some of the men below decks, for I had talked often with the carpenter and the printer in having extra crates and labels made for the fancy French poultry we were bringing home, and I saw a little of the ship's life, in my daily visits to the gaily crowing roosters, and to the hens, who laid eggs busily, undismayed by the novelty and commotion of their surroundings.

I had seen the cooks before their great cauldrons of porcelain, and the bakers turning out the huge loaves of bread, a hamper of which was later brought on deck to supply the lifeboats.

In accepting some gold coins, the ship's carpenter said: 'It is such good luck to receive gold on a first voyage!' Yet he was the first of the *Titanic*'s martyrs, who, in sounding the ship just after the iceberg was struck, sank and was lost in the inward-rushing sea that engulfed him.

Who can imagine the earthly purgatory of anguish endured by Captain Smith during the pitifully short time vouchsafed him to prepare for death – whose claim upon him, he, more than all others, must acknowledge?

Who exchanged a last word with any of the joyous bridal couples, to whom each day at sea had brought a deeper glow of happiness? Expectant, they stood at the threshold of earthly life, yet they passed together that night through the gates of Eternity to a fairer day than that which dawned for those left to face an unknown fate.

What scenes were enacted to immortalize forever the engineers who kept the ship lighted and afloat, giving a last chance of escape to passengers and even officers? How can we ever realize what it meant to find courage to reject the thought of beloved dependants on shore, and to face death in stoke-hold and engine room?

The 'greater love' that lays down life that another may live burnt in many a heart in the *Titanic*'s list of dead, and those who survive owe them a debt, only to be acknowledged and wiped out by a flawless record of lives nobly lived, because so cruelly bought.

Vivid and endless are the impressions of that great night. They remain as closely folded in the brain as the shock of the discharge of guns, the cries of the drowning and the sobs of the broken-hearted.

Clearest of all is the remembrance of the eighteen self-controlled women in our boat (Number 8), four of whom had parted, bitterly protesting, from their husbands.

In those hours spent face to face with the solemn thoughts of trials still to undergo before possible rescue, it was inspiring to see that these twentieth-century women were, in mentality and physique, worthy descendants of their ancestors who had faced other dire perils in Colonial and Revolutionary periods. Women rowed all night, others in the bow waved the lantern light in the air as a signal to the ship towards whose light our boat crept slowly till dawn, with only a young girl at the tiller to keep the boat headed straight in spite of the jerky, uneven rowing.

Treasured above all else was the electric light in the handle of a cane belonging to Mrs J. Stuart White, who waved it regularly while counting strokes for the haphazard crew.

The assurance that its light would burn continuously for thirty hours helped comfort many minds, aghast at the possibility of another night to be endured before rescue. We had no knowledge of wireless response to the *Titanic*'s frantic calls for help nor of the glorious rush through the sea of ice which was bringing near the fearless little *Carpathia*. If we, the survivors, spent a night of exhausting struggle, of emotion, and of prayer, what of the captain, the crew, and the awakening passengers of the rescue ship?

Nevertheless we turn to a brighter side of the picture, for hope must have filled all the hearts of those who turned back so promptly at the first distress signal. The United States Senate investigation brought to the world's notice a document containing Captain Rostron's written orders to his officers and crew, a copy of which should be framed on every ship as a model of perfect organisation in time of stress. No detail of careful preparation was omitted. All the reading world knows now that, after answering the *Titanic*'s wireless appeal, Captain Rostron put an additional officer on the *Carpathia*'s bridge, doubled his lookouts in the crow's nest, and called out an extra fire-room force.

But of his final and complete preparations, enough cannot be said. His three physicians – English, Italian and Hungarian – were detailed to look after the different classes of rescued passengers; his passengers were supplied with food, medicine and blankets, and they were ready to lower as soon as he should approach the wreck, which alas! he was indeed never to see.

He ordered his own crew to be fed and fortified for the coming hours of strain, and they promised their brave commander to show the world of what stuff the British seaman is made.

His own steerage passengers were placed in closer quarters, and their natural excitement quieted by a few judicious words. And these given instances of careful forethought are but a few, remembered at random, and only a suggestion of the great work accomplished by Captain Rostron in the cause of humanity.

When the *Carpathia* reached the scene of the disaster, finding fifteen boats, some only half-filled, the survivors of the tragedy that had been enacted between the setting and the rising sun were lifted on board with pity and tenderness almost divine in their gentleness.

The details of the shipwreck, its perils, horrors and uncertainties, have filled the magazines and newspapers, but of the wonderful, unique days that followed, little has been said.

Many of the survivors were dazed by the paralyzing events of the night, the shock of collision, and the terror of the realization that their only chance for life was in escaping in the lifeboats. The perilous descent into these boats, their ignorant handling, the immediate sinking of the *Titanic*, the heartrending cries of the dying, the night spent adrift on the bitterly cold sea, and finally the hazardous ascent in the boatswain's seat from the lifeboat to the *Carpathia*'s gangway, were all experiences to haunt and tax the most stoical.

For those who had lost members of their families, friends or servants, it was a bitter moment when, at ten o'clock on Monday morning, April 15, Captain Rostron steamed away from the scene of the wreck, leaving two tardy and cruelly negligent steamers to watch the scene of the greatest maritime tragedy.

The day was cold, but brilliant. All morning the *Carpathia* passed a field of ice, 40 miles in length, and extending northward as far as the eye could see.

After food and blankets had been distributed amongst the survivors, their names were carefully noted. Then the weary task began, lasting for days, of sending them by wireless to an awestricken, listening, longing world. The *Carpathia*'s own exhausted operator was relieved by the equally worn-out second operator (Harold Bride) from the *Titanic*, who had been lifted more dead than alive from the ocean.

Meanwhile, the *Carpathia*'s sympathetic passengers were sharing rooms and clothing with those rescued; every possible berth was assigned, and all available space in the library and dining saloon used for sleeping quarters. Mattresses were laid on the dining tables, and at night, old and young 'made up' beds on the library floor, a most informal proceeding consisting of spreading a folded steamer rug on the floor, with a second rug to sleep under, and, perhaps, if one had luck, a sofa cushion for a pillow.

Such beds were smilingly and uncomplainingly occupied. One bright old lady, who slept thus beside her sister's bed on a bench, called it the 'lower berth in the *Carpathia* Pullman!'

No such makeshift, however, for the President of the White Star Line – hidden in the English physician's comfortable room, he voyaged to New York, as heedlessly indifferent to the discomfort of his company's passengers as he had been to the deadly peril that had menaced them. Richer, far, in experience, were those who mingled freely in that ship's company.

There were lessons to be learnt in every hour of that voyage. Who could ever forget the splendid work of one young girl whose father was a missionary? After giving garments of her own to many survivors, she collected more clothing to supply further needs – she cut out dresses for the many forlorn babies, and spent days ministering to the terrified emigrants of the steerage.

Cruel indeed was the plight of these foreigners. Many of them were young mothers, with wailing babies who refused food – widowed, penniless, ignorant of the language of an unknown country, they faced the New World. But indeed, the wind was truly tempered to these shorn lambs, for North and South, East and West were gathering together a golden store for their needs on landing and for their future assistance.

The last three days of the voyage were taxing because rain kept the passengers crowded in the library, the wail of the foghorn sounding continuously, strained overwrought nerves, as the *Carpathia* steered cautiously and slowly towards New York with her doubly precious freight of human souls.

Many were the experiences and tales of adventures on sea and land exchanged in those penned-in, irksome hours; hot and bitter were the denunciations of the criminal neglect of those whose authority could and should have averted the disaster.

Inevitable were the collections and disagreements over loving cups and votes of thanks, to be presented to the embarrassed, bashful, but truly heroic captain.

Fire Island! Ambrose Channel! Welcoming sirens of hundreds of tugs, newspaper boats, steamers and yachts! And the lights of New York!

Hardly were the many telegrams from our friends handed us, before we neared the Cunard docks; never was homecoming so sweet, as on that immortal night of nights, when again the world waited, hushed, for the coming epic of abysmal horror, of consuming, unending grief, and of sublime heroism.

Even now, one must doubt whether the terrible lesson to be learnt from such an appalling tragedy has been given due consideration by those who govern the courses of the ocean liners. One reads of steamers again venturing over the northerly course, and reporting ice in sight. The captains of the best patronized lines state they would have followed Captain Smith's route, under similar conditions, apparently preferring insane speeding among icebergs to taking a more southerly course.

Almost from the time of the world's creation, men have 'gone down to the sea in ships'. Human intelligence has laboured long to conquer the elements, and today inventive genius seems to triumph over all that vexed the soul and brain of the sturdy adventurers who discovered our land. But man can never be omnipotent. An unsinkable ship will never cross the sea. Granting that the *Titanic* was a triumph of construction and appointments, even she could not trespass upon a law of nature, and survive.

Helplessly that beautiful and gallant ship struggled to escape from the hand of God, but was only an atom in the hold of inexorable justice.

Majestically she sailed; but bowed, broken and crouching, she sank slowly beneath the conquering ocean – a hidden memorial shaft to the unburied dead she carried with her, and to the

incredible wickedness of man, until the coming of the day when
'there shall be no more sea.'

(*National Magazine*, October 1912)

SINKING OF *TITANIC* STILL HORROR TO COUPLE HONEYMOONING ON SHIP

It was a strange honeymoon for Mr and Mrs Edward Beane of 44 Michigan Street when on April 14, 1912 they fled the doomed *Titanic* and from the temporary safety of a rowboat saw the gallant ship and its human cargo go crashing down to Davy Jones' locker.

Looking back on the event after nineteen years with two eager young sons to prod reluctant memory, the event is a hideous nightmare, they say. Mrs Beane, a bride of 17, longed in that midnight hour of disaster for the secure shelter of her home in Norwich, England.

'For years I didn't want to talk about it,' she said yesterday as her sons bent their heads over yellowed newspapers which described the event. 'Wherever we went, people pointed at us curiously, and made us aware that death had brushed us by. We must have been a mile away in the rowboat when the *Titanic* went down. We could hear the band playing and then just before the crash of sinking the anguished cries of those on board which was like one great human wail. It was years before I could forget that terrible scream.'

Mr Beane had been in the United States some years and had made several crossings before he sailed with his bride on the maiden voyage of the great *Titanic*, new mistress of the seas. They loved the beauty of the new ship and waved goodbye to their friends with happy pride. And yet they confessed to a fear of foreboding when the *Titanic* narrowly avoided a collision in the Southampton harbour.

The night of the thirteenth was stormy and dark, but the fourteenth dawned clear and bright. The boat was ripping through the water at 21 knots an hour, under orders to make a new record, when near midnight she struck an iceberg. It was some time before all the passengers realized the situation. The Beanes were, at first, not alarmed and received the news that the boat was sinking calmly, suspecting the commotion was only a boat drill. Indeed they were so laconic that a woman in the next state room came back twice to warn them. And then they were caught up in the terror of the event and went rushing up the stairs to the deck, the jewels on the night-stand forgotten and the beautiful linens and embroideries in the bride's trousseau, just neglected trappings.

'The crew had their rifles to keep the men back until the women and children could get into the boats,' explained Mr Beane. 'A man never knows what he'll do in an emergency or what tricks his nerves will play on him. I saw a man shot down for trying to break through the lines. I saw Charles Williams, the prize fighter, coming over for a tag match drop back when the rifle fire scorched his fingers for overeagerness. He was a big brute of a man, too.'

Mrs Beane was hustled into one of the lifeboats, dazed and stricken, and a little hypnotized by the terrifying beauty of that torchlit deck and its cowering humans; and strengthened too by the sturdy valour of a crew which went down with their ship.

Mr Beane, like the other men on the boat, could find no place in the lifeboats, and so jumped overboard. After swimming about in the water for hours he was picked up by one of the small rowboats and eventually put on board the *Carpathia* with the other survivors.

'All any of us wanted was solid ground under our feet and forgetfulness,' they added.

Neither Mr nor Mrs Beane have been on an ocean-going ship since they disembarked from the *Carpathia*.

(Rochester Democrat and Chronicle, 15 April 1931)

PASSENGER AND CREW LISTS

There is no definitive list for passengers and crew aboard the *Titanic* when she went down since the official lists contain many discrepancies and do not take into account the presence of stowaways, people travelling under assumed names or substitutes. This, therefore, is about as accurate a list as can be obtained although no doubt there are still a number of errors. Survivors are in bold.

PASSENGERS

FIRST CLASS

Allen, Miss E. W.
Allison, H. J.
Allison, Mrs H. J.
Allison, Miss H.
Allison, Master H.
Anderson, Mr H.
Andrews, Miss K.
Andrews, Thomas
Appleton, Mrs E. D.
Artagaveytia, R.
Astor, Col. J. J.
Astor, Mrs J. J.
Aubart, Mme L.
Barber, Miss E.

Barkworth, A. H.
Bauman, J.
Baxter, Mrs J.
Baxter, Mr Q.
Bazzoni, Miss A.
Beattie, Mr T.
Beckwith, Mr R. T.
Beckwith, Mrs R. T.
Behr, Mr K. H.
Bidois, Miss R.
Birnbaum, Mr J.
Bird, Miss E.
Bishop, Mr D. H.
Bishop, Mrs D. H.
Bissette, Miss A.
Bjornstrom-Steffanson, Mr M. H.

Blackwell, Mr S. W.
Blank, Mr H.
Bonnell, Miss C.
Bonnell, Miss E.
Borebank, Mr J. J.
Bowen, Miss G.
Bowerman, Miss E.
Brady, Mr J. B.
Brandeis, Mr E.
Brayton, Mr G.
Brew, Dr A. J.
Brown, Mrs J. J.
Brown, Mrs J. M.
Bucknell, Mrs W.
Burns, Miss E.
Butt, Major A.
Cairns, Mr A.
Calderhead, Mr E. P.
Candee, Mrs E.
Cardeza, Mrs J. W .M.
Cardeza, Mr T. D.
Carlson, Mr F.
Carrau, Mr F.
Carrau, Mr J.
Carter, Miss L.
Carter, Master W.
Carter, Mr W. E.
Carter, Mrs W. E.
Case, Mr H. B.
Cassebeer, Mrs H. A.
Cavendish, Mr T. W.
Cavendish, Mrs T. W.
Chaffee, Mr H.
Chaffee, Mrs H.
Chambers, Mr N. C.
Chambers, Mrs N. C.
Chaudanson, Miss V.

Cherry, Miss G.
Chevré, Mr P.
Chibnall, Mrs E. M.
Chisholm, Mr R.
Clark, Mr W. M.
Clark, Mrs W. M.
Cleaver, Miss A.
Clifford, Mr G.
Colley, Mr E.
Compton, Mrs A. T.
Compton, A.T. Jnr
Compton, Miss S.
Cornell, Mrs R. C.
Crafton, Mr J.
Crosby, Mr E. G.
Crosby, Mrs E. G.
Crosby, Miss H.
Cumings, Mr J. B.
Cumings, Mrs J. B.
Daly, Mr P.
Daniel, Mr R. W.
Daniels, Miss S.
Davidson, Mr T.
Davidson, Mrs T.
Dick, Mr A. A.
Dick, Mrs A. A.
Dodge, Mr W.
Dodge, Mrs W.
Dodge, Master W.
Douglas, Mrs F. C.
Douglas, Mr W.
Douglas, Mrs W.
Duff Gordon, Sir C.
Duff Gordon, Lady
Dulles, Mr W. O.
Earnshaw, Mrs B.
Endres, Miss C.

Eustis, Miss E.
Evans, Miss E.
Farthing, Mr J.
Flegenheim, Mrs A.
Fleming, Miss J. M.
Flynn, Mr J. L.
Foreman, Mr B. L.
Fortune, Miss A.
Fortune, Miss E.
Fortune, Miss M.
Fortune, Mr M.
Fortune, Mrs M.
Francatelli, Miss L.
Franklin, Mr T. P.
Frauenthal, Dr H.
Frauenthal, Mrs H.
Frauenthal, Mr I.
Frolicher, Miss H. M.
Frolicher-Stehli, Mr M.
Frolicher-Stehli, Mrs M.
Fry, Mr J.
Futrelle, Mr J.
Futrelle, Mrs J.
Gee, Mr A.
Geiger, Miss A.
Gibson, Miss D.
Gibson, Mrs L.
Giglio, Mr V.
Goldenberg, Mr S. L.
Goldenberg, Mrs S. L.
Goldschmidt, Mr G.
Gracie, Col. A.
Graham, Mr G.
Graham, Miss M. E.
Graham, Mrs W.
Greenfield, Mrs L. D.
Greenfield, Mr W.

Guggenheim, Mr B.
Harder, Mr G. A.
Harder, Mrs G. A.
Harper, Mr H. S.
Harper, Mrs H. S.
Harrington, Mr C. H.
Harris, Mr H. B.
Harris, Mrs H. B.
Harrison, Mr W.
Hassah, Mr H.
Haven, Mr H.
Hawksford, Mr W. J.
Hays, Mr C. M.
Hays, Mrs C. M.
Hays, Miss M.
Head, Mr C.
Hilliard, Mr H. H.
Hippach, Mrs I. S.
Hippach, Miss J.
Hogeboom, Mrs J. C.
Holverson, Mr A. O.
Holverson, Mrs A. O.
Hoyt, Mr F. M.
Hoyt, Mrs F. M.
Hoyt, Mr W. F.
Icard, Miss A.
Isham, Miss A.
Ismay, Mr J. B.
Jones, Mr C. C.
Julian, Mr H. F.
Keeping, Mr E.
Kent, Mr E.
Kenyon, Mr F. R.
Kenyon, Mrs F. R.
Kimball, Mr E. N.
Kimball, Mrs E. N.
Klaber, Mr H.

Kreuchen, Miss E.

Leader, Mrs A.

Le Roy, Miss B.

Lesueur, Mr G.

Levy, Mr E. G.

Lindeburg-Lind, Mr E.

Lindstrom, Mrs J.

Lines, Mrs E. H.

Lines, Miss M. C.

Long, M. C.

Longley, Miss G.

Loring, Mr J.

Lurette, Miss E.

Madill, Miss G. A.

Maguire, J. E.

Maioni, Miss R.

Maréchal, Mr P.

Marvin, Mr D. W.

Marvin, Mrs D. W.

Mayné, Mlle B.

McCaffry, Mr T.

McCarthy, Mr T. J.

McGough, Mr J.

Melody, Mr A.

Meyer, Mr E. J.

Meyer, Mrs E. J.

Millet, Mr F. D.

Minahan, Miss D.

Minahan, Dr W. E.

Minahan, Mrs W. E.

Mock, Mr P.

Molson, Mr H. M.

Moore, Mr C.

Natschm, Mr C.

Newell, Mr A. W.

Newell, Miss A.

Newell, Miss M.

Newsom, Miss H.

Nicholson, Mr A. S.

Nourney, Mr A.

Oliva y Ocana, Mr D.

Omont, Mr A.

Ostby, Mr E. C.

Ostby, Miss H.

Ovies, Mr S.

Parr, Mr M. H.

Partner, Mr A.

Payne, Mr V.

Pears, Mr T.

Pears, Mrs T.

Penasco, Mr V.

Penasco, Mrs V.

Perrault, Miss A.

Peuchen, Major A.

Porter, Mr W. C.

Potter, Mrs T. Jnr

Reuchlin, Mr J. G.

Rheims, Mr G.

Robert, Mrs E. S.

Roebling, Mr W. A.

Romaine, Mr C.

Rood, Mr H.

Rosenbaum Miss E.

Rosenshine, Mr G.

Ross, Mr J. H.

Rothes, Countess of

Rothschild, Mr M.

Rothschild, Mrs M.

Rowe, Mr A.

Ryerson, Mr A.

Ryerson, Mrs A.

Ryerson, Miss E.

Ryerson, Master J.

Ryerson, Miss S.

Saalfeld, Mr A.

Sagesser, Mlle E.

Saloman, Mr A.

Schabert, Mrs P.

Schutes, Miss E. W.

Serreplan, Miss A.

Seward, Mr F.

Shutes, Miss E.

Silverthorne, Mr S.

Silvey, Mr W. B.

Silvey, Mrs W. B.

Simonius, Col. A.

Sloper, Mr W. T.

Smart, Mr J. M.

Smith, Mr J. C.

Smith, Mr L. P.

Smith, Mrs L. P.

Smith, Mr R. W.

Snyder, Mr J.

Snyder, Mrs J.

Spedden, Mr F. O.

Spedden, Mrs F. O.

Spedden, Master R.

Spenser, Mr W. A.

Spenser, Mrs W. A.

Stalelin, Dr M

Stead, Mr W. T.

Stengel, Mr C. E. H.

Stengel, Mrs C. E. H.

Stephenson, Mrs W. B.

Stone, Mrs G. M.

Straus, Mr I.

Straus, Mrs I.

Sutton, Mr F.

Swift, Mrs F.

Taussig, Mr E.

Taussig, Mrs E.

Taussig, Miss R.

Taylor, Mr E. S.

Taylor, Mrs E. S.

Thayer, Mr J. B.

Thayer, Mrs J. B.

Thayer, Mr J. B. Jnr

Thorne, Mrs G.

Tucker, Mr G. Jnr

Uruchurtu, Mr M.

Vanderhoef, Mr W.

Walker, Mr W. A.

Ward, Miss A.

Warren, Mr F. M.

Warren, Mrs F. M.

Weir, Mr J.

White, Mr J. S.

White, Mrs J. S.

White, Mr P. W.

Wick, Mr G.

Wick, Mrs G.

Wick, Miss M.

Widener, Mr G. D.

Widener, Mrs G. D.

Widener, Mr H.

Willard, Miss C.

Williams, Mr D.

Williams, Mr N. M. Jnr

Williams-Lambert, Mr F.

Wilson, Miss H.

Woolner, Mr H.

Wright, Mr G.

Young, Miss M.

SECOND CLASS

Abelson, Mr S.

Abelson, Mrs S.

Aldworth, Mr C.

Andrew, Mr E.

Andrew, Mr F.

Angle, Mr W.

Angle, Mrs W.

Ashby, Mr J.

Bailey, Mr P.

Baimbrigge, Mr C.

Ball, Mrs M.

Banfield, Mr F.

Bateman, Rev. R. J.

Beane, Mr E.

Beane, Mrs E.

Beauchamp, Mr H.

Becker, Mrs A.

Becker, Miss M.

Becker, Miss R.

Becker, Master R.

Beesley, Mr L.

Bentham, Miss L.

Berriman, Mr W.

Botsford, Mr W. H.

Bowenur, Mr S.

Bracken, Mr J.

Brito, Mr J.

Brown, Miss A.

Brown, Miss E.

Brown, Mr T. W. S.

Brown, Mrs T. W. S.

Bryhl, Mr J.

Bryhil, Miss D.

Buss, Miss K.

Butler, Mr R.

Byles, Rev. T.

Bystrom, Mrs K.

Caldwell, Mr A. F.

Caldwell, Mrs A. F.

Caldwell, Master A.

Cameron, Miss C.

Campbell, Mr W.

Carbines, Mr W.

Carter, Rev E. C.

Carter, Mrs E. C.

Chapman, Mr C.

Chapman, Mr J. H.

Chapman, Mrs J. H.

Christy, Mrs A.

Christy, Miss J.

Clarke, Mr C. V.

Clarke, Mrs C. V.

Coleridge, Mr R.

Collander, Mr E.

Collett, Mr S.

Collyer, Mr H.

Collyer, Mrs H.

Collyer, Miss M.

Cook, Mrs A.

Corbett, Mrs W.

Corey, Mrs P.

Cotterill, Mr H.

Cunningham, Mr A. F.

Davies, Mr C. H.

Davies, Miss J. M.

Davies, Master J. M. Jnr

Davis, Miss M.

Deacon, Mr P.

del Carlo, Mr S.

del Carlo, Mrs S.

Denbury, Mr H.

Dibden, Mr W.

Doling, Miss E.

Doling, Mrs J. T.

Downtown, Mr W. J.

Drew, Mr J. V.

Drew, Mrs J. V.

Drew, Master M.

Duran y More, Miss A.

Duran y More, Miss F.

Eitemiller, Mr G.

Enander, Mr I.

Fahlstrom, Mr A.

Faunthorpe, Mr H.

Faunthorpe, Mrs E.

Fillbrook, Mr J.

Fox, Mr S.

Frost, Mr A.

Funk, Miss A.

Fynney, Mr J. J.

Gale, Mr H.

Gale, Mr S.

Garside, Miss E.

Gaskell, Mr A.

Gavey, Mr L.

Gilbert, Mr W.

Giles, Mr E.

Giles, Mr F.

Giles, Mr R.

Gill, Mr J. W.

Gillespie, Mr W. H.

Givard, Mr H.

Greenberg, Mr S.

Hale, Mr R.

Hamalainen, Mrs W.

Hamalainen, Master W.

Harbeck, Mr W.

Harper, Miss A.

Harper, Rev J.

Harris, Mr G.

Harris, Mr W.

Hart, Mr B.

Hart, Mrs B.

Hart, Miss E.

Herman, Miss A.

Herman, Miss K.

Herman, Mr S.

Herman, Mrs S.

Hewlett, Mrs M.

Hickman, Mr L.

Hickman, Mr L. M.

Hickman, Mr S. G.

Hiltunen, Miss M.

Hocking, Miss E.

Hocking, Mrs E.

Hocking, Mr R. G.

Hocking, Mr S.

Hodges, Mr H.

Hold, Mr S.

Hold, Mrs S.

Hood, Mr A.

Hosono, Mr M.

Howard, Mr B.

Howard, Mrs B.

Hunt, Mr G. H.

Ilett, Miss B.

Jacobson, Mr S. S.

Jacobson, Mrs S. S.

Jarvis, Mr J.

Jefferys, Mr C. T.

Jefferys, Mr E.

Jenkin, Mr S. C.

Jerwan, Mrs A.

Kantor, Mr S.

Kantor, Mrs S.

Jarnes, Mrs J. F.

Keane, Mr D.

Keane, Miss N.

Kelly, Mrs F.

Kirkland, Rev. C. L.

Knight, Mr R. J.

Kvillner, Mr J.

Lahtinen, Rev W.

Lahtinen, Mrs W.

Lamb, Mr J. J.

Laroche, Mr J.

Laroche, Mrs J.

Laroche, Miss L.

Laroche, Miss S.

Lehmann, Miss B.

Leitch, Miss J.

Lemore, Mrs A.

Lévy, Mr R.

Leyson, Mr R.

Linnane, Mr J.

Louch, Mr C. A.

Louch, Mrs C. A.

Mack, Mrs M.

Malachard, Mr N.

Mallet, Mr A.

Mallet, Mrs A.

Mallet, Master A.

Mangiavacchi, Mr S.

Matthews, Mr W. J.

Maybery, Mr F.

McCrae, Mr A.

McCrie, Mr J.

McKane, Mr P. D.

Mellinger, Mrs E.

Mellinger, Miss M.

Mellors, Mr W. J.

Meyer, Mr A.

Milling, Mr J.

Mitchell, Mr H.

Montvila, Rev J.

Moraweck, Mr E.

Morley, Mr H.

Mudd, Mr T.

Myles, Mr T.

Nasser, Mr N.

Nasser, Mrs N.

Navratil, Master E.

Navratil, Master M.

Navratil, Mr M.

Nesson, Mr I.

Nicholls, Mr J.

Norman, Mr R. D.

Nye, Mrs E.

Otter, Mr R.

Oxenham, Mr P.

Padron, Mr J.

Pain, Dr A.

Pallas y Castello, Mr E.

Parker, Mr C.

Parker, Mr F.

Parrish, Mrs S.

Pengelly, Mr F.

Pernot, Mr R.

Peruschitz, Rev J.

Phillips, Miss A.

Phillips, Mr E.

Phillips, Miss K.

Pinsky, Mrs R.

Ponesell, Mr M.

Portaluppi, Mr E.

Pulbaum, Mr F.

Quick, Mrs F.C.

Quick, Miss P.

Quick, Miss W.

Reeves, Mr D.

Renouf, Mr P. H.

Renouf, Mrs P. H.

Reynaldo, Miss E.

Richard, Mr E.

Richards, Master G.
Richards, Mrs S.
Richards, Master W.
Ridsdale, Miss L.
Rogers, Mr R.
Rugg, Miss E.
Sedgwick, Mr C. F.
Sharp, Mr P. J. R.
Shelley, Mrs I.
Silven, Miss L.
Sincock, Miss M.
Sinkkonen, Miss A.
Sjostedt, Mr E.
Slayter, Miss H.
Slemen, Mr R. J.
Schmidt, Mr A.
Smith, Miss M.
Sobey, Mr S.
Stanton, Mr S.
Stokes, Mr P. J.
Swane, Mr G.
Sweet, Mr G.
Toomey, Miss E.
Troupiansky, Mr M.
Trout, Miss E.
Trout, Mrs W. H.
Turpin, Mr W. J. R.
Turpin, Mrs W. J. R.
Veal, Mr J.
Walcroft, Miss H.
Ware, Mr J. J.
Ware, Mrs J. J.
Ware, Mr W. J.
Watson, Mr E.
Watt, Mrs J.
Watt, Miss R.
Webber, Miss S.

Weisz, Mr L.
Weisz, Mrs L.
Wells, Mrs A.
Wells, Miss J.
Wells, Master R.
West, Miss B.
West, Miss C.
West, Mr E. A.
West, Mrs E. A.
Wheadon, Mr E.
Wheeler, Mr E.
Wilhelms, Mr C.
Williams, Mr C.
Wright, Miss M.
Yvois, Miss H.

THIRD CLASS

Abbing, Mr A.
Abbott, Master E.
Abbott, Mr R.
Abbott, Mrs S.
Abelseth, Miss K.
Abelseth, Mr O.
Abrahim, Mrs J.
Abrahamsson, Mr A.
Adahl, Mr M.
Adams, Mr J.
Ahlin, Mrs J.
Aihimona, Mr N.
Aks, Master F. P.
Aks, Mrs S.
Alexander, Mr W.
Alhomaki, Mr I.
Ali, Mr A.
Ali, Mr W.
Allen, Mr W.

Allum, Mr O. G.
Andersen, Mr A. K.
Andersen, Miss C.
Andersson, Mr A. J.
Andersson, Mrs A. J.
Andersson, Miss E. A.
Andersson, Miss E. A. M.
Andersson, Miss E. I.
Andersson, Miss I.
Andersson, Miss I. A.
Andersson, Mr J.
Andersson, Master S.
Andersson, Miss S.
Andreasson, Mr P.
Angelhoff, Mr M.
Arnold-Franchi, Mr J.
Arnold-Franchi, Mrs J.
Aronsson, Mr E.
Asim, Mr A.
Asplund, Mr C.
Asplund, Mrs C.
Asplund, Master C. E.
Asplund, Master C. G. H.
Asplund, Master F.
Asplund, Master F. O.
Asplund, Mr J. C.
Asplund, Miss L.
Assaf, Mr G.
Assaf, Mrs M.
Assam, Mr A.
Attalah, Miss M.
Attalah, Mr S.
Augustsson, Mr A.
Ayoub, Miss B.
Baccos, Mr R.
Backstrom, Mr K. A.
Backstrom, Mrs K. A.

Baclini, Miss E.
Baclini, Miss E. L.
Baclini, Miss M.
Baclini, Mrs S.
Badman, Miss E.
Badt, Mr M.
Balkic, Mr K.
Barbara, Mrs C.
Barbara, Miss S.
Barry, Miss J.
Barton, Mr D. J.
Beavan, Mr W. T.
Bengtsson, Mr J.
Berglund, Mr K.
Betros, Master S.
Betros, Mr T.
Bing, Mr L.
Birkeland, Mr H.
Bjorklund, Mr E. H.
Bostandyeff, Mr G.
Boulos, Master A.
Boulos, Mr H.
Boulos, Mrs J.
Boulos, Miss N.
Bourke, Mr J.
Bourke, Mrs J.
Bourke, Miss M.
Bowen, Mr D.
Bradley, Miss B.
Braf, Miss E.
Braund, Mr L.
Braund, Mr O.
Brobeck, Mr K.
Brocklebank, Mr W.
Buckley, Mr D.
Buckley, Miss K.
Burke, Mr J.

Burns, Miss M.
Cacic, Mr J.
Cacic, Mr L.
Cacic, Miss Marija
Cacic, Miss Manda
Calic, Mr J.
Calic, Mr P.
Canavan, Miss M.
Canavan, Mr P.
Cann, Mr E. C.
Carlsson, Mr A. S.
Carlsson, Mr C. R.
Carr, Miss E.
Carr, Miss J.
Carver, Mr A.
Celotti, Mr F.
Charters, Mr D.
Chip, Mr C.
Christmann, Mr E.
Chronopoulos, Mr A.
Chronopoulos, Mr D.
Coelho, Mr D.
Cohen, Mr G.
Colbert, Mr P.
Coleff, Mr S.
Coltcheff, Mr P.
Conlon, Mr T.
Connaughton, Mr M.
Connolly, Miss K.
Connolly, Miss K.
Connors, Mr P.
Cook, Mr J.
Cor, Mr B.
Cor, Mr I.
Cor, Mr L.
Corn, Mr H.
Coutts, Master N.

Coutts, Master W.
Coutts, Mrs W.
Coxon, Mr D.
Crease, Mr E. J.
Cribb, Mr J.
Cribb, Miss L.
Culumovic, Mr J.
Daher, Mr S.
Dahl, Mr C. E.
Dahlberg, Miss G.
Dakic, Mr B.
Daly, Mr E.
Daly, Miss M.
Danbom, Mrs E.
Danbom, Master G.
Danoff, Mr Y.
Dantcheff, Mr R.
Davies, Mr A.
Davies, Mr E.
Davies, Mr J.
Davies, Mr J. S.
Davison, Mr T. H.
Davison, Mrs T. H.
Dean, Mr B. F.
Dean, Mrs B. F.
Dean, Master B.
Dean, Miss E.
Delalic, Mr R.
Demessenaeker, Mr G.
Demessemaeker, Mrs G.
De Mulder, Mr T.
De Pelsmaeker, Mr A.
Demetri, Mr M.
Denkoff, Mr M.
Dennis, Mr S.
Dennis, Mr W.
Devaney, Miss M.

Dika, Mr M.
Dimic, Mr J.
Dintcheff, Mr V.
Doharr, Mr T.
Dooley, Mr P.
Dorking, Mr E.
Dowdell, Miss E.
Doyle, Miss E.
Drazenovic, Mr J.
Dropkin, Miss J.
Duquemin, Mr J.
Dwan, Mr F.
Dyker, Mr A. F.
Dyker, Mrs A. F.
Edvardsson, Mr G.
Eklund, Mr H.
Ekstrom, Mr J.
Elias, Mr D.
Elias, Mr J.
Elias, Mr J. Jnr
Elias, Mr T.
Elsbury, Mr W. J.
Emanuel, Miss V.
Emir-Farres, Mr C.
Everett, Mr T. J.
Farrell, Mr J.
Finoli, Mr L.
Fischer, Mr E.
Fleming, Miss H.
Flynn, Mr James
Flynn, Mr Joseph
Foley, Mr J.
Foley, Mr W.
Foo, Mr C.
Ford, Mr A.
Ford, Miss D. M.
Ford, Mr E. W.

Ford, Mrs E. W.
Ford, Miss R.
Ford, Mr W.
Fox, Mr P.
Franklin, Mr C.
Gallagher, Mr M.
Garfirth, Mr J.
Gerios, Mr Y.
Gheorgheff, Mr S.
Gilinksi, Mr E.
Gilnagh, Miss K.
Glynn, Miss M.
Goldsmith, Mr F. J.
Goldsmith, Mrs F. J.
Goldsmith, Master F. J.
Goldsmith, Mr N.
Gonçalves, Mr M. E.
Goodwin, Mr C. E.
Goodwin, Mr C. F.
Goodwin, Mrs F.
Goodwin, Master H.
Goodwin, Miss J.
Goodwin, Miss L.
Goodwin, Master S.
Goodwin, Master W.
Green, Mr G.
Gronnestad, Mr D.
Guest, Mr R.
Gustafsson, Mr A. O.
Gustafsson, Mr A. V.
Gustafsson, Mr J.
Gustafsson, Mr K.
Haas, Miss A.
Hagland, Mr I.
Hagland, Mr K.
Hakkarainen, Mr P.
Hakkarainen, Mrs P.

Hampe, Mr L.

Hanna, Mr M.

Hannah, Mr B.

Hansen, Mr C. P.

Hansen, Mrs C. P.

Hansen, Mr H. D.

Hansen, Mr H. J.

Hargadon, Miss C.

Harknett, Miss A.

Harmer, Mr A.

Hart, Mr H.

Hassan, Mr G. N.

Healy, Miss N.

Hedman, Mr O.

Hee, Mr L.

Hegarty, Miss N.

Heikkinen, Miss L.

Heininen, Miss W.

Hellstrom, Miss H.

Hendekovic, Mr I.

Henry, Miss D.

Henriksson, Miss J.

Hirvonen, Mrs A.

Hirvonen, Miss H.

Holm, Mr J.

Holthen, Mr J.

Honkanen, Miss E.

Horgan, Mr J.

Howard, Miss M.

Humblen, Mr A.

Hyman, Mr A.

Ilieff, Mr I.

Ilmakangas, Miss I.

Ilmakangas, Miss P.

Ivanoff, Mr K.

Jalsevac, Mr I.

Jansson, Mr C.

Jardin, Mr J.

Jensen, Mr H.

Jensen, Mr N.

Jensen, Mr S.

Jermyn, Miss A.

Johannesen, Mr B. J.

Johanson, Mr J.

Johansson, Mr E.

Johansson, Mr G.

Johansson, Mr K.

Johansson, Mr M.

Johansson, Mr N.

Johansson, Mr O.

Johansson Palmqvist, Mr O.

Johnson, Mr A.

Johnson, Miss E.

Johnson, Master H.

Johnson, Mrs O.

Johnson, Mr W. C.

Johnston, Mr A. E.

Johnston, Mrs A. E.

Johnston, Miss C.

Johnston, Master W.

Jonkoff, Mr L.

Jonsson, Mr C.

Jonsson, Mr N.

Joseph, Mrs C.

Joseph, Mr M.

Joseph, Miss M.

Jussila, Mr E.

Jussila, Miss K.

Jussila, Mrs M.

Kallio, Mr N.

Kalvik, Mr J.

Karajic, Mr M.

Kareem, Mr J.

Kareem, Mrs J.

Karlsson, Mr E.
Karlsson, Mr J.
Karlsson, Mr N.
Kassem, Mr F.
Katavelas, Mr V.
Keane, Mr A.
Keefe, Mr A.
Kelly, Miss A.
Kelly, Mr James (boarded
  Southampton)
Kelly, Mr James (boarded
  Queenstown)
Kelly, Miss M.
Kennedy, Mr J.
Khalil, Mr B.
Khalil, Mrs B.
Kiernan, Mr J.
Kiernan, Mr P.
Kilgannon, Mr T.
Kink, Miss M.
Kink, Mr V.
Kink-Heilmann, Mr A.
Kink-Heilmann, Mrs A.
Kink-Heilmann, Miss L.
Klasen, Miss G.
Klasen, Mrs H.
Klasen, Mr K.
Korun, Mr F.
Korun, Miss M.
Kraeff, Mr T.
Krekorian, Mr N.
Lahoud, Mr S.
Laitinen, Miss K.
Laleff, Mr K.
Lam, Mr A.
Lam, Mr L.
Landergren, Miss A.

Lane, Mr P.
Lang, Mr F.
Larsson, Mr A.
Larsson, Mr B.
Larsson-Rondberg, Mr E.
Leeni, Mr F.
Lefebre, Mrs F.
Lefebre, Master H.
Lefebre, Miss I.
Lefebre, Miss J.
Lefebre, Miss M.
Leinonen, Mr A.
Lemberopolos, Mr P. L.
Lemon, Mr D.
Lemon, Miss M.
Leonard, Mr L.
Lester, Mr J.
Lievens, Mr R.
Lindahl. Miss A.
Lindblom, Miss A.
Lindell, Mr E. B.
Lindell, Mrs E. B.
Lindqvist, Mr E.
Linehan, Mr M.
Linhart, Mr W.
Ling, Mr L.
Lithman, Mr S.
Lobb, Mr W. A.
Lobb, Mrs W. A.
Lockyer, Mr E.
Lovell, Mr J. H.
Lulic, Mr N.
Lundahl, Mr J.
Lundin, Miss O.
Lundstrom, Mr T.
Lyntakoff, Mr S.
Mackay, Mr G.

Madigan, Miss M.
Madsen, Mr F.
Maenpaa, Mr M.
Mahon, Miss B.
Maisner, Mr S.
Makinen, Mr K.
Mamee, Mr H.
Mangan, Miss M.
Mannion, Miss M.
Mardirosian, Mr S.
Markun, Mr J.
Markoff, Mr M.
Masselmani, Mrs F.
Matinoff, Mr N.
McCarthy, Miss C.
McCormack, Mr T. J.
McCoy, Miss Agnes
McCoy, Miss Alice
McCoy, Mr B.
McDermott, Miss B.
McElroy, Mr M.
McGovern, Mrs H.
McGowan, Miss A.
McGowan, Miss K.
McMahon, Mr M.
McNamee, Mr N.
McNamee, Mrs N.
McNeill, Miss B.
Meanwell, Miss M.
Mechan, Mr J.
Meek, Mrs T.
Meo, Mr A.
Mernagh, Mr R.
Midtsjo, Mr K.
Miles, Mr F.
Mineff, Mr I.
Minkov, Mr L.

Mionoff, Mr S.
Mitkov, Mr M.
Mocklare, Miss E.
Moen, Mr S.
Moor, Mrs B.
Moor, Master M.
Moore, Mr L. C.
Moran, Miss B.
Moran, Mr D. J.
Moran, Mr J.
Morley, Mr W.
Morrow, Mr T. R.
Moubarek, Mrs G.
Moubarek, Master G.
Moubarek, Master H.
Moss, Mr A.
Moussa, Mrs M.
Moutal, Mr R.
Mullen, Miss K.
Mulvihill, Miss B.
Murdlin, Mr J.
Murphy, Miss C.
Murphy, Miss M.
Murphy, Miss N.
Myrhman, Mr P.
Naidenoff, Mr P.
Najib, Miss A.
Nakid, Miss M.
Nakid, Mr S.
Nakid, Mrs S.
Nancarrow, Mr W. H.
Nankoff, Mr M.
Nasr, Mr M.
Naughton, Miss H.
Nenkoff, Mr C.
Nicola, Master E.
Nicola, Miss J.

Nieminen, Miss M.

Niklasson, Mr S.

Nilsson, Mr A.

Nilsson, Miss B.

Nilsson, Miss H.

Nirva, Mr I.

Niskanen, Mr J.

Nofal, Mr M.

Nosworthy, Mr R. C.

Nysten, Miss A.

Nysveen, Mr J.

O'Brien, Mr D.

O'Brien, Mr T.

O'Brien, Mrs T.

O'Connell, Mr P.

O'Connor, Mr M.

O'Connor, Mr P.

Odahl, Mr N.

O'Donoghue, Miss B.

O'Driscoll, Miss B.

O'Dwyer, Miss E.

Ohman, Miss V.

O'Keefe, Mr P.

O'Leary, Miss N.

Olsen, Master A.

Olsen, Mr H.

Olsen, Mr K.

Olsen, Mr O.

Olsson, Miss E.

Olsson, Mr N.

Olsvigen, Mr T.

Oreskovic, Miss J.

Oreskovic, Mr L.

Oreskovic, Miss M.

Osen, Mr O.

Osman, Mrs M.

O'Sullivan, Miss B.

Palsson, Master G.

Palsson, Mrs N.

Palsson, Master P.

Palsson, Miss S. V.

Palsson, Miss T. D.

Panula, Master E.

Panula, Mr E. A.

Panula, Master Jaako

Panula, Master Juha

Panula, Mrs J.

Panula, Master U.

Pasic, Mr J.

Patchett, Mr G.

Paulner, Mr U.

Pavlovic, Mr S.

Peacock, Master A.

Peacock, Mrs B.

Peacock, Miss T.

Pearce, Mr E.

Pedersen, Mr O.

Peduzzi, Mr J.

Pekoniemi, Mr E.

Peltomaki, Mr N.

Perkin, Mr J.

Persson, Mr E.

Peters, Miss K.

Petersen, Mr M.

Petranec, Miss M.

Petrov, Mr N.

Petrov, Mr P.

Petterson, Mr J.

Pettersson, Miss E.

Pickard, Mr B.

Plotcharsky, Mr V.

Pokrnic, Mr M.

Pokrnic, Mr T.

Radeff, Mr A.

Rasmussen, Mrs R.

Razi, Mr R.

Reed, Mr J. G.

Rekic, Mr T.

Reynolds, Mr H. J.

Rice, Master Albert

Rice, Master Arthur

Rice, Master Eric

Rice, Master Eugene

Rice, Master G.

Rice, Mrs W.

Riihivuori, Miss S.

Rintamaki, Mr M.

Riordan, Miss H.

Risien, Mr S.

Risien, Mrs S.

Robins, Mr A. A.

Robins, Mrs A. A.

Rogers, Mr W. J.

Rommetvedt, Mr K.

Rosblom, Miss S.

Rosblom, Mr V.

Rosblom, Mrs V.

Roth, Miss S.

Rouse, Mr R. H.

Rush, Mr A.

Ryan, Mr E.

Ryan, Mr P.

Saad, Mr A.

Saad, Mr K.

Saade, Mr J.

Sadlier, Mr M.

Sadowitz, Mr H.

Sage, Master A.

Sage, Miss C.

Sage, Miss D.

Sage, Mr D.

Sage, Miss E.

Sage, Mr F.

Sage, Mr G.

Sage, Mr J. G.

Sage, Mrs J.

Sage, Miss S.

Sage, Master T.

Salander, Mr K.

Salkjelsvik, Miss A.

Salonen, Mr J.

Samaan, Mr E.

Samaan, Mr H.

Samaan, Mr Y.

Sandstrom, Miss B.

Sandstrom, Mrs H.

Sandstrom, Miss M.

Sap, Mr J.

Sather, Mr S.

Saundercock, Mr W.

Sawyer, Mr F. C.

Scanlan, Mr J.

Sdycoff, Mr T.

Shaughnessy, Mr P.

Sheerlinckx, Mr J.

Shellard, Mr F.

Shine, Miss E.

Shorney, Mr C.

Simmons, Mr J.

Sirayanian, Mr O.

Sirota, Mr M.

Sivic, Mr H.

Sivola, Mr A.

Sjoblom, Miss A.

Skoog, Master H.

Skoog, Master K.

Skoog, Miss Mabel

Skoog, Miss Margit

Skoog, Mr W.

Skoog, Mrs W.

Slabenov, Mr P.

Slocovski, Mr S.

Smiljanic, Mr M.

Smith, Mr T.

Smyth, Miss J.

Soholt, Mr P.

Somerton, Mr F.

Spector, Mr W.

Spinner, Mr H. J.

Stanev, Mr I.

Stankovic, Mr I.

Stanley, Miss A.

Stanley, Mr E.

Storey, Mr T.

Stoychoff, Mr I.

Strandberg, Miss I.

Stranden, Mr J.

Strilic, Mr I.

Strom, Miss S.

Strom, Mrs W.

Sunderland, Mr V.

Sundman, Mr J. J.

Sutehall, Mr H.

Svensson, Mr J.

Svensson, Mr J. C.

Svensson, Mr O.

Tenglin, Mr G.

Theobald, Mr T.

Thomas, Master A.

Thomas, Mrs A.

Thomas, Mr C. P.

Thomas, Mr J.

Thomas, Mr T.

Thomson, Mr A.

Thorneycroft, Mr P.

Thorneycroft, Mrs P.

Tikkanen, Mr J.

Tobin, Mr R.

Todoroff, Mr L.

Tomlin, Mr E.

Torber, Mr E.

Torfa, Mr A.

Tornqvist, Mr W.

Toufik, Mr N.

Touma, Mrs D.

Touma, Master G.

Touma, Miss M.

Turcin, Mr S.

Turja, Miss A.

Turkula, Mrs H.

van Billiard, Mr A.

van Billiard, Master J.

van Billiard, Master W.

Van den Steen, Mr L.

Van de Velde, Mr J. J.

Vandercruyssen, Mr V.

Vanderplanke, Miss A.

Vanderplanke, Mr J.

Vanderplanke, Mrs J.

Vanderplanke, Mr L.

Van de Valle, Mr N.

Van Impe, Miss C.

Van Impe, Mr J. B.

Van Impe, Mrs J. B.

Van Melkebeke, Mr P.

Vartanian, Mr D.

Vendel, Mr O.

Vestrom, Miss H.

Vook, Mr J.

Waelens, Mr A.

Ware, Mr F.

Warren, Mr C. W.

Webber, Mr J.
Wennerstrom, Mr A.
Whabee, Mrs G.
Widegren, Mr C.
Wiklund, Mr J.
Wiklund, Mr K.
Wilkes, Mrs J.
Willer, Mr A.
Willey, Mr E.
Williams, Mr H. H.
Williams, Mr L.
Windelov, Mr E.
Wirz, Mr A.
Wiseman, Mr P.
Wittevrongel, Mr C.
Yasbeck, Mr A.
Yasbeck, Mrs A.
Youssef, Mr B.
Youssef, Mr G.
Yousif, Mr W.
Zabour, Miss H.
Zabour, Miss T.
Zakarian, Mr M.
Zakarian, Mr O.
Zimmermann, Mr L.

MUSICIANS

Brailey, Mr W.
Bricoux, Mr R.
Clarke, Mr J.
Hartley, Mr W.
Hume, Mr J.
Krins, Mr G.
Taylor, Mr P.
Woodward, Mr J.

CREW

Smith, Mr E. J. (Captain)
Wilde, Mr H. T. (Chief Officer)
Murdoch, Mr W. M. (First Officer)
Lightoller, Mr C. H. (Second Officer)
Pitman, Mr H. J. (Third Officer)
Boxhall, Mr J. G. (Fourth Officer)
Lowe, Mr H. G. (Fifth Officer)
Moody, Mr J. P. (Sixth Officer)
O'Loughlin, Dr W. (Surgeon)
Simpson, Dr J. (Assistant Surgeon)
Hutchinson, Mr J. (Joiner)
Maxwell, Mr J. (Carpenter)
Nichols, Mr A. (Boatswain)
Haines, Mr A. (Boatswain's Mate)
Bailey, Mr J. (Master-at-Arms)
King, Mr W. (Master-at-Arms)
Phillips, Mr J. G. (Telegraphist)
Bride, Mr H. S. (Assistant Telegraphist)

QUARTERMASTERS

Bright, Mr A.
Hichens, Mr R.
Humphrey, Mr S.
Olliver, Mr A.
Perkis, Mr W.
Rowe, Mr G.
Wynn, Mr W.

LOOKOUT MEN

Evans, Mr A. F.
Fleet, Mr F.

Hogg, Mr G.
Jewell, Mr A.
Lee, Mr R.
Symons, Mr G.

ABLE SEAMEN

Anderson, Mr J.
Archer, Mr E.
Bradley, Mr F.
Brice, Mr W.
Buley, Mr E.
Clench, Mr F.
Clench, Mr G.
Couch, Mr F.
Davis, Mr S.
Evans, Mr F.
Forward, Mr J.
Holman, Mr H.
Hopkins, Mr R.
Horswell, Mr A. E. J.
Jones, Mr T.W.
Lucas, Mr W.
Lyons, Mr W.
Matherson, Mr D.
McCarthy, Mr W.
McGough, Mr G.
Moore, Mr G. A.
Osman, Mr F.
Pascoe, Mr C.
Peters, Mr W. C.
Poingdestre, Mr J.
Scarrott, Mr J.
Smith, Mr W.
Taylor, Mr C.
Terrell, Mr B.
Vigott, Mr P.
Weller, Mr W.

ENGINEERS

Bell, Mr J.
Coy, Mr F.
Creese, Mr H.
Dodd, Mr E. C.
Dodds, Mr H.
Dyer, Mr H.
Farquharson, Mr W.
Fraser, Mr J.
Harrison, Mr N.
Harvey, Mr H.
Hesketh, Mr J.
Hodge, Mr C.
Hodgkinson, Mr L.
Hosking, Mr G.
Kemp, Mr T.
Mackie, Mr W.
McReynolds, Mr W.
Millar, Mr R.
Millar, Mr T.
Moyes, Mr W.
Parsons, Mr F.
Shepherd, Mr J.
Smith, Mr J.
Ward, Mr A.
Wilson, Mr B.

LEADING FIREMEN

Barrett, Mr F.
Davies, Mr T.
Ferris, Mr W.
Ford, Mr T.
Hendrickson, Mr C.
Keegan, Mr J.
Mason, Mr J.

Mayo, Mr W. P.
Pugh, Mr P.
Small, Mr W.
Threlfall, Mr T.
Ward, Mr J.
Webber, Mr F.

FIREMEN

Abrams, Mr W.
Adams, Mr R.
Allen, Mr H.
Bailey, Mr G.
Barlow, Mr C.
Barnes, Mr C.
Barnes, Mr F.
Barrett, Mr F. W.
Beauchamp, Mr G.
Bendell, Mr F.
Bennett, Mr G.
Benville, Mr E.
Bessant, Mr W.
Biddlecombe, Mr C.
Biggs, Mr E.
Black, Mr A.
Black, Mr D.
Blackman, Mr H.
Blake, Mr T.
Blaney, Mr J.
Blann, Mr E.
Bradley, Mr P.
Brown, Mr J. J.
Brown, Mr J.
Burroughs, Mr A.
Burton, Mr E. J.
Butt, Mr W.
Camner, Mr J.

Carter, Mr J.
Cherrett, Mr W.
Chorley, Mr J.
Clark, Mr W.
Collins, Mr S.
Combes, Mr G.
Cooper, Mr H.
Copperthwaite, Mr B.
Corcoran, Mr D.
Couper, Mr R.
Crimmins, Mr J.
Cross, Mr W.
Cunningham, Mr B.
Curtis, Mr A.
Diaper, Mr J.
Dilley, Mr J.
Doel, Mr F.
Doyle, Mr L.
Dymond, Mr F.
Flaherty, Mr E.
Fraser, Mr J.
Geer, Mr A.
Godley, Mr G.
Golder, Mr M.
Graham, Mr T.
Graves, Mr S.
Grodidge, Mr E.
Hagan, Mr J.
Hall, Mr J.
Hallett, Mr G.
Hands, Mr B.
Hannam, Mr G.
Harris, Mr E.
Harris, Mr F.
Hart, Mr T.
Head, Mr A.
Hodges, Mr W.

Hosgood, Mr R.

Hunt, Mr T.

Hurst, Mr C.

Hurst, Mr W.

Instance, Mr T.

Jacobson, Mr J.

James, Mr T.

Jarvis, Mr W.

Joas, Mr N.

Judd, Mr C.

Kaspar, Mr F.

Kemish, Mr G.

Kerr, Mr T.

Kinsella, Mr L.

Knowles, Mr T.

Lahy, Mr T.

Light, Mr C.

Light, Mr W.

Lindsay, Mr W. C.

Lloyd, Mr W.

Major, Mr W.

Marrett, Mr G.

Marsh, Mr F. C.

Mason, Mr F.

May, Mr A.

May, Mr A. W.

Mayzes, Mr T.

McAndrew, Mr T.

McAndrews, Mr W.

McCastlen, Mr W.

McGarvey, Mr E.

McGaw, Mr E.

McGregor, Mr J.

McQuillan, Mr W.

McRae, Mr W.

Milford, Mr G.

Mintram, Mr W.

Moore, Mr J.

Morgan, Mr T.

Murdock, Mr W.

Nettleton, Mr G.

Noon, Mr J.

Norris, Mr J.

Noss, Mr B.

Noss, Mr H.

Nutbean, Mr W.

Oliver, Mr H.

Othen, Mr C.

Paice, Mr R. C.

Painter, Mr C.

Painter, Mr F.

Pearse, Mr J.

Podesta, Mr J.

Pond, Mr G.

Priest, Mr A.

Pusey, Mr R. W.

Reeves, Mr F.

Rice, Mr C.

Richards, Mr J.

Rickman, Mr G.

Roberts, Mr G.

Sangster, Mr C.

Saunders, Mr T.

Saunders, Mr W.

Scott, Mr A.

Self, Mr E.

Senior, Mr H.

Shea, Mr T.

Shiers, Mr A.

Smither, Mr H. J.

Snellgrove, Mr G.

Sparkman, Mr H.

Stanbrook, Mr A.

Street, Mr T.

Stubbs, Mr H.
Sullivan, Mr S.
Taylor, Mr John
Taylor, Mr James
Taylor, Mr T.
Taylor, Mr W. H.
Thomas, Mr J.
Thompson, Mr J.
Thresher, Mr G.
Tizard, Mr A.
Triggs, Mr R.
Turley, Mr R.
van der Brugge, Mr W.
Vear, Mr H.
Vear, Mr W.
Wardner, Mr F.
Wateridge, Mr E.
Watson, Mr W.
Williams, Mr E.
Williams, Mr R.
Witcher, Mr A.
Witt, Mr H.
Wyeth, Mr J.
Young, Mr F.

TRIMMERS

Allen, Mr E. F.
Avery, Mr J. F.
Bevis, Mr J.
Billows, Mr J.
Binstead, Mr W.
Blake, Mr P.
Brewer, Mr H.
Brooks, Mr J.
Calderwood, Mr H.
Carr, Mr R. S.

Casey, Mr T.
Cavell, Mr G.
Coe, Mr H.
Cooper, Mr J.
Cotton, Mr A.
Crabb, Mr H.
Dawson, Mr J.
Dickson, Mr W.
Dillon, Mr T.
Dore, Mr A.
Eagle, Mr A. J.
Elliott, Mr E.
Evans, Mr W.
Ferrari, Mr A.
Ford, Mr H.
Fredericks, Mr W.
Fryer, Mr A.
Gordon, Mr J.
Gosling, Mr B.
Gosling, Mr S.
Green, Mr G.
Harris, Mr F.
Haslin, Mr J.
Hebb, Mr A.
Hemming, Mr S.
Hill, Mr J.
Hinton, Mr W. S.
Hunt, Mr A.
Ingram, Mr C.
Kearl, Mr G.
Lee, Mr H.
Long, Mr F.
Long, Mr W.
Maskell, Mr L.
McGann, Mr J.
McIntyre, Mr W.
Mitchell, Mr L.

Moore, Mr R.
Morrell, Mr R.
Morris, Mr W.
O'Connor, Mr J.
Pelham, Mr G.
Perry, Mr E.
Perry, Mr H.
Preston, Mr T. C.
Proudfoot, Mr R.
Read, Mr J.
Reed, Mr R.
Saunders, Mr W.
Sheath, Mr F.
Shillaber, Mr C.
Skeats, Mr W.
Smith, Mr E. G.
Snooks, Mr W.
Snow, Mr E.
Steel, Mr R.
Stocker, Mr H.
Webb, Mr S.
White, Mr F.
White, Mr W. G.
Wilton, Mr W.
Witt, Mr F.
Woods, Mr H.

GREASERS

Baines, Mr R.
Bannon, Mr J.
Beattie, Mr J.
Bott, Mr W.
Castleman, Mr E.
Couch, Mr J.
Eastman, Mr C.
Fay, Mr T.

Gardner, Mr F.
Goree, Mr F.
Gregory, Mr D.
Jago, Mr J.
Jukes, Mr J.
Kanchensen, Mr F.
Kearl, Mr C. H.
Kelly, Mr J.
Kirkham, Mr J.
McInerney, Mr T.
Moores, Mr R.
Morris, Mr A.
Olive, Mr C.
Pallas, Mr T.
Phillips, Mr G.
Pitfield, Mr W.
Prangnell, Mr G.
Ranger, Mr T.
Scott, Mr F.
Self, Mr A.
Stafford, Mr M.
Tozer, Mr J.
Veal, Mr A.
White, Mr A.
Woodford, Mr F.

STOREKEEPERS

Foley, Mr J.
Foster, Mr A.
Kenzler, Mr A.
Kieran, Mr M.
Morgan, Mr W.
Newman, Mr C.
Parsons, Mr E.
Prentice, Mr F.
Ricks, Mr C.

Rogers, Mr E. J.
Rudd, Mr H.
Thompson, Mr H.
Williams, Mr A.

MESS STEWARDS

Blake, Mr S.
Coleman, Mr J.
Fitzpatrick, Mr C. W.
Gumery, Mr G.
Mathias, Mr M.
Tamlyn, Mr F.

STEWARDS

Abbott, Mr E. O.
Ahier, Mr P.
Akerman, Mr J.
Akermann, Mr A.
Allan, Mr R.
Allen, Mr F.
Allsop, Mr F.
Anderson, Mr W.
Andrews, Mr C. E.
Ashe, Mr H.
Back, Mr C.
Baggott, Mr A.
Bagley, Mr E.
Bailey, Mr G.
Ball, Mr P.
Barker, Mr E.
Barker, Mr R. L. (Assistant Purser)
Barlow, Mr G.
Barrett, Mr A.
Barringer, Mr A. W.
Barrows, Mr W.

Barton, Mr S.
Baxter, Mr T.
Beedem, Mr G.
Benham, Mr F.
Bessant, Mr E.
Best, Mr A.
Bishop, Mr W.
Bogie, Mr L.
Bond, Mr W. J.
Boothby, Mr W.
Boston, Mr W.
Boughton, Mr B.
Boyd, Mr J.
Boyes, Mr J. H.
Bradshaw, Mr J.
Brewster, Mr G.
Bristow, Mr H.
Bristow, Mr R.
Brookman, Mr J.
Broom, Mr H.
Broome, Mr A.
Brown, Mr E.
Brown, Mr W.
Bulley, Mr H.
Bunnell, Mr W.
Burke, Mr R.
Burke, Mr W.
Burr, Mr E. S.
Burrage, Mr A.
Butt, Mr R.
Butterworth, Mr J.
Byrne, Mr J. E.
Carney, Mr W.
Cartwright, Mr E. J.
Casswill, Mr C.
Cave, Mr H.
Cecil, Mr C.

Chapman, Mr J.
Charman, Mr J.
Cheverton, Mr W.
Chitty, Mr A.
Christmas, Mr H.
Clark, Mr T.
Coleman, Mr A.
Conway, Mr P. W.
Cook, Mr G.
Corben, Mr E.
Cox, Mr W.
Crafter, Mr F.
Crawford, Mr A.
Crisp, Mr A. H.
Crispin, Mr W.
Crosbie, Mr J.
Crowe, Mr G. F.
Crumplin, Mr C.
Cullen, Mr C.
Cunningham, Mr A.
Daniels, Mr S.
Dashwood, Mr W.
Davies, Mr G.
Davies, Mr R.
Dean, Mr G.
Deeble, Mr A.
Derrett, Mr A.
Deslands, Mr P.
Dineage, Mr J.
Dodd, Mr G. (Chief Second
  Steward)
Dolby, Mr J.
Donoghue, Mr T.
Doughty, Mr N.
Dunford, Mr W.
Dyer, Mr W.
Edbroke, Mr F.

Ede, Mr G. B.
Edge, Mr J. W.
Edwards, Mr C.
Egg, Mr W.
Ennis, Mr W.
Etches, Mr S.
Fairall, Mr H.
Faulkner, Mr W.
Fellows, Mr A. J.
Finch, Mr H.
Fletcher, Mr P.
Foley, Mr W.
Ford, Mr E.
Ford, Mr F.
Fox, Mr W.
Franklin, Mr A.
Freeman, Mr E.
Geddes, Mr R.
Gibbons, Mr J. W.
Gill, Mr J. S.
Goshawk, Mr A.
Gunn, Mr J.
Guy, Mr E.
Halford, Mr R.
Hamblyn, Mr E.
Hamilton, Mr E.
Harding, Mr A.
Hardy, Mr J.
Harris, Mr C.
Harris, Mr C. W.
Harris, Mr E.
Harrison, Mr A.
Hart, Mr J. E.
Hartnell, Mr F.
Hawkesworth, Mr J.
Hawksworth, Mr W.
Hayter, Mr A.

Heinen, Mr J.

Hendy, Mr E.

Hewitt, Mr T.

Hill, Mr H.

Hill, Mr J.

Hinckley, Mr G.

Hiscock, Mr S.

Hoare, Mr L. J.

Hogg, Mr C. W.

Hogue, Mr E.

Holland, Mr T.

Holloway, Mr S.

Hopkins, Mr F.

House, Mr W.

Howell, Mr A. A.

Hughes, Mr W. T.

Humby, Mr F.

Humphreys, Mr T. H.

Hyland, Mr J.

Ide, Mr H.

Ingrouille, Mr H.

Jackson, Mr J.

Janaway, Mr W.

Jenner, Mr H.

Jensen, Mr C. V.

Johnson, Mr J.

Jones, Mr A.

Jones, Mr A. E.

Jones, Mr R.

Keene, Mr P.

Kelland, Mr T.

Kerley, Mr W.

Ketchley, Mr H.

Kiernan, Mr J.

King, Mr A.

Kingscote, Mr W.

Kitching, Mr A.

Knight, Mr G.

Knight, Mr L.

Lacey, Mr B.

Lake, Mr A.

Lake, Mr W.

Latimer, Mr A. (Chief Steward)

Lawrence, Mr A.

Lefebvre, Mr P.

Leonard, Mr M.

Levett, Mr G.

Lewis, Mr A.

Light, Mr C.

Littlejohn, Mr A.

Lloyd, Mr H.

Longmuir, Mr J.

Lucas, Mr W.

Lydiatt, Mr C.

Mabey, Mr J.

Mackay, Mr C.

Mackie, Mr G.

Major, Mr T. E.

Mantle, Mr R.

Marks, Mr J.

Marriott, Mr J.

McCarthy, Mr F.

McCawley, Mr T. W.

McElroy, Mr H. (Purser)

McGrady, Mr J.

McMicken, Mr A.

McMullen, Mr J.

McMurray, Mr W.

Mellor, Mr A.

Middleton, Mr M.

Mishelany, Mr A.

Moore, Mr A. E.

Morris, Mr F.

Moss, Mr W.

Muller, Mr L.
Mullin, Mr T.
Nicholls, Mr S.
Nichols, Mr A.D.
Nichols, Mr W.
O'Connor, Mr T. P.
Olive, Mr E.
Orpet, Mr W. H.
Osborne, Mr W. E.
Owen, Mr L.
Pacey, Mr R.
Paintin, Mr J.
Parsons, Mr R.
Pearce, Mr A.
Pearcey, Mr A.
Pennell, Mr F.
Penny, Mr W. C.
Penrose, Mr J.
Perkins, Mr S.
Perren, Mr W.
Perriton, Mr H.
Petty, Mr E.
Pfropper, Mr R.
Philimore, Mr H.
Pook, Mr P.
Port, Mr F.
Prideaux, Mr J.
Prior, Mr H.
Pugh, Mr A.
Pusey, Mr J.
Pryce, Mr W.
Randall, Mr F. H.
Ransom, Mr J.
Rattenbury, Mr W.
Ray, Mr F.
Reed, Mr C. S.
Revell, Mr W.

Rice, Mr P.
Ridout, Mr W.
Rimmer, Mr G.
Roberts, Mr H.
Robertson, Mr G.
Robinson, Mr J. W.
Rogers, Mr M.
Rowe, Mr E.
Rule, Mr S. J.
Russell, Mr R.
Ryan, Mr T.
Ryerson, Mr W.
Samuel, Mr O.
Saunders, Mr D.
Savage, Mr C. J.
Scott, Mr J.
Scovell, Mr R.
Sedunary, Mr S. F.
Seward, Mr W.
Shea, Mr J.
Siebert, Mr S.
Simmons, Mr F. G.
Sivier, Mr W.
Skinner, Mr E.
Slight, Mr H.
Smillie, Mr J.
Smith, Mr C. E.
Smith, Mr F.
Smith, Mr R.
Stagg, Mr J.
Stebbings, Mr S.
Stewart, Mr J.
Stone, Mr E.
Stone, Mr E.T.
Stroud, Mr E.
Stroud, Mr H. J.
Strugnell, Mr J.

Swan, Mr W.
Symonds, Mr J.
Talbot, Mr G.
Taylor, Mr C.
Taylor, Mr L.
Taylor, Mr W.
Terrell, Mr F.
Teuton, Mr T.
Thaler, Mr M. D.
Thessinger, Mr A.
Thomas, Mr A.
Thomas, Mr B.
Toms, Mr F.
Tucker, Mr B.
Turner, Mr L.
Veal, Mr T.
Walpole, Mr J.
Ward, Mr E.
Ward, Mr P.
Ward, Mr W.
Wareham, Mr R. A.
Warwick, Mr T.
Watson, Mr W.
Weatherston, Mr T.
Webb, Mr B.
Wheat, Mr J.
Wheelton, Mr E.
White, Mr J.
White, Mr L.
Whiteley, Mr T.
Whitford, Mr A.
Widgery, Mr J.
Williams, Mr W. J.
Willis, Mr W.
Winser, Mr R.
Witter, Mr J. W.
Wittman, Mr H.

Wood, Mr J.
Wormald, Mr F.
Wrapson, Mr F.
Wright, Mr F.
Wright, Mr W.
Yearsley, Mr H.
Yoshack, Mr J.

STEWARDESSES

Bennett, Mrs M.
Bliss, Mrs E.
Caton, Miss A.
Gold, Mrs K.
Gregson, Miss M.
Jessop, Miss V.
Lavington, Miss B.
Leather, Mrs E.
Marsden, Miss E.
Martin, Mrs A.
McLaren, Mrs H.
Pritchard, Mrs A.
Roberts, Mrs M.
Robinson, Mrs A.
Sloan, Miss M.
Slocombe, Mrs M.
Smith, Miss K.
Snape, Mrs L.
Stap, Miss S.
Wallis, Mrs C.
Wallis, Mrs R.

GALLEY STAFF

Allen, Mr G.
Ayling, Mr G.
Barker, Mr A.

Barnes, Mr F.
Barrow, Mr C.
Bedford, Mr W.
Beere, Mr W.
Bochatay, Mr J.
Buckley, Mr H.
Bull, Mr W.
Burgess, Mr C. R.
Caunt, Mr W.
Chitty, Mr G.
Colgan, Mr J.
Collins, Mr J.
Coombs, Mr C.
Davies, Mr J. J.
Ellis, Mr J.
Farendon, Mr E.
Feltham, Mr G.
Giles, Mr G.
Gill, Mr P.
Gollop, Mr F.
Hall, Mr F.
Hardwick, Mr R.
Hatch, Mr H.
Hensford, Mr H.
Hine, Mr W.
Hutchison, Mr J.
Ings, Mr W.
Johnstone, Mr H.
Jones, Mr H.
Joughin, Mr C. J.
Kennel, Mr C.
King, Mr G.
Leader, Mr A.
Locke, Mr A.
Lovell, Mr J.
Martin, Mr F.
Maynard, Mr M.

Maytum, Mr A.
Mills, Mr C.
Neal, Mr H.
Orr, Mr J.
Parker, Mr T.
Platt, Mr W.
Proctor, Mr C. (Chef)
Roberts, Mr F.
Ross, Mr H.
Shaw, Mr H.
Simmons, Mr A.
Simmons, Mr W.
Slight, Mr W.
Smith, Mr C.
Smith, Mr J.
Stubbings, Mr H.
Thorley, Mr W.
Topp, Mr T.
Wake, Mr T.
Welch, Mr W. H.
Wiltshire, Mr W.
Windebank, Mr A.

RESTAURANT STAFF

Allaria, Sig. B.
Asperlach, Mr G.
Bamfi, Sig U.
Basilico, Sig. G.
Bazzi, Sig. N.
Bernardi, Sig. B.
Bertoldo, Sig. F.
Beux, Sig. D.
Bietrix, Mr G.
Blumet, Mr J.
Bochet, Sig. P.
Bolhuis, Mr H.

Bowker, Miss R.
Casali, Sig. G.
Charboisson, Mr A.
Cornaire, Mr M.
Coutin, Mr A.
Crovella, Sig. L.
Debreucq, Mr M.
Desvernine, Mr L.
Donati, Sig. I.
Dornier, Mr L.
Fei, Sig. C.
Gatti, Sig. G. A. (Manager)
Gilardino, Sig. V.
Grosclaude, Mr G.
Jaillet, Mr H.
Janin, Mr C.
Jeffery, Mr W.
Jouannault, Mr G.
Martin, Miss M.
Marsico, Sig. G.
Mattman, Mr A.
Maugé, Mr P.
Monoros, Mr J.
Monteverdi, Mr G.
Nannini, Sig. F.
Pachera, Mr J.
Pedrini, Sig. A.
Peracchio, Sig. A.
Peracchio, Sig. S.
Perotti, Sig. A.
Phillips, Mr W.
Piatti, Mr L.
Piazzo, Sig. P.
Price, Mr E.
Ratti, Sig. E.
Ricaldone, Sig. R.
Rigozzi, Sig. A.

Rotta, Sig. A.
Rousseau, Mr P. (Chef)
Saccaggi, Sig. G.
Salussolia, Sig. G.
Sesea, Sig. G.
Testoni, Sig. E.
Tietz, Mr C.
Turvey, Mr C.
Urbini, Sig. R.
Valvassori, Sig. E.
Vicat, Mr A.
Villvarlange, Mr P.
Vine, Mr H.
Vioni, Sig R.
Vogelin-Dubach, Mr H.
Zanetti, Mr M.
Zarracchi, Sig. L.

POSTAL CLERKS

Gwinn, Mr W.
March, Mr J.
Smith, Mr J.
Williamson, Mr J.
Woody, Mr O.

BARBERS

Klein, Mr H.
Weikman, Mr A. H.
White, Mr A.

ELECTRICIANS

Allsop, Mr A.
Chisnall, Mr G.
Ervine, Mr A.

Fitzpatrick, Mr H.
Jupe, Mr H.
Kelly, Mr W.
Middleton, Mr A.
Sloan, Mr P.

Duffy, Mr W.
King, Mr W.
Rice, Mr R. J.
Rous, Mr A.
Turner, Mr G.

CLERKS

Ashcroft, Mr A.
Campbell, Mr D.

WINDOW CLEANERS

Harder, Mr W.
Sawyer, Mr R.

DISCHARGED CREW

The following signed on as crew members but, for various reasons, were not on board the *Titanic* at the time of collision:

Blake, Mr C.
Bowman, Mr F. T.
Brewer, Mr B.
Burrows, Mr W.
Carter, Mr F.
Coffey, Mr J.
Dawes, Mr W.
Dawkins, Mr P.
Di Napoli, Mr E.
Ettlinger, Mr P.
Fish, Mr B.
Fisher, Mr R.

Haveling, Mr A.
Holden, Mr F.
Kilford, Mr P.
Manby, Mr A.
Mew, Mr W.
Penney, Mr V.
Sartori, Mr L.
Shaw, Mr J.
Sims, Mr W.
Slade, Mr A.
Slade, Mr B.
Slade, Mr T.

GLOSSARY

TERMS

Abaft – Nearer the stern than.

Aft – Towards the stern of a ship.

Amidships – In the middle of a ship.

Berth – A ship's place at a wharf. Also a sleeping-place on board ship.

Bow – The fore-end of a ship.

Bridge – The raised platform from where a ship is steered.

Bulkhead – The upright partition dividing a ship's watertight compartments.

Collapsible – A boat with canvas sides, allowing for easy storage.

C.Q.D. – The international maritime distress call, standing for 'Come Quick, Danger.'

Crow's nest – A shelter for look-outs fixed to the mast-head of a ship.

Davit – One of a pair of cranes used for hanging or lowering lifeboats.

Dry-dock – A basin from which water has been pumped out in order to allow the building or repair of a ship.

Falls – The ropes of hoisting-tackle, used in lowering lifeboats.

Forward – Towards the bow.

Gunwale – The upper edge of a boat's side.

Hull – A ship's frame.

Knot – Unit of speed equivalent to one nautical mile per hour. There are 6,080ft in a nautical mile.

Painter – Rope attached to the bow of a boat for making it fast to a ship or a stake.

Poop – The after-most and highest deck on the stern of the ship.

Port – The left-hand side of a ship, looking forward.

Slipway – The artificial slope down which a ship is launched.

Starboard – The right-hand side of a ship, looking forward.

Steerage – The area of a ship allocated to the passengers paying the cheapest fares. In the case of the *Titanic*, this was third-class.

Stern – The rear part of a ship.

Stoker – A member of the ship's crew who tends the furnace.

Strake – Continuous line of planking or plates from stem to stern of ship.

Thwart – Oarsman's bench in a rowing boat.

Tiller – The lever fitted to the head of a ship's rudder to aid steering.

SHIPS

Amerika – German liner which reported to the US Navy's Hydrographic Office in Washington at 1.45 p.m. on 14 April that she had passed two large icebergs at 41:27 north 50:8 west.

Baltic – White Star liner which warned the *Titanic* of ice at 1.42 p.m. on 14 April.

Californian – Leyland Line freighter which left Liverpool for Boston on 5 April 1912. Intrigue and speculation continue to surround her lack of response to the stricken *Titanic* despite being less than 20 miles from the sinking vessel. Did she see, but ignore, the *Titanic*'s distress rockets and was she the mystery ship seen on the horizon by some survivors? The *Californian* finally went to the *Titanic*'s aid just after 6 a.m. – nearly four hours after she went down – but by then it was too late. The *Californian* – and her Captain, Stanley Lord – were painted as the villains of the piece by both the US and British inquiries. She was sunk by a German submarine in 1917.

Caronia – Cunard liner journeying east from New York to Liverpool and which was the first to warn the *Titanic* of ice in the vicinity. The *Titanic* received the wireless message at 9 a.m. on 14 April even though it had been sent two days previously.

Carpathia – Mediterranean-bound Cunard liner which, although 58 miles away, sped to the assistance of the *Titanic* and ferried survivors to New York. Like the *Californian*, she was sunk by a German submarine during the First World War.

Frankfurt – German steamer in the area of the sinking but which had difficulty establishing radio contact with the *Titanic*.

Mackay-Bennett – Cable ship which set out from Halifax, Nova Scotia, to retrieve the bodies from the sea. Carrying over 100 coffins, she arrived at the scene of the disaster on 20 April 1912. Corpses with distinguishing features were embalmed and brought back to Halifax for identification but those which had deteriorated beyond recognition were weighted into sacks and buried at sea.

Mesaba – Westbound vessel which reported a number of large icebergs in the area to the *Titanic* at 9.40 p.m. on 14 April. It was the sixth ice warning given to the *Titanic* that day and pinpointed the precise location where the *Titanic* was to meet her doom. Yet because the *Titanic*'s wireless operator, Jack Phillips, was busy dealing with a backlog of messages, this warning was never delivered to either Captain Smith or the bridge.

Minia – Cable ship which assisted the *Mackay-Bennett* in retrieving bodies.

Mount Temple – Westbound Canadian vessel which was some 49 miles west of the *Titanic* at the time of the sinking.

New York – Liner involved in a near-miss with the *Titanic* as the latter left Southampton on 10 April.

Olympic – Sister ship of the *Titanic*, situated about 512 miles west of her at the time of sinking.

Virginian – Allan liner situated some 170 miles from the *Titanic* at midnight on 14/15 April.

PEOPLE AND PLACES

Abelseth, Olaus – Norwegian-born livestock farmer who had settled in South Dakota in 1908. In the autumn of 1911 he visited relatives in Norway, returning home on the *Titanic*. After the sinking he travelled around for a bit before eventually resuming work on his farm. In 1915 he married a Norwegian girl, Anna Grinde, who bore him four children. She lived to be over a hundred (dying in 1978) and he passed away two years later at the age of ninety-two.

Andrews, Miss Kornelia – A native of Hudson, New York State, where she was one of the managers of the City Hospital, sixty-three-year-old Miss Andrews was returning to the United States on the *Titanic* with her sister Anna Hogeboom and their twenty-one-year-old niece Gretchen Longley. They boarded at Southampton and travelled first-class. After the sinking Miss Andrews filed a claim for $480.50 against the White Star Line for a variety of lost possessions including fur coats, antique lamps and 'one velvet hat with ostrich plumes'. She died in December 1913 from pneumonia.

Andrews, Thomas – The nephew of Lord Pirrie, the principal owner of shipbuilders Harland & Wolff, Belfast-born Andrews left school at sixteen to join the firm as an apprentice. By 1910 he had become managing director of Harland & Wolff with special responsibility for design. In his final letter to his wife Elizabeth he wrote: 'The *Titanic* is now about complete and will, I think, do the old firm credit tomorrow when we sail.' One of the last sightings of him was sitting in the sinking ship's smoking room, staring blankly at the wall, his life jacket in front of him. He was thirty-nine.

Asplund, Mrs Selma – Steerage passenger from Sweden who was emigrating with her family to Worcester, Massachusetts. While Mrs Asplund, six-year-old daughter Lillian and baby Felix all survived their ordeal at sea, husband Carl and sons Gustaf, Oscar and Carl were lost. Mrs Asplund died on 15 April 1964 – the fifty-second anniversary of the sinking of the *Titanic*.

Astor, Colonel John Jacob – One of the richest men in the world in 1912 with a personal fortune estimated at $87 million. At the age of forty-six, he had scandalized New York society by choosing as his second wife Madeleine Force, who, at eighteen, was younger than his son Vincent. The newlyweds had fled to Egypt to escape the gossip but headed back to New York on the *Titanic* when Madeleine discovered that she was pregnant. After helping his wife into a lifeboat, he met his fate with great dignity in company with his Airedale terrier, Kitty. In August 1912 Astor's widow gave birth to a son, whom she named after him.

Astor, Mrs Madeleine – During the First World War, she married New Yorker William K. Dick (thus relinquishing all claim to the Astor fortune) and had two sons by him, but the union ended in divorce in 1933. That same year she married professional boxer Enzo Firemonte but that marriage lasted just five years before it too ended in divorce. She died in Palm Beach, Florida, in 1940, aged forty-seven.

Barrett, Frederick – Liverpool-born crew member who had previously served on the *New York*. As a leading fireman on the *Titanic*, he earned a monthly wage of £6. 10s. Shortly after testifying to the Board of Trade Inquiry, twenty-eight-year-old Barrett was back at sea working on the *Titanic*'s sister ship, the *Olympic*.

Beane, Edward – Although born in Norwich, England, he worked in New York as a bricklayer before returning to his home town to marry wife Ethel in April 1912. A few days later he returned to New York with his bride on board the *Titanic*. They travelled second-class and both were rescued in lifeboat No. 13. Mr Beane died in 1948, aged sixty-seven, but his wife lived until 1983, reaching the age of ninety.

Beesley, Lawrence – Educated at Cambridge, Beesley was

given his first teaching post at Wirksworth Grammar School, Derbyshire. By 1912 he was a science master at Dulwich College in south London, and provided the press with one of the most graphic accounts of the *Titanic* disaster. He died in 1967, aged eighty-nine.

Bentham, Miss Lillian – One of a party of eleven Americans on their way home from a trip to Europe, she travelled second-class from Southampton, paying £13 for her ticket. After her rescue, she was unable to be met in New York by her family because her brother had contracted typhoid. In 1918 Lillian married John Black. She died in 1977.

Bishop, Dickinson – Wealthy resident of Dowagiac, Michigan, who was returning to the US after honeymooning in Europe with his second wife Helen. They escaped on the first boat to leave the *Titanic* and twenty-five-year-old Bishop was thereafter the subject of unfounded rumours that he had dressed as a woman to secure his place in the boat. Fortune rarely smiled on them again. The baby that Helen was carrying at the time of the sinking died when just two days old, they were

caught up in an earthquake, and then Helen was involved in a car crash from which she never fully recovered. They were divorced in 1916 and she died later that year. He quickly remarried and lived until 1961.

Bjornstrom-Steffanson, Lt. Mauritz Hakan – A military man as well as being a leading light in the Swedish pulp industry, twenty-eight-year-old Bjornstrom-Steffanson paid £26 11s. for his first-class ticket. He was drinking hot lemonade in the first-class smoking room immediately prior to the collision. He and other survivors later presented an inscribed silver cup to Captain Rostron and medals to each of the 320 members of the *Carpathia*'s crew in appreciation of their bravery. In 1917 Bjornstrom-Steffanson married Mary Pinchot Eno to whom he had been introduced by fellow *Titanic* survivor Helen Churchill Candee. They set up home in Manhattan but had no children. He died in 1962, nine years after his wife.

Bonnell, Miss Caroline – Aged thirty from Youngstown, Ohio, Miss Bonnell travelled on the *Titanic* with her aunt Lily and the Wick family. She shared cabin C7 with Natalie

Wick. Rescued in lifeboat No. 8, among the wreckage in the water she spotted a man's glove and a baby's bonnet. She later married and had two children. She died in 1950.

Boxhall, Joseph – A twenty-eight-year-old from Hull, Yorkshire, Boxhall was the *Titanic*'s Fourth Officer and the man responsible for calculating the ship's precise position. He survived the disaster and acted as technical consultant on the making of the 1958 film *A Night to Remember*. When he died in 1967, his ashes were scattered at the point where the *Titanic* went down.

Brayton, George – Minnesota-born professional gambler George Brereton sailed on the *Titanic* under the alias of 'Brayton', presumably to avoid detection. Even on the *Carpathia* he tried to involve fellow survivor Charles Stengel in a horse-racing scam. Tragedy dogged his later years. Grieving over the death of their son, his wife shot herself dead in Los Angeles in 1922. Twenty years later in the same house, sixty-seven-year-old Brereton took his own life in similar fashion.

Bride, Harold – Twenty-two-year-old junior wireless operator aboard the *Titanic*, born

in Nunhead, South London. Despite selling his story at the time, he subsequently shunned publicity and went to live in Scotland where he worked as a travelling salesman. He died there quietly in 1956.

Brown, Miss Edith – A native of South Africa, fifteen-year-old Edith Brown was travelling with her sister and father to Seattle, but was the only survivor. Afterwards she went to live in Cape Town and in 1917 married Frederick Thankful Haisman following a whirlwind, six-week romance. They had ten children. She ended her days in Southampton where she died in 1997.

Brown, Mrs Margaret Tobin – Born in Hannibal, Missouri, in 1867 to an Irish immigrant family, she married impoverished miner James Joseph Brown in 1886 and, when he struck it rich, she became one of the most prominent citizens of Denver, Colorado. By 1912, however, they were virtually estranged since he did not share her enthusiasm for the high life. She had been holidaying with the Astors in Cairo when she learnt that her first grandchild was ill. So she booked on the first available ship back to the

United States – the *Titanic*. Her heroics in boat No. 6 and her indomitable spirit made her a national figure. She tried to run for Congress, became a keen supporter of women's rights and in 1932 was awarded the French Legion of Honour. She died in that same year of a brain tumour. Although she has gone down in history as 'Molly' Brown, the name was purely a Hollywood invention, *The Unsinkable Molly Brown* becoming a hit movie starring Debbie Reynolds.

Buckley, Daniel – Twenty-one-year-old from County Cork, he boarded at Queenstown and paid £7 15s. 17d. for his third-class ticket. He survived the *Titanic* but could not survive the First World War and was killed in service in 1918.

Buss, Miss Kate – One of a family of seven from Sittingbourne in Kent, Kate worked in a village grocer's shop owned by her brother Percy. She was going to America to marry her fiancé, Samuel Willis, in San Diego and transported assorted wedding gifts on the *Titanic*. The couple married later in 1912 and had a daughter Sybil. Kate Buss died in 1972, aged ninety-six.

Butt, Major Archibald – Hailing from a prominent Augusta, Georgia, family, Archie Butt graduated from the University of Tennessee in 1888 and went on to work as a journalist in Louisville, Kentucky, and Washington, DC. He joined the United States Army in 1898 as a lieutenant during the Spanish–American War and later became military aide to President Theodore Roosevelt. He held the same post with Roosevelt's successor, William H. Taft, but by 1912 his health had begun to suffer as a result of the stress caused by the ongoing feud between Roosevelt and Taft. To recuperate, Butt took six weeks' leave from the White House and went to Europe with his friend, the artist Frank Millet. Before leaving for Europe, Butt made a will, having apparently been told that he would meet his death on the trip. The return journey was aboard the *Titanic*. Butt hosted a party in the Café Parisien on the evening of the disaster and went down with the ship. He was forty-five.

Candee, Mrs Helen Churchill – A fifty-three-year-old New York writer and lecturer (married to Edward Candee), she journeyed alone on the *Titanic*. Shortly after the collision she gave an antique cameo of her mother to fellow first-class passenger Edward Kent in the belief that he was more likely to survive than her. In the event Kent died and she was rescued. When his body was recovered, the cameo was found on his clothing and returned to Mrs Candee. She eventually died in 1949.

Cardeza, Mrs Charlotte – A wealthy fifty-eight-year-old Philadelphian who, in her younger days, was a noted yachtswoman (twice sailing around the world) and fearless big game hunter. Married to attorney James Cardeza, she sailed on the *Titanic* with her son Thomas and maid Anna Ward, both of whom also survived. They brought with them fourteen trunks, four suitcases, three crates and a medicine chest, the contents including seventy dresses, ten fur coats, thirty-eight feather boas, twenty-two hatpins and ninety-one pairs of gloves. She later filed a fourteen-page claim against the White Star Line for loss of property amounting to $177,352.75. She died in 1939.

Carlisle, Alexander – General manager of shipbuilders Harland & Wolff and the leader of the team that designed the *Titanic*. He retired in 1910.

Carter, Billy – A prominent Philadelphian, aged thirty-six, who travelled with his wife Lucile and children Lucile and William. Their entourage also numbered Mrs Carter's maid, Mr Carter's manservant and his personal chauffeur for his luggage included two dogs and a brand new Renault car. The Carter family survived; the car didn't. He later claimed $5,000 for the loss of the car and $300 for the loss of the dogs. He reached the *Carpathia* before the rest of his family and did not recognize son William, who was hidden under a lady's hat, said to have been placed on his head by his mother in response to an order that no more boys were to be allowed in the lifeboat. Billy Carter died in 1940.

Cavendish, Mrs Julia – Born in Chicago, although she lived much of her life in Staffordshire, England. She was twenty-five when she boarded the *Titanic* with husband Tyrell and her maid Nellie Barber. She and the maid were rescued but Mr Cavendish perished when the ship went down. Mrs Cavendish died in Uttoxeter, Staffordshire, in 1963.

Cherbourg – Town in northern France, the first port of call for the *Titanic* on her transatlantic journey. Having left Southampton an hour late, she arrived at Cherbourg at 6.35 p.m., local time. Twenty-two passengers got off and 274 got on, among them Benjamin Guggenheim, the Duff Gordons and 'Molly' Brown.

Cherry, Miss Gladys – The thirty-year-old cousin of the Countess of Rothes with whom she shared first-class cabin B77 aboard the *Titanic*. After the disaster she married George Pringle and died at Godalming, Surrey, in 1965.

Chevré, Paul – Born in Brussels to French parents in 1867 (his father ran a foundry), Paul Chevré made his name as a sculptor, staging his first exhibition in Paris in 1890. His best-known work is the sculpture of Samuel de Champlain, Canada's founder, which stands in Quebec City. Commissioned by Charles Hays to do a bust of Canadian Prime Minister Sir Wilfrid Laurier for the lobby of the Grand Trunk Pacific Railway's Chateau Laurier Hotel in Ottawa, Chevré joined Hays on the *Titanic* to return to Canada for the hotel's official opening on 26 April 1912. He boarded at Cherbourg and on the evening of the disaster was playing cards in the Café Parisien with Pierre Maréchal, Alfred Omont and Lucien Smith. Chevré survived the night but died in Paris two years later.

Cottam, Harold Thomas – Twenty-one-year-old Nottinghamshire-born wireless operator on the *Carpathia* (for which he was paid £4. 10s. a month plus board) and the man who took the first call for assistance from the *Titanic*. Cottam went on to serve on many other ships and renewed his friendship with *Titanic* operator Harold Bride. He died in 1984.

Crosby, Mrs Catherine – A resident of Milwaukee, she travelled on the *Titanic* with her husband, Captain Edward Gifford Crosby, and their daughter Harriette. Their son Fred stayed behind in the US. Captain Crosby was drowned but Catherine and Harriette were rescued. Catherine Crosby died in 1920, aged seventy-one.

Daly, Eugene – Twenty-nine-year-old steerage passenger from Athlone in Ireland who was emigrating to the US. He played 'Erin's Lament' on his bagpipes as the *Titanic* left Queenstown and later filed a claim for $50 to cover their loss in the sinking.

He settled in New York where he died in 1965.

Daniel, Robert W. – Philadelphia banker who leapt from the sinking ship wearing only a bathrobe and lived to tell a colourful tale. Aboard the rescue ship *Carpathia* he met Mary Eloise Smith whose husband Lucien had gone down with the *Titanic*. Daniel and the newly widowed Mrs Smith struck up a romance and married within two years.

Dodge, Dr Washington – Assessor for the port of San Francisco and a first-class passenger on the *Titanic*. He, his wife and four-year-old son – Washington Jnr – all survived. But in 1919 Dr Dodge suffered a mental breakdown and shot himself.

Douglas, Mrs Mahala – American first-class passenger who travelled with husband Walter and her French maid Berthe Le Roy. She and the maid were rescued, but Mr Douglas was not among the survivors. She later went to live in California and died in 1945 at the age of eighty. She is buried in Cedar Rapids, Ohio.

Drew, Marshall – The son of a Cornish marble sculptor who emigrated to the United States, Marshall was born in Suffolk County, New York. His mother died two weeks after he was born and his aunt and uncle became the boy's adoptive parents. The three sailed on the *Olympic* to England to visit his father and uncle's family, returning to America on the *Titanic*, by which time Marshall was eight years of age. Surviving the ordeal, he married in 1930 and went on to teach fine arts at a New York high school. He died in 1986 and is buried in Rhode Island where the inscription on his headstone reads: 'Teacher, Artist, Friend – Survivor of the Titanic Disaster 15 April 1912'.

Duff Gordon, Sir Cosmo – Eton-educated husband of international dress designer Lucy, Lady Duff Gordon, with whom he travelled on the *Titanic* under the names of Mr and Mrs Morgan. A noted fencer who represented Britain at the 1908 Olympics, allegations about his lack of bravery on the night haunted him right up until his death in 1931 at the age of sixty-eight.

Duff Gordon, Lady Lucy – The daughter of a Toronto engineer, at eighteen she married James Wallace by whom she had a child. They were divorced in 1888, after which she found herself in dire financial straits. To support herself and her child, she set up a dressmaking business and rented a shop in London's West End – 'Maison Lucile'. The shop became so successful that in 1897 she moved to larger premises in Hanover Square. Within three years her enterprise had turned it into one of the leading London fashion houses and branches were subsequently opened in New York and Paris. Work commitments meant that she and Sir Cosmo tended to lead separate lives but they were reunited on the *Titanic* for an urgent business trip to New York which required her to take the first available crossing. Her business hit hard times in the early 1930s and she died in 1935.

Evans, Cyril Furmstone – Wireless operator on the *Californian*.

Fleet, Frederick – Twenty-four-year-old lookout on the *Titanic*, the man who sent the chilling message: 'Iceberg right ahead.' He remained at sea until the 1930s before landing a job as a shipbuilder with Harland & Wolff, the firm that built the *Titanic*. He later found work as a nightwatchman and then sold newspapers on street corners in his native Southampton. In 1965, devastated by the death of his wife, he hanged himself.

Franklin, Philip A. S. – Forty-one-year-old American vice-president of International Mercantile Marine, the parent company of the White Star Line.

Frauenthal, Dr Henry – The son of German immigrants, Frauenthal was born in Pennsylvania. He qualified as a doctor in 1890 and in 1905 set up the Hospital for Joint Diseases in Madison Avenue, New York. On 26 March 1912 he married Clara Heinsheimer in Nice and two weeks later the newlyweds boarded the *Titanic* at Southampton for their return journey to the US. At Cherbourg they were joined by his brother Isaac. All three survived, but Henry's mental health began to suffer and in 1927, aged sixty-four, he committed suicide by jumping from the seventh floor of the hospital he had founded. In his will he requested that his ashes be scattered from the roof of the same hospital building on its fiftieth birthday. This ceremony was duly performed in 1955.

Frauenthal, Isaac – Had travelled to Europe for his brother's wedding. Sailing home on the *Titanic*, he revealed a dream he had experienced shortly before boarding the liner. 'It seemed to me that I was on a big steamship that suddenly crashed into something and began to go down. I saw in the dream as vividly as I could see with open eyes the gradual settling of the ship, and I heard the cries and shouts of frightened passengers.' So when he got out of bed on the night of 14 April and discovered that the *Titanic* had hit an iceberg, he was aware of the impending danger. While his brother insisted that the ship was too big to sink, Isaac masterminded their escape. Isaac, a lawyer, never married and died in Manhattan in 1932.

Frolicher-Stehli, Max – In 1885 he married Margaretha, the daughter of his boss at the Swiss silk factory where he worked as managing clerk. Together they had five children and in 1912, sixty-one-year-old Frolicher-Stehli, accompanied by his wife and daughter Hedwig, sailed on the *Titanic* to visit old friends in the United States and Canada. All three were rescued but he died the following year of heart failure.

Futrelle, Jacques – Born in Pike County, Georgia, to a family of French descent, Futrelle, thirty-seven, was a successful mystery writer when he went down with the *Titanic*. His last novel, *My Lady's Garter*, was published posthumously. Beneath his photo in the book, his wife May wrote: 'To the heroes of the *Titanic*, I dedicate this my husband's book.'

Futrelle, Mrs May – Wife of Jacques. Born in Atlanta, Georgia, she was thirty-five at the time of the sinking. Her son, Jacques Jnr, later became night news editor of the *Washington Post*. May Futrelle died in Massachusetts at the age of ninety-one.

Gibson, Dorothy – twenty-two-year-old model and silent movie star from New York who, in March 1912, sailed with her mother for a holiday in Italy after completing the film *The Easter Bonnet*. But their stay was cut short when the film company wired for her to return to the US. They came home on the *Titanic* and, after escaping in lifeboat No. 7, Dorothy co-wrote and starred in the first *Titanic* movie, *Saved From the Titanic*. This was released on 14 May 1912 – just one month after the disaster – and was heavily criticized for its insensitivity at a time when so many were still coming to terms with their grief. She gave up her acting career shortly afterwards and, following a brief flirtation with marriage, she moved to Europe, dying in Paris in 1946.

Gracie, Colonel Archibald – US historian, the author of an acclaimed book on the American Civil War. He travelled back to his Washington home on the *Titanic* having been in England conducting research into the war of 1812. The thrilling story of his escape was one of the first survivors' tales to appear in book form but Gracie did not live to reap the profits, dying barely six months after the disaster from the after-effects of his ordeal.

Guggenheim, Benjamin – Forty-seven-year-old American mining baron who travelled first-class while his chauffeur, René Pernot, sailed second-class. With the ship doomed, Guggenheim and his valet, Victor Giglio, appeared on deck in full evening dress with Guggenheim declaring: 'We've dressed up in our best and are prepared to go down like gentlemen.' They did.

Harder, George – Chairman of a foundry, the twenty-six-year-old New Yorker sailed first-class on the *Titanic* with his new bride Dorothy. Both survived. Dorothy died from kidney

trouble in 1926 and George remarried – his second wife Elizabeth being fifteen years his junior. He died in 1959.

Harland & Wolff – Belfast ship-building firm which built the *Titanic*. Founded in 1862 by Yorkshire engineer Edward Harland and German engineer Gustav Wolff, the Queen's Island yard quickly became a major player in international shipbuilding. In 1864 the gross tonnage of ships built at the yard was 30,000; by 1884 the figure had risen to 104,000.

Harris, Henry B. – St Louis-born Broadway producer who managed such stars of the day as Lily Langtry. After travelling to London to arrange a play for another actress client, Rose Stahl, Harris and his wife René planned to return to New York on the *Titanic*. He never made it, helping his wife into the last lifeboat before going down with the ship. He was forty-five.

Harris, Mrs René – Thirty-five-year-old wife of Henry B. Harris (they married in 1898), she struggled to carry on his crumbling theatrical business after his death. She re-married on three occasions and died in 1969.

Hart, Eva – Seven-year-old British girl who was travelling second-class to Winnipeg with her parents. The Harts had been due to sail on another ship – the *Philadelphia* – but were forced to switch to the *Titanic* as the result of a coal strike in Britain. Eva's mother, Esther, had grave misgivings about the new liner and declared: 'It will never get to the other side of the Atlantic.' Even as they boarded the ship at Southampton, she begged her husband to turn back, but he refused. Reluctantly she joined him and little Eva but, convinced that disaster would strike the ship at night, opted to sleep during the day and remain awake during the hours of darkness. It was her vigilance which saved her and Eva's lives. Mr Hart was less fortunate. Eva Hart went on to become one of the last British survivors, dying in 1996.

Hartley, Wallace – Thirty-three-year-old violinist and leader of the eight-man band on the *Titanic*. The band famously played on until the bitter end, although argument still rages as to the identity of their final tune. Hartley's funeral in his home town of Colne, Lancashire, was almost a state occasion with thousands of people turning out to pay their last respects.

Hays, Charles M. – Illinois-born president of the Grand Trunk Pacific Railroad, the Canadian company which had recently built a bridge over the Niagara River at Niagara Falls. Keen on expanding into hotels, he travelled to London in April 1912 for a board meeting. Returning on the *Titanic*, he was relaxing in the first-class lounge with Colonel Archibald Gracie and Captain Edward Crosby on the fateful evening. An hour before the ship struck the iceberg he had expressed the view that 'the trend to playing fast and loose with larger and larger ships will end in tragedy'. Nevertheless he did not think the liner would sink so quickly and as he put his wife Clara and daughter Margaret into a lifeboat, he assured them that the *Titanic* would stay afloat for 'at least ten hours'. He gallantly went down with the ship, aged fifty-five. The town of Hays in Alberta is named after him.

Hichens, Robert – Thirty-year-old Cornish quartermaster who was at the wheel of the *Titanic* when she struck the iceberg and whose surly behaviour in boat No. 6 infuriated Arthur Peuchen and 'Molly' Brown. In 1914 he moved to South Africa to work as a harbour-master. On returning to the UK, he was sentenced to five years' imprisonment in 1933 for the attempted murder of a man in Torquay. He was killed in 1941 during a German air-raid on the south coast.

Hippach, Miss Gertrude – Born in Chicago, sixteen-year-old Gertrude Hippach had been touring Europe with her mother Ida. They boarded the *Titanic* at Cherbourg and occupied a first-class cabin. In the years following the disaster, she married and had three children. The union ended in divorce and she settled in Massachusetts before her death in 1974.

International Mercantile Marine (IMM) – Parent company of the White Star Line. Its proprietor was American financier John Pierpont Morgan.

Ismay, Joseph Bruce – Forty-nine-year-old chairman and managing director of the White Star Line and president of International Mercantile Marine Company. Ismay occupied luxury suite B52 – the best on the ship – after the *Titanic*'s owner, J. Pierpont Morgan, mysteriously withdrew from the trip at the last minute. Ismay's opportunist escape from the sinking ship – sneaking into a lifeboat as it was being lowered – coupled with allegations that he had demanded a transatlantic speed record from the *Titanic* and had deliberately withheld ice warnings from Captain Smith, made him the ideal scapegoat for the American press who labelled him 'J Brute Ismay'. Although exonerated by the British Court of Inquiry, he was left a broken man. He retired as chairman of the White Star Line in 1913, later sold his country home near Liverpool and retreated to County Galway in Ireland. He died from a stroke in 1937.

Lightoller, Charles Herbert – Second Officer on the *Titanic* and the senior surviving officer. At thirty-eight, Lightoller already boasted twenty-five years' experience at sea and his no-nonsense approach, particularly his strict adherence to 'women and children first', was a feature of the evacuation. He retired in the early 1920s to run a chicken farm. Then in 1940 his yacht *Sundowner* formed part of the fleet of 'little ships' at Dunkirk, where he single-handedly rescued 131 British soldiers. It is claimed that one soldier, hearing that he had been rescued by an officer who had served on the *Titanic*, immediately threatened to jump overboard because he thought it would be safer! Lightoller died in 1952, aged seventy-eight.

Lord, Stanley – Thirty-five-year-old captain of the *Californian*, born in Bolton, Lancashire. The US Senate Investigation into the disaster was severely critical of Lord's failure to respond and said that he had incurred 'a grave responsibility'. The British inquiry also concluded that the *Californian* could have saved the lives of most of those on board the *Titanic*. Lord was forced to resign from the Leyland Line in August 1912 but served with another London shipping company until his retirement in 1927. The 1958 film *A Night to Remember*, starring Kenneth More, stirred up the controversy again and Lord sought to clear his name. Before being able to do so, he died in 1962.

Lowe, Harold – Twenty-eight-year-old Welshman, the Fifth Officer on the *Titanic*. He admitted firing his gun to deter steerage passengers from storming the lifeboats and was forced to apologize to the Italian ambassador in the US for using 'Italian' as a synonym for 'coward'. Despite the fact that his coolness in marshalling lifeboats into a flotilla had saved many lives on the night and that his was the only lifeboat to return for survivors, he was overlooked for promotion by White Star and his career drifted into decline. After serving in the Royal Navy during the First World War, he retired to Wales.

Maioni, Roberta – Born in Norfolk, England, twenty-year-old Cissy – as she was known to her friends – served as maid to the Countess of Rothes. Apparently Cissy struck up a romance with a young *Titanic* steward who gave her a White Star badge from his uniform as a token of his affection. After her rescue she always kept it with her although she never revealed the steward's identity. She subsequently married Yorkshire author Cunliffe Bolling but in later years was stricken with severe arthritis which she attributed to prolonged exposure to freezing temperatures in the lifeboat. She died in 1963 and her beloved badge was auctioned in 1999.

Marvin, Daniel Warner – Son of Henry Marvin, the founder of Biograph, one of the earliest motion picture production companies. Legendary filmmaker D. W. Griffith perfected his technique at Biograph with

Henry Marvin. In 1912, Daniel, aged nineteen, married Mary Farquarson. Their ceremony was restaged for filming and was thus reported as the world's first wedding to be 'cinematographed'. They honeymooned in Europe and were returning to their native New York on the *Titanic* when disaster struck. Mary survived, but her young husband went down with the ship.

McGough, James – A thirty-sex-year-old buyer from Philadelphia who boarded at Southampton and shared first-class cabin E25 with fellow buyer John Flynn. Both men survived the sinking, McGough returning to live in Philadelphia until his death in 1937.

Mersey, Lord – Head of the British Court of Inquiry into the *Titanic* disaster.

Meyer, Mrs Leila – While holidaying in Europe with her husband Edgar J. Meyer, twenty-five-year-old Leila received a cable informing her that her father, prominent New York merchant Andrew Saks, had died on 9 April 1912. The couple, who had been married for just over two years, made immediate plans to return home for the funeral and booked a reservation on the first available ship – the *Titanic*.

They boarded at Cherbourg. She survived and was reunited with their young daughter who had stayed behind in the US, but he was lost at sea. Mrs Meyer later remarried and died in 1957.

Millet, Frank D. – The son of a Massachusetts surgeon, Frank Millet became city editor of the *Boston Courier* before embarking on a career as an artist. He won a gold medal in only his second year as a student at the Royal Academy of Fine Arts in Antwerp and went on to earn great acclaim. Sixty-five-year-old Millet accompanied Major Butt on board the *Titanic* and met the same fate. In a letter to a friend posted from Queenstown, he wrote of his fellow passengers: 'Queer lot of people on the ship. There are a number of obnoxious, ostentatious American women, the scourge of any place they infest and worse on shipboard than anywhere.'

Minahan, Miss Daisy – A thirty-three-year-old schoolteacher from Green Bay, Wisconsin, the daughter of Irish immigrants. She travelled first-class on the ill-fated liner with her doctor brother William and sister-in-law Lillian. Dr Minahan went down with the ship. His last words to his wife and sister were: 'Be brave.' Daisy never recovered from her ordeal and less than a month later was admitted to a sanatorium to be treated for pneumonia. She moved to Los Angeles but died there in 1919.

Mocklare, Miss Ellen – Hailing from Galway, Ellen Mocklare was sailing to New York to join her sisters Bridget and Margaret. She went on to work for the National Biscuit Company in New York before becoming a nun in 1917. Taking the name Sister Mary Patricia, she moved to Worcester, Massachusetts, where she taught in a number of schools. She died in a retired nun's convent on 1 April 1984, her ninety-fifth birthday.

Moody, James P. – Born in Scarborough, Yorkshire, twenty-four-year-old Moody was the *Titanic*'s Sixth Officer. He was last seen at 2.18 a.m. by Second Officer Lightoller trying to launch the collapsible boats.

Morgan, John Pierpont – Aggressive American steel tycoon who acquired the White Star Line in 1902 and was thus the real owner of the *Titanic*. Morgan curiously backed out of the ship's maiden voyage at the last minute, citing ill health. But two days after the disaster a reporter tracked the seventy-five-year-old down to a hotel in France where he was found to be in perfectly good health and enjoying the company of his French mistress. However, Morgan died the following year.

Murdoch, William – Scottish-born First Officer of the *Titanic*. forty-one-year-old Murdoch took over on the bridge from Second Officer Lightoller at 10 p.m. on 14 April and issued the orders which avoided a head-on collision with the iceberg. He was last seen, in the company of Chief Officer Wilde, trying to free one of the collapsible boats, and it is believed that he went down with the ship. However some accounts state that Murdoch committed suicide on the bridge by shooting himself because he felt he was partly to blame for the collision, and when this suggestion was repeated in James Cameron's *Titanic* movie, residents of Murdoch's home town – Dalbeattie – were angered by the slur on his character and demanded an apology.

Navratil, Michel – The last male survivor of the *Titanic*, he died in January 2001 at his home in Nice at the age of ninety-two.

Four-year-old Michel and his brother Edmond were travelling on the *Titanic* with their Czech father under the names of Hoffman because his father was separated from his French wife and did not have permission to take the children to the United States. The father saved the boys' lives by passing them to passenger Margaret Hays in one of the lifeboats. Michel, who went on to lecture in philosophy at Montpelier University, later recalled his father's parting words: 'My child, when your mother comes for you, as she surely will, tell her that I loved her dearly and still do. Tell her I expected her to follow us, so that we might all live happily together in the peace and freedom of the New World.'

Nye, Mrs Elizabeth – The daughter of a Folkestone Salvation Army bandsman, she lost her husband Edward in 1911 after seven years of marriage. After landing a job for the Salvation Army in its uniform department in New York, she decided to visit her parents in England. Elizabeth was due to return to the United States on the *Philadelphia* but the coal strike in Britain meant that the voyage was cancelled and she was

transferred to the *Titanic* instead. She was twenty-nine at the time of the sinking and later married a Salvation Army colonel, George Darby, by whom she had a son George. She died in 1963.

Olsen, Arthur – Following the death of his mother in 1906, young Arthur Olsen remained in his native Norway while his father Karl went to America and remarried. Arthur lived with his grandmother but when she, too, died in 1911, Karl Olsen returned to collect the boy and take him to the United States. Father and son were originally booked to sail on the *Philadelphia* but were transferred to the *Titanic* on which they travelled third-class. Karl went down with the ship, but eight-year-old Arthur survived. Showing no fear of the sea, he later joined the navy but ultimately worked as a house-painter in St Petersburg, Florida. He had a brief, unhappy marriage and died on 1 January 1975.

Peuchen, Major Arthur – Born in Montreal, Peuchen served as a marshalling officer at the coronation of George V and made frequent trips to Europe in his capacity as president of the Standard Chemical Company.

He considered himself to be an expert sailor and on hearing that Captain Smith was in charge of the *Titanic*, is said to have remarked: 'Surely not that man!' As it became clear that the ship was listing, he snatched three oranges from his cabin but left behind $200,000 in stocks and bonds. He repeated this feat in the 1920s when he lost a considerable sum of money through bad investments. He died in Toronto in 1929 at the age of sixty-nine.

Phillips, Jack – Twenty-four-year-old senior Marconi wireless operator on board the *Titanic*. He remained at his post until the last but, although he managed to reach one of the collapsible boats, he died from exposure. His body was never recovered.

Pitman, Herbert John – Thirty-four-year-old from Somerset, the *Titanic's* Third Officer. He remained at sea, serving with the Merchant Navy during the Second World War. In 1946 he was awarded the MBE for 'long and meritorious service at sea and in dangerous waters during the war.' He died in 1961, aged eighty-four.

Queenstown – Town in southern Ireland (renamed Cobh), the last scheduled port of call for the *Titanic* before New York. She arrived at 11.30 a.m. on 11 April and left two hours later. Since Queenstown was too small to accommodate the huge liner, anchor was dropped two miles off shore and a flotilla of small boats sailed out to the *Titanic* to offer goods for sale. From one of these enterprising vendors, Colonel John Jacob Astor bought a £165 lace shawl for his young wife.

Robert, Mrs Elisabeth – Born in Pennsylvania, Elisabeth McMillan married the elderly Judge Madill but in 1901, after just six years together, she found herself a widow. Three years later, she married Edward Scott Robert, a pallbearer at her first husband's funeral, but in December 1911 he, too, died. To recover from the shock of being a widow for the second time at the age of forty-three, Elisabeth went to Europe, accompanied by Georgette (her daughter from her first marriage), niece Elisabeth and maid Emilie Kreuchen, the party returning home on the *Titanic*. Following her rescue, she lived to a ripe old age in St Louis, Missouri, eventually dying in 1956.

Romaine, Charles Hallace – Forty-five-year-old sometime gambler from Georgetown,

Kentucky, who travelled under the alias of C. Rolmane. He survived the disaster and went to work in a New York bank. He was killed after being knocked down by a taxi cab in 1922.

Rostron, Arthur Henry – Lancashire-born captain of the rescue ship *Carpathia*. He was subsequently awarded the Congressional Medal of Honor and the American Cross of Honor and went on to command many other ships, notably the *Mauretania*. In 1926 he was knighted and awarded the freedom of New York. Sir Arthur retired from the sea in 1931 and went to live in Southampton where he died of pneumonia in 1940.

Rothes, Countess of – Redoubtable aristocrat who took the tiller on lifeboat No. 8 and also assisted with the rowing. Londoner Lucy Dyer-Edwards married the Nineteenth Earl of Rothes in 1900 and they had two sons, Malcolm and John. The Countess was thirty-three when she boarded the *Titanic* at Southampton with cousin Gladys Cherry and maid Roberta Maioni, bound for Vancouver. The Earl of Rothes died in 1927 and nine months later the Countess remarried.

She died in Hove, Sussex, in 1956.

Rowe, George – Quartermaster who served on the *Titanic* for a monthly wage of £5. Three months after the disaster he signed on to the *Oceanic* and when he quit the life at sea, he worked as a ship repairer in Southampton until he was over eighty. His devotion to duty earned him the British Empire Medal. He died in 1974, aged ninety-one.

Ryerson, Arthur – Sixty-one-year-old Philadelphia steel magnate who boarded the *Titanic* at Cherbourg with his wife and three children, the family hurrying back to New York after learning of the death of son Arthur Jnr. Arthur Ryerson senior finished a game of cards on board the doomed liner before going to his death.

Smith, Edward John – sixty-two-year-old Staffordshire-born captain of the *Titanic* who was planning to retire after the ship's maiden voyage. Smith had been in charge of her sister ship, the *Olympic*, when she collided with the cruiser HMS *Hawke* off the Isle of Wight in 1911, sustaining considerable damage. Nevertheless he had an excellent reputation and many passengers said they would only cross the Atlantic on a ship in his command. His precise fate remains shrouded in mystery. Some said he was last seen with a child in his arms; others that he reached a collapsible boat but chose to return to the sinking ship. The most reliable witnesses stated that he stayed on the bridge before going down with his ship in the finest tradition. He was subsequently criticized by the US inquiry for his failure to reduce speed knowing that there was ice in the vicinity. Senator William Alden Smith castigated his namesake for his 'indifference to danger, overconfidence, and neglect to heed the oft-repeated warnings of his friends'. In 1914 a statue of Captain Smith was unveiled in Lichfield, Staffordshire, even though he had been born at Hanley, Stoke-on-Trent, some 20 miles away. Rumours circulated that Stoke-on-Trent wished to disassociate itself from the captain of the *Titanic*. Smith's widow Eleanor died in 1931 after being knocked down by a taxi outside her London home.

Smith, Senator William Alden – Republican lawyer from Michigan who conducted the US Senate investigation into the *Titanic* disaster.

Snyder, John P. – Born in Minneapolis, John Pillsbury Snyder, twenty-six, was returning to America on the *Titanic* with his new bride Nelle. Some newspapers reported that a crewman called out, 'Put in the brides and grooms first' and so the couple felt justified in climbing into a lifeboat. After becoming a father of three, John P. Snyder died in 1959 while playing golf.

Stead, William T. – British journalist and editor who was travelling to America to address a peace conference at the specific request of President Taft. A noted spiritualist, Stead may have foreseen his own death. For in 1892 he had written a novel, *From the Old World to the New*, in which a ship sank after hitting an iceberg in the North Atlantic. In Stead's tale, survivors were picked up by a vessel captained by E. J. Smith. The captain of the *Titanic* was also named E. J. Smith.

Stengel, Charles Emil Henry – Patent-leather manufacturer from Newark, New Jersey, who boarded at Cherbourg with his wife Annie. He was saved from the *Titanic* but died in 1914, aged fifty-six.

Stengel, Mrs Annie – Forty-three-year-old wife of Charles Stengel, of whom she said in an interview: 'The nearest thing I've ever known to Heaven on earth was meeting my husband again on the deck of the *Carpathia*.' She died in 1956.

Stone, Herbert – Second Officer on the *Californian* and the watch officer between midnight and 4 a.m. on 15 April 1912.

Straus, Ida – Elderly wife of Isidor Straus who co-owned Macy's department store in New York with his brother. Isidor had begun to slow down by 1912 and enjoyed travelling with his wife. They had decided that the perfect way to round off their spring holiday was to return home on the maiden voyage of the *Titanic*. She famously refused to escape the stricken ship in a lifeboat, preferring to stay and die with her beloved husband.

Thayer, John B. – Second vice-president of the Pennsylvania Railroad Company. The Thayer family had been in Berlin as guests of the United States Consul and returned home on the *Titanic*. On the fateful evening, they joined Captain Smith at a dinner party. John Borland Thayer died on the *Titanic*, but his wife Marion and son Jack survived.

Thayer, Jack – Known as Jack, John Borland Thayer Jr was seventeen at the time of the disaster. Reunited with his mother on the *Carpathia*, he subsequently graduated from the University of Pennsylvania and went into banking. He duly married but when his son Edward was killed while serving in the Pacific during the Second World War, Jack sank into depression and committed suicide in 1945.

Warren, Mrs Anna – Sixty-year-old wife of Frank Warren with whom she had been on a tour of Europe. They boarded the *Titanic* at Cherbourg, but only she survived the sinking. A resident of Portland, Oregon, she became a prominent member of the Young Women's Christian Association and following her death in 1925, she left $14,000 to various religious organisations.

White Star Line – Leading British steamship company, the owners of the *Titanic*. The White Star flag was first flown around 1850 by a line of sailing vessels which ferried hopeful British emigrants to Australia following the discovery of gold in that continent. Under the leadership of Thomas Henry Ismay, son of a Cumberland shipbuilder, the company concentrated on the more profitable transatlantic routes. Following Ismay's death in 1899, he was succeeded by his son, J. Bruce Ismay.

Widener, George – Fifty-year-old head of a Philadelphia banking and railroad family with a personal wealth estimated at $30 million. His wife Eleanor travelled with a pearl necklace insured for $600,000, the equivalent of $4 million today. The Wideners had been staying at the Paris Ritz Hotel and had the distinction of hosting the last great dinner party aboard the *Titanic* – in honour of Captain Smith. George Widener and his twenty-seven-year-old son Harry were both lost in the tragedy.

Wilde, Henry Tingle – Liverpool-born Chief Officer of the *Titanic*, switched from the *Olympic* at the last minute because of his knowledge of huge liners. It was he who suggested that the officers might need guns and ammunition to control the passengers. Thirty-nine-year-old Wilde went down with the ship.

Willard, Miss Constance – A twenty-one-year-old from Duluth, Minnesota. At first she refused to get into a lifeboat whereupon the officer in charge said: 'Don't waste time – let her go if she won't get in.' Finally she reconsidered. She never married

and died in California in 1964.

Wright, Miss Marion – Farmer's daughter Marion Wright from Yeovil, Somerset, boarded the *Titanic* as a second-class passenger at Southampton to sail to America to marry her sweetheart Arthur Woolcott. The latter had relocated to the US in 1907, initially as a draughtsman and then as an Oregon fruit farmer. The pair married in New York within a week of the disaster and stayed together on their Oregon farm for another fifty-three years, raising three sons. Arthur Woolcott died in 1961, his wife four years later at the age of eighty.

Young, Miss Marie – An accomplished musician once employed as music teacher to Theodore Roosevelt's daughter, Ethel. She shared first-class quarters with Mrs J. Stuart White who remained in her cabin for the entire voyage. Miss Young's luggage included a number of valuable live chickens and she befriended one of the ship's carpenters, John Hutchinson, who took her below decks each day to check on the fowl. When she rewarded him with gold coins, he remarked: 'It's such good luck to receive gold on a first voyage.' She died in 1959, aged eighty-three.